THE CHILD IN CHRISTIAN THOUGHT

The Child in Christian Thought

Edited by

Marcia J. Bunge

WILLIAM B. EERDMANS PUBLISHING COMPANY
GRAND RAPIDS, MICHIGAN / CAMBRIDGE, U.K.

Wm. B. Eerdmans Publishing Co.
255 Jefferson Ave. S.E., Grand Rapids, Michigan 49503 /
P.O. Box 163, Cambridge CB3 9PU U.K.

Printed in the United States of America

05 04 03 02 01   7 6 5 4 3 2 1

Library of Congress Cataloging-in-Publication Data

The child in Christian thought / edited by Marcia J. Bunge.
p.   cm.
Includes bibliographical references.
ISBN 0-8028-4693-9 (pbk.)
1. Children (Christian theology) — History of doctrines.
I. Bunge, Marcia J. (Marcia JoAnn), 1954-

BT705.C45 2001
261.8'3423 — dc21

00-041732

www.eerdmans.com

To Isaac

Contents

Contents

Series Foreword

The Religion, Marriage, and Family series evolves out of a research project located at the University of Chicago and financed by a generous grant from the Division of Religion of the Lilly Endowment, Inc. The first phase of the project lasted from 1991 to 1997 and produced eleven books on religion and family. In late 1997, the Lilly Endowment gave the project an additional major grant that supports a second phase of research and publication. The books in the Eerdmans Religion, Marriage, and Family series come directly or indirectly from the initiatives of this second phase.

In some cases, the books will evolve directly out of the University of Chicago project. In other cases, they will be books written in response to that project or in some way stimulated by it. In all cases, they will be books probing the depth of resources in Judaism and Christianity for understanding, renewing, and in some respects redefining current expressions of marriage and family. The series will investigate issues of parenthood and children, work and family, responsible fatherhood, and equality in the family; the responsibility of the major professions in promoting and protecting sound marriages and families; the biblical, theological, philosophical, and legal grounds of Western family systems; selected classics of these traditions; and the respective roles of church, market, and state in supporting marriages, families, parents, and children.

The Religion, Marriage, and Family series intends to go beyond the sentimentality, political manipulation, and ungrounded assertions that characterize so much of the contemporary debate over marriage and family. It plans to develop an intelligent and accessible new literature for colleges and seminaries, churches and other religious institutions, questing individuals and families. Marriage and family issues are not just preoccupations of the United States;

they have become worldwide concerns as modernization, globalization, changing values, emerging poverty, and changing gender roles disrupt traditional families and challenge the very idea of marriage throughout the world. It has been predicted that the emerging marriage and family crisis will be the central issue of the twenty-first century. The Religion, Marriage, and Family series hopes to contribute to more balanced and well-informed public debate on this issue, both in the United States and around the globe.

*   *

This book, *The Child in Christian Thought,* edited by Marcia J. Bunge, is a stunning collection of essays that fills an enormous gap in contemporary family studies. We are bold enough to suggest that it launches a new field of inquiry: the study of Christian theological approaches to children and the responsibilities of families and society toward them. While there has been a groundswell in new scholarship on children from psychologists, sociologists, historians, and philosophers, contemporary theologians have on the whole neglected childhood as a serious intellectual or moral concern. These essays demonstrate not only that childhood has been a deep and abiding concern in Christian theology in the past — for example, in Augustine, Aquinas, Luther, Calvin, Schleiermacher, Edwards, the Jesuits, and the Pietists — but also, and even more importantly, that a complex and robust new theology of children is possible, one that combines systematic theology, ethics, history, and pastoral studies in a rich conversation about the nature and meaning of childhood and the obligations toward children in families, church, and society.

The essays here, among other things, challenge a flat association of Christianity with children's original sin; critique a contemporary culture of child devaluation, commodification, and neglect; probe the responsibilities of parenting as a serious calling and spiritual discipline; and examine the interconnecting responsibilities toward children of families, churches, the market, and the state. In short, this book is a wake-up call for theology to find its voice in a growing international debate for which it has profound yet so far largely untapped resources.

Don S. Browning *and* John Wall,
series editors

Acknowledgments

This book is part of a larger project entitled "The Child in Christian Thought," which I directed from 1998 to 2000. The main purpose of the project has been to strengthen contemporary reflection on children by critically examining ideas within the history of Christian thought about children and childhood. In addition to bringing together the scholars who contributed to this volume, the project encouraged them to offer public presentations of their ideas and to publish further research on issues regarding children and religion.

There are many people to thank for their contributions to this volume and to the project as a whole. First of all, I would like to thank the Lilly Endowment for supporting this project. I especially want to thank Christopher Coble (Program Director) and Craig Dykstra (Vice President of the Endowment's Religion Division) for their encouragement and for their own abiding commitment to children and young people. The Lilly Endowment grant enabled the contributors of the volume to meet together twice in order to discuss their work, thereby strengthening all of the essays, and it supported activities that disseminated and developed ideas formulated in this volume.

I also want to express my deep appreciation to all of the authors of this volume. They are excellent scholars in their various fields, and they share a common passion for the subject of children and religion. At our two meetings together, they freely exchanged ideas, carefully evaluated one another's manuscripts, and worked together in a spirit of genuine collaboration. My work as the editor of this volume was greatly eased because of their diligent research, goodwill, and sense of humor.

The volume and project as a whole benefited greatly from the ideas and advice of several people. Dorothy Bass (Valparaiso University), Don Browning

(University of Chicago), and Michael Welker (University of Heidelberg) served as the project's consultants, and each one of them provided invaluable advice at various stages of the project. I also want to thank the guest speakers who attended one of the contributors' meetings and who shared their insights into the situation of families and children today: Herbert Anderson (Catholic Theological Union), Don Browning, Mason Scholl (former Vice President of ChildServ), and Shannon Daly Harris (former Director of Religious Affairs at the Children's Defense Fund). Sheila Briggs (University of Southern California) participated in both of the meetings and offered insightful comments on several theological issues. My own essay and the introduction were strengthened by the comments and suggestions of Michael Welker, Dorothy Bass, Carol Roberts (Indiana University — Purdue University Fort Wayne), Leonard Hummel (Vanderbilt University), Walter Wangerin Jr. (Valparaiso University), Barbara Pitkin (Stanford University), Udo Sträter (Director of the *Interdisziplinäres Zentrum für Pietismusforschung*), and Thomas Müller-Bahlke (Director of the Archives at the *Franckesche Stiftungen*).

Several members of the Christ College and Valparaiso University community enabled me to make the most of the time and resources provided by the grant. The Dean of Christ College, Mark Schwehn, fully embraced the project and generously allowed me to reduce my teaching load in order to work on it. Roy Austensen (Provost of the University) and Alan Harre (President) also supported the project, and members of the finance office, particularly Nancy Stalbaum, helped provide financial reports. Members of the dining staff graciously served meals at one of the contributors' meetings. Paula Strietelmeier, administrative assistant for the project, contributed to it in numerous ways, especially by arranging meetings and keeping accurate records of the project's budget and activities. I also want to thank the Christ College students who participated in my seminar entitled "Children, the Family, and Faith" (fall semester, 1998). They affirmed the importance of paying more attention to issues regarding children and deepened my own thinking through their lively and serious discussions and papers.

During the past year, I also participated in an interdisciplinary consultation on the subject of children and religion. Although this book was just being completed when the consultation began, some of the questions and concerns that were raised in our initial conversation are reflected in the introduction. I therefore want to thank Robert A. Orsi (Indiana University, Bloomington), the director of the consultation, and all of its participants for their contributions to that conversation. Members of the consultation were Vigen Guroian (Loyola College), H. Ray Hiner (University of Kansas), James Kincaid (University of Southern California), Martha Manning (writer and clinical psychologist), Jon Pahl (Lutheran Theological Seminary at Philadelphia), Sarah Pike (California

State University, Chico), William J. Reese (University of Wisconsin, Madison), and Karen-Marie Yust (Christian Theological Seminary, Indianapolis).

I am deeply grateful to Eerdmans Publishing Company and its executive editor, Jon Pott, who supported the project from the beginning. I also want to thank Mary Hietbrink, the editor for the volume, who worked diligently, carefully, and cheerfully to bring the manuscript into its final form.

Finally, I want to thank members of my family for their insight and support. My mother, Myrene Bunge, was a school counselor and has nurtured four children and nine grandchildren, and I highly value her understanding of and compassion for children. Although my father, Richard Bunge, died in 1977, I continue to be grateful for and influenced by his love and wisdom. My spouse, Gary Dulin, shares with me all the delights and challenges of parenting and is my most intimate conversation partner about children. Our six-year-old son, Isaac, brings joy and enthusiasm to almost any endeavor and has enriched our lives in countless ways. Gary, Isaac, and other members of my family surround me with love and support, and I thank God for each one of them.

I sincerely hope that by providing a critical examination of both the limitations and the possibilities of past theological perspectives regarding children, this present volume will contribute to current interdisciplinary discussions about children and provide an occasion for re-examining our parental and communal responsibilities toward all children.

Marcia J. Bunge
Christ College, Valparaiso University
April 14, 2000

Introduction

MARCIA J. BUNGE

W hether or not we have children of our own, we are concerned about children in our midst and in our wider culture. Are they being raised with love and affection? Are they receiving a good education? Are they being exposed to good role models? How do we account for the serious problems many of them are facing, such as abuse, depression, teenage pregnancy, and poverty?[1] Our concerns and questions are reflected in the growing number of public debates across liberal and conservative lines about children. Diverse political parties, non-profit agencies, and religious groups are focusing more attention on a number of issues, including child health and safety, education, child poverty, juvenile crime, child neglect and abuse, and the moral development of children. Certainly, the severity of these problems is highly debated, and there is disagreement about whether the present situation of children is better or worse than it was in the past. Nevertheless, broad public concern for children and heightened recognition of the tremendous challenges they face are unmistakable.

This widespread concern is one of the many reasons that interest in children is growing in a range of academic disciplines, reaching well beyond those fields that have typically devoted attention to children, such as education and

---

1. Even today in the United States, as this country enjoys an overall strong economy, 18.9 percent of children under eighteen are poor. This percentage is cited from data provided by the United States Census Bureau. See its Web site at www.census.gov. Here, poverty is defined as an income under $13,003 for a three-person family. Studies have shown that poor children face greater disadvantages in a number of areas, such as lower academic test scores, less education, and lower wages in their adult years. See *The State of America's Children: Yearbook 2000* (Washington, D.C.: Children's Defense Fund, 1998), x-xiii.

1

child psychology.[2] For example, beginning with the influential 1960 study by Philippe Ariès,[3] a number of historians have been directly exploring the history of childhood in the West.[4] Recently, studies on the history of childhood in non-Western cultures have emerged as well.[5] During the past ten years, several studies have also emerged in the field of philosophy, particularly on philosophical conceptions of childhood, on children's cognitive and philosophical capacities, and on children's rights.[6] In addition, there is a lively debate among sociologists regarding children, especially in relation to the effects of divorce and single parenting on children.[7] Certainly, studies in the area of psychology continue to explore many aspects of children's lives. For example, classic works such as those by Lawrence Kohlberg and Carol Gilligan have attempted to paint a more sophisticated picture of the moral development of children.[8] Other studies

2. For a review of interest in children in a number of disciplines, see Scott Heller, "The Meaning of Children Becomes a Focal Point for Scholars," *The Chronicle of Higher Education*, 7 August 1998, A14-16.

3. Philippe Ariès, *L'Enfant et la vie familiale sous l'Ancien Régime* (Paris: Librairie Plon, 1960); translated by Robert Baldick as *Centuries of Childhood: A Social History of Family Life* (New York: Vintage Books, 1962).

4. See, for example, Hugh Cunningham, *Children and Childhood in Western Society since 1500* (New York: Longman Publishing, 1995); Linda Pollock, *Forgotten Children: Parent-Child Relations from 1500-1900* (New York: Cambridge University Press, 1983); Barbara Hanawalt, *The Ties that Bound: Peasant Families in Medieval England* (New York: Oxford University Press, 1986); James A. Schultz, *The Knowledge of Childhood in the German Middle Ages, 1100-1350* (Philadelphia: University of Pennsylvania Press, 1995); Shulamith Shahar, *Childhood in the Middle Ages* (London: Routledge, 1990); and Karin Calvert, *Children in the House: The Material Culture of Early Childhood, 1600-1900* (Boston: Northeastern University Press, 1992). This list could be expanded considerably. See the recent review essay by Hugh Cunningham, "Histories of Childhood," *The American Historical Review* 103 (October 1998): 1195-1208.

5. See, for example, *Chinese Views of Childhood,* ed. Anne Behnke Kinney (Honolulu: University of Hawaii Press, 1995); and Avner Gil'adi, *Children of Islam: Concepts of Childhood in Medieval Muslim Society* (New York: St. Martin's Press, 1992). See also *Children in Historical and Comparative Perspective: An International Handbook and Research Guide,* ed. Joseph M. Hawes and N. Ray Hiner (New York: Greenwood Press, 1991).

6. See, for example, Gareth Matthews, *Philosophy and the Young Child* (Cambridge: Harvard University Press, 1980), and *The Philosophy of Childhood* (Cambridge: Harvard University Press, 1994); and Michael Pritchard, *On Becoming Responsible* (Lawrence: University Press of Kansas, 1985).

7. See, for example, David Popenoe, *Disturbing the Nest: Family Change and Decline in Modern Societies* (Hawthorne, N.Y.: Aldine de Gruyter, 1988); Sara McLanahan and Gary Sandefur, *Growing Up with a Single Parent: What Hurts, What Helps* (Cambridge: Harvard University Press, 1994); and Paul R. Amato and Alan Booth, *A Generation at Risk: Growing Up in an Era of Family Upheaval* (Cambridge: Harvard University Press, 1997).

8. See, for example, Lawrence Kohlberg, *Philosophy of Moral Development* (New

have focused more directly on the religious perceptions and faith development of children.[9]

Studies such as these are helping us to reflect more seriously on a number of questions regarding the nature of children and the obligations of parents and the wider community to children. The historical studies highlight conceptions of childhood and how they can change over time, and they prompt us to reflect on our own current attitudes toward and assumptions about childhood. The psychological and philosophical studies shed light on the complex emotional, intellectual, moral, and spiritual lives of children, and they raise a number of important questions about the development of children, about our treatment of them, and about their religious worlds. Studies in these and other disciplines, particularly sociology and law, have also challenged us to think not only about the obligations of parents toward their own children but also about the responsibilities of schools, religious organizations, local communities, and the state for nurturing children.

The Current State of Theological Reflection on Children

When we ask what Christian theology might contribute to this wider public and academic debate about children or how it might help us to reflect on our notions about the nature of children and our obligations to them, one can easily suspect that it has very little to offer and is perhaps even destructive. The grounds for this suspicion are compelling and are twofold.

In the first place, until very recently, issues related to children have tended to be marginal in almost every area of contemporary theology. For example, systematic theologians and Christian ethicists have said little about children, and they have not regarded serious reflection on children as a high priority. What Todd Whitmore has claimed about the Catholic Church can be applied to Christian theology in general: there is no well-developed social teaching on the

---

York: Harper & Row, 1981); and Carol Gilligan, *In a Different Voice* (Cambridge: Harvard University Press, 1982). See also the earlier work of Jean Piaget, *The Moral Judgment of the Child* (New York: Free Press, 1932); and the recent work of Robert Coles, *The Moral Life of Children* (New York: Atlantic Monthly Press, 1986).

9. For children's religious perceptions, see, for example, David Heller, *The Children's God* (Chicago: University of Chicago Press, 1986); Ana-Maria Rizutto, *The Birth of the Living God: A Psychoanalytic Study* (Chicago: University of Chicago Press, 1979); and Robert Coles, *The Spiritual Life of Children* (Boston: Houghton Mifflin, 1990). Although recent studies have criticized aspects of the work of James Fowler, his book entitled *Stages of Faith: The Psychology of Human Development and the Quest for Meaning* (San Francisco: Harper & Row, 1981) opened a door to greater interest in the faith development of children.

nature of children and why we should care about and for them.[10] Although the church has highly developed teachings on other issues, such as abortion, economic justice, and moral conduct in war, theologians have not offered sustained reflection on the nature of children or on the obligations that parents, the state, and the church have to nurture children. Furthermore, children do not play a role in the way that systematic theologians think about central theological themes, such as the human condition, the nature of faith, language about God, the task of the church, and the nature of religion. Certainly, issues regarding children have sometimes been addressed in theological reflection on the family. However, as Whitmore points out, "For the most part, church teaching simply admonishes the parents to educate their children in the faith and for children to obey their parents."[11] The absence of well-developed and historically and biblically informed teachings about children in contemporary theology helps explain why many churches often struggle to create and to sustain strong programs in religious education and in child-advocacy ministry.[12]

In the second place, since little serious attention has been given to children in contemporary theology, assumptions about Christian perspectives on children are often shaped mainly by recent and disturbing studies about the re-

10. See Todd David Whitmore with Tobias Winright, "Children: An Undeveloped Theme in Catholic Teaching," in *The Challenge of Global Stewardship,* ed. Maura A. Ryan and Todd David Whitmore (Notre Dame: University of Notre Dame Press, 1997), 161-85. This essay is discussed more fully in the essay in this volume by Mary Ann Hinsdale.

11. Whitmore, "Children: An Undeveloped Theme in Catholic Teaching," 162.

12. Although almost all churches offer religious education for children, and although some programs are excellent, the materials offered are often theologically weak and uninteresting to children. Many churches also have difficulty recruiting and retaining enough qualified teachers for these programs. Furthermore, many churches often implicitly treat reflection on religious education and the moral and spiritual formation of children as "beneath" the job of systematic theologians or ethicists, and thus attention to children is left solely to pastoral theologians and religious educators. Mainline Protestant churches have also hesitated to contribute significantly to public debate about children and families. In contrast, Protestant evangelical and conservative churches have been more vocal in nationwide debates about familial issues and have established practical programs to address the needs of children and their families. However, their theological reflection on children often overemphasizes a narrow selection of biblical passages and focuses on the sinfulness of children, their need for obedience and instruction, and the protection of the rights of parents to raise children without governmental intrusion. Thus, these churches do not always adequately address the spiritual questions of children themselves, what children might teach adults, and the responsibilities of parents, the church, and the state to protect and support children. Furthermore, although these churches certainly do not condone the physical abuse of children, some of them either continue to justify the physical punishment of children (despite medical studies that cite its dangers) or do not explicitly reject it.

ligious roots of child abuse. Some of the most familiar studies have exposed what has been called a "poisonous pedagogy" in some past and present strains of European and American Protestantism.[13] This type of inhumane pedagogy stresses the absolute obedience of children to parents, the sinful nature or depravity of children, and the need to "break their wills" at a very early age with harsh physical punishment. According to some of these studies, the idea that children are sinful and thus must have their wills "broken" is often supported by the notions that since God punishes his people, parents must punish their children, and that obedience to God demands absolute obedience to parents, even if they are acting unjustly. This kind of religious reasoning and the emphasis on the depravity of children have apparently led, in some cases, to the physical abuse and even death of children, including infants. Most of these studies recognize that the Christian tradition is diverse and that Christianity has at times protected children and helped them to achieve wholeness. However, without further knowledge about what the church yesterday and today has said about children, and without focused attention on children in contemporary theology, it is easy to assume that what Christian theology offers to contemporary reflection on children is at best irrelevant and at worst destructive. If one believes that viewing children as sinful often fosters inhumane treatment of them, and if one observes that many theologians, both in the present and in the past, regard children mainly as sinful, then one will assume that most forms of Christianity are potentially destructive. Furthermore, even if theologians were to rule out explicitly the physical punishment of children, the view of children as sinful can appear to be hopelessly out of touch with common psychological conceptions of children that emphasize their potential for development and their need for loving nurture.

Several recent studies, however, are beginning to provide a fuller picture of Christian views of children and to enrich theological reflection on children, thereby enabling theologians to contribute more fully to the debate about children today. This is especially the case in the areas of pastoral care,

13. See, for example, Alice Miller, *Am Anfang war Erziehung* (Frankfurt: Suhrkamp, 1980), translated by Hildegarde and Hunter Hannum as *For Your Own Good: Hidden Cruelty in Child-Rearing and the Roots of Violence* (New York: Noonday, 1983); Philip Greven, *Spare the Child: The Religious Roots of Punishment and the Psychological Impact of Physical Abuse* (New York: Alfred A. Knopf, 1991); Donald Capps, *The Child's Song: The Religious Abuse of Children* (Louisville, Ky.: Westminster John Knox Press, 1995); and "Religion and Child Abuse: Perfect Together," *Journal for the Scientific Study of Religion* 31 (1992): 1-14. See also Philip Greven's work entitled *The Protestant Temperament: Patterns of Child-Rearing, Religious Experience, and the Self in Early America* (New York: Alfred A. Knopf, 1977). Here he ties methods of child rearing to three distinctive religious "temperaments" he finds in the seventeenth and eighteenth centuries.

ethics, and the history of Christianity. For example, several ethicists and pastoral theologians, especially through the Religion, Culture, and Family Project headed by Don Browning, have generated a number of new studies that focus directly on the family and in this way are shedding light on issues regarding children.[14] Others are combining attention to gender equity or reproductive issues with concerns for children and the family.[15] Some pastoral theologians, such as Herbert Anderson and Susan Johnson, are focusing more attention directly on the church's attitudes toward and treatment of children.[16] They are also exploring more fully the spiritual formation of children and the role of parents in this formation.[17] In the area of the history of Chris-

14. See, for example, Don Browning, Bonnie J. Miller-McLemore, Pamela D. Couture, K. Brynolf Lyon, and Robert M. Franklin, *From Culture Wars to Common Ground: Religion and the American Family Debate* (Louisville, Ky.: Westminster John Knox Press, 1997); *Faith Traditions and the Family,* ed. Phyllis D. Airhart and Margaret Lamberts Bendroth (Louisville, Ky.: Westminster John Knox Press, 1996); *The Family Handbook,* ed. Herbert Anderson, Don Browning, Ian S. Evison, and Mary Stewart Van Leeuwen (Louisville, Ky.: Westminster John Knox Press, 1998); and *Religion, Feminism, and the Family,* ed. Anne Carr and Mary Stewart Van Leeuwen (Louisville: Westminster John Knox Press, 1996). See also other recent studies on the family outside the work of the Religion, Culture, and Family Project, such as Gilbert Meilaender, "What Are Families For?" *First Things* 6 (October 1990): 34-41; and Stephen Post, *Spheres of Love: Toward a New Ethics of the Family* (Dallas: Southern Methodist University Press, 1994).

15. See, for example, Bonnie Miller-McLemore, *Also a Mother: Work and Family as Theological Dilemma* (Nashville: Abingdon, 1994); *The Family,* ed. Lisa Sowle Cahill and Dietmar Mieth (special issue of *Concilium,* 1995); Lisa Sowle Cahill and Thomas A. Shannon, *Religion and Artificial Reproduction* (New York: Crossroads, 1988); Ted Peters, *For the Love of Children: Genetic Technology and the Future of the Family* (Louisville, Ky.: Westminster John Knox Press, 1996); and Christine E. Gudorf, "Dissecting Parenthood: Infertility, in Vitro, and Other Lessons in Why and How We Parent," *Conscience* 15, no. 3 (Autumn 1994): 15-22.

16. See Herbert Anderson and Susan B. W. Johnson, *Regarding Children: A New Respect for Childhood and Families* (Louisville, Ky.: Westminster John Knox Press, 1994).

17. Previous theological studies regarding faith formation in children offered few distinctive insights because they relied heavily on psychological models of development. Recent and more informed studies are combining a more critical appropriation of psychological research with theological ideas. In contrast to earlier studies that focused on "mature" faith, they are also exploring religious experiences of children under twelve years of age. Several of these studies, such as Jerome Berryman's *Godly Play: An Imaginative Approach to Religious Education* (San Francisco: HarperSanFrancisco, 1991), build on the work of Sofia Cavalletti. She has written several books, including *The Religious Potential of the Child* (New York: Paulist Press, 1983). Her work and that of Gianna Gobbi have also shaped a particular approach to religious education called the "Catechesis of the Good Shepherd." For an introduction to this approach, see, for example, Tina Lillig, *The Catechesis of the Good Shepherd in a Parish Setting* (Chicago: Liturgy Training Publications, 1998). For studies that discuss the role of parents in the religious formation of children, see, for

tianity, several important studies have discussed children in the context of theological views of motherhood or the family.[18] The number of historical studies devoted specifically to children and their treatment in the church has also been increasing.[19]

The Necessity, Purpose, and Scope of This Book

Although research regarding children is beginning to emerge within several areas of theology, the current literature still lacks a full account of past theological perspectives on children and our obligations to them. Beyond material provided in the above-mentioned research on the religious roots of child abuse and other recent historical studies, we know little about what theologians in the past have actually said about children or how they have treated them, especially when compared to other themes or ethical concerns in theology. Furthermore, some studies about the views of past theologians regarding children can be misleading because they do not always take into account either the larger theological framework of a particular theologian or his or her specific social and historical context. Thus, a fuller account of past theological perspectives on children could help amplify and provide a corrective to the current literature. Such an account could also prompt more serious theological reflection on children among theologians and ethicists today, because they depend on strong accounts of past theological perspectives whenever they attempt to construct meaningful responses to contemporary challenges.

The main purpose of this volume is to offer a critical examination of past theological perspectives on children in order to strengthen ethical and theological reflection on children today and to contribute to the current academic and broader public discussion on children. In this sense — although the contribut-

---

example, Marjorie Thompson, *Family: The Forming Center: A Vision of the Role of Family in Spiritual Formation* (Nashville: Upper Room Books, 1996); Merton P. Strommen and Richard Hardel, *Passing on the Faith: A Radical New Model for Youth and Family Ministry* (Winona, Minn.: St. Mary's Press, 2000); and texts and materials offered by the Youth and Family Institute of Augsburg College and by the Search Institute. Thanks to Karen-Marie Yust, Jerome Berryman, and Richard Hardel for attention to some of the literature cited here and to issues in religious education.

18. See, for example, Clarissa Atkinson, *The Oldest Vocation: Christian Motherhood in the Middle Ages* (Ithaca, N.Y.: Cornell University Press, 1991); Steven Ozment, *When Fathers Ruled: Family Life in Reformation Europe* (Cambridge: Harvard University Press, 1983); and Gerald Strauss, *Luther's House of Learning: Indoctrination of the Young in the German Reformation* (Baltimore: The Johns Hopkins University Press, 1978).

19. See, for example, *The Church and Childhood*, ed. Diana Wood (Oxford: Blackwell, 1994).

ing authors come from the fields of ethics, the history of Christianity, pastoral care, and systematic theology — the volume can most accurately be described as a study within the area of historical theology. The main task of historical theologians is to examine carefully and critically past theological positions and to outline their implications for today. Thus, the authors in this volume have examined the theological perspectives of a number of influential theologians and movements in the history of Christian thought with regard to the following central question: What resources do they provide, if any, for reconsidering our views of children and our obligations to children? The essays therefore address the following specific questions:

1. How do these selected theologians and the leaders of these movements speak about the nature of children?
2. How do they speak about the responsibilities and obligations of parents, the state, and the church to nurture children?
3. How are their ideas about children and obligations to them related to the larger theological framework and the central theological concerns of each theologian or movement?
4. How are their ideas related to their particular social, cultural, and political contexts?
5. What are the implications of these ideas for our contemporary views of children and our obligations to them?

Since the contributing authors examine a variety of periods, thinkers, and movements, and since they work with diverse kinds of sources, their approaches and emphases vary. However, since the book as a whole is a study within the area of historical theology, all of the authors attempt to combine historical integrity, theological insight, and resonance with contemporary issues.

More particularly, the volume examines the ideas of the following individuals and movements: (1) selected theologians, such as Augustine, Thomas Aquinas, Martin Luther, and John Calvin, who have significantly shaped theology and the church; (2) selected theologians, such as Jonathan Edwards and Horace Bushnell, who have influenced many of the ways we still think about children and child rearing in the United States today; and (3) selected groups and movements — such as the Jesuits and Ursulines of the seventeenth century, the Pietists of the early eighteenth century, and the black women's clubs of the nineteenth century — that worked closely with children. The mixture of theologians and movements generates a richer theological discussion about children and helps reveal a variety of attitudes and behaviors toward children in the history of Christianity. The book does focus mainly on highly influential theologians, some of whom touched on the themes of children only marginally. The history of Christianity contains many other sources that have reflected more extensively — and, in some cases, with more insight — on children. However, it is important to examine these influential figures because they have greatly informed cultures and Christian theology and continue to shape the beliefs and practices of living communities of faith today. Just as feminist and womanist theologies have recognized that a critical examination of views of women within the Christian tradition must include the study of some of its most influential figures, a study of both the possibilities and the limitations of Christian perspectives on children must include an account of how some of the most influential figures in the tradition have thought about and acted toward children. It is hoped that this study, which does not aim to be exhaustive but which is wide-ranging and thought-provoking, will prompt further research into the ideas of other theologians and into the religious worlds of children themselves.[20]

Claims and Contributions of This Volume

By carefully examining selected theological perspectives of the past, this book as a whole makes three general claims and thereby offers three significant contributions to the discussion of children today.

First and most generally, by using childhood as a "lens" to examine the past, the study uncovers neglected aspects of the ideas and practices of theologians and movements and thus contributes to the history of Christian thought and of conceptions of childhood. The essays reveal a range of attitudes and behaviors toward children within Christian thought that is broader than much of the current literature suggests, and they indicate that childhood has not always been a marginal theme in Christian theology.

Second, the volume reveals varied perspectives among theologians on the nature of children, particularly in regard to the notion of the child as sinful. More specifically, it shows that notions of original sin and "breaking the will" are complex and do not automatically lead to the harsh punishment of children, and that the idea of original sin, set within a particular larger theological framework, has in some cases fostered the more humane treatment of children. The essays also make it clear that several theologians radically reinterpret or even reject the notion of original sin as something children inherit, and they provide alternative

20. The study of the ideas, experiences, and religious worlds of children themselves is an important and growing area of historical research. It is far more difficult to explore the religious lives of children than adult perspectives on children, in part because we often do not have extensive records from the past of the voices of children themselves. Although this kind of research was beyond the scope of most of the essays in this volume, the authors recognize the importance of attempting to uncover these voices.

perspectives on sin and the nature of children. By examining these various perspectives on the nature of children, the study provides a partial corrective to the current discussion of religion and child abuse, and it offers both "more negative" and "more positive" views of the nature of children that challenge many contemporary and often oversimplified conceptions of children.

Third, the study finds that several theologians took obligations and responsibilities toward children seriously: they emphasized the role of parents in the religious formation of children, outlined particular obligations of the church and the state, and understood care of and advocacy for children as central to Christian life and faith. By outlining some of these perspectives, the study can help to strengthen contemporary theological reflection on parenting and to foster further discussion about the responsibilities of the church, the community, and the state to children. The study also offers those within the church several theological grounds for child advocacy and prompts all readers — whatever our religious or philosophical commitments — to re-evaluate our own convictions about parental and communal responsibilities toward children and perhaps to discover obstacles that are preventing us from treating more children with care and compassion.

The following three sections provide a more complete discussion of each of these general claims and contributions of the volume and in this way highlight some of the most significant themes found within particular essays.

I. Contributions to the History of Christian Thought and of Conceptions of Childhood

By using childhood as a "lens" to examine the past, all of the essays in this volume reveal significant yet often ignored aspects of the ideas and practices of theologians and movements in the history of Christian thought. Just as when scholars have used gender as a category of analysis for understanding the past, when one uses the category of children, as the essays in this volume show, one is able to disclose neglected areas in the history of Christianity. This was the case especially with some of the most influential theologians. Authors found that although secondary literature exists on almost every aspect of the thought of these theologians, surprisingly little is written about their views of children, even when they had much to say about them. In the case of Friedrich Schleiermacher, for example, much more secondary literature has been devoted to his views of gender than to his views about children, even though he wrote as much or more about children than about relationships between men and women.

In general, the essays reveal a broader range of attitudes and behaviors toward children within Christian thought and often even within the work of a particular theologian than current secondary literature suggests. These varied attitudes and behaviors are based in part upon the diverse and sometimes seemingly contradictory notions about children that one finds in Scripture, as several essays recognize and as the essay by Judith Gundry-Volf fully addresses. Some biblical texts speak of children as gifts of God, signs of God's blessing, and sources of joy. Others depict children as ignorant and capricious and in need of education and strict discipline. Still others urge parents to love children with Christ-like compassion and not to provoke them to anger. In the Gospels, children are depicted in striking and even radical ways. At a time when children occupied a low position in society, Jesus receives children, blesses them, touches them, and heals them, and he is indignant toward those who have contempt for them. As Gundry-Volf emphasizes, Jesus identifies with a child and equates welcoming a little child in his name to welcoming himself and the One who sent him. Furthermore, he depicts children as models for adults of entering the reign of God, as models of greatness in this reign, and even as vehicles of divine revelation. The ways in which theologians wrestle with these diverse biblical texts and the particular texts that they eventually either incorporate into their theology or neglect determine in large part their particular perspectives on children and our obligations to them.

In addition, the study of past theological perspectives discloses that childhood has not always been a marginal theme in theology. Although references to children are often scattered throughout a theologian's writings and not discussed in a systematic way, many theologians, especially prior to the mid-nineteenth century, seriously reflected on issues of child rearing, education, and moral and spiritual formation. Several theologians wrote catechisms and were directly involved with the education of children and more practical concerns of the church. In the sixteenth century, for example, Luther and Calvin wrote catechisms for use in the home and encouraged parents, especially fathers, to take responsibility for the moral and spiritual formation of their children. We see attention to children even in the work of some nineteenth-century theologians, such as Horace Bushnell and Friedrich Scheiermacher, who both considered teaching children a crucial aspect of their ministry and theological reflection. However, this is generally not the case among most twentieth-century systematic theologians. Certainly the ideas of some central twentieth-century theologians, such as Karl Rahner and Karl Barth, can have rich implications for our view of children today, as the essays in this volume indicate. However, even they, like most theologians today, did not develop full-fledged teachings about children or their spiritual formation, and their attention to children is minimal.[21]

21. There are many reasons for this general lack of attention to children — reasons too complex to explore fully here. Two possible factors that developed during the nine-

By providing a fuller account of past theological perspectives on children, the essays also contribute to our understanding of the history of conceptions of childhood. In general, they offer a more nuanced and theologically informed picture of significant figures in Western thought regarding children than many historical studies have been able to provide. More particularly, a few essays also correct some common and inaccurate interpretations of specific figures. Several other essays also contribute to the discussion among historians regarding necessary correctives to the research of Philip Ariès regarding European attitudes toward children. As noted above, Ariès is an important scholar in the history of conceptions of childhood. According to Hugh Cunningham, he showed that "childhood has a history": "that over time and in different cultures, both ideas about childhood and the experience of being a child had changed."[22] Although his work is valued and has motivated other scholars to explore conceptions of childhood in various periods of history, historians have also challenged some of his findings. For example, he claimed that the "discovery of childhood" begins in the thirteenth century and that evidence of its development becomes more significant at the end of the sixteenth century and throughout the seventeenth.[23] Ariès also argued that prior to the late sixteenth and early seventeenth centuries, Europeans tended to treat children with indifference and a lack of affection.[24] Historians contesting these findings have shown that notions of childhood did exist in medieval thought[25] and that in the Reformation period adults were deeply interested in and affectionate toward children.[26] Several es-

---

teenth century were changes in the family and a deepening struggle with methodological questions in theology. As mothers took on more responsibility for the care and the moral and spiritual development of children, and as theologians focused more attention on philosophical issues regarding method, religious education itself became "feminized" and was seen as somehow "beneath" the job of the serious systematic theologian.

22. Cunningham, "Histories of Childhood," 1197.

23. Ariès, *Centuries of Childhood*, 47. Although, as Cunningham has shown, Ariès did not go so far as to say that the idea of childhood did not exist in medieval society (this is based on a mistranslation of Ariès), Ariès does argue that in the medieval world there seemed to be no place for childhood and little awareness of a particular nature of children that distinguishes them from adults. See Cunningham, "Histories of Childhood," 1197; and Ariès, *Centuries of Childhood*, 33, 128.

24. Ariès, *Centuries of Childhood*, 38-39. He claims that this was due in part to the high mortality rate of children. He also says that in the early eighteenth century, the relation between parents and children became increasingly sentimental and affectionate (Ariès, 370).

25. See, for example, Shahar, *Childhood in the Middle Ages*, and Schultz, *The Knowledge of Childhood in the German Middle Ages, 1100-1350*.

26. See, for example, Ozment, *When Fathers Ruled*, and Strauss, *Luther's House of Learning*.

says within this study — especially those on medieval and Reformation theologians by Cristina Traina, Barbara Pitkin, Jane Strohl, and Keith Graber Miller — build upon and contribute to this kind of historical work.

II. Perspectives on the Nature of Children

Theologians throughout history have held varied perspectives on the nature of children, particularly in regard to the notion of children as sinful. In their views of the nature of children, they have taken into account a number of issues that we continue to address today, such as the distinctive qualities of infants, the stages of child development, the differences between boys and girls, the differences between adults and children, approaches to discipline, the responsibilities of children to their parents, and levels of accountability for wrongdoing. Therefore, although one might be tempted to judge theologians on the basis of whether or not they view children as inherently sinful, as naturally good, or as possessing the potential for both good and evil, their positions are much more nuanced and diverse and can be neither easily criticized nor applauded.

Re-evaluating Original Sin and Punishment

One can appreciate the diversity of these perspectives by closely examining views of punishment among those theologians who believe that children in some sense inherit original sin. Although the majority of theologians represented in this volume claim that children are affected by original sin, they present distinctive perspectives on the nature of children and varied recommendations regarding their treatment. Some theologians use highly negative terms to describe the sinful nature of children and have a low estimate of the human ability to seek God or to love the neighbor, yet they do not recommend physically punishing children. For others, claiming that children inherit original sin goes hand-in-hand with harsh physical discipline of children. In still other cases, the idea of original sin, set within a particular larger theological framework, has fostered the more humane treatment of children, especially the poor.

For example, although Augustine and Calvin view children as affected by original sin, and although their views have been used in some cases to justify the harsh treatment of children, they speak about the nature of children in distinctive ways and do not recommend physically punishing children. Martha Stortz's essay, for example, reveals that although Augustine claims infants are born sinful and express sinful tendencies, he also recognizes they are physically unable to sin and thus are not yet guilty of specific sins. He claims that infants are in a state of what Stortz describes as "non-innocence": they are affected by original sin and thus not born innocent, but they are not yet guilty because they are unable physically to commit actual sins. As they grow, they gain speech and reasoning abilities, and gradually move from a state of non-innocence to a state of growing accountability for their actions. Furthermore, despite Augustine's near obsession with seeing evidence of sinful tendencies in very young children, he criticizes the physical punishment of children and emphasizes baptism, the example of others, and God's grace and God's love — not physical punishment — as vehicles for turning the corrupted will to God.

Barbara Pitkin's essay reminds readers that Calvin's view of the extent of sin and human depravity was more pessimistic than that of any of his predecessors and contemporaries. In keeping with this view, he claims that the "whole nature" of infants is a "seed of sin," and "thus it cannot be but hateful and abominable to God."[27] Despite these harsh words, Calvin, unlike Augustine before him or Edwards after him, does not dwell on evidences of corruption in small children. Furthermore, building on biblical passages, he says that infants are gifts of God and examples to adults and can proclaim God's goodness. Thus we see that Calvin, the theologian of "total depravity," is more appreciative of the positive character of children than are many Christians influenced by him. As Pitkin shows further, although Calvin's notion of the child's nature as a "seed of sin" was taken up by later Calvinists and other Protestants and used in some cases to justify the harsh treatment of children, Calvin himself did not argue for the physical punishment of children.

Although Jonathan Edwards, an eighteenth-century American Calvinist, appropriates and intensifies Calvin's severe language of the sinful child and is often accused of treating children harshly, even here the picture is more complicated, as the essay by Catherine Brekus indicates. Edwards is well-known for preaching openly and forcefully about infant damnation and childhood depravity, and he speaks directly and vividly to children themselves about the pains of hell and God's terrible wrath. However, although Edwards emphasizes the sinful nature of children, he also believes that they have rich spiritual lives and the potential for grace, and he claims that Christ loved even the poorest, humblest child. Furthermore, contrary to several historical studies, Brekus's study finds no concrete evidence that Edwards recommends the physical punishment of children. Although Brekus is critical of several aspects of Edwards's view and treatment of children, she concludes that he is neither as saintly nor as sinister as historians have often depicted him to be.

27. *Institutes of the Christian Religion: 1536 Edition,* trans. Ford Lewis Battles (Grand Rapids, Mich.: Eerdmans, 1975), 97. Quoted by Pitkin, 167.

In contrast to these positions, there are, of course, many clear cases in the history of Christianity in which original sin plays a role in supporting the harsh and even brutal treatment of children. This is especially clear in the essay by Clarissa Atkinson on the work of French Jesuits and Ursuline missionaries in the seventeenth century among the Huron Indians in Canada. Here, both theological ideas and cultural assumptions played a role in the physical punishment of Huron children. Atkinson claims that conversion of the Huron Indians was identified in large part with acceptance of French culture. Although the papal bull *Sublimis deus* of 1537 declared the indigenous peoples of the "New World" to be "true men," differences of dress, habit, and language caused the Jesuits and Ursulines to have some lingering doubts about the "full humanity" of the indigenous peoples. The missionaries were especially critical of the affection of the Huron toward their children and their rejection of physical punishment. In contrast to the Huron, the missionaries were enthusiastic proponents of corporal discipline in their schools, and they believed that one of the signs of accepting the Christian message among the Huron was that newly converted parents would begin physically punishing their children. Atkinson argues that one of the main reasons the missionaries insisted that children be taught in boarding schools away from home was to allow them to be "properly trained — that is, subjected to the corporal punishment that was taken for granted in French homes and schools."[28] This approach to children was supported not only by cultural assumptions but also by a view of human nature that depended heavily on Augustine and that departed significantly from the more Aristotelian and humanistic traditions of the Jesuit order. Thus, the approach of the French Jesuits toward the Huron children differed significantly from the approach of Spanish Jesuits who worked among indigenous peoples in Latin America during the previous century.

In still other cases, the idea of original sin, set within a particular theological framework, has fostered the more humane treatment of children. For example, my own essay on August Hermann Francke, an important German Pietist of the eighteenth century, shows that although he, like Augustine, Calvin, and others, believed that children are born with a fallen nature and even claimed that their "self-will" must be "broken," his particular understanding of "breaking the self-will" within the context of his major theological convictions led him not only to treat children with respect and kindness but also to pay attention to the needs of poor children. In contrast to John Locke and to many other contemporaries in his highly class-conscious period, Francke showed a concern for children that extended to orphans and children of the poor, and he built an extensive complex of charitable and educational institutions to address their needs. One of the most radical aspects of his schools was that he allowed poor students and orphans to be

---

28. See the essay in this volume by Clarissa W. Atkinson, 237.

educated according to their talents, and thus he allowed gifted students among them to prepare for a university education alongside children of the middle and upper classes. My essay shows that, when set within a rich theological context, original sin can provide a kind of positive, egalitarian framework of thought that opens a door to responding creatively and effectively to the needs of poor children and seeing them as individuals with gifts and talents that can be cultivated.

These essays and others in the volume add greater complexity to the picture of relationships between original sin and the treatment of children and in this sense provide a partial corrective to the current literature on the religious roots of child abuse. As noted above, this literature and other historical studies on children often assume that original sin is a key obstacle to the humane treatment of children.[29] The essays in this volume remind us that any judgments about the effect of the idea of original sin on the treatment of children must be made cautiously and always within the context of a thinker's larger philosophical, theological, cultural, and historical framework. Although some Christians who regard children as sinful have severely punished them, viewing children as sinful does not necessarily lead to the harsh treatment of children, and it is not always either the only or even the largest obstacle to their humane treatment.

Reconsidering Original Sin and Baptism

Several essays in this volume also illustrate the complexity of theological views of the nature of children and original sin by focusing on a theologian's view of baptism. (See especially those on Chrysostom, Augustine, Aquinas, Luther, Calvin, Simons, the Jesuits and the Ursulines, and Edwards.) For example, Cristina Traina shows how Aquinas incorporates into his view of children and baptism both the Augustinian notion that human beings are "fatally flawed by original sin" and the Aristotelian vision of "the rational person with the natural capacity to grow in virtue and wisdom."[30] Although he agrees with Augustine that because of original sin unbaptized infants are unworthy of salvation, he is also influenced by an Aristotelian view of human development and claims that infants are incapable of actual sin because they cannot yet reason or practice virtue. Thus, Aquinas believes that infants who die before baptism are sent to limbo. The influence of Aristotle led Aquinas to believe that infants are spared the pains of hell; it also

29. See, for example, Hugh Cunningham, *Children and Childhood in Western Society since 1500* (New York: Longman, 1995), 61-62. He claims that decline in belief in original sin, prompted in large part by the rise of secularism and by the ideas of Jean-Jacques Rousseau in the mid-eighteenth century, opened the door to the more sympathetic and humane treatment of children that many historians claim to find in the eighteenth century.

30. See the essay in this volume by Cristina Traina, 106.

16

shaped his understanding of differences between boys and girls. He assumed that girls are less rational than boys and therefore are inherently inferior. This mixture of Aristotelian and Augustinian ideas also led Aquinas to disregard biblical passages that speak of children as models for adults and to regard children mainly as incomplete and irrational beings who lack wisdom and virtue.

Menno Simons, a sixteenth-century Anabaptist leader, also articulated his understanding of the nature of children in relation to baptism, as Keith Graber Miller illustrates. Like his Protestant opponents, Simons acknowledged that children inherit "an Adamic nature predisposed toward sinning."[31] However, unlike his opponents, Simons rejected infant baptism. Furthermore, Simons distinguished between inherited sin and actual sinning, believing that "until the age of discretion," children remain "innocent" through the grace of Christ. His position becomes even more complex when one discovers that he was reluctant, along with other Anabaptists, to identify a precise age of discretion or accountability. As Graber Miller claims, for early Anabaptists and their present-day descendants, spiritual maturity does not always coincide with chronological maturity.

Providing Alternative Perspectives on Sin and Children

Other essays explore the ideas of theologians who reinterpret or even reject the notion of original sin as something children inherit and who provide alternative perspectives on sin and the nature of children. Instead of emphasizing the corrupt and sinful nature of children, some of these theologians focus on unjust familial and social structures that can negatively influence children, while others emphasize that children have the potential for both good and evil. As Margaret Bendroth claims, for example, Horace Bushnell, while not absolving children of sin, does state that children "by nature" do not need to choose evil, but they probably will because parental sins and unjust social structures are bound to negatively influence them. Thus, for Bushnell, children prompt reflection not so much on the dangers of a child's sinful nature but rather on elements in a child's culture or family life that could corrupt him or her; accordingly, he almost eliminates any discussion of a child's own responsibility. In her essay on Friedrich Schleiermacher, Dawn DeVries claims that he believed that children are born with as much potential for salvation as for sin, and that it is the duty of the parents to nurture their children's "higher self-consciousness," which connects them to the transcendent and thereby opens their hearts to love of others. In his essay, William Werpehowski discusses Karl Barth's view of sin and claims that although Barth takes human evil seriously, he rejects outright

31. See the essay in this volume by Keith Graber Miller, 194.

the "hereditary transmission of sin as an 'extremely unfortunate and mistaken' doctrine that would rule out a human agent's responsibility for the evil he or she does or becomes."[32]

Holding Up Children as Models of Faith

Among both those theologians who do and those who do not believe that sin is inherited, several take up the theme from the Gospels that children are models of faith and of entering the reign of God. Of course, these theologians provide distinctive — and in some cases inadequate — interpretations of the ways in which children are such models for adults. Nevertheless, their interpretations often lead them to regard children as something more than merely sinful and in need of instruction and thereby tend to complicate and enrich their discussions of the nature of children. Their ideas about children as models of spiritual maturity are based mainly on famous Gospel passages such as the following: "[Jesus] called a child, whom he put among them, and said, 'Truly I tell you, unless you change and become like children, you will never enter the kingdom of heaven. Whoever becomes humble like this child is the greatest in the kingdom of heaven. Whoever welcomes one such child in my name welcomes me'" (Matt. 18:2-5); "Jesus said, 'Let the little children come to me, and do not stop them; for it is to such as these that the kingdom of heaven belongs'" (Matt. 19:14); and "Whoever does not receive the kingdom of God as a little child will never enter it" (Luke 18:17). Thus, several essays in this volume discuss diverse interpretations of these and other biblical passages by particular theologians.

Of the theologians represented in this volume, the two who paid the most serious attention to the Gospel sayings of Jesus and who emphasized what children can teach adults are Friedrich Schleiermacher and Karl Rahner. Their theological positions led them to regard children both as human beings worthy of respect and dignity and as models for adults. Rahner, for example, incorporates several Gospel sayings in a very rich and striking view of the nature of children, which Mary Ann Hinsdale outlines. In contrast to those who, today and in the past, claim that children are not quite fully human — are beings "on the way" toward humanity — Rahner asserts that children have value and dignity in their own right and are fully human from the beginning. As a child's history unfolds, he or she realizes what he or she "already is." This view of children implies that we are to respect them and have reverence for them from the start and that they are a "sacred trust" to be nurtured and protected at every stage of their existence. Rahner also recognizes that Jesus uses children as examples of

---

32. See the essay in this volume by William Werpehowski, 391.

entering the reign of God. For Rahner, they are examples because they lack false ambition and artificiality, they do not seek honors or fame, and they are guileless and serene. Thus, as Rahner sees it, childhood is not only one stage of existence but also a "spiritually mature state" which is required to enter the reign of God and in which one has an attitude of "infinite openness" and wonder.

Re-examining Contemporary Conceptions of Children

By discussing the nature of children in such varied ways, the essays in this volume offer both "more negative" and "more positive" views that challenge some contemporary and often oversimplified conceptions of children. On the one hand, the views of those theologians who explore the sinful tendencies of children might be seen on the surface as "more negative" than current and commonly held views of children as innocent or as possessing the potential for both good and evil. However, these theologians recognize that children sometimes devote themselves to activities that are not always life-giving but instead are self-centered and harmful to themselves and others. By trying to take into account children's "sinful nature," these theologians at the same time are struggling to speak about the responsibilities of children and the possible levels of their accountability. Although one may not agree with their theological perspectives on sin and responsibility, theologians of the past might help readers question perspectives on children today that cannot adequately take into account a child's capacity to do harmful acts or to accept some degree of responsibility for those acts.

On the other hand, those theologians who lift up "more positive" conceptions of the nature of children by speaking of them as gifts of God, signs of divine blessing, images of God, vehicles of revelation, and examples to adults challenge us to re-examine other common attitudes toward children in the church and in contemporary culture. By speaking of children in such striking ways, these theologians warn those within the church not to be satisfied with theological teachings of children that depict them solely as sinful or in need of instruction. They also challenge all readers — whether inside or outside the church — to examine common yet harmful attitudes toward children in contemporary culture. For example, some scholars have argued that although we live in an apparently child-centered culture, our dominant attitude toward them is one of indifference and even contempt, as our treatment of poor children indicates.[33] Others assert that our attitude toward children is shaped pri-

33. Anderson and Johnson, *Regarding Children,* 13-18. Here they base some of their ideas on the work of sociologist Floyd M. Martinson. They also suggest that contempt for

marily by the logic of capitalism, and thus we view children not as beings with intrinsic worth but rather primarily as commodities, consumers, or economic burdens.[34] Much of the popular literature tends to depict infants and young children as pure and innocent beings whom we adore and teenagers as hidden and dark creatures whom we must fear. By examining such common contemporary attitudes in conversation with past theological perspectives, all readers might find ways to foster new conceptions of children; to treat them with respect and dignity; to explore the gifts they offer to families and communities; and to articulate more sophisticated theological and philosophical perspectives of them.

III. Insights into Obligations to Children

Although obligations toward children have been a marginal theme in contemporary theology, several essays in this volume find that a number of theologians in the past devoted attention to it, and they outlined specific responsibilities not only of parents but also of the church and the state. Furthermore, many of them understood care of and advocacy for children to be central to Christian faith and life.

Theological Reflections on Parenting

Although theologians today and in the past have at times neglected the vocation of parenting in favor of articulating a vision of the celibate life, several theologians examined in this volume recognize that parenting is a serious calling and a significant spiritual discipline, and they outline particular goals and duties of parenting. This emphasis on the vocation of parenting can be found in almost all of the essays, especially those on Chrysostom, Aquinas, Calvin, Luther, Simons, Francke, Schleiermacher, Bushnell, and feminist theologians. The essay by Vigen Guroian, for example, describes in detail the perspectives on parenting of John Chrysostom, an important figure both in the early church and for Eastern Orthodox communities of faith today. Chrysostom's understanding of the role of parenting and the home, which is grounded in his views of the Trinity, Christ, and the church, is described in rich metaphorical terms.

---

children is fostered within a culture that values strength and self-sufficiency and rejects human weakness and vulnerability.

34. Whitmore, "An Undeveloped Theme in Catholic Teaching," 167-75.

For example, he speaks of parents as "artists" who sculpt statues with great precision, for they are helping to restore the image of God in their offspring and thereby forming them into "wondrous statues for God." He also likens the task of parents to Christ's action for all of humanity. Just as Christ is the teacher for all of humankind, parents are to be teachers of their children. He also speaks of the family as a "little church" or "sacred community." Furthermore, he outlines in detail the obligations of parents, such as reading their children the Bible, praying with them, and being good examples. He ranks the neglect of children among the greatest evils and injustices, and he makes the striking claim that the salvation of parents is dependent on the virtue of their children.[35] Guroian offers this quote from Chrysostom: "One's own virtue is not enough for salvation, but the virtue of those for whom we are responsible is also required."[36]

Theologians of the Reformation represented in this volume also outline in detail the obligations of parents toward their children, and thus they confirm the claim of Steven Ozment, a Reformation historian, that "never has the art of parenting been more highly praised and parental authority more wholeheartedly supported than in Reformation Europe."[37] Jane Strohl's essay on Luther, for example, describes how he rejects the idea, common in his day, that certain states of life and occupations are religiously superior or more spiritual, such as taking up the vocation of the priesthood or monasticism. Instead, he insists that all believers are equal members of the priesthood of all believers.[38] Thus, they can exercise this priesthood in a wide variety of socially productive vocations. He clearly articulates the importance of the vocation of parenting when he says, "Most certainly father and mother are apostles, bishops, and priests to their children, for it is they who make them acquainted with the gospel. In short, there is no greater or nobler authority on earth than that of parents over their children, for this authority is both spiritual and temporal."[39] Luther wants parents to help their children to become mature confessors of the faith and responsible members of the community, and he outlines specific duties of parents. They are, for example, to baptize their children, expose them to the Word and the sacraments, read the Bible with them, pray with them, teach them about the faith, provide them with a good education that prepares them for ser-

35. He builds on Matthew 18:6 and the biblical story of Eli, who had two disobedient sons, to support his position (1 Sam. 2:12-36 and 4:12-18).

36. John Chrysostom, *On Marriage and Family Life,* trans. Catherine P. Roth and David Anderson (Crestwood, N.Y.: St. Vladimir's Seminary Press, 1986), 72.

37. Ozment, *When Fathers Ruled,* 132.

38. See the essay in this volume by Jane Strohl, 139.

39. Cited in Jane Strohl's essay, 140. Quoted from *Luther's Works,* ed. Jaroslav Pelikan and Helmut Lehmann, 55 vols. (St. Louis: Concordia Publishing House, 1955-1986), 45:46.

vice in the world, and help them find a proper mate. Luther also wrote cate-chisms to aid parents in cultivating the life of faith among the young. In Lu-ther's emphasis on parenting we see a striking paradox. Although Luther strongly emphasized that faith comes only through God's grace and God's ac-tivity, and although he was not as certain as Chrysostom before him and Bushnell after him that a proper upbringing results in faith, he did believe that nurturing faith in children is an urgent task and that faith comes in large part as a result of the diligent work of parents, teachers, and other adults.[40]

Bushnell and Schleiermacher, two nineteenth-century theologians, also emphasize the vocation of parenting and the importance of daily rituals and practices in the home for nurturing faith. Schleiermacher, a Reformed theolo-gian, believes that the Christian home is the "first and irreplaceable school of faith," for only here can children actually experience the full range of Christian religious affections and come to a living faith in Christ. As Dawn DeVries ex-plains, Schleiermacher sees faith as something "caught" more than "taught." Thus, the best way to enter the religious life is by observing the good example of parents and by participating in family worship and Bible study. Schleiermacher, a keen observer of children, urges parents to build trust in their relationships with children by taking their concerns and interests seriously, by responding empathetically to their needs, and by resisting the temptation to live out their own dreams and aspirations through their children. He also advises parents to control their own emotional responses to children; to allow children to play; and to teach them to obey. Lifting up Gospel sayings, Schleiermacher also em-phasizes that children are models who teach adults to live simply and in the present and to be flexible and forgiving.

Like Chrysostom, Bushnell, a leading Congregationalist pastor and scholar, also speaks of the family as a "little church." Although he sees the im-portant role that the church plays in the faith development of children, he be-lieves that the primary agent of grace is the family, not the church. "Religion never thoroughly penetrates life," he says, "until it becomes domestic."[41] His popular book *Christian Nurture* envisions spiritual formation as a natural pro-cess that adults encourage not merely by reading the Bible and teaching chil-dren aspects of the faith but also through everyday practices and routines and the examples of adults. Thus, he stresses the heroic importance of "small things" and claims that "it requires less piety . . . to be a martyr for Christ than it

40. As Gerald Strauss succinctly concludes and as Strohl confirms, only in the for-mal theology of Luther and other Reformers was "a sharp and final distinction made be-tween human effort and divine grace" (*Luther's House of Learning*, 39).

41. Horace Bushnell, *Christian Nurture* (New York: Charles Scribner, 1861; reprint, Cleveland: Pilgrim Press, 1994), 63. Quoted by Bendroth, 356.

does to . . . maintain a perfect and guileless integrity in the common transactions of life."[42] He also encourages parents to interweave lessons about the faith with play and a variety of fun activities. Like Chrysostom, Bushnell also has high expectations for parental influence. He believes that it would be almost impossible for a child who has been properly nurtured to reject the Christian faith. In the face of criticism by several of his contemporaries who claim that godly parents sometimes produce ungodly children for no apparent reason, Bushnell responds that there are so many ways to account for the failure of child rearing that doubts about his argument are unwarranted. He also claims that parents who neglect the spiritual well-being of their children will be judged by God.

Although a child's obedience to parents is clearly a biblical theme that is echoed in the work of most of the theologians represented in this volume who discuss the vocation of parenting, it is important to note that the grounds for this obedience vary, and in most cases obedience is not absolute. Several theologians who explicitly emphasize obedience and parental authority also cite specific reasons why children should not obey their parents. Calvin, for example, states that if parents lead their children to violate God's law, then children should regard their parents as strangers. Furthermore, citing Ephesians 6:4, many of them remind parents not to provoke their children to anger. For example, although Barth believes that parents are "God's natural and primary representatives" for children,[43] he claims that raising children "'in the discipline and instruction of the Lord' excludes provoking them to the anger, resistance and rebellion that emerges through the 'assertion of Law, or the execution of judgment.'" Instead, parents are "joyfully" to invite children to "rejoice" with them in God.[44]

By examining the theme of children from a theological perspective, this volume opens the door to more serious theological reflection on the vocation of parenting and the spiritual dimensions of the experience of raising children. Many parents recognize that parenting is a deeply spiritual endeavor that challenges them to rethink central theological concepts such as God, creation, and sin. It also allows many opportunities for parents to reflect upon and practice central Christian virtues, such as charity, patience, forgiveness, and humility. However, theology today offers few resources and little encouragement for articulating these themes. These essays and recent studies on the role of parents in

---

42. "Living to God in Small Things," in *Sermons for the New Life* (New York: Charles Scribner's Sons, 1904), 291-92. Quoted by Bendroth, 356.

43. Barth, *Church Dogmatics* III/4, trans. G. W. Bromiley (Edinburgh: T. & T. Clark, 1961), 242, 245; as cited in the essay by William Werpehowski, 395.

44. See the essay in this volume by William Werpehowski, 399, 405.

the faith formation of children might also help to urge parents to take a more active role in the spiritual formation of their children. Many people in the church today believe that programs offered in their congregations provide the primary place for the faith formation of children, and congregational leaders themselves have erred in allowing the focus of faith development to shift away from the family and to become centered in the congregation.[45] As recent studies show and as several essays in the volume argue, however, the family has the most potential of any institution for shaping the spiritual and moral lives of children.[46] Thus, the best vehicles for the transmission of faith to children are family rituals, family service projects, and meaningful conversations with children in the home.

Responsibilities of the Church, the State, and the Community

Although many essays in this volume emphasize the importance of parents in the nurturing of children, almost all of them show that in most periods not only the parents but also the church and the state are seen as playing significant roles in the protection and even the moral and spiritual formation of children. Raising and educating children are often seen as important tasks that require a cooperative effort between the home, the church, the community, and the state. Several essays speak about the state's role in providing for children and protecting them. For example, Calvin believed that it was society's duty to provide the right conditions for raising children to godliness and believed that all children should attend schools. Luther also urged civil authorities to provide universal education for both boys and girls, and he doubted that most parents "have the competence, breadth of knowledge or time" to educate their own children.[47] Other essays emphasize that moral and spiritual messages received at home must be supported by church and state so that these messages will take root in the hearts of children. Several other theologians also recognize that the state, the church, and the schools need to participate in the protection and the moral formation of children because they acknowledge that some parents are bad ex-

45. Merton Strommen, "A Family's Faith, a Child's Faith," *Dialog* 37 (Summer 1998): 177.

46. Merton Strommen, the founder of both the Search Institute and the Youth and Family Institute at Augsburg College, claims that "the family is the most powerful institution in promoting faith in children and youth." See "A Family's Faith, a Child's Faith," 177. See also Browning et al., *From Culture Wars to Common Ground*, 308. See also the work of Marjorie Thompson, *Family: The Forming Center: A Vision of the Role of Family in Spiritual Formation* (Nashville: Upper Room Books, 1996).

47. See the essay in this volume by Jane Strohl, 150-53.

amples and even neglect their children. Schleiermacher and Francke, for example, address the problem of bad parental role models, and Aquinas provides at least theoretical grounds for civil protection of children from negligent parents.

In her essay, Bonnie Miller-McLemore claims that although feminist theologians have spoken more indirectly than directly about children, they have had much to say about our obligations to children and the task of "widening the communal parameters of adult accountability in bearing and rearing children in terms of the roles of both the church and the state."[48] For example, in addition to arguing for "radical revision of paternal responsibility"[49] and the shared responsibilities of parents to nurture their children, feminist theologians have also urged the church to take seriously the needs of children and families. Some have suggested retrieving a religious motif of "adoption" that can transcend common structures of family and create covenants of extra-biological, extra-legal kinship. Others have recommended revitalizing the practice of naming godparents. Feminist theologians have also written frankly about parental struggles and family strife and the urgent need for congregations to address openly such struggles and to provide support for families. Several feminist theologians have also focused attention on the responsibilities of the state to create an environment and a legal system that are supportive of families. Many of them believe that religious commitment calls for serious engagement with public policies on pressing issues that affect children, such as welfare, poverty, and health-care benefits for families.[50]

Child Advocacy: Central to a Vision of Christian Faith and Life

As they articulate responsibilities of parents, the church, and the state toward children, some theologians strongly connect care of and advocacy for children to their vision of Christian life and faith. The calls to love the neighbor, to seek justice, to help the poor, to serve others, and to heal the sick are common themes within the Christian tradition as a whole but are not always applied to the needs of children. Several of the essays in this volume, however, clearly tie a view of the Christian life and service to the care of children. For example, although John Wesley's statements about the discipline of children are harsh and appear to follow the severe recommendations of his mother, his understanding of Christian life and discipleship led him to show a strong commitment to poor children, as Richard Heitzenrater shows. Like Francke and other Pietists who

48. See the essay in this volume by Bonnie Miller-McLemore, 468.
49. See Miller-McLemore's essay, 469.
50. See Miller-McLemore's essay, 469.

influenced Methodism, Wesley believed that a central part of the Christian life is service to the poor. Thus, he refused to accept many of the common assumptions of class and gender of his period. He provided education for poor students and for girls, and he mixed students from different social and economic backgrounds in his schools. In addition, he helped establish several institutions to care for the sick and the poor. His strong commitment to serving the needs of the poor still influences the educational and social programs in the Methodist Church today.[51]

The essay by Marcia Riggs shows how black women's clubs of the nineteenth century clearly connected caring for children with the mandate to work for social justice. The black women's clubs were a social-religious movement that worked for reform in society. One of their major emphases was the welfare of children. They provided children and young people with schooling and training for jobs and educated parents and teachers about the moral and spiritual development of children. Much of the impetus for the movement came from the struggles of the African American community, from the leadership of women like Mary Church Terrell, and from the ideas of the Social Gospel movement, which was responding to social problems and working for social justice for the oppressed. Drawing on all these influences, the black women's clubs emphasized the justice of God and the need to change individual lives and social structures to create a just society for all people, including children.

The Gospels themselves closely tie discipleship to care for and service of children. As Judith Gundry-Volf argues, in a dispute among the disciples about who is the greatest, Jesus takes a little child in his arms and teaches his disciples to "welcome" or "receive" *(dechomai)* one such little child in his name. Here, welcoming or receiving is more than a display of affection; it is a demonstration of service and hospitality. Jesus' teaching is striking because at that time children occupied the lowest rung on the social ladder, and caring for them was regarded as an undistinguished activity that belonged to the domain of women. His teaching about true greatness among the disciples places children at the center of the Christian community's attention "as prime objects of its love and service" and "requires of all who would be great in the community to serve children."[52]

---

51. See, for example, the United Methodist Church's *Bishops' Initiative on Children and Poverty.*

52. See the essay in the volume by Judith Gundry-Volf, 43-44.

Contemporary Reflections on Communal Obligations to Children and Grounds for Advocacy

By discussing the responsibilities of parents, the church, and the state to children, and by tying Christian faith and life to care of and advocacy for children, these essays invite all readers to reflect on their own understanding of communal obligations to children and to explore their own grounds for child advocacy. For those inside the church, the essays provide several theological foundations for making child ministry, religious education, and child advocacy vital parts of church ministry. Although many churches have developed effective and creative programs to address the needs of children,[53] the church as a whole has not taken a strong leadership role in child advocacy. Education about the situation of children today and about theological grounds for child advocacy may well be a key to solving this problem. We can recall that the church began taking more of an active role in the ecological movement once environmental problems and theological foundations for environmental responsibility were clear. Similarly, educating the church about the theological foundations for concern for children might help motivate the church to do more to address the challenges that children face today; to pay more attention to their spiritual and moral formation; to contribute more significantly to the public debate on children; and to help enact state and federal legislation and programs that can help families and children.[54] The essays prompt all readers — whatever our philosophical or religious commitments — to re-evaluate our own convictions about communal responsibilities toward children and perhaps to discover obstacles that are preventing us from treating more children with care and compassion.

---

53. Some of this work is taking place through several creative initiatives, such as through the work spawned by the *Bishops' Initiative on Children and Poverty* of the United Methodist Church, through the Search Institute, and through the Youth and Family Institute at Augsburg College in Minnesota. Many churches also serve communities by offering day-care facilities. According to one study, 98 percent of church-housed day-care programs are open to all members of the community; see Eileen W. Lindner, Mary Mattis, and June Rogers, *When Churches Mind the Children: A Study of Day Care in Local Parishes* (Ypsilanti, Mich.: High/Scope Press, 1983), 37.

54. Marian Wright Edelman, president and founder of the Children's Defense Fund, has made eloquent and powerful appeals on behalf of children and has urged churches to help address the challenges that children face today in these and others ways. The Children's Defense Fund offers several programs that work with churches to strengthen child advocacy ministry.

Conclusion

By critically examining both the problems and the possibilities of past theological perspectives on children, this book provides an occasion to re-examine the limits and the possibilities of our own current assumptions about children and our obligations to them. Like other historical studies of childhood, it also helps to provide a more complete and, in some cases, more accurate account of past perspectives on children. Furthermore, it exposes the inadequacy of current theological perspectives that either ignore children altogether or define them too narrowly as sinful, disobedient, and in need of instruction. By examining the complex relationships between ideas about children and central theological themes, such as baptism, sin, faith, and discipleship, this study also provides resources for strengthening theological and ethical reflection on children and helps establish it as a legitimate area of theological inquiry. Like the growing studies of children in many other disciplines outside theology, these essays also remind us that any accurate and meaningful account of human beings and their relationships cannot be built solely on the thoughts and actions of adults but must also take into account the development and the full humanity of children.

1. The Least and the Greatest:
Children in the New Testament

JUDITH M. GUNDRY-VOLF

The New Testament teaching on children forms the background for much of the Christian thought about children to be discussed in the present book. The main purpose of this essay is to introduce the reader to the material on children in the New Testament[1] in such a way that its main aspects come to light and the disparate traditions are set in a plausible relation to each other (though I will not be considering the possible influence of one tradition on the other). In particular, I am interested in how one may relate the profounder and more striking aspects of the New Testament material, which appear in Jesus' teaching on the reign of God and discipleship and in his ministry of healing and exorcism, to the more mundane (though not unimportant!) aspects, which appear in apostolic reflections on the family. Various studies have already been written on children in the New Testament as well as on individual New Testament texts dealing with children, and the material in the Synoptic Gospels has received the most attention.[2] But to my knowledge no study exists that attempts to do precisely what I have proposed.

1. I will exclude texts that refer only to adult children, speak of children metaphorically rather than literally (with a couple of exceptions), or refer to Jesus as an infant or a child. When the Synoptic Gospels share the same material on children, I will discuss the Markan versions, although Matthew's special or significantly redacted material will receive separate treatment. The Greek terms for children that appear in the texts discussed below are *brephos* (baby, infant), *pais* (child, son), *paidion* (little child), *teknon* (child), *kosarion* (little girl), and *nepios* (infant, minor).

2. See Kurt Aland, "Die Stellung der Kinder in den Frühen christlichen Gemeinde — und ihre Taufe," in *Neutestamentliche Entwürfe*, Theologische Bücherei Neues Testament 63 (München: Chr. Kaiser, 1979), 198-232; James Francis, "Children and Childhood

An investigation that shows what traditions about children were available in the New Testament to subsequent Christian thinkers and how one may relate those traditions to each other will enable readers of this volume better to assess the use of the New Testament tradition in the history of Christian thought: Which traditions have been ignored or de-emphasized? Which stressed? And how have they been adapted to new needs and purposes? This kind of investigation will also help New Testament specialists interested in the interrelationships between traditions on children in the New Testament.

In what follows I will give first a brief sketch of the understanding and roles of children in Greco-Roman antiquity, then an analysis of the material on children in the Gospels, followed by that in the epistles. "Jesus" in the following text means not the "historical Jesus" — a historical reconstruction of the earthly Jesus — but the *Jesus of the Gospels.* A *historian* should place all the references to Jesus in quotation marks: "Jesus."

---

in the New Testament," in *The Family in Theological Perspective,* ed. Stephen C. Barton (Edinburgh: T. & T. Clark, 1996), 65-85; G. R. Beasley-Murray, "Church and Child in the New Testament," *Baptist Quarterly* 21 (1965-66): 206-18; R. E. Clemens, "The Relation of Children to the People of God in the Old Testament," *Baptist Quarterly* 21 (1965-66): 195-205; John Dominic Crossan, *The Historical Jesus: The Life of a Mediterranean Jewish Peasant* (San Francisco: Harper, 1991), 265-302; S. Légasse, *Jésus et L'Enfant: "Enfant," "Petits" et "Simples" dans la Tradition Synoptique* (Paris: Lecoffre, 1969); J. Kodell, "Luke and the Children," *Catholic Biblical Quarterly* 49 (1987): 415-30; Peter Müller, *In der Mitte der Gemeinde: Kinder im Neuen Testament* (Neukirchen-Vluyn: Neukirchener, 1992); Hans-Hartmut Schroeder, *Eltern und Kinder in der Verkündigung Jesu: Eine hermeneutische und exegetische Untersuchung,* Theologische Forschung 53 (1972); Hans-Ruedi Weber, *Jesus and the Children: Biblical Resources for Study and Preaching* (Geneva: World Council of Churches, 1979). The following articles in *Semeia* 29 (1983) address the issue of Jesus and children: John Dominic Crossan, "Kingdom and Children: A Study in the Aphoristic Tradition," 75-95; Daniel Patte, "Jesus' Pronouncement about Entering the Kingdom Like a Child: A Structural Exegesis," 3-42; Vernon Robbins, "Pronouncement Stories and Jesus' Blessing of the Children: A Rhetorical Approach," 43-77. The question of infant baptism has received special treatment; see Joachim Jeremias, *Infant Baptism in the First Four Centuries* (Philadelphia: Westminster, 1960); Kurt Aland, *Did the Early Church Baptize Infants?* trans. G. R. Beasley-Murray (London: SCM, 1963); and others (see the summary in Beasley-Murray, "Church and Child in the New Testament," 208-9). Works devoted to individual New Testament texts discussed here are listed in the notes below.

Children in Greco-Roman Antiquity

To be properly understood, the New Testament material on children must be viewed within its historical and cultural setting.[3] Below I will sketch the basic contours of the understanding and roles of children in Greco-Roman antiquity that are significant for reading the New Testament texts. The material is divided up according to two social and religious contexts, the Hellenistic context and the Jewish context, which significantly overlap with, as well as differ from, each other. Additional background material relevant to particular texts will be incorporated into the exegetical discussions that follow.

The Hellenistic Context

There were two contrasting sentiments toward children in a first-century Greco-Roman context.[4] On the one hand, parents loved and took pleasure in their children, as ancient letters and funerary inscriptions attest;[5] they valued children as necessary to their economic survival and well-being and as heirs in whom they would live on after death. The state considered children indispensable for eco-

3. As many Christian scholars writing on the family in the New Testament have already noted, the New Testament partly shares the basic patriarchal and androcentric framework of its wider cultural setting; for further discussion on this point, see, for example, Carolyn Osiek, "Families in Early Christianity," *The Family Handbook*, ed. Herbert Anderson et al. (Louisville, Ky.: Westminster John Knox, 1998), 287-90; Scott Bartchy, "Families in the Greco-Roman World," in *The Family Handbook*, 282-86.

4. For a more detailed discussion of this background material, the reader should consult the specialized works in the notes. Major treatments include K. R. Bradley, *Discovering the Roman Family* (New York: Oxford University Press, 1991); James Casey, *The History of the Family* (Oxford: Basil Blackwell, 1989); Suzanne Dixon, *The Roman Family* (Baltimore: The Johns Hopkins University Press, 1992); Peter Garnsey and Richard Saller, *The Roman Empire: Economy, Society, and Culture* (Berkeley and Los Angeles: University of California Press, 1987); A. Oepke, παῖς, κτλ., *Theological Dictionary of the New Testament* (Grand Rapids, Mich.: Eerdmans, 1968), 5.636-654 (639-45); *The Family in Ancient Rome: New Perspectives*, ed. Beryl Rawson (Ithaca, N.Y.: Cornell University Press, 1986); Richard P. Saller, *Patriarchy, Property, and Death in the Roman Family* (Cambridge: Cambridge University Press, 1994); W. Stegemann, "Lasset die Kinder zu mir kommen: Socialgeschichtliche Aspekte des Kinderevangeliums," in *Traditionen der Befreiung*, vol. 1, ed. W. Schottroff and W. Stegemann (Munich: Kaiser; Gelnhausen, Berlin, Stein: Burckhardthaus-Laetare, 1980), 114-44; Thomas Wiedemann, *Adults and Children in the Roman Empire* (New Haven and London: Yale University Press, 1989).

5. See the letters of Cicero (discussed in Wiedemann, *Adults and Children in the Roman Empire*, 84-89); Seneca *De Consolatione ad Marciam* 9.2; *Epistulae* 9.7, 99.23; Fronto *Ad amicos* 1.12; cf. Garnsey and Saller, *The Roman Empire*, 139.

nomic, cultural, and military purposes.[6] On the other hand, childhood was viewed largely negatively as a state of immaturity to outgrow. The standard of measurement was the free adult male Roman citizen. Apart from the so-called rediscovery of the child in Hellenism, in which poets, painters, sculptors, and the rich showed an interest in children and their antics for their own pleasure,[7] people considered children fundamentally deficient and not yet human in the full sense.[8] They were physically small, underdeveloped, and vulnerable.[9] They were mentally deficient and ignorant; they spoke nonsense and failed to think and plan rationally; they were capricious, foolish, and quarrelsome. In a word, they lacked the prime Roman virtue of reason and could not participate in the rational world of Roman citizens. The Roman philosopher Cicero wrote concerning childhood, "the thing itself cannot be praised, only its potential," and categorically denied the desirability of reverting in any sense to the state of childhood.[10]

In light of these attitudes, it is not surprising that children occupied a low rung on the social ladder.[11] The most powerful evidence for this low status is the legal position of children and the brutal practices toward children allowed by Ro-

6. Wiedemann, *Adults and Children in the Roman Empire*, 25-26, 32-43; Garnsey and Saller, *The Roman Empire*, 141-45. Cf. the speech attributed to Augustus by Cassius Dio (*Roman History* 56.3): "Is it not a joy to acknowledge a child who possesses the qualities of both parents, to tend and educate a person who is both the physical and the mental mirror of yourself, so that, as he grows up, another self is created? Is it not a blessing, when we leave this life, to leave behind as our successor an heir both to our family and to our property, one that is our own, born of our own essence, so that only the mortal part of us passes away, while we live on in the child who succeeds us?" The speech was designed to encourage Roman aristocrats, who needed only one male heir, to have more children so as to ensure the future of the aristocracy. But the emperor's attempt to increase the aristocratic population failed, which suggests that his views were not widely shared. The state also encouraged marriage and procreation in the general populace in order to gain future laborers and (male) soldiers.

7. See Oepke, παῖς, 639. Oepke cites the Hellenistic rediscovery of the child as an exception to the decline in the classical period (under discussion here) from the more positive views of the child found in the pre-Greek Mediterranean world and the early Greek world (640-41).

8. See Müller, *In der Mitte der Gemeinde*, 89-110, 161-64.

9. Infant and child mortality was high in the classical city, and children were thought to have a greater liability to sickness and fright (Wiedemann, *Adults and Children in the Roman Empire*, 11-21).

10. Cicero *De Republica*, p. 137.3 ed Ziegler frag. incert. 5; cf. also *On Old Age*, 83; cf. Wiedemann, *Adults and Children in the Roman Empire*, 7, 21-25.

11. Stegemann suggests that the social status of children can be compared with that of slaves. The use of the same or etymologically related terms for "child" and "slave" (see *The Greek-English Lexicon of the New Testament*, s.v. παῖς; παιδίσκη) mirrors the social similarities between the two (Stegemann, "Lasset die Kinder zu mir kommen," 123; cf. Müller, *In der Mitte der Gemeinde*, 190-92, 195).

man law. Children had no rights of their own and were legally subject to their father, who had almost absolute power over them. According to Dionysius of Halicarnassus, "the law-giver of the Romans gave virtually full power to the father over his son, whether he thought proper to imprison him, to scourge him, to put him in chains, and keep him at work in the fields, or to put him to death."[12]

The Roman father's authority was supremely demonstrated in his "power of life and death" over his children. He could decide whether to recognize a newborn and raise it, or to expose it (cast it out in a public place). Although the frequency of exposition is debated, it was practiced at every sociocultural level in the Roman world, and, as Peter Garnsey and Richard Saller argue, continued until the late fourth century.[13] Ancient writers certainly assumed, as Thomas Wiedemann shows, "that belief in the exposition of unwanted babies was widespread"; "the fulminations of Stoic moralists, Jews, and Christians . . . suggest that infanticide and exposition were sufficiently widespread for these groups to need to express their moral outrage."[14] Some pagan writers were, in fact, surprised that Jewish parents did not adopt these practices.[15] Females were especially vulnerable to exposition, as a letter from a husband to his pregnant wife (ca. 100 C.E.) suggests: "If by chance you bear a child, if it is a boy, let it be, if it is a girl, cast it out."[16] Exposed infants would die, unless they were (as expected)[17] picked up by strangers, in which

---

12. Dionysius of Halicarnassus *Rom. Ant.* 2.26.4; cf. Beryl Rawson, "Children in the Roman *Familia*," in *The Family in Ancient Rome*, 170-200; J. E. Boswell, "*Expositio* and *oblatio:* The Abandonment of Children and the Ancient and Medieval Family," *American Historical Review* 89 (1984): 10-33; Garnsey and Saller, *The Roman Empire*, 136-41; Müller, *In der Mitte der Gemeinde*, 107-8.

13. Garnsey and Saller, *The Roman Empire*, 136 (further literature in n. 35); cf. Rawson, "Children in the Roman *Familia*," 246 (further literature there). The ancient Spartan practice of exposing deformed children is referred to by Plutarch *Lycurgus* 16.1ff. Poverty as a common motive is indicated by Stobaeus *Eclogae* 75. Yet the rich also practiced exposition (see Weber, *Jesus and the Children*, 6-7).

14. Wiedemann, *Adults and Children in the Roman Empire*, 36. Cf. Dionysius of Halicarnassus *Roman Antiquities* 2.27.1; Pseudo-Plutarch *De Liberis Educandis* 12; Quintilian 7.4.27; Ps.-Phocylides 207-9; Plutarch *Moralia* II 8F-9A; Menander in Stobaeus, IV 26.3ff. = Hense II, p. 650.1ff.; Philo, *De Specialibus Legibus* 3.108-19; *Hypothetica* 7.7; Josephus, *c. Ap.* 2.24 § 202; Ps.-Phocylides 184-85. Cf. Andrew Lincoln, *Ephesians*, WBC Series, vol. 42 (Dallas: Word, 1990), 399-400; Ernest Best, *Ephesians*, ICC Series (Edinburgh: T. & T. Clark, 1998), 568.

15. Cf. Menahem Stern, *Greek and Latin Authors on Jews and Judaism*, 3 vols., Fontes Ad Res Judaicas Spectantes (Jerusalem: The Israel Academy of Sciences and Humanities, 1976-84), 1.33-34, 2.41.

16. POxy IV 744, cited by J. L. White, *Light from Ancient Letters* (Philadelphia: Fortress, 1986), 111-12.

17. Garnsey and Saller, *The Roman Empire*, 138.

case they might be raised for profit as slaves, prostitutes, or beggars (sometimes having been mutilated for this purpose). (Ironically, children's marginalized status also made them suitable mediators with the divine world and suited them for special roles in cultic settings for which normal adults were unsuited,[18] although children's less rational nature and sexual purity have also been proposed as reasons for these roles.)[19]

Childhood was viewed above all as a training ground for adult life, not as a valuable stage of life in itself.[20] This accounts for the great stress placed on education. A. Oepke comments that "there is hardly any word which better denotes the ancient estimation of children than *erudire*. Plut Lib. Educ., II, 1-14 everywhere presupposes that only by strenuous educative effort, and only then with normal gifts and the right technique, can something be made of the raw material."[21] "The right technique" included strict discipline and often painful corporeal punishment to ensure results.[22]

The Old Testament-Jewish Context

Children have a fundamentally positive significance and role in Old Testament-Jewish tradition.[23] We find, first of all, testimonies to parental love and pleasure in children, such as 4 Maccabees 15:4 ("O how may I express the passionate love of parents for children . . . ?"[24]) and anecdotes suggesting the same. For instance, according to a second-century rabbinic tradition, a rabbi who was observed crawling on his hands and feet with a reed in his mouth and following his son explained his behavior by saying, "You see that when a man loves to have children, he acts like a fool" (*Midrash* Ps. 92,14.206b §

18. Cf. Müller, *In der Mitte der Gemeinde*, 117-123; Oepke, παῖς, 640-45.

19. Cf. Wiedemann, *Adults and Children in the Roman Empire*, 176-86; Oepke, παῖς, 643-45.

20. Cf. Oepke, παῖς, 640.

21. Oepke, παῖς, 642.

22. Cf. Seneca *De Constantia Sapientis* 12.3, who justifies admonishing children "with pain and ill" which "overcomes their obstinacy"; Marcus Aurelius *Reflections* 5,9; 11,6; 10,36, who assumes an association between beating and the schooling of children. By contrast, Quintilian (*Institutio Oratoria* I, 1, 20) condemned flogging in Roman schools and advocated praising pupils for good performance and other humane educational practices. Cf. Wiedemann, *Adults and Children in the Roman Empire*, 9-10, 27-30; Weber, *Jesus and the Children*, 7.

23. For more detailed discussion on the following, see Oepke, παῖς, 645-48; Joachim Jeremias, *New Testament Theology*, vol. 1: *The Proclamation of Jesus* (London: SCM, 1971), 227-28; Müller, *In der Mitte der Gemeinde*, 123-61.

24. See Francis, "Children and Childhood in the New Testament," 71n. 11.

13).[25] Children are, more fundamentally, a divine gift and sign of God's blessing, in accordance with the very blessing of the Creator upon humanity in primal history: "Male and female he created them. God blessed them and God said to them, 'Be fruitful and multiply, and fill the earth . . . !'" (Gen. 1:27-28). Abundant children were an abundant blessing and a great source of joy (Pss. 127:3-5; 128:3-6), as well as the hope of life after death (through one's descendants: see Gen. 48:16; 2 Sam. 18:18). Childlessness was wretched, and unusual measures were taken to overcome it (Gen. 30:1-22; 1 Sam. 1; Deut. 25:5-10; cf. Mark 12:19-23). Children were, notably, a central feature of God's promise to Abraham to bless him and make of him "a great nation" (though he was childless at the time of the promise) by giving him descendants as innumerable as the dust of the earth and the stars in the heavens (Gen. 12:2; 13:16; 15:5).

Infant males received the sign of the covenant — circumcision (cf. Gen. 17:10-14) — and Jewish parents were to teach their children the commandments: "Recite them to your children and talk about them when you are at home and when you are away, when you lie down and when you rise" (Deut. 6:7). Children were thus members of God's covenant with Israel — in rabbinic teaching, even those still in the womb[26] — and it was expected that they would assume covenantal responsibilities.

On the other hand, children were not romanticized. In the Old Testament, including the Apocrypha, children are viewed as ignorant, capricious, and in need of strict discipline (see 2 Kings 2:23-24; Isa. 3:4; Wisd. 12:24-25; 15:14; Prov. 22:15; Sir. 30:1-13). In rabbinic literature their status under religious law "is paraphrased by the constantly recurring triad 'deaf and dumb, weak-minded, under age' (Erub. 3.2; Shek. 1.3; Sukk. 2.8; 3.10. . . . The three mentioned in the triad have in common the fact that they are not in full possession of their intellectual powers)."[27] Along the same lines, a Talmudic anecdote states, "Morning sleep, mid-day wine, chattering with children and tarrying in places where men of the common people assemble, destroy a man."[28] Such comments indicate a view of children as falling short of the ideal represented by the adult male law-observant Israelite. The fundamentally positive significance of children, however, is not thereby negated. Indeed, Jews distinguished themselves from many of their contemporaries by rejecting brutal practices toward children, including abortion and the expo-

25. See Weber, *Jesus and the Children*, 11-12.
26. See Hecataeus of Abera, in Diodorus Siculus 40,3.8; Josephus, *contra Apionem* 1,60 (cf. Wiedemann, *Adults and Children in the Roman Empire*, 37).
27. Jeremias, *The Proclamation of Jesus*, 227n. 2.
28. M. *'Abot* 3.10; cf. Oepke, παῖς, 646.

sure of newborns,[29] which can be traced to less positive views of children, and by placing limits on the Jewish father's power over his children.[30]

New Testament scholarship has sometimes overestimated the low estimation and ill treatment of children in the first-century Mediterranean world. Nevertheless, as seen above, the evidence is twofold. Children were both appreciated in various respects and viewed negatively in others. This complex picture of children in Greco-Roman antiquity, including Judaism, forms the background for the New Testament teaching on children. And, as we shall see, the New Testament picture itself is complex, while its most positive aspects are quite striking for the time.

Children in the Gospels

There are five main ways in which the significance of children is underscored in Jesus' teaching and practice. He blesses the children brought to him and teaches that the reign of God belongs to them. He makes children models of entering the reign of God. He also makes children models of greatness in the reign of God. He calls his disciples to welcome little children as he does and turns the service of children into a sign of greatness in the reign of God. He gives the service of children ultimate significance as a way of receiving himself and by implication the One who sent him. He is acclaimed by children as the "Son of David." Some of these points are present in more than one text, so my discussion, which proceeds text by text rather than point by point, will contain some slight overlaps. I will begin with Mark 10:13-16 and Matthew 18:1-5 on the relationship of children and childlikeness to the reign of God. Then I will look at Mark 9:33-37 on the relationship between serving children, being great in the reign of God, and welcoming Jesus. Finally, I will turn to Matthew 21:14-16 on children and the knowledge of Jesus.[31]

---

29. See Tacitus *Histories* 5.5; Strabo 18.824. Cf. Garnsey and Saller, *The Roman Empire*, 138.

30. Despite Philo, who says that a Jewish father "is empowered to upbraid or beat his children, to impose harsh punishments on them and keep them locked up. But in case the children nevertheless remain obdurate . . . the Law has even authorized parents to go so far as to impose the death penalty" (*De Specialibus Legibus* 2.232; cf. also *Hypothetica* 7:2). Nevertheless, actual practice is not necessarily reflected in Philo's statement.

31. It is impossible within the scope of this essay to address the problem of Jesus' seemingly inimical stance toward children in Mark 10:29-30; 13:12; Luke 9:59-62; 12:51-53; and 14:26, where he requires disciples to "leave" and "hate" family members, including

Children as Recipients of the Reign of God

People were bringing little children[32] to him in order that he might touch them;[33] and the disciples spoke sternly to them. But when Jesus saw this, he was indignant and said to them, "Let the little children come to me; do not stop them; for it is to such as these that the kingdom of God belongs. Truly I tell you, whoever does not receive the kingdom of God as a little child will never enter it." And he took them up in his arms, laid his hands on them, and blessed them. (Mark 10:13-16; parr. Matt. 19:13-15; Luke 18:15-17)[34]

In this pericope *Jesus blesses the children who are brought to him and teaches that the reign of God belongs to them.* The backdrop for this teaching and practice is his disciples' rebuke of those who were bringing the children and the disciples' attempt to hinder them.[35] We are not told why the disciples react this way; and whether their reaction should be understood as entailing a pejorative view of children is open to question.[36] In any case, Jesus forcefully overrides the disciples' intervention. He becomes indignant — one of only two references to Jesus' anger in the New Testament (cf. also Mark 3:5), which fact suggests the seriousness of excluding children from the blessings of the

---

children, for the sake of following him. (Cf. Stephen Barton, "Jesus — Friend of Little Children?" in *The Contours of Christian Education*, ed. Jeff Astley and David Day [Great Wakering, Essex: McCrimmons, 1992], 30-40; also his monograph noted in n. 82 below.) These texts — which have in view children in general rather than young children or infants in particular — require separate treatment, and must be seen in relation to the material treated here. I will reserve such discussion for a later occasion.

32. Luke reads "infants" (18:15). According to Barton, the word *infants* in Luke may reflect that Gospel's emphasis on divine grace for the poor and weak (Barton, "Jesus — Friend of Little Children?" 37-38).

33. Matthew reads "that he might lay his hands on them and pray" (19:13).

34. The story of Jesus' blessing of the children has played an important role in theological discussion of children's baptism, but it is very unlikely that the practice is reflected here. The view that Mark's text mirrors a dispute about baptizing children in the early church at the time the Gospel was written has been discredited. (See Joachim Gnilka, *Das Evangelium nach Markus*, Evangelisch-katholischer Kommentar zum Neuen Testament, vol. 2 [Zürich, Einsiedeln, Köln: Benziger; Neukirchen-Vluyn: Neukirchener, 1979], 81). For a discussion of this pericope in relation to Old Testament practices, cf. J. Duncan M. Derrett, "Why Jesus Blessed the Children (Mk 10:13-16 par.)," *Novum Testamentum* 25 (1983): 1-18.

35. Some scholars have suggested that the Jewish custom of bringing children to the elders or scribes for blessing and prayer following the Day of Atonement lies behind this scene, although the practice is attested to not in the New Testament but only later in the Talmudic tractate *Soferim* 18.5. (Cf. Weber, *Jesus and the Children*, 15; Jeremias, *Infant Baptism in the First Four Centuries*, 49.)

36. For possible reasons, see the discussion in Robert H. Gundry, *Mark: A Commentary on His Apology for the Cross* (Grand Rapids, Mich.: Eerdmans, 1993), 549.

reign of God[37] — and he issues the double command, "Let the little children come to me; do not stop them." Then he takes the children up into his arms, lays his hands on them, and blesses them. These actions are followed by his teaching that the reign of God belongs to children. A more emphatic statement of children's reception into the reign of God by Jesus could hardly be made. Why is it, we can ask, that Jesus so vigorously counters the disciples on this matter and insists on welcoming the children into God's reign?

His teaching on the reign of God elsewhere suggests an answer. According to the Beatitudes, the lowly and powerless are the primary beneficiaries of that reign: "Blessed are you who are poor, for yours is the kingdom of God. Blessed are you who are hungry now, for you will be filled. Blessed are you who weep now, for you will laugh" (Luke 6:20-23; cf. Matt. 5:3-12). Now children shared the social status of the poor, the hungry, and the suffering, whom Jesus calls "blessed." For this reason, apparently, he insists on receiving children into the reign of God. John Dominic Crossan may be overstating his case when he asserts that Jesus taught a "kingdom of children" in the sense of a "kingdom of *nobodies*," for "to be a child was to be a *nobody*"[38] (italics added) — an overstatement because children were emphatically not "nobodies" in the Old Testament-Jewish tradition. Nevertheless, it is probably correct to say that children's vulnerability and powerlessness seem to lie at the heart of Jesus' extension of the reign of God to them. Children *qua children* in this sense — referring presumably to children within the covenant community — are the *intended* recipients of the reign of God. It has come for them.[39]

Children as Models of Entering the Reign of God

Not only are children recipients; they are also *models of entering the reign of God*, as Jesus also states in the pericope cited above: "Whoever does not receive

---

37. Weber, *Jesus and the Children,* 15-16.

38. Crossan, *The Historical Jesus,* 269; cf. 265-302.

39. It can be argued that Jesus' healing of children and exorcism of evil spirits from them in Mark's narrative are concretizations of his teaching that the reign of God belongs to children (cf. Mark 5:22-23, 35-43; 7:24-30; 9:14-29). It is noteworthy that Jesus helps children of both sexes. In a letter to me dated October 6, 1999, Adela Yarbro Collins objects to the first point, however, saying that it seems "that Jesus heals and exorcises children as a blessing or benefit for the parents more directly than for the children themselves." While it is true that Jesus performs these miracles *at the request of parents*, one need not conclude that the parents benefit more directly than the children. After all, it is the children, not the parents, who are healed or delivered. Rather, the parents also benefit — namely, by receiving their children back from the clutches of sickness and death.

the reign of God as a child will not enter it" (Mark 10:15).[40] This claim is striking, for nowhere in Jewish literature are children put forward as models for adults,[41] and in a Greco-Roman setting, comparison with children was highly insulting. In what sense are children models, and what does it mean to receive the reign of God "as a child"?[42] The question is a difficult one, for the text seems open to various interpretations.

There are two basic options, each of which can be spelled out in various ways. Either Jesus is referring to adults' adopting a *childlike status,* similar to his telling the rich young ruler to exchange his wealth for poverty by selling all he has and giving the money to the poor (Mark 10:17-22) — and the key to entering the reign of God is a matter of lowly status corresponding to the child's. Or Jesus is referring to emulating some presumed *childlike quality.*[43] But what kind of childlike status or quality?

In considering these options and trying to define them more precisely, the argument of Willi Egger, based on the form of Jesus' teaching, must be taken into account. Egger argues that Jesus takes a typical Jewish formula about what was necessary for entering the reign of God and turns it on its head by stating not *what works of the Law* are required for entrance but rather "whoever does not receive the reign of God *as a child* will never enter it."[44] Since children were not even *required* to follow the Law, much less did they actually fulfill it, Jesus can be taken to challenge the perception that adults who are under obligation to the Law, and do fulfill it, are thereby qualified to enter the reign of God. Egger thus concludes that the phrase "as a child" means "as one who has neither obedience nor obligation to the Law."

This argument both takes into account the connotations of Jesus' saying

40. Cf. F. A. Schilling, "What Means the Saying about Receiving the Kingdom of God as a Little Child?" *Expository Times* 77 (1965): 56-58.

41. W. D. Davies and Dale Allison, *A Critical and Exegetical Commentary on the Gospel of Matthew,* ICC Series (Edinburgh: T. & T. Clark, 1991), 2: 759. They account for this phenomenon by noting that knowledge of and obedience to the law is the essence of piety in Judaism; thus in this tradition an unlearned child can scarcely be an illustration of religious greatness.

42. Grammatically speaking, there are two ways to take the phrase "as a child." It can modify "the reign of God," in which case receiving the reign of God is being compared with receiving a child. Or it can function as a subordinate clause to be paraphrased: "whoever does not receive the reign of God as a child receives the reign of God. . . ." With most interpreters, I take the latter view.

43. Proposed qualities are innocence, trust, humility, nonresistance, and so forth; see the discussion in Gundry, *Mark,* 548-51.

44. Willi Egger, παιδίον, *Exegetical Dictionary of the New Testament* 3.4 (appealing to Hans Windisch, "Die Sprüche vom Eingehen in das Reich Gottes," *Zeitschrift für die neutestamentliche Wissenschaft* 27 [1928]: 163-92).

evoked by its form and appeals to social and religious conventions of the time for the interpretation of the child's significance, and therefore seems to have the edge over interpretations that do not do so. It will not do, of course, to interpret the pericope along the lines of a Pauline critique of the works of the Law and the notion of justification of the ungodly by faith alone.[45] No rejection of the works of the Law is implied here, simply the acceptance of those without obedience to the Law into the reign of God, which implies the similar irrelevance of obedience to the Law on the part of those who already fulfill it. This too is a provocation, of course, but less so than in Paul's teaching.

Some interpreters have seen this pericope as teaching that the reign of God is a "gift" that comes "in a totally gratuitous way," which is not far from the interpretation of Egger that I am following here. We might thus also say that the idea of entering the reign of God "as a child" means "as one who is solely dependent on divine favor."[46] This interpretation fits the portrayal of the children in this pericope as doing nothing to obtain Jesus' blessing: they are simply brought to him, and he takes them into his arms and blesses them.

If the interpretation advocated here is correct, then in this pericope Jesus teaches that adults should become like children by relinquishing the-Law-as-the-basis-for-entering-God's-reign and by asserting instead simple dependence on God's mercy. Entering the reign of God "as a child" thus seems to involve *both* a certain status — actual dependence on God — *and* a corresponding quality — trust — that are both "childlike." (It should be noted that no contrast between Jesus' teaching and Judaism is necessarily implied; rather, Jesus identifies the *child within Judaism*, rather than the adult, as the one who exemplifies how to enter the reign of God.)

Humble Like a Child

At that time the disciples came to Jesus and asked, "Who is the greatest in the kingdom of heaven?" He called a child, whom he put among them, and said, "Truly I tell you, unless you change and become like children, you will never

---

45. Adela Yarbro Collins even doubts that the original meaning of the text had anything to do with the works of the Law (in a letter to me dated October 6, 1999).

46. Cf. Weber, *Jesus and the Children*, 19, 29; similarly, Davies and Allison, in *A Critical and Exegetical Commentary on the Gospel of Matthew*, 2:34, commenting on the parallel text in Matthew 19:14; Bruce Chilton and J. I. H. McDonald, *Jesus and the Ethics of the Kingdom* (Grand Rapids, Mich.: Eerdmans, 1987), 85-86; Gnilka, *Das Evangelium nach Markus*, 81. This interpretation does not deny Jewish dependence on the grace of election and God's faithfulness to the covenant, but views Jewish stress on obedience to the Law as the horizon of Jesus' teaching here.

enter the kingdom of heaven. Whoever becomes humble like this child is the greatest in the kingdom of heaven. And whoever receives one such child in my name receives me." (Matt. 18:1-5)[47]

Matthew has Jesus teach about childlikeness, not in the context of people bringing children to Jesus for blessing (as in Mark), but in connection with the disciples' asking him who is the greatest in the reign of God.[48] That is, here *Jesus teaches childlikeness for the great in particular* (church leaders in Matthew's audience)[49] as well as for all. What special connotations does childlikeness have here as an essential quality for the great, and why single them out as needing to show childlikeness?

Childlikeness is defined explicitly as humility in this pericope: "Change and become like children" is explicated in the immediately following statement, "Whoever becomes humble like this child. . . ."[50] As in the Markan parallel, it could refer *both* to a condition typical of children (who by virtue of their weakness and vulnerability are "humble") *and* to a corresponding quality or frame of mind (humility as trust in divine favor). Still, what special connotations does it have for the great, and why do they need to exemplify such humility?

On the basis of the immediately following verses, we can suggest that Jesus targets the great in particular with his requirement of humility because they stand most in danger — on account of their status in the community — of thinking highly of themselves at the expense of others, especially those of low status. In Matthew 18:6, 10-14, Jesus warns his disciples of divine judgment for despising and creating stumbling blocks for "little ones":

> If any of you put a stumbling block before one of these little ones who believe in me, it would be better for you if a great millstone were fastened around your neck and you were drowned in the depth of the sea. . . . Take care that you do not despise one of these little ones; for, I tell you, in heaven their angels continually see the face of my Father in heaven. What do you think? If a shepherd has a hundred sheep, and one of them has gone astray, does he not leave the ninety-nine on the mountains and go in search of the one that went astray? And if he finds it, truly I tell you, he rejoices over it more than over the

47. On the parallel text, Mark 9:33-37, see below.
48. The question reflects the prevalence of discussions among Jesus' contemporaries about rank in the coming reign of God. Cf. Mark 10:35-37, where James and John petition Jesus: "Grant us to sit, one at your right hand and one at your left, in your glory."
49. Eschatological greatness (future) and greatness in the community (present) are both in view here.
50. Robert H. Gundry, *Matthew: A Commentary on His Literary and Theological Art,* 2d ed. (Grand Rapids, Mich.: Eerdmans, 1994), 360.

ninety-nine that never went astray. So it is not the will of your Father in heaven that one of these little ones should be lost.

Whether we take the "little ones" *(mikroi)* here as the "little children" *(paidia)* of 18:1-4 (as may be suggested by *hen ton mikron touton,* "one of these little ones" [18:14], which agrees in gender with *ta paidia* of 18:1-4 [both are neuter]) or whether the "little ones" refers, more generally, to socially weak disciples like children and including children (as suggested by *hena ton mikron touton,* "one of these little ones" [18:6], which has the masculine gender and is therefore broader in scope[51])[52] — that is, whether this text refers explicitly or implicitly to children, its relation to the preceding is clear. Just as "little ones" are special objects of divine care and protection, and to despise and mistreat them is to put oneself at cross-purposes with the God of the weak and oppressed and at risk of divine judgment (cf. also Matt. 25:37-40), so also to humble oneself and "receive"[53] little children as Jesus does is to be great in the reign of God. Jesus' warning against mistreating the "little ones" and his instruction to receive little children in childlike humility are two sides of the same coin.

The humility of the great thus consists particularly in their stooping humbly to serve children; and it is necessary precisely because Jesus and God have taken this part toward the little ones, so one can hardly expect to be great in the reign of God and treat children otherwise. (Indeed, one can expect judgment for doing so!)

In summary, Matthew's Jesus teaches childlikeness as *humility toward children* on the part of *church leaders* in particular and *for the sake of children* who are at the mercy of those greater than themselves in the community.[54]

Jesus' teaching about greatness in the reign of God as manifested in how one treats children is also found in Mark 9:33-37, though not in connection with "childlikeness." So I will now explore that teaching in its Markan context.

51. Will Deming takes the masculine gender literally, to refer to males, rather than in a generic sense as referring to all disciples. See Deming, "Mark 9.42–10.12; Matthew 5.27-32, and *B. Nid.* 13b: A First-Century Discussion of Male Sexuality," *New Testament Studies* 36 (1990): 130-41.

52. Davies and Allison, *A Critical and Exegetical Commentary on the Gospel of Matthew,* 2:753-54, 762, favor the second option because of the shift in terminology from *ta paidia* in 18:1-4 to *hoi mikroi* in 18:6-10.

53. On this notion, see the discussion on Mark 9:33-37 below.

54. This teaching suggests a church with a hierarchical structure (cf. also 10:40-42; see Gundry, *Matthew,* 203) in which, nevertheless, those with power are to use it in humble and loving service of the powerless. Compare the more egalitarian-sounding teaching in Matthew 23:8-10: "But you are not to be called rabbi, for you have one teacher, and you are all brothers. And call no man your father on earth, for you have one Father, who is in heaven. Neither be called masters, for you have one master, the Christ."

Serving Children and Being Great

> Then they came to Capernaum; and when he was in the house he asked them, "What were you arguing about on the way?" But they were silent, for on the way they had argued with one another who was the greatest. He sat down, called the twelve, and said to them, "Whoever wants to be first must be last of all and servant of all." Then he took a little child and put it among them; and taking it in his arms, he said to them, "Whoever welcomes one such child in my name welcomes me, and whoever welcomes me welcomes not me but the one who sent me." (Mark 9:33-37; parr. Matt. 18:1-2, 4-5; Luke 9:46-48)[55]

To settle the disciples' dispute about which of them is the greatest, Jesus takes a little child and puts it in their midst. Then he takes the child in his arms and teaches his disciples similarly to "receive one such little child in his name." "Receive" or "welcome" (dechomai) in the New Testament is used especially for hospitality to guests, which implies serving them (see, e.g., Luke 10:8; 16:4). Jesus' taking the child into his arms demonstrates such service. The action is more than a display of affection.[56] Thus, to be great in the reign of God, disciples have to love and serve children.[57]

The teaching is, of course, ironic, for children occupied the lowest rung on the social ladder, and caring for children was a low-status activity. But according to the principle of the eschatological reversal — "whoever wants to be first must be last of all and servant of all" — the humblest service characterizes the greatest. Jesus thus redefines care for children as a mark of greatness.

Two Hellenistic texts contemporaneous with the New Testament similarly view the taking of children into the arms[58] in order to love and serve them as an exemplary action by which great distinction accrues to their subjects. In Moralia 492D Plutarch describes a Roman festival at which women "take in their arms and honor their sisters' children" in commemoration of Leucothea, who took her sister's child under her care when her sister died. Diodorus (3.58.1-3) speaks of Cybele, who was exposed on a mountain as a newborn, was

---

55. Cf. Matthew Black, "The Marcan Parable of the Child in the Midst," Expository Times 59 (1947): 44-57; R. Leaney, "Jesus and the Symbol of the Child (Luke ix.46-8)," New Testament Studies 27 (1981): 287-94; and David Wenham, "A Note on Mark 9.33-42/Matt 18.1-6/Luke 9.46-50," Journal for the Study of the New Testament 14 (1982): 113-18.

56. With Gnilka, Das Evangelium nach Markus, 57. Oepke rightly distinguishes Jesus' welcome of children (which is characterized by service) from the so-called rediscovery of the child in Hellenism (see above).

57. Weber (Jesus and the Children, 50) compares the Old Testament prophets' call for justice and charity toward orphans, whose defender is God (Exod. 22:22ff.; Isa. 1:23).

58. The same term for "take into the arms," enangkalizomai, found in Mark 9:36, is used in these texts.

saved from death through the intervention of providence, became the savior of others, and was named "mother of the mountain." Diodorus notes in particular that babies "were saved from death by her spells, and were generally taken up into her arms."

There is a significant difference between these Hellenistic texts and Jesus' teaching, however. While Plutarch and Diodorus depict memorable or legendary *women* as taking children into their arms and as exemplary in this respect for other *women*, Mark depicts Jesus, a *man*, taking a little child into his arms as an example for his *male* disciples in particular, and *all* disciples in general. There is no gender stereotyping here: welcoming children is the responsibility of all, male and female, who would be "great." Jesus thus redefines the service of children as a sign of greatness for all disciples. What appeared to be an undistinguished activity — care for children, belonging to the domain of women, similarly marginalized people — becomes a prime way for all disciples to demonstrate the greatness that corresponds to the reign of God.

Jesus' teaching about receiving children as the mark of true greatness places children at the center of the community's attention as prime objects of its love and service, and requires of all who would be great in the community to serve children.

Welcoming Children and Welcoming Jesus

In the concluding saying of the same pericope, Jesus raises the stakes. Not only is welcoming children a mark of the great; it is a mark of welcoming Jesus himself and, by implication, his divine Sender: "Whoever welcomes one such child in my name welcomes me, and whoever welcomes me welcomes not me but the one who sent me" (9:37).[59] Welcoming children thus has ultimate signficance. It is a way of receiving and serving Jesus and thus also the God who sent him. Conversely, failing to welcome children implies rejection of Jesus and God. On what basis are these claims made, and what do they imply about the relation between social practices and responses of faith?

The little child in this scene is Jesus' representative and therefore to be received. But the child is not sent to speak in the name of Jesus as the disciples are sent into the towns and villages to preach in his name and to be received by the people there.[60] The child represents Jesus in another manner. The child is to be

---

59. The closest Old Testament parallel is the identification of Yahweh with the lowly in Proverbs 19:17: "The one who is kind to the poor lends to the Lord."

60. The sending of the disciples is to be understood against the background of the Jewish tradition of the *shaliah*, or authorized representative of the sender.

taken into the arms and welcomed, for the child is weak and needy. *The child thus represents Jesus as a humble, suffering figure.* Welcoming the child signifies receiving Jesus and affirming his divinely given mission as the suffering Son of Man.

This new explanation of the child's representation of Jesus that I am proposing is supported by the immediate context in conjunction with familiar practices toward children in Greco-Roman antiquity. First Jesus' teaching about the little child as his representative is to be seen in light of his teaching about his passion in the immediately preceding pericope (Mark 9:30-33). Mark narrates that Jesus taught the disciples while passing through Galilee on the way to Capernaum: "The Son of Man is to be betrayed into human hands, and they will kill him, and three days after being killed, he will rise again." But the disciples "did not understand what he was saying and were afraid to ask him." Instead they engaged in a dispute about which of them was the greatest. When they arrived in Capernaum, Jesus gave the teaching about the little child in response to their dispute — but also in response to their incomprehension and fear at the passion prediction, for Mark points out that both the dispute and the passion prediction took place "on the way." Thus we can conclude that Mark intentionally parallels Jesus' identification with the little child with his self-reference as the suffering Son of Man.

But what justifies such a parallel? As noted above, infants and children were sometimes the objects of extreme brutality in the first-century Hellenistic world, as seen in the Greco-Roman practice of the exposure of newborns by their own parents. A loose parallel can be drawn to the Son of Man's betrayal into human hands by one of his own and his killing. In other words, we can construe both the little child and the Son of Man as suffering figures and explain Jesus' self-identification with the little child in light of this parallel. One might object that Jews did not practice the exposure of infants. Yet the protests of many Jewish as well as Greco-Roman writers against exposure and other brutal practices toward children attest to familiarity with the problem (see above). Therefore, it is not too much to assume that Mark's audience would have caught an allusion to the suffering child in Jesus' teaching.

To welcome a little child in Jesus' name, I therefore propose, is to welcome Jesus himself in the sense that he humbled himself like a little child and endured the worst lot of the little child in carrying out his God-given mission. This is not to say that Mark suggests that acceptance of children in the name of Jesus makes acceptance of Jesus as the suffering Son of Man superfluous. After all, welcoming children needs to take place *in Jesus' name*. But when such welcoming does take place, Jesus himself is welcomed.

As suggested by Mark's larger narrative, welcoming children may also *enable* one to welcome the Jesus who became like a little child. Here is how one

45

can construe Mark's passion account to illustrate a case of positive interrelationship between social practices and faith responses.

It is often noted that women play an important role in Mark's passion narrative. They are the disciples who keep solidarity with Jesus and continue ministering to him in his hour of suffering. Mark narrates that "there were also some women looking on from afar [at the crucified Jesus], among whom were Mary Magdalene, and Mary the mother of James the Less and Joses, and Salome . . . [who] used to follow him and minister to him; and there were many other women who had come up with him to Jerusalem" (15:40-41). Further, Mark tells us that Mary Magdalene and Mary the mother of Joses went to the tomb "to see where he was laid" (15:47). They bought spices and came back the next morning to anoint his corpse (16:1-2). Mark also mentions Joseph of Arimathea as showing solidarity with Jesus (15:43-46); yet his closest male disciples betray, deny, and flee from him. It is possible that social practices played a role in the women's responses to Jesus during his passion. Women, whose traditional role involved caring for children, similarly cared for Jesus as he suffered, died, and was buried. Men, who were not traditionally charged with caring for children (and, it will be remembered, tried to prevent children from coming to Jesus for blessing), similarly abandoned Jesus in his passion. Thus particular social practices (toward children in particular) may be seen as helping to shape reponses of faith here.

In conclusion, Jesus' teaching on welcoming children (1) informs *social practice* toward children and (2) suggests that these social practices serve to strengthen faith in Jesus and are themselves a form of this faith.

Children and Knowledge of Jesus

> The blind and the lame came to him in the temple, and he cured them. But when the chief priests and the scribes saw the amazing things that he did, and heard the children crying out in the temple, "Hosanna to the Son of David," they became angry and said to him, "Do you hear what these are saying?" Jesus said to them, "Yes, have you never read, 'Out of the mouths of infants and nursing babies you have prepared praise for yourself'?" (Matt. 21:14-16)

In this pericope children play the striking role of those who have true insight about Jesus, in contrast to the chief priests and scribes, who not only fail to recognize him but object to the children's acclamation. When the children observe Jesus' miraculous deeds in the temple, which identify him as the expected Messiah,[61] they acclaim him as "the Son of David." The chief priests and

61. Cf. Ulrich Luz, *Das Evangelium nach Matthäus* 1.3 (Zürich/Düsseldorf: Benziger; Neukirchen-Vluyn: Neukirchener, 1997), 185, 188n. 81.

scribes, however, are scandalized by the application of this Messianic title to Jesus: "Do you hear what these are saying?" The scene is, of course, ironic. The chief priests and scribes, who, of all people, are in a position as religiously trained Jewish adults to see the significance of Jesus' deeds, recognize him as the Messiah, and lead the people in acclaiming him, do not do so; rather, the children, who are ignorant and untrained in religious matters and the least likely to play this role, in fact take it up.

The explanation for the children's surprising role is evident in Jesus' response to the Jewish leaders. Citing Psalm 8:3 (in the Septuagint), he says, "Have you never read, 'Out of the mouths of infants and nursing babies you have prepared praise for yourself'?" Just as the cries of infants can be taken as praise that God has prepared for Godself, so also the children's hosannas to Jesus in the temple are to be seen as *praise that God has put in their mouths*. Ignorant children can speak truly about Jesus because God has given them this insight and opened their mouths.

The notion of children who utter divinely inspired speech is not unparalleled in Greco-Roman antiquity. In fact, W. D. Davies and Dale L. Allison suggest that Matthew is alluding here to the tradition of the supernatural singing of Israelite children by the Red Sea when Moses led the people out of Egypt (cf. Wisd. 10:21), and also note that Greeks and Romans viewed the shouts of children at play — especially in the vicinity of pagan temples, where revelation was likely to take place — as omens.[62] Matthew has already attributed to "infants" in a metaphorical sense (referring to unsophisticated and untrained minds)[63] insight about Jesus' deeds and identity through divine revelation in 11:25. There Jesus prays, "I thank you, Father, Lord of heaven and earth, because you have hidden these things[64] from the wise and the intelligent and have revealed them to infants" (par. Luke 10:21). In the pericope on the children in the temple, literal children speak divinely revealed knowledge about Jesus.

In the gospel tradition, children are not mere ignoramuses in terms of spiritual insight. They know Jesus' true identity. They praise him as the Son of David. They have this knowledge from God and not from themselves, and because they do, they are living manifestos that God is the source of all true

62. Davies and Allison, *A Critical and Exegetical Commentary on the Gospel of Matthew,* 3.141. Cf. also 1 En. 106.3, 11; Ladder of Jacob 7.6-7; Aelian *De Natura animalium* 11.10; esp. Plutarch *Isis and Osiris* 14.356E. Similarly, in the Old Testament Yahweh chooses children or youth as servants, highlighting the divine power at work through them (cf. 1 Sam. 3:1, 8; 1 Kings 3:7; Jer. 1:6).

63. Gundry, *Matthew,* 216.

64. Referring to the works of Christ mentioned in 11:2, 5, 19; see Gundry, *Matthew,* 216, who also notes other biblical or Jewish literature with the motif of education by divine revelation.

knowledge about Christ. Jesus' affirmation of the children's praise of him in this pericope is thus an affirmation that children who "know nothing" can also "know divine secrets" and believe in him.

Children in the Epistles

Although there are a number of metaphorical references to children in the Epistles, they mention actual children rarely, and only in relation to parents. In 1 Corinthians 7 Paul makes a passing, but important, reference to children in a discussion on marriage and divorce, where he describes the children of a marriage between a believer and an unbeliever as "holy" (7:14). Colossians and Ephesians exhort children to obey their parents and fathers not to provoke their children but "to bring them up in the discipline and instruction of the Lord" (Col. 3:20-21; Eph. 6:1-4). The Pastorals make fathers' success in these roles into qualifications for church leadership (1 Tim. 3:4-5, 12; Titus 1:6).

All of these texts use the word *teknos* for children, which simply denotes a physical descendant and is not age-specific; it can refer to adult children as well as small or young children, depending on the context. There are reasons to think that small or young children are particularly in view in some of these texts, so I will include them in the present discussion. I will try to show not only what these texts teach about children and the treatment of children, but also, in light of the preceding discussion, how one might relate this material to the teaching and practice of Jesus.

"Your Children . . . Are Holy"

> If any believer has a wife who is an unbeliever, and she consents to live with him, he should not divorce her. And if any woman has a husband who is an unbeliever, and he consents to live with her, she should not divorce him. For the unbelieving husband is made holy through his wife, and the unbelieving wife is made holy through her husband. Otherwise, your children would be unclean, but as it is, they are holy. (1 Cor. 7:12-14)

Paul's statement about children in 1 Corinthians 7:14b[65] is embedded in a larger argument about divorce — more specifically, about Christians divorcing

65. Cf. the discussions by Gerhard Delling, "Nun aber sind sie heilig," 237-69; "Lexikalisches zu τέκνον," 270-80; "Zur Exegese von 1. Kor. 7,14," in *Studien zum Neuen Testament und zum hellenistischen Judentum: Gesammelte Aufsätze, 1950-1968* (Göttingen:

non-Christian spouses, as seen in the quotation above. The structure of the argument is as follows:[66] (1) The Christian should not divorce a non-Christian spouse (out of fear of being "defiled," it is implied), assuming the latter consents to live together, (2) for the non-Christian spouse "is made holy" *(hegiastai)* through the Christian spouse (rather than the Christian spouse being defiled by the non-Christian spouse), (3) which claim is supported by the fact that, if it were not the case that the non-Christian spouse is made holy by the believer, then their children would be unclean *(akatharta)*; in fact, however, the children are "holy" *(hagia)*.[67] Scholars often take the text to mirror a Corinthian concern about spiritual defilement through the relationship with an unbelieving spouse (perhaps particularly through sexual relations with the unbeliever) — less commonly, a concern also about defilement through the children born of such a marriage — and see Paul as countering the assumption that the believer can "catch" the unbeliever's impurity with the view that the unbeliever "is sanctified" through the believer.[68] To support his position, Paul appeals to the fact that the children of the couple are not unclean (unclean, namely, because of the unbelieving parent)[69] — which view he presumes the Corinthians also to hold, since they were not arguing for dissociating themselves from these children; rather, the children are holy. The second assertion is not necessarily one that the Corinthians held in common with Paul — it seems to go beyond their powers of imagination — but one which he uses to further the argument that the non-Christian spouse is made holy, and to which he assumes the Corinthians will at least assent.[70] The assertions about children here, which Paul neither argues for nor explains, must be interpreted in light of this larger discussion.

"Unclean" *(akathartos)* and "holy" *(hagios)* are originally cultic terms[71] that describe on the one hand what is common or belongs to the world, and on

---

Vandenhoeck & Ruprecht, 1970); Will Deming, *Marriage and Celibacy in 1 Corinthians 5–7* (Cambridge: Cambridge University Press, 1995), 131-48.

66. Cf. Friedrich Lang, *Die Briefe an die Korinther,* Das Neue Testament Deutsch 7 (Göttingen/Zürich: Vandenhoeck & Ruprecht, 1986), 94.

67. In prohibition of divorce by two believing spouses, Paul simply cites Jesus' prohibition of divorce in 7:10.

68. Cf. Wolfgang Schrage, *Der erste Brief an die Korinther. 2. Teilband. 1 Kor 6,12–11,16,* Evangelisch-katholischer Kommentar zum Neuen Testament VII/2 (Solothurn/Düsseldorf: Benziger; Neukirchen-Vluyn: Neukirchener, 1995), 107-9.

69. Jewish views about impurity through intermarriage might be relevant to this discussion; cf. the recent discussion by Christine Hayes, "Intermarriage and Impurity in Ancient Jewish Sources," *Harvard Theological Review* 92 (1999): 3-37.

70. This distinction between the two assertions in v. 14b is not made in the literature; cf., e.g., Müller, *In der Mitte der Gemeinde,* 360.

71. See, e.g., Leviticus 10:10.

the other, what is set apart for God and belongs to God. "Unclean" with reference to people can thus denote unbelievers (see 2 Cor. 6:17, citing Isa. 52:11). "Holy" describes Israel or the church as people set apart for God (see Exod. 19:6; 1 Pet. 2:9), and "holy ones" (*hagioi,* usually translated "saints") is used throughout the New Testament to denote Christian believers. In these texts the terms "unclean" and "holy" have not primarily moral holiness or unholiness in view but, more fundamentally, consecration to God or its opposite.[72] So also in 1 Corinthians 7:14b the notion that children are not "unclean" but "holy" is to be understood in the sense that they are consecrated to God as opposed to belonging to the world.

But how are we to take these claims? Is Paul saying that the children are saved, or that they will be saved, or simply that they are somehow different from mere unbelievers? This question is more easily answered after examining the basis for Paul's assertion. There are two basic explanations for why Paul can affirm that the children of a "mixed marriage" are not unclean but holy. First, it is conceivable that the children are believers or baptized, and on that basis Paul asserts they are not unclean but holy, despite the association with the unbelieving parent. Just as the unbelieving parent cannot undo the children's consecration to God through faith and baptism, so also the unbelieving spouse cannot undo the believing spouse's consecration to God on the same basis; since the believing/baptized children are and remain "holy," so also the believing spouse remains holy and is not defiled.[73] Yet this explanation is unlikely, for Paul's assertion about the children grounds the claim *not* that the Christian spouse is holy and not defiled by the non-Christian (a claim which is merely implied rather than stated) *but* that the "unbelieving husband is made holy through his wife" and "the unbelieving wife is made holy through her husband." That is, Paul is aiming to argue more than that non-Christian uncleanness cannot infect Christians; he wants to show even that Christian holiness is transferred to non-Christians — in other words, just the opposite of what the Corinthians thought.

In order for Paul's assertion about the children to work as an argument supporting the non-Christian spouse's *holiness through the Christian,* it seems to entail the children's *holiness through the Christian parent.* This is the second explanation of the holiness of the children of a mixed marriage. In this case the supporting assertion ("Otherwise, your children would be unclean, but as it is, they are holy") is illuminated by the very point that it substantiates ("the unbeliever is made holy through the wife/husband"). In light of verse 14a, we can in-

---

72. Lang, *Die Briefe an die Korinther,* 93-94.

73. The widespread use of *teknos* for children of any age (cf. Delling, "Lexikalisches zu τέκνον") makes this interpretation possible.

fer that the basis for Paul's assertion that the children are not "unclean" but instead "holy" is their relationship to the believing parent, not their faith or baptism. Whether the children are believers or baptized is an open question, although a better parallel with the unbelieving spouses would be achieved if the children are unbelievers/unbaptized.

How then are we to understand the claim that the children are not unclean but holy, if not as a simple reaffirmation of their Christian status but as an affirmation that — even apart from belief or baptism — they are holy through the Christian parent? Clearly, "holy" is used here differently from normal Pauline usage, where it refers to consecration to God and sanctification of *believers by God*.[74] "Holy" in 1 Corinthians 7:14 does not imply the present participation in salvation that can be predicated of believers, for Paul writes concerning the same unbelieving spouses who are "made holy" through the Christian wife or husband: "Wife, for all you know, you might save *[sōseis]* your husband. Husband, for all you know, you might save *[sōseis]* your wife." This text presents the salvation of the unbelieving spouse now "made holy" through the believing spouse as a future possibility rather than a present reality and gives the believer a role in such salvation.

Similarly, in Romans 11 Paul argues that his contemporary non-Christian Jews are "holy," which he deduces from the fact that their ancestors are "holy": "If the part of the dough offered as first fruits is holy *[hagia]*, then the whole batch is holy; and if the root is holy *[hagia]*, then the branches also are holy"(v. 16).[75] Paul is, of course, referring to the fact that the promises of God received by the ancestors in faith are valid for their descendants, though unbelieving. Ultimately, therefore, God's faithfulness to the promises is the guarantee of the holiness of the unbelieving Jews.[76] What is useful for our discussion, however, is that Paul makes the believing ancestors themselves (as recipients of the promises) the basis for his assertion that unbelieving Jews are "holy." Furthermore, he envisions their future faith and salvation both through the agency of the apostle (11:13-14) and the agency of God (as implied in 11:23-24, 26a).

This secondary usage of the terminology of "holiness" in Paul for unbelievers who are nevertheless consecrated to God through their familial or genealogical relationship to believers supplies the background for interpreting Paul's statement that the children of a mixed marriage are "holy" and suggests

74. Cf. *hagios* in Rom. 1:7; 1 Cor. 1:2, *et passim; hagiazo* in Rom. 15:16; 1 Cor. 1:2; 6:11; 1 Thess. 5:23, etc.

75. The operative principle here is that the part sanctifies the whole; Beasley-Murray, "Church and Child in the New Testament," 209-10.

76. Cf. Rom. 11:28-29: "As regards the gospel they are enemies of God for your sake; but as regards election they are beloved, for the sake of their ancestors; *for the gifts and the calling of God are irrevocable*" (my italics).

that Paul anticipates their coming to faith and salvation. How this works is not spelled out, but presumably Paul is thinking of believers as agents of God for the salvation of those unbelievers with whom they share the intimacy of the household.[77] Moral or spiritual influence is presumably included[78] but may not exhaust the meaning of the believer's agency here; magical working can be ruled out as un-Pauline.[79] I concur with Gordon Fee in his conclusion that in 1 Corinthians 7 "Paul is setting forth a high view of the grace of God at work through the believer toward members of his/her own household (cf. 1 Pet 3:1)."[80] Finally, it is important to note that Paul does not simply *assume* the salvation of children *qua* children, yet he asserts the consecration to God of these particular children of believers, which portends their salvation.[81]

In summary, Paul believes that the children of believers are consecrated to God, which presents the possibility of their salvation, if not portends their salvation, and that God works out the consecration and salvation of these children through the familial bond with the believing parent — that is, in the social context of the family where one parent at least is a Christian.

It is not clear whether Jesus' teaching that family and household ties should be subordinated to the bond with him played any role in the tensions between Christian and non-Christian members of Corinthian families presupposed in this text.[82] What is clear is that, if Paul knew Jesus' teaching about

---

77. Gordon Fee thus cautiously translates 1 Cor. 7:14: the unbeliever "is sanctified in (the relationship with)" the believer. See Fee, *The First Epistle to the Corinthians,* New International Commentary on the New Testament Series (Grand Rapids, Mich.: Eerdmans, 1987), 300n. 24. Cf. Rodney Stark on the phenomenon of "secondary conversions" in exogamous marriage, in particular, on the conversions of husbands of Christian wives to Christianity as a factor accounting for the rise of the movement (Stark, *The Rise of Christianity: A Sociologist Reconsiders History* [Princeton: Princeton University Press, 1996], 111-17).

78. Cf. Lang, *Die Briefe an die Korinther,* 94.

79. Contrast Schrage, *Der erste Brief an die Korinther,* 2.107-9.

80. Fee, *The First Epistle to the Corinthians,* 302. Similarly, Aland, "Die Stellung der Kinder in den Frühen christlichen Gemeinde — und ihre Taufe," 208-12.

81. Some have suggested that Jewish proselyte language illuminates the argument: in rabbinic texts the children of a proselyte born after conversion are born "in holiness" (but if before conversion, "in unholiness"). But there are significant problems with this suggestion. See Delling, "Nun aber sind sie heilig," 264-66.

82. Cf. Mark 10:29-30: "There is no one who has left house or brothers or sisters or mother or father or children or fields, for my sake and for the sake of the good news, who will not receive a hundredfold now in this age — houses, brothers and sisters, mothers and children, and fields with persecutions — and in the age to come eternal life"; Luke 14:26: "Whoever comes to me and does not hate father and mother, wife and children, brothers and sisters . . . , cannot be my disciple"; cf. also Mark 13:12; Luke 9:59-62; 12:51-53. Stephen Barton discusses the Matthean and Markan material in relation to the phenomenon of familial tension resulting from conversions to the Christian faith in the early Christian

leaving family members for his sake, he did not think it applied to the Corinthian context, a sedentary life in households rather than an itinerant ministry requiring literal following of Jesus. Paul's response instead latches onto a teaching of Jesus that is suited to this social context, namely, his prohibition of divorce (7:10-11), and extends it to the situation of a family divided over the gospel (7:12-16). The believer is not called to leave in order to maintain purity but to remain and be the leaven of the gospel. The believer should be concerned not for her own holiness but for the holiness of the unbelieving family members. If she stays, then God will be at work through her, sanctifying and saving the unbelievers.

Paul's teaching about children has both affinities to and differences from Jesus' teaching and practice. While Jesus gave the general teaching that the reign of God belongs to children, Paul explicitly teaches only that children of a believing parent are "holy." Both Jesus and Paul, on the other hand, give adult believers important roles in the children's access to eschatological blessings. Paul implies that children are "holy" through their relationship to a believer, and Jesus blesses the children brought to him by other members of the believing community.

More obviously similar are Paul's and Jesus' restraint concerning procreation — which contrasts with conventional Jewish stress on marriage and sex for procreation — derived from their shared outlook of eschatological expectation. Paul favored celibacy in light of "the impending crisis" (1 Cor. 7:26) — so long as it did not lead to immorality — and remained silent on procreation in his discussion of marriage in 1 Corinthians 7. Jesus pronounced "woe to those who are pregnant and to those who are nursing infants in those days" (Mark 13:17), referring to the coming eschatological distress.

Responsibilities of Children and Parents

> Children, obey your parents in everything, for this is your acceptable duty in the Lord. Fathers, do not provoke your children, or they may lose heart. (Col. 3:20-21)

> Children, obey your parents in the Lord, for this is right. "Honor your father and mother" — this is the first commandment with a promise: "so that it may be well with you and you may live long on the earth." And fathers, do not

---

movement. (See Barton, *Discipleship and Family Ties in Mark and Matthew* [Cambridge: Cambridge University Press, 1995].) I will not treat the texts here for the reason given in n. 31.

provoke your children to anger, but bring them up in the discipline and instruction of the Lord. (Eph. 6:1-4)

The references to children in Colossians and Ephesians[83] cited above occur in a series of instructions to the members of Christian households regarding their mutual obligations — the so-called household codes.[84] They incorporate views about children and their relationship to parents that were widely held in the first-century Mediterranean world, but they also have distinctly Christian elements. After pointing out the basic similarities with other such codes, I will analyze the Christian character of the Colossian and Ephesian codes in relation to Jesus' teaching on children.

The Colossian and Ephesian household codes exhort children to obey their parents, and fathers not to provoke their children but to educate them.[85] For these exhortations we can find parallels in Greco-Roman and Jewish writings. First, children's obligation to obey their parents was universally accepted,[86] not surprisingly, given the prevailing hierarchical model of the family, where children were subordinate to parents and the father was the head of the family. The command to obey one's parents in Colossians and Ephesians appeals both to general recognition of this duty — "for this is right" and "for this is your acceptable duty" — and to the Fifth Commandment (Exod. 20:12; cf. Deut. 5:16).[87] Second, while Roman law granted fathers almost absolute authority over their children, the abuse of paternal authority brought forth pleas for moderation by Roman and Jewish writers alike.[88] Similarly, the household codes exhort fathers not to provoke their children lest they lose heart. Third, the exhortation to fathers to bring their children up in the discipline and instruction of the Lord has parallels in Judaism, where fathers bore primary responsibility for educating children toward the goal of fulfilling the covenant obligations, as well as in a Greco-Roman milieu, where fathers were the chief

83. The close similarity here and elsewhere between Colossians and Ephesians has been explained in terms of a literary dependence, usually conceived as the dependence of Ephesians on Colossians. Both letters have been taken by many scholars as pseudonymous letters written by a disciple of Paul after his death, and thus as providing a window onto the church in a post-Pauline situation.

84. Also found in Greco-Roman and Hellenistic Jewish writings.

85. The command to obey could include adult children, but the commands not to provoke children but to educate them suggest young children or youth.

86. Among Jews, cf. Sir. 3.1-9; Philo *De Decalogo* 120; among Greeks and Romans, cf. Aristotle *Nicomachean Ethics* IX 2 = 1165a; Plutarch *Moralia* 479f. (Cf. Best, *Ephesians*, 562-63.)

87. Also cited in Matt. 15:4; 19:19; Mark 7:10; 10:19; Luke 18:20.

88. Cf. Ps.-Phocylides 207-9; Stobaeus, *Anthologion* 4.26.7, 13. (Cf. Lincoln, *Ephesians*, 406.)

educators for most of the children's lives, the goal being to enable children to be contributers to culture.[89]

What makes the Colossian and Ephesian household codes *specifically Christian* in their teaching about children, and how are they *related to Jesus' teaching and practice?* At first glance it seems that the relation to Jesus' teaching and practice is one of simple contrast and that the Christian features are superficial. Yet it would be more accurate to say that there are both contrasts and parallels or affinities to Jesus and that the Christian features entail some significant departures from the milieu of the time.

First, the household codes enjoin children to obey their parents ("in everything," Col. 3:20), whereas Jesus sets children up as models for adults and even commands that one must "hate" father and mother in order to follow him. It would be wrong, however, to conclude that the codes merely mimic the surrounding culture's emphasis on children's subordination and obedience to parents, and that Jesus advocates the social equality of children. While he elevates children to models of entering the reign of God, he actually presupposes their social inequality when he instructs his disciples to serve the *least* and welcome *little children*. Everything in the Gospels suggests that *Jesus would have expected children to obey parents,* unless it conflicted with the obligations of discipleship.

Second, the household codes appeal to divine authority in support of children's obedience: "obey your parents *in the Lord*"[90] (Eph. 6:1); "this is your acceptable duty *in the Lord*" (Col. 3:20). The qualifying phrase "in the Lord" does more than simply provide religious legitimation for a general ethical ideal carried over into a Christian context. *"In the Lord" qualifies obedience as taking place within the larger framework of one's relationship to Christ.*[91] This phrase

---

89. In Judaism children were given religious instruction first in the home and then later (boys at age seven) in the synagogue (Lincoln, *Ephesians*, 406). Instruction was given in the traditions of Israel (Deut. 4:9), the Law (Deut. 11:19), and practical religious and moral wisdom (Prov. 4:1ff.); see Oepke, παῖς, 647-48; and Weber, *Jesus and the Children*, 37-42. In Roman society the mother reared the child until the age of seven, at which time the father assumed the main responsibility for educating the child, with the help of a pedagogue or other servants. The household was the primary locus of education, while formal education (borrowed from the Greeks) played a secondary role; see Oepke, παῖς, 642; Wiedemann, *Adults and Children in the Roman Empire*, 143; and Weber, *Jesus and the Children*, 34-37. In general, cf. W. Barclay, *Educational Ideals in the Ancient World* (London: Collins, 1959); S. F. Bonner, *Education in Ancient Rome* (London: Methuen, 1977); W. Jentsch, *Urchristliches Erziehungsdenken: Die Paideia Kyriou im Rahmen der hellenistisch-jüdischen Welt* (Gütersloh: G. Mohn, 1951); and H. I. Marrou, *A History of Education in Antiquity* (London: Sheed & Ward, 1956).

90. *En kyrio* ("in the Lord") is missing in some manuscripts but is probably original. The phrase modifies "obey," not "parents."

91. Cf. Lincoln, *Ephesians*, 401-2; Müller, *In der Mitte der Gemeinde*, 268.

and similar ones occur frequently in the Pauline corpus to denote the believer's relationship to Christ as that which fundamentally defines and qualifies her life in all respects. In this light it becomes clear why the household codes do not parallel parents with God/gods in order to motivate the appropriate behavior, as do some ancients.[92] Parents stand alongside children *under* the Lord. The obedience enjoined upon children in the household codes is thus not simply derived from but also subordinate to obedience to the Lord. Moreover, the "Lord" is not simply an empty marker of divine authority but the Lord Jesus Christ, who is the model for Christians to imitate. Hence, in principle, *children's relationship to the Lord could fulfill a critical function in relation to that to parents* and, in particular cases, release children from the obligation toward parents (as in Jesus' teaching), although the codes do not explicitly envision such a conflict.

Third and related to the preceding point, the household codes address children directly, as they do adults, and ground children's ethical obligations, as those of adults, in their relationship with the Lord: "*Children*, obey your parents *in the Lord*" (Eph. 6:1); "*Children*, obey your parents in everything, for this is your acceptable duty *in the Lord*" (Col. 3:20)."[93] By contrast, in Stoic household codes the adult male is usually addressed with instructions regarding the obedience of children.[94] Although children participated in the Greco-Roman religions, they did not do so on the basis of a relationship with the deity shared with adults.[95] *In that they presume children's unmediated relationship to the Lord, the household codes are structurally parallel with Jesus' teaching and practice,* rooted in Old Testament-Jewish tradition. He welcomed little children and did not privilege adults; rather, he privileged children and welcomed adults who became like children.

Fourth, though the household codes prohibit fathers from provoking their children[96] (in line with some of their contemporary cultural critics), they

---

92. Cf. Aristotle *Nicomachean Ethics* 1165a 24; Philo *De Specialibus Legibus* 2.225, 226; *De Decalogo* 119, 120; Hierocles, in Stobaeus, *Anthologion* 4.25.53. For further references, see Müller, *In der Mitte der Gemeinde*, 320; Lincoln, *Ephesians*, 399, 401; Best, *Ephesians*, 565.

93. For adults' ethical obligations as grounded in their relation to the Lord in the household codes, cf. Col. 3:18, 22; 4:1; Eph. 6:5-9.

94. Müller, *In der Mitte der Gemeinde*, 330; similarly, James D. G. Dunn, "The Household Rules in the New Testament," in *The Family in Theological Perspective,* ed. Stephen C. Barton (Edinburgh: T. & T. Clark, 1996), 52.

95. In Greco-Roman religions, however, children were incorporated into the cultic fellowship as newborns and participated in family worship and in the public cultus; some exercised special roles in cultic ceremonies. (See Oepke, παῖς, 643-45.)

96. Patrick Miller contrasts the implicitly reciprocal character of the parent-child relationship in Ephesians 6:1-4 to the Decalogue, which simply enjoins children to obey parents. See Miller, *Deuteronomy* (Louisville: John Knox, 1990), 86.

lack any exhortation to love and serve children; by contrast, Jesus taught that the great should *welcome* little children. Ephesians does spell out the husband's duty toward the wife in a way that comes close to how Jesus enjoined his disciples to treat children: "Husbands, love your wives. . . . He who loves his wife loves himself. For no one ever hates his own body, but he nourishes and tenderly cares for it, just as Christ does for the church" (Eph. 5:25, 28-30).[97] Nevertheless, children are not mentioned as recipients of the same kind of action.

Yet even here the differences from Jesus are not as pronounced as they may seem at first sight. Ephesians 5:21 prefaces the household code with the command "Submit to one another in the fear of Christ!" which can be taken to imply that not only are children to submit to parents but parents are to submit to children, though in a different way — for example, by not provoking children but treating them with kindness and respect. Colossians prefaces the household code with general instructions to manifest Christ-like compassion and love to fellow believers in one's debt, which includes children, even though they are not specifically mentioned: "Put on then, as God's chosen ones, holy and beloved, compassion, kindness, lowliness, meekness, and patience, forbearing one another and, if one has a complaint against another, forgiving each other; as the Lord has forgiven you, so you also must forgive. And above all these put on love, which binds everything together in perfect harmony" (Col. 3:12-14). In Colossians and Ephesians, therefore, *children are subsumed — but hopefully not lost! — under the general category of fellow members of the community to be shown the compassion and care which each owes the other in imitation of Christ,* who welcomed little children and taught all his disciples to do so.

Fifth, although Ephesians agrees with other ancients about children's need for education and the role of fathers in this task, it nevertheless gives the education prescribed a specifically Christian character: "the discipline and instruction *of the Lord*."[98] The phrase refers either to (1) the instruction *from the Lord* mediated by fathers (similar to the "discipline of the Lord" [*paideia kyriou*] in LXX Prov. 3:11 as the discipline that the Lord exercises), or (2) the instruction *in the light of the Lord* given by fathers. Andrew Lincoln concludes that fathers are to "teach their children the apostolic tradition about Christ and help to shape their lives in accordance with it."[99]

It is by virtue of children's need for Christian instruction that Ephesians also uses children as a metaphor for the spiritually ignorant and unsophisti-

---

97. The hierarchy presupposed in the relationship between husband and wife here parallels that between parents and children.

98. The terms *paideia* and *nouthesia,* translated "discipline" and "instruction," are not clearly distinguishable and together denote the educative process.

99. Lincoln, *Ephesians,* 408.

cated: "We must no longer be children, tossed to and fro and blown about by every wind of doctrine . . ." (4:14). Jesus uses children similarly to illustrate foolish misunderstanding of the hour of salvation (Matt. 11:16-19; Luke 7:31-35).[100] Yet in the pericope on the children in the temple, he casts children in the opposite role of the spiritually insightful through divine revelation. Children cannot have this dual signifiance in Ephesians, however, since this Epistle reserves the revelation of the knowledge of "the mystery of Christ" for "his holy apostles and prophets" (3:5), who make it known to others (3:9). In Ephesians there is a chain of mediation of the knowledge of Christ in which children are the last link. The order is God to apostles and prophets, apostles and prophets to other believers, fathers (included in other believers) to children.[101]

In summary, the household codes reflect some of the emphases of Jesus' teaching on children, but not the most radical valorizations of children. In Colossians and Ephesians children are viewed as members of the community of believers but not as models for adult believers or as spiritually insightful. These roles that children have in Jesus' teaching have been eclipsed by the roles of others in the early church and by children's own roles in the family.

Managing the Household and Managing the Church

> . . . He [a bishop or deacon] must manage his own household well, keeping his children submissive and respectful in every way — for if someone does not know how to manage his own household, how can he take care of God's church? . . . Let deacons . . . manage their children and their households well. (1 Tim. 3:4-5, 12)

> [An elder is to be] . . . someone . . . whose children are believers, not accused of debauchery and not rebellious. (Titus 1:6)

The Pastorals are interested in children's relationship to parents as a model of the relationship between church members and leaders. To qualify for

100. Weber attributes this saying to Jesus' realism based on his actual observation of children. See Weber, *Jesus and the Children*, 1, 13.
101. 1 Clem 21:6ff., however, suggests that by the early second century the church included children in the catechumenate, or instruction of believers in the Christian faith: "Let our children be partakers of the instruction which is in Christ; let them learn how lowliness of mind prevaileth with God, what power chaste love hath with God, how the fear of Him is good and great and saveth all them that walk therein in a pure mind with holiness." (Cf. Beasley-Murray, "Church and Child in the New Testament," 215.) On Christian training for children in early Christianity, cf. also Polycarp *Philippians* 4:2; Shepherd of Hermas, *Visions* 1.3.1, 2; 2.3.1.

the ministry of bishop, deacon, or elder in the church, a man[102] must "manage his own household well, keeping his children submissive and respectful in every way" (1 Tim. 3:4; cf. v. 12). In addition, he must be someone whose children are exemplary believers (Titus 1:6).[103] These comments suggest that the church is seen along the lines of a hierarchically ordered family whose "heads" must be able successfully to rule over subordinate members by pastoring them in the Christian faith and life. The Pastorals reflect the ideals for children and parents seen in the household codes and relate those ideals to church leadership. Beyond this, they contribute nothing new. If we go by what these texts actually say about children — rather than what we may speculate that they assume — the distance from the teaching and practice of Jesus on our topic seems the greatest.

Conclusion

As the preceding discussion has shown, there are diverse and to some extent contrasting traditions on children in the New Testament. Some of these traditions have exerted more influence on later Christian thinking than others, and different Christian thinkers and groups have taken up different aspects of the New Testament teaching. From the essays that follow in this volume, it appears that the Epistles' teaching on children as subordinate to parents and on parents' responsibility toward children, especially for their Christian formation, has played a dominant role in shaping Christian thought on children, though this teaching has sometimes been understood in a limited way. For example, children's obedience to parents has received far more emphasis than parents' responsibility to show Christ-like gentleness toward their children. Jesus' teaching on children as objects of Christian care and service is reflected in some traditions (e.g., the Pietist tradition and black women's clubs), while his more provocative teaching on children as co-recipients and model entrants of the reign of God has generated significant theological discussion (cf. esp. John Calvin, Friedrich Schleiermacher, and Karl Rahner), not least in connection with infant baptism, in which case the texts are read with heavily invested theological interests. The similarly provocative teaching about children as recipients of divine insight and representatives of Jesus seems to have had the least *Wirkungsgeschichte*.

---

102. Women are not considered for such tasks in the Pastorals, in contrast to Pauline texts such as Rom. 16 and Phil. 4:2-3.

103. Cf. Rom. 1:30 and 2 Tim. 3:2, where disobedience to parents is an indication of depravity or a sign of the last days.

In light of the traditional reception of the New Testament teaching, the most significant challenge before us is to recapture in our own particular contexts the radicalness of Jesus' teaching on children. Children are not only subordinate but sharers with adults in the life of faith; they are not only to be formed but to be imitated; they are not only ignorant but capable of receiving spiritual insight; they are not "just" children but representatives of Christ. What makes that challenge so difficult is that it would entail changing not only how adults relate to children but how we conceive of our social world. Jesus did not just teach how to make an adult world kinder and more just for children; he taught the arrival of a social world in part defined by and organized around children. He cast judgment on the adult world because it is not the child's world. He made being a disciple dependent on inhabiting this "small world." He invited the children to come to him *not* so that he might initiate them into the adult realm but so that they might receive what is *properly theirs* — the reign of God.[104]

104. I would like to express my sincere thanks to several colleagues who read and made helpful comments on previous versions of this article: Adela Yarbro Collins, Robert Gundry, Miroslav Volf, and co-participants in the Lilly Project on Perspectives on Children in Christian Thought, including Marcia Bunge, Catherine Brekus, and Margaret Bendroth. Thanks also to Tamara Warhol for various and sundry tasks in getting this article into final form.

2. The Ecclesial Family: John Chrysostom on Parenthood and Children

VIGEN GUROIAN

In our day hyper-individualism and exaggerated notions of personal autonomy flourish culturally and have influenced law. The religious sociologist Robert Bellah calls this ontological individualism — a belief that the individual is primary and that the individual's claims take precedence over community, which is thought to be derivative and artificial.[1] This individualism is reflected conspicuously in current attitudes and opinions about marriage and divorce, abortion, and physician-assisted suicide, to name a few. Thus many see marriage as strictly a contract between two autonomous selves who happen to have strong feelings for one another. A woman's decision to have an abortion, whether she is single or married, is judged as solely her prerogative. And Dr. Jack Kevorkian has conducted his crusade for the legalization of physician-assisted suicide and euthanasia with the cunning calculation that the logic of the principle of autonomy, deeply imbedded in modern people's minds, ultimately will prevail over traditional moral objections to the practice.

To the extent that these notions of individualism and autonomy influence contemporary thought on childhood, there is a tendency to define childhood apart from serious reflection on the meaning of parenthood. Yet a moment's pause might lead one to recognize that there is hardly a deeper characteristic of human life than the parent-child relationship. This essay was completed on the heels of the tragic killings at Columbine High School in Littleton, Colorado, in April of 1999, where two students ruthlessly gunned down fellow classmates and teachers. The violence at Columbine High School was followed by much

---

1. Robert Bellah et al., *Habits of the Heart* (Berkeley and Los Angeles: University of California Press, 1985), 334.

lamentation in the press and in other media about the so-called crisis of child-hood in our culture. Commentary focused on individuals and their roles in the events and external influences on youthful behavior such as television and the Internet. Far less attention was given to the statistics on the diminished time that parents are able or willing to spend with their children or the failure of the society as a whole to transmit fundamental rules of manners and morals to young people.

The Christian faith would have us look more closely at the fundamental parent-child nexus. Yet in the churches far too little discussion is given over to the vocation of parenthood and the child's obligations to parents. Instead, churches ape the culture's obsessive interest in individual psychology and, as I have mentioned, personal autonomy. In Christian education these habits are reflected in the strict divisions of instruction by age group and the dominance of developmental models of child psychology that overemphasize autonomy and cognitive capabilities. The latter has led to a neglect of effective socializa-tion of children into the community of believers using the church's own re-sources of narrative and sacramental theology.[2]

My aim here is to present one of the great figures of the early church and of Eastern Christianity specifically, St. John Chrysostom (c. 347-407), and to let him enter this discussion. For St. John Chrysostom emphasized the solidarity of human community, the need for socialization of the young into the church, and the powerful unitive and communicative love that the parent-child nexus infuses into human society. Chrysostom often addressed parents of his day on these matters, and he speaks to us powerfully even in the present about the la-cunae in our religious and moral understandings of parenthood and child-hood. His views are solidly grounded in the Trinitarian and Christological teachings of the church, and so he integrates both the communal and personalist aspects of the Christian faith in his advice on parenting. In his ser-mons and tracts, Chrysostom proposes that the Christian family is itself an ecclesial (or churchly) entity wherein adults and children rehearse for member-ship in the kingdom of heaven. He advances a strong moral teaching about the virtues and responsibilities of parenthood and invests that role with a powerful soteriological significance.

As a priest in Antioch and bishop of Constantinople, the highest episco-pal see in the Christian East, Chrystostom often raised this question: "What are the attributes of a good Christian parent and, in turn, what is the nature of the parent-child relationship?" He would have understood our contemporary con-

2. John L. Boojamra strikes chords that resonate with Chrysostom's own pastoral insights and is critical of prevailing models and methods of Christian education in *Foun-dations for Christian Education* (Crestwood, N.Y.: St. Vladimir's Seminary Press, 1989).

cern that childhood is in crisis. He witnessed and addressed a similar phenomenon in his own time. But he would also remind us that when and wherever there is a crisis of childhood there is bound also to be a crisis of parenthood. And he would encourage us in our circumstances to examine closely the parental side of the parent-child relationship especially. Thus, without neglecting to consider the meaning of childhood, I here endeavor to present Chrysostom's virtually unique contribution to a Christian understanding of parenthood.

The Context of John Chrysostom's Ministry

St. John Chrysostom lived at a time of great monastic activity; but as he became involved in priestly and episcopal responsibilities within the great urban centers of ancient Antioch and Constantinople, he turned his attention to the family and the domestic life of his parishioners. He applied what he had learned of the monastic discipline to the secular realm and insisted that even the highest Christian virtues embodied in the Beatitudes of the Sermon on the Mount (Matthew 5–7) are binding upon all Christians and not reserved solely for monks.[3]

The society in which John Chrysostom lived and preached was diverse and in flux, not unlike our own. The pagan culture of antiquity was in distress and decline. Moral standards were deteriorating, and the old pagan religion was losing force in the lives of many, especially in the cities. In the midst of this change, the Christian church had begun to exert a formative influence upon state and society. In 313 the Emperor Constantine issued the Edict of Milan, which granted the Christian church legal toleration and freedom of worship within the Empire. And during Chrysostom's own lifetime, Theodosius I, Roman emperor from 379 to 395, established Christianity as the official religion of the state.

3. Addressing married person who were making excuses for themselves, Chrysostom responded, "And if these beatitudes were spoken to solitaries only, and the secular person cannot fulfill them, yet He [Christ] permitted marriage, then He has destroyed all men. . . . And if persons have been hindered by their marriage state, let them know that marriage is not the hindrance, but their purpose which made an ill use of marriage." See John Chrysostom, "Homilies on the Hebrews," in *Chrysostom: Homilies on the Gospel of John and the Epistle to the Hebrews*, vol. 14 of *A Select Library of the Nicene and Post-Nicene Fathers of the Christian Church*, first series, ed. Philip Schaff (New York: Christian Literature Co., 1890), 402. The Eastern Church has never formally declared a hierarchy of Christian life in which celibacy is designated a higher state of Christian living than marriage. Chrysostom's views are echoed by other Eastern Christian writers such as Clement of Alexandria in his *Stromateis*. For further discussion and references, see chapter 4 of my book *Incarnate Love: Essays in Orthodox Ethics* (Notre Dame: University of Notre Dame Press, 1987).

However, this success of the church also presented temptations of crippling compromise. The purity of the faith was in jeopardy as Christians increasingly took up responsibilities in the secular world. Belonging to the church was beginning to be seen as routine and advantageous for worldly success. Chrysostom abhorred a cake-frosting variety of Christianity. Constantly he inveighed against the moral laxity of self-professed Christians and their excessive preoccupation with material possessions, entertainment, social status, and political influence. He was especially troubled, even outraged, by the eagerness of some Christian parents to propel their children into the secular professions, while neglecting their spiritual and moral formation. Thus he felt especially moved to speak about the role and responsibilities of parents.

Communal Christianity and the Ecclesial Family

As I have mentioned, John Chrysostom's understanding of parenthood was biblically inspired and deeply grounded in the Trinitarian and Christological teaching of the church. Human parenthood and childhood mirror the life of the Divine Persons of the Trinity. The Fatherhood of God and the Sonship of the Divine Word are founded in love and reciprocity, and the Holy Spirit intends and carries that love toward and between the two. When one reflects on the Holy Trinity, one begins with the Father. Fatherhood points to Sonship, and then the Spirit lovingly energizes and liberates the relationships of all those upon whom the Spirit rests. Thus parents who are worshippers of the triune God are called upon to emulate God the Father's love for his Son, while children should love and obey their parents as the Son loves and obeys the Father through the Spirit. Together, through love, parents and children participate in the triune Life of God.

Likewise, the godly family is an image of the church, in so much as all of its members rehearse the redeemed and sanctified life, worthy of Christ, that the church continually offers to God in sacrifice. In a famous passage from his homily on Ephesians 5:22-23, the great preacher draws this comparison of the Christian household with the church:

> If we regulate our households [properly] . . . we will also be fit to oversee the Church, for indeed the household is a little church. Therefore, it is possible for us to surpass all others in virtue by becoming good husbands and wives.[4]

4. John Chrysostom, *On Marriage and Family Life,* trans. Catherine P. Roth and David Anderson (Crestwood, N.Y.: St. Vladimir's Seminary Press, 1986), 57.

Chrysostom employs a typological reading of the Old Testament to fill out this ecclesial analogy. For example, in a homily on the book of Acts, he maintains that the Abrahamic household kept and practiced the virtues of the kingdom of God in an exemplary and prophetic manner that should be imitated by Christian families. All the members of a household, adults and children, must ready their home and themselves to receive divine visitors and Christ himself. Thus, like the church, the home must be made a house fit for the presence of God. "Abraham received the strangers in the place where he abode himself; his wife [Sarah] stood in the place of a servant, the guests in the place of masters. He knew not that he was receiving Christ; knew not that he was receiving Angels; so that had he known, he would have lavished his whole substance. But we, who know that we receive Christ, show not even so much zeal. . . . Let our house be Christ's general receptacle."[5]

Because the physical dwelling is to be "Christ's general receptacle," the members of the household must strive to make it a place worthy of the Holy One. In another homily on Acts, Chrysostom exhorts his listeners to "let the house be a Church, consisting of men and women. . . . 'For where two,' He saith, 'are gathered together in My Name, there am I in the midst.'"[6] The Christian family, under the headship of the husband and father, are to be engaged in a spiritual discipline of holiness and embody in their relations the virtues of charity and hospitality. Indeed, the woman who is chosen for a wife should possess these virtues. Abraham sent his servant to his own country to find a wife for Isaac, and the servant looked for the woman who offered water not only to him but for his camels (Gen. 24:11-14). This was done, writes Chrysostom, because, "everything good" that happened to the household "came because of hospitality."[7] This hospitality is a form and expression of charity and neighbor love. Chrysostom insists that charity begins at home in the care that parents give their children to bring them up "in the Lord" and prepare them as heirs of the kingdom of God.

---

5. John Chrysostom, "Homilies on the Acts," in *St. John Chrysostom: Homilies on the Acts of the Apostles and the Epistle to the Romans*, vol. 11 of *A Select Library of the Nicene and Post-Nicene Fathers of the Christian Church*, 277.

6. Chrysostom, *Homilies on the Acts of the Apostles*, 127.

7. Chrysostom, *On Marriage and Family Life*, 103-4.

The Image of God, Original Sin, and
the Divine Model of Parenthood

Early in his adult life, Chrysostom emphasized these communal and soteriological principles in his defense of monasticism. But later, as a pastor and bishop, he argued with equal vigor that the health and mission of the church crucially depends upon the vitality of the Christian family; and he gave himself over to clarifying the normative character of the family and prescribing appropriate child-rearing practices.

According to Chrysostom, the character of the ecclesial family is decided largely by the relationship of husband and wife as father and mother to their children. In my estimate, St. John Chrysostom's richest theological statement about parenthood and raising children appears in his homily on Ephesians 6:1-4:

> Let us bring them [our children] up in the discipline and instruction of the Lord. Great will be the reward in store for us, for if artists who make statues and paint portraits of kings are held in high esteem, will not God bless ten thousand times more those who reveal and beautify His royal image (for man is the image of God)? When we teach our children to be good, to be gentle, to be forgiving (all these are attributes of God), to be generous, to love their fellow men, to regard this present age as nothing, we instill virtue in their souls, and reveal the image of God within them. This, then, is our task: to educate both our children and ourselves in godliness; otherwise what answer will we have before Christ's judgment seat? If a man with unruly children is unworthy to be bishop [Titus 1:6], how can he be worthy of the kingdom of heaven? What do you think? If we have an undisciplined wife, or unruly children, shall we not have to render an account for them? Yes, we shall, if we cannot offer to God what we owe Him, because we can't be saved through individual righteousness.[8]

In this paragraph, Chrysostom introduces the important metaphor of parents as artists — a metaphor that he uses throughout his writings to explore and to explain the vocation of Christian parenthood and the significance of children in the life of the church. The paragraph also includes a related theme in his discussion of parenthood: parents are to reveal the image of God in their children.

These central notions of his vision of parenthood are best understood in relation to Chrysostom's particular theological anthropology. This anthropology is thoroughly informed by the doctrine of the *imago Dei:* that every human being is created in the image and likeness of God. Chrysostom follows the lead of Irenaeus, Athanasius, and the Cappadocian fathers in attributing to the di-

8. Chrysostom, *On Marriage and Family Life,* 44.

vine image reason, free will, moral responsibility, and reciprocity in love and to the likeness mastery of the passions and the exercise of virtue. According to Chrysostom, the *imago Dei* also supercedes differences in sex and age. In his homily on Ephesians 5:22-23, he broaches the subject in this manner: "[God] did not, on the one hand, fashion woman independently from man; otherwise man would think of her as essentially different from himself."[9] Instead, male and female are equally created in the image and likeness of God (Gen. 1:26-27).

Chrysostom also believes that through the physical union and loving communion of male and female, parents pass on the image and likeness of God to their offspring. Chrysostom did not enjoy our scientific and biological understanding of conception. Nevertheless, the theological and soteriological meaning he attributes to marriage, procreation, and child rearing is profound, richly Trinitarian and Christological. He employs the language of *perichoresis* (coinherence) and consubstantiality when speaking of the marital union and the community of being it brings into existence:

> How do they become one flesh? As if she were gold receiving purest gold, the woman receives the man's seed with rich pleasure, and within her it is nourished, cherished, and refined. It is mingled with her own substance and she then returns it as a child! The child is a bridge connecting mother to father, so the three become one flesh. . . . And here the bridge is formed from the substance of each! Just as the head and the rest of the body are one, so it is with the child. That is why Scripture does not say, "They shall be one flesh." But they shall be joined together "into one flesh," namely the child. But suppose there is no child; do they then remain two and not one? No; their intercourse effects the joining of their bodies, and they are made one, just as when perfume is mixed with ointment.[10]

Although he claims that all human beings are made in the image of God, Chrysostom believes that original sin has brought about corruptability and death and weakened the capacity to grow into God's likeness in virtue and loving communion. He is a major voice within a consensus of Greek patristic writers who interpret the Fall "as an inheritance essentially of mortality rather than sinfulness, sinfulness being merely a consequence of mortality."[11] This Greek patristic understanding of original sin stems from their translation of Romans

9. Chrysostom, *On Marriage and Family Life*, 44.

10. Chrysostom, *On Marriage and Family Life*, 76. In his homily on Ephesians 5:22-33, Chrysostom makes an explicit Christological analogy: "The child is born from the union of their seed, so the three are one flesh. Our relationship to Christ is the same; we become one flesh with Him through communion" (51).

11. John Meyendorff, *Byzantine Theology: Historical Trends and Doctrinal Themes* (New York: Fordham University Press, 1976), 144.

5:12, where Paul, speaking of the Genesis story, writes, "As sin came into the world through one man, and through sin, death, so death spread to all men *because all men have sinned* [*eph ho pantes hemarton*]." John Meyendorff, who quotes this text in his book *Byzantine Theology,* explains:

> In this passage there is a major issue of translation. The last four Greek words were translated in Latin as *in quo omnes peccaverunt* ("in whom [i.e., in Adam] all men have sinned"), and this translation was used in the West to justify the doctrine of guilt inherited from Adam and spread to his descendants. But such a meaning cannot be drawn from the original Greek — the text.[12]

Eph ho was translated and interpreted in and from the Latin as "in whom," not as "because," which is the correct Greek meaning. Thus, theological interpretation in the Latin West has stressed that sin is passed on by Adam to all of humankind, and with it guilt also; whereas in the Greek East, death is seen as the punishment of Adam's sin passed on to all his descendants and sin its inevitable consequence. Thus Adam's mortal illness corrupts nature, and the deep habit of sin afflicts and weakens the human will.

Consistent with this Eastern understanding, Chrysostom believes that although the essential image of God in man has not been touched, the likeness and capacity to grow in divine similitude has been severely weakened. Humankind is subject to a kind of regression so that the image is soiled rather than brought to a heavenly luster. Thus God takes the initiative in Jesus Christ to heal and restore corrupted human existence. Christ by the very nature of being fully God and fully human invites a synergy of grace and human striving to purify the image and bring humanity into communion with the divine life.

These ideas about the image of God and increase in likeness to God are the basis for Chrysostom's claim that parents can help restore and refine this image in their children. Chrysostom argues that when parents educate their children in virtue, they assume a role comparable to Christ's action for all of humanity. For in word and deed Christ revealed himself to be the express Image of God, the prototype of that image of God given to human beings at their creation and from which the race has declined due to sin. Parents are not the saviors of their children, but they are, according to God's will and design, their natural teachers, as Christ is the divine teacher for all of humankind. "This, then, is our task," Chrysostom urges parents: "to educate both ourselves and our children in godliness."[13]

In *An Address on Vainglory and the Right Way for Parents to Bring Up*

---

12. Meyendorff, *Byzantine Theology,* 144.
13. Chrysostom, *On Marriage and Family Life,* 71.

Their Children, a landmark in Christian pastoral theology devoted to the religious education and formation of children, Chrysostom expands upon his favorite metaphor. He says to parents,

> To each of you fathers and mothers, I say, just as we see artists fashioning their paintings and statues with great precision, so we must care for these wondrous statues of ours. Painters when they have set the canvas on the easel paint on it day by day to accomplish their purpose. Sculptors, too, working in marble, proceed in a similar manner; they remove what is superfluous and add what is lacking. Even so must you proceed. Like the creators of statues so you give all your leisure to fashioning these wondrous statues for God.[14]

In this way Chrysostom assigns to parents a sacred responsibility for the religious and moral formation of their offspring. He attributes to children complete human status (the image of God), but he also reminds parents and adults that much remains for the completion (increase in likeness to God) of these "wondrous statues of ours." They are God's greatest work, made in his very own image and intended by God to participate in the divine life (2 Pet. 1:4). Parenthood is right in the thick of a web of human relations, obligations, and the synergy of human and divine wills that contributes to salvation. Thus parents hold not only an ecclesial office but also a soteriological one, a salvific one.[15] God has put parents in care of their children's souls, and whether a child inherits the kingdom of heaven relies upon the care he or she receives from parents.[16]

Baptism

Chrysostom's ideas about sin and the image of God are also reflected in his understanding of baptism. His interpretation is consistent with much that is said in the Christian East. It differs in important respects, however, from the familiar Augustinian and Reformed interpretations in the West. As I have stated, Chrysostom understands original sin not in terms of inherited or personal guilt, but in terms of an inherited mortality that causes human beings to sin. In

14. *An Address on Vainglory and the Right Way for Parents to Bring Up Their Children,* in M. L. W. Laistner, *Christianity and Pagan Culture in the Later Roman Empire* (Ithaca, N.Y.: Cornell University Press, 1967), 96. The "Address" is appended to the back of Laistner's volume.

15. Margaret Bendroth finds in Horace Bushnell's writing a similar attribution of soteriological character to Christian parenthood. (See her essay in this volume.)

16. Chrysostom nowhere suggests that God cannot find other means to save his "children." Children of bad parents are still related to a gracious and merciful God.

her essay on St. Augustine, Martha Ellen Stortz ably explores how the former interpretation of original sin is reflected in Augustine's justification of infant baptism. She explains that Augustine believes that even newly born infants participate in Adam's sin. Augustine attributes their relative innocence, or the absence of personal sin, solely to the "physical weakness" of infants, "i.e. being unable to harm anyone else."[17] But he commends infant baptism in the belief that infants are, nevertheless, born into the grasp of Satan and that baptism is principally for repossessing the child for Christ.[18]

By contrast, Chrysostom maintains that newborn infants are innocents, wholly without sin. Infants may belong to a corporate human nature, which in its wholeness is mortally wounded by original sin and the will of which is weakened and prone to personal sin, but they are still innocents. In the fourth of his catechetical lectures on baptism, he freely states, "We do baptize infants. Although they are not guilty of any sins."[19] But if it is true that infants are sinless, then we might ask Chrysostom why the church baptizes them? Like Augustine, Chrysostom attributes a remedial power to baptism. But for him this is a single aspect of the sacrament and does not exhaust its whole meaning. Baptism, above all else, is an acceptance by the church and entrance of the baptized person into the redeemed and sanctified body of Christ. Baptism is the beginning of a life spent in spiritual combat (askesis) and instruction in holiness and godliness and on a deepening journey into the kingdom of heaven. Infants and children are especially needful of being incorporated and socialized into the church because they benefit from the care and discipline of adults experienced in the spiritual struggle.

Salvation, Parenting, and Children

Related to Chrysostom's ideas about the image of God and the parents' role in restoring this image in their children is his belief in the corporate nature of salvation. "We can't be saved through individual righteousness," Chrysostom insists in his homily on Ephesians 6:1-4. And he continues, "If the man who buried his one talent gained nothing, but was punished instead, it is obvious that one's own virtue is not enough for salvation, but the virtue of those for whom

17. Martha Ellen Stortz, "'Where or When Was Your Servant Innocent?' Augustine on Childhood," 82.

18. Stortz, "'Where or When Was Your Servant Innocent?'" 96-97.

19. In *The Later Christian Fathers,* ed. and trans. Henry Bettenson (Oxford: Oxford University Press, 1977), 165.

we are responsible is also required."[20] The implications for parenthood are striking. Though a parent may lead an otherwise virtuous life, if he or she neglects the needs of the child and fails to instruct the child in godliness, then that virtue does not count for much in the eyes of God. "Not only does God punish children who behave badly toward their parents, not only does he receive favorably those who are good," Chrysostom writes, "but he also does the same thing to the parents, severely punishing those who neglect their children, but honoring and praising those who care for them."[21]

If God is not a monad but rather a triune community of being whose ecstatic communion brings into existence creatures to love, and if humankind is created in God's very own image and likeness, then genuine virtue is an unselfish service of love toward others. And what is more natural and imitative of God's love than the love of parents for their children? Chrysostom's view of love, however, is free of sentimentalism and romanticism. It is a teaching about what we today would call "tough love." In Chrysostom's view the love of God is correlative with the fear of God, the respect and honor due to God because God is holy. Something analogous, he says, must obtain in the parent-child relationship. Filial love necessarily includes obedience to Christ, who is perfectly obedient to the Father. Thus St. Paul exhorts, "Children, obey your parents in the Lord, for this is right. 'Honor your father and mother' (this is the first commandment with a promise) 'that it may be well with you and that you may live long on the earth'" (Eph. 6:1-3, RSV).[22] As for parents, St. Paul instructs fathers, "Do not provoke your children to anger, but bring them up in the discipline and instruction of the Lord" (Eph. 6:4, RSV). Chrysostom adds, "[Paul] does not say, 'love them.' He would regard such a commandment as superfluous; trusting that nature will draw even the unwilling parent to the love of their children. What does he say? 'Do not provoke your children to anger.'"[23] It fol-

---

20. Chrysostom, *On Marriage and Family Life*, 72.

21. John Chrystostom, *A Comparison between a King and Monk/Against the Opponents of the Monastic Life*, translated and with an introduction by David G. Hunter (Lewiston, N.Y.: Edward Mellen Press, 1988), 132.

22. Filial obedience is not an absolute. In his homily on Ephesians 6:1-4, Chrysostom raises the question "What if my parents command me to do things that are wrong?" He answers the would-be inquirer as follows: "St. Paul has left us a provision in this case, by saying, 'Obey your parents *in the Lord*,' that is, whenever they tell you to do what is pleasing to God. So if your father is an unbeliever, or a heretic, and demands that you follow him, you ought not to obey, because what he commands is not in the Lord." See Chrysostom, *On Marriage and Family Life*, 66.

23. Chrysostom, *On Marriage and Family Life*, 66-67. In several of the essays in this volume, corporal punishment is mentioned. Some of the figures that are discussed strongly approve of it and even explain in detail how it might be administered. See, for example, Keith Graber Miller's essay on Menno Simons in this volume. I have not found any

lows that parents must not treat their children as slaves or instruments for their own pleasure.

The kind of love to which God calls parents is above natural love and transcends every corruption of it. It is the deepest sort of respect for the child as a divine "statue," an icon of God. This respect obligates parents to bring up their children "in the discipline and instruction of the Lord." Chrysostom proposes the highest doctrine of the parent-child relationship, rooted in the agapeic love (and fear) of God.

John Chrysostom also believed that the relative weakness and dependency of children set certain conditions for the salvation of both them and their parents. Parents and children together suffer when the former do not assume responsibility for the latter. In his early tract entitled *Against the Opponents of the Monastic Life,* Chrysostom endeavors to drive home this hard truth through a consideration of the life of the priest Eli, whose story is related in 1 Samuel. Eli's valuable service to God and Israel is beyond dispute, but he failed to discipline adequately and to correct the behavior of his two adult sons. Their crimes were fornication and gluttony (1 Sam. 2:12-36). For this failure God did not spare Eli a violent death.[24] Chrysostom judges Eli and his sons severely. He makes not even the slightest allowance that a parent might not be wholly responsible for the behavior of his or her children. This judgment appears in *Against the Opponents of the Monastic Life,* which in all likelihood Chrysostom wrote just before or about the time of his ordination to the priesthood in 386. The hard edge of his monastic training had not been softened by his later experience in the pastorate.

> What, then, did God say to Samuel? *He knew that his sons cursed God, and he did not correct them* [1 Sam. 3:13]. However, this is not exactly true because Eli certainly did correct his sons, but God says that his was not true correction. God condemned his warning because it was not sufficiently forceful. Therefore, even if we show concern for our children, if we fail to do what is necessary, it will not be true concern, just as Eli's correction was not a true one. After God had stated the charge against Eli, he added the punishment with great wrath: *For I have sworn,* he said, *to the house of Eli that the iniquity of Eli's house shall not be expiated by sacrifice or offering for ever* [1 Sam. 3:14]. Do you see God's intense anger and merciless punishment? Eli must perish utterly, he says, not only him and his children, but also his entire household with him, and there will be no remedy to heal his wound. Except for the

---

such preoccupation in Chrysostom. He does mention corporal punishment on one or two occasions that I am aware of and advises parents to use it when it is needed. But this is not unusual in his day or ours.

24. Keith Graber Miller mentions that Menno Simons also held the story of Eli and his sons in special regard as an admonition to Christian parents. (See his essay in this volume.)

man's negligence in regard to his children, however, God had no other charge to make against the elder at that time; in all other respects Eli was a marvelous man.[25]

Since the value of children is so great in God's estimate and their weakness equally evident, parental neglect ranks among the gravest evils and injustices. "I would say that these parents [who put their own needs before their children's needs and neglect the good of their children's souls] (and I am not speaking out of anger) are even worse than those who kill their children. I say these things now," Chrysostom adds, "so that we may realize that God will not easily tolerate those who neglect the ones so dear to him. He cannot labor on behalf of their salvation, while others disdain to show concern for them. . . . When parents are concerned only with their own affairs and do not wish to give priority to their children's, they necessarily neglect their children, as well their own souls."[26]

We might question Chrysostom's judgment about what constitutes parental neglect of children. On this matter there was no consensus in his day any more than there is in ours. It is clear, however, that the very high standard to which he holds parents responsible for their children rests upon several religious and moral principles that he has drawn from the Christian gospel. The most important of these is love of the neighbor. Neighbor love entails much more than goodwill: it requires an active interest in the neighbor's salvation. "The Judge demands of us with the same strictness both our own and our neighbor's salvation. That is why Paul everywhere urges everyone to seek not merely their own interest, but also the interest of the neighbor." My salvation and the salvation of my neighbor are inextricably tied together, Chrysostom argues. And our children are our most proximate neighbors. Furthermore, children are among the weakest and most vulnerable members of society. Therefore, the obligation of neighbor love is that much stronger in the parent-child relationship. "Writing to the Romans, Paul ordered them to exercise great care in this matter, urging the strong to be like parents to the weak and persuading the former to be anxious for the salvation of the latter." Paul does not say such things "on his own authority, but on instruction from the Teacher." Chrysostom continues, "For the Only-begotten of God, wishing to teach that this is a necessary duty, and that great misfortunes await those who do not wish to fulfill it, said: *Whoever should scandalize one of these little ones, it would be better for him to have a great millstone fastened around his neck and to be drowned in the depths of the sea* [Matt. 18:6]."[27]

25. Chrysostom, *Comparison/Against the Opponents*, 128-29.
26. Chrysostom, *Comparison/Against the Opponents*, 132-33.
27. Chrysostom, *Comparison/Against the Opponents*, 124-25, 125, 125-26.

On the basis of gospel passages such as this, Chrysostom concludes that God has seen fit to establish parents' obligation for the care and nurture of their own offspring through nature as well as by divine statute. First, God "has endowed nature with a powerful desire which by a kind of inescapable necessity leads parents to care for their children"; and, second, he has left commandments which fortify this natural bond and make care for one's children every bit as much a duty as caring for oneself.[28]

Parental Responsibility for the Christian Formation of Children

As I have said, John Chrysostom did not believe that the image of God is destroyed or that it has been so radically distorted by sin that we are forbidden to think about how it might be humanly repaired or refurbished. It is just this optimism about reform and perfectibility (*theosis* or divinization) that moved Chrysostom to exhort parents unremittingly to take up their responsibility to influence and shape the lives of their children by example and through common worship, discipline, and religious education.

Chrysostom harshly chastised Christian parents more concerned with secular standards of success and goals for living than with the church's standards of right living. Over and against the commercialism and hedonism of his own day, Chrysostom affirms a "worldly" Christian asceticism that he would have reach into every corner of the secular world.

> If a child learns a trade, or is highly educated for a lucrative profession, all is nothing compared to the art of detachment from riches; if you want to make your child rich, teach him this. He is truly rich who does not desire great possessions, or surrounds himself with wealth, but who requires nothing. . . . Don't worry about giving him an influential reputation, for worldly wisdom, but ponder deeply how you can teach him to think lightly of this life's passing glories, thus he will become truly renowned and glorious. . . . Don't strive to make him a clever orator, but teach him to love true wisdom. He will suffer if he lacks clever words, but if he lacks wisdom, all the rhetoric in the world can't help him. *A pattern of life is what is needed, not empty speeches; character, not cleverness; deeds, not words* [my emphasis]. These things will secure the Kingdom and bestow God's blessings.[29]

28. Chrysostom, *Comparison/Against the Opponents*, 131-32.
29. Chrysostom, *On Marriage and Family Life*, 68-69.

Throughout his preaching on the subject of Christian character, John Chrysostom has in mind this "pattern of life." By what means are children to learn this pattern? Chrysostom leaves us a long list, including instruction in the Commandments, worship, and the habit of prayer. Interestingly, storytelling also ranks high on the list. Chrysostom, of course, prefers stories from Scripture; but he does not exclude pagan stories, which can be used to prepare the child's appetite and imagination for instruction in the Bible. "The child . . . learns the story of raising from the dead. If in pagan legend such marvels are told, one says: 'he made the soul the soul of a hero.' And the child believes and, while he does not know what a hero is, he knows that it is something greater than a man. And as soon as he hears, he marvels. Much more will he do so when he hears of raising from the dead and the younger brother [Abel] went up to heaven."[30]

Chrysostom is confident also that the biblical stories can communicate powerful and important truths to children. He goes to great lengths in *An Address on Vainglory* to explain to parents how they might accomplish this in their own homes. For example, he suggests juxtaposing the story of Cain and Abel with that of Jacob and Esau. Parents should first draw out the distinct lessons of each story and then compare them so as to identify the common themes of sibling rivalry, envy, and fratricide, and the importance of obedience to God and parents. He urges parents to tell these stories to their child not once but often and repeatedly. Then they should say to the child,

> "Tell me the story of those two brothers." And if he begins to relate the story of Cain and Abel, stop him and say: "It is not that one that I want, but the one of the other two brothers [Jacob and Esau] in which the father gave his blessing." Give him hints but do not as yet tell him their names. When he has told you all, spin the sequel of the yarn, and say: "Hear what occurred afterwards. Once again the elder brother, like in the former story, was minded to slay his brother."[31]

Chrysostom is even attentive to what we today refer to as "age appropriateness." Thus he advises parents that when a child is older, they may tell him more fearful tales — but not too soon, "for thou shouldst not impose so great a burden on his understanding while he is still tender, lest thou dismay him." When a child is "ten or eight or even younger let him hear of the flood, the destruction of Sodom, the descent into Egypt . . . stories full of divine punishment. When he is older let him hear also the deeds of the New Testament —

30. Chrysostom, *Address on Vainglory,* 104.
31. Chrysostom, *Address on Vainglory,* 106. See also "Family and Christian Virtue," chapter six in my book entitled *Ethics after Christendom: Toward an Ecclesial Christian Ethic* (Grand Rapids, Mich.: Eerdmans, 1994).

deeds of grace and deeds of hell." He explicitly advises that a child should not hear of hell until "he is fifteen years old or older."[32]

In the same work, Chrysostom also discusses at length biblical models of the parent-child relationship and sibling relations. To parents, as we have seen already, he commends the examples of Abraham and Sarah for their great virtues of hospitality and obedience to God. He also holds up Hannah, the mother of Samuel, especially as an exemplar of unselfish parenthood whose first concern was to see that her only son was fit for the kingdom of heaven and available to the Lord. Hannah fulfilled the community's office of parenthood by unselfishly giving her only son to the temple to become a priest. Godly parents raise their child for God, to be God's servant. Hannah "gave Samuel to God, and with God she left him, and thus her marriage was blessed more than ever, because her first concern was for spiritual things."[33] Likewise, Chrysostom encourages parents to name their children after the righteous and to teach them their lives. Every child should be taught the great lives, whether of believers or unbelievers. "Let us guide the conversation to the kingdom of heaven and to those men of old, pagan or Christian, who were illustrious for their self-restraint. Let us constantly flood his ears with talk of them,"[34] he exhorts. Last but not least, he insists upon a discipline of prayer and worship. Parents must teach their children "to pray with great fervor and contrition," and he adds with the voice of the strong pastor to a human lot with which we all are too familiar, "and do not tell me that a lad never will conform to these practices."[35]

Conclusion

In the last analysis, John Chrysostom set forth in some of his many writings an impressive theology of parenthood and a recipe for what we of late call the education of character. It is, indeed, striking how so many of the metaphors he employs to exhort parents to seize responsibility for the religious and moral education of their children have to do with leaving an "impression" on the soul or person of a child. "If good precepts are *impressed* [my emphasis] on the soul while it is yet tender, no man will be able to destroy them when they have set firm, even as does a waxen *seal* [my emphasis],"[36] he states. The means by which

32. Chrysostom, *Address on Vainglory,* 109.
33. Chrysostom, *On Marriage and Family Life,* 68.
34. Chrysostom, *Address on Vainglory,* 118.
35. Chrysostom, *Address on Vainglory,* 119.
36. Chrysostom, *Address on Vainglory,* 95.

an impression of good character may be set firm in a child are various, and Chrysostom visits and revisits these in his sermons and tracts. Various as these means are, however, the end is clear. Chrysostom raises parenthood to cardinal importance in the Christian religion as a moral and ecclesial calling, and he justifies doing so solidly on Trinitarian and Christological grounds. Another way of putting this — not Chrysostom's but my own — is that parents are fellow workers [*synergoi*] with Christ (1 Cor. 3:9) in the garden of childhood. They are called upon by the Son of God to raise their sons and daughters to the full stature of maturity in Christ (Eph. 4:13; Col. 1:28), as members of his body, the one holy, catholic, and apostolic church.

It is possible that Chrysostom is a far more contemporary figure than he at first appears to be. For example, when he chastises parents for their obsession with educating their children in skills for worldly success — vainglory, as he calls it — is he not also speaking to us? Or when he advises that parents pay serious attention to the moral education of their children by judiciously selecting the images and examples of life that reach their children's eyes and ears, is he not striking a contemporary theme brought sadly and tragically to mind by the plague of violence committed by children against children on the streets and in our schools? As he closes *An Address on Vainglory*, Chrysostom addresses the education of boys — but we may apply his advice to our daughters also: "First train his soul and then take thought for his reputation,"[37] he insists. Not bad advice for any age and, maybe, especially our own.

---

37. Chrysostom, *Address on Vainglory*, 119. When he is not talking about children in general and is more specific, Chrysostom's regular practice is to speak of sons and boys, not girls or daughters. Similarly, he more often than not addresses himself to fathers, but he does have things to say about the mother's role in raising children. For example, he freely speaks of mothers reading and telling stories to their children. This is not only a presumed practice but something he encourages.

3. "Where or When Was Your Servant Innocent?" Augustine on Childhood

MARTHA ELLEN STORTZ

Introduction

The plight of the Holy Innocents loomed large in the imagination of Christian men and women in late antiquity. Sermons on Herod's cruel slaughter of the newly born (Matt. 2:16) proliferated in the Latin West.[1] Shortly after his ordination as presbyter of the North African city of Hippo in 396, Augustine (354-430) turned to this grisly incident in a discussion on free will. At that time, Augustine regarded all the children as "martyrs," although they had not been baptized. He was certain God had some "good compensation" reserved for them.[2]

Only a few years later, in the course of reviewing his own infancy, Augustine reversed himself. He raised grave questions about the innocence of children: "Who reminds me of the sin of my infancy? for 'none is pure from sin before you, not even an infant of one day upon the earth' (Job 14:4-5 LXX). Who reminds me? Any tiny child now, for I see in that child what I do not remember in myself. . . . So the feebleness of infant limbs is innocent, not the infant's mind."[3] Writing to Jerome in 415, Augustine retracted his earlier judgment of the Holy Innocents. Because they died unbaptized, they were condemned. He professed profound dismay over the solution: "But when we come to the penal

---

1. Paul A. Hayward, "Suffering and Innocence in Latin Sermons for the Feast of the Holy Innocents, c. 400-800," in *The Church and Childhood,* ed. Diana Wood (Oxford: Blackwell Publishers, 1994), 67-80.

2. Augustine, "On Free Will" 3.23.68, in *Augustine: Earlier Writings,* vol. 6 of Library of Christian Classics, ed. John H. S. Burleigh (Philadelphia: Westminster Press, 1953), 211.

3. Augustine, *Confessions* 1.7, trans. Henry Chadwick (New York: Oxford University Press, 1991), 9.

sufferings of children, you must believe that I experience great difficulties for which I have no answer."[4]

Controversy with the Pelagians (420-430), particularly with fellow bishop Julian of Eclanum (d. circa 455), occupied Augustine in the last period of his life and turned his attention once again to infants, children, and baptism. Augustine was convinced that these followers of the British monk Pelagius (d. circa 418) presented an overly optimistic view of human capacity and denied the grace of God. He summoned to his defense earlier interpretations of Romans 5:12, which he now understood as a summary judgment applying even to infants. *All* had sinned in Adam. At the same time, however, Augustine supplemented judgment with promise: baptism erased the burden of Adam's sin. Arguing from Romans 6:3 and from the practice of baptism itself, he insisted that all who were baptized were baptized into Christ's salvific death. Augustine claimed that Julian threatened to exclude infants from their promised salvation. Julian claimed that Augustine impugned the justice of God.

This controversy with Julian over baptism determined Augustine's final interpretation of childhood. His emerging thinking on sin and his own conversion experience informed his observations of children. In brief, Augustine's final argument could be outlined as follows:

1. Even infants show sinful tendencies;
2. Adam's transgression, which implants in his progeny an alien sin, accounts for these tendencies;
3. Baptism remedies these damnable tendencies and should be conferred as early as possible.

Herein lie the "great difficulties" that Augustine encountered when confronted with the suffering of the Holy Innocents.

The first task of this essay is to take Augustine at his word, examining each stage of his argument: the status of childhood, the nature of the human, and the role of baptism. Such investigation grants access to the understanding of children in a theology that has formed and informed, transformed and deformed Christian attitudes toward children.

The second task of this essay is to push beyond Augustine as he follows his own theological logic to its inevitable and tragic conclusions. Lest we be "orphaned of our own past," in Adrienne Rich's words, we need to sift Augustine's convictions, allowing his past to illumine our present. With equal rigor we must allow present knowledge to revise his past judgments.[5]

4. Augustine, "To Jerome, Letter 166," in *Letters of St. Augustine,* trans. and ed. John Leinenweber (Tarrytown, N.Y.: Triumph Books, 1992), 190.

5. Rich is quoted in Mary Pellauer's detailed essay entitled "Augustine on Rape: One

Situating Augustine's Perspectives on Childhood

Any examination of Augustine's theology of childhood must interrogate his point of view: what did he know about children and how did he know it? For his *Confessions* he drew on memories of his own childhood, embellished with careful observation of infants as an adult. For Augustine and his contemporaries, childhood prefigured the Christian life as a whole. Conversion returned individuals physically and experientially to childhood. Regardless of their age, candidates for baptism were regarded as "infants" *(infantes)*, because baptism signaled their spiritual rebirth.[6]

In addition, Augustine's responsibilities as bishop of Hippo afforded him different perspectives on the world of childhood. It acquainted him with the issue of abandoned children. Although Augustine censured the cruelty of this act, his overall attitude could be characterized as one of "ambivalent resignation": this "does not mean that he lacked concern for children: he simply recognized . . . that most parents had little choice about abandoning, and he directed his disapproval at those cases where he assumed there was choice."[7] Where he sensed parents had a choice, Augustine could be quite strict. When a pious woman wrote asking if she could leave both her husband and her children to become a nun, Augustine reminded her forcefully of her prior obligations as mother and wife.[8] In addition to such pastoral counsel, Augustine the bishop supervised instruction and initiation into the church, producing catechetical manuals that have deeply influenced traditions of the religious instruction of children to the present.[9] His episcopal duties offered insight into the situation of children in the ancient world.

Augustine also had more intimate experience with children. He was himself the father of one son, Adeodatus, probably born in 372, when Augustine

---

Chapter in the Theological Tradition," in *Violence against Women and Children: A Christian Theological Sourcebook,* ed. Carol J. Adams and Marie M. Fortune (New York: Continuum, 1995), 228. Analyzing Augustine's treatment of the rape of Lucretia in *The City of God,* Pellauer takes a revisionist approach similar to the one proposed in this essay.

6. Cf. J. D. C. Fisher, *Christian Initiation: Baptism in the Medieval West: A Study in the Disintegration of the Primitive Rite of Initiation* (London: SPCK, 1965), 5-6.

7. John Boswell, *The Kindness of Strangers: The Abandonment of Children in Western Europe from Late Antiquity to the Renaissance* (New York: Pantheon Books, 1988), 170.

8. Cf. Gillian Clark, "The Fathers and the Children," in *The Church and Childhood,* 4-5.

9. Cf. Augustine, *Teaching Christianity,* trans. Edmund Hill, O.P., in *The Works of St. Augustine,* Part I, vol. 11, ed. John Rotelle, O.S.A. (Hyde Park, N.Y.: New City Press, 1996). For discussions of Augustine's catechetical writings, see Eugene Kevane, *Augustine the Educator: A Study in the Fundamentals of Christian Formation* (Westminster, Md.: Newman Press, 1964); William Harmless, *Augustine and the Catechumenate* (Collegeville, Minn.: Liturgical Press, 1995).

was eighteen. The child was the issue of a long relationship with an unnamed woman who lived with Augustine as his concubine.[10] Although he declared the relationship to have been the product of lust, he was nonetheless faithful to this woman for fourteen years.[11] He could have married her, but ambition directed him to a more worthy match.[12] When he dismissed her, she returned to North Africa, vowing to know no other man. The church required the continence of such "repudiated women" if they were to receive baptism, and it is clear that Augustine's concubine was a catechumen at least by the time of her dismissal and possibly long before then.[13]

Concubinage, lust, and ambition are unremarkable in the world of late antiquity. Augustine's situation, however, was unique in two respects. First, he was faithful to his concubine, and this stands out in an age of promiscuity to challenge his own self-confessed sexual excess. Second, he was faithful to his son, and this was unusual at a time when Roman law remanded custody of the children of concubinage to their mother. Upon his mother's dismissal, Adeodatus remained with his father, an arrangement that publicly acknowledged Adeodatus as Augustine's legitimate progeny and also promised the child better material security than his mother could provide. In pledging continence, Adeodatus's mother in effect barred herself from entering other relationships of concubinage or marriage that might have provided for her and the boy. Although he acquiesced in the engagement arranged by his mother Monica, Augustine lamented for years the loss of the woman "who was torn from my side."[14] The effect on mother and child can only be imagined.

---

10. Concubinage was an acceptable relationship in late antiquity and occupied the middle ground between marriage, on the one hand, and promiscuity, or *stuprum,* on the other. The term "mistress," often used by translators of Augustine's *Confessions,* does not do justice to the prevalence and relative respectability of concubinage. Cf. Kim Powers, "*Sed unam tamen:* Augustine and His Concubine," *Augustinian Studies* 23 (1992): 50ff.; Aline Rousselle, *Porneia,* trans. Felicia Pheasant (Oxford: Basil Blackwell, 1988), 91ff.

11. "Nevertheless, she was the only girl for me, and I was faithful to her" (Augustine, *Confessions* 4.2, 53).

12. Powers points out that the boundaries between marriage and concubinage were fluid. The church tended to regard concubinage as marriage if the couple intended fidelity, procreation, and lifelong commitment. The Council of Toledo (397-400) permitted an unmarried man with one concubine to receive communion. Cf. Powers, "*Sed unam tamen,*" 50ff.

13. Peter Brown speculates that Augustine's concubine was a catechumen throughout her partner's "Manichaean enthusiasms." Brown thinks that Augustine was probably a Manichaean "hearer" for nine of their fourteen years together. Cf. Peter Brown, *Augustine of Hippo: A Biography* (Berkeley and Los Angeles: University of California Press, 1969), 62-63; Powers, "*Sed unam tamen,*" 52.

14. Augustine, *Confessions* 6.15, 109.

Although Augustine wrote little either about his son or about his direct experience of fatherhood, his general comments on parenting and marriage reveal much. He contrasted marriage, a relationship contracted for the purpose of raising children, and concubinage, a relationship struck up for the purpose of satisfying lust. In the latter, "the birth of a child is contrary to their intention — even though, if offspring arrive, they compel their parents to love them."[15] Indeed, Augustine's love for his own son deepened as the boy matured. An early dialogue, *The Teacher*, featured a conversation between father and son, and the father recorded no small degree of pride in noting that "he was responsible for all the ideas there attributed to him in the role of my partner in the conversation. He was 16 at the time. . . . His intelligence left me awestruck."[16] Adeodatus died soon afterwards, in 390. Within the space of four years Augustine suffered the loss of his son, his concubine, his mother, and his good friend Nebridius. This surplus of grief may account for the theologian's silence surrounding his son, but the experience of fatherhood undoubtedly shaped Augustine's theology of childhood.

The Non-Innocence of Children: Augustine on the Status of Childhood

Augustine spent much time in his *Confessions* probing the innocence of childhood, and his conclusion was resolute: "I ask you, my God, I ask, Lord, where and when your servant was innocent?"[17] With this he dismissed any claims for the innate innocence of infants and children. Nor did he come to the opposite conclusion, arguing for an innate depravity in infants and children. Between innocence and depravity Augustine posed a third possibility: non-innocence. Any innocence in childhood resided in physical weakness — that is, in being unable to harm anyone else (*in-nocens*, literally "not harming").[18]

15. Augustine, *Confessions* 4.2, 53. For a recent study of Augustine's view on marriage, see *St. Augustine on Marriage and Sexuality*, ed. Elizabeth Clark (Washington, D.C.: Catholic University Press of America, 1996).

16. Augustine, *Confessions*, 9.6, 164. Cf. Augustine, "The Teacher," in *Augustine: Earlier Writings*, 64-101.

17. Augustine, *Confessions* 1.7, 10.

18. Gillian Clark, "The Fathers and the Children," 23. Clark argues etymologically that *innocence* literally means "not harming." "Non-innocence" is my own term to express what I believe to be Augustine's view. He believed that even infants are tainted with original sin, though no opportunity for actual sin has occurred. Thus, their only "innocence" resides in the fact of their physical frailty and their lack of language. As children grow,

Just as infants gain physical strength as they mature, so they assume greater accountability for their actions. A child learns to speak by associating sounds with objects, and speech introduces the ability to distinguish right from wrong. Rewards and punishments reinforce this learning. With maturity, reason grows stronger and allows children gradually to discern a basic human equity that undergirds civil society. Augustine adopted a view of the human life-cycle that featured graduated guilt for one's actions: with age one moved from non-innocence into greater accountability.

Following a common classical trope, Augustine proposed six stages of human life.[19] *Infancy,* the first stage, extended from birth to the acquisition of language. For Augustine, it was simultaneously the most treacherous and the most transparent stage in all of human life. Two decisions followed immediately upon birth. Midwives routinely examined newborns for physical imperfections. If the newborn passed inspection, the midwife cut the umbilical cord at the specified length of four fingers from the stomach and knotted it. If judged defective, the infant was left to hemorrhage to death.[20] Fathers made a second decision about the infant's fate. In raising or "taking up" *(tollere)* the infant to a vertical position, the father claimed it as his own. Girls were not raised up by their fathers, and there is evidence that girls were exposed more frequently than boys. But a boy who was raised up would be safe from the threats of abandonment and disinheritance.[21]

Augustine watched infants closely and attempted to put into words this world without language. Perhaps no other author in the ancient world showed such attention. For someone so dependent upon language, infancy framed both beauty and terror. Augustine described tenderly the smiles of sleep and the comfort of nursing, but juxtaposed these occasions of serenity with a newborn's jealous rage when, even after it had been fed, it saw another infant at a

---

gaining language, strength, and reason, they become more and more responsible for their actions.

19. Cf. "Aetas," in *A Latin Dictionary,* ed. Charlton T. Lewis and Charles Short (Oxford: Clarendon Press, 1975). See also Boswell, *The Kindness of Strangers,* 30.

20. Galen specified both the length at which the umbilical cord was to be cut and the order of the events: "The umbilical cord shall be cut at a distance of four fingers from the stomach of the newborn, that is of course if he is perfect in all respects" (quoted in Rousselle, *Porneia,* 50).

21. Rousselle, *Porneia,* 51. John Boswell argues that this practice was more a matter of custom than of law (*The Kindness of Strangers,* 34n. 64). This practice of a father "raising up" a child as his true son may stand behind Paul's discussion of sonship and adoption in Romans 8:15-17ff. Paul is suggesting that such children rightly respond with a cry of "Abba! Father!" to one who has already raised them up as true sons. Both secular practice and its Pauline interpretation echo throughout Augustine's description of his conversion in the *Confessions,* as I shall argue later.

nurse's breast. Augustine judged the tantrum that followed unworthy of punishment: without language the infant could not understand the rebuke.[22] But he chose infants' tantrums and not their periods of serenity and sweet sleep as emblematic of this first stage. For Augustine, these epitomized the non-innocence of infancy: a baby already fed and in no hunger still grasping for the breast.

The acquisition of speech inaugurated the second stage of the life cycle: *childhood*. Words introduced a child to a rational world whose limits disobedience tested. Language ushered a child "more deeply into the stormy society of human life."[23] With childhood came rebuke and punishment as the child trespassed boundaries created by language and policed by adults. The non-innocence of infancy that resided in a grasping insatiability beyond all physical need phased into increased accountability. Language introduced the difference between obedience and disobedience, for which a child was accountable.

Despite this increasing accountability, Augustine could not condone the many beatings he had received as a child. He archly observed that both adults and children played games, yet children were the ones who got punished for playing them![24] That basic inequity between children and adults marked his childhood: "The schoolmaster who caned me was behaving no better than I was."[25] Though childhood was full of reprehensible actions, Augustine did not favor punishing children as severely as adults. Hopefully with maturity "reason begins to take hold," and the rationale behind the rules becomes clearer, making willing obedience a possibility.[26]

Puberty marked the next stage of development: *adolescence*. Augustine recorded the pride his father, Patricius, registered in observing obvious signs of

22. Colin Starnes, *Augustine's Conversion: A Guide to the Argument of Confessions I-IX* (Waterloo, Ont.: Wilfrid Laurier University Press, 1990), 10.

23. Augustine, *Confessions* 1.8, 11.

24. "But we loved to play, and punishments were imposed on us by those who were engaged in adult games. For 'the amusement of adults is called business.' But when boys play such games they are punished by adults, and no one feels sorry either for the children or for the adults or indeed for both of them" (Augustine, *Confessions* 1.9, 12).

25. Augustine, *Confessions* 1.9, 12.

26. "But who would dare assert that thefts, lies, and false oaths are not sins except one who wishes to commit such sins with impunity? Yet these sins are more common in childhood, although it seems that they should not be punished in children as severely as in adults, because one hopes that with the passing years, as reason begins to take hold, these children will be able to understand better the precepts pertaining to salvation and to give them willing obedience." See Augustine, "The Literal Meaning of Genesis" 10.13.23, in *Ancient Christian Writers*, vol. 42, ed. Johannes Quasten, Walter J. Burghardt, and Thomas Comerford Lawler, and trans. John Hammond Taylor, S.J. (New York: Newman Press, 1982), 112-13. Cf. Clark, "The Fathers and the Children," 24.

his son's emerging virility. His mother quaked, fearing incontinence.[27] Yet Augustine characterized this next stage of childhood not with sexual sin but with the gang-theft of pears from a neighbor's yard.[28] In choosing puberty to mark the onset of this third stage of the life cycle, Augustine led his reader to expect some salacious sexual encounter, but theft rather than incontinence better served the narrative.

The deed expanded on and intensified the account of increasing accountability Augustine had been building. Another encounter with food, it echoed eerily the infant's tantrum, because the youths were not hungry and in no physical need. Unlike that initial display of an infant's non-innocence prompted by jealousy, however, deliberate malice appeared to be the motive in the theft of the pears. A child erred in disobeying a verbal command; these youths knowingly violated a basic code of human decency. No one had to tell them not to steal the pears: they knew it was wrong. They stole for the sheer delight of doing something wrong. In this they disobeyed not a rule arbitrarily set by an adult but a certain bedrock equity in the world of human society. Not surprisingly, Augustine followed his description of the escapade with a catalogue of vices: pride, ambition, cruelty, lust, curiosity, ignorance, stupidity, idleness, luxury, prodigality, avarice, envy, anger, fear, and regret.[29] The increasing accountability of adolescence was illustrated by voluntary violation of divine and human natural justice for which the youth must be held accountable.

The meaning of accountability shifted throughout these three initial stages of the life cycle. While the infant's non-innocence might be judged premoral due to its lack of physical strength, the child's developing language skills conferred both an ability to communicate and increasing accountability for behavior. A child was held accountable if he or she violated a verbal rule — often an arbitrary one. Adolescence heralded the emergence of reason, and a youth faced even greater accountability for his or her behavior. With maturity and the acquisition of speech and reason, the non-innocence of an infant phased into the increasing accountability of childhood and adolescence. Greater accountability brought with it a greater sense of guilt. Augustine read into these first three stages of childhood a certain moral nuance.

Traditional division of the life cycle ended with three final stages: young adulthood *(juventus)*, the middle age of the *seniores*, and old age *(senectus)*.

27. "Indeed, when at the bathhouse my father saw that I was showing signs of virility and the stirrings of adolescence, he was overjoyed to suppose that he would now be having grandchildren, and told my mother so. . . . She shook with a pious trepidation and a holy fear" (Augustine, *Confessions* 2.6, 26-27).

28. Augustine, *Confessions* 2.4, 28-29.

29. Augustine, *Confessions* 2.6, 31-32.

Writing in the last years of his own life, Augustine refused to trade the chronic debilities of old age for a second childhood: "Infancy . . . starts this life not with smiles but with tears; and this is, in a way, an unconscious prophecy of the troubles on which it is entering."[30] Infancy epitomized "the wretchedness of the human condition."[31]

Despite this rather dour assessment of childhood, however, Augustine did not lobby for harsh treatment of children.[32] On the contrary, he treated his own son Adeodatus with exceptional care. Moreover, he did not believe children should be punished as harshly as he himself had been.

Rather, Augustine observed children closely for insights into adult behavior. Infancy revealed a non-innocence that phased into increasing accountability as children matured into adulthood. The infant grasping for the breast even after it had been fed became symbolic of a habit of concupiscence that would intensify throughout the life cycle. An adult merely replicated and amplified the sins of the child: "Behavior does not change when one leaves behind domestic guardians and schoolmasters, nuts and balls and sparrows, to be succeeded by prefects and kings, gold, estates, and slaves, as one advances to later stages in life."[33] Although maturity altered the objects of desire, from "nuts and balls" to "gold and estates," the continuity of concupiscence haunted Augustine. Interestingly, he concluded his observation not with judgment but with sympathy: "But when boys play such games they are punished by adults, and no one feels sorry either for the children or for the adults or indeed for both of them."[34] He matched the increasing moral accountability with increasing sympathy.[35]

Talking about infancy as "the epitome of human wretchedness" told only half of Augustine's story. Another infancy narrative in the *Confessions* complicated the picture considerably. Book 8 found Augustine once again sobbing uncontrollably in a garden, inarticulate as any infant. Now, however, he stood at the threshold of conversion, not infancy. As Margaret Miles observes with in-

30. Augustine, *City of God* 21.14, ed. David Knowles and trans. Henry Bettenson (New York: Penguin Books, 1972), 991.

31. R. A. Markus, *Saeculum: History and Society in the Theology of St. Augustine* (Cambridge: Cambridge University Press, 1970), 24.

32. Barbara Pitkin's essay on Calvin in this volume stresses this point: a low anthropology of childhood, encouraged in this case by a strong doctrine of original sin, is not at all inconsistent with the positive treatment of children.

33. Augustine, *Confessions* 1.19, 22.

34. *Confessions* 1.19, 22. I am grateful to Margaret Miles for pointing out the nuance in Augustine's reaction to the observation that adults and children are driven by similar desires.

35. Cf. Margaret R. Miles, *Desire and Delight: A New Reading of Augustine's "Confessions"* (New York: Crossroad, 1992), 21.

sight, the scene deliberately parallels Augustine's description of the first months and years of his life.[36]

The similarity in the two accounts is striking. Augustine credited his mother, Monica, with two births: his birth in the flesh and his birth in the spirit.[37] His second birth reproduced the tears and flailing limbs of a newborn. In this state of physical and spiritual chaos, Augustine saw a vision of Continence as "a fruitful mother of children." She urged him to take a few steps toward her, a scene that deliberately echoed the process of learning to walk. As any parent would do, Continence encouraged him, assuring him that God would not let him stumble and fall.[38] Suddenly, the voice of a child at play broke into his dream: "*Tolle et lege*" — "Take up and read." At this direction, Augustine picked up a Bible, opened it, and read from Romans 13. As he read, he experienced a peace he had probably only known before at the breast. A reader of late antiquity would have doubtless noted the symmetry that Augustine's story shared with the ancient ritual enacted at the birth of a child. A newborn whom a father had ritually "taken up" *(tollere)* and officially claimed as his own would be protected by that gesture from abandonment or disinheritance in the future.[39] In the *Confessions* Augustine's narrative of infancy frames the narrative of his conversion.

In addition, infancy provided the metaphors for the subsequent life of a Christian. Throughout his writings Augustine described himself as "sucking milk" at the breast of the Church.[40] Childhood embodied the perfect state of humility that characterized Christian discipleship.[41] The language, of course, revealed Augustine's deep debt to Paul, but it also bore the unique stamp of his own theology.

36. Margaret R. Miles, "Infancy, Parenting, and Nourishment in Augustine's *Confessions*," *Journal of the American Academy of Religion* 50 (September 1983): 349-64.

37. Augustine observed that Monica "suffered greater pains in my spiritual pregnancy than when she bore me in the flesh" (*Confessions* 5.9, 83).

38. Augustine, *Confessions* 8.11, 151-52.

39. On this practice, see Rousselle, *Porneia*, 50-51, who observes, "A girl would not be raised up by her father. But a son who was taken up into his father's arms in this way would be safe from the threat of abandonment thereafter" (51). Cf. Boswell, *The Kindness of Strangers*, 64, 145, 156, 164, 194.

40. "When all is well with me, what am I but an infant sucking your milk and feeding on you, 'the food that is incorruptible' (John 6:27)?" (Augustine, *Confessions* 4.1, 52). "The food which I was too weak to accept he mingled with flesh, in that 'The Word was made flesh' (John 1:14), so that our infant condition might come to suck milk from your wisdom by which you created all things" (*Confessions* 7.18, 128). Cf. Starnes, *Augustine's Conversion*, 80.

41. Augustine, *Confessions* 1.11, 13-14.

Adam's Transgression and the Nature of the Human

In the *Confessions* Augustine had observed that with childhood one "entered more deeply into the stormy society of human life."[42] Tempests raged in human society for a reason. For Augustine all creatures stood in the shadow of Adam, and the goodness of creation had been vitiated for all who follow him, including those newly born. Late in Augustine's life, Julian, follower of Pelagius and the bishop of Eclanum, pressed him hard on this point. How could two baptized parents pass on what they themselves no longer possessed: the burden of original sin? In a debate that has been described as "an unintelligent slogging match," Julian brought out the worst in Augustine.[43] In formulating his answer, Augustine drew upon a lifetime of theological reflection and a long exegetical journey through the writings of Paul.[44] He returned in his deliberations to childhood and to two passages involving children: Romans 9 and the two infants Jacob and Esau, and Romans 5:12 and the sons of Adam.

The twin sons of Isaac and Rebekah caught Augustine's attention early in his theological career, and he examined the fate of the infants in three separate writings toward the end of the fourth century. Why was Jacob favored and not Esau? For a culture that believed people were driven by stars and spirits, the question was a pressing one. In a treatise from 388 addressing eighty-three questions about Scripture, Augustine appealed to "the deeply hidden merits of souls" to explain why Jacob was favored and not his brother.[45] Later in 394, pressed by a group of Carthaginian Christians, he returned to the fate of the infants a second time. Now he cited Jacob's "merit of faith" to explain why he had been favored and not his brother Esau.[46] But when asked in 398 by Bishop

42. Augustine, *Confessions* 1.9, 11.

43. Brown, *Augustine of Hippo*, 387.

44. The late fourth century in the Latin West marked a resurgence of interest in Paul, with commentaries on the Pauline corpus from Marius Victorinus, Ambrosiaster, Pelagius, Jerome, and Rufinus's translation of Origen's commentary. In addition, there were unfinished attempts from Augustine, who, in the critical decade after his conversion, studied both Romans and Galatians. Cf. Brown, *Augustine of Hippo*, 151; Maurice Wiles, *The Divine Apostle: The Interpretation of St. Paul's Epistles in the Early Church* (Cambridge: Cambridge University Press, 1967), 13ff.; Andreas Lindemann, *Paulus im altesten Christentum* (Tübingen: Paul Siebeck/J. C. B. Mohr, 1979); and Ernst Benz, "Das Paulus-Verstandnis in der morgenlandischen und abendlandischen Kirche," *Zeitschrift fur Religions-und Geistesgeschichte* 3 (1951): 289ff.

45. Augustine, "Eighty-Three Different Questions" 68.3, in *The Fathers of the Church*, vol. 70, trans. David L. Mosher (Washington, D.C.: Catholic University of America Press, 1982), 162.

46. ". . . but that mercy was given to the preceding merit of faith *(merito fidei)*, and that hardening precedes impiety." Cf. Augustine, "Propositions from the Epistle to the

Simplicianus of Milan to explain Jacob's good fortune, Augustine admitted that he was not content with his earlier exposition.[47] This time he identified no difference on the part of the twins, either in capacity or belief, that could account for Jacob's favored status. Rather, Augustine now cited a certain "hidden equity" on God's part by which Jacob was favored.[48] He concluded his exegesis by appealing to another passage from Romans: "O the depth of the riches and wisdom and knowledge of God! How unsearchable are his judgments and how inscrutable his ways!" (11:33).[49]

In his emerging exegesis of the fate of these two infants, Jacob and Esau, Augustine shifted from an analysis that turned on creaturely ability and creaturely choice to one that turned on the Creator and divine choice. The shift entailed a distinction between the God who created and the God who judged. Drawing on a passage from the prophet Malachi, ". . . I have loved Jacob but I have hated Esau" (Mal. 1:2-3), Augustine gave the words his own interpretation. As Creator, God loved everything that is created; as Judge, God hated sin. Both Jacob and Esau were sinners: as descendants of Adam, both were part of the one mass of sinning that originated in Adam *(una massa omnium)*. God could have justly condemned both of them. But by a certain "hidden equity" residing in God alone, God chose to hate sin in Esau and to love in Jacob "not the sin which he had blotted out, but the grace which he had freely given him."[50] Against the Pelagians, Augustine argued that God arrived at both decisions apart from any consideration of future merit in the twins.[51]

Romans" 62.12, in *Augustine on Romans,* ed. and trans. Paula Fredriksen Landes (Chico, Calif.: Scholars Press, 1982), 35.

47. Augustine, "To Simplician — on Various Questions" 1.1, preface, in *Augustine: Earlier Writings,* 376.

48. "Let us believe that this belongs to a certain hidden equity that cannot be searched out by any human standard of measurement" (Augustine, "To Simplician — on Various Questions" 1.2.16, 397).

49. Augustine's conclusion is pure doxology; he reaches beyond the limits of human understanding: "Only let us believe it, if we cannot grasp it, that he who made and fashioned the whole creation, spiritual and corporeal, disposes of all things by number, weight and measure. But his judgments are inscrutable and his ways past finding out. Let us say Halleluia and praise him together in song; and let us not say, What is this? or, Why is that? All things have been created each in its own time" ("To Simplician — on Various Questions" 1.2.22, 406).

50. "To Simplician — on Various Questions" 1.2.18, 400. In this same exegesis, cf. "Then, of all was formed one mass *(una massa omnium)* coming from inherited sin and the penalty of mortality, though God formed and created what was good" (1.2.20, 403-4).

51. In this struggle with the fate of two infants, Augustine arrived at an exegetical rationale that John Calvin would take to its logical conclusion: a doctrine of double predestination. Scholars differ as to whether or not Augustine himself had a thoroughgoing doctrine of double predestination. According to John Wright, Augustine frequently speaks of God's fore-

What so compromised human nature even in a newborn infant? In dealing with the knotty question of Jacob and Esau prior to the Pelagian controversy (c. 412-430), Augustine had already distinguished between two natures: the first nature was created nature; the second was fallen nature. The distinction was not unique. Almost two hundred years earlier, another African theologian, Tertullian (d. circa 220), had arrived at the same conclusion.[52] But Augustine's battles with the Donatists and the Pelagians focused all his theological attention on the second nature. He wove various strands of tradition into a synthesis uniquely his own.

For Augustine, any discussion of creaturely nature was discussion of this second, corrupt, and fallen nature. It was the only nature remaining after the Fall, and it was composed of a single mass of sinning that encompassed all the descendants of Adam. Embedded in this nature was a will that without the intervention of divine grace tended toward sinning. As a result of the Fall, humans could no longer even do the good that they might will to do. Their disordered desire attached voraciously to earthly pleasures.[53] Augustine found

---

knowledge and preparation of people for the fixed number of saints in heaven. Wright adds, "In one place he speaks also of God predestining others to eternal death: 'He is also the most just dispenser of punishment to those whom he predestined to eternal death, not only because of the sins which they add of their own will, but also because of original sin even if, being infants, they add nothing of their own'" (John H. Wright, S.J., "Predestination," in *The New Dictionary of Theology,* ed. Joseph A. Komonchak, Mary Collins, and Dermot A. Lane [Collegeville, Minn.: Liturgical Press, 1991], 798). Since all could justly be condemned for possessing original sin, Augustine focuses on why some people, like Jacob, were then saved, and he explores the mysterious workings of divine grace. This raises a corollary question: Why is divine grace not extended to all? Augustine's belief that there were a fixed number of saints in heaven forced him to decide against universal salvation, but this was not really Augustine's predominant concern. Jaroslav Pelikan states the ambiguity: "Even in his most explicit statements about double predestination, however, Augustine spoke of that grace as a mystery. . . . It was an unfathomable mystery why one should receive grace and another not receive it, when neither of them deserved to receive it. The words of Romans 11:33 were his consistent reply to those who wanted the mystery resolved" (Pelikan, *The Emergence of the Catholic Tradition [100-600],* vol. 1 of *The Christian Tradition* [Chicago: University of Chicago Press, 1971], 298). See Barbara Pitkin's article in this volume.

52. Cf. J. N. D. Kelly, *Early Christian Doctrines* (London: A. & C. Black, 1958), 176.

53. Following Paul, Augustine agreed that the entire Decalogue could be reduced to the single commandment "Thou shalt not covet" *(non concupisces).* The Law revealed concupiscence and intensified it by forbidding it, which only added the crime of transgression. "The consequence was that concupiscence was even increased, since it could not be resisted when grace was not yet received. For concupiscence acquires greater strength when in addition there is violation of a law. It is aggravated when it is done against the law, and becomes a worse sin than if there had been no law prohibiting it. . . . Sin, then, existed before the law, but did not reach its full sinfulness because there was so far no violation of a law" (Augustine, "To Simplician — on Various Questions" 1.1.3, 377).

evidence of disordered desire especially in the first three stages of the life cycle: an infant grasping for the breast, a child quarreling in play, a gang of youths stealing pears. Even the infant was not innocent!

In the wake of the condemnation of Pelagius in 418, Julian of Eclanum pressed Augustine hard on precisely *how* this second nature was transmitted to newborns, particularly from parents who had themselves been baptized. Augustine countered with a twofold understanding of sin: sin was both exemplary and essential. In its exemplary character, sin consisted in repetition of sinful acts or personal sins, variously described as a habit of sinning *(moles consuetudinis)*, a frequency of sinning *(frequentatio peccandi)*, or the continuation of pleasure *(adsiduitas voluptatis)*. With this exemplary character of sin Augustine's contemporaries had no quarrel: they would have regarded this as sin in full.[54] Because the newborn had neither time nor opportunity to develop habits of any kind, it could scarcely be accused of sinning. Julian of Eclanum subscribed to this exemplary understanding of sin and was outraged over Augustine's condemnation of Pelagius.

But at this point Augustine introduced what he saw as an essential aspect to sin: all of Adam's progeny were born into the one mass of sinning. He insisted that even infants, who could hardly be said to have sinned by force of habit, belonged to this mass of sinning and were corrupted by original sin. They possessed and manifested evidence of a vitiated will; one needed only to observe them carefully. Infants were non-innocent and assumed greater accountability for their actions as they matured. For precisely this reason it would be cruel to exclude infants from baptism: they too needed access to baptism for the forgiveness of sin.

Augustine argued the existence of this essential aspect of sin on the basis of Romans 5:12.[55] It is clear that he and Pelagius both had different Latin translations of the verse.[56] Pelagius read that "sin came into the world *[introire]*."

54. The Pelagian Celestius announced that infants were born in exactly the same state as Adam before the Fall. Pelagius regarded all subsequent sin as the result of a habit of sinning *(consuetudo)*, which adhered to the soul like a corroding rust, but could be scraped off.

55. Cf. J. Patout Burns, "The Interpretation of Romans in the Pelagian Controversy," *Augustinian Studies* 10 (1979): 43-54; William S. Babcock, "Augustine's Interpretation of Romans: A.D. 394-396," *Augustinian Studies* 10 (1979): 55-74.

56. Bruce Metzger observes that "various people, at various times, and in various places, with varying degrees of success had translated various parts of the Bible into Latin. The result was chaos. The different versions had become so mixed and corrupt that no two manuscripts agreed" (Metzger, *The Early Versions of the New Testament: Their Origin, Transmission, and Limitations* [Oxford: Oxford University Press, 1977], 330). It is worth noting that both Augustine and Pelagius had inaccurate readings of the Greek on one point. Both read from texts that found Adam to be the one "in whom all have sinned" *(in*

The text supported him, supplying the Latin *introire*, literally meaning "to come into." On the basis of this, he fashioned a sort of travel diary of sin and death. In his commentary on the Epistles of Paul, Pelagius argued that sin "came into the world" *(advenire)* through Adam and "passed on" *(pertransire)* to Moses.[57] Pelagius had a strong theological investment in sticking with the travel metaphors. In the back of his mind was the Manichaean heresy, which posited cosmic dualism and identified creation, the body, and nature with the forces of evil. Arguing against this heresy, he would not concede that sin could penetrate a nature that was created good, or that the Creator created somehow imperfectly. A sinful creation implied an unjust God. Pelagius asserted to the contrary in lapidary fashion: "God is, and God is just."[58]

Augustine simply had a different Latin text. In his version of Romans 5, he read that "sin penetrated *[intrare]* the world," and the translation confirmed an essential aspect to sin and his image of a God whose justice exceeded human

---

quo omnes peccaverunt). The Greek *eph ho* would have more accurately been translated *propter quod* or "because of whom" all had sinned. If Adam is merely the one "because of whom all have sinned," one had grounds to argue an exemplary understanding of sinning. The creature could choose to follow Adam's poor example — or not! But if Adam is the one "in whom *[in quo]* all have sinned," one had grounds for arguing a more essential understanding of sinning. The creature cannot escape its nature. Both theologians had Latin texts that argued for a more essential understanding of sinning, but Pelagius refused this understanding on the basis of the context of the passage, as argued above.

57. Pelagius on Romans 5:12: "*Therefore, just as through one person sin came* [introiit] *into the world, and through sin death. By example or by pattern. Just as through* Adam sin came *[advenit]* at a time when it did not yet exist, so in the same way through Christ righteousness was recovered at a time when it survived in almost no one. And just as through the former's sin death came in *[intravit]*, so also through the latter's righteousness life was regained. *And so death passed on* [pertransiit] *to all people, in that all sinned.* As long as they sin the same way, they likewise die. For death did not pass on *[pertransiit]* to Abraham and Isaac and Jacob, concerning whom the Lord says: 'Truly they are all living.' But here he says all are dead because in a multitude of sinners no exception is made for a few righteous." [*Propter ea sicut per unum hominem in hunc mundum peccatum introiit et per peccatum mors.* Exemplo vel forma. Quo modo, cum non esset peccatum, per Adam advenit, ita etiam, cum paene aput nullum justitia remansisset, per Christum est revocata; et quo modo per illius peccatum mors intravit, ita et per hujus justitiam vita est reparata. *Et ita in omnes homines pertransiit, in quo omnes peccaverunt.* Dum ita peccant, et similiter moriuntur: non enim in Abraham et Isaac et Jacob pertransiit, de quibus dicit dominus: "omnes enim illi vivunt." Hic autem ideo dicit omnes mortuos quia in multitudine peccatorum non excipiuntur pauci justi, sicut ibi: "Non est qui faciat bonum, non est usque ad unum," et "omnis homo mendax."] Cf. *Pelagius's Commentary on St. Paul's Epistle to the Romans,* ed. and trans. Theodore de Bruyn (Oxford: Clarendon Press, 1993), 92.

58. Pelagius on Romans 1:19: "What can be known by nature about God, that he exists and that he is just." [Quod potest naturaliter sciri de deo, quod sit et quod justus sit.] See *Pelagius's Commentary on St. Paul's Epistle to the Romans,* 64.

comprehension. Romans 11:33 echoed throughout his later writings: "O the depth of the riches and wisdom and knowledge of God! How unsearchable are his judgments and how inscrutable his ways!" Divine justice was real but inaccessible to human reason. Through Adam sin did not simply "come into" the world but "penetrated" *(intrare)* it.[59] Augustine concluded that "all men are understood to have sinned in that first 'man,' because all men were in him when he sinned."[60]

For Augustine the word *intrare* dripped with sexual meaning: the contamination spread from Adam's semen! Goaded by Julian of Eclanum into further specifying the site and circumstances of Adam's sin, Augustine did not disappoint. He pulled the various pieces of his exegetical writings together into a neat and terrible bundle. Peter Brown describes his inexorable theological logic:

> Thus, while many Catholics in Africa and in Italy already believed that the "first sin" of Adam had somehow been inherited by his descendants, Augustine will tell them precisely where they should look in themselves for abiding traces of this first sin. With the fatal ease of a man who believes that he can explain a complex phenomenon simply by reducing it to its historical origins, Augustine will remind his congregation of the exact circumstances of the Fall of Adam and Eve. When they had disobeyed God by eating the forbidden fruit, they had been "ashamed": they covered their genitals with fig-leaves. That was enough for Augustine: "Ecce unde! That's the place! That's the place from which the first sin was passed on."[61]

Augustine could thus maintain the goodness of nature created by God as well as the corruption of nature by Adam's sin: creatures possessed a good creation but a corrupt propagation.[62] The sin of Adam penetrated all of human nature, even the newborn baby. Birth from two baptized parents did not exempt the newborn: one exception proved the rule. One infant alone escaped this contamination: the one who was "born of a woman" and created without

---

59. Augustine on Romans 5:12: "For just as through one man sin entered into [intravit] the world and death through sin." [*Sicut enim per unam hominem peccatum intravit in hunc mundum et per peccatum mors.*] See Paula Fredriksen Landes, *Augustine on Romans,* 10-11.

60. Augustine, "Against Two Letters of the Pelagians" 4.4.7, in *St. Augustin: Anti-Pelagian Writings,* vol. 5 of *The Nicene and Post-Nicene Fathers,* First Series, ed. Philip Schaff (New York: Christian Literature Company, 1887), 419.

61. Brown, *Augustine of Hippo,* 388.

62. Augustine, "Reply to Faustus the Manichaean" 24.2, in *St. Augustin: The Writings against the Manichaeans and against the Donatists,* vol. 4 of *The Nicene and Post-Nicene Fathers,* First Series, ed. Philip Schaff (New York: Christian Literature Company, 1887), 319.

male semen, Christ. Ancient biology colluded in this desperate conclusion.[63] Male sperm contained the creature intact, while the female remained a passive receptacle for fertilization of the tiny homunculus. Conception by the Holy Spirit and a virgin birth spared the Son of God from the corruption of the sons of Adam. Christ possessed the pure humanity of nature before the Fall: the first nature. Christology conspired with biology to buttress Augustine's emerging doctrine of original sin.[64]

What did this do to the creature? From conception the creature was trapped in a second nature penetrated by sin and driven by a vitiated will. Moreover, from conception the creature was crippled by a kind of sinning that was infinitely more damaging than mere habit. We see here not simply the non-innocence of newborns but the non-innocence of the fetus *in utero*. Here too is the origin of terrifying medieval devices that allowed for baptism in the womb. Augustine's understanding of the nature of the human was one more plank in his argument for non-innocence of infants. The argument reveals what Margaret Miles identified as "the totalitarian scope of his anxiety," and he applied that anxiety in an equally totalitarian fashion to all creatures from conception to crypt.[65]

The Role of Baptism

The Roman Emperor Constantine, who converted himself and his empire to Christianity, was baptized in May of 337 on his deathbed, wearing the white robes of a catechumen. There would be no sinning after baptism for the emperor. Augustine himself was not baptized until he was thirty-three, despite a grave childhood illness that threatened to convince his mother that the sacrament should be hastened.[66] Yet the logic of his thinking on childhood and human nature compelled him to argue for the baptism of infants. Although they had accumulated nothing to repent of or to rejoice in, although they had acquired no evil habits, they bore the burden of sin passed on to them by

63. Cf. Jaroslav Pelikan, *The Emergence of the Catholic Tradition,* 289-90.

64. Cf. G. M. Lukken, *Original Sin in the Roman Liturgy* (Leiden: E. J. Brill, 1973), 276ff.; Thomas Laquer, *Making Sex: Body and Gender from the Greeks to Freud* (Cambridge: Harvard University Press, 1990).

65. Miles, *Desire and Delight,* 8.

66. He writes of this in the *Confessions:* "My cleansing was deferred on the assumption that, if I lived, I would be sure to soil myself; and that after that solemn washing the guilt would be greater and more dangerous if I then defiled myself with sins" (Augustine, *Confessions* 1.11, 14).

Adam.[67] Baptism removed this burden, but it did not restore the first nature in which Adam had originally been created.

Augustine's theology of baptism is crucial to understanding his theology of childhood. In the religious landscape of North Africa, where persecution had been intense and martyrdom frequent, baptism signified a renunciation of the world and its ways. Local churches boasted of huge baptisteries.[68] In North Africa the rite of baptism was long a focal point of North African theology and spirituality. Not surprisingly, it featured prominently in the controversies that consumed Augustine during the last years of his life: Donatism and Pelagianism.

In each of these struggles, Augustine battled robust interpretations of baptism. Donatist Christians persisted in the martyrs' spirit of opposition even after persecution had ceased. They declared themselves to be "the righteous of God" *(justi)* and the one "true church."[69] Pelagius's late antique version of small-group Christianity offered believers an option that was less combative but equally flattering: the possibility of being "the authentic Christian" *(integrus christianus).*[70] For him baptism effected real change in the believer, scraping off the rust of the habit of sinning *(consuetudo)* and affording the possibility of a life of holiness.

By contrast, Augustine's alternative theology of baptism is decidedly unattractive. Baptism did not sacramentally create either "the righteous of God" or "the authentic Christian." It did not admit one into a visible and true church. Augustine was neither so optimistic about human nature nor so confident about the possibility of knowing God's purposes. For him the baptized Christian was a pilgrim *(peregrinus).*[71] Baptism admitted one into the hospital of grace, where one spent a lifetime convalescing. Augustine's repeated references to Christ "the Physician" reinforced this metaphor of healing. Baptism only pointed to final deliverance from a terminal disease; the corrosive effects of a sin had penetrated human nature to its core.

Baptism as it was practiced in the huge baptisteries throughout North Africa was his final defense against Julian of Eclanum. When Augustine had exhausted his arsenal of exegetical weaponry, theological logic, and *ad hominem* attack, he turned to the rite of baptism itself in defending his position on origi-

---

67. Augustine, "The Punishment and Forgiveness of Sins and the Baptism of Little Ones," in *Answer to the Pelagians: I,* trans. Roland J. Teske, S.J., in *The Works of St. Augustine,* Part I, vol. 23, ed. John Rotelle, O.S.A. (Hyde Park, N.Y.: New City Press, 1997), 45-48.

68. W. H. C. Frend, *The Rise of Christianity* (Philadelphia: Fortress Press, 1984), 653.

69. Frend, *The Rise of Christianity,* 656-57.

70. Cf. Brown, *Augustine of Hippo,* 347.

71. Brown, *Augustine of Hippo,* 324. Brown makes much of this notion of the Christian as *peregrinus,* "pilgrim" or "resident alien."

nal sin and the necessity of baptism for newborns. Pieces of the ancient rite that Augustine knew echo in contemporary celebrations, but understanding them the way he did makes a familiar rite strange.

In his final works against Julian, Augustine repeatedly appealed to parts of the rite that featured exorcism. The *exsufflatio* literally meant blowing or spitting on Satan. Adult catechumens turned to the West, thought to be the dominion of Satan, and blew or spat with contempt on the king of demons. In infant baptism, the priest blew three times into the child's face, saying, "Depart from him, impure spirit, and make way for the Holy Spirit." The *consignatio* followed the *exsufflatio,* in which the child was marked with the sign of the cross. Afterward salt was placed on the infant's tongue. The act called to mind the biblical injunction for Christians to be "the salt of the earth" (Matt. 5:13). In addition, the ancients believed that salt possessed medicinal properties to ward off corruption and sickness. Greek doctors, whose expertise was highly regarded in the Latin world, recommended rubbing newborns with fine salt.[72] Augustine remembered that he was "blessed regularly from birth with the sign of the Cross and was seasoned with God's salt."[73] In a world that believed in demons, such protection was essential: denying it to infants, who were most at risk and least able to defend themselves, would be cruel.

Belief that the newborn lay in the grasp of Satan undergirded these practices, and the rite of baptism signified first and foremost Christ's repossession of the child. The fourth century saw the first explicit statements linking the ancient sin of Adam with possession by Satan, but it was in Augustine "that reflection on original sin and Satan's dominion attain[ed] its peak."[74] Controversy with the Pelagians and Julian of Eclanum brought the bishop's argument to its inexorable conclusion: all the unbaptized, including newborns, were "under the power of the devil."[75] Similarly, controversy with the Pelagians forced Augustine to his inalterable judgment with regard to the Holy Innocents: they had been consigned to eternal damnation, though he hoped their punishment would be gentle.[76] Driven to this conclusion by the juggernaut of his mature

72. Rousselle, *Porneia,* 52.

73. "I was already signed with the sign of the cross and seasoned with salt from the time I came from my mother's womb" (Augustine, *Confessions* 1.11, 13). Boswell records the medieval confusion over abandoned children found with a packet of salt in their swaddlings. Did the salt indicate that the child had already been baptized or that the infant required baptism? Cf. Boswell, *The Kindness of Strangers,* 322-23.

74. Lukken, *Original Sin in the Roman Liturgy,* 198.

75. Augustine, "On Marriage and Concupiscence" 1.11, in *St. Augustin: Anti-Pelagian Writings,* 273.

76. Cited in Eugene Portalie, S.J., *A Guide to the Thought of Saint Augustine,* trans. Ralph Bastian, S.J. (London: Burns & Oates, 1960), 212.

thinking on childhood and conversion, human nature, and the rite of baptism itself, Augustine nonetheless professed dismay over the plight of all infants newly born. However certain he sounded in the controversies with Julian of Eclanum, Augustine registered anguish in a letter to his friend Jerome:

> Children are wasted by sickness, racked by pain, tormented by hunger and thirst, mangled and crippled, deprived of their senses and abused by evil spirits.
>
> What has to be shown is how they suffer these things justly without any wickedness on their part as a cause. It is not allowable to say that God is unaware of these things, or that he cannot put an end to the causes of these evils, or that he does them or allows them to be done unjustly. . . . God is good. God is just. God is almighty. Only a mad person would doubt this. And so let the just reason why such terrible things happen to children be stated. When adults suffer such things we are accustomed to say that they are being put to the test like Job, or that they are being punished for their sins like Herod; and from the examples God has chosen to make manifest we are allowed to guess at others that are obscure. But this holds only for adults. Explain to me what we can say of children, if they have no sins to be punished by such sufferings — for of course at that age they have no righteousness to be put to the test.[77]

The statement calls for modest revision of Krister Stendahl's proposal regarding Augustine's "introspective conscience."[78] We credit Augustine as being "the first modern man" and forget that he inhabited a world populated with demons and that he knew people who had been possessed. Evil was an external, palpable, personified presence. We too easily project onto Augustine's world the scientific sensibilities of our own, a world from which all spirits have departed. In doing so, we fail to acknowledge the spirits he saw. There could be a besetting evil that did not belong to an infant but still plagued it with disease, discomfort, and demons. It is from the very foreign terrain of this world that we must judge Augustine's final conflict with Julian of Eclanum, which largely revolved around infant baptism. Julian stubbornly maintained the innocence of infants: when the infant matured, baptism would be required. Augustine found ample evidence that even infants were non-innocent. Although possessed of no personal sin, they were clearly infected by some evil. To withhold baptism from them was cruel and unjust punishment.

Yet even as Augustine argued on theological and liturgical grounds for the baptism of infants, he wrote detailed catechetical manuals for those who had not been baptized as infants. One treatise offered the catechist specific

---

77. Augustine, "To Jerome, Letter 166," in *Letters of St. Augustine,* 190-91.
78. Krister Stendahl, *Paul among Jews and Gentiles* (London: SPCK, 1977).

counsel in teaching the faith to a group that might include young and old, educated and uneducated persons, rural and city folk — even "grammarians and rhetoricians"![79] Augustine urged appeal to the imagination, directing the catechist to place himself in the position of the student and to receive the student's delight in learning as if it were his own.[80] In these and other writings, a conscious pedagogy directed the will toward true happiness.[81]

Probing the outlines of Augustine's *"paideia Christi,"* Eugene Kevane challenges the judgment that "education is a theme which Augustine rarely broaches."[82] Kevane argues to the contrary, identifying Augustine's treatise *On Christian Doctrine* as "the entire plan of a Christian education designed to be a 'safe way for youth' in contrast with the corruptions of the *paideia* which St. Augustine had experienced as a student and teacher in the educational institutions of imperial Rome."[83] Augustine's consecration as bishop of Hippo effectively made him director of catechetics for his episcopate. In this capacity he engaged in a serious study of the Bible, the result of which is *On Christian Doctrine.* The treatise took up the classical education, in particular the sciences of grammar and rhetoric, applying them to the understanding of the scriptures.

On Christian Doctrine was Augustine's philosophy of education with the Christian scriptures as its subject. In addition to advising catechists, the treatise provided a *ratio studiorum* for the cathedral school that Augustine maintained in Hippo. Entrusted with the responsibility for developing a well-educated body of clergy, Augustine established an institution that was simultaneously a monastery and a school for those who would be involved in the various ministries of the church. It housed Augustine's large library as well as a scriptorium, where manuscripts could be copied and repaired. To the teachers and ministers trained here fell the education of the laity. Because the people they served were largely illiterate, Christian education proceeded largely through worship, biblical preaching, and reading Scripture aloud.

Augustine's arguments on infant baptism, his catechetical instruction,

79. The catechumens might include men and women, boys and girls. Augustine commented on their diversity: ". . . a highly educated man, a dull fellow, a citizen, a foreigner, a rich man, a poor man, a private individual, a man of honours, a person occupying some position of authority, an individual of this or the other nation, of this or the other age or sex, one proceeding from this or the other sect, from this or the other common error . . ." (Augustine, "On Catechising the Uninstructed," in *The Works of Aurelius Augustine, Bishop of Hippo,* vol. 9, ed. Marcus Dods [Edinburgh: T. & T. Clark, 1892], 284-300).

80. Augustine, "On Catechising the Uninstructed," 292.

81. Eugene Kevane notes that many of Augustine's early dialogues at Cassiciacum (*de ordine, de beata vita*) explore a *paideia Christi.* Cf. Kevane, *Augustine the Educator,* 101.

82. Frederik Van Der Meer, *Augustine the Bishop,* trans. Brian Battershaw and G. R. Lamb (London: Sheed & Ward, 1961), 188.

83. Kevane, *Augustine the Educator,* 137. Cf. Augustine, *Teaching Christianity.*

and his educational pedagogy reveal the mixed practices of a church that included "cradle Christians," converts, and people who simply wanted to postpone baptism as long as possible. The gradual move Augustine made toward baptizing infants would gradually pull apart rites that had once been incorporated in the liturgy of the Easter Vigil. Originally the liturgy included baptism and chrismation of catechumens who had undergone a lengthy period of instruction in the faith. It concluded with celebration of the Eucharist, which the newly baptized would receive for the first time. Eastern practice still holds baptism, chrismation, and First Communion together — even for infants. Churches that observe believers' baptism delay baptism until children have some knowledge of the faith they are entering.[84] The impact of Augustine's argument for infant baptism lingers, as churches practicing infant baptism struggle to catechize the baptized and inculcate in them the faith.

Conclusion

These three strands of Augustine's thought — the status of childhood, the nature of the human, and the ritual of baptism — frame a theology of childhood. They are so tightly braided together as to seem inseparable. They constitute a highly ambiguous legacy for the history of Christian attitudes toward childhood.

Augustine observed children with care, attention, and empathy. He lamented their extreme vulnerability to diseases, which in the absence of medical treatments and technologies were often fatal. Much of the writing about his own infancy and childhood radiated warmth and insight. Yet over the course of his career and in the midst of controversies with the Pelagians, Augustine hardened his conviction that from the moment of conception children were non-innocent. When pressed on the tragic fate of the Holy Innocents, he sadly consigned them to eternal punishment.

How can we sift Augustine's judgments, allowing for a mutually critical dialogue between his insights and our own? If we could imaginatively create such a conversation, we might issue the following challenges to a long-dead saint whose ideas continue to have such impact today.

1. We would want to charge Augustine with overly theologizing and mor-

---

84. On the Eastern traditions, see Vigen Guroian's essay on Chrysostom in this volume; on believers' baptism, see Keith Graber Miller's essay on Anabaptism in this volume. In *Christian Initiation*, J. D. C. Fisher documents the "distintegration" of baptism, confirmation, and first communion.

alizing childhood. What we regard as developmental issues he examined for evidence of the burden of a sin that had infected all of Adam's progeny. We take the narcissism of an infant more lightly, hopeful that the child will grow out of it. Augustine found in it seeds of selfishness that he discovered in adults on a larger, more sinister scale.

At the same time, however, we must applaud Augustine's belief that children have a moral life, and we must acknowledge that he presented it with insight. Although his understanding of nature tainted with sin led later thinkers to doctrines of innate depravity, his own thinking was remarkably nuanced. He refused the romantic option of seeing children as completely innocent, born with a nature as pure as Adam's before the Fall. He equally refused the cynic's view of infants as miniature demons in desperate need of discipline. Non-innocence fairly characterizes his attitude toward infancy. As they matured and acquired the abilities to speak and reason, children assumed a gradually increasing accountability for their actions.

Augustine understood the small cruelties that ricochet through children's play without even rising to a level of deliberate malice. Were he called in to adjudicate a playground dispute that had dissolved into tears and recriminations, he might have the wisdom not to ask who was at fault. He saw between guilt and innocence a great gray area of non-innocence and nuanced accountability. As infants acquired language, as children learned to reason and to love aright, as adolescents practiced the discipline of self-restraint, Augustine assigned greater moral responsibility. For him non-innocence remained a realistic appraisal of what was morally at stake in infancy, the first stage of the life cycle.

2. The somatic determinism of Augustine's understanding of "human nature" repulses us today. Augustine found the decisive and identity-forming event to be one's conception in the stream of Adam's transgression. Accordingly, baptism was the defining and identity-reforming event in the life of a Christian. We excavate different terrain for identity formation: childhood events or experiences, positive or negative.

When Augustine did focus on character, he overplayed the negative. He wrestled with his own fascination with evil rather than good and projected this fascination onto the whole of humanity. Habits of sinning received far more attention from him than virtues. What if he could have combed through childhood for traces of the image of God or vestiges of the Trinity as closely as he watched for traces of Adam's sin?

3. As Margaret Miles has skillfully argued, Augustine saw his conversion through the lens of childhood. Unfortunately, the reverse is also true: Augustine saw his childhood through the lens of conversion. Did this point of view allow him an accurate vision of childhood? Or did he merely see there the after-image of the adult sins that had prompted his own conversion?

Certainly there is projection, and Augustine's had tragic consequences. What he saw in infancy and childhood from the fresh perspective of his conversion only confirmed a growing conviction in the non-innocence even of infancy. What we perceive as "narrowness" in his portrayal of childhood warns us of the terrible dangers in speaking for a population that cannot speak for itself. Parenthood exercises the imagination, as parents must train themselves to imagine how a child encounters the world so that they can pad sharp corners, lock enticing closets, and place dangerous chemicals out of reach. One wonders how much practice Augustine really had in that vocation.

But children fascinated Augustine. He did not portray them as miniature adults. Rather, Augustine portrayed adults as grown-up children — only more complex. Perhaps he watched children closely because they seemed to him so much more transparent than adults. They taught him much about ordinary impulses and desires. Childhood provided him a hermeneutic for understanding adults, as one traded "nuts and balls and pet birds" for "money and estates and servants."[85]

One wonders about the way our own culture sees children. We too rapidly point children toward the adults they will become, scrutinizing their play for signs of a future profession. Children of privilege quickly develop schedules that require secretaries to manage and chauffeurs for transport. On the other end of the economic spectrum, children without privilege become regarded as burdens on a society that is really an economy in disguise. Recent "welfare reform" measures in effect punish these children for having only one parent and banish them to day-care facilities of unregulated quality. Their mothers are required to realize the only worth they and their offspring will have in this world: as workers, not as parents — and certainly not as professionals. Whether privileged or disprivileged, childhood is something that happens on the way to becoming an adult. Sadly, the adulthood that is the end product of an instrumental childhood turns out to be empty indeed. Augustine's respect for childhood and his sense that it was an end in itself challenge us to examine our own explicit and implicit attitudes toward an irreplaceable and unrepeatable stage in the life cycle.

4. Augustine saw a continuity between childhood and adulthood that was dictated by nature. But he also observed discontinuity. He recognized boundaries between the various stages of the life cycle and found in each stage a level of accountability that was chronologically and experientially appropriate. In particular, he evaluated the first stages of the life cycle in terms of increasing levels of moral accountability. Although they were non-innocent, infants assumed little or no accountability: they had neither language nor reason. It was fruitless to rebuke them because they could not understand language. With the acquisition of lan-

85. Augustine, *Confessions* 1.19, 40.

guage and reason came greater accountability. He expected children to obey verbal commands and adolescents to understand the basic demands of human decency. These graduated levels of accountability implied graver consequences for transgressions. Looking back on a gang-stealing of pears, Augustine lamented the sins of his youth — but at least he knew when it was over!

By contrast, we confuse the boundaries between infancy, childhood, and adulthood. The Jonesboro shootings in March 1998 prompted a Texas legislator to propose extending the death penalty to eleven-year-olds. Meanwhile, parents wander out of families and marriages to find people they should have located decades earlier: themselves. They leave behind children who have probably spent their own adolescence parenting parents. As a culture we are constantly blurring the distinctions between various stages of life. We could learn from the boundaries Augustine saw and observed in the cycle of life.

5. Finally, a faulty grasp of biology, the theological imperative of original sin, and the rite of baptism informed Augustine's theology of childhood. His logic was inexorable. Infants show sinful tendencies that can be accounted for by Adam's transgression, an alien sin implanted in them in conception. Therefore, baptism should be conferred as early as possible to remedy these damnable tendencies.

But if the first premise can be challenged, the argument arrests there. Certainly claims of Christ's sinlessness based on his being born "of a woman" and without any male involvement vanish in view of contemporary scientific understandings of conception. Sin and sinlessness are both more and less complex than Augustine figured. Augustine's biological determinism cannot grasp why an African-American male infant born in West Oakland will be so much more likely to face incarceration than his white "brother in Christ" born three miles to the east. In this situation, race, gender, and class pose complex issues beyond the scope of Augustine's biological explanations. But while we would be analyzing data and consulting the experts, Augustine would have been out searching for demons and demanding exorcism.

The questions Augustine leaves us with are these: How can we attend to children in a world that is driven by adult concerns? How shall we understand and nurture the moral lives of children? How can we educate for virtue? How can we exorcise the demons in our own cultural environment: racism, poverty, and neglect? How can we tend and nourish the lives of children?[86]

86. Barbara Pitkin, Jane Strohl, Cris Traina, and Marcia Bunge generously read and commented on prior drafts, and I thank them for their particular care. I am also deeply indebted to careful readings from my Graduate Theological Union colleagues; Margaret R. Miles, dean at the GTU; and Mary Ann Donovan, professor of church history at the Jesuit School of Theology in Berkeley.

4. A Person in the Making:
Thomas Aquinas on Children and Childhood

CRISTINA L. H. TRAINA

One day, while Thomas was still a babe unweaned, his nurse was about to give him a bath, and as she was taking off his clothes he put out his hand and seized and held on to a piece of paper that was lying unnoticed on the ground. And when the nurse tried to open his hand and remove the paper, so that she might finish washing him, the child began to cry loudly; but when she let him keep it he was quiet again. And while she washed, dried and clothed him, he still clutched the paper. But his mother, in spite of his protests, at last extracted it from his grasp; and she found written on it nothing but the angel's greeting, Ave Maria, gratia plena. . . . And surely it was appropriate, that in this way Providence should indicate in the boy what was to be so conspicuous in the man, a love of the doctrine of salvation which it would be his vocation to teach. It was the divine Spirit that led him to find that paper.[1]

1. Bernard Gui, "The Life of St. Thomas Aquinas," in *The Life of St. Thomas Aquinas: Biographical Documents,* trans. and ed. Kenelm Foster, O.P. (London: Longmans, Green; Baltimore: Helicon Press, 1959), para. 2, 25-26.

Special thanks for advice, encouragement, and bibliographic help to Richard Kieckhefer, Barbara Newman, Jean Porter, Sister Rita Stalzer, and the other authors in this volume — especially Clarissa Atkinson, Marcia Bunge, Mary Ann Hinsdale, Barbara Pitkin, and Martha Stortz, whose painstaking comments corrected and improved the essay in countless ways.

Custom and ecclesiastical approbation have guaranteed the Dominican theologian St. Thomas Aquinas (1224?-1274) a profound influence upon Roman Catholic theology up to the present day. Hence the significance of his vision of childhood for Christian thought and practice is as much contemporary as historical. Even this account of his infancy, penned by Bernard Gui not quite fifty years after Thomas's death, is a marvelous example of the rich riddles that the sparse but powerful medieval writings on children (many of which echo current debates) still pose.[2] For instance, the tale coheres with Thomas's convictions that all persons are susceptible to the unexpected and exceptional manipulation of the Spirit and that baptized children can be endowed with the spiritual maturity of adults.[3] The nurse's failure to wrest the paper from Thomas's hand may also subtly reflect the medieval ecclesiastical opinion that mothers, and not wet nurses or nannies, were the most astute and appropriate caretakers of young children.[4] Gui likely counts on the fourteenth-century reader's agreement that a person's future character is typically evident in his infancy (presumably after baptism),[5] an assumption that to some degree runs

2. On the sparseness of medieval material, see David Herlihy, "Medieval Children," in *Essays on Medieval Civilization*, The Walter Prescott Webb Memorial Lectures, XII, ed. Bede Karl Lackner and Kenneth Roy Philp (Austin and London: University of Texas Press, 1978), 109-41. On the conflicts within medieval imagery of childhood and the doctrinal problems these created, see Janet L. Nelson, "Parents, Children, and the Church," in *The Church and Childhood*, Studies in Church History 31, ed. Diana Wood (Oxford: Blackwell, 1994), 81-114.

3. See Thomas Aquinas, *Summa Theologica*, trans. the Fathers of the English Dominican Province (1948; reprint, Westminster, Md.: Christian Classics, 1981), III.72.9; because "the various ages of the body do not affect the soul," "perfect spiritual age" is attainable "in youth or childhood" *(juventutis et pueritiae)*. It is unclear whether by *pueritiae* Thomas means childhood in general or the span from seven to fourteen in particular; his usage elsewhere in the *Summa* suggests the former.

The *Summa*'s proper title is *Summa Theologiae*, hereafter *ST.*

4. Mary Martin McLaughlin, "Survivors and Surrogates: Children and Parents from the Ninth to the Thirteenth Centuries," in *The History of Childhood*, ed. Lloyd deMause, 101-81 (New York: The Psychohistory Press, 1974), 115-17. For the reasons, see Lloyd deMause, "The Evolution of Childhood," in *The History of Childhood*, ed. Lloyd deMause, 1-73 (New York: The Psychohistory Press), 34-35; Danièle Alexandre-Bidon and Didier Lett, *Les Enfants au Moyen Age: V^e-XVe Siècles*, rev. ed. ([n.p.]: Hachette Littératures, 1997), 123-25; Shulamith Shahar, *Childhood in the Middle Ages* (London: Routledge, 1990), chapter 4 and 75-83; and Clarissa Atkinson, *The Oldest Vocation: Christian Motherhood in the Middle Ages* (Ithaca, N.Y.: Cornell University Press, 1991), 157-58. The disapproval of optional wet-nursing was not unanimous. (No one objected to wet nursing that was necessary for survival.)

5. On the development of this idea in Germany, and on its implications for child rearing, see James A. Schultz, *The Knowledge of Childhood in the German High Middle Ages, 1100-1350*, Middle Ages Series (Philadelphia: University of Pennsylvania Press, 1995).

against Thomas's own vision of infants as spiritually and morally unformed. Another of Thomas's beliefs produces an arresting contrast between this picture of precocious, postbaptismal sanctity and the unbaptized: "all who are not baptized are subject to the power of the demons" — infants and young children included — and therefore in need of exorcism as well as of the remission of original sin.[6] Infancy seems fraught with extraordinary degrees of both spiritual peril and spiritual potential.

Tension and Transition

The complex tensions within Thomas's thought reflect two issues that persist in Christian thought today. The first is the problem of original sin. The history of the theology of childhood might well be cast as the history of the struggle to preserve and express Augustine's doctrine of original sin without eroding beliefs in both divine justice and divine mercy toward the weak and vulnerable. Thomas's curious hybrid solution to this problem grew out of the cross-pollination between his primary theological authority, Augustine, and his central philosophical authority, Aristotle. Medieval authors on childhood, although they may not have attributed these visions to Augustine and Aristotle so explicitly, embraced in varying proportions the same two contradictory theological anthropologies.[7] In the Augustinian model, as we saw earlier, infant victims of original sin are "non-innocent" only because they lack the physical strength to do harm. Masses of inordinate desires, they are essentially sinful, selfish, and repulsed by all things good and holy. Christian maturation is their gradual "convalescence" from original sin and its effects through the sacraments, prayer, and tutelage, which — through the aid of grace — curb, heal, and redirect these desires, producing virtue and devotion.[8] The Aristotelian

---

6. *ST* III.71.2.1, 71.4. Unbaptized children were thought particularly susceptible to replacement by demonic changelings. On changelings, see McLaughlin, "Survivors and Surrogates," 120 and 155-56, n. 100; and Jean-Claude Schmitt, *The Holy Greyhound: Guinefort: Healer of Children since the Thirteenth Century,* trans. Martin Thom (New York: Cambridge University Press, 1983), especially 74-82. Belief in changelings persisted well into the sixteenth century — for instance, in the works of Martin Luther (Schmitt, *The Holy Greyhound,* 76, 81-82). For a contemporary rendering of the theft of a baby and its replacement by a changeling, see Maurice Sendak's children's book, *Outside Over There* (New York: Harper & Row, 1981).

7. See Shahar, *Childhood in the Middle Ages,* 14-20; and McLaughlin, "Survivors and Surrogates," 136-39.

8. See Martha Stortz's essay in this volume.

model, on the other hand, more resembles our contemporary developmental understanding of childhood: the child as pure, innocent, uncultivated potential. On this view, children are immature and simpleminded, but their basic inclinations and desires are not evil. They simply await ordering by children's as yet undeveloped capacity for reason. Childhood is then just a stage in a person's life-long progress in virtue. For example, in the sixth century St. Benedict of Nursia had, guided partly by this assumption about the relative guilelessness of youth, directed that abbots be elected by the whole community and that older monks make a practice of respecting the opinions of younger monks, to whom "the Lord often reveals the best course."[9]

To adopt an extreme version of either of these convictions would be to choose one of two heretical positions: deterministic nihilism, the belief that the human will is essentially and irretrievably evil and sinful; or Pelagianism, the belief that people are essentially good and can save themselves through good works. Thomas, refusing the choice, attempted the apparently impossible: he embraced simultaneously the pessimistic Augustinian vision of the human will fatally flawed by original sin and the optimistic Aristotelian vision of the rational person with the natural capacity to grow in virtue and wisdom. Although he agrees with Augustine that original sin renders the unbaptized unworthy of salvation,[10] Thomas envisions grace as completing rather than correcting nature. Thus he tends to emphasize children's potential for spiritual growth with the aid of grace rather than, like Augustine, their incapacity for true devotion and virtue in the absence of grace. Yet Thomas's refusal completely to discard a strong doctrine of original sin in favor of developmentalism is evident in many places — for instance, in his theory of limbo (below). It may also play a part in his refusal to decide whether, by advising parents to "bring [children] up in the discipline and correction of the Lord," St. Paul recommends spankings and remonstrations or simply encouragement to good and restraint from evil.[11] Thus Thomas bequeaths the Augustinian-Aristotelian tension to later writers, all of whom resolve it differently, in some cases by nearly eradicating one pole.

Thomas's work also mirrors a slow evolution in the medieval vision of the person in the family. On the one hand, he nearly always discusses children in

9. St. Benedict of Nursia, *The Rule of St. Benedict,* trans. Anthony C. Meisel and M. L. del Mastro (Garden City, N.Y.: Image Books, 1975), chapter 64 (99-100) and chapter 3 (51).

10. *ST* III.68.1.

11. St. Thomas Aquinas, *Commentary on Saint Paul's Epistle to the Ephesians,* translated and introduced by Matthew L. Lamb, O.C.S.O., Aquinas Scripture Series, vol. 2 (Albany, N.Y.: Magi Books, 1966), 230-31. Later chapters in this volume will debunk the myth that strong doctrines of original sin can be correlated with harsh discipline and weak doctrines with gentle treatment. Quite often the opposite is the case; other factors supervene.

their familial or ecclesiastical contexts; in fact, unfolding the shape and obligations of the perduring connection between parent and child *(filiatio)* is at least as important to him, practically and symbolically, as describing childhood *(pueritia)* in itself. In the tradition Thomas received, the young child was in many respects the possession of the family and could be given away, to God in oblation or to another family in betrothal; Thomas himself was a Benedictine oblate, presented by his parents to the monastery at Monte Cassino when he was five or six years old.[12] Thomas's presentation of the child as an extension of the parents is likewise traditional; literally of the same substance as they, the child is their natural successor.[13] Thomas also thinks it perfectly natural that parents — mainly fathers — take full credit for their children's successes and failures, that they expect obedience, that they might wish to control their offspring's adult lives, and that they desire their sons to follow their advice in marrying.[14]

On the other hand, Thomas also lived in an age that was beginning to prize the integrity and independence of the individual conscience over families' designs for their children. In the late twelfth century and the first half of the thirteenth century, new ecclesiastical policies dictated that oblates who wished to leave the monastic life be released at puberty, before taking solemn vows.[15]

12. James A. Weisheipl, O.P., *Friar Thomas D'Aquino: His Life, Thought, and Work* (Garden City, N.Y.: Doubleday, 1974), 10.

Oblation was the donation by parents of a minor child — usually accompanied by a monetary gift — to a convent or monastery. Until the late twelfth century, oblation was irreversible. On the history of child oblation in the West, see Mayke De Jong, *In Samuel's Image: Child Oblation in the Early Medieval West* (New York: E. J. Brill, 1996); and Patricia A. Quinn, *Better than the Sons of Kings: Boys and Monks in the Early Middle Ages,* Studies in History and Culture, vol. 2 (New York: Peter Lang, 1989), chapter 2.

13. *ST* II-II.101.2.2.

14. Thomas Aquinas, *Commentary on Saint Paul's Epistle to the Galatians,* trans. Fabian R. Larcher, O.P., introduction by Richard T. A. Murphy, O.P., Aquinas Scripture Series, vol. 1 (Albany, N.Y.: Magi Books, 1966), 109; *ST* Suppl. 47.6.

15. On canonical debates over oblation, see John Doran, "Oblation or Obligation? A Canonical Ambiguity," in *The Church and Childhood,* ed. Diana Wood, Studies in Church History 31 (Oxford: Blackwell, 1994), 127-42; see also John Boswell, *The Kindness of Strangers: The Abandonment of Children in Western Europe from Late Antiquity to the Renaissance* (New York: Pantheon Books, 1988), 296-321. Oblation was heavily debated in the thirteenth century, with many orders establishing minimum ages of puberty or higher for entry and with official proscription of irreversible commitments of young children to monasteries (Shahar, *Childhood in the Middle Ages,* 191-92). Parents' expressed aims in oblation were religious, and it was not as a rule a form of abandonment. The practical consequence of oblation was the cementing of ties between the family and the monastery rather than the cutting of ties between parent and child; quite frequently there would be many members of the same extended family in a monastery or convent, and visits from secular

107

Thomas agrees, adding that children who have reached puberty may also, against their parents' wishes, break a betrothal or enter marriage or holy orders.[16] Even the filial obligation to honor father and mother does not bar older children from holy orders unless their parents are completely without other means of support.[17] In fact, "if our parents incite us to sin, and withdraw us from the service of God, we must, as regards this point, abandon and hate them."[18] When Thomas declares that parents may persuade their children to marry, he intimates that children should be swayed not by raw parental authority but by worthy arguments; elsewhere he opines that good fathers appeal, exhort, and encourage their children rather than commanding or ruling them.[19] Even where parents have jurisdiction, their authority is not limitless: a father may dictate "matters relating to the conduct of [a son's] life and the care of the household" but not whether he marries or how many children he may have.[20] In these examples Thomas presents children's independence from parental control not as special or exceptional but as one instance of the still-accepted general principle that no subordinate need obey commands not directly related to his responsibilities to his superior.[21]

Here as well, Thomas's experience no doubt influenced his writing: in his late teens, he left the prestigious Benedictine order to become a Dominican mendicant, apparently dashing his mother's hopes that he would become abbot of the prominent monastery at Monte Cassino. His family's wrath at this disobedient flouting of family alliances was so great that they kidnapped and held him for

---

family members were common. See Nelson, "Parents, Children, and the Church," 107-12, and Alexandre-Bidon and Lett, *Les Enfants au Moyen Age,* 89. Still, many parents offered to convents or monasteries children who for want of good health, congeniality, intelligence, legitimate parentage, or money were unmarriageable. See Boswell, chapters 5 and 8, for this interpretation and numerous concrete examples; children of priests were heavily represented among the latter group. Thomas's exclusion of men of illegitimate parentage from the priesthood may thus have been motivated as much by political or prophetic as by canonical considerations: according to his rule, priests could not quietly provide for their sons by setting them up as clerics.

16. Parents may override the private vows of young children; see *ST* II-II.88.8-9, 189.5.

17. *ST* II-II.101.2.2, 101.4.4; see II-II.189.6 for another perspective on the same question.

18. *ST* II-II.101.4.1.

19. *ST* Suppl. 47.6; Thomas Aquinas, *Commentary on Saint Paul's First Letter to the Thessalonians and the Letter to the Philippians,* trans. Fabian R. Larcher and Michael Duffy, Aquinas Scripture Series, vol. 3 (Albany, N.Y.: Magi Books, 1969), 16.

20. *ST* II-II.104.5.

21. John Finnis, *Aquinas: Moral, Political, and Legal Theory* (Oxford: Oxford University Press, 1998), 170-76 and 184-85, note "el."

over a year before finally permitting him to return to the Dominicans and travel to Paris for theological education.[22] Gui underscores Thomas's perseverance in resisting his family with two powerful stories: Thomas drove out the "lovely but shameless girl" whom his brothers sent to tempt him away from religious life; and he managed to preserve Dominican dress during his confinement by having a Dominican brother bring him "changes of clothing by the expedient of coming dressed in two habits, one of which, as soon as they were alone, he would take off and give to Thomas."[23] Hagiography confirms theory: Thomas approved of conscientious disobedience. For older children as for all people of mature reason, the conscience — formed responsibly around the hierarchy of ultimate and temporal goods — trumps other ostensible obligations.[24]

Thus, where Thomas reflects the social order, he reflects not only the established social and political hierarchies but also the tension of conflict and change. For instance, the clash between "child as family property" and "child as independent subject" is corroborated in hagiographical literature generally, which alternately praises absolute filial obedience and rewards independent-mindedness.[25] As in other cases, Thomas sets his own course,[26] insisting that

---

22. Weisheipl, *Friar Thomas D'Aquino,* 10, 26-36.

Boswell suggests that parental accusations of "brainwashing" of adolescents were as commonly made against the new mendicant orders of the thirteenth century as they were against the American "cults" of the 1970s (*The Kindness of Strangers,* 318).

These problems were not new. Patricia Quinn shows how, in the ninth century, the monastery design recommended in the St. Gall plan organized — apparently intentionally — the oblates' space in a way that would have made escape or parental kidnap nearly impossible. See Quinn, *Better than the Sons of Kings,* 54-55.

23. Gui, *The Life of St. Thomas Aquinas,* paras. 7-8, 30-31.

24. See *ST* I-II.19.5-6.

25. Shahar, *Childhood in the Middle Ages,* 205-6. For the conflict between proprietary and independent images of children, see McLaughlin, "Survivors and Surrogates," 140. For ambivalence toward family as a theme in Christian spirituality up to the thirteenth century, see Jennifer Carpenter, "Juette of Huy, Recluse and Mother (1158-1228): Children and Mothering in the Saintly Life," in *Power of the Weak: Studies on Medieval Women,* ed. Jennifer Carpenter and Sally-Beth MacLean (Urbana and Chicago: University of Illinois Press, 1995), 57-93; and Barbara Newman, "'Crueel Corage': Child Sacrifice and the Maternal Martyr in Hagiography and Romance," in *From Virile Woman to WomanChrist: Studies in Medieval Religion and Literature,* Middle Ages Series (Philadelphia: University of Pennsylvania Press, 1995), 76-107.

26. See, for instance, Alasdair MacIntyre, "Natural Law as Subversive," *Journal of Medieval and Early Modern Studies* 26 (Winter 1996): 61-83. For a dissenting voice, see Katherine Archibald, "The Concept of Social Hierarchy in the Writings of St. Thomas Aquinas," *Aquinas,* vol. 1, ed. John Dunn and Ian Harris, Great Political Thinkers Series, vol. 4 (Lyme: Elgar Reference, 1997), 166-92; originally published in *The Historian* 12 (Autumn 1949): 28-54.

older children, at least, have some capacity — accompanied by a proportionate right and obligation — to make significant choices for themselves.

Thomas's Developmental Anthropology

Philippe Ariès's complaint about the absence of a medieval perception of the "particular nature which distinguishes the child from the adult"[27] finds no support in the writings of Thomas Aquinas. Thomas envisions childhood — if not precisely as contemporary Westerners do — as a developmental stage with peculiar and evolving needs and characteristics. As we shall see, it is an image that incorporates but occasionally strains uncomfortably against Augustine's more pessimistic vision. According to Thomas's theological anthropology, human beings are created for a twofold but consistent end: an earthly life of prayer and virtue, and perfection of knowledge and love in posthumous heavenly union with God. Human beings are created with a desire for both the intermediate goods of human earthly flourishing and the ultimate good of union with God. The natural or acquired virtues, which smooth earthly life, are more or less within human power. The supernatural virtues, which are proportionate to the heavenly goal, require salvific grace, which in turn cooperates with and perfects human nature, guiding the will toward the highest good.[28]

Grace is no respecter of age; the habits (capacities or tendencies) of the theological virtues are infused in even the tiniest infant at baptism.[29] But growth in grace — preferably assisted by the now-separate sacrament of confirmation — is not the only prerequisite to human spiritual perfection.[30] One

27. Philippe Ariès, *Centuries of Childhood: A Social History of Family Life,* trans. Robert Baldick (New York: Alfred A. Knopf, 1962), 128; originally published as *L'Enfant et la Vie Familiale sous L'Ancien Régime* (Paris: Librairie Plon, 1960). Ariès's treatment is heavily weighted toward France. An unfortunate translation in the English version of this work has led some scholars to interpret his claim about a lack of sensibility or perception of childhood as a lack of an idea of childhood. See Hugh Cunningham, "Histories of Childhood," *The American Historical Review* 103 (October 1998): 1195-1208 at 1197.

28. On the virtues, see *ST* I-II.55-66. See also Cristina L. H. Traina, *Feminist Ethics and Natural Law: The End of the Anathemas* (Washington, D.C.: Georgetown University Press, 1999), chapter 2.

29. *ST* II-II.47.14.3.

30. The early rite of Christian initiation typically combined what are now the sacraments of baptism and confirmation with first Eucharist. Thomas, like his contemporaries, assumed infant baptism as the standard for the faithful, stressed the importance of confirmation as a separate, subsequent sacrament, but stopped short of claiming that it was indispensable for salvation. For a discussion of Thomas's place in the medieval debate over

must develop the acts of the supernatural virtues just as one would the natural or acquired virtues.[31] To act virtuously requires the capacity to reason practically (recognizing and acting appropriately for good ends), and to think virtuously requires the capacity to reason speculatively (making connections among necessary truths). Neither capacity is present in the baptized newborn child. But as the inchoate passions that stir up young minds are tamed, reason gradually gains a foothold, and children become increasingly capable of the acts of the virtues.[32]

Thomas thus measures the process of human maturation largely by the capacity to reason, including the ability to make and act on responsible choices. Children lack this capacity. But they are not a separate, lower species: "When . . . imperfection is not inseparable from the imperfect thing, the same identical thing which was imperfect becomes perfect. Thus childhood is not essential to man, and consequently the same identical subject who was a child, becomes a man."[33] Children are only temporarily incomplete, not essentially inferior, for childhood imperfection is something one outgrows.[34] Thus Thomas embraces a notion of graded responsibility much like Augustine's. Increasing age, grace, and virtue order one's passions and one's actions, bringing one closer either to perfection or to damnation. But this is not strictly a matter of time.[35] Prudence, the keystone of the moral and intellectual virtues, entails careful reflection on past events, consultation with peers, and a whole host of other factors for which a fund of social experience is an indispensable prerequisite. This suggests that

---

confirmation, see J. D. C. Fisher, *Christian Initiation: Baptism in the Medieval West: A Study in the Disintegration of the Primitive Rite of Initiation* (London: SPCK, 1965), 125-30.

31. The natural virtues are habits of thought and action — good with respect to the common good — developed individually through disciplined repetition of acts but without special benefit of grace. It is possible to possess one of these virtues to an appreciable degree and to lack many others, but it is not possible to perfect any. (Technically, grace elevates and transforms natural virtue rather than perfecting it.) Supernatural or theological virtues, on the other hand, are infused by God as a group in the form of habits — transformed ends and motivations for action — but without any new discipline of right action. A person who already had acquired natural virtues would not have any difficulty acting well when granted the habits of the infused virtues, but a person with no acquired virtues — like a newly baptized infant — or with a heavy burden of acquired vices will have to make a highly disciplined effort to manifest these virtues in acts. See *ST* I-II.51-53 (acquisition of natural virtues); I-II.65.3.2-3; II-II.47.14; and III.69.4-5. See also Traina, *Feminist Ethics and Natural Law,* chapter 2.

32. See *ST* III.69.6 and 69.8.2.

33. *ST* II-II.4.4.

34. For similar themes in Middle High German texts, see Schultz, *The Knowledge of Childhood in the German High Middle Ages,* especially chapter 9.

35. *ST* II-II.47.15.2. See also Finnis, *Aquinas,* 88, and 101-2, note w.

reason and its first principles develop slowly in children not only because of their need to organize the internal "multiform movements" of their bodies but also because they must accumulate material to analyze.[36] Thus, reason is social and experiential.

The Phases of Childhood

Like Augustine, Thomas divides human life into a series of stages, but he distinguishes these explicitly with regard to the capacity to reason. The first three comprise what we might today think of as childhood and youth:

> The first is when a person neither understands by himself nor is able to learn from another; the second stage is when a man can learn from another but is incapable by himself of consideration and understanding; the third degree is when a man is both able to learn from another and to consider by himself. And since reason develops in man by little and little, in proportion as the movement and fluctuation of the humors is calmed, man reaches the first stage of reason before his seventh year; and consequently during that period he is unfit for any contract, and therefore for betrothal. But he begins to reach the second stage at the end of his first seven years, wherefore children at that age are sent to school. But man begins to reach the third stage at the end of his second seven years, as regards things concerning his person [e.g., marriage], when his natural reason develops; but as regards things outside his person [e.g., property], at the end of his third seven years.[37]

36. On the need to calm "the movement of the sensitive passions," see *ST* II-II.47.15.2; also St. Thomas Aquinas, *On the Truth of the Catholic Faith: Summa Contra Gentiles*, Book Two: *Creation*, trans. James F. Anderson (Garden City, N.Y.: Hanover House, 1956), 60.11, pp. 186-87. Thomas quotes Aristotle, *Physics*, VII, 3 (248a 1): a child does not have understanding, not because he "has not yet the nature enabling him to understand," but because of "the multiform movements in him." See also *ST* I-II.94.1 on the gradual knowledge of the first principles of practical reason.

37. *ST* Suppl. 43.2. Thomas abandoned the *Summa Theologiae* before he finished the treatise on the sacraments, and for the sake of completeness others pieced together questions and answers from earlier writings. These are known as the Supplementum. They therefore do not always represent his most mature thought. I have drawn on the Supplementum in this essay in cases where (1) I believe that it is consistent with Thomas's later thought, and (2) the opinions, whether or not the mature Thomas would have accepted them, are consistent with and have influenced the doctrines and practices of the Roman Catholic Christian tradition.

For more information on medieval visions of the life cycle, see Shahar, *Childhood in the Middle Ages*, chapter 2; and Shulamith Shahar, "The Boy Bishop's Feast: A Case-Study

Thomas, like many other authors, is not particularly concerned to employ the technical labels for these stages;[38] he typically calls children *pueris,* whether they occupy the stage classically labeled *infantia* (one to seven years of age), *pueritia* (seven years to puberty), or *adolescentia* (puberty to young adulthood). He rarely makes use of Augustine's term *parvuli* (reserved for the unbaptized) or of the fourth stage, youth or *juventus,* unless quoting another source. Instead, he asks about the children's rational sophistication and its implications for their accountability. For a person of any age can fall into actual sin or practice true virtue only to the degree that she can reason about ends and pursue them.

Infantia

Infancy presents the greatest challenge to Thomas's Aristotelian-Augustinian synthesis. As we have seen in an earlier chapter, according to Augustine unbaptized infants are infected by original sin and excluded from salvation but lack both the will and the understanding to do anything about it. Their inability to cause harm is a practical rather than a theoretical one: they are too small and weak to inflict significant damage. The problem facing Thomas is the apparent contradiction between Augustine's belief in original sin as an impediment to salvation and his own confidence in the manifest actual innocence of the

---

in Church Attitudes towards Children in the High and Late Middle Ages," in *The Church and Childhood,* ed. Diana Wood, Studies in Church History 31 (Oxford: Blackwell, 1994), 251-62; Michael E. Goodich, *From Birth to Old Age: The Human Life Cycle in Medieval Thought, 1250-1350* (Lanham, Md.: University Press of America, 1989), chapter 3; and René Metz, "L'Enfant dans le Droit Canonique Médiéval: Orientations de Recherche," in *La Femme et L'Enfant dans le Droit Canonique Médiéval,* 9-96 (London: Variorum Reprints, 1985), 11-23. Shahar notes that the markers of adolescence and young adulthood — inheritance, management, and gradual financial independence — were typically unavailable to girls, so that they for most purposes passed directly from *pueritia* to adulthood (Shahar, *Childhood in the Middle Ages,* 30).

To twentieth-century eyes, Thomas might seem to avoid or deflect questions by relying on civil or canon law. However, in the thirteenth century there was arguably more systematization of Christian canonical and moral thought, and more comfortable coherence between these and the stipulations of civil, positive law, than at any time before or since. Thus Thomas sees civil and ecclesiastical rulings as preferably continuous with — not unrelated to — systematic theology.

38. On the loose use of these terms, see David Nicholas, "Childhood in Medieval Europe," in *Children in Historical and Comparative Perspective: An International Handbook and Research Guide,* ed. Joseph M. Hawes and N. Ray Hiner (New York: Greenwood Press, 1991), 33-34.

unbaptized child. Babies or young children, lacking reason, are not intentional moral agents: they cannot sin, practice virtue, or make vows or contracts — in short, they cannot be held accountable for anything. They are essentially incapable of actual sin. This medieval confidence in actual infantile innocence is confirmed by medieval sacramental theology. Thomas taught that young children need not receive the sacraments of penance[39] or extreme unction because they could not have sinned.[40] Other medieval theologians' opinion that Masses need not be held for the souls of dead infants is now thought by some to reflect not the infants' irrelevance but a similar claim about their moral purity.[41]

On the one hand, Thomas's interpretation of divine justice leads him to agree with Augustine that no one with original sin deserves salvation, but on the other, it prevents him from believing that anyone deserves condemnation who through no fault of her own dies unbaptized but innocent of all actual sin. Thomas proposes an innovative solution to the problem for adults and older children: the baptism of desire. Rational persons who by God's grace genuinely wish to be baptized but are prevented from participating in the sacrament receive all the grace of sacramental baptism, including the remission of original and actual sin, simply through this wish.[42]

Because this solution does not answer the needs of infants — who, although as likely as not to die before they were old enough to request baptism, were unable to understand or desire it[43] — Thomas urged parents to arrange baptism for newborns speedily.[44] Yet this patch too leaves holes in the dike. What about infants who die unbaptized despite these measures? They cannot receive even the baptism of desire. Are they are excluded from heaven? Thomas declares that, although they are undeserving of damnation, since they are incapable of *actual* sin, they are also undeserving of salvation, since they still bear the stain of *original* sin. They are therefore consigned to the *limbus puerorum,* or children's limbo. Here they are denied intimate union with God but spared

39. Implied in *ST* Suppl. 16.1.

40. *ST* Suppl. 32.4. Thomas presumed that physical suffering in illness was at least partially a result of sin. Extreme unction was effective against the actual sin that caused adult suffering, but not against the remnants of original sin that caused juvenile suffering.

41. For evidence of this belief in the early Middle Ages, see Rob Meens, "Children and Confession in the Early Middle Ages," in *The Church and Childhood,* ed. Diana Wood, Studies in Church History 31 (Oxford: Blackwell, 1994), 59; and Nelson, "Parents, Children, and the Church," 87.

42. *ST* III.68.2: "The sacrament of Baptism may be wanting to anyone in reality but not in desire . . . which desire is the outcome of *faith that worketh by charity,* whereby God, Whose power is not tied to visible sacraments, sanctifies man inwardly."

43. *ST* III.68.8-9.

44. *ST* III.68.3. Infants are baptized not on account of their own faith but on account of the faith of their parents and the Church; see *ST* III 68.9, 71.1.

the physical, spiritual, and psychological pain of hell. The chilling implications of this interpretation of the inexorable logic of divine justice are unmistakable in its bizarre psychology. In two articles on limbo that were compiled from Thomas's early works and are now read as an appendix to the *Summa Theologiae*, Thomas argues matter-of-factly that in limbo, unbaptized children — then possessing the natural perfection of reason — will recognize but not protest their separation from God: "If one is guided by right reason one does not grieve through being deprived of what is beyond one's power to obtain, but only through lack of that which, in some way, one is capable of obtaining."[45] Innocent bearers of original sin, they neither deserve nor expect heaven. This conclusion held in the Roman Catholic Church until the mid-twentieth-century work of Karl Rahner.

Thomas's treatment of young children's care is even sparser than his piecemeal discussion of their salvation. Nurture by the family — specifically, the mother — is appropriate for children at this pre-rational stage, although he does not seem to notice the incongruity between the tending of infants by supposedly "irrational" and physical women and the fact that infants emerge from their care rational enough to be morally — if not legally — accountable.[46] Thomas takes the injunction to keep children under parental care so seriously that in the *Summa Theologiae* he twice insists it would be a greater transgres-

---

45. *ST* Appendix 1, 1.2; see also Appendix 1, 1.1 and Suppl. 69.6. These treatments were compiled from earlier writings. Evidence that Thomas retained the belief in children's limbo when he wrote the *ST* can be found in I-II.89.6. See also Thomas Aquinas, *De Malo* 5.3; and Thomas Aquinas, *Commentary on the Sentences* I.2.33.2.2. On the origins and history of the doctrine, see Shahar, *Childhood in the Middle Ages*, 45; Boswell, *The Kindness of Strangers*, 398; and Herlihy, "Medieval Children," 126. The perfection of natural reason should, on Thomas's logic, lead to a desire for God. Thus it is hard to understand how separation from God in limbo could be "painless," even when the justice of that separation is clearly understood.

Infants in the womb — or infants in danger of dying in childbirth — may not be baptized until their heads emerge, but neither may a living mother be cut open that her endangered child may be baptized (*ST* III.68.11). The logic of the first claim seems to be that one must be physically able to receive the sacramental washing of baptism; the logic of the second is that evil means — killing — may not be used to a good end — baptism. Thomas's additional intriguing suggestion is that "children while in the mother's womb . . . can, however, be subject to the action of God, in Whose sight they live, so as, by a kind of privilege, to receive the grace of sanctification" (*ST* III.68.11.1). Thus God may have a way of saving even stillborn children.

46. On the maternal and paternal roles, see Shahar, "The Boy Bishop's Feast," 255; and *ST* II-II.154.2. For a discussion of paternal and maternal roles in procreation, see Kari Elisabeth Børreson, *Subordination and Equivalence: The Nature and Role of Women in Augustine and Thomas Aquinas*, trans. Charles H. Talbot (Washington, D.C.: University Press of America, 1981), 192-96.

sion to baptize young Jewish children forcibly than it would be to risk their dying unbaptized.[47] This opinion may seem a welcome nod to religious freedom, but the central point appears to be that family authority trumps child welfare, even when salvation — the greatest good of all — is at stake.

Yet this authority was not intended as license to behave cruelly: although unwanted children were often neglected or abandoned, medieval records of both theory and practice suggest a regnant ideal of comparatively gentle, indulgent treatment of wanted children, especially those under seven.[48] Thomas concurs. Young children do not attend school, should not fast, and ought generally to be only gradually introduced to the rigors of the moral and intellectual virtues and the spiritual life.[49]

Like most medieval theologians, Thomas says next to nothing about young children's behavior, development, or spiritual life. This lacuna may have to do with the fact that he, like other monastic theologians who had entered monasteries as children, simply had no adult experience of children who were below the age at which their own monasteries accepted oblates (generally five or six, for children who were not abandoned, and in some cases much older). Whatever impressions of infancy they did preserve were then necessarily childish, likely reflective of the attitudes and practices of the nobility, and possibly colored by their sentimental longing for their own involuntarily truncated childhoods.[50] In addition, because infants could receive baptism without catechesis, priests needed to have no intimate or extended contact with a child until the first celebration of the sacrament of penance, at about age seven. Texts like

47. *ST* II-II.10.12, III.68.10. See the replies to III.68.10.1 and 3: "Neither should anyone infringe the order of the natural law, in virtue of which a child [*filius*] is under the care of its father, in order to rescue it from the danger of eternal death"; "a child [*puer*], before it has the use of reason, is ordained to God, by a natural order, through the reason of its parents, under whose care it naturally lies, and it is according to their ordering that things pertaining to God are to be done in respect of the child." In any case, the responsibility for their spiritual welfare rests entirely on their parents' shoulders, not on those of outsiders, and the children can choose baptism themselves once they reach the age of reason. Interestingly, although the parents' intention is the prerequisite for infant baptism, it is through the action of the whole Church rather than simply of the parents or sponsors that the child is baptized (*ST* III.68.9).

48. Among others, see Shahar, "The Boy Bishop's Feast," 253-54.

49. Thomas cautions that "all who have been lately baptized should be drilled into righteousness, not by penal, but by easy works, so as to advance to perfection by taking exercise" (*ST* III.68.5.2; italics in translation removed). On fasting, see *ST* II-II.147.4. Note that the rigors of which Thomas speaks would have been physically harmful to children; for example, the Lenten fast involved taking only one meal a day and abstinence from all flesh, eggs, and milk products.

50. McLaughlin, "Survivors and Surrogates," 134-35.

the *Summa Theologiae,* meant to prepare seminarians for the priesthood, may not have been intended to address a stage of life for which there were no priestly responsibilities. But whatever the reason, this gap in Thomas's thinking leaves us with a first stage of life that is as mysterious developmentally as it is complex soteriologically.

Pueritia

The second stage of childhood begins with the dawning of rational thought. Somehow one emerges at about the age of seven with the rudiments of reason in place. With reason come the incipient capacities for formal learning, moral accountability, sin, and virtue, and consequently the need for the sacrament of penance. Children in this age group can desire and request baptism, can have devotion to and receive the Eucharist, and can even make simple vows that are morally binding if not annulled by their fathers.[51] Reason and self-discipline develop during this period, at the close of which one has the capacity to be accountable in relationships with others — in Thomas's terms, to dispose of one's own body — and so to choose or reject marriage or holy orders. Thomas believes that this rational ability coincides with the physical changes of puberty (along with reason, the prerequisites for marriage): typically, but not necessarily, at the age of twelve for girls and fourteen for boys.[52]

Despite the child's new accountability, the soteriological intrigue continues, and the Augustinian anthropology of the corrupt will receives another decisive (if tantalizingly undeveloped) blow. Thomas believes that rational self-consciousness matures at a particular — if not easily discernible — moment. If the unbaptized "child that is beginning to have the use of reason"[53] immediately "direct[s] himself to the due end, he will, by means of grace, receive the remission of original sin: whereas if he does not then direct himself to the due end, as far as he is capable of discretion at that particular age, he will sin mortally, through not doing that which is in his power to do."[54] Apparently, then, for children to receive the baptism of desire and the remission of original sin, it

51. On the Eucharist, see *ST* III.80.9; on vows, *ST* II-II.88.8-9, 189.5. Thomas's condition for a binding simple vow seems to be (1) attainment of the use of reason, plus parental agreement, or (2) puberty. Solemn vows (of marriage or commitment to the religious life) and oaths may not be made before puberty; on the latter, see *ST* II-II.89.10.

52. *ST* Suppl. 43.2.3, 58.5.

53. *ST* I-II.89.6.3.

54. *ST* I-II.89.6; see also St. Thomas Aquinas, *Quaestiones Disputatae et Quaestiones Duodecim Quodlibetales,* vol. 5: *Quaestiones Quodlibetales* (Rome: Domus Editoriales Marietti, 1942), 11.22.

may be enough that they turn — with the aid of grace — toward the good at the first moment when they can rationally choose it. If they do not, they will have to repent and be baptized formally in order to avoid damnation. This tiny opening foreshadows Reformation Calvinist and twentieth-century Catholic disengagement of the remission of original sin from baptism, which then becomes primarily a rite of incorporation and a source or sign of further, sustaining grace.[55]

Thomas's developmental vision of *pueritia* also supports a degree of self-determination that actually exceeds that of some later periods and authors. He strikes a double blow at early, forced, and arranged marriages: first, since marriage is a matter of mutual consent rather than of ceremonial rectitude, a coerced "expression of words without inward consent makes no marriage"; and, second, a secret marriage between children who have reached puberty is valid.[56] Likewise, as we have seen, he held that at puberty children had the right to leave the monastic life or to disobey their parents in order to enter it. The latter case is easy to explain, the religious life being a higher good than the secular life, but the former emphasizes Thomas's acknowledgment of older children's rationality and moral accountability — as well as of the disturbances that resentful monks and nuns created in monastic communities. In all these cases Thomas's purpose is to articulate and justify children's right to decide for themselves whether and when to marry or enter the religious life.

Yet Thomas provides little other concrete guidance for raising older children. He does opine that many things allowed to children would be scandalous in virtuous adults, and in at least one case he stretches his permissiveness to young adulthood: Job sends his blessings to his sons and daughters as they feast, perhaps performs sacrifices to expiate sins that his sons might have committed while feasting, but declines to join them.[57] This pattern of indulgence of the young suggests that Thomas would have adhered to a thirteenth-century French movement that pegged both the matter and the method of education to the special needs and character of children.[58] If so, he would have been slightly ahead of monastic practice, in which concessions to oblates' youth were mostly

---

55. Note that Calvinists — though not the reformer John Calvin himself — have turned this understanding of baptismal grace in narrower, more predestinarian directions than have recent Roman Catholics. See the chapters on Calvin and Karl Rahner in this volume.

56. *ST* Suppl. 45.4-5; see also Suppl. 47.3-4, 6.

57. Thomas Aquinas, *The Literal Exposition on Job: A Scriptural Commentary Concerning Providence,* trans. Anthony Damico, Classics in Religious Studies, no. 7 (Atlanta: Scholars Press, 1989), 73-75.

58. Nicholas Orme, *From Childhood to Chivalry: The Education of the English Kings and Aristocracy, 1066-1530* (London and New York: Methuen, 1984), 90-94.

physical rather than spiritual, social, or psychological.[59] But, as we shall see, it is also likely that his concern to fit means to the different ends inscribed in the natures of the sexes would have led him to support the medieval practice of sending boys to school or apprenticeships and educating girls in households.[60]

Yet Thomas might have said much more. From his own experience as an oblate, university student, and teacher, he could have ruled explicitly on the content and philosophy of French and Italian education.[61] His experience as a priest and confessor would have been pertinent: penitentials, even from the early Middle Ages, detail separate, milder penalties for children.[62] He might have commented on guides for parents and monasteries that recommend both a certain brutality in the treatment of errant children — owing to their increasing ability to sin — and a mitigation of that brutality — owing to their incomplete rationality and to the dawning realization that violence might not beget virtue in its victims.[63] But in his theological writings Thomas tells us little more than that older children's minds, spirits, and bodies continue to grow and that allowances should be made for them.

Adolescentia

Because the real milestones of rationality fall at the beginning and end of *pueritia,* Thomas treats children past the age of puberty as adults in ecclesiastical and moral matters. This does not mean that he thought adolescents were fully mature: they lacked the shrewdness to control property and — if boys —

59. Despite some relaxation of standards for eating, sleep, and labor, play and bantering were severely curtailed when they were not forbidden, and oblates, like older monks and nuns, were punished physically for transgressions. See Shahar, *Childhood in the Middle Ages,* 193-97; McLaughlin describes a life of "almost intolerable rigor and confinement" for young oblates ("Survivors and Surrogates," 130).

60. On gender differences in education, see Shahar, *Childhood in the Middle Ages,* chapters 9-12 passim; Nicholas, "Childhood in Medieval Europe," 37-38; and Alexandre-Bidon and Lett, *Les Enfants au Moyen Age,* 133-248 passim.

61. On medieval Italian and Renaissance formal education, see Robert Black, "Italian Renaissance Education: Changing Perspectives and Continuing Controversies," in the *Journal of the History of Ideas* 52 (1991): 315-34. On British education, see Nicholas Orme, *Education and Society in Medieval and Renaissance England* (London: Hambledon Press, 1989).

62. Meens, "Children and Confession in the Early Middle Ages," 60-63.

63. Shahar, "The Boy Bishop's Feast," 254-58. Contemporary research on Benedictine monasteries gives evidence of both the rigor and the order of early medieval oblates' lives and the ways in which that rigor was mitigated; see Quinn, *Better than the Sons of Kings,* chapter 5. For evidence of this particular combination of indulgence and brutality, see Benedict's *Rule,* especially chapters 30, 40, 63, and 70 (on punishment of children), and chapters 36, 37, 39, 22, and 64 (on gentle and appropriate treatment of oblates generally).

may have been years from marriage and householding.[64] It is true that Thomas gives little evidence of the lenience with which medieval "adolescents" were normally penalized for infractions of civil laws or ecclesiastical sexual codes. But his insistence on accounting for circumstances, for the actors' degree of rationality, and for their level of knowledge suggests that a Thomistic, developmental view of childhood may want to make special allowances for adolescents, even if Thomas rarely does so himself.[65]

In sum, Thomas's discussions of children contain neither direct advice about child rearing nor even the sort of evocative imagery of children that we find in Augustine. What we take from Thomas is primarily a sense of the soteriological, rational, and legal status of the developing child.

Childhood as Relation, Human and Divine

Human Parents and Their Children

Historians' arresting statistics on child mortality (as high as 50 percent before the age of five in pre-industrial Europe), John Boswell's relentless recounting of the unbroken, almost ubiquitous European tradition of child abandonment, and Philippe Ariès's claims about self-defensive parental detachment from children should not lead us to assume that the thirteenth-century parents that Thomas had in mind were universally indifferent toward their children.[66] Clerical admonitions against excessive spoiling and mourning suggest the opposite.[67] Medieval authors, like their contemporary counterparts, made declarations about the value and proper treatment of children against the backdrop of a society in which desired children seem to have been loved and treated well but

64. *ST* Suppl. 43.2; Shahar, *Childhood in the Middle Ages*, 27-31.

65. *ST* I-II.18-19 (circumstances, ends, conscience, and the goodness of the will), 76-77 (ignorance and the passions).

66. For mortality rates, see the estimate in Shahar, *Childhood in the Middle Ages*, 149 and 305n. 50. Alexandre-Bidon and Lett report that in a study of the cemetery of Notre Dame de Cherbourg (tenth and eleventh centuries), 45 percent of the burials were of persons less than eighteen years old; of these, 58 percent were under four, and 25 percent were less than a year old (*Les Enfants au Moyen Age*, 63). See Ariès, *Centuries of Childhood*, 38. See also Boswell, *The Kindness of Strangers*.

67. On spoiling, see the accounts of Jean Gerson in Shahar, *Childhood in the Middle Ages*, 151; see also Herlihy, "Medieval Children," 125-26. On mourning, see Shahar, *Childhood in the Middles Ages*, 149-55; and Meens, "Children and Confession in the Early Middle Ages," 59. These admonitions may have been made to people of the upper classes; spoiling and excessive mourning would have been more difficult for the poor.

unwanted children were not. Possibly in (thickly veiled) response to this problem, Thomas builds on the "natural" human obligation toward and love of our own "productions," implying that rejection or neglect of one's own child would be "unnatural" and irrational.

Thomas's vision of the natural relation between parent and child exhibits none of the anxieties about the waywardness of natural impulses that would later worry thinkers like Menno Simons and A. H. Francke. Rather, he relies heavily on Aristotle's confident account of rational, proper family relationships.[68] Thomas's image flows first from his Aristotelian belief in the natural affinity of identical or closely related natures. We love and wish well those most closely related to us, for "the union arising from natural origin is prior to, and more stable than, all others, because it is something affecting the very substance, whereas other unions supervene and may cease altogether."[69] Strictly speaking, we should love our parents more than we do our children, in recognition of their having given us life; but "from the standpoint of the lover" the affective love of parent for child is appropriately among the most intense, intimate, long-lasting human attachments.[70] No one is nearer to us than our children, whom we love "as being part of" ourselves.[71]

Second, "nature has taught to all animals . . . sexual intercourse, education of offspring and so forth."[72] Again, by nature — rather than by divine revelation — people have responsibilities toward their children and are aware of them: "If we do not care for our own," he declares, "we are worse than infidels."[73] Chief among their responsibilities seem to be provision for children's material welfare and, significantly, for their education,[74] although, as we have

68. Aristotle, *The Ethics of Aristotle: The Nichomachean Ethics,* trans. J. A. K. Thompson (New York: Penguin Books, 1976), 8.vii (pp. 269-70), 8.xii (p. 279).

For an illuminating analysis of Thomas's vision of the family as a whole, with emphasis on the marital relationship, see Don S. Browning, Bonnie J. Miller-McLemore, Pamela D. Couture, K. Brynolf Lyon, and Robert M. Franklin, *From Culture Wars to Common Ground: Religion and the American Family Debate,* Religion, Family, and Culture Series (Louisville: Westminster John Knox Press, 1997), chapter 4.

69. *ST* II-II.26.8-9.

70. Thomas always ranks active principles and origins over derivations and products. Thus one's parents deserve more honor (as sources of one's goodness and being) than one's children (as mere products) (*ST* II-II.26.9); the same sort of paradox gives parents precedence over spouses, strictly speaking (II-II.26.11).

71. *ST* II-II.26.9.

72. *ST* I-II.94.2.

73. *ST* II-II.26.7.

74. *ST* II-II.26.7, 26.9.1; Suppl 45.5.1. Thomas's repeated insistence on the parental obligation to educate reflects the increasing "psychological and economic investment" by medieval families in their children. See Herlihy, "Medieval Children," 112, 124.

seen, they include religious instruction and sacraments as well. Although Thomas may seem to take parental responsibilities lightly (Boswell complains that his thorough treatment of vice in the *Summa Theologiae* does not explicitly address the rampant problem of abandonment, for instance), Thomas's insistence upon the comprehensiveness and longevity of the essential parental obligation toward children is arresting.[75] The "debt" of "influence and care" that parents owe to their "effects" is lifelong:[76]

> Since a father stands in the relation of principle, and his son in the relation of that which is from a principle, it is essentially fitting for a father to support his son: and consequently he is bound to support him not only for a time, but for all his life, and this is to lay by.[77]

As we have seen, this obligation extends beyond economic support: parents are to influence their adult offspring (well and rationally, of course) in their decisions about marriage and, as in Job's case, to admonish them and to intercede before God on their behalf. Nor do these parental responsibilities cease if parents decide to follow the higher path of the religious life.[78]

Finally, as Todd David Whitmore and Tobias Winright have argued, Thomas's case for the care of children extends beyond instincts shared with other animals to particularly human rational arguments. Love *(amor)* may be inspired merely by another's attractiveness or closeness, but care *(cura)* is the rational and obligatory human response to another's genuine need. On the intimate level, the distinction between love and care implies that parents must respond to their children's needs, no matter what their degree of affection. The distinction has social implications as well, for those to whom a person owes care may lie far outside the circle of her intimate love. Thus adults' responsibility to care for others also helps them to calculate how they should divide their attention between their own children and needy, unrelated others and, as will be suggested again below, implies a corporate, societal obligation to care for all who are needy — many of whom are children.[79]

75. Boswell, *The Kindness of Strangers*, 334. But Boswell's interpretation of Thomas's teaching may be overstated. For similar complaints against Thomas, see Carpenter, "Juette of Huy," 89n. 74.

76. *ST* II-II.26.9.1.

77. *ST* II-II.101.2.2. There does not seem to be a distinction in this matter between sons and daughters, although it may be that Thomas would have considered arrangement of an agreeable and prosperous marriage adequate payment of the parental debt to a daughter.

78. *ST* II-II.189.6.

79. Todd Whitmore with Tobias Winright, "An Undeveloped Theme in Catholic Teaching," in *The Challenge of Global Stewardship*, ed. Maura A. Ryan and Todd David Whitmore (Notre Dame: University of Notre Dame Press, 1997), 180-81.

The gravity of the parental obligation clarifies yet another difference between Augustine and Thomas. For both, fornication is a mortal sin, a symptom of disorder and irrationality. But for Thomas, this is not primarily because fornication is a surrender to the power of lust (sometimes the case even in marriage) but because it irrationally and unjustly jeopardizes the life and moral education of the child who could be conceived: birth out of wedlock deprives the child of the fatherly rational influence that is so necessary for children (probably especially boys) after *infantia*. In addition, such a child will almost certainly be abandoned (Boswell's interpretation) or grow up in poverty and, if male, arrive at adulthood without the right to inherit or be ordained.[80]

But this general obligation to offspring does not take the same shape for all children. Thomas took for granted gross divergences — by both gender and class — in the medieval fulfillment of it. Medieval parents had practical reasons for preferring sons to daughters: they were more likely to remain attached to the household and to support their parents. Thomas observes, "Parents usually prefer sons to daughters, both because that which is more perfect is more desirable and males are compared to females as the perfect to the imperfect, and because sons are usually more ready than daughters to help in managing business affairs."[81] To be rid of an economically unproductive adolescent daughter required an investment without expectation of return: a dowry or a gift to a convent. Boys were more productive. That Job has seven well-to-do sons and only three dependent daughters is evidence to Thomas of Job's favor with God, and he and his daughters are even more fortunate that the sons willingly provide for them.[82]

Thomas reinforces these calculated practical preferences for boys with claims about girls' inherent inferiority: girls' tendencies toward emotional volatility make them by and large less rational than boys and therefore less perfect and desirable in the absolute sense.[83] These claims, while not used by him to

80. *ST* II-II.154.2; Thomas is concerned mainly about the father's role in the child's moral education, but he implies that material provision is important; see also Thomas, *Commentary on Saint Paul's Epistle to the Ephesians*, 227. Boswell's interpretation is plausible but requires significant extrapolation; see *The Kindness of Strangers*, 315, 334. See also Nicholas, "Childhood in Medieval Europe," 39. On illegitimacy and holy orders, see *ST* Suppl. 39.5. Thomas must struggle mightily to explain why, if "nature" and "essence" are the links between parent and child, the illegitimate child does not have stronger claim on the father. In the end this seems to be a matter of decorousness and convention: illegitimacy is shameful. Yet fathers do have a moral responsibility to provide for their natural offspring, and they can (and perhaps should?) take advantage of legal mechanisms that can restore illegitimate sons' rights of inheritance (*ST* Suppl. 68.2-3).

81. Thomas, *The Literal Exposition on Job*, 72.

82. Thomas, *The Literal Exposition on Job*, 73.

83. On this see Børreson, *Subordination and Equivalence*, 174-78.

justify cruel treatment of girls, nonetheless reflect assumptions that supported such treatment. For instance, medieval female infants tended to be abandoned or killed more frequently than boys, weaned earlier (to their detriment), and ignored in censuses. Girls were generally denied formal education, for learning domestic skills — in their own homes for ordinary girls, or in other noble households for wealthy ones — was thought to be the best preparation for their future roles.[84]

Thomas also heartily approved of the rigid class differences that produced gross disparities in education. Medieval European people enjoyed "equal opportunity" only with respect to heaven;[85] on earth one was expected to keep to one's place in a strict social hierarchy in which levels of dignity corresponded to degrees of perfection.[86] Therefore, one required only the degree and sort of education that matched one's expected station. These divisions had some advantages for poor children, who, remaining at home, likely developed and maintained closer ties with their parents and siblings than children of nobles and the well-to-do; but they also shut most poor children of both sexes out of advanced study.[87]

On the details of parents' concrete duties to children, Thomas is again woefully general. By contrast, the preoccupation with mistreatment of children evidenced in medieval sermons, guides for parents, legal codes, and penitentials corroborates the general ecclesiastical anxiety over high rates of abandonment, exposure, infanticide, overly harsh beatings, fatal "trials" of suspected changelings, and suspicious overlaying of children in bed.[88] Less objectionable but still

84. On these differences, see, for example, Alexandre-Bidon and Lett, *Les Enfants au Moyen Age*, 116-18; Herlihy, "Medieval Children," 117; Nicholas, "Childhood in Medieval Europe," 37-39; and Shahar, *Childhood in the Middle Ages*, chapters 9-12. Existence of instructions for increasing the likelihood of conceiving a girl indicates that some parents — or at least some mothers — preferred girls (Shahar, *Childhood in the Middle Ages*, 43-45). There is debate over what proportion of low census figures for girls reflects a devaluation of living girls and what proportion indicates their early death.

85. Archibald argues that the advantaged had an edge even here, for in Thomas's scheme, power, reason and intellect, and virtue tend to be correlated ("The Concept of Social Hierarchy in the Writings of St. Thomas Aquinas," 188).

86. Archibald, "The Concept of Social Hierarchy in the Writings of St. Thomas Aquinas," 172.

87. On class differences in education and child rearing, see Nicholas, "Childhood in Medieval Europe," 42-45; Alexandre-Bidon and Lett, *Les Enfants au Moyen Age*, 129-248; McLaughlin, "Survivors and Surrogates," 136-39; and Shahar, *Childhood in the Middle Ages*, chapters 9-12.

88. On changelings, see note 6. Overlaying, or suffocation of an infant in the parental bed, was generally considered to be either bad luck or an unfortunate result of parental carelessness. (Drunkenness was a common accusation.) But, as in SIDS deaths today, par-

frowned upon by these sources was the practice of sending unwanted children to distant wet-nurses, where inadequate, unmonitored treatment and feeding were often fatal.[89] Here again, Thomas, by his silence on these topics, excludes practical, concrete reflection on parenting from the job description of the systematic theologian.[90]

The aims of Thomas's scattered treatments of parental responsibility seem to be twofold. First, he clearly means to justify social and familial hierarchies theologically: because they are part of the natural order created by God, genuine social and spiritual growth necessarily occur through (willing and obedient) adherence to them rather than rebellion against them. But, second, he attempts to mitigate the likelihood of exploitation by drawing on this same created order, which, he believes, also contains evidence of a strong natural tendency toward parental responsibility and benevolence. He is less interested in describing exactly what form parenting should take, quite possibly because he relies heavily on these natural tendencies to guide parents' hands.

Children and Their Parents

There seems no end in Thomas to parents' (or principles') debt to offspring (or effects). Children, on the other hand, owe their parents merely obedience (within the limits of the right and good) and the sort of honor, reverence, and service due to principles:[91] "[Children] must venerate [their parents] as elders; show obedience to them as teachers; and give them sustenance as the ones who had nourished them when they were strong."[92] All other obligations are contingent applications of these essential "debts" in particular circumstances: parental illness or poverty, for instance:[93] "For the son to bestow something on his fa-

---

ents were sometimes suspected of suffocating their children intentionally and then claiming them to be victims of overlaying.

89. Nelson, "Parents, Children, and the Church," 92; McLaughlin, "Survivors and Surrogates," 120-21; Meens, "Children and Confession in the Early Middle Ages," 5, 56; and Schmitt, *The Holy Greyhound.* Medieval sources disagree on beating; some advocate the practice in moderation, and fewer others call for its abolition. See Herlihy, "Medieval Children," 124-25; Nicholas, "Childhood in Medieval Europe," 41; McLaughlin, "Survivors and Surrogates," 136. On wet-nursing, see Shahar, *Childhood in the Middle Ages,* chapter 4; and Atkinson, *The Oldest Vocation,* 59-61.

90. Thomas is not so reticent on all moral matters: war, self-defense, theft, sexual ethics, truth-telling, and many other subjects receive thorough coverage in the *Summa Theologiae.*

91. *ST* II-II.26.9.1.

92. Thomas, *Commentary on Saint Paul's Epistle to the Ephesians,* 228.

93. *ST* II-II.101.2.

ther is accidental, arising from some momentary necessity, wherein he is bound to support him, but not to lay by as for a long time beforehand, because naturally parents are not the successors of their children, but children of their parents."[94] At the same time, that this duty is not "essential" to sons and daughters does not mean they can ignore it with impunity. As we have seen, for instance, one may not enter religious life if one's parents are destitute. This special burden arises out of the duty of filial service, "out of favors received," and out of the intensity of filial love, not simply from the parents' needs; one does not have the same sort of obligation to anonymous others.[95]

Thus, in the end, Thomas's circumspection is less hard-hearted toward parents than it at first appears. Still, paradoxically, the higher and more perfect love that children owe their parents entails more limited and conditional obligations than the lower, less perfect love that parents owe their offspring. The premise — that children have no absolute or essential material obligations to parents — is strikingly modern.

Yet Thomas's vision of parent-child relations has an invidious flip side. Social rights of children in relation to their parents depended on age. As we have seen, Thomas grants pubertal children remarkable freedom from parental control but cedes parents exclusive authority and thus absolute power over the care of their young children. In this respect a child under the age of reason "differs not from an irrational animal"; as animals are used according to their masters' wishes, so children are raised according to their parents' desires.[96] The comparison loses a bit of its horror when we realize that in the thirteenth century, control and care implied each other, and subordination and domination were the rule rather than the tolerated exception. Nearly everyone spent a significant portion or even all of life under the power of others: wives under husbands; oblates under monks, who in turn were under abbots; nuns under abbesses; slaves under masters; peasants under nobles.[97] Yet unlike adults, who normally both submitted to and exerted control, children were always at the bottom of the heap. Parents, like all superiors, had a moral obligation of benevolence: "The father manages his child for the child's advantage."[98] But it is not clear that Thomas expected human (or civil) law to enforce this obligation. Most laws that Thomas mentions protect men, men as heads of households, or the internal or external political security of a com-

94. *ST* II-II.101.2.2.

95. *ST* II-II.26.9.3, 189.6.

96. *ST* II-II.10.12.

97. Archibald, "The Concept of Social Hierarchy in the Writings of St. Thomas Aquinas," 181, 185; Finnis, *Aquinas*, 174.

98. Thomas, *Commentary on Saint Paul's Epistle to the Ephesians*, 230.

monwealth.[99] Thus Thomas's vision of government seems to leave few *actual* openings for children to make direct claims on society.

Yet he does provide *theoretical* grounds for the civil protection of children from negligent or malevolent parents. First, rulers are to make laws that protect the common good of the social whole, presumably including children.[100] Second, laws can be circumvented for the same reason. Order and subordination, intended to serve the common good, are to be subverted when they cause suffering: "manifest and urgent" need justifies the taking of another's property, and "the injury of the multitude" justifies revolution.[101] But in both these latter cases the need must be excruciating, and the burden is on the victim. Children — who identify with their families, lack political leverage, and possess only rudimentary moral sensibility — cannot be expected to recognize and demand their due. Thomas's theoretical seeds can bear fruit, then, only if children have vocal and powerful adult advocates.[102]

Childhood and the Divine

Thomas's discussions of mortal parents and children produce unique, if by now unsurprising, twists on the imagery of spiritual childhood. For Thomas, chronological childhood is an ambivalent theological metaphor. Although, as for Augustine, chronological childhood *(pueritia)* most often recalls childbirth, the symbol of spiritual regeneration in baptism,[103] only rarely does Thomas tout the innocence and humility of childhood as a model for the adult spiritual life.[104] This reserve separates him from popular medieval devotional traditions like the Cistercian cult of the Child Jesus, which linked childish simplicity with wisdom rather than ignorance. Some mystics and visionaries of both sexes

99. Exceptions already mentioned include laws regarding the age for marriage or religious vows, the rights of children presented at monasteries, the limited rights of illegitimate children, and the proscription of fornication.

100. Law in general is "an ordinance of reason for the common good, made by him who has care of the community, and promulgated" (*ST* I-II.90.4). Human — or positive — law is designed with the common social good in mind.

101. *ST* II-II.66.7, II-II.42.2.3.

102. See also Finnis, *Aquinas,* 233; and Whitmore with Winright, "An Undeveloped Theme in Catholic Teaching," 179. Both use Thomistic arguments to underline the contemporary need for government to ensure child welfare.

103. Thomas Aquinas, *Commentary on the Gospel of St. John*, Part I, trans. James A. Weisheipl, O.P., S.T.M., and Fabian R. Larcher, O.P., Aquinas Scripture Series, vol. 4 (Albany, N.Y.: Magi Books, 1980), 186-90. See also *ST* III.66.9, 68.9.

104. Thomas, *Commentary on Saint Paul's First Letter to the Thessalonians and the Letter to the Philippians,* 15.

imagined themselves as infants nursing at the breast of Jesus or of Mary; in a fascinating twist, a number of nuns envisioned themselves suckling the infant Jesus. In stark contrast to Augustinian anthropology, all of these devotions celebrated children's "natural" joy and humility and entailed a decidedly non-Thomistic idealization of physical, lusty constructions of childhood and maternity.[105]

Rather, for Thomas, the ignorance and irrationality of infancy cast a pejorative shadow — "childishness" — over what was for some of his contemporaries (and would be for later thinkers like Friedrich Schleiermacher and Karl Rahner) an image of spiritual perfection — "childlikeness."[106] Even innocent children are poor spiritual role models because they are incomplete, lacking both wisdom and active virtue. Childhood in Thomas is typically a metaphor for "imperfection of knowledge" and seeing "through a mirror in a dark manner."[107] In Galatians, Thomas argues, Paul suffers "in labour again" because his children "are not perfectly formed." Here he opines that spiritual regression causes people to "become small": unworthy of the honorific "sons," they are reduced to "little children."[108] A further sign of the incompleteness of childhood is Thomas's opinion that the fleeting perfection of the body comes not, as in our cultural ideal, in the teens, but at about thirty.[109] Thomas values maturity, the fruit of virtuous living, more highly than raw potential, which can be bent toward good or evil.

Far more common and more positive — if troublingly gendered — is im-

105. On the cult of the Child Jesus, see Herlihy, "Medieval Children," 127-30. On mystical lactation, see Caroline Walker Bynum, *Holy Feast and Holy Fast: The Religious Significance of Food to Medieval Women* (Berkeley and Los Angeles: University of California Press, 1987), especially chapter 5, chapter 9, and plates. See also Rosemary Drage Hale, "'Taste and See, for God Is Sweet': Sensory Perception and Memory in Medieval Christian Mystic Experience," in *Vox Mystica: Essays on Medieval Mysticism in Honor of Professor Valerie M. Lagorio,* ed. Anne Clark Bartlett, Thomas H. Bestul, Janet Goebel, and William F. Pollard, 3-14 (Cambridge: D. S. Brewer, 1995). Here the body becomes a vehicle for — not an obstacle to — union with God. See Caroline Walker Bynum, "The Female Body and Religious Practice in the Later Middle Ages," in *Fragmentation and Redemption: Essays on Gender and the Human Body in Medieval Religion* (New York: Zone Books, 1991), 181-238.

106. See Nelson, "Parents, Children, and the Church," 85.

107. Thomas, *Commentary on Saint Paul's Epistle to the Galatians,* 109.

108. Thomas, *Commentary on Saint Paul's Epistle to the Galatians,* 132. See also the pejorative use of "childhood" on 109: the incompleteness of the Old Law and the present life are as children in comparison with perfection, the New Law in Christ and the future, perfect knowledge of God.

109. On the fleeting beauty of the youthful body, see Thomas, *The Literal Exposition on Job,* 223. On the perfection of the body at thirty, see *ST* Suppl 81.1. There are Christological reasons for this claim, however.

agery of the natural sonship *(filiatio)* of Jesus Christ and the adoptive sonship of the believer. Christ, the "true and natural Son of God,"[110] is "naturally begotten of the Father"[111] and therefore is — just as a human being would be — of precisely the same nature as his father.[112] Human beings by definition cannot be the "natural sons" of God, for they lack both divinity and perfect knowledge of God[113] as well as literal direct divine parentage.[114] Still, they are God's offspring analogously, by participation, through the "spirit of adoption";[115] they are called "sons of light" because they abound in Christ, "the light of the world."[116] The filial relation and accompanying likeness to the Father even ground claims of justice upon God: "it is not fitting for an image of God, namely, man, to be excluded from the kingdom of God except for some obstacle . . . sin."[117] Thus for Thomas adoptive sonship conjures images of maturity, fulfillment, and rightful inheritance rather than of the helpless if innocent dependency of infancy.

Legacy

What Thomas bequeaths first of all is a theological justification for a developmental model of childhood. This not only sets the sort of historical precedent for developmentalism that is important to Christians for whom theological tradition is a standard of contemporary orthodoxy. It also provides a needed, credible theological interpretation of the developmental theories that are our

110. *ST* III.23.4. See also Thomas Aquinas, *The Sermon-Conferences of St. Thomas Aquinas on the Apostles' Creed*, ed. and trans. Nicholas Ayo, C.S.C. (Notre Dame: University of Notre Dame Press, 1988), IV (46-53).

111. Thomas, *Commentary on the Gospel of St. John*, 92, 369.

112. See *ST* I.42.4, 6.

113. See, for example, Thomas, *Commentary on the Gospel of St. John*, 104-5.

114. In the sixth and seventh centuries, Isidore of Seville argued that "legitimate" fatherhood implies that the child is of the same blood — or semen — as the father. See Thomas Laqueur, *Making Sex: Body and Gender from the Greeks to Freud* (Cambridge and London: Harvard University Press, 1990), 55-57. Therefore, especially given the ancient and medieval belief that semen contained a *homunculus,* an entire human being who needed merely the nourishment of the womb, it would have been impossible for human beings to be literal, genuine sons or daughters of God.

115. Thomas, *Commentary on the Gospel of St. John*, 128; also 92, 168. See also *ST* III.23.2-4.

116. Thomas, *Commentary on Saint Paul's First Letter to the Thessalonians and the Letter to the Philippians*, 44; see also 89.

117. Thomas, *Commentary on the Gospel of St. John*, 189.

de facto cultural authorities. Theology has not kept up with psychology here; for instance, the dour Augustinian view of infant rages that still prevails in many pulpits is due for replacement, and an updated version of Thomas's vision provides a credible alternative. For Thomas, childhood is not simply a phase to be tolerated on the way to true personhood. Rather, it is an appropriate and necessary stage within the lifelong journey toward perfection in which adults too are engaged. The person who is "unnatural" — thanks to sin or to divine intervention — is the one who skips childhood, stalls there, or returns to it after having outgrown it.

Thomas's theory will disappoint those who envision the child as a fully conscious and dignified religious subject; his child is incomplete, imperfect, and (because she is irrational) still growing into her humanity. In order to be useful today, Thomas's sketch of development must be filled in with color and detail. Jean Porter, for instance, has fused Thomas's image of children with contemporary psychology and virtue theory to create a suggestive and credible account of children's social acquisition of virtue and moral knowledge.[118] The developmental model might also be able to reinforce a flagging theory of juvenile personal accountability while slowing the frightening downward slide of the age of financial and criminal accountability. For example, Thomas insists on young adolescents' ability to commit themselves to marriage or the religious life. But he also stresses the importance of postponing control of property and households until they are older, and he seems to concur with the custom of lenient sentences and penances for adolescents. Furthermore, adoption of the Aristotelian emphasis upon rationally ordering (rather than castigating) children's chaotic, innocent, but generally good impulses may well be one prerequisite for the end of violence against children, although — as later chapters in this book show — it is certainly not a sufficient condition. In addition, Thomas's concern to articulate parents' obligations toward children, his genuine (if backhanded) appreciation of the irreplaceability of early familial nurture, and his placement of the family within the network of an interdependent social order provide ample openings for moral arguments in support of children's welfare. These marks, which concur with much contemporary wisdom, need not be partisan; they can be used in a politically conservative way, as John Finnis shows when he argues for loving, permanent, heterosexual unions, or they can suggest more general and flexible critical standards, like the need of foster children for consistent care in a single home.[119]

118. Jean Porter, *Moral Action and Christian Ethics* (Cambridge: Cambridge University Press, 1995), chapter 5.

119. Finnis, *Aquinas,* 152; see also chapters vii.4, vii.6. For feminist assertions of the importance of family indebted to Aristotle and Thomas — but construed with somewhat

Thomas's theological anthropology of childhood also sets a precedent for middle-of-the-road solutions to the depravity/innocence debate. As later chapters will show, the distinction between "pessimistic" and "optimistic" estimates of children's moral and spiritual condition often has less to do with the theologians' reading of the deepness of the wound of original sin than with their understanding of the subsequent availability of healing grace. Be that as it may, the distinction has merit as a tool for comparing theologians' estimates of the spiritual capacities of children, whether graced or "natural." Thomas — like Menno Simons and, arguably, even Augustine — struggles mightily to strike a balance between the poles of depravity and innocence. First, for Thomas, children are bearers of actual — but not existential — innocence: afflicted with a fault that does not automatically consign them to hell, neither are they models of purity or virtue. Second, Thomas comes to the thoroughly modern conclusion that no one goes to hell who has not consciously, rationally chosen to do wrong when he could have done otherwise.[120] Divine justice excludes such persons from both heaven and hell. The continuing power of these two claims is unmistakable in the persistence of the doctrine of limbo, which maintained its grip until Karl Rahner rejected it in the middle part of the twentieth century in an attempt to prevent divine justice from swallowing divine mercy.

Some apparent and oft-quoted dangers in Thomas's treatment of children may simply be correctable archaisms. For instance, a thoroughgoing misogynism, rooted in a narrowly defined rationalism that both depends upon and is suspicious of the body and its passions, can be avoided by expanding our gauge of development. Others, like Thomas's matter-of-fact declaration that the condition of slavery is hereditary,[121] lose their power in an era in which we see social roles as the flexible products of human ingenuity rather than as the evidence of divine design working through heredity.

Thomas's ideal of family structure — a faithful, monogamous marriage with offspring — also appears anomalous in an era when so few families achieve it. But this ideal loses its air of antiquity when we realize that the gap between

---

more breadth and flexibility than in Finnis's account — see Jean Bethke Elshtain, *Public Man, Private Woman: Women in Social and Political Thought* (Princeton, N.J.: Princeton University Press, 1981); and Lisa Sowle Cahill, *Sex, Gender, and Christian Ethics,* New Studies in Christian Ethics (Cambridge: Cambridge University Press, 1996). As we will see in this book's chapter by Bonnie J. Miller-McLemore, concern for the family and children in the family extends far beyond political conservatism and moderate feminism.

120. This way of stating the matter is redundant with respect to Thomas, for whom wrongdoing always implies the rejection of a better path; the point is that he would not have accepted Luther's doctrine of the bondage of the will, under which a person can do only evil until he is released through justification.

121. *ST* II-II.10.12, Suppl. 52.4.

ideal and reality was just as wide in thirteenth-century families as in families in the twenty-first century. Large numbers of children were born outside marital relationships and were abandoned or were supported with struggle by mothers and sometimes by fathers; parents died, orphaning children and setting the stage for stepfamilies, adoptions, and servitude; young children were sent away to learn skills or trades. The purported disarray of contemporary families is not, it turns out, a sufficient argument against the ideal of the stable, monogamous union. Rather than justifying an easy dismissal of the ideal as an archaism, a close look at Thomas in his context forces us instead to ask why it has persisted against such apparently high practical odds in both Thomas's era and our own.[122]

The deepest flaws in Thomas's teachings on children have much to do with what he did not say. In light of thirteenth-century debates over the needs and treatment of children, it is remarkable that Thomas did not treat children's issues in more concentrated ways or at greater length. This is especially surprising given his detailed attention to other moral questions. Mentions of children are instead scattered through his works, appearing obliquely whenever his theological systematic seems logically to raise them. His vagueness on developmental details and his lack of direct interest in particular issues of child rearing qualify his immediate usefulness for a contemporary theology or ethic of childhood. This failure is especially damaging when, as for example in the cases of child neglect and abandonment, absence of direct condemnation may well have combined with his opinions on the inferiority of women to bend clerical and parental opinions against female offspring. This is hardly a constructive, substantive precedent for contemporary reflection on the care of children.

Another serious danger of Thomas's brand of developmentalism is equally hard to dismiss. Thomas anticipates the later Western image of the child as a whole person with a free will. Yet this image touched off a conflict whose reverberations are felt today: the conflict between this autonomous child and the paternalistic view of the child as the obedient possession and responsibility of the family. Then and now, children have been viewed as persons who, measured by their potential, are on equal footing with adults and make remarkably strong moral claims on parents.[123] Then and now, the developmental model has committed us to the claim that children are not fully developed, cannot be responsible for themselves, and must be entrusted to others. Paradoxically, their good care requires that limits be placed on their autonomy.[124]

122. See Browning et al., *From Culture Wars to Common Ground,* for some contemporary arguments in favor of the ideal.

123. For a contemporary affirmation of this claim, see Finnis, *Aquinas,* 171.

124. On the importance of this claim for contemporary Roman Catholic teaching on children, see Whitmore with Winright, "An Undeveloped Theme in Catholic Teaching," 178.

Thomas saw the fundamental potential for exploitation, and he partially corrected it by absolving rational older children legally and morally from absolute obedience to parents. But he left young children vulnerable to their families' whims.

Unfortunately, the delicate task of articulating and enforcing young children's legal rights within families remains unfinished over seven centuries later. But Thomas's thought on childhood is not therefore a theological or political blind alley, for it contains many raw materials for constructing these protections: a developmental anthropology, a theory of justice, and a doctrine of the *imago dei.* These elements, which in the thirteenth century were eclipsed by Thomas's acquiescence to an overdrawn medieval preference for family autonomy and patriarchal hierarchy, can exert their full power in support of children's rights in our more individualistic, more democratic age.[125]

---

125. Whitmore and Winright note that the subsumption of children under the rubric of the family is a fault that still plagues Roman Catholic social teaching ("An Undeveloped Theme in Catholic Teaching," 161).

5. The Child in Luther's Theology: "For What Purpose Do We Older Folks Exist, Other Than to Care for . . . the Young?"

JANE E. STROHL

The theology of Martin Luther (1483-1546) is characterized by paradox. He defined the believer as *simul iustus et peccator*, simultaneously saint and sinner, for although in God's sight we have been made wholly righteous by the grace of Christ, the sin that deformed our nature at the Fall continues to ensnare us. The believer experiences a twofold reign of God throughout her earthly life — in the structures governing the creation on the one hand, and in the proclamation of the gospel on the other. Thus the Word of God also makes itself known in a twofold fashion, as command (law) and unconditional promise (gospel). An acute eschatological tension drives each of these doctrines — that is, only with the second coming of Christ will the paradoxes be resolved so that the Christian is wholly saint, living in the fullness of God's reign, where the distinction between law and gospel is no longer necessary. The turbulence of his times convinced Luther that the victorious return of Christ, with its attendant cataclysm for the sinful world, was imminent.

Understanding such paradoxes requires a certain experience of the ambiguities of life and a degree of mental and spiritual sophistication that are not characteristic of children. Insofar as children occupied Luther's theological attention, it was primarily in terms of what they should become: mature, seasoned confessors of the evangelical faith and responsible members of family and community. Children depended upon commitment and care from adults to achieve this goal. Luther regarded the work of mothers and fathers as a most holy calling and obligation. He also recognized what contemporary society struggles to internalize: that it takes more than a family to raise a child. For Luther, the wider community and the civil authorities played critical roles in the vocation of parenting. This chapter will examine a selection of Luther's writings illustrative of the main perspective from which he regards children theologically — that is, in the context of the parent-child relationship. We will begin by exploring the experiences of Luther himself as a child. We will then consider some specific implications of Luther's thought for children and child-rearing practices, and conclude with a discussion of Luther as a father.

Luther the Son

In his study *Young Man Luther,* Erik Erikson makes bold to press the scanty crop of information about Luther's childhood to yield a heady vintage of psychoanalytic speculation. He is particularly intrigued by Martin's relationship with his father, Hans:

> Hans Luder in all his more basic characteristics belonged to the narrow, suspicious, primitive-religious, catastrophe-minded people. He was determined to join the growing class of burghers, masters, and town fathers — but there is always a lag in education. Hans beat into Martin what was characteristic of his own past, even while he meant to prepare him for a future better than his own present. This conflictedness of Martin's early education, which was *in* and *behind* him when he entered the world of school and college, corresponded to the conflicts inherent in the ideological-historical universe which lay *around* and *ahead* of him. The theological problems which he tackled as a young adult of course reflected the peculiarly tenacious problem of the domestic relationship to his own father; but this was true to a large extent because both problems, the domestic and the universal, were part of one ideological crisis: a crisis about the theory and practice, the power and responsibility, of the moral authority invested in fathers: on earth and in heaven; at home, in the market-place, and in politics; in the castles, the capitals, and in Rome. But it undoubtedly took a father and a son of tenacious sincerity and almost criminal egotism to make the most of this crisis, and to initiate a struggle in which were combined elements of the drama of King Oedipus and the passion of Golgotha, with an admixture of cussedness made in Saxony.[1]

This is not the type of material upon which historians build with confidence, but neither can it be dismissed from consideration. Critics of Luther charged from the outset that his theology represented not an insight into the biblical

1. Erik H. Erikson, *Young Man Luther: A Study in Psychoanalysis and History* (New York: W. W. Norton, 1958), 77.

witness of universal import but a peculiar neurosis writ large and imposed as a hermeneutic upon the Christian tradition. Contemporary voices, impelled by ecumenical perspectives rather than partisan polemics, express similar concerns.[2] Whatever reservations one has about the potential extravagances of the kind of psycho-history Erikson produced, it is clear that Luther's own experience as a child, particularly in the parent-child relationship, influenced his reflections on children and the life of Christian faith.

Late medieval Europe has been described as enduring a crisis of the symbols of security. While every era is in some sense in crisis, this period witnessed unprecedented upheaval in social, political, and economic life.[3] The citation from Erikson is notable for placing the personal struggle of a father and son coming of age in the context of the wider societal struggle with issues of autonomy and authority. The success of the Reformation has been attributed to its appeal to the laity, its acknowledgment of the capacity of those heretofore under the church's guardianship to weigh the evidence and draw their own conclusions regarding the faith.[4] This concern for self-determination and the respect accorded one's decisions appears in Luther's writings concerning the obligations of the parent-child relationship. At points he explicitly addresses the conflict that his own vocational choices precipitated with his father.

Hans Luther was vehemently opposed to his eldest son's decision to abandon his course of university study in law and enter the Augustinian cloister at Erfurt. He withheld his blessing and broke off relations with Martin. A reconciliation followed at the time Luther celebrated his first mass, but his recollection of the event shows it to have been less than satisfying. In the letter of November 21, 1521, addressed to Hans Luther and dedicating the treatise "On Monastic Vows" to him, Luther writes,

> For I remember very well that after we were reconciled and you were [again] talking with me, I told you that I had been called by terrors from heaven and

2. See, for example, B. A. Gerrish, *Continuing the Reformation: Essays on Modern Religious Thought* (Chicago: University of Chicago Press, 1993), 236.

3. Carter Lindberg, *The European Reformations* (Oxford: Blackwell, 1996), 25. See also Merry E. Wiesner, *Women and Gender in Early Modern Europe* (Cambridge: Cambridge University Press, 1993), who points out that these convulsions of change that inaugurated the early modern period stopped short of transforming gender relations: "Of all the ways in which society was hierarchically arranged — class, age, rank, occupation — gender was regarded as the most 'natural' and therefore the most important to defend" (255). Wiesner states that the causes of this rigid enforcement of gender hierarchy have not yet been fully explained, although clearly in part it served as a defensive mechanism in the face of so much social dislocation. For further discussion of sixteenth-century developments, see the chapters in this volume by Barbara Pitkin and Keith Graber Miller.

4. Euan Cameron, *The European Reformation* (Oxford: Clarendon Press, 1992), 312.

that I did not become a monk of my own free will and desire, still less to gain any gratification of the flesh, but that I was walled in by the terror and the agony of sudden death and forced by necessity to take the vow. Then you said, "Let us hope that it was not an illusion and a deception." That word penetrated to the depths of my soul and stayed there, as if God had spoken by your lips, though I hardened my heart against you and your word as much as I could. You said something else too. When in filial confidence I upbraided you for your wrath, you suddenly retorted with a reply so fitting and so much to the point that I have hardly ever in all my life heard any man say anything which struck me so forcibly and stayed with me so long. "Have you not also heard," you said, "that parents are to be obeyed?" But I was so sure of my own righteousness that in you I heard only a man, and boldly ignored you; though in my heart I could not ignore your word.[5]

The conflict over how finally to judge the meaning of Martin's decision, which so traumatically affected the lives of both father and son, is resolved for Luther in this letter. He acknowledges his father's authority over him as a son and grants that Hans's desire that Martin be removed from the monastery has prevailed by God's own design. At the same time, Luther insists that his original decision to defy his father's wishes and embrace monastic vows was also in fulfillment of the divine will.[6]

According to Luther, he and his father were both right in principle that the commandments of God are to be put before all things, *and* each needed to learn an ironic lesson about what that meant in actuality. He acknowledges that his vow was illegitimate, since by it he withdrew himself from the authority and guidance of his parents, thus violating the Fourth Commandment ("Honor your father and your mother"). He now sees that he acted in accordance with human doctrines and hypocritical superstitions. Nonetheless, Luther marvels at how much good God has made to come out of all the error and sin of his original decision and asks his father, "Would you now not rather have lost a hundred sons than not have seen this good?"[7] He concedes Hans's enduring pa-

---

5. *Luther's Works,* ed. Jaroslav Pelikan and Helmut Lehmann, 55 vols. (St. Louis: Concordia Publishing House, 1955-1986), 48: 332. Citations to the American edition of Luther's works will be designated by the letters LW followed by the volume and page number(s).

6. "But it was the Lord's will, as I now see, that the wisdom of the schools and the sanctity of the monasteries should become known to me by my own actual experience, that is, through many sins and impieties, so that wicked men might not have a chance, when I became their adversary, to boast that I condemned something about which I knew nothing. Therefore I lived as a monk, indeed not without sin but without reproach" (LW 48: 333).

7. LW 48: 333.

ternal authority insofar as the monastic life is concerned; however, that life is of no importance to Luther anymore. God, whose authority is superior to all earthly claims, has called Luther to the ministry of the Word.

> Nevertheless [God], who has taken me out of the monastery, has an authority over me that is greater than yours; you see that he has placed me now not in a pretended monastic service but in the true service of God. Who can doubt that I am in the ministry of the Word? And it is plain that the authority of parents must yield to this service, for Christ says, "He who loves father or mother more than me is not worthy of me." Not that this word destroys the authority of parents, for the Apostle [Paul] often insists that children should obey their parents; but if the authority of parents conflicts with the authority or calling of Christ, then Christ's authority must reign alone.[8]

As a reformer, Luther often insists on filial obedience as a foundation of evangelical discipleship.[9] His cagey way of besting his father on this issue, however, shows that his concept of Christian freedom, by which the believer is lord of all and servant of all,[10] allowed children some means to counter their parents' demands based on the Fourth Commandment.[11]

Scott Hendrix, a contemporary Luther scholar who has practiced as a licensed family therapist, also concerns himself with the "family system" that shaped Luther.[12] Although he recognizes significant lacunae in Erikson's analysis — for example, the fact that it gives scant attention to the influence of Luther's mother and her family and does not account for the anger and bitterness of the older Luther — Hendrix does agree with Erikson that the conflict between father and son was of great significance for Martin's development as a person and a theologian. However, whereas Erikson presents the conflict as generating mental illness in the reformer, Hendrix concludes that Luther resolved the problem in a nonpathological way — indeed, almost too well: "Luther not only healed the rift with his father; that healing unleashed a new devotion to Christ alone that resulted in his radical claim to own the rights to the only true reformation."[13] Luther's absolute obedience to Christ proved to be delayed obedience to his father in the matter of monastic life as well, but this

8. LW 48: 335.

9. See below, 155-56.

10. Martin Luther, "The Freedom of a Christian," in *Martin Luther's Basic Theological Writings,* ed. Timothy F. Lull (Minneapolis: Fortress Press, 1989), 596.

11. The reader will note that the theme of legitimate exceptions to the commandment prescribing filial obedience recurs in a number of the essays in this volume.

12. Scott Hendrix, "Beyond Erickson: The Relational Luther," *Lutheran Theological Seminary Bulletin* 75:1 (Winter 1995): 3-12.

13. Hendrix, "Beyond Erikson," 7.

resolution was very costly in emotional, relational, and professional terms. The long-term consequence, in Hendrix's judgment, was Luther's frequent immaturity in dealing with disappointment and vicious attacks on those who rejected "his" gospel.

Family Life

The medieval church distinguished between secular and spiritual estates. Persons who took upon themselves the counsels of perfection — poverty, chastity, and obedience — obtained a higher righteousness than those immersed in the affairs of the world, and merited special grace on the church's behalf. This was the particular vocation of priests and monks.[14]

Luther rejected the idea that certain states of life and occupations were religiously superior or more spiritual. Just as he taught that one emerged from the waters of baptism "priest, bishop, and pope," an equal member of the priesthood of all believers, so he insisted that one could honorably exercise that priesthood in a wide variety of socially productive vocations. The Christian life was to be lived in Christ through faith and for the neighbor in love.[15] God deliberately created the human realm to be social — everyone is born as someone's child, "educated as someone's pupil, governed as someone's subject, supplied as someone's customer, married as someone's spouse, nurtured as someone's parishioner," and usually becomes someone's parent in turn, thus starting the cycle over.[16] The foundation for this mission of service, the staging platform for the advance of the gospel, is the home.

In Luther's first writings extolling the married state over enforced celibacy, his rejection of the latter and embrace of the former are focused on the problem of lust. He lauds marriage as a defense against the threat posed by this sin to both the individual and society. Celibacy, when it is imposed as a legal requirement rather than received as a divine charism, is an invitation to disaster. Luther later complements this view of marriage as a remedy against sin with a more positive understanding of the marital relationship as an estate of faith in which the gospel's gifts of mercy and righteousness bear social fruit.[17]

While recognizing the goodness of love and sexual compatibility in the

14. Lindberg, *The European Reformations,* 99.
15. Luther, "The Freedom of a Christian," 623.
16. William H. Lazareth, *Luther on the Christian Home: An Application of the Social Ethics of the Reformation* (Philadelphia: Muhlenberg Press, 1960), 132.
17. Lazareth, *Luther on the Christian Home,* 217.

husband-wife relationship, Luther chiefly extols the vocation of marriage because it produces family life:

> But the greatest good in married life, that which makes all suffering and labor worth while, is that God grants offspring and commands that they be brought up to worship and serve him. In all the world this is the noblest and most precious work, because to God there can be nothing dearer than the salvation of souls. Now since we are all duty bound to suffer death, if need be, that we might bring a single soul to God, you can see how rich the estate of marriage is in good works. God has entrusted to its bosom souls begotten of its own body, on whom it can lavish all manner of Christian works. Most certainly father and mother are apostles, bishops, and priests to their children, for it is they who make them acquainted with the gospel. In short, there is no greater or nobler authority on earth than that of parents over their children, for this authority is both spiritual and temporal.[18]

Marriage not only presents the pre-eminent arena for the exercise of sanctification, but also allows a deep experience of the creative, sustaining power of faith.

The vocation of parents exemplifies Luther's theology of the cross, the way in which God's life-giving grace must be discerned under contradictory appearances:

> Now you tell me, when a father goes ahead and washes diapers or performs some other mean task for his child, and someone ridicules him as an effeminate fool — though that father is acting in the spirit just described and in Christian faith — my dear fellow you tell me, which of the two is most keenly ridiculing the other? God, with all his angels and creatures, is smiling — not because that father is washing diapers, but because he is doing so in Christian faith. Those who sneer at him and see only the task but not the faith are ridiculing God with all his creatures, as the biggest fool on earth. Indeed, they are only ridiculing themselves; with all their cleverness they are nothing but devil's fools.[19]

The daily grind of childcare appears to "that clever harlot, our natural reason"[20] to be insignificant, distasteful, and despicable. Yet Christian faith looks upon these duties and beholds them "adorned with divine approval as with the costliest gold and jewels."[21] For Luther, parental responsibility to serve one's children as their "apostle and bishop" manifests itself in four crucial duties: to provide the sacrament of baptism for infants, to form children in the true faith as

18. LW 45: 46.
19. LW 45: 40-41.
20. LW 45: 39.
21. LW 45: 39.

they mature, to attend to their education for vocation, and to provide them with a suitable spouse in a timely fashion (i.e., before lust puts them at significant risk of sin).

Baptism

Luther was a ferocious defender of the practice of infant baptism. He had no patience with reformers who insisted that the biblical saying "He who believes and is baptized will be saved" (Mark 16:16) required that the sign of cleansing be given only to those who could offer conscious confession of their faith and deliberate demonstration of their intent to live according to the believing community's discipline.[22] Luther plays with the possibility that infants do indeed have faith; he argues that the witness of Scripture at least does not sustain his opponents' claim that they are incapable of it. Ultimately, it does not much matter, for what makes any baptism valid is not the faith of the recipient, whatever her age, but the promise of God attached to the sign. Luther argues that an infant's need for the grace of the sacrament is just as urgent as any other person's, for a child comes into the world already damnably infected with original sin — that is, the inherent inability to trust, fear, or love God.[23]

In his 1528 treatise "Concerning Rebaptism," he writes that infant baptism is the most certain form of baptism, precisely because children are incapable of the kinds of conscious discernments that come with maturity:

> For an adult might deceive and come to Christ as a Judas and have himself baptized. But a child cannot deceive. He comes to Christ in baptism, as John

22. Concerning sixteenth-century Protestant debates over the practice of baptism, see also the essays by Barbara Pitkin and Keith Graber Miller in this volume.

23. "Apology of the Augsburg Confession," in *The Book of Concord: The Confessions of the Evangelical Lutheran Church,* trans. and ed. Theodore G. Tappert (Philadelphia: Fortress Press, 1959), 103. In responding to mothers who fear for the salvation of their miscarried or stillborn infants, Luther assures them that their prayers, even in the form of inconsolable sighs, will find a hearing with God, and that their faith will serve God's purpose to save, even in the absence of baptism. Luther reminds them that God's power is not constrained by the sacrament; that the Word, by which God unites God's self with humanity, acts through the sacraments certainly but not exclusively. Baptism is necessary for salvation, and its absence condemns those who reject or despise it. Those who are deprived of the sacrament through no fault of their own (such as premature death) constitute a different case. See *Werke,* Kritische Gesamtausgabe, Series 1, 62 vols. (Weimar: H. Boehlau, 1883-), 53: 205-8. Citations to the critical edition of Luther's writings will be designated by WA followed by the volume and page number(s).

came to him, and as the children were brought to him, that his word and work might be effective in them, move them, and make them holy, because his word and work cannot be without fruit. Yet it has this effect alone in the child. Were it to fail here it would fail everywhere and be in vain, which is impossible.[24]

Thus infant baptism becomes a measure for Luther of the graciousness of the gospel and the depth of the Christian community's trust in God to bring to fruition the good work God has initiated in the sacrament. Having received the command to offer the gospel and baptism to everyone, the church must include children.

Baptism was the linchpin of Lutheran piety. The whole of the Christian life could be described as a daily return to baptism, and death itself as the completion of its promises. Now the old Adam does indeed die, never again to drag the believer down into sin, and the new Adam rises with no further fear of falling. Luther comforted himself in times of temptation and despair with the assurance that he was baptized, and he counseled others to do the same.[25]

The primary task of discipleship is to learn to "use Baptism aright,"[26] to practice making its gifts one's own and to forge a life that confidently builds on them. This, for Luther, can only be accomplished within the church — that is, "the assembly of all believers among whom the Gospel is preached in its purity and the holy sacraments are administered according to the Gospel."[27] Baptism, "through which we are first received into the Christian community,"[28] speaks not only to the individual receiving it but also to the whole believing community celebrating the sacrament. The effect of baptism is to bestow God's Holy Spirit, and the chief work of the Spirit is to create and sustain the church, as Luther makes clear in his explanation of the third article of the creed:

24. LW 40: 244.

25. "To appreciate and use Baptism aright, we must draw strength and comfort from it when our sins or conscience oppress us, and we must retort, 'But I am baptized!' And if I am baptized, I have the promise that I shall be saved and have eternal life, both in soul and body. This is the reason why these two things are done in Baptism: the body has water poured over it, though it cannot receive anything but the water, and meanwhile the Word is spoken so that the soul may grasp it" ("Large Catechism," in *The Book of Concord: The Confessions of the Evangelical Lutheran Church*, trans. and ed. Theodore G. Tappert [Philadelphia: Fortress Press, 1959], 442).

26. Large Catechism, 442.

27. "Augsburg Confession," in *The Book of Concord: The Confessions of the Evangelical Lutheran Church*, trans. and ed. Theodore G. Tappert (Philadelphia: Fortress Press, 1959), 32.

28. Large Catechism, 436.

I believe that by my own reason or strength I cannot believe in Jesus Christ, my Lord, or come to him. But the Holy Spirit has called me through the Gospel, enlightened me with his gifts, and sanctifies and preserves me in true faith, just as he calls, gathers, enlightens, and sanctifies the whole Christian church on earth and preserves it in union with Jesus Christ in the one true faith. In this Christian church he daily and abundantly forgives all my sins, and the sins of all believers, and on the last day he will raise me and all the dead and will grant eternal life to me and to all who believe in Christ. This is most certainly true.[29]

One can say that, for Luther, salvation occurs when baptism is received, as long as one recognizes that what makes it saving is the ongoing reorientation of human life that it effects. Luther's emphasis on the daily return to baptism shows that the claim "I am baptized" does not so much identify a specific event in time as describe a lifelong condition. The two most defining relationships in a baptized person's life are with the God of the gospel and with the church. To use baptism aright is to immerse oneself in the various means of grace — worship, prayer, proclamation, sacraments — so that one is constantly exposed to the working of the Spirit. Apart from the church, this is impossible.[30]

---

29. "Small Catechism," in *The Book of Concord: The Confessions of the Evangelical Lutheran Church,* trans. and ed. Theodore G. Tappert (Philadelphia: Fortress Press, 1959), 345.

30. A recent commentary on the Lutheran confessions makes this point clearly: "The Christian life is dynamic in another sense as well. Salvation is not automatic and baptism does not guarantee it regardless of how the Christian lives. Along with God's promise baptism gives Christians access to the means whereby the Holy Spirit continually fights their sin, forgives it, strengthens their faith, produces good works, and preserves them unto eternal life. These means are prayer, preaching, and the sacraments, and they are available in the Christian community. The confessions would never condone the statement: 'I am baptized and read the Bible; I do not have to go to church.' The means provided by God need to be used or else Christians run the risk of having sin overcome their faith to the point that they stop repenting and are lost. The certainty that believers have is not that God will save them no matter what they do, but that God will save them as they repent and use the means offered to keep their faith alive. That happens in the church, where the Holy Spirit 'daily and abundantly forgives all my sins, and the sins of all believers, and on the last day will raise me and all the dead and will grant eternal life to me and to all who believe in Christ. This is most certainly true' (SC 2.6)." See Guenther Gassmann and Scott Hendrix, *Fortress Introduction to the Lutheran Confessions* (Minneapolis: Fortress, 1999), 173-74.

The Formation of Children and Luther's Catechisms

"When faith comes, baptism is complete," writes Luther.[31] Although the growth must be left to God, the church, and particularly parents, are responsible for planting and watering. Luther provided his catechisms as aids for this cultivation of the life of faith among the young. As Gerald Strauss succinctly concludes, "Only in formal theology was a sharp and final distinction made between human effort and divine grace."[32] Luther and his followers were convinced that a systematic program of religious and ethical indoctrination would have results. Only God could create a human being, but right-thinking and right-living people were in large part the products of disciplined, hard human work.

Luther's theological perceptions of childhood and youth were complex. On the one hand, he could hold children up in their very neediness and simplicity as the model of faith.[33] Those "high and mighty" adults who dismiss the catechism as a "simple, silly teaching which they can absorb and master at one reading" are far inferior to the receptive, diligent children they patronize:

> These dainty, fastidious fellows would like quickly, with one reading, to become doctors above all doctors, to know all there is to be known. Well, this too, is a sure sign that they despise both their office and the people's souls, yes, even God and his Word. They need not fear a fall, for they have already fallen all too horribly. What they need is to become children and begin learning their ABC's, which they think they have outgrown long ago.[34]

Yet he also portrayed these appearances as deceiving, for original sin infected the child as much as the adult. He did, however, recognize developmental stages; sin had a history in the life of each individual.[35] It lies dormant at first, but between the ages of five and seven this changes as the ego begins to assert itself: "Children under seven years of age have not developed real thoughts. We

---

31. LW 40: 246.

32. Gerald Strauss, *Luther's House of Learning: Indoctrination of the Young in the German Reformation* (Baltimore: The Johns Hopkins University Press, 1978), 39.

33. In discussing Luther's catechisms, Strauss writes, "Catechism is *Kinderlehre* — doctrine for children — but in a profound sense, not literally; for becoming a Christian demands a return to one's childhood, that is to say to the guilelessness, candor, and docility of one's early years before reason and ambition destroyed innocence. True Christians are always 'children and simple-minded people'" (Strauss, *Luther's House of Learning*, 159, footnote omitted).

34. Large Catechism, 359.

35. Strauss, *Luther's House of Learning*, 99-101. See also the discussion of Augustine's notion of a graduated responsibility and guilt in Martha Stortz's essay in this volume.

know this because they do not feel the urge to kill and commit adultery. Still, sin has begun to stir in them, as is evident in their tendency to steal, snatch sweets, and so on."[36] The child quickly lays claim to her inheritance of sin, the acting out of which is an ineluctable part of growing up.

Luther shared the perception common in his time that human development was marked by crises, occurring in a seven-year cycle, that tested and propelled the process of maturation.[37] The most disconcerting of these turning points grew out of the awakening of the sex drive at age fourteen. Thereafter the child became aggressive and defiant of authority. Of course, teachers and parents had no control over the biological onset of sexual maturity, but they often did try to delay the psychological confrontation with this new phase of personhood, hoping thereby to prolong the relative tractability of childhood to good influences. In contrast, Luther recognized the futility of such efforts in the face of the natural, necessary, and God-given force of sexual desire. Luther feared the snares for consciences, comparable to those set by enforced monastic vows of celibacy, that such denial would impose on adolescents. Since it is impossible and unhealthy to sublimate the body's needs (as much so with sexual urges as with the processes of elimination), the proper response is to get on with the arrangement of a suitable marriage.[38] Luther did agree, however, that discipline and teaching in the receptive years of childhood were crucial if the person was to make the passage through puberty and into full adulthood successfully. With age, concupiscence only took more vile and devious forms.

This question remains: For Luther and his colleagues, what constituted success in the process of rearing a child? On this issue the Small Catechism and the Large Catechism provide much helpful information. Prepared by Luther himself in 1529, both documents are included in the Lutheran church's collection of official confessional writings, *The Book of Concord* (1580).

Here in practice is one of the most noteworthy paradoxes of Luther's reform. He was convinced that the end was at hand, yet he expected families and governments to invest significant energy and resources in establishing structures to inculcate the faith and prepare Christian subjects for a future of useful service. Catechizing was important for all ages, but Luther and his followers focused on children as being the most susceptible to formation. Luther was at first rather insouciant, confident of the power of the gospel rightly preached to move hearts and generate energy for its cause. He saw the family as the natural

36. Martin Luther, *Tabletalk* (WA Tr 1, no. 660), cited in Strauss, *Luther's House of Learning*, 100.

37. The following summarizes the thorough discussion in Strauss, *Luther's House of Learning*, 100-104.

38. See below, 155-56.

locus of education: parents catechizing their children and household dependents, joining them in prayers, teaching them their proper duties, and administering discipline. But Luther's naiveté was dispelled by the radicalism of the 1520s and the depressing results of the church visitations in Saxony in the latter half of the decade. Gerald Strauss has argued that the result was a transfer of responsibility for education from negligent parents to the superior paternal authority, the ruler and his instruments of governance.[39] Catechizing was part of the school curriculum and was to be the constant subject of pastoral teaching and preaching in parishes. Ironically, learning about the freedom of a Christian became for Lutherans a highly regimented process.

The preface to Luther's Small Catechism makes clear that he wrote it in response to crisis. It now seemed that the greatest threat to the evangelical movement came from within its own ranks:

> The deplorable conditions which I recently encountered when I was a visitor constrained me to prepare this brief and simple catechism or statement of Christian teaching. Good God, what wretchedness I beheld! The common people, especially those who live in the country, have no knowledge whatever of Christian teaching, and unfortunately many pastors are quite incompetent and unfitted for teaching. Although the people are supposed to be Christian, are baptized, and receive the holy sacrament, they do not know the Lord's Prayer, the Creed, or the Ten Commandments, they live as if they were pigs and irrational beasts, and now that the Gospel has been restored they have mastered the fine art of abusing liberty.[40]

Luther insists that "young and inexperienced people must be instructed on the basis of a uniform, fixed text and form."[41] He exhorts teachers to choose whatever form of evangelical catechism pleases them and to adhere to it strictly thereafter, not altering a single syllable in the recitation from year to year.

According to Lutheran theology, the gospel is not a carrot and a stick to drive the wayward creature; it is just a carrot. Yet in the midst of disappointing realities, the angry Luther thrashed his audience with scorn and harsh threats. As for those who refuse to study the catechism, he says they should be reviled for denying Christ, barred from participation in any Christian privileges, and turned over to the devil. Moreover, parents and employers should refuse to provide them with food and drink and should threaten them with the possibility of banishment by the prince.[42]

---

39. Strauss, *Luther's House of Learning*, 123-31.
40. Small Catechism, 338.
41. Small Catechism, 339.
42. Small Catechism, 339.

The catechism clearly concerns itself with issues of social order and civic virtue as well as doctrine and piety. Indeed, Luther believed that faith was wholly a gift, the working of the Holy Spirit in the believer so that she might not just hear the Word but cling to its promise of mercy with her whole heart. No matter how carefully constructed and controlled the process of catechizing, it could not guarantee this result. The goal of socialization, however, was within human reach:

> Although we cannot and should not compel anyone to believe, we should nevertheless insist that the people learn to know how to distinguish between right and wrong according to the standards of those among whom they live and make their living. For anyone who desires to reside in a city is bound to know and observe the laws under whose protection he lives, no matter whether he is a believer or, at heart, a scoundrel or knave.[43]

Luther instructs teachers to emphasize those commandments or other sections of the catechism that are of particular significance for their students. For example, he recommends concentrating on the Seventh Commandment ("You shall not steal") with laborers and shopkeepers, and on the Fourth ("Honor your father and your mother") when instructing "children and the common people in order that they may be encouraged to be orderly, faithful, obedient, and peaceful."[44]

In the Large Catechism's section on the Decalogue, the discussion of the Fourth Commandment is by far the longest. It makes clear that for Luther, the command to honor is primarily about obedience,[45] not only to fathers by blood but also to fathers of a household (masters of servants and apprentices), fathers of the nation (the prince), and spiritual fathers (the pastor). He states that if God's will is observed, nothing is more important than the will and word of our parents, with the proviso that these too are subordinated to obedience to God and do not violate the first three commandments ("You shall have no other gods"; "You shall not take the name of God in vain"; "You shall sanctify the holy day").[46] Although the Fourth Commandment specifically addresses the duties of children to parents, Luther's interpretation makes clear that he regards the obligations as reciprocal.[47] He sternly reminds parents of their responsibilities

---

43. Small Catechism, 339.

44. Small Catechism, 340.

45. "Learn well, then, how important God considers obedience, since he so highly exalts it, so greatly delights in it, so richly rewards it, and besides is so strict about punishing those who transgress it" (Large Catechism, 384).

46. See above, 136-38, for the discussion of Luther's own conflict with his father on the issue of obedience.

47. The ethicist Paul Lehmann makes much of Luther's elaboration of such reciprocal responsibilities. See *The Decalogue and a Human Future: The Meaning of the Com-*

as well. God will hold them accountable for the discharge of their duty as "superiors" to bring up their children "to usefulness and piety." Their obedience in these matters will be amply rewarded:

> If this were done, God would richly bless us and give us grace so that men might be trained who would be a benefit to the nation and the people. We would also have soundly instructed citizens, virtuous and home-loving wives, who would faithfully bring up their children and servants to be godly.[48]

Luther's often apocalyptic proclamation of the breaking of the gospel's dawn upon the darkened and suffering world produces here rather unremarkable domesticated fruit.

Scholars have debated the effect of the programs of catechesis that became so central to the Lutheran reformation. To the historian Gerald Strauss, the stultifying pedagogical method seems incapable of conveying the complexity of the confessional self-understanding. Rejecting works as the means of salvation but delineating the rules for conduct in the world with a clarity far easier to grasp than the ambiguities of justification by faith, the catechism most likely left consciences confused rather than comforted.[49] Despite its radical theology of grace, the Lutheran movement allied itself with the status quo and may well have proven more successful at the task of socialization than evangelization.[50]

Another Reformation historian, Steven Ozment, counters this pessimistic

---

mandments for Making and Keeping Human Life Human (Grand Rapids, Mich.: Eerdmans, 1995).

48. Large Catechism, 388-89.

49. Strauss writes of the extensive Lutheran catechetical literature: "Nothing was asserted in the catechism that was not, in the explanation, blurred. Nothing was promised that was not somewhere taken back. Justification by faith alone — announced as a blissful release from the burden of works, a great heartease and liberator of the conscience, was at the same time presented as a most difficult and rare achievement. . . . Encouraged to think that no more was required of him than trust and faith, the simple Christian was at the same time forever being thrown back upon his own strength and resources and cautioned that success in this most fateful of all his tasks was far from assured" (*Luther's House of Learning*, 235-36).

50. "Lutheran theologians, preachers, and pedagogues were clear, consistent, and all but unanimous. They accepted the institutions and conventions of the emerging bourgeois society sheltering their movement even while they deplored its defects and its inherent incompatibility with evangelical principles. Seeing in the established order the only alternative to social disintegration and moral chaos, they were determined to reinforce its structures and maintain its operations. Acting from this resolve, they set to work to persuade their followers to take their places in society and participate in its processes as a duty dictated by their Christian conscience" (Strauss, *Luther's House of Learning*, 236).

evaluation of the catechetical process as an assault on the freedom and autonomy of children. He points to the fundamentally subversive element of the confession, which urges its hearers to abandon the faith of their ancestors. The catechism, rather than inculcating social mores, may instead have been the chief instrument of liberation from the internal bonds of authoritarian religion.[51] Ozment rejects the imposition on the sixteenth century of contemporary values with regard to individual autonomy and the rights of children vis-à-vis parents. Pervasive concern for morals and discipline characterized the sixteenth and seventeenth centuries; the vision of the good life was one of clear boundaries, good order, and social duty. Being born into the species did not make one a *human* being in the eyes of the adult world; a child "was a creature in search of humanity."[52] The major fear of those responsible for the rearing of children was that they might grow up to pursue their individual desires at the expense of their community's common good.[53] They were equally concerned about parents who placed their own interests above the welfare of their offspring.

One must also consider the catechism's potential for supporting spiritual growth.[54] It initiated those young in the faith into the believing community's vision of life and distinctive discourse; it gave them a clear point of orientation in the world. It provided for them a conceptual vocabulary with which to test and construe their experience as they matured. Undoubtedly for many, engagement with these texts remained superficial, but their effectiveness in sustaining a distinctive piety cannot be simply dismissed.

51. Steven Ozment, *When Fathers Ruled: Family Life in Reformation Europe* (Cambridge: Harvard University Press, 1983), 172-73.

52. "'Singularity of temperament' — that is what differentiated human from animal character. Although each child was thought to have an inner disposition to rationality and moral virtue, Erasmus and his contemporaries also believed that the bestial could triumph over rationality in a child. On this issue Erasmus and Luther agreed, and it was not by chance that each characterized unacceptable behavior as animal-like. The modern reader will not begin to fathom sixteenth-century childrearing and family dynamics until he appreciates the depth of this fear. A child was not believed to be truly human simply by birthright; he was a creature in search of humanity — unpredictable, capable of animal indolence, selfishness, and savagery — traits that would dominate his adult life if they were not controlled in childhood. The rational and moral self-control that raised humans above animals did not come as an inalienable endowment of nature; it was a state of maturity into which each child had to grow by hard, persistent exercise under vigilant parental and tutorial discipline" (Ozment, *When Fathers Ruled*, 138-39).

53. Ozment, *When Fathers Ruled*, 177.

54. For an appreciative evaluation of Luther's baptismal pedagogy, see Timothy J. Wengert, "Luther on Children: Baptism and the Fourth Commandment," *Dialog* 37:3 (Summer 1998): 185-89.

Schooling

Luther recognized that parents, in addition to their obligations to promote the spiritual health of their children, had responsibilities for their social welfare, especially in the area of education. During the medieval period the church had been the chief provider of education. Through its monastic and cathedral schools it served both children preparing for church vocations and those of various classes destined for life in society. University students were dependent upon the receipt of benefices — the income from appointments to ecclesiastical posts — to defray the costs of study. By restricting educational opportunities to those entering the church or the professions (law, medicine), the church reinforced the attitude that education was otherwise a waste of time and contributed to the social division between the learned and the common people.[55]

During the Reformation, the abandonment of monastic life by many religious and the forcible closure of monasteries by Protestant civil authorities had a devastating effect on schooling. In addition, the disdain for formal education continued in German society. Radicals interpreted Luther's doctrine of the priesthood of all believers to imply an egalitarianism that made formal education for clerical office unnecessary, even offensive to the Holy Spirit, which blows where it wills. The wider society became increasingly utilitarian in its values. The only learning that mattered, besides preparing for the professions of law, medicine, and theology, was that which pertained to the world of commerce and trade.[56]

In his 1524 treatise "To the Councilmen of All Cities in Germany That They Establish and Maintain Christian Schools," Luther contemptuously dismisses both the content and the methods of late medieval pedagogy.[57] He recommends instead a liberal arts program, including biblical languages, history, singing, and music "together with the whole of mathematics,"[58] a curriculum reflective of the humanist reforms of his day. Moreover, Luther proposes that this education be universal:

---

55. Lindberg, *The European Reformations,* 127.

56. LW 46: 209-10.

57. "It is perfectly true that if universities and monasteries were to continue as they have been in the past, and there were no other place available where youth could study and live, then I could wish that no boy would ever study at all, but just remain dumb. For it is my earnest purpose, prayer, and desire that these asses' stalls and devil's training centers should either sink into the abyss or be converted into Christian schools." See "To the Councilmen of All Cities in Germany . . . ," in *Martin Luther's Basic Theological Writings,* ed. Timothy F. Lull (Minneapolis: Fortress, 1989), 709.

58. Luther, "To the Councilmen," 726.

So you say, "But who can thus spare his children and train them all to be young gentlemen? There is work for them to do at home," etc. . . . My idea is to have the boys attend such a school for one or two hours during the day, and spend the remainder of the time working at home, learning a trade or doing whatever is expected of them. In this way, study and work will go hand-in-hand while the boys are young and able to do both. . . . In like manner, a girl can surely find time enough to attend school for an hour a day, and still take care of her duties at home.[59]

Students who showed great promise would, according to Luther, continue in school longer or even be dedicated to a life of study.

In his 1530 treatise "A Sermon on Keeping Children in School," Luther soundly chastises parents for putting their own economic interests before their offspring's vocational opportunities. By keeping them out of school to work, parents not only sin against their children. They also wrong the wider community and their ruler by withholding human resources that can be of great service to church and society. Finally, they wrong God, who requires a properly prepared pool of talent to govern the creation and to proclaim the word of salvation.[60]

As noted above, Luther also lobbied for the education of girls, but the curriculum offered in Lutheran circles reflects the fact that women were for the most part barred from participation in the public realm.[61] Destined for neither

---

59. Luther, "To the Councilmen," 727.

60. "We shamefully despise God when we begrudge our children this glorious and divine work and stick them instead in the exclusive service of the belly and of avarice, having them learn nothing but how to make a living, like hogs wallowing forever with their noses in the dung-hill, and never training them for so worthy an estate and office. Certainly we must either be crazy, or without love for our children" (LW 46: 241).

61. Merry Wiesner provides this summary of the educational opportunities for Protestant girls: "In the sixteenth century, about forty Protestant church ordinances in Germany called for the establishment of girls' schools, though it is difficult to tell how many schools were actually opened, for many areas do not have good records. . . . Because of these girls' schools, it was long held that the Protestant Reformation increased opportunities for female education. More recent historians, especially Susan Karant-Nunn, have noted the continuation of a large gap between boys' and girls' opportunities for learning in even the most enlightened German states. She points out that the opening of girls' schools must be balanced against the closing of convent schools which had served noble and upper middle-class girls, and the prohibition of unlicensed 'cranny schools' which had been places not only for poorer girls to learn, but for women to teach.

"Even where schools were established, the education they offered was meager. Girls attended for an hour or so a day, for one to two years, and were to learn 'reading and writing, and if both of these can't be mastered, at least some writing, the catechism learned by heart, a little figuring, a few psalms to sing.' What did Protestant authorities see as the aim

church nor government, girls were prepared for the vocation of wife and mother. Their studies focused on matters of importance for the maintenance of a household and the performance of domestic duties. Chief among these was competence in the catechism so that they might exemplify and teach orthodox piety in the home.

Civil Authority and Children's Welfare

Luther expected the schools to be public, sustained by government supervision and support. He appeals to the authorities to act *in loco parentis* when the natural parents prevent able youngsters from pursuing an education. The interests of the state he recognizes as superior to the rights of the parents in such cases.[62] Moreover, even when the will to educate their children is present, Luther doubts that parents generally have the competence, breadth of knowledge, or time to do so.[63] Some families may employ private tutors, but, Luther points

---

of girls' education? 'To habituate girls to the catechism, to the psalms, to honorable behavior and Christian virtue, and especially to prayer, and make them memorize verses from Holy Scripture so that they may grow up to be Christian and praiseworthy matrons and housekeepers.' While boys were engaged in competitions in Latin rhetoric, the best student in the Memmingen girls' school in 1587 was chosen on the basis of her 'great diligence and application in learning her catechism, modesty, obedience, and excellent penmanship.' Along with reading, writing, and religion, sewing and other domestic skills were also often part of the curriculum at these schools, which worked to the advantage of female teachers, who were also hired in preference to male because they could be paid less; scholarships set up for poor girls read: 'To be sent to school, and especially to learn to sew.' A potential teacher's intellectual abilities often came third in the minds of city councils establishing girls' schools, after her 'honorable lifestyle' and ability to teach domestic skills" (*Women and Gender in Early Modern Europe,* 121-22, footnotes omitted).

62. "It therefore behooves the council and the authorities to devote the greatest care and attention to the young. Since the property, honor, and life of the whole city have been committed to their faithful keeping, they would be remiss in their duty before God and man if they did not seek its welfare and improvement day and night with all the means at their command. Now the welfare of a city does not consist solely in accumulating vast treasures, building mighty walls and magnificent buildings, and producing a goodly supply of guns and armor. Indeed, where such things are plentiful, and reckless fools get control of them, it is so much the worse and the city suffers even greater loss. A city's best and greatest welfare, safety, and strength consist rather in its having many able, learned, wise, honorable, and well-educated citizens. They can then readily gather, protect, and properly use treasure and all manner of property" (Luther, "To the Councilmen," 712-13).

63. "But, you say, everyone may teach his sons and daughters himself, or at least train them in proper discipline. Answer: Yes, we can readily see what such teaching and

out, that is not an option for orphans or the children of the poor. "Necessity compels us, therefore, to engage public schoolteachers for the children,"[64] lest promising students be overlooked.

The 1523 ordinance of a common chest for the city of Leisnig, which was drawn up in consultation with Luther and approved by him,[65] is representative of the efforts of Lutheran communities to address such issues of civic welfare.[66] In his preface to the document, Luther makes a number of suggestions on how to deal with ecclesiastical property in the now reformed area. The governing authorities should close the monasteries by encouraging the resident monastics to leave of their own free will and by preventing the admission of future applicants. Those who choose to stay "because of their age, their bellies, or their consciences"[67] are not to be forced out. Luther advises the authorities to take over monastic and other ecclesiastical properties for use in three ways: (1) to provide for the needs of such remaining monastics until they die; (2) to provide those who leave with sufficient funds to make a fresh start in life; and (3) to devote all the rest "to the common fund of a common chest, out of which gifts and loans could be made in Christian love to all the needy in the land, be they nobles or commoners."[68] Luther further suggests that mendicant houses located in cities be converted into schools or housing as needed.

---

training amount to. Even when the training is done to perfection and succeeds, the net result is little more than a certain enforced outward respectability; underneath, they are nothing but the same old blockheads, unable to converse intelligently on any subject, or to assist or counsel anyone. But if children were instructed and trained in schools, or wherever learned and well-trained schoolmasters and schoolmistresses were available to teach the languages, the other arts, and history, they would then hear of the doings and sayings of the entire world, and how things went with various cities, kingdoms, princes, men, and women. Thus, they could in a short time set before themselves as in a mirror the character, life, counsels, and purposes — successful and unsuccessful — of the whole world from the beginning; on the basis of which they could then draw the proper inferences and in the fear of God take their own place in the stream of human events. In addition, they could gain from history the knowledge and understanding of what to seek and what to avoid in this outward life, and be able to advise and direct others accordingly. The training we undertake at home, apart from such schools, is intended to make us wise through our own experience. Before that can be accomplished we will be dead a hundred times over, and will have acted rashly throughout our mortal life, for it takes a long time to acquire personal experience" (Luther, "To the Councilmen," 725-26).

64. Luther, "To the Councilmen," 712.

65. LW 45: 162.

66. However, implementing the ordinance in Leisnig proved to be a difficult and disappointing business. See LW 45: 161-68.

67. LW 45: 171.

68. LW 45: 172. Luther does not see the formation of a common chest as a misappropriation of designated funds: "In this way, too, the will and testament of the founders

The "Fraternal Agreement on the Common Chest of the Entire Assembly at Leisnig" proposes to support the chest through receipts from various church properties and incomes, donations of food, voluntary gifts, and the imposition of a graduated annual tax "on every noble, townsman, and peasant living in the parish," when necessary.[69] The order includes an article on disbursements for the schools. The ten directors of the common chest, in consultation with Leisnig's pastor and other religious leaders, are given the authority to call and appoint "a pious, irreproachable, and learned man" as schoolmaster for young boys and "an upright, fully seasoned, irreproachable woman" for instructing young girls under the age of twelve.[70] Both teachers may, with the approval of the directors, charge appropriate fees to pupils who come from outside of the parish; otherwise they are neither to solicit nor to accept compensation additional to that paid from the common chest. Moreover, students coming from outside the parish of Leisnig must do so at their own expense and are strictly forbidden to beg. The directors are charged with overseeing the work of the schools and supervising the teachers. They are also responsible for making provision from the common chest for the maintenance and/or improvement of school buildings.

The Leisnig ordinance includes a number of other provisions that would have affected the welfare of children. The directors of the common chest are to take care of the material needs of poor and neglected orphans within the parish until such time as they can work. The boys are to be trained for "labor, handicrafts, and other suitable occupations."[71] Young boys, either orphans or the children of impoverished parents, who show an aptitude for arts and letters will continue their education at public expense. The common chest will also be used to fund suitable dowries for both orphaned and poor girls. Further provisions for loans to residents of the parish unable to work and to newcomers in need of assistance in establishing themselves would also have benefitted the children of the families involved.[72]

---

would be carried out. For although they erred and were misled when they gave this property to monasteries, their intention certainly was to give it for the glory and service of God; but their purpose was not realized. Now there is no greater service of God than Christian love which helps and serves the needy, as Christ himself will judge and testify at the Last Day, Matthew 25[:31-46]." Moreover, he makes allowance for the property to revert to the heirs of the founder if they are impoverished.

69. LW 45: 192.

70. LW 45: 188-89.

71. LW 45: 190.

72. "Disbursements for home relief: To artisans and others suffering in private, whether married or widowers, who are residents of the city and villages within our parish and who are honestly unable to ply their trade or other urban or rural occupation, and have no other source of help, the directors shall advance an appropriate amount out of the common chest, to be repaid at some future date. In cases where despite honest and diligent

Marriage

Parents had a crucial role to play in their children's entrance into the married state. Protestant and Roman teaching held the free mutual consent of the parties in an exchange of vows to be the constitutive act of marriage, although the reformers did not continue to regard the rite as a sacrament. They also parted ways on the validity of so-called secret marriages — that is, the freely exchanged promises between two parties of legally marriageable age, without public witnesses or parental consent. Whereas Roman canon law recognized such unions, Luther and other Protestant reformers vehemently opposed them, largely on the grounds that they violated the Fourth Commandment. Luther believed that a child should not become engaged or marry without parental knowledge and consent, and that if she or he did so, the parents had the authority to dissolve such a union. However, he also insisted that such interference must be for substantive reasons. He did not concede to parents the authority to prevent a child's marriage arbitrarily, and he condemned any attempt to compel a child to marry against his or her will:

> Now Paul says in I Corinthians 16:3 that even the very highest authority, namely, to preach the gospel and govern souls, was granted by God for building up and not for destroying. How much less, then, should the authority of parents, or any other authority, have been given for destroying rather than exclusively for building up.
>
> It is quite certain therefore that parental authority is strictly limited; it does not extend to the point where it can wreak damage and destruction to the child, especially to its soul. If then a father forces his child into a marriage without love, he oversteps and exceeds his authority.[73]

The question remains whether the child so wronged must obey the parents and suffer the injury.

Luther's answer is equivocal. A true Christian would neither refuse nor resist such a forced marriage but would render filial obedience, trusting in

---

toil they are unable to make repayment, the debt shall be forgiven for God's sake as a contribution to their need. Such circumstances shall be carefully investigated by the directors.

"Disbursements for the relief of newcomers from without: In the case of newcomers to the parish of whatever estate, be they men or women, if they are in Christian and brotherly harmony with our general assembly and wish to seek their livelihood within the city or villages of our parish by their labor, toil, and industry, the ten directors shall encourage them, and even offer them help through loans and gifts out of our common chest, as circumstances dictate, so that the strangers too may not be left without hope, and may be saved from shame and open sin" (LW 45: 190-91).

73. LW 45: 386.

Christ to preserve her from the potentially disastrous consequences. But then Luther asks, Where are there such Christians? He insists he must teach only what is Christian but advises weak souls unable to face the risks of such obedience to appeal to the civil realm for help. Princes, city officials, or other authorities should intervene to forestall the injustice. "Although a Christian is in duty bound to tolerate injustice, the temporal authority is also under obligation to punish and prevent such injustice and to guard and uphold the right."[74] If the civil authorities fail to do their duty, Luther grants that, as a last resort, the child may flee to another land, abandoning both parents and government, "just as in former times certain weak Christians fled from tyrants into the wilderness."[75] Luther is unable to grant that opposing an abusive parent might be the higher form of discipleship in such a situation, but he is at least humane enough to offer a theological loophole to those so oppressed. And then there is always the promise of God's grace for bold sinners to help such children summon the courage to break the commandment.

Parents ought not compel their children to marry; neither may they forbid them to do so altogether. To force a child into a life of celibacy is another way of violating the child's soul and placing him at high risk, rather than protecting him from temptation and sin. Indeed, because parents have primary responsibility for the care of their children's souls (as their apostles and bishops), they are duty bound to get the child "a good mate who will be just right for him, or who seems to be just right for him."[76] If they fail to do so, the child is justified in taking the initiative in the matter himself. However, once parents have faithfully offered their counsel, their consciences are clear. If children reject it and persist in their intention to make a match their parents find objectionable, the parents are free to leave their offspring to their own devices and commit the matter to God.

Luther the Father

There has been significant scholarly debate about the status of children in early modern society.[77] Some interpreters have argued that families of that time were largely without affection. They attribute the failure of parents to invest emo-

74. LW 45: 389.
75. LW 45: 389.
76. LW 45: 392.
77. See the article entitled "Family" by Thomas Max Safley in the *Oxford Encyclopedia of the Reformation*, ed. Hans J. Hillerbrand, 4 vols. (New York: Oxford University Press, 1996), 2: 93-98.

tionally in their children to the high infant mortality rate. A certain degree of detachment would limit the grief that parents endured in the event of a loss. However, there is also ample evidence of deep affectional ties between parents and children, one of the most moving examples coming from Martin Luther himself.

Luther was the father of three sons and three daughters. He and his wife also brought up four orphaned children from among their relatives. Of the six biological children, four survived to adulthood. The Luthers lost their first daughter, Elisabeth, at nine months of age and their second daughter, Magdalena, at age thirteen. Letters Luther wrote at the time of Magdalena's death provide a glimpse of his own experience of parenthood. Here is a moving excerpt:

> I believe the report has reached you that Magdalena, my dearest daughter, has been reborn into the everlasting kingdom of Christ, and although I and my wife ought to do nothing but joyfully give thanks for such a felicitous passage and blessed end, by which she has escaped the power of the flesh, the world, the Turk and the devil, nevertheless, so great is the force of our love that we are unable to go on without sobs and groanings of heart, indeed without bearing in ourselves a mortal wound. The countenance, the words, the gestures of our daughter, so very obedient and respectful both while she lived and as she died, remain firmly fixed in the old heart so that the death of Christ (in comparison to which what are all other deaths?) is unable to drive out sorrow from our inmost depths as it ought to do. You therefore give thanks to God in our stead![78]

A month later in another letter Luther emphasizes the fact that Magdalena fell asleep "full of faith in Christ" and once again gives expression to his own overpowering grief: "I loved her fervently."[79] As time passes, Luther is able to write with more conviction of the comfort he finds in the manner of Magdalena's death and its timing. She becomes for him one of those saints whose precipitate departure is a sign of the impending end times. He has grounds to be thankful that she lived long enough to develop a strong faith in the gospel and was carried off to safety before the world could harm her.[80] Three years later, however,

---

78. Martin Luther, *Briefwechsel*, Kritische Gesamtausgabe, Series 4, 18 vols. (Weimar: H. Boehlau, 1883-), 10: 3794, 20-29. Hereafter references to Luther's letters will be denoted by WA Br followed by the number and line designations. The translations in this section are by the author.

79. WA Br 10: 3797, 18, 20.

80. "But now I rejoice that she lives in a most sweet sleep with her Father until the last. And our times being what they are, and they will degenerate even more, I pray from the depths of my heart that a similar hour of departure might be granted to me and mine

he confesses that his sorrow still lingers: "It is astonishing how much the death of my Magdalena torments me, which I have not yet been able to forget."[81]

All the desirable attributes of the parent-child relationship are here for Luther. Magdalena distinguished herself by her obedience and respect, even in her final sufferings. She was sustained in life and in death by faith in the gospel of Christ and was able to make confession of this faith with pious, holy words.[82] Her father had served her well as "apostle and bishop," and she had proven an able disciple. But the parent-child relationship, defined in terms of mutual duties and obedience to the Fourth Commandment, was for them suffused through and through with love.

Conclusion

The distance between the world of our children and parenting and that of Luther's is vast, sometimes stunningly so. We work with a wealth of understanding about the nature and pitfalls of child development simply not available in the sixteenth century. And Luther was, after all, a theologian, not a social scientist. From his perspective, the most important contribution he made to the welfare of children was his lifelong struggle for right understanding of the gospel and the freedom it created. One could not navigate the way of salvation by moral perfection or religious activities. The work of securing our lives in God lay with Christ alone. Because of his presence for us, we are empowered to focus our energies on our neighbors, letting our light so shine before others that they may see our good works and glorify our Father in heaven. For Luther, there is no neighbor closer than one's own children, no claim upon society more pressing than that of the young. Whether or not they have biological children, all adults must exercise the vocation of parenting in one way or another. In "To the Councilmen of All Cities in Germany," when Luther urges his readers to consider the command of God enjoining parents to instruct their children, he is

---

and to you and to all whom we hold dear. That is, that with such great faith and peaceful repose we too might truly fall asleep in the Lord, neither seeing nor tasting death nor feeling a bit of fear. I hope that now is and will be the time of which Isaiah spoke: 'For the righteous are gathered together and they enter peacefully into their resting chambers,' so that when he has gathered the grain into his barn, he consigns the chaff to his fire, which fate the world has merited and still deserves on account of its ingratitude, contempt, and horrible hatred of the word of grace. Conditions are such that it is disgusting to live and see anything in this dreadful Sodom" (WA Br 10: 3805, 4-14).

81. WA Br 11: 4122, 9-10.

82. WA Br 10: 3829.

addressing "every citizen."[83] Attending to children's physical welfare, their vocational prospects, their need to learn of God's grace not only through preaching and catechesis but also through the experience of human care and protection — this is an essential part of all Christian discipleship. "Indeed, for what purpose do we older folks exist, other than to care for, instruct, and bring up the young?"[84] Luther's question is still acutely pertinent, probing not only the values espoused by individuals but also the priorities established by public policy. And Luther's uncompromising answer, rooted in his theological understanding of vocation and love for the neighbor, continues to challenge others to go and do likewise.

83. Luther, "To the Councilmen," 707.
84. Luther, "To the Councilmen," 710.

6. *"The Heritage of the Lord":*
Children in the Theology of John Calvin

BARBARA PITKIN

Wishing to clear himself from the charge of a want of natural affection brought against him, [Bauduin] reproaches me with my lack of children. God had given me a little boy: God took [him] away. This he reckons among my misdeeds, that I have no children. And yet I have myriads of children throughout the Christian world.

John Calvin, *Responsio ad Balduini convicia* (1562)[1]

Introduction

Writing just two years before his death and at the end of a long career as a pastor in Geneva, the Protestant reformer John Calvin (1509-1564) alludes to both his biological child, a son who died shortly after premature birth in July 1542, and his ecclesiastical children spread throughout Europe.[2] His application of

1. John Calvin, *Responsio ad Balduini convicia*, in *Ioannis Calvini Opera Quae Supersunt Omnia*, ed. G. Baum, E. Cunitz, and E. Reuss, 59 vols., Corpus Reformatorum, vols. 29-87 (Brunswick and Berlin: C. A. Schwetschke and Son [M. Bruhn], 1863-1900), 9:576 (hereafter abbreviated CO).

2. For a discussion of Calvin's family life, see Richard Stauffer, *Calvins Menschlichkeit* (Zurich: EVZ-Verlag, 1964), 11-20. Calvin refers to the death of this son in a letter to Pierre Viret of August 1542 (CO 11:430). There are several references to this child or others in subsequent correspondence, although it is not at all clear that these indicate that Calvin had more than one biological child. In May 1554 he notes in a letter to William Farel that a daughter is ill (CO 11:722); this may refer to one of the children from

160

the image of "children" to his followers in the Reformed faith conforms to the largely symbolic character of children in most of his writings, especially his extensive and influential commentaries on Scripture. Of course, he is not alone in viewing children as metaphor for the religious life of adult Christians. Following the lead of Scripture, especially Paul (e.g., 1 Cor. 13:11; 14:20), and traditional and contemporary patterns of biblical interpretation, he writes for adults and provides only brief hints at the lives, religious or otherwise, of children.[3] Calvin himself, unlike Martin Luther, does not provide details about his personal acquaintance with children. Little is known about his relationship with the two children of his wife's first marriage, aside from his pledge to her upon her deathbed (in 1549) to care for them. It is likewise difficult to construct much from the scattered references in his correspondence to other youth, including the children of his brother Antoine, living in his household.[4] In most of his writings, his attitudes toward children are expressed indirectly and are often only implicit in discussions of other topics.

To conclude, however, that Calvin was insensitive or indifferent to real children or that his writings were of no consequence to them would be unjustified. His writings, along with the social and ecclesial changes he participated in and sought to effect, bear witness to the importance of children in church and society. Serious implications for children's lives and important assumptions

---

the first marriage of Idelette de Bure, Calvin's wife, who had a daughter named Judith and a son whose name is not known. In April 1546 Calvin thanks Monsieur de Falais for an offer made for the baptism of "our baby" (CO 12:322). Finally, in August 1547 he mentions to Farel an incident that had occurred at the baptism of Calvin's son, Jacobus (CO 12:580). Most scholars have taken Calvin's 1562 reference to but one son as indication that he and Idelette had only one child — namely, Jacobus. Even if there were others who died in infancy, William Bouwsma's argument from Calvin's virtual silence about family matters assumes too much: "Like his contemporaries in an age of high infant mortality, Calvin could not afford to be sentimental about children whose acquaintance he had never made, and he was compelled to satisfy his paternal instincts elsewhere" (*John Calvin: A Sixteenth-Century Portrait* [New York: Oxford University Press, 1989], 23).

3. For example, Matthew 18:3 was used traditionally as a springboard for discussing adult behavior rather than children's nature. Gerald Strauss notes that little was made of potential arguments for children's innocence in sixteenth-century sermons and pedagogical writing: "Childlike qualities acclaimed in this [Matt. 18:3] and many other gospel passages tended to be invoked as corrective to adult trespasses, constantly in sermons, frequently in pedagogical writings" (*Luther's House of Learning: Indoctrination of the Young in the German Reformation* [Baltimore: The Johns Hopkins University Press, 1978], 53).

4. For a concise overview of Calvin's life, see the introduction to David C. Steinmetz, *Calvin in Context* (New York: Oxford University Press, 1995), 3-22. Selections of Calvin's correspondence appear in English in *Letters of John Calvin*, 4 vols., ed. Jules Bonnet, vols. 1 and 2 translated by David Constable, vols. 3 and 4 translated by Marcus Gilchrist (Edinburgh: Thomas Constable & Co., 1855-1858; reprint, New York: Burt Franklin, 1972).

about their nature emerge in his radically theocentric theology of grace, especially in his understandings of providence, covenant, baptism, and human nature as created and fallen. Moreover, when one takes into account the full range of his reforming activity, especially his preparation of ordinances for regulation of the Genevan church (1541), his two catechisms (1537 and 1541-2), and his promotion of school reforms in Geneva, it becomes clear that Calvin, like many intellectuals and reformers of his day, was intensely interested in children and child rearing. The following discussion will delineate this interest as it emerges in his scriptural commentaries, in his reforming work in the spheres of home, society, and the church, and in the theological convictions underlying his doctrine of baptism and his understanding of Christian education.

Recent studies of attitudes toward children in sixteenth-century Germany have challenged some of the views of historians inspired by Philippe Ariès's *Centuries of Childhood*.[5] These perspectives, like that of Ariès, generally assume a gradual evolution in attitudes toward children in Europe, from indifference and neglect in the Middle Ages to a fuller appreciation of children and an awareness of childhood as a distinct stage of life sometime in the seventeenth to nineteenth century. While there is much to support the notion of a change in family life in the early modern period, some scholars have sought to refute the idea that adults in medieval and early modern times were largely indifferent or hostile toward children.[6] For example, Gerald Strauss and Steven Ozment, although they draw different conclusions about the effectiveness of Protestant pedagogy, have demonstrated that adults in Reformation times were not indifferent to but rather profoundly interested in — and often deeply affectionate

5. Phillipe Ariès, *L'enfant et la vie familiale sous l'Ancien régime* (Paris: Librairie Plon, 1960); in English, *Centuries of Childhood: A Social History of Family Life*, trans. R. Baldick (New York: Alfred A. Knopf, 1962). For a summary of Ariès, see Carmen Luke, *Pedagogy, Printing, and Protestantism: The Discourse on Childhood* (Albany: SUNY Press, 1989), 36-40; and Linda Pollock, *Forgotten Children: Parent-Child Relations from 1500 to 1900* (New York: Cambridge University Press, 1983), 1-28. Lawrence Stone traces an evolution in the nature of the family and characterizes sixteenth-century parent-child relations in England as brutal when compared with the "affectionate" attitude that emerges in the latter half of the seventeenth century. See *The Family, Sex, and Marriage: England, 1500-1800* (London: Weidenfeld and Nicolson, 1977).

6. See especially Linda Pollock, *Forgotten Children;* Sandra Lee Piercy, "The Cradle of Salvation: Children and Religion in Late Sixteenth- and Seventeenth-Century England" (Ph.D. diss., University of California, Santa Barbara, 1982); and Louis Haas, *The Renaissance Man and His Children: Childbirth and Early Childhood in Renaissance Florence, 1300-1600* (New York: St. Martin's Press, 1998). Hugh Cunningham has noted that these efforts were in part "galvanized" by a misleading translation on page 215 of the English version of Ariès's book. See "Histories of Childhood," *The American Historical Review* 103, no. 4 (October 1998): 1197.

toward — children. This interest, moreover, was not new; sixteenth-century authors drew on classical models to distinguish different stages of childhood and shape theories of child rearing and education. They advanced the physical well-being of children through a burgeoning body of literature on birth and pediatrics, attended to their intellectual and social formation through school reforms and pedagogical treatises, and enthusiastically supported the spiritual nurture of children. Most importantly, with few exceptions, Protestant preachers and educators did not use the doctrine of original sin to underscore the sinful character of children or legitimate harsh treatment of them. No less disappointed than later generations in the failings of the young, especially adolescents, sixteenth-century writers did not generally condone physical abuse and violence as means of correction and discipline. Without a doubt, children were subject to corporal punishment, and catechists and preachers repeatedly reminded parents of their obligation to correct and discipline their children.[7] Nevertheless, as Strauss notes, most German catechisms "were moderate on the subject of sin and generous with promises of eternal bliss."[8]

With respect to his attitude toward children, Calvin was a man of his times. But the fact that he is typical should not diminish interest in what he has to say. Given his widespread influence in Western religion and politics, his understanding of children, about which there turns out to be a surprising wealth of information, gains importance and even relevance. Hence this investigation aims first to fill out the historical picture by delineating his understanding of children and the nature of childhood, and the place of children in the family, society, and the church. This investigation will show that Calvin was involved, often quite personally, in the implementation of public policies that had important implications for children. Furthermore, the study will demonstrate that although Calvin undoubtedly had a low estimate of human ability to seek God on its own power and initiative, he did not use his convictions about the

7. For evidence, see Robert James Bast, *Honor Your Fathers: Catechisms and the Emergence of a Patriarchal Ideology in Germany, 1400-1600,* Studies in Medieval and Reformation Thought (Leiden: E. J. Brill, 1997), 60-65. The biblical proof text traditionally cited in support of physical discipline is Sirach 30:1. It would be interesting to determine whether this passage continued to be invoked by Protestants who rejected the canonicity of this book.

8. Strauss, *Luther's House of Learning,* 214; Steven Ozment, *When Fathers Ruled: Family Life in Reformation Europe* (Cambridge: Harvard University Press, 1983), 163-64. For discussions of family in the sixteenth century, see Merry Wiesner-Hanks, "Family, Household, and Community," in *The Handbook of European History, 1400-1600: Late Middle Ages, Renaissance, and Reformation,* 2 vols., ed. T. A. Brady, H. A. Oberman, and J. D. Tracy (Leiden and New York: E. J. Brill, 1994), 1:51-78; and the *Oxford Encyclopedia of the Reformation,* 4 vols., ed. Hans J. Hillerbrand (New York: Oxford University Press, 1996), 2: 93-98.

sinfulness of all humans (including infants and children) and divine "double" predestination (whereby some people, including infants, are reprobate because of a divine decree) to argue for or justify harsh treatment of children. Although some later Calvinists (and others) may have emphasized the presence of original sin even in very young children, Calvin himself decidedly did not. While he did not go so far as to idealize the faith of children, as did his own spiritual descendant, Friedrich Schleiermacher, he did consider the youngest infants capable of not merely manifesting but indeed *proclaiming* God's glory. Finally, he based his theology of baptism on the conviction that the elect are from birth full inheritors of God's covenant and members in the church.

Each of these insights must, of course, be understood critically and within context, and hence the most important and immediate purpose of this investigation is to lift out the images of children in the thought and work of a theologian whose historical and theological significance some may regret but few will deny. After this task of reconstruction, it will be possible to suggest ways in which these images, critically reappropriated, might enrich current theological discussion of children and, ultimately, enhance children's well-being.

The Child and Childhood

Like many of his contemporaries and classical and medieval predecessors, Calvin divides childhood into three stages, each lasting approximately seven years.[9] He also expresses the prevailing opinions of each period's character. In his interpretation of Psalm 8:2, which states that God has founded a bulwark "out of the mouths of babes and infants," he says that children are called "babes" or "infants" until they reach their seventh year.[10] This "tender age," he argues in his comments on Matthew 18:1-5, "is distinguished by simplicity to such an extent, that [little children] are unacquainted with the degrees of honor, and with all the incentives to pride."[11] For this reason, Jesus holds up a young child as an emblem of humility. Infancy ends with the onset of reason, at about age six. Here the child enters into the period of intellectual, spiritual, and moral maturation. In his comments on 1 Corinthians 13:11, in which Paul claims to have

9. For a discussion of Luther and Erasmus, see Strauss, *Luther's House of Learning,* 34-35, 54-56, 99-100; cf. Ozment, *When Fathers Ruled,* 144. See also the discussions of Augustine, Thomas Aquinas, and Luther earlier in the present volume.

10. CO 31:89; in English in *Calvin's Commentaries,* 46 vols. (Edinburgh: Calvin Translation Society, 1843-1855); reprint in 22 vols. (Grand Rapids, Mich.: Baker Books, 1989). The discussion appears in the Commentary on the Psalms, 1:96.

11. CO 45:500; Commentary on the Harmony of the Evangelists, 2:332-33.

put away childish things, Calvin provides as an example the fact that education is necessary for childhood, but does not suit those who have already reached maturity (in the Latin commentary) or have already attained the age of discretion (in the French commentary).[12] Furthermore, the awakening of reason in this period also involves a lapse from earlier simplicity. Commenting on Genesis 8:21, which states that imagination of the human heart is "evil from youth," Calvin remarks, "The clause which is added, 'from youth,' more fully declares that men are born evil; in order to show that, as soon as they are of an age to begin to form thoughts, they have radical corruption of mind."[13] The third stage of childhood encompasses adolescence, beginning at about fourteen, perhaps slightly earlier for girls. Calvin and many of his contemporaries and predecessors viewed this as an age of pride and rebelliousness fired by the awakening sex drive. In his interpretation of Genesis 34:4, in which Shechem demands that his father obtain for him Dinah, the daughter of Jacob, Calvin actually lifts up as an example for adolescents of his day Shechem's filial modesty. Shechem had fallen victim to lust in raping Dinah, but he now returns to the order of nature and seeks his father's permission to marry her. "So much the more ought young men to take heed to themselves, lest in the slippery period of their age, the lusts of the flesh should impel them to many crimes. For, at this day, greater license everywhere prevails, so that no moderation restrains youths from shameful conduct."[14]

Calvin's comments on the divisions of childhood are not that extensive and, in the end, for him as for many of his contemporaries, the lines between them are fluid. Nonetheless, he is surprisingly clear, especially in the commentaries, that the younger the child, the less he or she manifests the effects of sin. Like Augustine, Calvin assumes a graduated guilt as one moves with age to greater accountability for acts of wrongdoing. However, he does not dwell on evidences of corruption in small children, as Augustine does in his analysis of the grasping insatiability of the newborn.[15] Although young children are corrupted by original sin, when compared to older children and adults, they demonstrate a lack of malice that their elders ought to emulate. The biblical basis for this view is 1 Corinthians 14:20, where Paul urges believers to be children not in understanding but in malice. Calvin cites this verse as a key to his interpretation of Matthew 18:1-5 and 19:13-15 to account for Jesus' commendation of children. Adult believers ought to imitate children's natural simplicity but not their lack of understanding.

---

12. CO 50:513; Commentary on 1 Corinthians, 428-29.
13. CO 23:141; Commentary on the Book of Genesis, 1:285.
14. CO 23:457; Commentary on Genesis, 2:219.
15. See the essay by Martha Stortz in this volume, 83-84, 86.

Calvin's appreciation of what we might call the "spiritual maturity" of children goes deeper than the praise of their natural ignorance of preferment and lack of pride. The lack of understanding is blameworthy in older children and adults, but apparently not so in young children; in fact, Calvin views very young infants as mature proclaimers of God's goodness. Having granted in his comments on Psalm 8:2 that infancy extends until age seven, he argues that this verse refers only to the very young who still nurse at the breast. Even though older children are considered "babes" and "infants," the passage in question speaks literally of the very young who do not yet have the power of articulate speech. Calvin also rules out understanding "babes and infants" allegorically for the faithful.[16] The tongues of real, nursing infants "even before they pronounce a single word, speak loudly and distinctly in commendation of God's liberality toward the human race." Like Augustine in Book One of the *Confessions,* Calvin is impressed by the testimony to God's providence that nursing infants afford. However, Augustine saw also in such infants manifestations of sin and in his Psalms commentary determined that this verse could be interpreted allegorically only for new converts. Calvin, in contrast, argues that David attributes to the testimony of nursing infants "mature strength." "It means the same thing as if he had said, these [babies] are invincible champions of God, who, when it comes to the conflict, can easily scatter and discomfit the whole host of

16. This symbolic interpretation of the passage was advanced by Augustine, who, though mentioning the dominical application in Matthew 21:15-16, understood "babes" to refer to the "babes in Christ" of 1 Corinthians 3:1-2 (Augustine of Hippo, *Expositions on the Book of Psalms,* vol. 13 of A Select Library of the Nicene and Post-Nicene Fathers [1888; rpt., Grand Rapids, Mich.: Eerdmans, 1983], 28). Following Nicolas of Lyra's "literal explanation," the fourteenth-century exegete Denis the Carthusian offers as "literal" explanation of the passage the application of this to the children praising Jesus upon his entrance to Jerusalem (*Super librum Psalmorum,* in vols. 5 and 6 of *Doctoris estatici D. Dionysii Cartusiani Opera Omnia,* 42 vols. in 44, ed. by the Monks of the Carthusian Order [Montreuil-sur-Mer, Tournai: S. M. de Pratis, 1896-1913; Parkminster: S. Hugonis, 1935], 5:452). Martin Luther, like Denis, sees multiple levels of meaning, none of which, however, understand "babes" and "sucklings" to mean actual infants. In his first lectures on the Psalms, Luther states explicitly that "babes" and "sucklings" are not taken literally but refer to those who are weaker in faith, just as were the children praising Jesus in Matthew 21:15 (*First Lectures on the Psalms: I: Psalms 1–75,* ed. Hilton C. Oswald, vol. 10 of *Luther's Works* [St. Louis: Concordia Publishing House, 1974], 86). In his second exegetical work on the Psalms, Luther explicitly rejects the idea that the literal sense refers only to the children in Matthew 21:15 and argues that there is a more general application to all simple believers. He is most concerned to see here an example of his theology of the cross, according to which God is proclaimed by what the world counts as lowly. He thus interprets the phrase "out of the mouths of babes" with respect to what it suggests about how preachers ought to preach (*Operationes in Psalmos,* part 2, ed. G. Hammer and M. Biersack, vol. 2 of *Archiv zur Weimarer Ausgabe der Werke Martin Luthers* [Cologne: Bohlau, 1981], 455-69).

the wicked despisers of God. . . . [David] imposes on infants the office of defending the glory of God."[17]

These findings are all the more interesting when one takes into account that Calvin's understanding of sin was more pessimistic than that of any of his predecessors or contemporaries. Against the dominant patristic and medieval traditions, Calvin and some of his contemporaries, especially Luther and Melanchthon, understood original sin itself to consist of an inherited corruption of the entire human nature, especially of the will *and* the understanding.[18] With certain earlier traditions, these theologians also understood sin to have negative effects on the mind, the will, the senses, and the body, and they argued that, apart from God's grace, humans could do nothing to rid themselves of sin and be restored to divine favor. But Calvin's estimate of the effects of sin on the mind was harsher than that of any of his predecessors or contemporaries.[19] Infants are not excepted from his dim appraisal of human inability in the arena of salvation. In a passage written in 1536 and carried throughout all subsequent editions of the *Institutes* unchanged, he says, "Even infants bear their condemnation with them from their mother's womb; for, though they have not yet brought forth the fruits of their own iniquity, they have the seed enclosed within themselves. Indeed, their whole nature is a seed of sin; thus it cannot be but hateful and abominable to God."[20] Children of all ages are subject to this harsh curse of fallen nature, the remedy to which is baptism and faith. In light

17. CO 31:89-90; Commentary on the Psalms, 1:96-97.

18. These patristic and medieval traditions were shaped largely by Augustine, Anselm of Canterbury (1033-1109), Peter Lombard (c. 1095-1160), Hugh of St. Victor (c. 1096-1141), Albert the Great (c. 1200-1280), and Thomas Aquinas (c. 1225-1274). For a discussion of these traditions and Calvin's relationship to them, see Barbara Pitkin, "Nothing but Concupiscence: Calvin's Understanding of Sin and the *via Augustini*," *Calvin Theological Journal* 34, no. 2 (November 1999): 347-69.

19. David Steinmetz has demonstrated this through comparative analysis of Calvin's interpretation of Romans 1:19-23. Most other Western interpreters held, with Paul, that humans perceive God in the created order and then proceed to suppress this knowledge because of sin. Calvin, however, argues that because of sin, fallen human beings misperceive God's self-revelation in nature, and this culpable misperception in turn leads them to further suppression of the knowledge of God. For details, see Steinmetz, *Calvin in Context*, 29-32.

20. *Christianae religionis Institutio* (1536), in *Ioannis Calvini Opera Selecta*, 5 vols., ed. Peter Barth (Munich: Christian Kaiser, 1952-1962), 1:131 (hereafter abbreviated OS); in English, *Institutes of the Christian Religion: 1536 Edition*, trans. Ford Lewis Battles (Grand Rapids, Mich.: Eerdmans, 1975), 97. All translations are taken from this English edition. English translations for the 1559 edition are taken from John Calvin, *Institutes of the Christian Religion*, ed. John McNeill and trans. Ford Lewis Battles, vols. 20-21 of the Library of Christian Classics (Philadelphia: Westminster Press, 1960), and are referenced by book, chapter, and section. The passage referenced earlier appears in *Institutes*, 4.15.10.

of Calvin's extreme judgment, it is important to underscore that he does not view children as *more* sinful and depraved than anyone else.

This point is worth stressing in light of continuing misconceptions surrounding Calvin's doctrine of election, which sometimes imply that his views were unusually harsh, especially in his insistence that children, too, were sinful and therefore that some of them were to be numbered among the reprobate.[21] Although we will revisit this topic when we take up the question of baptism, it is important to note here that Calvin did not understand God to be damning *innocent* newborns but rather, with the vast majority of Western theologians since Augustine, held that all humans from conception on were corrupted by original sin, a failing for which even they themselves were culpable. Therefore, they were not innocent but sinful and would not be saved unless grace intervened. Although Calvin followed Augustine and a few late medieval theologians in explicitly attributing reprobation — even of tiny babies — to God's active will, in effect this view is little different from the common medieval scholastic idea that God predestines some to salvation though his elective purpose, leaving the rest to their deserved damnation by failing to elect them to salvation.[22] The significant difference between the two views lies not in their assessments of the relative sinfulness of human beings but rather in their understandings of divine activity — namely, whether or not God actively reprobates particular people. Hence Calvin's insistence on the sinfulness of infants cannot be attributed to his understanding of election, nor can it be considered unique to him or unusually harsh in the premodern era. Even theologians such as Thomas Aquinas (who held that God predestines some people to salvation but actively reprobates no one) understood that newborns were not innocent and without God's predestination would not be saved. Thomas, to be sure,

21. This is often achieved by quoting out of context a statement that appears in Calvin's *On the Secret Providence of God,* suggesting that Calvin believed that "God . . . hurls innocent new born babes, torn from their mother's breast, into eternal death"; see, for example, Peter Slater, *Children in the New England Mind: In Death and in Life* (Hamden, Conn.: Shoe String Press, 1977), 26; citing from an article defending Calvin against the charge that unbaptized infants are eternally damned (Charles Eugene Edwards, "Calvin on Infant Salvation," *Bibliotheca Sacra* 88 [1931]: 328). Calvin did indeed teach that God reprobated and damned some infants, but he also held the traditional Western view that because of original sin, they were not innocent and therefore were justly damned. In this quotation, however, he is speaking rhetorically to refute as ludicrous the idea that those whom God damns are innocent.

22. The only late medieval theologians who advocated the controversial, late Augustinian view of "double-particular predestination" (i.e., that God elects both to salvation and to damnation through his active will) were Gregory of Rimini, Pierre d'Ailly, and Marsilius of Inghen. For details, see James L. Halverson, *Peter Aureol on Predestination: A Challenge to Medieval Thought* (Leiden: E. J. Brill, 1997), 7-10.

along with many other medievals, held that young children who died before baptism did not suffer the physical torments of hell.[23] But this argument rested on the assumption not that children were innocent but rather that they were only a little less sinful, since they had not yet had opportunity to commit actual sin.

Far from contradicting this assumption, Calvin's views imply agreement with medieval judgments that newborns and young children were not as sinful as their elders. Although Calvin does not share Thomas's view of a neutral final destination ("limbo") for infants who die unbaptized, he does hold that young children manifest a simplicity that is worthy of emulation, testify to divine providence, and, as he writes in his comments on Deuteronomy 1:39, do not consciously and willfully provoke God's wrath. Nevertheless, he makes clear in this same discussion that they are not exempt from original sin.[24] Children in the earliest stages of childhood are no less than those in the "slippery years" in need of divine grace. These seemingly contradictory notions about the nature of children run throughout the Christian tradition, reflecting in part the diversity of Scripture, from the potentially negative implications of Genesis 8:21 and Romans 5:12 to the positive implications of the Synoptic accounts of Jesus' embrace of children. Expressing this plurality of views, Calvin, the theologian of "total depravity," is more appreciative of the positive character of children, dwelling less on their sinfulness than some of his forebears (such as Augustine) or successors (such as Jonathan Edwards).

Children and Families

In the sixteenth century, the family was the primary context for the moral, intellectual, social, spiritual, and physical nurture of children. Recent scholarship has demonstrated the complexity of family life and has often arrived at conflicting conclusions about the relationship between domestic relations and religious, economic, and social changes.[25] Some historians, such as Strauss, have argued that the tasks of spiritual and intellectual development of children fell increasingly under ecclesiastical and political purview in the Reformation era.[26] Calvin clearly ascribed responsibility for caring for children to both the domes-

---

23. See the essay by Cristina Traina in this volume.

24. CO 25:207; Commentary on the Last Books of the Pentateuch, 4:86-87.

25. For a survey of current scholarship, see Wiesner-Hanks, "Family, Household, and Community"; *Oxford Encyclopedia of the Reformation*, s.v. "Family."

26. Strauss, *Luther's House of Learning*, 7-10.

tic and the public spheres, as one can see when one considers his views on the place of children in the family and on parental obligations toward children.[27]

Calvin's interpretation of Psalm 127 provides a fruitful point of departure. Verses 3-5 of this brief psalm claim that children are a "heritage from the Lord" and "the fruit of the womb [is] a reward." Children are like the arrows in a warrior's quiver; the man who has many of them is indeed happy and will not be put to shame by his enemies. Calvin remarks that all of human life is guided by divine providence; children are not "begotten of a secret instinct of nature" or the "fruit of chance" but rather are the gifts of God. Underscoring this point elsewhere, he notes that the birth of offspring tends to conciliate spouses and increases their love for each another.[28] He can also speak quite tenderly of the relationship between parents and their children. In April 1541, while Calvin was attending the Colloquy at Regensburg, he received word of the death of Charles Richebourg, a young man who had been living in Calvin's house while studying in Strasbourg. In his long letter of consolation to the boy's father, Calvin speaks of his own affection for the deceased boy, taken away in the "very flower of his age." He seeks to console the father with the awareness that the boy had, nevertheless, "grown ripe in the sight of the Lord." Taking comfort in God's providence and in the blessing of his surviving brother does not mean that the father should lay aside all grief, but only that he should "shed those tears . . . due to nature and fatherly affection, [but] . . . by no means give way to senseless wailing."[29] Although the tone of the letter is quite formal, one nevertheless senses Calvin's understanding of the depth of parental affection. Just a little over a year later, he would personally experience a similar loss, and write to Pierre Viret: "The Lord has certainly inflicted a severe and bitter wound in the death of our infant son. But he is himself a Father, and knows best what is good for his children."[30] Consoling parents over the loss of a child was undoubtedly a common pastoral task in an age in which the mortality of children ranged between 30 and 50 percent.[31]

Regarding children as gifts of God's providence implies several things

27. Determination of whether his views are original or typical and the extent to which they conform to reality awaits more detailed demographic and qualitative analysis of the Genevan and wider European situations in Calvin's day.

28. See Calvin's comments on Genesis 29:31 and 30:20 (CO 23:405, 412; Commentary on Genesis, 2:135, 148). See also Calvin's comments on Genesis 30:2, 33:5 (CO 23:405, 408, 450; Commentary on Genesis, 2:134-35, 141, 208).

29. Calvin to Monsieur de Richbourg, CO 11:188-94; Bonnet, *Letters of John Calvin*, 1:222-29.

30. Calvin to Pierre Viret, August 19, 1542, CO 11:430; Bonnet, *Letters of John Calvin*, 1:320.

31. Ozment, *When Fathers Ruled*, 216, n. 7.

about parental attitudes and obligations. In his comments on Psalm 127, Calvin notes that "the majority of children are not always a source of joy to their parents." In response to such inevitable disappointment, parents must consider that God's special favor also extends to forming their children's minds, dispositions, and character. Far from absolving parents of all responsibility for raising their children, this recognition of God's role in child rearing actually inspires and enhances parental care. Calvin remarks, "*Unless* men regard their children as the gift of God, they are careless and reluctant in providing for their support, just as on the other hand this knowledge contributes in a very eminent degree to encourage them in bringing up their offspring."[32] Such parents will also be careful with whatever inheritance they have to leave to their children. From their children parents can expect the "arrows" of virtue and moral integrity, by which they "protect" their parents. The psalmist teaches that "the children we ought to wish for are not such as may violently oppress the wretched and the suffering, or overreach others by craft and deceit, or accumulate great riches by unlawful means, but such as will practice uprightness, and be willing to live in obedience to the laws, and prepared to render an account of their life."[33]

This image of the ideal child reveals something about Calvin's understanding of parenting. The primary obligation of parents, especially fathers but also mothers, is to teach godliness. Calvin makes this point frequently in his biblical commentaries. For example, in his interpretation of Genesis 18:19, Calvin claims that God spoke to Abraham concerning Sodom and Gomorrah because Abraham "would faithfully fulfill the office of a good householder, in instructing his own family." Although all parents have the duty of communicating what they have learned from the Lord to their children, many stifle this knowledge.[34] Similarly, in his comments on Psalm 78:3-6, Calvin remarks that even the unlearned and babes can benefit from the Word of God. He stresses paternal obligation to fulfill God's command and diligently instruct the children in the family.[35] Linked to this is the duty of Christian parents to baptize their children. In the *Institutes*, Calvin concludes his discussion of baptism by arguing that the sacrament assures parents by word and sight that their offspring are in God's care. Without this testimony of God's grace, parents would become ungrateful toward God and negligent in instructing their children in piety.[36]

This same image also sheds light on Calvin's perceptions of children's ob-

32. CO 32:325; Commentary on the Psalms, 5:111 (my emphasis).
33. CO 32:325; Commentary on the Psalms, 5:112.
34. CO 23:258; Commentary on Genesis, 1:481.
35. CO 32:722-23; Commentary on the Psalms, 3:228-32; cf. Calvin's comments on Psalm 44:2 (CO 31:437; Commentary on the Psalms, 2:152).
36. *Institutes* (1559), 4.16.32 (OS 5:341).

ligations, which reflect assumptions and concerns typical of his age. Children ought to be morally upright, submissive to authority, and self-critical. His treatments of the commandment to honor father and mother in his commentary on the Decalogue, the catechism, and the *Institutes* underscore the duty of children to submit to parents and, by extension, the duty of all people to submit to their divinely ordained superiors. He characterizes the superiority of parents over children as "by nature most amiable and least invidious."[37] In the commentary on Genesis, Calvin frequently remarks on the duty of children to adhere to their parents' wishes when contracting marriage.[38] Calvin's abhorrence of anarchy and chaos manifests itself in the fact that he worries more about subordinates violating the authority of their superiors than about superiors exploiting those submitting to them. In the *Institutes,* he warns that God in the law prescribes the death penalty for those who curse or disobey their parents. Nevertheless, he recognizes both there and elsewhere a limit to parental authority: if parents lead their children to violate God's law, children should regard them not as parents but as strangers.

Some have used Calvin's mention of the biblical statutes concerning the punishment by death of those who disobey their parents to imply that Calvin instituted a law in Geneva to this effect and that his views reflect a harsh attitude toward children that justified physical mistreatment in his own day and among later Calvinists.[39] Yet if we inquire more closely into Calvin's attitudes, especially with respect to the most difficult passage, we find no evidence to justify either of these implications. The biblical test-case for parental authority appears in Deuteronomy 21:18-21, which (echoing similar judgments in Exodus 21:15, 17 and Leviticus 20:9) prescribes the death penalty for incorrigible sons. According to the Deuteronomic statute, the parents themselves must function as the accusers of their child. Raymond Blacketer has thoroughly analyzed Calvin's 1555 sermonic treatment of this passage in the context of earlier and contemporary interpretations.[40] More than these others, Calvin emphasizes the duties of parents, devoting nearly two-thirds of his sermon to this topic. He stresses the need for both fathers and mothers to provide proper instruction for

37. *Institutes* (1559), 2.8.35 (OS 3:377).

38. See Calvin's comments on Genesis 21:20, 24:3, 34:4 (CO 23:306, 331, 457; Commentary on Genesis, 1:551; 2:14, 219). Here, too, Calvin is following sixteenth-century trends; see Strauss, *Luther's House of Learning,* 122, and the literature cited in his n. 81.

39. See Arthur W. Calhoun, *A Social History of the American Family: From the Colonial Times to the Present,* 3 vols. (1917; reprint, New York: Barnes and Noble, 1945), 1:47, 120-21. Cf. Stone, *The Family, Sex, and Marriage: England, 1500-1800,* 175. See also Catherine Brekus's chapter on Jonathan Edwards in the present volume.

40. Raymond Andrew Blacketer, "*L'École de Dieu:* Pedagogy and Rhetoric in Calvin's Interpretation of Deuteronomy" (Ph.D. diss., Calvin Theological Seminary, 1998), 315-58.

their children, not merely to restrain them from evil and not in order to fulfill the parents' personal ambitions. Parents ought to consider that children in the home constitute a "mirror of God's grace," a sign that God cares for the family, and from this consideration be moved to fulfill their parental obligations. Only when these have been met can the statute be invoked; indeed, if parents have been deficient in their instruction, they are themselves to blame for the result and should share any punishment. Turning to the question of punishment itself, Calvin stresses first the need for parents to be patient and exercise forbearance in dealing with rebellious offspring. Although he admits that parents must in some cases apply harsh discipline ("put the bit" in their children's mouths), he emphasizes also that this must be done with love and gentleness, not with wickedness and cruelty. The question remains open whether he actually sought to implement the divine statute prescribing capital punishment for truly incorrigible children. As Blacketer concludes, "The most that can be surmised is that Calvin does believe that irreformable individuals should be executed, particularly when they are guilty of such heinous crimes as blasphemy." However, nothing in either Calvin's interpretation or the historical record supports the "malicious slander," perpetuated no less in popular writings than in the recent *Oxford Children's Encyclopedia*, that little children were actually executed in Geneva for disobeying their parents.[41]

Ozment has observed, "Never has the art of parenting been more highly praised and parental authority more wholeheartedly supported than in Reformation Europe."[42] If this is so, then the utter seriousness with which Calvin took family life fits well within the spirit of his times. He stressed the dignity and importance of bearing and rearing children by designating these not merely divinely ordained but activities of God himself, who providentially gives children and forms their character. He understood the essence of good parenting to be instruction in piety. Calvin shares also the widespread concern for order, especially social order, that characterized the sixteenth century. His delineation of children's duty to honor, obey, and love and care for their parents

---

41. Blacketer, *"L'École de Dieu,"* 358. The perpetuation of the false assertion that a boy was executed for striking his parents is so troubling that Blacketer's footnote merits citation: "Examples of such nonsense include that found in the *Oxford Children's Encyclopedia*, 7 vols. (Oxford: Oxford University Press, [1991] 1995), VI:43. . . . See also the fabrications of Paul Johnson in *A History of Christianity* (London: Weidenfeld and Nicolson, 1976): 286-292; and the facile, secondary-source derived stereotypes of William Manchester, *A World Lit Only By Fire: The Medieval Mind and the Renaissance* (Boston: Little, Brown, and Company, 1992): 189-190, 128, 176, 188, and esp. 190-193. . . . These fictions are irresponsibly perpetuated by Philip Yancey, *What's So Amazing about Grace?* (Grand Rapids: Zondervan, 1997): 234-235."

42. Ozment, *When Fathers Ruled*, 132.

is extremely typical.[43] While the stress on responsibilities of children over their rights may trouble us today, this is but an indication of the distance between the sixteenth century and our own. As Ozment notes, "The great fear [in Reformation Europe] was not that children would be abused by adult authority but that children might grow up to place their own individual wants above society's common good."[44] For Calvin as for others, the task of rearing children to place the common good above their individual desires fell not just to the family, but was in fact a coordinated effort of family, government, and church.

Children and Society

In Calvin's view, it was society's duty to provide the right conditions for raising children to be godly. The attempts at social reform, especially the "control of morals," in the Geneva of Calvin's day are well-known, even if few appreciate the fact that many of the laws regulating morality were already on the books before Calvin's arrival in 1536, or that many early modern cities expended similar efforts at social improvement (but were less successful than Geneva). Robert Kingdon has argued that the explanation for the moral seriousness and austerity of Calvinism lies in the successful enforcement of morality in Geneva through the creation, at Calvin's suggestion in 1541, of a new body, the Consistory.[45] The Geneva Consistory was an ecclesiastical court made up of the members of the Company of Pastors and elders, who were elected from the various hierarchical councils of the Genevan government. It was, therefore, a standing committee of the government, even though it included the pastors, who were not elected officials. Several issues that came before the Consistory during Calvin's career have relevance for children — in particular, cases having to do with marriage and baptismal policies. The two other ecclesiastical offices (in addition to elders and pastors) called into existence by Calvin's *Ecclesiastical Ordinances* (1541) — namely, the deacons and the teaching doctors — have even more immediate bearing on children's lives.[46] For though Genevan social wel-

43. Ozment, *When Fathers Ruled*, 150; see also Bast, *Honor Your Fathers*.
44. Ozment, *When Fathers Ruled*, 177.
45. See Robert M. Kingdon, "The Control of Morals in Calvin's Geneva," in *The Social History of the Reformation*, ed. L. P. Buck and J. W. Zophy (Columbus: Ohio State University Press, 1972), 3-16.
46. An English translation of the *Ecclesiastical Ordinances* appears in *The Register of the Company of Pastors of Geneva in the Time of Calvin*, ed. and trans. Philip Edgecumbe Hughes (Grand Rapids, Mich.: Eerdmans, 1966), 35-53. The Company's Register appears in the original languages as *Registres de la Compagnie des Pasteurs de Genève au Temps de*

fare (administered largely through the hospital) and public schooling were already in the process of being reformed prior to 1536, Calvin's support and shaping of these reforms, especially through the creation of the offices of deacon and doctor, were important. We are likely to learn more about the exact nature of his significance, and likewise to determine exactly how children themselves might have been affected by these endeavors, as the records of these bodies' activities become more easily accessible.[47] With an eye to these opportunities, I wish to probe the possibilities these sources may offer for uncovering information about children's lives in Genevan society.

In its weekly meetings, the Consistory dealt with an astounding variety of cases of suspected misconduct and domestic difficulty, including engagement disputes, marital problems, accusations of infidelity, charges of abuse, unfair business practices, strife between servants and their employers, and disputes between neighbors. The members of the Consistory heard a case, rendered a judgment, counseled the parties involved, and, if appropriate, determined a penalty. In cases of established misconduct, the most common was a "ritualized scolding" (or "bawling out"), which closed the case unless the guilty party resisted correction.[48] In such instances, the Consistory might excommunicate the individual and bar him or her from receiving communion at the next quarterly celebration. If the crime involved a violation of Genevan law, then the case would be referred to the Small Council (one of Geneva's elected governing bodies) to determine punishment, which ranged from public shaming and humiliation to execution.

Recent studies of the development and implementation of marriage policy in Geneva have unearthed a wealth of information with implications for children's lives. Having thrown out canon law with the Catholic faith, Geneva, like other reformed areas, needed to formulate policies for establishing, recognizing, preserving, and dissolving marital bonds. We have already seen Calvin (in his commentary on Genesis) expressing a common Protestant concern to

---

Calvin, ed. Jean-François Bergier (vol. 1) and Robert Kingdon (vol. 2) (Geneva: Librairie Droz, 1964, 1962).

47. For details on the Consistory registers, see Robert M. Kingdon, *Adultery and Divorce in Calvin's Geneva* (Cambridge: Harvard University Press, 1995), 204-5. Kingdon has been supervising the transcription and edition of these records, the first volume of which has recently appeared: *Registres du consistoire de Genève au temps de Calvin,* vol. 1 (1542-1544), ed. T. Lambert and I. Watt, with R. Kingdon and J. Watt (Geneva: Librairie Droz, 1996).

48. Kingdon, *Adultery and Divorce in Calvin's Geneva,* 18. For a fuller description of the kinds of cases the Consistory heard, see Kingdon, "Calvin and the Family: The Work of the Consistory in Geneva," in *Articles on Calvin and Calvinism,* ed. Richard C. Gamble (Hamden, Conn.: Garland Publishing, 1992), 13:93-106; and E. William Monter, "The Consistory of Geneva, 1559-1569," *Bibliothèque d'Humanisme et Renaissance* 38 (1976): 467-84.

do away with secret betrothals and insist upon parental consent as a necessary but not sufficient condition for a legal engagement.[49] In other areas as well marriage assumed a different character than under canon law, and these changes must have had lasting impact on the children involved. Most significantly, marriage was no longer a sacrament, and it was now possible, albeit extremely difficult, to divorce and remarry. The conclusions drawn from the cases discussed by John Witte and Robert Kingdon are suggestive of avenues for further research.[50] First, the Geneva Consistory and Small Council were extremely reluctant to dissolve any marriage and almost always attempted to reconcile the parties involved. Divorce was granted only on grounds of proven adultery or desertion. Ongoing current research of the Consistory records, the first volume of which has been recently published, may well reveal whether the existence of children and their ages played a role in these determinations, and whether the Consistory or Council ever entertained the effects of marital discord on children. Second, if a divorce was granted, there were in some cases subsequent complaints or even lawsuits about the management of property designated for children. In a case discussed by Kingdon, Benoite Ameaux lost the rights to her property inherited from her first husband when she was convicted of adultery and divorced from her second husband.[51] Although in this case the ex-husband continued to manage the property for the benefit of the children of Benoite's first marriage, there must have been other instances where the trustees of property designated for children were not so honorable. Finally, illustrated in the divorce case touching Calvin quite literally closest to home, there is the matter of the effect on children of a divorce granted, often with the immediate result of banishment or execution of one parent. In 1557, Calvin guided his brother Antoine through a second, successful divorce petition against his wife, Anne Le Fert. Antoine, Anne, and their four young children lived in Calvin's home. Convicted of adultery solely on circumstantial evidence, Anne Le Fert was sentenced by the Small Council to permanent banishment and given twenty-four hours to leave the city.[52] Her husband was granted his divorce and custody of

49. See note 38 earlier for specific references to the commentary on Genesis. For a detailed discussion of why Protestants objected to the medieval practice of "secret betrothals" and insisted on public declarations of intent and celebrations of marriage (preferably with parental consent), see Ozment, *When Fathers Ruled*, 25-44.

50. Kingdon, *Adultery and Divorce in Calvin's Geneva;* and John Witte Jr., *From Sacrament to Contract: Marriage, Religion, and Law in the Western Tradition* (Louisville: Westminster John Knox Press, 1997), 74-129. See the slightly expanded discussion in "Between Sacrament and Contract: Marriage as Covenant in John Calvin's Geneva," *Calvin Theological Journal* 33, no. 1 (April 1998): 9-75.

51. Kingdon, *Adultery and Divorce in Calvin's Geneva*, 63.

52. Kingdon, *Adultery and Divorce in Calvin's Geneva*, 87.

the couple's four children. Kingdon explicitly mentions the impact of the divorce on the children as deserving attention in this case.[53] Granted the singularity of this case involving the Calvin family itself, it nevertheless suggests that there may have been other cases in which the Consistory and Council's decisions about domestic matters left lasting marks on the children involved.

A second window into the place of children in society is provided by a long-standing controversy between the pastors and some of the Genevan citizenry over names given to children.[54] Starting in April 1546, the ministers began to refuse to recognize certain given names at baptisms, often baptizing the infants presented under other, acceptable names. Initially they had the support of the magistrates for their efforts to ban all names associated, in the minds of the French ministers, with Catholic "superstitions": names of popular saints with local shrines (especially "Claude"), names associated with the Godhead (such as "Jesus" and "Emmanuel"), names of feast days (such as Pentecost), and other nonbiblical names that simply "sound[ed] bad" (such as "Allemand").[55] However, the public outcry — sometimes resulting in riots — against what was perceived as ministerial arrogance subsequently led prominent citizens, some of them current or former members of the Small Council, to voice objections. As William Naphy observes, many of these were "not attached to Catholic superstitions, but people who strongly resented being forbidden, by foreigners, from giving their children traditional, family names."[56] Add to this the embarrassment of being told publicly that many of their own names were superstitious and sinful. The ministers, for their part, complained of public insolence

53. "Anne, as the guilty party, lost custody of her children, and they remained in the house of their father, uncle, and later stepmother. But they were so young that they must inevitably have been upset and bewildered by the divorce and the abrupt departure of their mother. As they grew older they may well have resented the forceful steps that had been taken to drive their mother away. This is the most obvious explanation for the 'disobedience' of his two sons from his first marriage about which Antoine Calvin complained bitterly at the time he reduced their inheritance portions in his final testament" (*Adultery and Divorce in Calvin's Geneva*, 94-95).

54. The controversy between 1546 and 1554 is immensely significant because it sheds light on the escalating resentment of many native Genevans toward the policies of their ministers, all of whom were French, and because it led to the first crisis between the ministers and the magistrates over the right of excommunication. See William G. Naphy, *Calvin and the Consolidation of the Genevan Reformation* (Manchester and New York: Manchester University Press, 1994), 144-53; this appears in abbreviated and slightly altered form as "Baptisms, Church Riots, and Social Unrest in Calvin's Geneva," *Sixteenth Century Journal* 26, no. 1 (Spring 1995): 87-97.

55. For an extract of the ordinance issued in November 1546, see *The Register of the Company of Pastors of Geneva in the Time of Calvin*, 71-72; cf. CO 10:49-50.

56. Naphy, *Calvin and the Consolidation of the Genevan Reformation*, 150.

and disobedience and urged the magistrates to punish offenders; they viewed this resistance to the baptismal policy as a serious threat to the establishment of true piety. Children thus became a public battleground in disputes over ecclesiastical power, parental rights and obligations, and "ethnic" resentments between Genevans and French. With respect to the latter, the controversy over the policy points to a potential hazard of Calvin's view of children as God's gifts. For the ministers, the very act of naming children ought to reflect this belief. For some parents, their right to name their children as they wished conflicted with their duty to present them for baptism and raise them in the Reformed faith. In such cases, the ministers and, ultimately, the magistrates felt the need to step in and resolve the conflict, even if this meant sacrificing familial to Christian identity.

In two other areas, social welfare and education, society exercised a less controversial and clearly more directly influential role toward children. Geneva's organization and expansion of both reflected the general trend in Protestant urban areas toward centralized, civic control of activities carried out previously in disparate fashion by various ecclesiastical bodies. The Geneva General Hospital, established by a consolidation of several existing hospitals in 1535, was an "all purpose institution" administering social welfare to those in need: the sick, but also orphans and foundlings, widows, other poor, and travelers passing through Geneva.[57] An elected board of *procureurs* approved allocations of food and resources, managed properties, arranged for children in the orphanage to enter society through apprenticeships (for boys) or dowries (for girls), and raised funds for the ongoing social welfare. A layman appointed as *hospitallier* and his wife carried out the daily operations. Eventually the *procureurs* and the *hospitallier* became the deacons established by Calvin's *Ecclesiastical Ordinances* — that is, lay ministers for the gathering and distributing of alms, although they continued to be referred to by their traditional titles.[58] From its beginnings, the newly centralized system of social benefice dealt mostly with situations affecting children.[59] In the early years, fifty of the hospital's seventy inmates were children.[60] These were for the most part orphans,

57. Robert Kingdon, "Social Welfare in Calvin's Geneva," *The American Historical Review* 76 (1971): 52; reprinted as chapter 6 of R. M. Kingdon, *Church and Society in Reformation Europe* (London: Variorum Reprints, 1985). See also William C. Innes, *Social Concern in Calvin's Geneva* (Allison Park, Penn.: Pickwick Publications, 1983).

58. Jeannine E. Olson, *Calvin and Social Welfare: Deacons and the Bourse française* (Selinsgrove: Susquehanna University Press, 1989), 32.

59. These are detailed by Alice Denzler in *Jugendfürsorge in der alten Eidgenossenschaft: ihre Entwicklung in den Kantonen Zürich, Luzern, Freiburg, St. Gallen und Genf bis 1798* (Zurich: Verlag des Zentralsekretariates Pro Juventute, 1925), 485-613.

60. Denzler, *Jugendfürsorge,* 537.

foundlings, the products of illegitimate relationships, or children whose parents were too poor to support them. Sometimes children were raised in the hospital, but many were housed with foster families until they were old enough to live on their own. The hospital also provided food, clothing, and even financial assistance for children living in large families or families of insufficient means. The aim of all this support, which was institutionalized also in other Swiss cities, was to enable children in difficult situations to become productive members of society. Geneva was particularly distinguished for its attention to vocational training for both boys and girls.[61]

As in other cities, the hospital care was intended specifically for locals. In Geneva, however, the large influx of religious refugees starting in the 1540s led to the creation of additional benevolent institutions. For example, the innovative French fund, or *Bourse française,* was created with donations to provide both short-term and long-term aid to French immigrants and refugees. By 1554, the administrators of the fund were also designated deacons. Initially, most of the refugees were single men or men who had left families behind.[62] However, the *Bourse* increasingly found itself dealing, like the hospital, with children's needs, arranging for wet nurses and foster families and paying their fees, making gifts of clothing and schoolbooks, paying for medical bills, and arranging for apprenticeships and other training.[63] Calvin was more directly involved with this organization than with the hospital, which was already established before his arrival and whose operations may well have shaped his understanding of social welfare.[64]

As with the hospital, school reforms coinciding with the political and religious reformation in Geneva built upon a long-standing local tradition and reflected general trends in urban society, especially in France and Germany. However, systematic schooling in Geneva apparently broke down during the struggle for independence between 1528 and 1535.[65] Hence the mag-

---

61. Denzler, *Jugendfürsorge,* 8. For more details on children, see Innes, *Social Concern in Calvin's Geneva,* 130-31.

62. E. William Monter, *Calvin's Geneva* (New York: John Wiley & Sons, 1967), 166; Innes, *Social Concern in Calvin's Geneva,* 207.

63. Olson, *Calvin and Social Welfare,* 42-43.

64. Innes, *Social Concern in Calvin's Geneva,* 103; Robert Kingdon, "The Deacons of the Reformed Church in Calvin's Geneva," in *Mélanges d'histoire du XVI siècle offerts à Henri Meylan,* Travaux d'Humanisme et Renaissance 110 (Geneva: Librairie Droz, 1970), 87; reprinted as chapter 7 of R. M. Kingdon, *Church and Society in Reformation Europe.*

65. For succinct summaries of these events, see William Naphy, "The Reformation and the Evolution of Geneva's Schools," in *Reformations Old and New: Essays on the Socio-Economic Impact of Religious Change, c. 1470-1630,* ed. Beat Kümin (Brookfield, Vt.: Ashgate Publishing Co., 1996), 183-94; and Robert W. Henderson, *The Teaching Office in the Reformed Tradition: A History of the Doctoral Ministry* (Philadelphia: Westminster Press, 1962), 16-24 and 41-56.

istrates included in the "Reformation decrees" of May 1536 a charge to establish schools for all Genevan children. In September 1535 the collège had reopened and was relocated in 1544 to the former Franciscan monastery as the Collège de Rive. The *collège* provided instruction in Latin, Greek, Hebrew, and French; various *petits écoles* also existed to provide more rudimentary education. These efforts to provide universal schooling were motivated by the desire to mold good citizens and to prepare educated leaders and civic employees. Included in this desire was the understanding that the schools would also provide religious instruction. In fact, primers for learning such things as the alphabet, numbers, and basic grammar were, as in medieval times, often combined with basic catechetical content, such as the Lord's Prayer and the Creed.[66]

Thus Calvin, arriving in Geneva in the late summer of 1536, did not initiate the concern for education of children or determine its precise character. However, he did shape it in two decisive ways, inspired in part through his work in Strasbourg between 1538 and 1541, during which the educational system in Geneva seems once again to have fallen on hard times.[67] First, in the *Ecclesiastical Ordinances,* Calvin established the office of teaching doctor and brought the selection of teachers under control of the pastors. Initially this move seems analogous to his designating the current hospital administrators and staff as deacons. Schools, especially the primary ones but also the secondary *collège,* functioned pretty much as before; public, post-secondary lectures by the pastors continued, and financial control of the schools remained with the magistrates.[68] However, there was also tension over the status and appointment of the teachers, apparently brought on in part by the clerical control, which the magistrates supported nevertheless. Moreover, like the diaconate, the doctoral office increased in role and importance in the 1550s. Second, Calvin also called in the *Ordinances* for the establishment of a centralized institution (with a separate school for girls), including a post-secondary Academy, to prepare children for careers in church and government.[69] In 1559 Calvin finally succeeded in establishing a new academy, which consisted of a lower-level Latin school (the *schola privata*) and a new, upper-level institution of higher education (the *schola publica*), which became renowned throughout Europe. This new institution served initially as a training ground for Reformed pastors, but from its early

66. See R. Peter, "L'abécédaire genevois ou catéchisme élémentaire de Calvin," *Revue d'Histoire et de Philosophie religieuses* 45 (1965): 15-16.

67. See Naphy, "The Reformation and the Evolution of Geneva's Schools," 195-96.

68. See Henderson, *The Teaching Office in the Reformed Tradition,* 48-70; and Naphy, "The Reformation and the Evolution of Geneva's Schools," 196-97 and 202.

69. *Ecclesiastical Ordinances,* in *The Register of the Company of Pastors of Geneva in the Time of Calvin,* 41.

days many of the magistrates supported (and fought for) a broadening of the curriculum.[70]

Children figure prominently in many of the social reforms implemented by the Genevan government as it restructured and centralized social and political life after achieving its independence. Few of these reforms were unique to Geneva, and Calvin played virtually no role in their initiation. Nevertheless, he supported and to various degrees transformed some of these social actions and institutions affecting children. In the arenas of morals, social welfare, and schooling, Calvin effectively "baptized" the civic legislation by designating the administrators lay ministers. His own involvement ranged from mere sanctioning of existing "ministries," as in the case of the hospital, to extensive leadership, as in the case of the Consistory. His activity may well have shaped the attitudes toward children expressed, for example, in the commentaries on Genesis and the Psalms that he wrote in the 1550s. Continued investigation of the records of such bodies as the Consistory, the hospital, and the councils will provide a much more nuanced and needed account of how the developments he inspired or supported actually affected children. They may also furnish more instances of specific actions taken to improve children's well-being, as, for example, Calvin's suggestion to the magistrates "that balconies be added to all Genevan buildings for the greater safety of children."[71] They will undoubtedly, of course, also provide additional evidence of the tension between public and private responsibility for children as illustrated in the controversy over the baptismal policy.

Children and the Church

The area of Calvin's literary activity most directly relevant for children concerns their role in the church. His writings on baptism and preparation of catechisms designed especially for the instruction of youth constitute his most important and lasting contribution to the topic of children in Christian thought.

Calvin upheld the traditional practice of infant baptism and, moreover, recognized the validity of baptism in the Roman church. Nevertheless, with Luther, he transformed the meaning of baptism and the sacraments in general and reduced the number of sacraments to two (baptism and eucharist), understood

70. These are detailed by Karin Maag in *Seminary or University? The Genevan Academy and Reformed Higher Education, 1560-1620* (Brookfield, Vt.: Ashgate Publishing Co., 1995).

71. Monter, *Calvin's Geneva*, 107.

as visible signs or seals of God's word, designed to aid human weakness. In further contrast to Roman teaching, baptism signified the full remission of *all* sin (original and actual, past and future). No further sacrament (i.e., penance) was needed for the remission of post-baptismal sin. Despite this apparently enhanced status of baptism, Calvin did not believe that the sacrament was strictly necessary for salvation. Salvation rests on God's promise and not on the sacramental sign of the promise. Christian parents have the duty to baptize children according to God's command but should not worry about their fate should they die unbaptized.

The grounds for Calvin's confidence both about the strength of baptism and concerning the fate of unbaptized children lie in his espousal of a traditional, Augustinian notion of predestination, combined with a Lutheran insistence that those justified by faith are certain of their salvation. With Augustine, he held that the grounds for salvation lie in God's eternal decree, according to which God determines to predestine some sinners to salvation apart from any consideration of their future merit or faith. Unlike Luther and his followers, Calvin (again siding with Augustine) also emphasized explicitly that God at the same time actively determined to reprobate those whom God did not elect to save. With Luther, but against Augustine and the medieval tradition, he held that one could be absolutely certain that one was among the elect and would be saved. For both Luther and Calvin, this does not mean that believers enjoy unbroken psychological certainty of their final destiny, for both clearly understood the role of doubt, fear, and temptation in the Christian life. However, both also emphasized that those justified by faith had complete assurance in God's promise that their personal salvation was secure. Far from seeking to justify spiritual laxity, Luther and Calvin thought this assurance was necessary to comfort believers in their weakness and deter them from seeking to earn their salvation from God by doing good works. Therefore, for Calvin, the doctrine of predestination itself was a comfort, since believers could rest assured that there was nothing they could do to thwart God's grace and jeopardize or lose their salvation. It is important to stress that while he held that one would be certain of one's own election, one could never judge whether anyone else was elect or reprobate. Despite this agnosticism concerning the state of others' souls, Calvin argues that Christian parents have good reason to trust that God's promise to save will be extended toward their children.

Significantly, however, Luther and Calvin drew slightly different conclusions about baptism's role in salvation from their common assumptions about the efficacy of God's grace and the certainty of salvation for those justified by faith. A grasp of these differences is important in order to appreciate the distinctive reasons by which Calvin defends infant baptism. More than Calvin, "Luther saw baptism as the concrete place *in time* where the believer is joined to the saving history of Jesus Christ."[72] As Jane Strohl points out, baptism for Luther effects an "ongoing reorientation of human life," and its promise is fulfilled only in death.[73] Yet Luther still spoke of baptism as the moment in which this salvation begins. He thus accepted the traditional view that, barring rare exceptions, baptism was necessary for salvation, although he rejected the medieval doctrine that the sacrament was effective through the administration of the rite.[74] For him, the word of promise, conjoined with the water, makes the sacrament efficacious by awakening faith. But if this is so, how can infants make proper use of the sacraments by responding in faith? Luther addresses this issue in his *Babylonian Captivity* (1520) by espousing the traditional notion that infants have vicarious faith through their sponsors and parents. In his *Concerning Rebaptism* (1528), however, arguing against Anabaptists' insistence that a personal faith precede the sacrament, he suggests that no one can prove that infants themselves do not believe. Luther is careful to stress that the efficacy of the sacrament depends not on the recipient's faith but only on God's word there proclaimed.[75] He believed that the Anabaptists, by understanding baptism as a confirmation of a prior experience of faith, diminished the importance of baptism as the place where the one baptized dies and is born again, and the experience out of which faith is born and nurtured.

Calvin's understanding of baptism as visible proclamation of the gospel and faith as the proper use of the sacrament is the same as Luther's; he also stresses the idea that through baptism believers are engrafted into Christ's death. However, he does not emphasize the idea of the sacrament as the concrete moment in time when salvation begins, nor does he stress the daily return to baptism to the same degree. This is not to say that Calvin does not think that baptism nourishes faith, for he clearly holds that this is one of the chief purposes of both sacraments, and writes at length in the *Institutes* about the comfort that remembrance of baptism affords.[76] However, he speaks more of the

---

72. Mark D. Tranvik, "The Other Sacrament: The Doctrine of Baptism in the Late Lutheran Reformation" (Th.D. diss., Luther Northwestern Theological Seminary, 1992), 213.

73. See Jane Strohl's essay in this volume, 141-43.

74. This view was formalized in the Augsburg Confession, which declares in article 9 that baptism is necessary for salvation.

75. See Tranvik, "The Other Sacrament," 28-31; cf. Timothy Wengert, "Luther on Children: Baptism and the Fourth Commandment," *Dialog* 37, no. 3 (July 1998): 185-89. On infant faith, see Eero Huovinen, *Fides Infantium: Martin Luthers Lehre vom Kinderglauben,* Veröffentlichungen des Instituts für Europäische Geschichte Mainz, vol. 159 (Mainz: Philipp von Zabern, 1997).

76. For example, Calvin criticizes the Roman sacrament of penance and writes, "Therefore, there is no doubt that all pious folk throughout life, whenever they are troubled by a consciousness of their faults, may venture to remind themselves of their baptism,

symbolic and spiritual character of the rite as a *token* of the cleansing, forgiveness, and union with Christ already promised to the elect. Baptism does not effect but signifies rebirth or regeneration for the elect. In baptism, as in the eucharist, the non-elect receive only the empty sign and not the promise. Calvin thus more explicitly links the efficacy of this sacrament to election than does Luther.[77] He also does not insist as strictly as Luther does on the necessity of baptism for salvation. Writing against the practice of emergency baptism, Calvin argues,

> Yet (you say) there is a danger lest he who is ill, if he die without baptism, be deprived of the grace of regeneration. Not at all. God declares that he adopts our babies as his own before they are born, when he promises that he will be our God and the God of our descendants after us [Gen. 17:7]. Their salvation is embraced in this word. No one will dare be so insolent toward God as to deny that his promise of itself suffices for its effect.[78]

These distinctive emphases are reflected in the arguments Calvin advances in his defense of infant baptism.

If salvation depends on predestination to grace in Christ, why ought Christian parents present their children for baptism? Although Calvin acknowledges the presence of original sin in children, designating their "whole nature . . . a seed of sin," he does not make this the basis of his defense of infant baptism. The motive for baptism is not to cleanse from original sin and thereby seek to avoid damnation. Rather, he, again like Luther (but to a much greater degree), Huldrych Zwingli, and Martin Bucer, draws an analogy between baptism and circumcision to argue that children have a *right* to baptism.[79] Elect children already have the promise and ought therefore not to be denied the sign. This one reason, Calvin claims, is alone sufficient to refute all opposition

---

that from it they may be confirmed in the assurance of that sole and perpetual cleansing which we have in Christ's blood" (*Institutes* [1559], 4.15.4; OS 5:288).

77. See François Wendel, *Calvin: The Origins and Development of His Religious Thought,* trans. Philip Mairet (New York: Harper & Row, 1963; reprint, Durham, N.C.: Labyrinth Press, 1986), 316.

78. *Institutes* (1559), 4.15.20; OS 5:301.

79. Martin Luther, *Concerning Rebaptism,* in *Martin Luther's Basic Theological Writings,* ed. Timothy F. Lull (Minneapolis: Augsburg Fortress, 1989), 356; W. P. Stephens, *The Theology of Huldrych Zwingli* (Oxford: Clarendon Press, 1986), 196; Willem Balke, *Calvin and the Anabaptist Radicals,* trans. W. J. Heynen (Grand Rapids, Mich.: Eerdmans, 1981), 102. For some implications of Calvin's view, see Arnie R. Brouwer, "Calvin's Doctrine of Children in the Covenant: Foundation for Christian Education," *The Reformed Review* 18, no. 4 (May 1965): 17-29. The proof text for the argument that children have a right to membership in the covenant is Genesis 17:7.

to the practice of infant baptism.[80] In other words, his primary justification for infant baptism is not the sinfulness of children, nor even their need for faith or perhaps their latent possession of it, but the fact that God has commanded it *because they are already members of the covenant.* Since one cannot determine who is elect and who is not, Calvin argues for the baptism of all children born of at least one believing parent.[81]

Calvin also justifies infant baptism by appealing to its benefits. By signifying children's place within the covenant, the baptism of infants nourishes parental faith. The rite confirms the promise given to believing parents that God will be God to them and to their descendants, and parents "see with their very eyes the covenant of the Lord engraved on the bodies of their children."[82] Obviously, baptism also benefits those baptized, since they are commended to other church members and (for Calvin as for Luther) have a basis for inspiring greater zeal for God by remembering their baptism. Moreover, in response to Anabaptist critiques that infants do not need baptism but remain "children of Adam" until the age of discretion, Calvin defends the need even for children to be regenerated by the Holy Spirit, implying that children who die young have been sanctified.[83] Moreover, Calvin suggests that infants may receive from the Spirit some small foretaste of the knowledge of God and a "seed" of future repentance and faith.[84]

Calvin's answer to the question of why infants ought to be baptized and how infants, who cannot understand preaching, can be saved contrasts with that of some of his contemporaries. For all their insistence on the necessity of baptism, Luther himself and Lutheran pamphleteers also sought to lessen parents' anxiety over the death of unbaptized infants by stressing, like Calvin, that baptism alone did not save. However, they also insisted on the need for faith and argued, unlike Calvin, that infants "not only can have faith, but infant faith is declared to be the most effective kind."[85] Whereas Luther came to advance a

---

80. *Institutes* (1559), 4.16.5; OS 5:309. This passage and nearly the entire defense of infant baptism in chapter 16 stems from the 1539 edition of the *Institutes.* The only major addition in 1559 is the refutation of Servetus in *Institutes* (1559), 4.16.31. In the *Institutes* much more than in his commentary, Calvin stresses the literal interpretation of Jesus' embrace of babes and children (Luke 18:15; Matt. 19:14; Mark 10:13) in justifying his position (*Institutes* [1559], 4.16.7).

81. Calvin writes, "The children of Christians are considered holy; and even though born with only one believing parent, by the apostle's [Paul's] testimony they differ from the unclean seed of idolators" (*Institutes* [1559], 4.16.6; cf. 4.15.22; OS 5:309; cf. 5:303).

82. *Institutes* (1559), 4.16.9; OS 5:313.

83. Calvin is likely responding to Balthasar Hubmaier, but for a related understanding of children's nature, see Keith Graber Miller's discussion of Menno Simons's notion of "complex innocence" in this volume.

84. *Institutes* (1559), 4.16.18-20; OS 5:321-25.

85. Ozment, *When Fathers Ruled,* 165.

notion of infant faith in his polemical writings against the Anabaptists, Calvin abandoned the notion of infant faith that he had advanced in the first edition of the *Institutes* in his efforts to address Anabaptist critiques that infants are incapable of faith and repentance. Even in his polemical treatise against the Anabaptists, his main justification lies in the fact that children are part of the covenant, sealed now with the sign of baptism and before in circumcision.[86] And while he speaks in the *Institutes* of a baptismal regeneration, a planting of the seed of faith, he says that this is not the same as the faith of mature believers — and, in fact, he prefers to leave undetermined whether their knowledge of God is the same as faith.[87]

In his theology of baptism, Calvin also adopted the innovative and controversial Lutheran notion that after baptism sin remains but is no longer imputed as sin.[88] Because faith and repentance are but a "seed" and because of remaining sin, children need to grow into an understanding of their baptism. Calvin is convinced that if they do, they will be "fired with greater zeal for renewal" when they learn of and meditate on their own baptism as infants.[89] Although the growth of the seed of faith and repentance, like its planting, is the work of the Holy Spirit, Calvin also held that the church had an obligation for a program of religious education in order to inspire and guide children to lives of piety. For this reason, he called in the *Articles Concerning the Organization of the Church* (1537) and again in the *Ecclesiastical Ordinances* (1541) for a program of weekly catechetical instruction and for teaching small children to sing psalms so that they might help lead congregational singing.[90] According to the *Ordinances,* catechism classes

---

86. CO 7:56-64; in English, John Calvin, *Brief Instruction . . . Against the Errors of the Common Sect of the Anabaptists* (1544), in *Treatises against the Anabaptists,* ed. and trans. Benjamin Wirt Farley (Grand Rapids, Mich.: Baker Books, 1982), 44-56. Calvin's position contrasts with that of later Lutherans, such as Johannes Wigand, who apparently did make the sinfulness of infants the primary justification for infant baptism (Mark D. Tranvik, "Defending Infant Baptism in the Lutheran Reformation," paper presented at the Sixteenth Century Studies Conference in Toronto, October 22-25, 1999).

87. *Institutes* (1559), 4.16.19; OS 5:323.

88. *Institutes* (1559), 4.15.10-11; OS 5:292-93.

89. *Institutes* (1559), 4.16.21; OS 5:325-26.

90. *Articles Concerning the Organization of the Church,* in *Calvin: Theological Treatises,* Library of Christian Classics, vol. 22 (Philadelphia: Westminster Press, 1954), 54; *Ecclesiastical Ordinances,* in *The Register of the Company of Pastors of Geneva in the Time of Calvin,* 40, 45, 47. The establishment of catechetical instruction may follow the Synod of Bern (1532); see Nubuo Watanabe, "Calvin's Second Catechism: Its Predecessors and Its Environment," in *Calvinus Sacrae Scripturae Professor: Calvin as Confessor of Holy Scripture,* ed. Wilhelm Neuser (Grand Rapids, Mich.: Eerdmans, 1994), 229. Of course, there was widespread interest in catechisms as a tool of instruction in the sixteenth century; see Strauss, *Luther's House of Learning,* 151-75.

would be held at noon on Sundays. Parents were required (and repeatedly reminded) to bring their children to lessons. The catechism was also studied in school, and the pre-Reformation tradition of writing alphabet primers containing basic catechetical information appears to have flourished.[91] Adults also were required to attend catechism if they showed insufficient understanding of proper teaching. Before a child was admitted to the Lord's Supper at about age eleven or twelve, he or she had to give a public confession of faith before the congregation. This confession was preceded by an oral interview with a pastor and consisted of a brief summary of the child's belief.

Calvin prepared his first catechism in 1537 and produced a Latin translation in 1538. After his return to Geneva in 1541, he wrote another, longer catechism, which he also subsequently translated into Latin.[92] In this second work, he adopted a question-and-answer format and divided the material into fifty-five lessons covering 373 questions. He also reordered the topics, now beginning not with the law, like Martin Luther, but rather with faith, like his former Strasbourg colleague, Martin Bucer.[93] This modification is significant and indicates both the centrality of faith for Calvin and his emphasis on the use of the law as a guide for Christian life. It also assumes that the catechumen is not brought to initial faith but rather to a deeper understanding of faith through catechesis. Under the section on faith, the catechism explores the Creed; this exploration is followed by the discussion of the law. The next topic is prayer, and includes discussion of the Lord's Prayer. The final sections cover worship, both Word and sacraments. There is no mention of election or predestination and little discussion of human sinfulness.[94] In fact, the assumption throughout is that the child is to be treated as a Christian, not converted to the true faith. The child is fully Christian, "not because the faith expressed in his answers has yet

91. R. Peter, "L'abécédaire genevois ou catéchisme élémentaire de Calvin."

92. Calvin prepared the catechism in 1541-1542. For an English translation of the Latin edition of 1545, see *The Catechism of the Church of Geneva* (1545), in *Calvin: Theological Treatises,* 88-139. On this catechism, see Watanabe, "Calvin's Second Catechism"; Olivier Millet, "Rendre raison de la foi: Le Catéchisme de Calvin (1542)," in *Aux origines du catéchisme en France,* ed. P. Colin et al. (Tournai: Desclée, 1989), 188-207; Guy Bedouelle, "Das Entstehen des Katechismus," *Internationale katholische Zeitschrift "Communio"* 12 (1983): 25-40; Peter Y. DeJong, "Calvin's Contributions to Christian Education," *Calvin Theological Journal* 2, no. 2 (November 1967): 162-201; Peter, "L'abécédaire genevois ou catéchisme élémentaire de Calvin," 11-45; Brouwer, "Calvin's Doctrine of Children in the Covenant"; and Marius B. Van't Veer, *Catecheses en Catechistische Stof bij Calvijn* (Kampen: J. H. Kok, 1942).

93. For discussions of the relationship between Calvin's catechism and those of others, see Millet, "Rendre raison de la foi"; and Watanabe, "Calvin's Second Catechism."

94. For a more detailed discussion of the contents of the catechism, see Monter, *Calvin's Geneva,* 103-7.

been experienced by him, but because it is his by right of God's gracious covenant, and it is his duty and privilege to lay claim to it."[95]

Despite the question-and-answer format, it appears that the ultimate aim of catechetical instruction was not rote memorization of the catechism, although this undoubtedly accounted for a large part of catechetical instruction. The *Ordinances* do not mandate this as a prerequisite for participation in the sacrament. Moreover, the length and complexity of many of the lessons (especially those treating the Trinity and the eucharist) are simply beyond the comprehension of even the most precocious child.[96] The Genevan catechism likely served as a "point of doctrinal reference" for the pastor or teacher, who may have availed himself of other, shorter texts to prepare pre-adolescents to make their public profession of faith.[97] Given the presence of more age-appropriate instructional texts (such as the ABC primers), it is probable that Calvin did not intend children, most of whom would have been under the age of thirteen, to learn the material by heart. Repetition and memorization, though surely not of the complete text, were likely tools employed to achieve a higher goal: to provide the young, through dialogue with the minister or teacher, with the vocabulary for articulating their growing faith.

No doubt political concerns for uniformity of belief and practical disappointment over the incomplete success of the catechetical endeavor mingled with these lofty aspirations in the reality of catechetical instruction in Geneva as elsewhere in sixteenth-century Europe. However, the fact that in practice catechesis may have been less effective than reformers and magistrates hoped ought not to diminish appreciation of the fundamental conviction motivating the attempts to provide solid religious education for the young. Catechetical instruction was more than "a conscious, systematic, and vigorous effort . . . to change the human personality through pedagogical conditioning."[98] There can be no denying that this was in part true. However, the main motivation appears to have been the same as the justification for baptism: this education was the right of Christian children, and it was the duty of their elders to provide them with the tools for nourishing their nascent faith. The seriousness with which Calvin himself took this duty is indicated in the attention he directed toward the catechism in the last years of his life. In 1563, he held two "congregations,"

95. Brouwer, "Calvin's Doctrine of Children in the Covenant," 26.

96. DeJong suggests that for this reason, perhaps, the Genevan catechism was replaced in the Reformed tradition by the Heidelberg Catechism and the two Westminster catechisms; see "Calvin's Contributions to Christian Education," 182-83.

97. Millet, "Rendre raison de la foi," 202; cf. Peter, "L'abécédaire genevois ou catéchisme élémentaire de Calvin." For a similar judgment concerning Luther's catechisms, see Strauss, *Luther's House of Learning*, 159-60.

98. Strauss, *Luther's House of Learning*, 175.

or public lectures, on the catechism.[99] In his deathbed farewell to his fellow pastors, Calvin claimed that the magistrates' pledge to maintain both catechism and discipline were the two conditions of his agreement to return to Geneva in 1541. He also recalled his hasty preparation of this catechism and regretted that he had never had a chance to revise it. Completely a man of his times in his conviction that "all change is dangerous," he urged his fellow pastors to change "nothing," even if the catechism, the prayers, and the baptismal formula had been hastily composed.[100] Without embracing this fear of change or even many of his recommendations concerning children and their place in society and the church, later generations might do well not to challenge his foundational assumption that the children of the Christian faithful, no matter how young, are fully Christian; they are not only the heritage given by God to their families but are themselves true inheritors of God's covenant.

Conclusion

Like many of the other figures and movements covered in this volume, John Calvin bequeaths to subsequent generations a mixed legacy on the topic of children. As noted, many of his seemingly contradictory notions about children originate in the variety of scriptural testimony and in the plurality of classical and contemporary understandings. Yet he combines these traditional insights in distinctive ways that hold for contemporary Christians both peril and promise.

The most obvious and broadest criticism to be leveled at Calvin applies to the Christian theological tradition as a whole. Despite the appreciation of children, their importance, and the concern for their physical, intellectual, and spiritual well-being, children do not constitute a major theme in Calvin's theology. Children are included, but marginally; they are subsumed under a notion of human nature that takes as its normative representative the adult male. Sin, for example, is understood as a failing in mind and will — something that hardly fits, as Calvin himself realizes, the experience of young children.

Another potential pitfall lies in the kinds of conclusions one might draw from the traditional notion of the sinfulness of infants. Calvin himself appears not to have advocated the use of physical force in response to sin in children; though he recognized the need for parental discipline, his explicit remedies for sin were baptism and education (albeit strict and structured) into faith and

---

99. *Deux congrégations et exposition du catéchisme: première réimpression de l'édition de 1563,* introduction and notes by R. Peter (Paris: Presses Universitaires De France, 1964).
100. For a translation, see Monter, *Calvin's Geneva,* 95-97.

morality. However, some scholars have claimed that the idea of children's nature as a "seed of sin" was taken up by later Calvinists and used in some cases to justify harsh treatment of children in order, literally, to beat the hell out of them.[101] Yet the essay by Catherine Brekus in this volume shows that these claims have been inappropriately (although innumerably) made in the case of the Calvinist Jonathan Edwards. Other studies find no logical connection between an emphasis on original sin and physical mistreatment. One in fact argues that despite the belief in original sin and double predestination among Calvinist Puritans, they no less than their Arminian Anglican contemporaries perceived sin in children as different from sin in adults, did not regard children as foul and loathsome, and adopted strikingly similar pedagogical and disciplinary strategies that downplayed the use of corporal punishment.[102] Another concludes that although some Puritan leaders advanced prescriptions for harsh discipline and justified these on the grounds of original sin, parents largely refused to follow them in the home, though they were implemented in the schools.[103] The point is that while in Calvin's case a pessimistic view of human nature did not lead to the sanctioning of extreme physical punishment, this connection had some currency, though perhaps limited, among some of his spiritual descendants. As Marcia Bunge argues in her essay in this volume, the language of depravity, original sin, and breaking the self-will (a phrase apparently not common in Calvin's writing) is complex and need not reflect or lead to harsh attitudes toward or abusive treatment of children. Moving in a constructive direction, I suggest that it is not the language itself or understandings of human nature as fallen that are the problem. But in articulating these concepts today, theologians ought to be explicit in ruling out possible misinterpretations of them that would diminish the fundamental humanity of children.

Calvin's concept of election, which holds that only some children receive God's promise and have a claim to membership in the covenant, might seem to justify unequal treatment of children, but even this was not so exclusive as it might have been. It is important to remember that Calvin held that one could not know whether a particular child was elect or reprobate and thus believed that one should treat all children as if they were members of the covenant. Practically this meant that children of one believing parent would be baptized and raised in the church. But it is not clear what this might have meant for treat-

101. See especially Anthony Fletcher, "Prescription and Practice: Protestantism and the Upbringing of Children, 1560-1700," in *The Church and Childhood*, ed. Diana Wood (Oxford: Blackwell, 1994), 325-46; and Stone, *The Family, Sex, and Marriage: England, 1500-1800*.

102. Piercy, "The Cradle of Salvation: Children and Religion in Late Sixteenth and Seventeenth Century England." See also Pollock, *Forgotten Children*.

103. Fletcher, "Prescription and Practice."

ment of an Anabaptist, Jewish, or Muslim child. Obviously, Calvin would not want these children baptized (unless one of their parents converted), but would he argue that society had certain obligations toward them, on a par with what would be provided for baptized children? Modern Christians must seek other foundations for the equal regard for children — foundations that provide more explicitly for humane and just treatment of all children, not just Christian ones. Perhaps one such foundation for egalitarian treatment can be sought in the very different assumption of Calvin's contemporary, Menno Simons, that every child, Christian or not, was protected by Christ up to a certain age.[104]

Finally, the very common recognition that children grow into their sin or their faith may imply in certain cases that young children are somehow incomplete and not quite fully human. The entire pedagogical strategy developed out of classical models and prevalent in Calvin's day is designed to form children into responsible adults: good citizens and godly Christians. Children are raised *into* humanness for their own good, for the good of society, and for the glory of God. Even where this does not result in attitudes like that of the seventeenth-century Puritan Lewis Bayly, that the infant is nothing but "a brute having the shape of a man," it *may* reflect the assumption that childhood is not essentially valuable in itself but rather a stage to be gotten through.[105] Our own age is itself caught up in an "instrumentalization" of childhood. As Martha Stortz has noted, we point children "too rapidly toward the adults they will become. . . . Childhood . . . is something you do on the way to becoming an adult."[106] Contemporary theological and ethical writing needs to be sensitive to these pitfalls when discussing spiritual development. I do not think that the language of growth and advancement must be given up completely. But theologians and ethicists ought also to find ways of expressing and appreciating the spiritual (and other) gifts of even young children. While other theologians in the Reformed tradition, notably Friedrich Schleiermacher and Horace Bushnell, provide a broader basis for this, one could also take seriously Calvin's claim that even nursing infants glorify God and, though lacking words and understanding, are mature defenders of the faith.[107]

Certainly sixteenth-century assumptions about society, family relations, and church limit the utility of many of the child-rearing strategies employed in Geneva in Calvin's day. But inasmuch as a general ignorance of children as children and the assumption of the normative character of adulthood shape our own

104. On Menno Simons, see the essay by Keith Graber Miller in this volume.

105. Lewis Bayly, quoted in Fletcher, "Prescription and Practice," 326.

106. Martha Ellen Stortz, "Whither Childhood?" *Dialog* 37, no. 3 (July 1998): 162.

107. On Schleiermacher and Bushnell, see the essays in this volume by Dawn DeVries and Margaret Bendroth.

mentality, we can see glimpses of our own reality in the Genevan situation. For example, underlying the battles over the baptismal policy and the admonishments to send children to catechism are tensions over the rights of parents and the duties of society that are no less prevalent in our day. In seeking to draw boundaries, it is important not to let children simply function as a battleground for adult conflicts over what is best for them, to view children as property. Further insights may be gleaned from Calvin's views on parental obligations. Calvin's concern for good parenting is praiseworthy. However, it suffers from a narrowness of focus on the parental duty to nourish children spiritually. In our day, advocates of "family values" often focus on moral and spiritual upbringing as the primary remedy to social ills. Yet especially in theological writing, as well as in the practice of faith communities, a concern for godliness and faith must be combined with more explicit attention to physical, emotional, and intellectual nurture as parental obligations if we are to combat the widespread contempt for and neglect of children in our society.[108] In addition, Calvin's argument that viewing children as gifts of God and baptizing them young are essential prerequisites for good parenting may well provide a positive foundation for Christian attitudes toward children and understandings of child rearing, but they must be carefully articulated in a religiously plural context. These notions support the idea that children are not private possessions and may indeed enhance a Christian parent's attitude toward and care of his or her child and of children in general. But certainly an atheist, a non-Christian, or an Anabaptist is solely for lack of these notions at no disadvantage when it comes to raising a child.

Happily there are also elements of promise in Calvin's understanding of children and even views that mitigate against the pitfalls, both potential and real, sketched above. Calvin's notion of spiritual maturity, unlike his understanding of sin, is not necessarily cast from an androcentric and adult-centered mold. Proclaiming God's goodness and glory is not even an exclusively human activity but the work of all creation. This activity is not something that people grow into but one that they, along with the entire order of nature, are called (indeed, designed) to engage in at every moment of existence. That even young children can *as* children fulfill their potential is confirmed in Calvin's literal interpretation of Psalm 8:2 and evident also in his attitude toward those who die young. Such a life is not incomplete; even though it may seem to us that the child was cut off in the "flower" of youth, he or she was already "ripe" in the sight of the Lord. Such insights may well contribute to an endeavor to construct a theology that takes seriously childhood as an end in itself.

108. On these attitudes, see Herbert Anderson and Susan B. W. Johnson, *Regarding Children: A New Respect for Childhood and Families* (Louisville: Westminster/John Knox Press, 1994), 2-4, 13-18.

Closely related to the idea of the fundamental humanity of children is the notion of their complete inclusion in the family of faith and the establishment of practices designed to reinforce this assumption. Once again, the rite of infant baptism need not be the necessary foundation for this view. However, Calvin's particular interpretation of the sacrament has great merit for those traditions furthering this practice. First, the primary justification for baptism lies not in sinful humanity's need for cleansing from sin but rather in the claim all Christians — children included — lay to God's promise of reconciliation. Second, baptism recognizes children as gifts of God and "mirrors of God's grace." How might present attitudes toward children's bodies (and especially the physical needs of poor children) be transformed and neglect and abuse of children challenged by taking seriously, with Calvin, the conviction that children bear in their very bodies the engravings of the divine covenant — that children's bodies are, in a sense, sacraments? Finally, baptism marks the formal recognition of the child in a community of covenant to which he or she already completely belongs. More than this, baptism also stands for the pledge and prayer of that community, the church, to take seriously the status of children as full inheritors of God's covenant. Baptism so understood is the rite signaling the church's calling to be a sanctuary for children.

Part of the fulfillment of that obligation lies in the duty to provide religious education and spiritual nurture for children as well as adults. Calvin and his contemporaries clearly perceived this need and sought to meet it through regular catechetical instruction utilizing materials considered in that day to be age-appropriate. In Geneva at least, children laid further claim to their inheritance through a public profession of faith at the culmination of catechetical instruction. While contemporary Christians will wish to avail themselves of a broader range of materials and methods of instruction, they would do well to emulate Calvin's commitment to the spiritual nurture of children by providing religious instruction that is stimulating, serious, and theologically and pedagogically sound. In so doing, they would affirm the fundamental humanity of children and share in Calvin's belief that Christians of all ages and abilities possess the capacity to testify to their faith and witness to the glory and goodness of God.

7. Complex Innocence, Obligatory Nurturance, and Parental Vigilance: "The Child" in the Work of Menno Simons

KEITH GRABER MILLER

"Dear reader," writes Menno Simons (1496-1561) in a Reformation-era treatise on Christian baptism, "if faith always brings forth good fruits . . . what fruits and righteousness which are evidence of faith do our little children bring forth?" The former Catholic priest, who committed himself to the Anabaptist movement in 1536, asserts that it may be "plainly observed" that children do not manifest "the fruits of faith, or of the new birth." Instead, "all they do is nurse, drink, laugh, cry, warm themselves, play, etc., as has been the nature of children from the beginning."[1] Throughout his voluminous writings during his quarter-century as an Anabaptist leader, Simons echoes this theme of what might be called "complex innocence," a recognition of the absence of both faithfulness and sinfulness in children, but an "innocence," as he describes it, tempered with the acknowledgment of an inherited Adamic nature predisposed toward sinning. Simons's perspective on the child's nature, shared by most other sixteenth-century Anabaptists before and after him, then utterly obligated parents and the Christian community to nurture children "in the fear of God by teaching, admonishing, and chastising them," serving also as models of an "irreproachable life," so that when their children come to the "years of dis-

---

1. Menno Simons, "Christian Baptism," in *The Complete Writings of Menno Simons, c. 1496-1561* (hereafter *CWMS*), translated from the Dutch by Leonard Verduin and edited by J. C. Wenger (Scottdale, Pa.: Herald Press, 1956), 240. Simons wrote this treatise in 1539, only three years after becoming an Anabaptist.

Student assistant P. Michael Zimmerman Freed assisted with the initial research for this chapter.

194

cretion," they may "hear, believe, and accept the most holy Gospel of Jesus Christ."[2]

Simons, whose followers came to be known as Mennonites,[3] came into leadership in the fledgling Anabaptist movement just over a decade after its inception. Contemporary Mennonites and other related groups, including the Old Order Amish and the Hutterites, trace their historical origins to this sixteenth-century movement, which was part of what has become known as the "left wing" of the Protestant Reformation, or as the Radical Reformation. The Anabaptists agreed with much of what the Reformers were seeking to do but believed that the Reformers were not going far enough on some issues. Of central importance to early Anabaptist leaders, including Simons, was the autonomy of the church from the state in matters of worship and religious practice; the separation of Christians from the "worldly" realm of politics; rejection of the use of "the sword"; and the necessity for baptism into the church to be voluntary, based on an adult commitment to follow in the way of Christ.[4]

In part, this study seeks to provide an accurate description of the early Anabaptists' theological rationale for rejecting infant baptism, a rejection often misunderstood by other sixteenth-century Reformers. The Anabaptists' practice of believers' baptism illuminates much about their views of children and childhood nurture as well as their perspective on the nature of Christian faith. The study also illustrates the degree to which the Catholic and Protestant persecution of Anabaptists affected their understanding of the earthly family and their recognition of the need for extended family networks. Simons, one of the core leaders and most prolific writers among the early Anabaptists, provides a window into the movement's theological convictions about children. Among his key contributions to our understanding of children are his notions that all children are covered by God's grace, whether or not they have made a commitment of faith, and that parents and the Christian community together are responsible for nurturing children toward voluntary commitments of faith and discipleship.

2. Simons, "Christian Baptism," *CWMS*, 257.

3. The larger Anabaptist family consists of more than a score of denominations. A sociological analysis of contemporary Mennonite families can be found in J. Howard Kauffman and Leo Driedger, *The Mennonite Mosaic: Identity and Modernization* (Scottdale, Pa.: Herald Press, 1991), especially chapter 5, "Changing Family Patterns."

4. Descendants of the sixteenth-century Anabaptists now number more than a million around the world.

The Family Life of Simons and the Anabaptists

In Simons's later years, in a controversy about the ban's disruption of families (those banned could have no physical contact with family members still in the church), he wrote that the heavenly marriage between Christ and the believer's soul was more important than the earthly marital relationship of husband and wife. Nonetheless, he married about a year after leaving the Catholic priesthood in 1536 and had at least three children with his wife Geertruyd, a former Beguine from his home village of Witmarsum.[5] Apparently only one of Simons's children, a daughter, outlived him; he was preceded in death by Geertruyd, his son Jan (named after Menno's brother, who also died young), and a daughter whose name is lost to the historical record.[6]

While little is known about Simons's family life, occasionally his letters include greetings from other family members, and he expresses regret that his family has to suffer along with him because of his mission work. "I with my poor, weak wife and children have for 18 years endured excessive anxiety, oppression, misery and persecution," he laments in an unusual moment of self-pity in 1554. "At the peril of my life I have been compelled everywhere to drag out an existence in fear," he says, while other preachers "repose on easy beds and soft pillows," being greeted as doctors, lords and teachers, while "our recompense and portion must be fire, sword and death."[7] The Anabaptist leader,

---

5. For more on Simons's views of women and marriage, which are dealt with in only a cursory way here, see, for example, Beth Kreitzer, "Menno Simons and the Bride of Christ," *Mennonite Quarterly Review* 70, no. 3 (July 1996): 299-318; John Klassen, "Women and the Family among Dutch Anabaptist Martyrs," *Mennonite Quarterly Review* 60, no. 4 (October 1986): 548-71; Betti Erb, "Reading the Source: Menno Simons on Women, Marriage, Children, and Family," *Conrad Grebel Review* 8, no. 3 (Fall 1990), 301-20; and William R. Wohlers, "The Anabaptist View of the Family in Its Relationship to the Church" (Ph.D. diss., University of Nebraska–Lincoln, May 1976).

6. The surviving daughter, who moved to Hoorn, gave some information about Simons to the historian and minister Pieter Jansz Twisck. Geertruyd apparently died in 1557, and though an editor's note in *CWMS* suggests that both daughters survived Menno, more recent sources suggest this is not the case. For the quite limited information about Menno's family, see *CWMS*, 25 and 250 (which contain contradictory information about whether one or two daughters survived Menno); Cornelius Krahn, "Menno Simons," in *The Mennonite Encyclopedia*, vol. 3, ed. Cornelius Krahn (Scottdale, Pa.: Mennonite Publishing House, 1973), 580; and Piet Visser and Mary S. Sprunger, *Menno Simons: Places, Portraits, and Progeny* (Altona, Manitoba: Friesens, 1996), 28, 38, 54. Simons was born in Witmarsum, Friesland, the son of a peasant named Simon. He apparently had three brothers: Peter, Tijd, and Jan.

7. Simons, "Reply to Gellius Faber," *CWMS*, 674. In his "Pathetic Supplication to All Magistrates" (1552), Simons writes that "some of us, and not a few, must naked and plun-

hounded and hunted throughout the quarter-century he spent in the movement, rarely stayed in one city more than a year or two. While evangelizing or on the run, Simons frequently was separated from his family. More than four thousand of his Anabaptist siblings experienced martyrdom at the hands of both Protestant and Catholic authorities,[8] a reality that destroyed families, orphaned countless children, and shaped Anabaptist theological convictions. Simons, fortunate enough to escape his pursuers throughout his life, died of natural causes in January 1561 and was buried in an unmarked grave in his garden. Simons's collected writings, compiled in a thousand-page tome titled *The Complete Writings of Menno Simons,* include theological treatises on baptism, the Incarnation, church discipline, the nurture of children, discipleship, and other doctrinal matters as well as replies to his many critics, prayers, hymns, and a handful of letters to friends and churches.

Most sixteenth-century Anabaptist sources reflect little of actual family life[9] or family affections, save the sparse references to greetings from one family to another embedded in correspondence. The exception is Thieleman J. van Braght's *Martyrs Mirror of the Defenseless Christians,* which identifies by name eight hundred Anabaptist martyrs, as well as hundreds of others throughout Christian history.[10] The text, still in print after more than three hundred years, graces many contemporary Mennonite homes, an ever-present symbol of faithfulness and fragility. In addition to detailing the executions of the sixteenth- and seventeenth-century martyrs — with tongue screws, torn flesh, burlap-sack drownings, and stake-burnings aplenty — *Martyrs Mirror* preserves letters from men and women awaiting their deaths, offering us rare, passionate, emotive glimpses into the affections of both fathers and mothers. Such letters are confirmation of Steven Ozment's assertion that sixteenth-century spouses and families evidenced tenderness, mutual respect, and love.[11] Among the Anabaptists whose correspondence is recorded, spousal and parental affection is unmistakable. In one testament from 1573, Janneken Munstdorp writes to her one-month-old child, born to her in prison:

---

dered wander in foreign lands with our poor, weak wives and little children, bereft of the fatherland, our inheritance, and the fruit of our heavy toil" (256).

8. Paul Schowalter, "Marytrs," *The Mennonite Encyclopedia,* vol. 3, 524.

9. Piet Visser and Mary Sprunger write, "We know very little about what daily life was like for the average Anabaptist or how they practised faith. It was too dangerous for those involved to record their activities on paper." See *Menno Simons,* 109.

10. John Klassen, in "Women and the Family among Dutch Anabaptist Martyrs," 549, notes that the text identifies 1,007 persons by gender. Of these, 288 — or 28.6 percent — were women. The gender of another 661 martyrs is not identified.

11. Steven Ozment, *When Fathers Ruled: Family Life in Reformation Europe* (Cambridge: Harvard University Press, 1983).

Oh, that it had pleased the Lord, that I might have brought you up . . . but it seems that it is not the Lord's will. . . . The Lord could still take me from you, and then, too, you should have to be without me, even as it has now gone with your father and myself, that we could live together but so short a time, when we were so well joined since the Lord had so well mated us, that we would not have forsaken each other for the whole world, and yet we had to leave each other for the Lord's sake. So I must also leave you here, my dearest lamb; the Lord that created and made you now takes me from you. . . . I herewith commend you to the Lord, and to the comforting Word of his grace. . . . I hope to wait for you; follow me, my dearest child. Once more, adieu, my dearest upon earth; adieu, and nothing more; adieu, follow me; adieu and farewell.[12]

Two months later, Munstdorp was burned with three others, leaving her orphaned child with her parents, who "had not yet come to the true faith."[13] Although Simons and his immediate family avoided the executioners, throughout his life as an Anabaptist he was keenly aware of the possibility of permanent familial separation and death. Later we will examine the impact that awareness had on Anabaptist commitments to children and families.

Complex Innocence and Infant Baptism

Anabaptists' enemies similarly elicited and thereby contributed to the preservation of Radical Reformation views of the nature of children. Simons writes

12. Thieleman J. van Braght, *The Bloody Theater or Martyrs Mirror of the Defenseless Christians* (Scottdale, Pa.: Herald Press, 1982), 985-87. The text, written by an elder in the Flemish Mennonite congregation at Dordrecht, was first published in Dutch in 1660, and has been translated and published repeatedly since that time. According to John Klassen, "Fifteen Anabaptist fathers and five mothers wrote at varying lengths about what kind of adults they wanted their children to become. An additional fourteen men mentioned children in letters to their wives but gave no descriptive counsel on upbringing, and another four men and one woman did not mention any children in their letters to their spouses." Klassen says thirty-nine letters were addressed to wives, and another three were addressed to "my chosen sister," which likely meant one's spouse as well ("Women and the Family among Dutch Anabaptist Martyrs," 567). Klassen helpfully identifies the *Martyrs Mirror* pages on which letters from men and women can be found: for men's letters, see pp. 469, 478, 516, 564-66, 581, 581-87, 626, 641-43, 652, 676-80, 699-702, 704-7, 709-11, 713-14, 715-21, 750-57, 760-61, 770-74, 798-809, 848-63, 877-80, 883-84, 909-16, 933-35, 947-51, 951-54, 954-60, 969-71, 1004, 1026-35, 1065-68, 1076-80, 1086-88; for women's letters, see pp. 646-69, 667-70, 926-29, 981-83, 984-86.

13. Editor's note, *Martyrs Mirror*, 987.

about baptism and childhood innocence repeatedly, in response to those who accused Anabaptists of being "murderers of infants' souls" because they refused to baptize their newborns. Sixteenth-century law, in some places, required that unbaptized infants who died be buried in pagan cemeteries alongside Turks and infidels.[14] Simons ardently argues, in the sharp rhetoric characteristic of Reformation writings, that one cannot find a single word in Scripture commanding "such monkeyshine and mockery" as infant baptism. His words, and the tradition's practice of adult baptism, reveal much about Anabaptists' sacramental theology as well as their views of the nature and nurture of children. Simons's concerns are that the practice of baptizing children is not only unbiblical but presents both theological and practical problems. As we will see below, he believes infant baptism is not necessary, since God's grace covers all children, nor is it efficacious in calling forth discipleship or changing the relationship between the child and God. Worse yet, it deceives its practitioners. Parents are comforted by thinking that through this baptismal transaction their children are Christians, and in this way they are raised from the cradle "without the fear of God, so that when they come to the years of discretion they have as yet no knowledge of the Word of God." Such people, says Simons, "walk all their lives, trusting in infant baptism, upon a dark and crooked way without confession, without faith and new birth, without Spirit, Word and Christ."[15]

Simons, accurately representing the tradition he both inherited and then shaped, insists that baptism be reserved only for those who have come to the

14. William Klassen, "The Role of the Child in Anabaptism," in *Mennonite Images: Historical, Cultural, and Literary Essays Dealing with Mennonite Issues,* ed. Harry Loewen (Winnipeg: Hyperion Press Ltd., 1980), 18. Anabaptist women sometimes had difficulty finding midwives to attend them in childbirth, since midwives often were the first to know whether children were baptized. In addition, midwives who espoused Anabaptist views alarmed authorities, who feared the women might dissuade parents from baptizing their newborns. Occasionally Anabaptist midwives were forbidden to practice their craft, though the need for such skilled assistance often mitigated such objections. On this, see Claus-Peter Clasen, *Anabaptism: A Social History, 1525-1618* (Ithaca, N.Y.: Cornell University Press, 1972), 148-49.

15. Simons, "Reply to False Accusations," *CWMS,* 570. Similar passages are found throughout Simons's writings, including "Christian Baptism," 250, 257, 263; "Reply to Gellius Faber," 710; and "The True Christian Faith," 390. Simons and other Anabaptists believed that Scripture trumped all other sources for theological or ethical reflection. In "Foundation of Christian Doctrine," Simons responds to the charge that Origen and Augustine said they received infant baptism from the apostles. "To this we answer by asking, Have Origen and Augustine proved this from the Scriptures? If they have, we would like to hear it, and if not, then we must hear and believe Christ and His apostles, not Augustine and Origen" (137). In "Reply to Gellius Faber," Simons writes, "As to [Gellius's] writing that children are reckoned as believers, this is merely reason and human opinion which cannot be substantiated by a single word of the Scriptures" (710).

age of discretion and professed their faith. "Little ones must wait according to God's Word until they can understand the holy Gospel of grace and sincerely confess it; and then, and then only is it time, no matter how young or how old, for them to receive Christian baptism."[16] Those who baptize children, says Simons, do so before that which is represented in baptism — *faith* — is found. "This is as logical," he says, "as to place the cart before the horse, to sow before we have plowed, to build before we have the lumber at hand, or to seal a letter before it is written."[17] In an earlier treatise he raises particular concerns about Luther's rationale for infant baptism. Simons consistently speaks vituperatively about the Catholic Church he once served as a priest, but most of his written arguments are with the Reformers, whom he believes stopped short of completing the movement they began. While honoring Luther as a "learned man," he cannot grasp why the Reformer

> holds that children without knowledge and understanding have faith, whereas the Scripture teaches so plainly that they know neither good nor evil, that they cannot discern right from wrong. Luther says that faith is dormant and lies hidden in children, even as in a believing person who is asleep, until they come to years of understanding. If Luther writes this as a sincere opinion, then he proves that he has written in vain a great deal concerning faith and its power.[18]

16. Simons, "Christian Baptism," *CWMS*, 241. Later in the same treatise, he says, with even more vigor, that "an infant so long as it is in its infancy will remain ignorant, simple, childish, and disposed to evil, even though it be baptized a hundred times and its baptism be still more subtly asserted by six times a hundred garbled Scriptures. It is plain to an intelligent person that with infants are found neither doctrine, faith, spirit, nor fruits of the divine commandment" (272). For an excellent recent account of Simons's debates with other Reformers on this and other issues, see Abraham Friesen's "Present at the Inception: Menno Simons and the Beginnings of Dutch Anabaptism," *Mennonite Quarterly Review* 72, no. 3 (July 1998): 351-88.

17. Simons, "Christian Baptism," *CWMS*, 259. In 1524 Johannes Kessler writes with similar punch regarding the baptism of unbelieving children: "A child is an unreasoning being and it would be like dipping any other unreasoning animal, like a cat or a stick, into the water." See *The Sources of Swiss Anabaptism: The Grebel Letters and Related Documents*, ed. Leland Harder (Scottdale, Pa.: Herald Press, 1985), 298.

18. Simons, "Foundation of Christian Doctrine," *CWMS*, 126. Simons clearly rejects his Protestant peers' arguments that infant baptism paralleled Hebrew circumcision. This is problematic, he says, because Abraham was in the covenant before he was circumcised; because children were in the covenant before they were circumcised on the eighth day; and because although only males were circumcised, women and female children also "had the promise in common in the promised seed, the promised land, the kingdom and glory." See Simons, "Foundation of Christian Doctrine," 132. See also, for example, "Reply to Gellius Faber," 706.

For Simons, baptism represents the believer's faith, while for Luther and Calvin baptism represents God's promise, a contrast Simons may not fully grasp or appreciate.

Implicit in Simons's understanding of the inappropriateness of infant baptism is his view of human nature, sin, grace, and faith, all of which have implications for the Christian nurturance of children. From his earliest writings as an Anabaptist to those near the end of his life, Simons acknowledged, in words similar to those of other Reformers and early church theologians, humans' inborn, sinful nature, "namely the lust or desire of our flesh," a sin "contrary to the original righteousness" that is "inherited at birth by all descendants and children of corrupt, sinful Adam, and is not inaptly called original sin."[19] Through the "first and earthly Adam," all people "became wholly depraved and children of death and of hell."[20] Simons seemingly shares, in part, the theological anthropology of Augustine, Luther, Calvin, and others, making his refusal to baptize infants all the more perplexing to his accusers. The Anabaptist leader does not espouse an optimistic view of humans' inherited nature. But neither is his view of human nature compatible with Augustine's non-innocence, which suggested that children had the will to do harm, but not the strength, so childhood innocence meant simply being *unable* to harm another.[21] Nor is it identical with other Reformers' notions of "total depravity," which suggested that all born of Adam's sin deserved condemnation for original sin apart from any willful sinning.[22] Simons delineates between a *nature* predisposed toward sin and actual *sinning*, disallowing the former to obliterate childhood innocence and identifying only the latter as that for which believers have responsibility before God. This distinction is similar to the one drawn by Thomas Aquinas in his discussion of *infantia*, as developed by Cristina Traina in this volume, though Simons clearly is less constrained by Augustine than is Aquinas in espousing his view. Such a perspective was shared not only by others in the Radical Reformation movement but also by Zurich reformer Huldrych Zwingli, with whom the Swiss Anabaptists first collaborated and then contested in the early years of the Reformation.

In his "Reply to False Accusations" (1552), Simons distinguishes between

19. Simons, "Reply to False Accusations," *CWMS*, 563.

20. Simons, "Foundation of Christian Doctrine," *CWMS*, 130. Simons notes repeatedly humans' Adamic nature. Among other places, see "The True Christian Faith," 391; "A Pathetic Supplication to All Magistrates," 527; "Reply to False Accusations," 563-64; and "The Nurture of Children," 948-50.

21. On this, see Martha Ellen Stortz's essay on Augustine in this volume.

22. See, for example, Barbara Pitkin's analysis of John Calvin in this volume. Pitkin notes that Calvin recognized that the younger a child, "the less he or she manifests the effects of sin." However, even young children are never entirely innocent, in Calvin's view.

four types of sins: (1) the inherited, original sin described above; (2) the fruits of the first sin, known as "actual sin" by theologians, some of which are adultery, fornication, avarice, drunkenness, hatred, envy, lying, theft, murder, and idolatry; (3) "human frailties, errors, and stumblings which are still found daily among saints and regenerate ones," including "careless thoughts, careless words, and unpremeditated lapses in conduct"; and (4) the sin of the committed disciple who has "tasted of the heavenly gifts" and is "born of God" but willfully "renounces all knowledge and grace, rejects the Spirit and Word of God" and "ejects [sic] the sweet, new wine which he had drunk," returning "to the broad way" and refusing "to be subjected."[23] While Simons is distressed by the second form of sin, and troubled by the third sort of "lapses," in which he appears to participate, he clearly is most exercised about the fourth kind of post-baptismal sin, which also was perceived as a greater problem in earlier parts of Christian history.

Where Simons differs from Augustine and his contemporaries, however, is on the soteriological ramifications of the corrupt, sinful nature, particularly as it is embodied in children. "Our entire doctrine, belief, foundation and confession," says Simons, "is that our innocent children, as long as they live in their innocence, are through the merits, death, and blood of Christ, in grace, and partakers of the promise."[24] In "Christian Baptism," Simons writes that children are given this promise "out of pure and generous grace, through Christ Jesus our Lord." He cites the Synoptic Gospel accounts of Jesus encouraging children to come to him,[25] "for such is the kingdom of heaven."

> Inasmuch as He has shown such great mercy toward the children that were brought to Him that He took them up in His blessed arms, blessed them, laid His hands upon them, promised them the kingdom of heaven and has done no more with them; therefore such parents have in their hearts a sure and firm faith in the grace of God concerning their beloved children, namely, that they are children of the kingdom of grace, and of the promise of eternal life through Jesus Christ our Lord . . . and not by any ceremony.[26]

23. Simons, "Reply to False Accusations," *CWMS*, 563-65. For treatments of this question of original and other sin, see, for example, Robert Friedmann, "The Doctrine of Original Sin as Held by the Anabaptists of the Sixteenth Century," in *Essays in Anabaptist Theology*, ed. H. Wayne Pipkin (Elkhart, In.: Institute of Mennonite Studies, 1994), 147-56; and Richard E. Weingart, "The Meaning of Sin in the Theology of Menno Simons," 157-73 in the same volume.

24. Simons, "Reply to Gellius Faber," *CWMS*, 708.

25. Matthew 19:14, Mark 10:14, and Luke 18:16. See also Judith Gundry-Volf's examination of these passages in her essay in this volume.

26. Simons, "Christian Baptism," *CWMS*, 280. Another Dutch Anabaptist leader, Dirk Philips, echoes Simons's teaching on this and other points related to children and

Even though children inherit original sin,[27] they remain innocent through the grace of Christ, which is efficacious in covering their sinful natures, leaving them innocent. Those who die "before coming to years of discretion," says Simons earlier in the same treatise, "die under the promise of God."[28] While such grace for children might come particularly for those of Christian parentage, he suggests at several points that Christ's grace is for children of both believing and unbelieving parents.[29] Christ's grace is not only for those within the Christian fold but for all children, apparently including even those of the Turks.

The Age of Discretion

Menno Simons, along with other Anabaptists and their twenty-first-century descendants, was reluctant to identify a precise age of discretion or accountability, which no doubt frustrated his opponents. As they grow, children often show

---

baptism: "But just as sin had its origin in disobedience and began with the knowledge of good and evil in Adam, in like measure it also occurs with children. For, though they all come from a sinful Adam, yet original sin (as people call it) is not imputed to them by God to damnation, for the sake of Jesus Christ. For they are in part like Adam and Eve were before the fall, namely this, that they being simply both good and bad, understand neither good nor evil. But as soon as they come to a knowledge of good and evil and step from simple ignorance into conscious wickedness, and they sin against the Lord through their own disobedience and transgression of the divine Word and command, then it is the proper and appointed time that they first be taught, yes, with the law of God be heartily admonished to penitence." See *The Writings of Dirk Philips, 1504-1568*, translated and edited by Cornelius J. Dyck, William E. Keeney, and Alvin J. Beachy (Scottdale, Pa.: Herald Press, 1992), 77.

27. Contemporary Mennonite theologian Marlin Jeschke, arguing like an Anabaptist, says, "Original sin is not a given or fixed quantity of evil brought like a load of karma into the world by a particular soul at its birth, a quantity of evil that can be removed by some liturgical act or rite. . . . Those who take original sin most seriously are not necessarily those who hasten children to the font, but rather those who nurture children and youth most effectively toward the actualization of the 'not I, but Christ' form of life in which the dominating influence of the Adamic nature is broken by God's love and power, so that even if that original fallen nature is not totally removed, the Spirit of God becomes the governing power of an individual's life." See Jeschke, *Believers Baptism for Children of the Church* (Scottdale, Pa.: Herald Press, 1983), 87-88.

28. Simons, "Christian Baptism," *CWMS*, 241.

29. This is evident in, for example, "Christian Baptism," *CWMS*, 280, and also in "Reply to Gellius Faber," 707, where he is expressing other Protestants' views of this broad grace, "which according to my opinion would not be altogether contrary to the Scriptures," and implicit in, for example, "Foundation of Christian Doctrine," 130-38.

"the evil seed of Adam," says Simons, and "as they get a little older, they manifest it still more."[30] Simons gives the reader little direct help as to when the age of discretion begins, though clearly faith "is not found in children of two, three, or four years, both the Scriptures and common sense teach us."[31] As noted above, in "Christian Baptism," Simons says "little ones" need to wait "until they can understand the holy Gospel of grace and sincerely confess it; and then, and then only is it time, *no matter how young or how old,* for them to receive Christian baptism."[32] What may be unique about Simons's understanding is a concern for spiritual maturity that does not always coincide with chronological maturity.

Contemporary Mennonite theologian Marlin Jeschke, speaking out of the tradition he inherited from Simons, suggests that although identifying a precise age of accountability is complex, we are obliged to recognize its reality. He notes that Pedobaptist churches acknowledge it through the ritual of confirmation; Judaism has bar mitzvahs and bas mitzvahs; secular society makes a distinction between juveniles and adults in law courts; minimum ages for marriage are established; children are protected through labor laws; and in most primitive societies, puberty rites mark a passage between childhood status and adult roles. "In short," says Jeschke, "the consensus of experience and wisdom of the entire human race establishes what theology has usually designated an age of accountability, an age of spiritual and moral responsibility."[33] Jeschke's argument is designed to support the convictions of Simons and other Anabaptists that children ought not be baptized until they are able to make commitments of discipleship, but he is perhaps clearer than Simons about the general

30. Simons, "Christian Baptism," *CWMS*, 240.

31. Simons, "Reply to Gellius Faber," *CWMS*, 709.

32. Simons, "Christian Baptism," *CWMS*, 241 (emphasis mine). Editor J. C. Wenger says in a footnote to the passage, "Menno recognizes that the age of accountability does not come at a uniform point in the maturation of children." In Wenger's own theology text, *Introduction to Theology* (Scottdale, Pa.: Herald Press, 1954), he says, "The Scriptures do not assign any age as the normal one in which to accept Christ. Intelligent Christian parents and leaders therefore do not precipitate conversion before the child has reached a sufficient degree of maturity, intellectual, moral, and spiritual. Only the Holy Spirit is able to know when the proper time has arrived in the life of the individual to turn to Jesus. It would appear that frequently the Holy Spirit does begin His gracious work of repentance in the life of the adolescent about the time he enters puberty. . . . It is cruel and unchristian to attempt to precipitate a conversion experience in those who are not sufficiently mature to experience conversion" (276).

33. Jeschke, *Believers Baptism for Children of the Church*, 112. Jeschke goes on to note that in a society when youths are kept in school by law until age sixteen, cannot drive until sixteen, and cannot vote until eighteen, "we are deluding ourselves if we ask them to make authentic decisions with respect to personal faith at a much earlier age."

period of accountability, which is only implicit in Simons and, as noted, is not always linked with a particular age.

In *Luther's House of Learning,* historian Gerald Strauss lays out the sixteenth-century understandings of a three-fold period of childhood and youth and their pedagogical implications.[34] Up until age seven, parents and teachers had many opportunities for molding because "receptivity of mind and malleability of character" were at their highest. Beginning at age seven, the age of "reason," the senses and memory were working, understanding was intact, and habits were still unset, though "even at that tender age the seeds of obstinacy and malice were ready to burst into full-grown weeds to choke the delicate fruits of good instruction." By age fourteen, the opportunity had passed "unless sound ideas, good habits, and correct responses had already been firmly implanted." Even then, though, the destructive force unleashed as the young person came to sexual maturity could throw a reconstructed personality.[35]

While Simons was reticent to identify such specific developmental categories, some of his faith peers did. A few Hutterites, the communal-living Anabaptists who emerged even before Simons made his commitment to the Radical Reformation movement, articulated stages of development similar to those of Augustine, Aquinas, Luther, Calvin, and other thinkers discussed in this volume. Peter Walpot (1521-1578), a powerful and effective Hutterite bishop in Moravia, detailed several stages of growth and designated appropriate discipline at each stage. He moved from those who were unable to talk, help, or understand, who therefore should hardly be punished at all; through those who have started school and whose self-will[36] needed to be broken; through those who could maintain a good conscience and had been given communal tasks, who should be diligently punished if they were derelict because they understood their obligations but were reluctant to meet them.[37] As we will see below, Hutterite bishop Peter Riedeman (1506-1556) similarly articulated a step-by-

---

34. These developmental categories have classical origins, of course. See Martha Ellen Stortz's essay on Augustine in this volume, for example.

35. Gerald Strauss, *Luther's House of Learning: Indoctrination of the Young in the German Reformation* (Baltimore: The Johns Hopkins University Press, 1978), 106.

36. As we will see in several of the following essays in this volume, including Marcia Bunge's work on August Hermann Francke (1663-1727), later theologians further develop and nuance this notion of breaking children's "self-will." Although we do not find a full description of this in Walpot, it seems to include moving the child away from self-direction and toward full obedience to the parents, and hence to God. Francke believes the self-will (which is the human fallen will that is self-centered) needs to follow God's will, and usually speaks in positive terms about this process of reorientation.

37. "A Hutterite School Discipline of 1578 and Peter Scherer's Address of 1568 to the Schoolmasters," trans. Harold S. Bender, *Mennonite Quarterly Review* 5, no. 4 (October 1931): 231-44.

step pedagogy for the developing child and youth. In a twentieth-century analysis of "Early Anabaptist Ideas about the Nature of Children," Hillel Schwartz suggests that Anabaptists established a variety of criteria which signified the shift from "child" to "youth." Among these, according to Schwartz, are the development of self-will; the ability to understand, and to choose between alternatives; and an exhibition of a "fear of God," or conscience.[38]

In practice, the age of accountability and hence baptism has varied dramatically among Anabaptist-Mennonite young people. Early Anabaptist leaders Hans Hut (d. 1527), Ambrosius Spittelmaier (c. 1497-1528), Hans Schlaffer (d. 1528), Peter Walpot, and some others thought that adults aged thirty and over qualified for believers' baptism. Their view was based in part on the desire to imitate Jesus, whose baptism at age thirty was an example for his followers.[39] At the other extreme, Balthasar Hubmaier (c. 1480-1528) saw age seven, when "the will is developed," as the minimum age for baptism. The *Martyrs Mirror* indicates that some Anabaptists, presumably baptized believers, were teenagers. Some children in Austrian lands were baptized by the ages of ten and eleven.[40] Among more recent Anabaptists, the age of accountability has seemingly settled in the mid-to-later teens. In a 1963 census of the Mennonite Church, the median age of baptism for those over fifty had been 16.5; for those thirty to forty-nine, the median age was 14.5; and for younger people (ages twenty to twenty-nine), it was 13.6.[41] Nonetheless, in 1959 one Mennonite scholar, im-

---

38. Hillel Schwartz, "Early Anabaptist Ideas about the Nature of Children," *Mennonite Quarterly Review* 47, no. 5 (April 1973): 107.

39. Rollin Stely Armour, *Anabaptist Baptism: A Representative Study* (Scottdale, Pa.: Herald Press, 1966), 55, 61, 93-95. I am grateful to John Klassen ("Women and the Family among Dutch Anabaptist Martyrs," 564) for calling my attention to these examples.

40. Noted in John Klassen, "Women and the Family among Dutch Anabaptist Martyrs," 564. Klassen also notes the impreciseness of medieval and early modern sources regarding the terms "childhood" and "youth." "*Puer* and *adolescens,* or 'child,' could mean one as old as 28," says Klassen, "and a *iuvenis,* or 'youth,' could mean one as old as 49 or 50, although normally no more than 21 or 28." Here Klassen draws on Klaus Arnold, *Kind und Gesellschaft in Mittelalter und Renaissance* (Paderborn: Schöningh, 1980), 20-26.

41. Melvin Gingerich, "The Mennonite Family Census of 1963," mimeographed report (Goshen, In.: Mennonite Historical and Research Committee, 1965). Another study a decade later identified the median age of baptism for those fifty and over at 16.2; for those thirty to forty-nine at 14.9; and for those twenty to twenty-nine at 14.2. See J. Howard Kauffman and Leland Harder, *Anabaptists Four Centuries Later: A Profile of Five Mennonite and Brethren in Christ Denominations* (Scottdale, Pa.: Herald Press, 1975), 71-72. Fear that the age of baptism was dropping prompted Mennonite Church leaders to pass a position statement entitled "The Nurture and Evangelism of Children," which sought to defend "early adolescence" as the usual beginning time of accountability. The statement was passed on 27 August 1959 and published in Ernest D. Martin, *The Story and Witness of the Christian Way* (Scottdale, Pa.: Mennonite Publishing House, 1971), 81-83.

plicitly suggesting a later date for baptisms, noted that Gregory of Nazianzus and Jerome, both of whom were nurtured in Christian homes, were baptized in their twentieth and thirtieth years, respectively.[42] Such recommendations were a response to the apparent decrease in age at baptism, a fact that chagrined many leaders in the church.

While Simons himself does not delineate clear stages of growth, he does address the various signifiers noted by Schwartz. For the most part, though, he is reluctant to attach these developments to particular ages, though it is clear such characteristics are not present in the first few years of life. Although it is difficult to specify a particular age of accountability, Simons's view is that grace covers children's sinful nature, with children taking increasing responsibility for their actual sins as they age.[43]

The Nature of Anabaptist Nurture

Such a view of the nature of children makes imperative the careful, intentional, aggressive, and vigilant nurturing of children in Christian faith. While God has determined the overall course of history, humans essentially have free will to choose between right and wrong, Simons and other Anabaptists believed. Along with most of his faith peers, Simons gives parents the primary responsibility for this nurturance toward righteousness. Because children are committed to parents' special care, says Simons, "Be sure that you instruct them from their youth in the way of the Lord, that they may fear and love God."[44] In a similar vein, but more forcefully, he says elsewhere: "It behooves true Christians to teach, to admonish, to reprove, and to chasten their children; to set them an example in all righteousness, to rear them in the fear of the Lord, and to care for their poor souls lest through their negligence they depart from the true path, die in their sins, and so perish at last in their unbelief."[45] Just as Moses had commanded Israel to teach their children the law, to talk of it when they sat in their houses and walked along the way, when they went to bed and rose up (Deut. 6:4), so ought the present chosen generation nurture their children's character and faith.

42. Gideon G. Yoder, *The Nurture and Evangelism of Children* (Scottdale, Pa.: Herald Press, 1959), 142.

43. Again, this is similar to the view espoused by Thomas Aquinas, as Cristina Traina notes in her essay in this volume.

44. Simons, "The Nurture of Children," *CWMS*, 950.

45. Simons, "The True Christian Faith," *CWMS*, 389. Similar passages can be found scattered throughout Simons's work. See also, for example, "Christian Baptism," 257, 281.

Such character-shaping did not take place, in Simons's view, through reading a specific catechism or a particular set of texts, but simply through parental guidance, clear boundaries, and an immersion in Scripture. The cover page of each of Simons's treatises features 1 Corinthians 3:11, a passage that many twenty-first-century Mennonites still know by heart: "For no other foundation can anyone lay than that which is laid, which is Jesus Christ." Parents were to help their children "fear God, do right and be saved."[46] Since the righteous will inherit eternal life, but the wicked will receive eternal death, Simons urges parents to lead their children on the straight path, the way of life, "watch[ing] over their salvation as over your own souls."[47]

According to Simons, parents are to seek their children's salvation just as Abraham, Tobit, and the Maccabean mother[48] did. "If they transgress, reprove them sharply," says Simons. "If they are childish, bear them patiently. If they are of teachable age, instruct them in a Christian fashion. Dedicate them to the Lord from youth."[49] Such a responsibility was borne by both fathers and mothers,[50] as

46. Simons, "The Nurture of Children," *CWMS*, 950.

47. Simons, "The Nurture of Children, *CWMS*, 951.

48. This is a reference to the Maccabean mother and her seven sons who were killed, one by one, by King Antiochus. All remained faithful, the brothers and the mother encouraging one another, making it clear they would rather die than transgress the laws of their ancestors. Just before the last brother was killed, the mother whispered in his ear, "My son, have pity on me. I carried you nine months in my womb, and nursed you for three years, and have reared you and brought you up to this point in your life, and have taken care of you. I beg you, my child, to look at the heaven and the earth and see everything that is in them, and recognize that God did not make them out of things that existed. And in the same way the human race came into being. Do not fear this butcher, but prove worthy of your brothers. Accept death, so that in God's mercy I may get you back again along with your brothers." The story is told in 2 Maccabees 7, and reads much like the accounts in *Martyrs Mirror.*

49. Simons, "The True Christian Faith," *CWMS*, 390. The only reference to children in the most recent *Confession of Faith in a Mennonite Perspective* (Scottdale, Pa.: Herald Press, 1995), adopted by both the Mennonite Church and the General Conference Mennonite Church, is on pp. 72-73: "Children are of great importance. Jesus saw them as examples of how to receive the reign of God. Children are to be loved, disciplined, taught and respected in the home and in the church. Children are also to honor their parents, obeying them in the Lord."

50. It bears mentioning that although Simons saw both fathers and mothers as actively involved in nurturing their children, he grossly misunderstood their roles in the process of conception. In several lengthy treatises, including "Brief Confession on the Incarnation," "The Incarnation of Our Lord," and "Reply to Gellius Faber," Simons propounds his problematic "heavenly flesh" incarnational theology. Drawing on Aristotelian notions about the passivity of the mother's seed, as well as John 6 and 1 Corinthians 15, Simons asserts that Mary nourished Jesus' humanity, but that its substance originated in heaven and was unaffected by Mary. The teaching, espoused by Dutch Anabaptist Dirk Philips as well, was not accepted by the Swiss Anabaptists and was dropped out fully by the Dutch by the

was true more generally for Reformation-era European families.[51] Children left to themselves, without reproof, are the shame and disgrace of both parents, believed Simons.[52] Training children toward making commitments of faith and being faithful disciples was the ever-present goal of childhood nurture. Such a life of discipleship was impossible without experiencing a new birth, being converted and changed, and parents needed to guide their children toward such conversions and commitments.

For Simons and other Anabaptists, as well as those in the tradition of Augustine, God's grace was assumed as precipitating this conversion. The Anabaptists focused their attention on what other Protestant traditions might call "sanctification" more than "justification," or at least on preparation for sanctified living.[53] The tension between nurture and conversion becomes evident for

---

mid-eighteenth century. Nonetheless, it has been an embarrassment to Mennonites throughout the centuries. Because Simons thought believers could be born anew through faith in the new Adam who had come down from heaven, he believed they could be re-created to a new state of obedience. As Marlin E. Miller notes, "This new creation manifests itself in the church without spot and wrinkle." And while the doctrine itself dropped out of Mennonite theological understandings early on, Miller says, "It may have influenced some Mennonite concepts of church, salvation, and Christian ethics considerably longer, perhaps until the present. The concept of the pure church, linked originally with the heavenly flesh Christology, has most likely contributed to both perfectionism and divisions among Anabaptists and Mennonites throughout their history" ("Christology," in *The Mennonite Encyclopedia*, vol. 5, ed. Cornelius J. Dyck and Dennis D. Martin [Scottdale, Pa.: Herald Press, 1990], 148). C. Arnold Snyder notes that Simons's earlier writings suggest that the "new being" came about through a process of change over time. He says, "This view suggests a less-than-perfect church made up of 'disciples in the making.' In the later writings Menno insists on a pure church. . . . This view suggests 'disciples already made.' The impression left by Menno's writings as a whole is that he moved progressively towards a more perfectionistic understanding of regeneration and the new being." See C. Arnold Snyder, "Keywords Relating to Discipleship in the Thought of Menno Simons," in *Discipleship in Context: Papers Read at the Menno Simons 500 International Symposium*, ed. Alle Hoekema and Roelf Kuitse (Elkhart, In.: Institute of Mennonite Studies, 1997), 105.

51. Shulamith Shahar suggests that in the Middle Ages, the prevailing belief "was that once a boy reached the age of 7, it was his father's task to educate him, while the mother continued the education of the daughters. Some writers demanded of the mother that she also provide a Christian education for her sons even after the age of 7 (and not merely that she refrain from pampering them), but her main function was always to raise her daughters — to furnish them with a religious education and to prepare them for their roles as mothers and housewives." See Shahar, *Childhood in the Middle Ages* (London: Routledge, 1990), 174.

52. Simons, "The Nurture of Children," *CWMS*, 952.

53. On this, see, for example, Cornelius J. Dyck, "Anabaptist-Mennonite Perspectives," in *Perspectives on the Nurturing of Faith*, ed. Leland Harder (Elkhart, In.: Institute of Mennonite Studies, 1983), 132-51.

those Anabaptists in the second and later generations. Anabaptist children, unlike their Catholic and most of their Protestant peers, are never assumed to be members of the church until they make their own commitments of faith. However, given that they are raised in Anabaptist homes, dramatic conversions are not expected, either: instead, the tradition calls for a gradual embracing of the faith and the Christian community through steady, integrative modeling and nurturing.

As Margaret Bendroth notes,later in this volume in her essay on Horace Bushnell (1802-1876), the nineteenth-century American theologian finds it "monstrous" and "unnatural," a form of "virtual abuse and cruelty," to "teach young children that they are depraved and fallen without offering them a genuine opportunity for conversion."[54] Such a criticism may apply to some contemporary descendants of the Anabaptists, who have been influenced by Evangelicalism and Pietism in addition to Anabaptism. This particular blending of several theological streams, some of which call for a greater awareness of depravity and earlier conversion and commitment than Anabaptism seems to desire, occasionally makes parents, if not children, anxious about their salvation. Contemporary Evangelicalism also often calls for an emotion-filled moment of decision that contrasts with the long-term training toward and commitment to discipleship inherent in early Anabaptism.

While Simons and other sixteenth-century Anabaptist parents were exceedingly cognizant of their children's bent toward sin, their admonitions to children were not unduly directed toward making them conscious of their depravity or sinful natures. Although they chastised and reproved sinful behavior, their energies, as noted above, were focused on nurturing children toward faithfulness and lives of discipleship — the formation of Christ-like character — which they genuinely believed to be possible. As would be true for most other early moderns, Anabaptist children were urged to love one another, bear with one another, do honorable work, not be prideful, flee from evil, fear God, and follow the example set by Christ. Making lifelong commitments of discipleship rather than momentary decisions for personal salvation is what was essential to the sixteenth-century Radical Reformers. Hence, children were nurtured toward this more positive, life-giving way of being, not simply left wallowing in their Adamic misery. Baptism was construed as a beginning, not an end.

Nonetheless, for the sixteenth-century Anabaptists, theological anxiety abounded for both children and parents. In a footnote to Simons's treatise "The True Christian Faith," editor J. C. Wenger remarks that the Swiss Mennonites of eastern Pennsylvania "used to have a traditional fear that their own salvation

---

54. See Margaret Bendroth's essay on Horace Bushnell in this volume.

would be imperiled or lost if their children went astray," and here "Menno teaches the same view."[55] The supreme anti-model for Simons and other early Anabaptists was the high priest Eli, who was "held responsible because he had not reproved his children enough."[56] Failure to train and nurture children toward eventual faith and baptism might have earthly as well as eternal consequences: those who did not live up to their commitment to Christ evidenced their inability to teach others. If we can't guide our children, says Simons, "we may verily lay our hands upon our mouths and keep still."[57] Christian parents are to be "as sharp, pungent salt, a shining light, an unblamable, faithful teacher, each in his own home."[58]

Some parents, Simons fears, have so much "natural affection" for their children that they fail to carry out their God-given responsibility to nurture and train their children. The predisposition toward sin is no illusion: those who do not keep a strict watch over their children, correcting and chastising them according to the Word of the Lord, may find their children's and their own souls required on the day of judgment.[59] From our youth we are "always inclined to the worst," finding nothing from "the heritage of our first birth but blindness, unrighteousness, sin, and death."[60] On his missionary trips, Simons had observed, apparently *within* as well as *beyond* Anabaptist communities, "more than enough how disorderly, improperly, yes, heathenish, many parents carry on with their children."[61] He instructs parents to keep their children away from "good-for-nothing" youngsters, "from whom they hear and learn nothing but lying, cursing, swearing, fighting and mischief."[62] It is better, says Simons in words that make many of his faith descendants squirm, to have one just child than a thousand who are unjust, and better "to die without children, than to have them that are ungodly."[63]

For Simons, obedience to parents was a cardinal virtue, and such obedience carried much theological and ethical freight for adult believers as well. In his 1558 treatise "Instruction on Excommunication," Simons refers to the "unusually strong and solemn commandment, Honor thy father and thy mother," noting that for the Hebrews those who cursed, struck, or disobeyed their parents had to die, according to the law of Moses.[64] To contemporary sensitivities,

55. Simons, "The True Christian Faith," *CWMS*, 390.
56. Simons, "The True Christian Faith," *CWMS*, 387.
57. Simons, "The Nurture of Children," *CWMS*, 950.
58. Simons, "The True Christian Faith," *CWMS*, 387.
59. Simons, "The True Christian Faith," *CWMS*, 387.
60. Simons, "The Nurture of Children," *CWMS*, 949.
61. Simons, "The Nurture of Children," *CWMS*, 952.
62. Simons, "The Nurture of Children," *CWMS*, 951.
63. Simons, "The Nurture of Children," *CWMS*, 951.
64. Simons, "Instruction on Excommunication," *CWMS*, 970.

many of Simons's injunctions, and those of his Reformation peers, seem unduly harsh. Parental modeling and instruction are significant forms of Christian nurture, but parents also are to demand obedience. Discipline from parents issues from God, and children are to obey unless the family's will conflicts with what can clearly be understood as God's will. If parents are too lenient with their child, responding with fear to every cry, the unrestrained child "becomes headstrong as an untamed horse." Citing almost verbatim the apocryphal book Sirach, which was often quoted by other sixteenth-century Reformers as well, Simons says parents should give a child "no liberty in his youth, and wink not at his follies," but instead "bow down his neck while he is young, lest he wax stubborn and be disobedient to thee."[65] Children's native disposition toward blindness and unrighteousness must be "broken, suppressed, and destroyed," and to achieve such brokenness one must not spare the rod if necessity requires it.[66] Historian Shulamith Shahar says that in medieval Christian society, the view that "he who spares the rod spoils the child" was "part and parcel of educational theory in the second stage of childhood."[67] According to Simons, again quoting Sirach, parents[68] who love their son will cause him to of-

---

65. Simons, "The Nurture of Children," *CWMS*, 951. The larger passage from Sirach 30, sometimes referred to as Ecclesiasticus or the Wisdom of Jesus, Son of Sirach, in the New Revised Standard Version is as follows: "He who loves his son will whip him often, so that he may rejoice at the way he turns out. . . . Whoever spoils his son will bind up his wounds, and will suffer heartache at every cry. An unbroken horse turns out stubborn, and an unchecked son turns out headstrong. Pamper a child, and he will terrorize you; play with him, and he will grieve you. . . . Give him no freedom in his youth, and do not ignore his errors. Bow down his neck in his youth, and beat his sides while he is young, or else he will become stubborn and disobey you, and you will have sorrow of soul from him."

66. In *Luther's House of Learning*, Strauss writes, "'Wild,' 'unbroken,' 'crude' were the adjectives most often applied to youths in their 'natural' condition, their undisciplined state. 'A child brought up at home is like an unbroken bull,' asserted a contemporary proverb; given his own way by permissive parents, a youngster will remain 'stubborn, obstinate, incapable of ruling himself, and bound to come to a bad end.' Man, 'who in his childhood is no more than a brute beast and has no other powers than those of anger and concupiscence,' needs to be tamed, and the earlier this is done the better" (96). Simons would agree with much of this perspective. He likely would temper the suggestion that in childhood youngsters are "brute beasts," though as they age they have that potential.

67. Shahar, *Childhood in the Middle Ages*, 110. In *Luther's House of Learning*, Strauss says sixteenth-century folk wisdom suggested that "the bigger the rod, the better the child." Objections were sometimes neutralized with the observation that God created the buttocks "with a generous amount of flesh so that no irreparable damage will be done when a child is whipped." Children sometimes intoned, under their masters' watchful eyes, a "hymn to the birch rod": "O, my dear rod, Teach me to fear God; Make me good, I beg, Or the hangman will have my neck" (180).

68. John Klassen helpfully notes, in "Women and the Family among Dutch Anabap-

ten feel the rod so that they may have "joy of him in the end."[69] Even though a firm hand does "smart [their children] in the flesh," well-intentioned parents will chastise and punish out of "unsullied, paternal love," to the benefit of their children.[70] For Simons, as for many of his contemporaries, this was to be "controlled beating": parents should apply the rod with restraint. "Constrain and punish them with discretion and moderation," he says, "without anger or bitterness, lest they be discouraged."[71] The precise nature of this moderation is not developed further in this treatise or elsewhere, though implicit in Simons's work is the understanding that infants and young children should be treated with more leniency. Simons and his Anabaptist peers who allow for the use of the rod also do not address the tension between this corporal punishment and their rejection of "the sword."

Simons suggests, in words amplified by the reality of Anabaptist persecution, that "properly believing parents" would rather see their children "jailed in a deep, dark dungeon" or "bound hands and feet and dragged before princes" or "exiled, burning at the stake, drowning or attached to a wheel" or "scourged from head to foot for the sake of the glory and holy name of the Lord" than to see them "with drunken dolts in taverns" or marrying "rich persons who fear not God" or adorning themselves "with silks, velvets, gold, silver, costly trimmed and tailored clothes," living "apart from God in all luxury and carnal pleasures."[72] If letters from jailed Anabaptists to their children are representative of Anabaptist sentiments, scores of Simons's followers were "properly believing" folks. Those death-awaiting parents whose letters to their children are preserved in van Braght's *Martyrs Mirror* frequently admonish their children, through and between Scripture citations (e.g., Sir. 6:18, 1 Pet. 2:11, 2 Tim. 2:22, Tob. 4:13, Matt. 11:12), to remain faithful, free themselves from impure thoughts, love not "dainties" or wine, pray for their persecutors, and obey the commandments of the Lord. The *Martyrs Mirror* became one of the primary pedagogical tools for nurture of young Anabaptists, and a large body of other devotional and didactic literature also emerged

---

tist Martyrs," that none of the women's letters to children in *Martyrs Mirror* mention using the rod. Says Klassen, "It would be interesting to know whether women in general at this time disapproved of beating and whether they understood that the use of force is not the most effective way to develop civilized and productive adults" (570).

69. Simons, "The Nurture of Children," *CWMS*, 951. Letters from imprisoned parents to their children in Thieleman van Braght's *Martyrs Mirror* often echo this sentiment. Thomas van Imbroeck writes to his wife that she should "give [their children] the rod, according to the command of the Lord, when they transgress and are obstinate; for this is also food for the soul, and drives out the folly which is bound up in their hearts" (581).

70. Simons, "The Cross of the Saints," *CWMS*, 615.

71. Simons, "The Nurture of Children," *CWMS*, 951.

72. Simons, "The True Christian Faith," *CWMS*, 386-87.

in the sixteenth and seventeenth centuries. Among these was van Braght's *School of Moral Virtues*, which first appeared in 1657 and was reprinted into the nineteenth century, and Pieter Jansz Twisck's *Instructions on How Parents and House Fathers Should Teach Their Children and Servants*.[73]

Peppered throughout the writings of Simons and many other Anabaptists are references to adult believers as "children of God," a carefully chosen descriptor. Such a reference indicated not followers' call to innocence but a call to submission.[74] Fellow Dutch leader Dirk Philips (1504-1568) says the "something good" in children is "a simple, unassuming, and humble bearing. . . . For this reason also Christ sets children before us as an example that we should in these respects become like them."[75] Just as children were to obey their earthly parents, so adult believers made a voluntary commitment to obey Christ and manifest the fruits of faithfulness in lives of discipleship.

This obedience, for children in relation to parents just as for adults in relation to God, was to be joyful and voluntary (particularly for the latter) — a cheerful form of compliance rather than disciplined drudgery.[76] For Simons, "our heavenly Father" also oftentimes chastened "His elect children" with his "paternal rod" so that they would "put into practice devout instruction and piety" and "fear God with sincerity of heart" so that they might "in this way as obedient and disciplined children of God at the end be made partakers of the promised kingdom and inheritance."[77] As Anabaptist parents chastised and re-

---

73. Both sources are noted in Dyck, "Anabaptist-Mennonite Perspectives," 141.

74. See, for example, Simons, "The New Birth," *CWMS*, 92.

75. From *Anabaptism in Outline: Selected Primary Sources*, ed. Walter Klaassen (Scottdale, Pa.: Herald Press, 1981), 185. Interestingly, the passage was included in a contemporary Mennonite devotional book, under the heading "The Breadth of Grace." See J. Craig Haas, *Reading from Mennonite Writings, New and Old* (Intercourse, Pa.: Good Books, 1992), 194-95.

76. Early Hutterite leader Peter Riedeman writes, "Thus this same Holy Spirit of God assureth us through the working of his strength in us that we are God's children. Through him we may well dare with joy and certainty to name him Father, and approach and cry to him in good confidence for all we desire, since we know that he loveth us, and in Christ hath given us all things, and that his ear is open to our cry and attentive to grant our request. Therefore we, having experienced his fatherly grace, have yielded ourselves in obedience to his will as children to our Father, that he may use all our members according to his own will and good pleasure. This his work we, as his obedient children, desire with a willing and attentive heart to endure and suffer, to let him guide our whole life and control our heart, mouth, eyes, ears, hands, feet, and all our members, so that now not we, but he, the Lord, may live and do everything in us. He also careth for us as a father for his children and doth shower upon and fill us with all good things. Therefore is God our Father and we his children." See *Account of Our Religion, Doctrine, and Faith* (Rifton, N.Y.: Plough Publishing House, 1970 [1545]), 18-19.

77. Simons, "The Cross of the Saints," *CWMS*, 615.

proved their children, they were no doubt aware of their own calling toward obedience and submission to God, and such a recognition conceivably shaped their motivations for both positive and negative discipline and tempered their responses. For Simons and other Reformers, admonition to use the rod carefully likely performed a mediating function, much as the Hebrews' "eye for an eye" did in its original context.

Woven into Simons's insistence on obedience also was a genuine love for children. "Oh, nurture and cherish your young children!" Simons writes. "Neither grieve them nor thrust them away. . . . In Christ gather the little chicks and neither scatter them nor peck at them . . . neither abuse nor disgrace them."[78] Implicit in the believers' commitment to God is the grace already received from God, and all parental discipline, reproving and nurturing, is framed within a context of loving children and desiring what is best for them. "If I love the salvation of my neighbors, many of whom I have never seen, how much more should I have at heart the salvation of my dear children . . . who are out of my loins, and are my natural flesh and blood," asks Simons.[79] Those who truly love their children will acquaint them rightly with God's Word "as soon as they have ears to hear and hearts to understand," says Simons.[80]

---

78. Simons, "Instruction on Excommunication," *CWMS*, 997. In "Women and the Family among Dutch Anabaptist Martyrs," 565, John Klassen notes the "considerable disagreement among commentators as to the nature of attitudes parents had toward children in medieval and early modern Europe": "Elisabeth Badinter sums up one side when she writes that before 1760 educators such as Juan Luis Vives (1492-1540) saw expressing playful affection and tenderness for children as proof of softness and sin. Indifference, reserve and brutality were the predominant attitudes of parents toward their children. Flandrin points out that until the middle of the sixteenth century, love between parent and child was not expected. French Catholic commentaries on the fourth commandment mentioned parent-child sentiments relating to hierarchy, such as respect, deference and contempt. When the word 'love' was used, it was used in a negative context, as in 'Have you not beaten any of your children excessively . . . because you did not love them?' But after 1574 there was only one commentary on the fourth commandment that did not prescribe parental love for children. Ozment, on the other hand, argues that far from treating the child with aloofness and cruelty, early modern parents tended to spoil their children. However, he says, their primary preoccupation was their offspring's morality and discipline. The richest and best inheritance a father could give his child was a training in self-discipline, usable skills, and a sense of honor." Evidence from the mid-to-latter-sixteenth-century Anabaptist records strongly supports Ozment's position. For the other sources besides Ozment, which was noted above, see Elisabeth Badinter, *Mother Love: Myth and Reality* (New York: Macmillan, 1981); Jean Louis Flandrin, *Families in Former Times: Kinship, Household, and Sexuality* (London: Cambridge University Press, 1979); and Lawrence Stone, *The Family, Sex, and Marriage in England, 1500-1800* (New York: Harper & Row, 1977).

79. Simons, "The True Christian Faith," *CWMS*, 386.

80. Simons, "The True Christian Faith," *CWMS*, 388.

From Simons's perspective, this is not a sentimental, overindulging sort of love. Such a "natural love," while valuable because it prompts reasonable parents to provide their children with essential food and clothing,[81] sometimes also spoils children. "The bad love of the flesh," which he had observed in his sixteenth-century context, blinds some with natural affections to the point that they can "neither see nor perceive any evil, error or defect in [their children] at all, notwithstanding they are frequently full of mischievous tricks and wickedness," disobedience to their parents, lying, quarreling, and name-calling.[82] An authentic spiritual love for children will correct problematic aspects of children's behaviors, weaknesses that need to be adjusted or eradicated for their own betterment. Such a love is expressed repeatedly, once again, in parents' letters to their children in *Martyrs Mirror*. Shortly before his death in Antwerp in 1560, Lenaert Plovier began a letter to his "dear and much beloved children" by explaining that when he was taken from them "it was not for any crime, but for the testimony of Jesus, and because I loved you unto death." Prompted by that love, Plovier writes that when his children "have reached the years of understanding," he hopes they will seek their salvation. Along with other specific charges rooted in Scripture, he admonishes them to be obedient to their mother, to not be deceitful or obstinate or quarrelsome, and to "take a Testament, and see what Christ has left and commanded us there."[83]

Apparently some of the Anabaptists were successful with their child rearing, if one can believe the occasional testimony of those outside the community. Sixteenth-century Nieuwvaert schoolmaster Pieter Claess van der Linden, an opponent of the Anabaptists, says that aside from their few heretical views, "their life and conversation is better than that of many others," and "they also seek to bring up their children in better discipline and fear of God, than many other people." The schoolmaster, who had had Anabaptist children under his tutelage, indicates they were "apter and learned more readily than others."[84] Such testimonies from outsiders are few, but the Anabaptists no doubt were warmed and encouraged by these affirmations of their child rearing.

---

81. Simons, "The True Christian Faith," *CWMS*, 338.

82. Simons, "The Nurture of Children," *CWMS*, 952.

83. Van Braght, *Martyrs Mirror*, 642-43. Such instructions are quite typical of the letters contained in the text. See also the little-known, book-length admonition by Anabaptist minister Pieter Jansz Twisck titled *A Father's Gift of 1622*, translated by Titus B. Hoover (Port Treverton, Pa.: T. B. Hoover, 1982). Twisck quotes extensively both from Scripture and from the ancient Greek philosophers in this loving "last will and testament."

84. This obscure account is found in *Martyrs Mirror*, 931, a text which obviously has its own biases. The account is noted in Wohlers, "The Anabaptist View of the Family in Its Relationship to the Church," 227. Wohlers says Anabaptists "often cited the infrequent but vocal support" of such individuals outside the brotherhood.

The Spiritual Family's Primacy over the Natural Family

Evident in the martyrs' letters, as well as Simons's writings, is the primacy of the faith community and one's faith commitments over the natural family. Along with other Reformers, Simons clearly believed that the family was ordained by God, and that the Roman church had wrongly promoted monasticism and celibacy over marriage and family. Commitments to the family are extraordinarily important, Simons appears to believe, but never should they stand in the way of the call to Christian discipleship, a costly calling which trumps other loyalties. In Matthew 10:34-38, Jesus says that a person's foes will be those in his or her household: "The one who loves father or mother more than me is not worthy of me; and the one who loves son or daughter more than me is not worthy of me." In Luke 14:26, Jesus calls on his followers to hate their parents and their spouses and their children and their siblings and even their own lives if they want to be his disciples. Strange and troubling as such injunctions seem in the twenty-first century, and contrary as they are to purported Christian "family values," the Anabaptists took seriously such counsel. In several places Simons cites such passages from the Synoptic Gospels. Urging his readers to test themselves, he asks whether they have the boldness and faith to forsake their families and take up the cross of Christ, denying themselves wholly.[85] Those in Christ's church must be ready to abandon not only money, goods, and their lives, but also their parents, spouses, children, and everything else, "if the honor of God requires it."[86]

For sixteenth-century Anabaptists, such commitments were not empty ones, but realities encountered daily. In a period of intense persecution, followers of Simons frequently were reminded that obedience to God might mean following Jesus to the cross. Either by fleeing civil authorities, which is what Simons often had to do, or by being jailed or martyred, Anabaptists often were forced to abandon their families. Historian William Wohlers says because of that, "it was not difficult for them to see this as a fulfillment of Christ's demand that they commit everything to him. It is not surprising that these conditions led them to place less emphasis on the stability of the family and more on the

85. Simons, "The True Christian Faith," *CWMS*, 394. See also 397 in the same treatise.

86. Simons, "Reply to Gellius Faber," *CWMS*, 645. Among other Anabaptists, Dutch leader Dirk Philips echoes this teaching in, for example, "The True Knowledge of God," in *The Writings of Dirk Philips*: "But now the love of God must take precedence, so that one must leave everything, every creature, everything that is visible, yes father, mother, brothers, and sisters, wife, and children, Deut. 33:9; Matt. 10:37, and our own life, Luke 14:26, for God's will, as the Scripture plainly indicates in great clarity with words and examples" (261).

firmness of their covenant with Christ."[87] This tension between competing loyalties is perhaps most poignantly — and horribly — expressed in a letter by Thomas van Imbroeck to his family shortly before he was beheaded in 1558. "Now I know that wife and children are visible, and though they are dear to me, yet I will count them as dung," says van Imbroeck, citing Philippians 3:8 and 2 Corinthians 5:16. Nonetheless, the twenty-five-year-old martyr exudes immense affection for his wife and children in this and a later letter, expressing hope that they will "appear together in the eternal joy."[88] The *Martyrs Mirror* recounts scores of stories about families being destroyed by persecution: the sword-death of Adriaen Pan while his wife was pregnant, and then her subsequent drowning after she had given birth; the killing of Peter the Spaniard, who had traveled to an Anabaptist fellowship in Antwerp and was about to return to Spain to his wife, children, friends, and acquaintances with the hope of bringing them "to the true knowledge of the truth," but who was apprehended and drowned before he could do so; and the burning at the stake of the "eloquent," "intelligent," and "kind" teacher Jacob the Chandler, whose several prison letters to his wife, children, and church leaders are preserved.[89]

For the Anabaptists, separation from families was caused by internal as well as external dynamics.[90] Simons was a strong proponent of the practice of "the ban" or "excommunication" of those who fell away from the church.[91] Simons sees the ban — which forbade common daily intimacy, conversation,

---

87. Wohlers, "The Anabaptist View of the Family in Its Relationship to the Church," 80-81. Claus-Peter Clasen, noting the hardship suffered by innocent relatives of the Anabaptists, says that with the breadwinners often gone, "sometimes those left behind had to be supported by the Poor Law, which implied great humiliation. At Nuremberg the wives of expelled Anabaptists were warned that they would also be driven out if they sent their husbands sectarian books. They had to notify the town council whenever they received or sent letters. Often the wives were badly shaken by the strain of these harrowing events. When an Anabaptist came to tell a woman at Augsburg that he had seen her husband at Strasbourg, he noticed how terribly frightened she was and left at once. The Anabaptists were too concerned with saving their souls to waste much time worrying about their families." See Clasen, *Anabaptism*, 411-12.

88. Van Braght, *Martyrs Mirror*, 578-82.

89. Van Braght, *Martyrs Mirror*, 618, 640, 714.

90. An additional external dynamic not noted in the text, but relevant as background, is the high mortality rate and the various plagues that decimated the European population during the medieval and early modern period. Some scholars have argued, though their arguments have been refuted, as noted above, that such a reality of loss forced parents to maintain emotional distance from their children to protect themselves from devastating grief.

91. The ban was imposed only on baptized church members, so unbaptized children, youth, or adults would not be subject to the ban, even though they might become quite wayward.

social or business transactions, and table fellowship with those excommunicated — as a work of divine love rather than as cruelty. Intended to be a way of chastising and correcting those who had apostatized, the ban often separated husbands from wives and children from parents. Responding to his own question "Should husband and wife shun each other on account of the ban, also parents and children?" Simons answers that, yes, when former believers become apostate, they should be shunned even by those most intimately related to them.[92] However, few Anabaptist leaders sympathized, at least for long, with marital shunning.[93] Near the end of his life, in "Final Instruction on Marital Avoidance" (1558), Simons himself makes some concessions for family members of excommunicants in the interests of spouses and children. If there be a houseful of children, he says, and the non-excommunicated parent believes they may grow up in evil and their souls be lost, the couple may stay together.[94]

Because of excommunication and even more so persecution and martyrdom, Simons and other Anabaptists broadened the nurturing community. While parents carried primary responsibility for their children, in their absence children sometimes were cared for by the extended family or others in the Christian community. Hutterites institutionalized this extended nurturing, perhaps to a fault. In his *Account of Our Religion, Doctrine, and Faith* (1545), one of the basic doctrinal statements of communal-living Anabaptists, Peter Riedeman describes the nurturing practices of Moravian Hutterites. Riedeman says that as soon as mothers weaned their children, they gave them over to the community's school. There, "competent and diligent" sisters trained the children until their fifth or sixth year, teaching them the Word of God and telling them of prayer. When they were able to read and write, they were entrusted to the schoolmaster, who further instructed them in the knowledge of God. By learning to be obedient to parents, they also learned obedience to God. "Thus we teach our children from babyhood to seek not what is temporal but what is eternal," says Riedeman. Youths were trained by the schoolmaster until they could be taught a particular practical skill, whereupon they contributed to the community through their work. After their education, upon confession of their faith, they were baptized.[95] Hutterite parents continued to have a role in raising their children, but this was a more passive role of modeling Christian disciple-

92. Simons, "Account of Excommunication," *CWMS*, 478-79. See also "Instruction on Excommunication," 971-72.

93. On this see, for example, Visser and Sprunger, *Menno Simons*, 52.

94. Simons, "Final Instruction on Marital Avoidance," *CWMS*, 1061.

95. Riedeman, *Account of Our Religion, Doctrine, and Faith*, 130-31. For a contemporary analysis of these practices, see, for example, John Hostetler and Gertrude Enders Huntington, *The Hutterites in North America: Case Studies in Cultural Anthropology* (Fort Worth: Harcourt Brace College Publishers, 1996).

ship for their offspring.[96] One contemporary Mennonite observer, William Klassen, says, "Whatever may be said against the Hutterite system of communal living, it probably represented the best alternative to the disintegration of family life which was a necessary concomitant of the first few generations of Anabaptism." Klassen asserts that while ruling authorities — who themselves often broke up Anabaptist families — accused the Hutterites of gross neglect and paganism for separating children from parents, "there is no doubt such an arrangement gave considerable freedom to the parents in their response to the Christian mission and under these circumstances probably was also best for the children."[97]

The majority of early Anabaptists were non-communal, however, with parents raising their children without the aid of parochial educational institutions. In their early decades in western Europe, they lived and worked and were often schooled alongside Catholic and Protestant members of their communities. However, unlike Thomas Aquinas, Martin Luther, and John Calvin, who expected much from "public" schools, sixteenth-century Anabaptist-Mennonites appeared to place little hope in any educational institutions beyond the family and the church. This was true even though many of their children attended state-run schools. Mennonites established few private schools in western Europe, even in later generations.[98] Simons, himself educated in a monastery after his parents consecrated him to the service of the Catholic Church as a youth, makes no reference in his voluminous writings to children's

96. Claus-Peter Clasen writes, "Clearly the Hutterite educational system imposed a great sacrifice on parents by separating them from their children. . . . Rigid rules were laid down concerning visits and gifts: parents had to ask permission even to take their children for a walk. The Hutterites mitigated the rigor of this system by allowing parents to have their children during the day for four weeks in the year. Some women could not endure the separation and returned with their children to Germany. . . . Obviously the Hutterite boarding schools were aimed at destroying such special bonds between parents and children, for such bonds were incompatible with life in a Hutterite community. People who reared their own children would naturally consider the interests of their children first and think of the community only afterward. They might even try to provide for their children's future by amassing property. As a result the old class distinctions would reappear. In the Hutterite community, by contrast, both parents and children would be emotionally attached to the congregation — at least that is what the leaders hoped. They even went so far as to bury children without notifying their mothers. However extreme their doctrines, it must be admitted that the Hutterites were consistent. Ultimately the institution of the family may very well not be compatible with the principles of a classless society." See Clasen, *Anabaptism,* 270-71.

97. Klassen, "The Role of the Child in Anabaptism," 28.

98. In Russia, North America, and elsewhere, Mennonites have established far more parochial schools than in Europe, partly because of the greater homogeneity of their settlements in these locations than in western Europe.

formal education outside the home or Christian community. Although Simons and a number of other first-generation Anabaptist leaders were educated, often in university or para-university settings, early in the movement's history a suspicion of scholarship and higher education developed. Scholarly devices such as syllogisms (logic) and synecdoche (literature and hermeneutics) were seen as contrivances "to blunt the clear, literal meaning and demands of Scripture."[99] Simons writes that "learnedness and proficiency in languages I have never disdained, but have honored and coveted them from my youth." However, he says, this is because the "precious Word of divine grace has come to us" through the knowledge of languages, and we should employ languages in "genuine humility and to the glory of God and the service of our fellows."[100] Many educated Anabaptist leaders were martyred in their early years, often after being convicted through the arguments of theologians and other educated authorities, and they were replaced with less educated church members. By the mid-sixteenth-century, most Anabaptists shared the same suspicions of scholarship that many other medieval laypersons had.

Partly because they placed little faith in state-run schools, Anabaptist believers recognized their dependence on the larger church for assisting with the shepherding of their children. Near the end of his "Instruction on Excommunication," Simons lauds the various persons who take care of the flock of Christ — shepherds and teachers in the church and fathers and nurses and "spiritual mother hens."[101] For the Anabaptists, others frequently needed to take on primary rather than secondary roles when biological parents were imprisoned or killed. Depending on the time period and the beneficence of civil authorities, Anabaptists sometimes were unable to choose those who cared for their children in their absence. In some cases, persecutors intentionally placed orphans with Catholic or Protestant families. In other cases they simply made no arrangements for the children, who then needed to fend for themselves until another family saw their plight and took them in. Thieleman J. van Braght notes that the children of Hans Meyli Jr. and his wife were "put out among strangers" after their parents' arrest in 1639, a fact which "must have caused no small sorrow and anxiety to the hearts of these imprisoned parents." In spite of their love for their afflicted children, the Meylis refused to apostatize. Finally, and unexpectedly, they were reunited with their children when they were released on Good Friday 1642, "keeping a good conscience."[102]

99. Walter Klaassen, "Scholarship," in *The Mennonite Encyclopedia*, vol. 5, p. 799.
100. Simons, "The Incarnation of Our Lord," *CWMS*, 790.
101. Simons, "Instruction on Excommunication," *CWMS*, 996-97.
102. Van Braght, *Martyrs Mirror*, 1110-11. Among the scores of tragic and powerful stories in the book of martyrs' tales is the description of Maeyken Wens's death. On 5 October 1573, Wens was burned at the stake after having her "tongue screwed up," a common

Other Anabaptists either were given the opportunity to choose their children's caretakers or spirited them away to relatives before authorities could take them into custody. Although the separation clearly was traumatic, as evidenced in the anguish-laden letters from prison, Anabaptist parents seemed comforted to know their children would be cared for, loved, and nurtured in the faith. While imprisoned in Zealand before he was burned at the stake on 9 February 1569, Hendrick Alewijns writes to his sisters and brothers in the fellowship, "O beloved church of God, take care of my three poor, dear little orphans, that are without parents, without possession, or inheritance." To his children he writes, in turn, about his regret that he cannot in these circumstances fulfill his "fatherly love and debt of discipline," but he commends them to God and to his fellow believers, "fully confident that you will be well, very well, taken care of, out of love, for God's sake and mine." Friends in the church will have guardianship over the three children, says Alewijns, "as though they were your parents," so he instructs them to "be subject most obediently, as dear children, to the friends, and you will endear yourselves to them all."[103] The father then writes several pages of "careful Scriptural instruction," charging his son to make copies for his younger sisters, encouraging them to show their love for each other in whatever ways they can, even though they are not living together but distributed among several families in the church.[104]

Soetgen van den Houte, whose husband had been martyred before she was put to death on 27 November 1560, counseled her "beloved lambs" Betgen and Tanneken to "obey your uncle and aunt, and your elders, and all who instruct you in virtue."[105] While perhaps little comfort by modern standards, the breadth of the nurturing community apparently allowed some Anabaptist parents to faithfully face their deaths, knowing that their children likely would receive care by parent-substitutes in the fellowship. Their theological convictions also assured them that, even if their earthly separation was permanent, if they and their children remained faithful, "we shall hereafter meet in one fold (John

---

practice to prevent Anabaptist testimonials during their public executions. Adriaen Wens, the woman's fifteen-year-old son, could not stay away from the place of execution, so he took his three-year-old brother and went to a bench "not far from the stakes erected, to behold his mother's death." Horrified by the sight, Adriaen lost consciousness during the actual burning, but afterward went to the place where she had been martyred and hunted in the ashes until he found "the screw with which her tongue had been screwed fast, which he kept in remembrance of her" (980). The gruesome scene is depicted in one of Jan Luyken's 105 etchings, which were first used in the 1685 edition of the text.

103. Van Braght, *Martyrs Mirror*, 749-51. Alewijns's wife had been martyred before him.

104. Van Braght, *Martyrs Mirror*, 757.

105. Van Braght, *Martyrs Mirror*, 649.

10:16) with all God's chosen children, at the resurrection of the just."[106] In any event, Simons and other Anabaptist parents believed faithfulness to the point of familial separation and death better served God, their children, and their religious community than did presence when such was possible only through recantation and apostasy.

Conclusion

In his article on the child in Anabaptism, William Klassen says it would be his forebears' wish "that we take from them the good and leave the rest in the same way that we regard the historically conditioned forms, which, having served them, we can now discard."[107] Whether or not Simons and other figures whose views are explicated in this volume had such a wish, any thoughtful reappropriation must distinguish between theological wheat and chaff. In Simons, as well as in the other historical characters in this volume, one finds plenty of both. From a contemporary perspective, most notable in the chaff category, perhaps, are the charges to bow down the necks of children, breaking, suppressing, and destroying their native dispositions. As Marcia Bunge illustrates in her chapter on German Lutheran Pietist August Hermann Francke (1663-1727), for some later theologians such "breaking" was more nuanced than it appears in Simons and some other sixteenth-century figures. We also should use care both in interpreting the language of "breaking the self-will" and in judging our theological predecessors, who rather consistently write about restraint in applying discipline.

Ironically, as I write this chapter, a debate rages on MennoLink, an e-mail chat group for heirs to Simons's tradition, about whether "breaking the will" of a child is desirable or sinful, and if the former, how it should be done. "I have believed for years and still believe that the will of the child must be broken without damaging the spirit," says one parent and church leader in his posting. "This takes loving and firm discipline which is painful without being harmful." Another parent, not recognizing his flawed account of origins, writes,

---

106. Van Braght, *Martyrs Mirror*, 587. The line is from a letter by Joris Wippe to his children before he was put to death at Dortrecht on 28 April 1558. The day following his drowning in a wine cask filled with water, Wippe was hanged by his feet from the gallows "as an object of derision to the people." Three of his letters came into the possession of van Braght, though he "doubtless would have written more," says the editor, if prison officials had not kept him from having ink. His final letter to his children, cited here, was written with mulberry juice. See 584-85.

107. Klassen, "The Role of the Child in Anabaptism," 32.

"'Breaking the will' bespeaks using fear and coercion rather than reason and love. The need to break the will comes from a 'total depravity' view of human Fallenness, which is a Fundamentalist perception." Yet another worries about how sharply the will may be curbed before the spirit breaks. "I also am a father," he says, "with a fabulously energetic and testosterone-overloaded six-year-old son. I'm doing the best I can to be the banks of the river rather than a dam, but ultimately, parenting is an act of faith on my part." A mother writes that breaking wills is "usually an abusive process": "We all agree that training children is a valid concept. But 'breaking' wills and training children are not interchangeable concepts." In the various MennoLink postings, even the "will-breakers" seem distanced from the apparent harshness of Simons's sixteenth-century admonitions.

Often those from outside the Mennonite tradition express surprise that sixteenth-century Anabaptists did not reflect on the apparent discontinuity between corporal punishment and rejection of "the sword." Indeed, though some contemporary Mennonites find physical punishment of children inconsistent with nonviolence, no sixteenth-century Anabaptist writer — nor any other pre-twentieth-century Mennonite, to my knowledge — makes this link. That may be due, in part, to the Anabaptist reluctance to write abstract treatises or to reflect philosophically beyond what could be known from the biblical text. In addition, they were primarily concerned with lethal violence, which they knew well from the receiving end, and which undoubtedly seemed decidedly different from their physical will-breaking. In any event, for Anabaptists in the early centuries, and for most of their peers in the Protestant and Catholic traditions, it was self-evident that training children to be obedient to their parents, and to God, necessitated corporal punishment.[108] While some twenty-first-century Mennonites still defend this principle, others suggest that spanking children is inappropriate for those committed to peacemaking and nonviolence. In our own household, which includes three zesty children under age eight, we have chosen not to spank so that we can tell our young sons and daughter, with integrity, "We don't hit you, and we don't want you to hit others. We're not the kind of people who hit." Such words, no doubt, would have seemed strange to Simons, who may well have perceived us as negligent parents.

More generally, Simons's expectations that youth and baptized disciples will move toward a kind of purity and near-perfection, wrought through their new birth and participation in Christ, may place unreasonable expectations on committed yet fallible believers, contributing to a nurturing process that is more restrictive and rigid than is reasonable. Related to this is Simons's prob-

---

108. I am grateful to Mennonite historian John D. Roth for confirmation of this historical information in e-mail correspondence.

lematic, intentional splitting of families through "the ban," which from a contemporary perspective likewise appears misguided, as it did to many of his sixteenth-century peers as well. One can appreciate, in Simons's context, that families will be divided because of persecution, but to purposefully add to those divisions, marginalizing and shunning family members when they fall short of community standards, is tragic.[109]

Instructive in the early Anabaptist experience, as evidenced in *Martyrs Mirror,* is the care that orphaned children received from the broader Christian community. In the contemporary world, peopled with millions of children orphaned by warfare, genocide, AIDS, and other natural and human causes, the compassion of Anabaptist families and communities is exemplary. Today, however, we need to be conscious of extending care, as well as protection and justice, far beyond "our own" children.

Instructive in Simons's own perspective is his calling for the intentional and vigilant nurturing of children. Children's character is malleable and can be shaped in various directions. Parents and others who care for children, therefore, have the responsibility to nurture diligently their offspring toward lives of integrity, discipleship, and faithfulness. Although descendants of Simons still do not baptize their children, in most Mennonite communities infants are "dedicated" during a church service, perhaps more formally than they were in the early years of Anabaptism. Such a dedication service, which varies widely in practice, reflects a theological understanding not all that distinct from that of other Reformers, including Calvin, for whom infant baptism signaled, in part, the faith community's responsibility for children, providing a foundation for the present view of the church as a sanctuary for children.[110] In Anabaptist-Mennonite child dedication services, parents publicly commit themselves to loving, instructing, and training their children. Further, all of those within the religious community are called to model lives of discipleship for their younger charges. Congregations often repeat, at the time of children's dedications, this pledge: "We promise, with humility and seriousness, to share in your child's nurture and well-being. We will support, by our example and words, your efforts to provide a loving and caring home, where trust in God grows and Christ's way is chosen." The statement concludes with the hope that "our shared life and witness" may make the parents' task "both joyful and fruitful."[111]

109. Some might suggest that one might apply a modified version of Simons's ban to those who commit the current familial sins of verbal, physical, or sexual abuse of a spouse or children, where a form of ceasing contact and a reluctance to reintegrate may be appropriate.

110. On this, see Barbara Pitkin's essay on John Calvin in this volume.

111. *Hymnal: A Worship Book,* ed. Rebecca Slough (Scottdale, Pa.: Mennonite Publishing House, 1992), no. 791.

Also to Simons's credit — in contrast with at least *some* of the other figures whose views are explored in this volume — he appears to recognize that children are not just small-framed adults, and that they should be given the freedom in their earliest years to "nurse, drink, laugh, cry, warm themselves, play, etc.," with few parental expectations and few worries about their imperfections. Implicit in his writings, at least with a generous reading of his treatises, is a valuing of childhood in its own right. Children ought not be trained in guilt too early on, made to feel depraved and despicable. Instead, they should be made conscious of the blessing and embrace of God, introduced to the Jesus who took them upon his knee and called adults to be as they are. In Simons's view, Christ's grace covers young children, frees them from immediate responsibility for their own natures, and gives them space and time to gradually develop and mature.[112] Moreover, for Simons, as for some of the other Reformers, this grace is broad, covering not only believers' children but *all* children. Physically, politically, and economically embodying this spiritual reality to the impoverished children in our midst, those who are abused, and the orphans we create or encounter is essential for those who represent the God manifested in Jesus. If God's grace covers all of God's children across the world, in every faith and nation, believers' treatment of their own children as well as those of outsiders, strangers, and enemies — their young neighbors at the gate — must reflect such grace.

112. This complex innocence does not, of course, negate the need for chastisement and correction, in Simons's view.

8. *"Wonderful Affection": Seventeenth-Century Missionaries to New France on Children and Childhood*

CLARISSA W. ATKINSON

Along with the gospel, Christian missionaries carried to the New World distinct and deeply held beliefs and assumptions about children and childhood. Such beliefs and assumptions are embedded in culture,[1] and in Christian contexts associated also with the theological anthropology of particular times, places, and religious subgroups or denominations. In the seventeenth century, the ideologies of childhood of Roman Catholic missionaries to New France were tested and developed in the harsh environment of a mission field that drew them into close and intense encounters with people of cultures radically unlike their own. To Jesuit and Ursuline missionaries, the indigenous people of eastern Canada held not only different but horrifyingly mistaken views about many things — notable among these, the nature, education, and discipline of children. At the outset, such matters were not of primary concern to the Jesuits, nor to this group of Ursulines, even though theirs was a teaching order. The missionaries came to the New World with the single, burning intention to bring souls to Christ, but their work made it necessary for them to deal with children,

1. I use the term in the sense of an embracing network of systems, signs, and symbols, following Clifford Geertz, *The Interpretation of Cultures* (New York: Basic Books, 1973).

I am grateful to Fay Martineau and Rochelle Mazar for research assistance and for talking with me about missionaries and children.

and with cultural differences concerning children, before they were long in the field.

These missionaries constituted one energetic component of the passionate movement of Catholic reform in seventeenth-century France. In their difficult, hazardous, and often discouraging enterprise, they were nourished and consoled by the tradition of Christian martyrdom and filled with the fervor of mystical encounter with the divine. Under the circumstances, identification with the martyrs was realistic: unlike Mexico, Canada was not "conquered," and the early missionaries accompanied fishermen and fur traders instead of armies. As a mission field, Canada was dangerous as well as difficult, resembling more nearly the ninth-century Germany of St. Boniface than Central America in the wake of the conquistadors.[2]

Any consideration of early encounters between Europeans and native Americans, including the missions, must reckon with the epidemics that ravaged the native people of North as well as South and Central America in the first century after contact. The early years of Jesuit settlement among the Huron coincided with the smallpox epidemic of 1634, closely followed by influenza in 1636, scarlet fever in 1637, and a devastating recurrence of smallpox in 1639. Population loss was enormous — as much as a quarter or a third — and the social, economic, political, and spiritual losses of the native people were catastrophic. Although the significance of these great New World epidemics, long ignored or underestimated by historians, is now appreciated, their social, political, economic, and religious implications are still not well understood.[3] What *is* known is that in the Canadian wilderness, as in the cities of Central America, Christian missionaries were dealing with sick and dying people, and this brutal fact shaped their strategies, their successes, and their failures.

In the 1630s and 1640s, the decades that comprise the chronological focus of this essay, outposts and schools were established by Jesuits and Ursu-

---

2. For the account of the martyrdom of the missionary Isaac Jogues, S.J., see *The Jesuit Relations and Allied Documents*, 73 vols, ed. Reuben Gold Thwaites (Cleveland: Burrows Bros., 1896-1901), 31: 227-33. (Hereafter this source will be designated by the abbreviation *JR*, and citations in the text will include volume and page numbers.) This classic narrative of martyrdom in the Canadian context resembles in several respects the traditional *Acta Martyrorum* of the ancient church.

3. The Jesuits began at once to blame the victims. In the first volume of the *JR*, Pierre Biard (see note 5 below) wrote, "It is maintained that they have thus diminished since the French have begun to frequent their country; for . . . they do nothing all summer but eat; and the result is that, adopting an entirely different custom and thus breeding new diseases, they pay for their indulgence during the autumn and winter by pleurisy, quinsy, and dysentery, which kill them off" (1:77). For a summary discussion of demographic and other losses, see Bruce Trigger, *Natives and Newcomers: Canada's "Heroic Age" Reconsidered* (Kingston, Ont.: McGill-Queens University Press, 1985), 229-51.

lines among the Huron, waves of epidemic disease broke over eastern Canada, and many kinds of sparks flew from the initial striking-together of such very different people and cultures. My research is based primarily on *The Jesuit Relations,* a series of annual reports from the field composed and sent to Paris by Jesuit missionaries from 1632 until the late eighteenth century.[4] The seventy-three volumes of the *JR* constitute our most important source for the history of Roman Catholic mission in Canada, and for the observations of Europeans about the habits and attitudes of the people they came to serve. As a source for theological anthropology and the history of childhood, however, the *JR* is frustrating as well as invaluable; the writers did not comment directly on their own view of childhood or that of the native people, leaving us to infer assumptions and attitudes from descriptive and anecdotal material. We learn a great deal about the intentions and activities of the missionaries, and about their perceptions of the native Canadians, but we miss any systematic discussion of theoretical matters, including theological questions as well as ideas about education and child development. In order to benefit from the partial and slanted light shed by the *JR* on the central questions addressed in this volume, we must examine material designed for very different purposes than our own — a rewarding but difficult and sometimes problematic endeavor.

The first substantial and enduring Jesuit settlement in Canada was established among the Huron of modern Ontario in 1634.[5] Because the Huron depended more on fishing and agriculture and less on hunting than other native groups, they were seen as attractive potential converts. A "settled" life was understood by the French to be basic to civilization and therefore to the Christianization of indigenous people. In 1639 the Jesuits were joined by three Ursuline nuns and their lay sponsor, Madame de la Peltrie,[6] who came to Can-

---

4. The Thwaites edition of the *JR* will be superseded by *Monumenta Novae Franciae,* ed. Lucien Campeau (Quebec: Les Presses de l'Université Laval, 1967-), when the new edition is complete.

5. Among the several earlier French ventures, mercantile and missionary, was that of Pierre Biard, S.J., who produced the first catechism designed for the native people of Canada and Acadia. For an account of French catechetics in the New World, see Raymond Brodeur and Nive Voisine, "Nouvelle France, Nouveau catéchisme: La reproduction d'un modèle européen par le catéchisme en Amerique française," in *Aux Origines du Catéchisme en France,* ed. P. Colin et al. (Paris: Relais-Desclée, 1989), 247-60. I am indebted to Mary Ann Hinsdale for this reference.

6. The impact of the *JR* on devout French people in the seventeenth century is evident in the obituary notice of Madame de la Peltrie, a wealthy widow who both sponsored and accompanied the Ursuline mission to Canada. When she read the *Relation* of 1635, she resolved at once "as far as the weakness of her sex would permit, at securing the conversion and salvation of all the nations of the world" (56:228).

ada to assist in the work of conversion, education, and salvation by establishing a school for native girls. Whatever their original strategy, the Jesuits discovered before long that they would have to work through children, girls as well as boys. They intended to promote Christian family life among the Indians, and such families, in Canada as in Europe, required young women trained to become Christian wives and mothers. In the seventeenth century the necessity of single-sex education and of female teachers for girls was self-evident.[7] The story of the Ursuline mission is recounted in *The Jesuit Relations* and available also in the letters and other writings of their remarkable leader, Marie de l'Incarnation (1599-1672).[8] Marie's call to serve overseas occurred in 1633, after a difficult year in the Ursuline novitiate at Tours. She reported later that "My body was in our monastery, but my spirit, united to that of Jesus, could not remain shut up there. This apostolic spirit carried me in thought to the Indies, to Japan, to America, to the East and to the West, to parts of Canada, to the country of the Hurons."[9] Like their Jesuit colleagues, Marie and her sisters in mission were called to save souls; the work of educating and "civilizing" children was undertaken in the service of that primary vocation.

Seventeenth-century Jesuits, products of humanist training, were thoroughly convinced of the crucial function of education, understood in terms of moral and spiritual formation as well as arts and letters.[10] By the first century after its foundation, the order had become a major force, perhaps *the* major force, in European education. Jesuit schools were recognized for their excellence and rigor; members of the order were in demand as tutors and schoolmasters as well as confessors in courts and cities. In Jesuit colleges in France, boys learned grammar and rhetoric, Latin and Greek, in an environment of careful religious practice from masters who insisted also upon the highest stan-

---

7. The teaching ministries of French religious women in the New World are discussed by Dominique Deslandres, "Femmes Missionnaires en Nouvelle-France," in *La Religion de ma Mère: Les Femmes et la Transmission de la Foi,* ed. Jean Delumeau (Paris: Éditions du Cerf, 1992), p. 211. See also Leslie Choquette, "'Ces Amazones du Grand Dieu': Women and Mission in Seventeenth-Century Canada," *French Historical Studies* 17 (1992): 627-55.

8. A recent edition of Marie's writings is available in *Marie of the Incarnation: Selected Writings,* ed. Irene Mahoney (Mahwah, N.J.: Paulist Press, 1989). For interpretations of this extraordinary woman's life, mission, and mystical experience, see, among others, Natalie Zemon Davis, "New Worlds," in *Women on the Margin: Three Seventeenth-Century Lives* (Cambridge: Harvard University Press, 1995); and Anya Mali, *Mystic in the New World* (Leiden: E. J. Brill, 1996).

9. Cited in *Marie of the Incarnation,* 112.

10. For a useful and concise account of the complex relationship between the early Jesuits and Renaissance humanism, see John W. O'Malley, *The First Jesuits* (Cambridge: Harvard University Press, 1993), chapter 10.

dards of moral behavior. Monthly confession and communion and weekly instruction in Christian doctrine were essential aspects of the curriculum.[11] The humanist interest in arts and letters, with its traditional emphasis on the Latin and Greek classics, was integrated with the strict moral teaching and discipline of the Catholic reform.

In the circumstances of the New World, however — particularly in the earliest missions — a very different level of Christian education was required: a simple catechism for adults and children alike, in which correct answers were rewarded with trinkets such as glass beads. Especially with women and children, who were assumed to be more simpleminded than men, the missionaries emphasized recitation of prayers, chanting, and making the sign of the cross. Instruction could not advance beyond the most elementary level until the Jesuits themselves gained some mastery of native languages, a task they set about immediately. Even the most basic theological teaching required substantial facility with language; the early missionary Jean de Brébeuf spent three years among the Huron before he could "recite Bible stories [and] explain simple theological matters."[12]

Since the Renaissance, humanists in Italy and northern Europe, Erasmus notable among them, had preached the importance of infancy and early childhood in the development of good Christians and good citizens. There were ample precedents in French moral teaching, too, for devoted attention to childhood. Preachers such as Jean Gerson, a fifteenth-century chancellor of the University of Paris, exhorted Christians to attend and respond to the nature and needs of children. In the later Middle Ages, the increasingly popular devotion to the Holy Family and the Child Jesus were effectively linked to reminders of Christian obligations to children, particularly the children of the poor.[13]

---

11. The curriculum and atmosphere of sixteenth-century French Jesuit colleges (comparable in terms of the pupils' age to modern American middle and high schools) are described by A. Lynn Martin in *The Jesuit Mind: The Mentality of an Elite in Early Modern France* (Ithaca, N.Y.: Cornell University Press, 1988), chapter 3. Martin points out that although the student population included some younger pupils, accepted reluctantly in French schools, and some older Jesuits in advanced classes, most of the students were boys between about ten and fourteen years of age.

12. Bruce Trigger, *The Children of Aataentsic: A History of the Huron People to 1660* (Kingston, Ont.: McGill-Queen's University Press, 1987), 408; see also 507-8. In addition, see Lucien Campeau, *La Mission des Jésuites chez des Hurons, 1634-1650* (Montréal: Éditions Bellarmin, 1987), 122.

13. See the discussion by Lawrence Wolff, "Parents and Children in the Sermons of Père Bourdaloue: A Jesuit Perspective on the Early Modern Family," in *The Jesuit Tradition in Education and Missions*, ed. C. Chapple (Scranton: University of Scranton Press, 1993), 81-94.

Certainly no children could have been more "poor" — more in need of devotion, literacy, and salvation — than the little *sauvages*[14] of the New World.

Formed in the humanist tradition, the Jesuits certainly acknowledged the importance of early childhood, but they understood their particular educational vocation as well as their inclination to be the teaching of older boys. Lynn Martin says that Jesuits "preferred mature students who had already learned to read and write," and quotes a discouraging report from the college at Lyons, where (according to the terms of the endowment) two teachers had to offer "one class a day" to 180 little boys. They found the boys "a great annoyance [who] show little results after much time, with even less honor to the college, because they are all small, barefooted brats and in very bad order."[15]

The children with whom the Jesuits worked in New France were not necessarily younger than their European counterparts but were at a much more elementary stage of education: they had first to learn their letters. The burden of primary education was joyfully shouldered, but it was still a sacrifice for those who had prepared to deal with more advanced students and studies. The missionaries reiterated their delight at this opportunity, but we should note that their *Relations* were fund-raising and recruiting instruments as well as annals and letters, and their enthusiasm may have been exaggerated. (I do not suggest that the reports were disingenuous, only that they presented public, official positions.) In 1632 the leader of the mission, Paul LeJeune (1592-1672), remarked that "teaching the alphabet is more rewarding than instructing sophisticated audiences in France," and later he commented, "Behold me at last returned to the A.B.C., with so great content and satisfaction that I would not exchange my two pupils for the finest audience in France" (*JR* 5:63).[16] The Jesuits originally intended — and undoubtedly would have preferred — to work through adult male leaders, but to the humanist conviction of the importance of "bending the twig" was soon added the practical necessity of recruiting the next generation, both boys and girls, for the work of conversion.

14. For the meanings of this term, see Gordon M. Sayre, *Les sauvages Americains* (Chapel Hill: University of North Carolina Press, 1997). "In French," Sayre explains, "the adjective *sauvage* means wild instead of domesticated" (p. xv), lacking the pejorative connotations of the English *savage*. In the seventeenth century, the term was used to refer to *all* the indigenous people of the New World — as Sayre points out, "a collective body of people defined only as and after they were united by a common experience of displacement, death, and discrimination" (p. xiv).

15. Martin, *The Jesuit Mind*, 58.

16. Paul LeJeune led the mission to New France for thirty years, working as superior in the field and later in Paris; his was the most influential single voice in the early years. As an important writer and editor, too, LeJeune had a major role in shaping the image of the mission and missionaries and of the native people transmitted through the *JR*.

As early as 1632, LeJeune was convinced and working to convince others of the central importance of residential schools for native children: "The means of assisting them, in my opinion, is to build seminaries [boarding schools], and to take their children, who are very bright and amiable. The fathers will be taught through the children" (*JR* 5:33). In Canadian as in European schools, the emphasis remained distinctly on *Christian* education. After the Jesuit seminary in Quebec was established, the boys were instructed in reading, writing, and catechism; they participated in prayers and heard daily mass.

*   *

The Ursuline order was founded in the fifteenth century for the purpose of teaching girls in the towns and cities of southern Europe, and the nuns were no less convinced than their Jesuit colleagues of the central role of children in any program of Christianization. Like the Jesuits, the Ursulines became a powerful force in education in the early modern world; their reputation and achievements remained significant to modern times. Their original mission was to poor children in Italian towns, but with the coming of the Counter Reformation and their expansion into France, the Ursulines, along with other women's orders, were pushed back inside the cloister by a hierarchy primarily concerned with the proper appearance and behavior of female religious. In the cloister, the educational efforts of the Ursulines had to be confined to boarding pupils and thus to the daughters of the middle and upper classes, and their aims were more narrowly identified with the training of such girls for Christian marriage and motherhood. According to a governing statement of the sisters at Lyons, their goals were to instruct students in Christian doctrine, confession, and the examination of conscience, to teach them to read devotional books and sing spiritual songs, to avoid occasions of sin and perform works of mercy, and to manage a household — everything required of a good Christian woman. Finally, "in order to attract students to their schools and to turn them away from heresy and impurity, they would teach them reading, writing, and needlework"; these secular activities, presumably, were included in order to persuade ambitious parents to send their children for preparation for middle-class marriage.[17]

Marie de l'Incarnation, the leader of the Ursuline mission to Canada, was the daughter of a baker of Tours. She had little formal education herself but received substantial religious instruction at home and at church. The education of middle-class French girls was directed toward moral and spiritual develop-

17. Quoted in Roger Chartier, *L'Éducation en France du XVIe au XVIIIe Siècle* (Paris: Société d'Édition d'Enseignement Superieur, 1976), 236, in the context of an important discussion of the education of girls.

ment, and with the ever-greater emphasis on family life in the seventeenth century among Protestants and Catholics alike, girls increasingly were recognized and appreciated as future teachers of the next generation and moral centers of the household of faith. The household, that central building-block of early modern church and society, was reinterpreted in the exotic circumstances of the New World. The missionaries were determined to promote Christian ideals of monogamy and domesticity among the Indians, and such families, in Canada as in Europe, required Christian wives and mothers. In 1633 LeJeune wrote, "I see that it is absolutely necessary to teach the girls as well as the boys . . . for the boys that we have reared in the knowledge of God, when they marry Savage girls or women accustomed to wandering in the woods, will, as their husbands, be compelled to follow them and thus fall back into barbarism, or to leave them, another evil full of danger" (*JR* 5:145). In 1637 he added, "For a little Savage girl comfortably settled and married to some Frenchman or Christian Savage, would be a powerful check upon some of her wandering countrymen" (*JR* 11:53). In the Canadian wilderness, conversion was identified with a settled agricultural way of life, with French culture, and with Christian domesticity, and the entire system was understood to rest on women.

The early missionaries tended to find *all* native people "childlike," and their characterizations of this condition provide some access to their ideas about the nature of children and the state of childhood. During a visit to Acadia in 1613, Pierre Biard wrote that the natives lacked "reason and maturity," interpreted as the absence of "language and reason" (*JR* 1:183). We should not identify such observations too closely with the familiar racism of the nineteenth and twentieth centuries; seventeenth-century Europeans tended to understand native differences from themselves less in terms of physical characteristics and more in terms of "deficiencies" in language, writing, civilization, and culture. To these French men and women, language — closely associated with reason itself — was the essential criterion of adulthood as well as civilization. "These miserable people," wrote Biard, "will always remain in a perpetual infancy as to language and reason . . . because it is evident that where words, the messengers and dispensers of thought and speech, remain totally rude, poor and confused, it is impossible that the mind and reason be greatly refined, rich, and disciplined. However, these poor weaklings and children consider themselves superior to all other men, and they would not for the world give up their childishness and wretchedness. And this is not to be wondered at, for as I have said, they are children" (*JR* 2:13).[18] In the service of mission, LeJeune was capable of turning the charge of childishness against himself: when the "savages" laughed at his

18. Here and elsewhere, the missionaries showed surprise and resentment when the Indians refused to recognize French superiority and insisted on their own!

pronunciation of *their* language, he said he "was a child and that children made their fathers laugh with their stammering; but in a few years [he] would become large, and then, when [he] knew their language, [he] would make them see that they themselves were children in many things, ignorant of the great truths of which [he] would speak to them" (*JR* 7:93).

The Jesuit Relations reveals lingering suspicions about the full humanity of the indigenous people of the New World, a question that supposedly had been settled in 1537 by the papal bull *Sublimis deus,* which declared them "true men." For excellent theological reasons, the enterprise of evangelization, unlike exploration and conquest, could not have existed at all without the assumption of full humanity. Christ came to save human beings and instructed the apostles to bring the message of salvation to all people; if the Indians were not human beings, there could be no mission. But doubts must have lingered, for a different tone tended to reappear in tense circumstances. The missionaries referred to the Iroquois, who threatened and killed Huron and missionary alike and eventually defeated the Huron, as "brutes," meaning brute beasts.[19] If racial differences were not perceived in modern terms, difference itself was certainly noticed, and rarely to the natives' advantage.[20]

To the French, the important differences between themselves and the Indians included language, dress, and domestic customs. It soon became obvious that such matters could be corrected more easily in children than in adults, and in mission schools rather than in longhouses. The "filth of the savage children" impressed and delighted the Ursulines with the opportunity for sacrifice and good works, and when visitors expressed surprise and disgust, they reflected on their own superior attitudes, as one of Marie's comments makes clear: "Still less did they understand how we could embrace these little orphans, holding them on our laps, when their bodies were heavily smeared with grease and covered only by a small greasy rag, giving them a terrible odor. For us all this was an un-

19. In *Friend and Foe: Aspects of French-Amerindian Cultural Contact in the Sixteenth and Seventeenth Centuries* (Toronto: McClelland & Stewart, Ltd., 1976), chapter 1, Cornelius Jaenen provides a thoughtful discussion of the question of "full humanity" in the Canadian environment.

20. Exceptions to this rule usually took the form of comments intended directly or indirectly for a French audience, praising the native people for virtues seen as lacking at home. (Montesquieu's essay "On Cannibals" is the classic representation of the "savage" who outshines the European.) In the spirit of traditional Christian preaching in favor of maternal breast-feeding and against wet nursing, for example, the Recollet missionary Gabriel Sagard wrote in praise of native women who, unlike some French women, always breast-fed their children; see *The Long Journey to the Country of the Hurons by Father Gabriel Sagard,* ed. G. M. Wrong (Toronto: Champlain Society, 1939), 128. Like Erasmus, the missionaries believed that Christianity could be absorbed through mothers' milk (*JR* 13: 179).

imaginable happiness. Once they had grown accustomed to us, we tried to clean them up over a period of a few days, for this grease with its strong smell clung to their skin like glue. Then we gave them some underwear and a little tunic to protect them from the vermin which covered them when they first came to us."[21] The native students learned Christian doctrine and French manners and were dressed like French girls.[22] In Ursuline accounts the girls' appearance tended to reflect their spiritual state: their clothing displayed their piety, innocence, and charm.[23] Accounts of girls' education, particularly in the *JR*, with its positive approach to the mission, tended to present them as easier to convert to Christianity and to make "French" than boys, who were wilder, more apt to run away, and less likely to look and act like French children. Marie's letter of 1668 offers a rare glimpse of the little girls as well as clues to the Ursuline curriculum and plans for the children in their care: "Like squirrels, they climb up our palisade (which is as high as a wall) and go running in the woods. There are also those who persevere and whom we raise in the French manner. Then marriages are arranged for them and they do very well. . . . Others return to their savage parents. They speak French well and are knowledgeable in both reading and writing."[24]

*   *

The most striking and significant comments by Jesuits on cultural difference concern the discipline, punishment, and "spoiling" of children. From the very

21. *Marie of the Incarnation*, 138-39. Some of the children may have been literal orphans, but the phrase "little orphans" refers to what the nuns perceived as the children's physical and spiritual plight. Compassion expressed in physical care and demonstrations of affection for those afflicted with repulsive manifestations of filth and disease belong to a tradition that derives in its late medieval form from St. Francis and was characteristic of very holy Christian women throughout the later Middle Ages and into modern times.

22. By 1668 the Ursulines had taken over the education of French girls of the colony and had to limit the number of their Indian pupils: "The savage girls both live and eat with the French girls, but it is necessary to have a special mistress for their instruction, and sometimes more than one, depending on their number. To my great sorrow I have just refused seven Algonquin boarders because we lack food." The nuns sent some of the French girls home for the same reason: Marie wrote to her son, "We are limited to sixteen French girls and three Indians, of whom two are Iroquois and one a captive to whom they want us to teach the French language. I say nothing of the poor who are here in great numbers and with whom we must share whatever we have left" ("Letter to Her Son" [August 9, 1668], in *Marie of the Incarnation*, 270-71).

23. There are many descriptions of the appearance of the girls, but not many of the boys: see, among other passages, *JR* 18:159.

24. "Letter to Her Son" (August 9, 1668), in *Marie of the Incarnation*, 272.

beginning, the missionaries were both struck by the Indians' love for their children and horrified at the way they raised them: "They treat their children with wonderful affection, but they preserve no discipline, for they neither themselves correct them nor allow others to do so" (*JR* 1:277). This attitude and behavior interfered with instruction and conversion. The theme is repeated over and over: children had to be taught in boarding schools away from home because their parents would not allow them to be properly trained — that is, subjected to the corporal punishment that was taken for granted in French homes and schools. LeJeune recognized the problem and proposed a solution in 1632:

> These people may be converted by means of seminaries; and how necessary it is to educate at Kebec the children of the Savages, who belong to settlements farther up the river. We shall have them [the children] at last; for they will give them, if they see that we do not send them to France. As to the children of this section, they must be sent up there. The reason is that the Savages prevent their instruction; they will not tolerate the chastisement of their children, whatever they may do; they permit only a simple reprimand. Moreover they think they are doing you some great favor in giving you their children to instruct, to feed, and to dress. (*JR* 5:197)[25]

The French never did comprehend or become resigned to the fact that corporal punishment of children was simply not acceptable to the Huron. The Jesuits, enthusiastic proponents of the widespread belief in physical discipline among early modern Europeans, insisted upon such punishment in their French schools. Neither their humanist tradition nor their dedication to education countered their acceptance of the general view that beating a child was a necessary and appropriate part of moral and intellectual training. Indeed, when it was suggested that they employ a lay person to administer beatings to recalcitrant boys, they objected on the grounds that students would lose respect for masters who did not wield the rod themselves.[26] With that attitude and such habits, it is not surprising that the Jesuits found the Huron treatment of children threatening as well as shocking. A striking example of this central cultural difference appears in the story of a French drummer boy who hit an Indian with his drumstick, apparently accidentally, but sharply enough to draw blood. The Indians demanded compensation, which they expected in the form of gifts;

---

25. Complaints about the "spoiling" of children abound in the *JR*; see, among many other examples, 6:153 and 9:103. Apparently the native mothers and grandmothers were most adamant in their refusal to allow children to be sent to France: in the matrilineal, matrilocal society of the Huron, children were most closely identified with their mothers' families. See Trigger, *The Children of Aataentsic*, 523.

26. Martin, *The Jesuit Mind*, 62.

the French version of appropriate compensation was to whip the child. The Indians begged them to desist, and one of them shielded the boy, offering his own body for the beating. According to the Jesuits' account of the incident, they were primarily concerned with the interference with proper discipline and its implication for their program: "All the Savage tribes of these quarters, and of Brazil, as we are assured, cannot chastise a child or see one chastised. How much trouble this will give us in carrying out our plans of teaching the young!" (*JR* 5:221).

Children had to be removed from their parents as far as possible "because these Barbarians cannot bear to have their children punished, nor even scolded, not being able to refuse anything to a crying child. . . . Upon the slightest pretext they would take them away from us, before they were educated" (*JR* 6:153). When the French inquired about this behavior, they were told by "some Savages . . . that one of the principal reasons why they showed so much indulgence towards their children, was that when the children saw themselves treated by their parents with some severity, they usually resorted to extreme measures and hanged themselves, or ate of a certain root . . . which is a very quick poison" (*JR* 14:37). This passage is difficult to interpret in the absence of more specific information, but we may infer at least that native parents understood the young to be extremely sensitive to adult disapproval and punishment, to which they did not subject their own children. Anecdotes in the *JR* make it clear that French schooling created problems of its own, for the missionaries frequently had to deal with depressed, sad children and with runaways. The Jesuits may have chosen to understand these behaviors as characteristic of native children rather than as consequences of their own teaching and discipline. Marie, too, interpreted the inability to endure "sadness" as a native characteristic, observing that some of the little girls were "like birds on the wing, staying with us only until they become sad, a condition which the character of the savages cannot endure. As soon as they grow sad their parents will take them away, fearful that they will die. On this score we leave them free, for we win more this way than by constraint."[27]

In relation to discipline, the *JR* reveals an important change over time. In later years, stories were reported about the behavior of native *Christian* parents, who did punish their children. In the account of 1670-71, the convert Marie Oendraka, presented as a marvelously holy woman and mother, became uneasy at the thought of her young son left alone in their cabin. When his older sister, also a Christian, was sent to check on him, she "caught her little brother, and one of his comrades of his own age, in an act of indecency bordering on impurity. Giving a loud scream, as if the house had been on fire, she assailed those

27. "Letter to Her Son" (August 9, 1668), in *Marie of the Incarnation*, 271-72.

two little culprits with feet and hands, and drove them into the street. The mother hastened home and ... caused a good handful of rods to be prepared, in order to inflict punishment at the close of Mass, in sight of all the people" (*JR* 55:29). She was interrupted by a relative who pitied the boy, pulled him away, took him to church to beg forgiveness, and gave him back to his mother, who would not speak to him or give him food until the priest intervened on his behalf. The mother said the child belonged in hell, taking pity on neither his physical nor his mental suffering. The account of her story may, of course, be exaggerated: it is presented as an exemplum of the converted parent. After forty years of mission, some (Christian) native parents had learned how to *make* their children good.

The missionaries sought to model and to teach the natives new ways to "love" children. The Ursulines were inclined to regard themselves as the "true" mothers of their pupils, and the Jesuits greatly admired their devotion: "I have never seen Mothers so solicitous for their children as are Madame de la Pelletrie [the nuns' lay sponsor] and the Ursulines for their little seminarists. The love that finds its source in God is more generous and more constant than the tenderness of nature" (*JR* 19:37). The missionaries reported the girls' behavior in the light of this ideology, as in the story of "a little Huron girl among the Algonquins; on being asked if she had still her mother, 'She whom I have in my country is no longer my dear mother,' answered the child, 'because she does not believe in God; it is you who are my true Mothers, since you instruct me'" (*JR* 20:137). Madame de la Peltrie is described as especially loved by the little girls, who are "not moved at seeing the Savage girls or women come and go, — they show no desire to follow them, they salute them in the French way, and leave them smilingly; it seems as if we were their natural mothers." She is quoted as saying, "I would not be satisfied if I did not tell you of the comfort that I daily experience in our little girls. I have all the pleasure that a mother can wish from her good children, — both in the obedience they render me, and in the tender and filial love they bear me" (*JR* 19:55). The nuns participated happily in this traditional form of "true" motherhood, understood as purely spiritual love, especially fervent because unsullied by biological relationship or "personal" attachment. These mothers and children loved each other in and through Christ.[28] The *Relation* of 1673-74 tells of a mother who invited "the most fervent Christians" among her people to the chapel to hear prayers recited over her

---

28. These attitudes are consistent with the Christian monastic ideology of "spiritual motherhood" developed during the patristic era and continued, in monastic contexts, through the Middle Ages and beyond. See Clarissa W. Atkinson, *The Oldest Vocation: Christian Motherhood in the Middle Ages* (Ithaca, N.Y.: Cornell University Press, 1991), chapter 3.

dead child, "the first among our Savage women who has had the courage to do so; for, as a rule, the mothers here think only of weeping at the death of their children" (*JR* 58:191). Christian love — the love that replaces physical and emotional ties and triumphs even over death — was offered as a consolation to bereaved parents. It also suggested an alternative to the "natural" parental love that was believed to result in excessive affection and in spoiling.

As we observe significant differences between the French and the Huron, it is essential to remember that the missionaries were not lay people with families but members of Roman Catholic religious orders, vowed to celibacy. Their sexual abstinence was remarkable and somewhat ludicrous to the Indians, who did not share the Christian veneration of virginity and celibacy. In regard to children, and the "wonderful affection" showed to children by their native parents, the missionaries, particularly the Ursulines, carried a very different set of values and rules not only from those they came to serve but from many of their fellow Christians at home. For these missionaries, human love could — and would, if one were not endlessly watchful — be in conflict with the love of God and thus perpetually problematic for those who had vowed to love God only. The conflict was exemplified in Marie de l'Incarnation herself, who left an eleven-year-old son when she entered religious life. She wrote in her "Relation of 1654" that she had prepared her son Claude for this separation from babyhood; when he vociferously protested her departure, "I was amazed at his deep affection, for since his infancy I had been determined to leave him in obedience to God. I had never fondled him as one does with children, despite my deep love. My intention was to detach him from me in view of the time when he would be old enough for me to leave him."[29] Not surprisingly, Claude was furious and wounded despite his "preparation." In fact, both mother and son interpreted her departure as abandonment, for which Marie was consoled, much later, by her son's Benedictine vocation: "All this year," she wrote in 1641, "I have been in great torment, imagining the pitfalls where you might stumble. But finally our gracious God gave me peace in the belief that his loving and fatherly goodness would never lose what had been abandoned for his love."[30]

The affection shown by native adults toward children looked to the mis-

29. *Marie of the Incarnation,* 97. Marie's story stands squarely in the tradition of St. Jerome's friend Paula, who left a young son behind when she joined the saint in the Holy Land, and (in Marie's own time) of the complicated relationship of Jane Frances de Chantal and her son, whom she left to enter the Order of the Visitation. For more on this chapter of Christian motherhood, see Atkinson, *The Oldest Vocation,* chapter 6.

30. *Marie of the Incarnation,* 221. As an adult, Claude wished martyrdom for his mother, and although according to their shared assumptions he was hoping for the best for her, I am inclined to agree with John Farina that "one is tempted to see beneath the pietistic language of self-abnegation the human realities of guilt and resentment" (2).

sionaries like spoiling, while French discipline looked to the natives like incomprehensible brutality. However, we should not exaggerate or attach modern assumptions to the Huron affection for children in the seventeenth-century Canadian context. And we should not make easy assumptions about what seems like the inconsistent treatment of orphans. Orphaned children without parents to take care of them were sometimes put to death, although the adults apparently were glad to find ways to avoid that harsh option: such cases were reported in the *JR* because the options included handing the children over to the French for care and education.[31] The Indians may have regarded killing orphans as a kindness to children who would otherwise be left alone, but it is difficult to determine whether this was a widely accepted practice or a rare occurrence in times of epidemic, famine, or war. In any case, it seems inconsistent with LeJeune's report of a point raised by a "sorcerer" in the course of an argument about monogamy. LeJeune said, "'It was not honorable for a woman to love anyone else except her husband; and that, this evil [adultery] being among them, he himself [the sorcerer] was not sure that his son . . . was his son.'" The sorcerer replied, "'Thou hast no sense. You French people love only your own children; but we love all the children of our tribe'" (*JR* 6:255). LeJeune was more interested in the issue of monogamy than that of love for children; he did not trouble himself to respond to the latter comment but simply laughed off the sorcerer's argument as an example of the typically weak reasoning of the Indians.

*   *

As mentioned above, *The Jesuit Relations* is a collection of annals and letters and reports from the field with a spin aimed at raising money and recruits; it is a source rich in observation, not in theological speculation. Some accounts are suggestive of certain assumptions underlying the enterprise of conversion, but generally one must depend on inference for insight into theological questions, including questions about childhood. Among seventeenth-century French Jesuits, a humanist optimism about the value of education and training co-existed with an Augustinian theology of grace and nature. The teaching and practice of the missionaries were rooted in a theological anthropology permeated by a dismal view of nature and of "natural man": one of its obvious implications was the conviction that the effective conversion of an adult required a complete break with the

---

31. ". . . a Savage gave an arquebus to our Pierre, telling him to kill this miserable child because, having no parents, he would be abandoned by every one during his lifetime. Our Savage, hearing that, had pity on the little one, took him, and fed him up to the time when he gave him to us" (5:137). Again (6:117), the natives are described as glad to accept the Jesuits' offer of care for an orphan.

past. They departed from the footsteps of their Jesuit predecessors in Latin America, whose theological anthropology, shaped by Aristotle as interpreted and modified by Aquinas, found human nature, including that of the native people of the New World, to be fundamentally good and worthy of study and attention in its own right.[32] The missionaries to North America, working in the next century and shaped for the most part by French instead of Spanish religious culture, were a good deal less optimistic about the value of cultural diversity and the probability of the "evolution" of New World people toward full Christianity. Peter Goddard has argued persuasively that French Jesuits departed from the humanist, Thomist, and (according to their enemies) lax traditions of their own order. Along with other branches of Reformed French Catholicism, these seventeenth-century Jesuits opted for a "bleak" Augustinianism that emphasized the total corruption of nature, lacking the characteristically Thomist expectation of the co-existence of nature and grace as well as any enthusiastic optimism about the possibility of change. LeJeune, the most influential Augustinian spokesman of the early decades of the mission, saw the lives of the Indians as exemplars of the fate of the natural man unrestrained by Christian teaching and practice; such instruction offered their only opportunity for rescue from the slavery to nature in which he found them.[33]

Notwithstanding the absence of systematic theological argument and reflection in the *JR*, its many references to baptism do shed a slanting light on the theological agendas of both missionaries and converts. Accounts and discussions of baptism offer useful glimpses into theological anthropology and pastoral practice, both because of the importance of that rite in accepting new Christians into the church and because of its central role as *the* sacrament of infancy in early modern Christianity. Furthermore, baptism quickly became an arena for acting out some of the confusions and misunderstandings that marked cultural and theological interactions between the French and the Huron.[34] In ac-

32. See Anthony Pagden, *The Fall of Natural Man: The American Indian and the Origins of Comparative Ethnology* (Cambridge: Cambridge University Press, 1986). See also Luis Martin, "The Peruvian Indian through Jesuit Eyes: The Case of José de Acosta and Pablo José de Arriaga," *The Jesuit Tradition in Education and Missions,* ed. C. Chapple (Scranton: University of Scranton Press), 201-13.

33. The strict Augustinian Louis Lallemant taught at the Jesuit College at Rouen from 1619 to 1631; Paul LeJeune was one of his pupils, as was the martyr Isaac Jogues. My discussion is based in part on Peter Goddard's excellent essay entitled "Augustine and the Amerindian in Seventeenth-Century New France," *Church History* 67 (1998): 662-81.

34. Most discussions by historians of the role of baptism in conversion and colonization attend to the Latin American experience. An exception is James Axtell's essay "Were Indian Conversions Bona Fide?" in *After Columbus: Essays in the Ethnohistory of Colonial North America* (New York: Oxford University Press, 1988), in which the topic is examined in a North American setting.

cordance with their Augustinian anthropology, the Jesuit program for the instruction of adults was serious and intense. The Jesuits required converts to be well-versed in Christian doctrine and practice, and they did not hesitate to use a variety of means, including economic advantage, to secure their long-term allegiance. In the short term, however, faced with raging epidemic disease, the Jesuits tended to overlook their own criteria for "true" conversion and to make use of the Indians' weakness, fear of death, and interest in the afterlife by preaching hellfire. It may be an exaggeration to claim with Goddard that "*most recipients of the sacraments experienced the sacred rites only as part of the trauma of terminal illness,*"[35] but it is certain that many adults who accepted baptism and managed to survive the early epidemics did turn against the Christians later, as people continued to die. In some instances, priests and their native converts were accused of spreading illness by witchcraft. Perceiving "backsliding" among the Indians, the Jesuits responded with a more strenuous program of instruction and economic pressure: for example, only baptized Indians were allowed to buy firearms.[36]

The baptism of young children was a different matter. In the first place, of course, neither instruction nor "conversion," in the sense of the total change of life and heart necessary for an adult, was required for the baptism of an infant or young child. The Jesuits announced their clear intentions at the outset: "Since we cannot yet baptize the adults, . . . there remain for us the children, to whom the kingdom of heaven belongs; these we baptize with the consent of their parents and the pledge of the god-parents" (*JR* 2:13). However, these intentions were not always realized in the drastic circumstances of the New World, where a sick, unbaptized baby was perceived as an emergency. The *JR* reveals (in sketchy, unsystematic fashion) that the missionaries shared the notion of limbo described by Thomas Aquinas (see Cristina Traina's essay in this volume): infants who die without baptism, although they do not suffer the pains of hell, are deprived of the presence of God for eternity.[37] In his *Relation* of 1638, LeJeune tells the story of a convert who appreciated this distinction: "When he had learned that his child, having died in infancy, did not feel the

---

35. Peter Goddard, "Converting the *Sauvage:* Jesuit and Montagnais in Seventeenth-Century New France," *Catholic Historical Review* 84 (1998): 231, italics mine.

36. Trigger, *Natives and Newcomers,* chapter 5.

37. In seventeenth-century Italy, the Holy Office charged and tried certain midwives with pretending to resuscitate infants long enough for them to be baptized. This practice, which was doubtless comforting to the parents but not acceptable to the Church, illustrates the passions aroused in the event of the death of an unbaptized infant. See Silvano Cavazza, "Double Death: Resurrection and Baptism in a Seventeenth-century Rite," in *History from Crime,* ed. Edward Muir and Guido Ruggiero (Baltimore: The Johns Hopkins University Press, 1994), 1-31.

pains of hell, not having committed any actual sin, he thanked us heartily for having taught him a doctrine so favorable" (*JR* 14:181). Others were not so grateful: some mothers who had their children baptized "weep bitterly when they hear it said that their children are in the flames, for not having wished to believe,[38] or . . . deprived of the pleasures of Heaven because they were not baptized" (*JR* 9:97).

The notion of limbo did not inhibit the missionaries from breaking their own rules about parental consent. There are several references in the *JR* to the baptism of terminally ill infants *against* the will of their parents. In 1637, "Father Pierre . . . baptized . . . an infant two months old, in manifest danger of death, without its parents being aware that he did so; not having succeeded in obtaining their permission, he made a feint of wishing to give it a little sugared water to drink and at the same time dipped his finger in the water; and seeing that its father showed some distrust and urgently requested him not to baptize the child . . . under pretext of seeing if it really slept, applied his wet finger to its face and baptized it; at the end of forty-eight hours, it went to heaven" (*JR* 14:41). For Father Pierre the eternal destiny of the child was paramount, overriding any other consideration. These eager and dedicated priests believed that baptism assured salvation for innocent infants. If such children, whether French or Indian, died shortly after baptism with no opportunity to sin, they not only avoided hell but became angels instantaneously: "We baptized four little children; two died the next day, and the third a few days afterward. What a favor from heaven for these little angels!" (*JR* 14:39).[39]

As the epidemics grew worse and literally hundreds of children were baptized at the point of death, it is not surprising that some of the Huron came to believe that baptism *caused* death: "Hence their affection for their children, which verges on folly, has always led them to devote all their efforts to preventing them from receiving that grace" (*JR* 58:225). Others, even some of those who had not accepted baptism for themselves, did accept it for their children, perhaps because they misunderstood the promise of salvation and hoped the rite itself, or the holy water, could work a cure in this life. But their acceptance put them in a terrible quandary. If the children died, the parents might be persuaded that baptism had sent them to the Christian heaven, as the missionaries assured them was the case. Since their own religious system placed great importance on an afterlife spent with one's ancestors and descendants, parents were

38. I believe this refers to the "baptism of desire"; see Traina, "A Person in the Making," 114-15, 117.

39. See also *JR* 7:285: a French layman baptized a baby he believed to be so close to death that a priest could not be called; his wife took care of the child and later saw in her sleep "a great troop of Angels coming to take it. . . . They were very glad that they had helped send to Heaven a soul that will bless God throughout all eternity."

faced with the terrible prospect of eternal separation. Sometimes this belief caused them to accept baptism for themselves, and the Jesuits were not reluctant to exploit their fear.[40] LeJeune wrote, "I mildly represented to [a Huron mother] the danger into which she was throwing herself of being forever separated from her child, whom she loved so passionately that, in my opinion, she was sick from grief and sadness. 'Thy daughter,' I said to her, 'is in Heaven, and thou wilt be at the bottom of the abyss. Thou sayest that thou lovest her, yet thou dost not wish to go with her; thou canst not follow her, if thou dost not believe and if thou art not baptized'" (JR 9:39). LeJeune used this threat as a strategy; in 1636 he wrote, "You see the inclination of the Hurons . . . to receive Christianity; and this will be greatly increased by the fact that we have already baptized many of their children. For they say, 'We do not wish to be separated from our children, we desire to go to Heaven with them'" (JR 10:31). Perhaps we may attribute the callous tone of this comment to LeJeune's Augustinian distrust of nature and thus of the "natural" love of parents for their children. For the unfortunate Huron, then, it was necessary in some cases to choose between the eternal society of their ancestors and that of their children. The torment of this choice was not soothed but exacerbated by Jesuit teaching and counseling: "The relatives [of a sick boy] seemed at first somewhat inclined to have this child go after death to that place where his dead relatives were; [later they] desired their son to go where it would be best for him" (JR 14:31).

*   *

In a short essay, it is impossible to begin to do justice to the abyss that gaped between French Catholic missionaries and the native people of the New World in terms of religion, culture, family relationships and ideologies, and care for children. The Jesuits and the Ursulines came to Canada with the passionate intention of saving souls from hell, and this single-minded purpose shaped their relationships with their hosts as well as every other aspect of their experience. In the passage quoted above about the "little angels" who died shortly after baptism, the writer continued, "And what a consolation for us to see that this divine goodness deigns to use us to wrest from the hands of the devil so many souls created in his [God's] image, and to apply to them the merits of the blood of his son!" (JR 14:39). When we read about disguised baptisms, or about attempts to take children away from their parents, to teach the adults to punish

---

40. From the beginning of their mission to the Huron, the Jesuits played on themes of heaven and hell and of the choice required or implied by true conversion. See Trigger, *The Children of Aataentsic*, 506-8, and Campeau, *La mission des Jésuites chez des Hurons*, 122.

245

and shame their children, or to frighten parents with the spectre of eternal separation, we need to remember this central intention and the theological passion that drove it. We must also be mindful of the context: modern readers horrified by missionary attitudes and activities would also find appalling the conditions and discipline in French households and boarding schools in the seventeenth century. It is our responsibility not to judge the missionaries but to observe that, as always, the theological message, the message of the gospel, was proclaimed within a specific culture, a distinct set of practices and ideologies.

For modern times it may be most important to note that Christian approaches to the people that they wished to save and serve were as deeply embedded in seventeenth-century European culture as was "wonderful affection" for children among the Huron. The missionaries' theology of childhood — if one can infer such a phenomenon when they themselves did not articulate or develop it — was enmeshed in a cultural system that strikes us today as harsh, arrogant, and misguided. From our perspective it is obvious that those they regarded as their cultural inferiors had much to teach, had European Christians been able or inclined to learn. In this essay I have endeavored to demonstrate that significant discrepancies between various cultural definitions of childhood and understandings of "human nature," as embodied in the young, have crucial implications for the ways in which infants and children are loved, raised, and educated. Theologies and theories of childhood live only within discrete and specific cultural systems, and I believe that the encounter between French Catholic missionaries and the decimated Huron families and villages of eastern Canada sheds light on some of the ways in which beliefs *about* children shape the ways in which we treat them. As we attempt to address and ameliorate the condition of children in our society, we will do well to struggle against our own cultural blindness. Warned by the mistakes of the missionaries, we may be inclined to pay attention to positive models and wise approaches wherever these can be found.

9. Education and the Child in Eighteenth-Century German Pietism: Perspectives from the Work of A. H. Francke

MARCIA J. BUNGE

Although Pietism is sometimes characterized as a religious movement that focused on individual salvation and a denial of worldly pleasures, German Pietism of the early eighteenth century emphasized not only the renewal of the individual believer but also the need to live out this renewal in love of the neighbor. Pietism in Germany developed in the late seventeenth century as a protest against Lutheran Orthodoxy, which tended to define faith as assent to precisely worded doctrinal statements. Because of its overemphasis on doctrine, Lutheran Orthodoxy generally neglected religious experience and ethical and social concerns. The Pietists helped to inspire a new religious vitality within the church by emphasizing the study of the Bible, the experiential nature of faith, the individual's personal relation to God and Christ, and the importance of living out one's faith in concrete acts of love and service to others.[1] German Pietism was part of a larger religious awakening in Europe during the seventeenth and eighteenth centuries and influenced several other Protestant reform movements, including Methodism and North American revivalism.

One of the most important leaders of German Pietism who directly tied

---

1. For an introduction to Pietism in English, see the following works by F. Ernest Stoeffler: *The Rise of Evangelical Pietism* (Leiden: Brill, 1971); *German Pietism during the Eighteenth Century* (Leiden: Brill, 1973); and *Continental Pietism and Early American Christianity* (Grand Rapids, Mich.: Eerdmans, 1976); see also Dale Brown, *Understanding Pietism* (Grand Rapids, Mich.: Eerdmans, 1978). For introductions in German, see *Geschichte des Pietismus,* volume 1 (1993) edited by Martin Brecht and volume 2 (1995) edited by Martin Brecht and Klaus Deppermann (Göttingen: Vandenhoeck & Ruprecht); Erich Beyreuther, *Geschichte des Pietismus* (Stuttgart: Steinkopf, 1978); and Martin Schmidt, *Pietismus* (Stuttgart: Kohlhammer, 1972).

love of neighbor to attention to the needs of children was August Hermann Francke (1663-1727). Francke was a Lutheran pastor at St. George's Church in Glaucha and a professor of Greek and Oriental languages at the nearby University of Halle. Here he established a large complex of charitable and educational institutions, including a school for poor children and an orphanage. The scale of the enterprise was "unheard of" at the time;[2] it covered about thirty-seven acres and involved almost three thousand students, teachers, and staff. His institutions became "one of the most important places in German educational life,"[3] sparking the establishment of other schools and orphanages throughout Germany as well as in other countries, including North America.[4]

Francke is acknowledged not only for his institutions and remarkable organizational skills but also for his innovative approach to education. He incorporated the ideas of several religious thinkers who were also concerned about education, such as François Fénelon (1651-1715), Johann Valentin Andrea (1586-1654), and especially Johannes Amos Comenius (1592-1670),[5] and he is

2. W. R. Ward, *The Protestant Evangelical Awakening* (Cambridge: Cambridge University Press, 1992), 62.

3. Koppel Pinson, *Pietism as a Factor in the Rise of German Nationalism* (New York: Columbia University Press, 1934), 135.

4. Although Klaus Deppermann claims that Halle was a model for new or renovated orphanages in Königsberg, Stargard, Bautzen, Zittau, Erfurt, Lemgo, Pyrmont, Wildungen, Kassel, Bayreuth, Darmstadt, Stuttgart, and the military orphanage in Potsdam, Udo Sträter provides a more detailed discussion of Halle's influence, distinguishing orphanages that followed Francke's model from those that were established primarily on economic grounds, depended on state funds, or used children for hard labor. See Klaus Deppermann, "August Hermann Francke," in *Orthodoxie und Pietismus,* ed. Martin Greschat (Stuttgart: Kohlhammer, 1982), 257; and Udo Sträter, "Pietismus und Sozialtätigkeit: Zur Frage nach der Wirkungsgeschichte des 'Waisenhauses' in Halle und des Frankfurter Armen-, Waisen- und Arbeitshauses," *Pietismus und Neuzeit* 8 (1982): 201-30. For the influence of Francke's institutes in other countries, see, for example, Wolf Oschlies, *Die Arbeits- und Berufspädagogik August Hermann Franckes (1663-1727): Schule und Leben im Menschenbild des Hauptvertreters des halleschen Pietismus* (Wittenberg: Luther-Verlag, 1969), 41-46; for their influence in the United States, see, for example, Hermann Winde, "Die Frühgeschichte der Lutherischen Kirche in Georgia" (unpublished dissertation, Martin-Luther-Universität Halle-Wittenberg, 1960), 135-48; and Thomas J. Müller, *Kirche zwischen zwei Welten: die Obrigkeitsproblematik bei Heinrich Melchior Muehlenberg und die Kirchengründung der deutschen Lutheraner in Pennsylvania* (Stuttgart: Steiner, 1994).

5. Francke was highly informed by Comenius; he mentions Comenius in his writings, and many texts by Comenius can be found in the library of Francke's institutes. For a discussion of Francke's relation to Comenius, see Erhard Peschke, "Die Reformideen des Comenius und ihr Verhältnis zu A. H. Franckes Plan einer realen Verbesserung in der ganzen Welt," in *Der Pietismus in Gestalten und Wirkungen,* ed. Heinrich Bornkamm, Friedrich Heyer, and Alfred Schindler (Bielefeld: Luther Verlag, 1975), 368-82; and Franz

recognized for putting these ideas into practice in a highly visible way. Instead of supporting the common educational approaches of the time, Francke advocated education for all children (including girls and the poor), rejected coercion and harsh disciplinary measures, paid attention to the individual needs and abilities of students, recommended teaching students in the vernacular (instead of Latin), and emphasized not only the acquisition of knowledge but also the development of character.

By carrying out these and other kinds of reforms, Francke's schools attracted many students and had an excellent reputation for preparing well-qualified pastors and teachers. Francke's ideas also influenced the rich debates about pedagogy in Europe during the eighteenth century, sometimes called "the pedagogical century,"[6] and helped establish pedagogy as a separate academic discipline.[7] In addition, Francke's ideas significantly shaped school reforms and social policies in Prussia. Largely as a result of his influence, wealthy citizens and nobility became interested in the establishment of public schools. And in 1717 Friedrich Wilhelm I of Prussia, who knew and respected Francke, decreed compulsory education for children between the ages of five and twelve and established about two thousand schools, modeling them after Francke's schools in Halle.[8]

Although Francke is acclaimed for promoting such educational reforms, he has also been criticized for stating that the will of the child must be "broken" and for emphasizing the need for religious conversion. One of the most common complaints raised by critics from the Enlightenment to the twentieth century is that by emphasizing the breaking of the will and conversion, he disregarded the individuality of children.[9] Like other Pietists, he is also often

---

Hofmann, "A. H. Franckes Idee der 'Universal-Verbesserung' und die Weltreformpläne des Comenius," in *Hallesche Universitätsreden* (Halle: Martin Luther Universität Halle-Wittenberg, 1964). See also the influence of Duke Ernest the Pious on Francke's ideas of education in Lowell Green, "Duke Ernest the Pious of Saxe-Gotha and His Relationship to Pietism," in *Der Pietismus in Gestalten und Wirkungen*, 179-91.

6. Willy Moog, *Geschichte der Pädagogik* (Ratingen: A. Henn Verlag, 1967), 2:30.

7. Oschlies, *Die Arbeits- und Berufspädagogik August Hermann Franckes*, 160.

8. Pinson, *Pietism as a Factor in the Rise of German Nationalism*, 137; Oschlies, *Die Arbeits- und Berufspädagogik August Hermann Franckes*, 42.

9. For a discussion of Enlightenment critiques of Francke, especially those of Christian Thomasius and Christian Wolff, see Carl Hinrichs, *Preussentum und Pietismus: Der Pietismus in Brandenburg-Preussen als religiös-soziale Reformbewegung* (Göttingen: Vandenhoeck & Ruprecht, 1971); and Martin Brecht, "August Hermann Francke und der Hallische Pietismus," in *Geschichte des Pietismus*, 1: 503-7. For later critiques, see Karl Richter, *A. H. Francke: Schriften über Erziehung und Unterricht* (Berlin: Julius Klönne, 1871), 152-55; and Franz Hofmann, "Die Stellung A. H. Franckes in der Geschichte der Pädagogik," in *August Hermann Francke: Das humanistische Erbe des grossen Erziehers*

characterized as an anti-intellectual who replaced critical thinking and rigorous scholarship with a focus on devotional life and spiritual edification.[10] Furthermore, because Francke required strict supervision of children and a rigorous daily schedule in his schools, his ideas about child rearing and education are criticized as too harsh, "rigid," and even "repressive,"[11] especially when compared to modern approaches or even to ideas of some of his near contemporaries who have been recognized for their more enlightened views of children, such as the English philosopher John Locke (1632-1704). Studies tend to judge Francke along with Pietism in general either as "regressive" or as leading toward more progressive views of children but nevertheless having serious limitations. Indeed, since he emphasized original sin and the breaking of the will, it would be easy to dismiss him as merely a precursor to the kind of "poisonous pedagogy" that the disturbing studies of Alice Miller and Philip Greven have uncovered in some later forms of Pietism and in strains of American Protestant thought influenced by Pietism.[12] This type of inhumane pedagogy stresses the absolute obedience of children to parents, the depravity of children, and the need to "break their wills" at a very early age with harsh physical punishment if necessary.

However, recent studies on Francke and Pietism and on the histories of childhood and the care of the poor enable a reassessment of his view of educa-

---

(Halle: Druckerie der Werktätigen, 1965), 9-18. Hofmann claims the limitations of Francke's pedagogy include his suppression of the "natural self-will" and "the individuality of children," his promotion of the constant supervision of children, and his mistrust of free time and play (14).

10. Erhard Selbmann, "Die gesellschaftlichen Erscheinungsformen des Pietismus hallischer Prägung," in *450 Jahre Martin-Luther-Universität Halle-Wittenberg*, edited by Leo Stern (Halle: Selbstverlag der Martin-Luther-Universität, 1952), 2:66.

11. Although Klaus Deppermann appreciates aspects of Francke's pedagogy, Deppermann claims that in order to break the will of the students without using corporal punishment, Francke kept the children under constant supervision, and the virtues of order, diligence, and obedience were taught at the cost of a child's own initiative, happiness, and self-confidence. Deppermann concludes that "in the context of the 18th century, Francke's pedagogy represented a system of extreme repression" (Deppermann, "August Hermann Francke," 252). He also claims that although Francke theoretically rejected any kind of method of conversion because conversion is the work of God, in practice he made conversion and sanctification the goal of his pedagogical method (253).

12. Philip Greven, *Spare the Child: The Religious Roots of Punishment and the Psychological Impact of Physical Abuse* (New York: Alfred A. Knopf, 1991) and *The Protestant Temperament: Patterns of Child-Rearing, Religious Experience, and the Self in Early America* (New York: Alfred A. Knopf, 1977); and Alice Miller, *For Your Own Good: Hidden Cruelty in Child-Rearing and the Roots of Violence*, translated by Hildegarde and Hunter Hannum (New York: Farrar, Straus & Giroux, 1983). For a summary of facets of "poisonous pedagogy," see Miller, *For Your Own Good*, 58-63.

tion and children. In this essay I will build on this research and conclude that although Francke does claim that the will must be "broken" and emphasizes religious conversion, he believes that children should be treated with compassion, and he asserts that the central aim of education is to foster in children a lively faith that expresses itself in love and service of others, especially the poor. Furthermore, by examining his approach to education in relation to his theological convictions, I will reveal specific ways in which it incorporated an appreciation of individuality and scholarship. Finally, although on the surface it might seem that the notions of original sin and breaking of the will necessarily would encourage the harsh treatment of children, I will show that in the context of Francke's theology, these notions not only fostered the humane treatment of children but also helped to provide a strong vision of concern for all children, regardless of class or gender.

This examination of Francke's view of the nature, rearing, and education of children provides both a richer picture of diverse conceptions of childhood in the eighteenth century and an important corrective to current discussions of "poisonous pedagogy" and the religious roots of child abuse. Although historians now resist the temptation to date the "discovery of childhood," and although some find more continuity than change in the history of childhood,[13] many still consider the eighteenth century to be a significant period in the transformation of ideas about childhood.[14] They find in this century, for example, a growing sensitivity to childhood and to children[15] and the development of institutions to serve poor children.[16] They also discover theories of childhood that tend to reject the notion of original sin, placing responsibility for a child's behavior primarily on environmental factors and parental guidance.[17] For some historians, the "key" to this greater sensitivity to children and the more humane treatment of them comes from secularization and the decline in the belief of original sin.[18] However, by closely examining Francke's career and

13. See, for example, Linda Pollock, *Forgotten Children: Parent-Child Relations from 1500-1900* (Cambridge: Cambridge University Press, 1983). Pollock claims that changes in the eighteenth century are minor compared to the continuity one sees in parent-child relationships from the sixteenth century to today. She does, however, notice increased emphasis on abstract thinking about children and parental care in the eighteenth century (269).

14. Hugh Cunningham, *Children and Childhood in Western Society since 1500* (New York: Longman, 1995), 61.

15. Cunningham, *Children and Childhood in Western Society since 1500,* 61.

16. Markus Meumann, *Findelkinder, Waisenhäuser, Kindsmord: Unversorgte Kinder in der frühneuzeitlichen Gesellschaft* (München: Oldenbourg, 1995).

17. W. M. Spellman, *John Locke and the Problem of Depravity* (Oxford: Clarendon, 1988), 203-4.

18. Ulrich Herrmann states, for example, that the more loving care of children that one finds in the eighteenth century could only take place once the "theological view" of

writings, this study reveals a more complex perspective on the religious language of "breaking the will" and on the relationship between views of original sin and the treatment of children. It also helps to differentiate the treatment of children among early Pietists and later religious groups influenced by Pietism and to reveal often-ignored commonalities between Enlightenment and Pietist views of children. Finally, this investigation shows that elements of Francke's theology led him to possess a deeper concern for the poor and underprivileged than many of even his most enlightened contemporaries and, indeed, many people today.

I begin this study of Francke with a brief historical background and a description of his institutions. I go on to explore some of the grounds for his creation of the institutions; examine his ideas about breaking the "self-will" and the aims of child rearing and formal education; and outline his proposals for carrying out these aims. I then conclude with a brief comparison to Locke and an evaluation of Francke's approach.

Historical Background and Development of Francke's Institutes

When Francke came to Halle and the nearby town of Glaucha in 1692 to take up his duties as pastor and professor, he found many children in tremendous need because of poverty, neglect, and poor educational opportunities. Halle had suffered during the Thirty Years' War and was devastated by the Plague (1682-83) and fires (1683-84).[19] This situation created economic hardships for

---

children as weak and depraved was replaced by the "pedagogical view" of children as individuals with open futures. See Ulrich Herrmann, "Kind und Familie im 18. Jahrhundert," in *Das Kind im 18. Jahrhundert: Beiträge zur Socialgeschichte des Kindes,* ed. Johannes Oehme (Lübeck: Hansisches Verlagskontor H. Scheffler, 1988), 12. See also Cunningham, *Children and Childhood in Western Society since 1500,* 62. In another book, Cunningham recognizes the complexity of this period. He states that although two strains of thought concerning children do battle with one another in the eighteenth century (one strain sees children as "conceived and born in sin" and often advocates firm discipline, and the other strain builds on "the Lockean conception of the child as a tabula rasa" and "the more positively sentimental idea that children are the embodiment of innocence"), it is misleading to place individuals in one camp or the other, since "those with the sternest views could be kind and loving in practice," and since some thinkers "seemed able to perceive of children as both innocent and sinful." See *Children of the Poor: Representations of Childhood since the Seventeenth Century* (Oxford: Blackwell, 1991), 47-49.

19. For a description of Glaucha in this period, see Brecht, "August Hermann Francke und der Hallische Pietismus," 1:456; Erich Neuss, "Das Glauchaische Elend 1692," in *August Hermann Francke: Das humanistische Erbe des grossen Erziehers,* 19-27; Mary

many families and a high number of orphans, and Francke often speaks of children forced to beg or steal. Glaucha was a small town with no school. Thirty-seven of its two hundred homes were taverns, and it had a reputation as a place to get drunk and a high rate of alcoholism.

In Halle and indeed throughout many areas of Germany at this time, overall conditions for children were grim. About 40 percent of infants died within the first year of life, and many others suffered chronic illnesses.[20] In addition, German educational life was still affected by the devastation of the war. Many libraries and school buildings were just being repaired, and there was still a shortage of teachers. Most children did not go to school. Poor children could not afford to attend school, and the prevailing attitude, even among the clergy, was that schooling was not useful for children of the lower classes.[21] Education that was available also had its critics. Among representatives of both Pietism and the Enlightenment there was widespread criticism of schoolteachers who disciplined children harshly and often beat them with rods, and of university students who lacked discipline, oppressed younger students, and drank heavily.[22] Furthermore, in regard to religious education and practice for young people, standards were minimal.[23]

Francke responded to this situation by starting religious instruction at his church, preaching about child rearing,[24] and establishing in Halle a number of institutes (in German, the *Franckesche Stiftungen*) to educate children and care for the poor.[25] Plans for a school for the poor began in 1695, when Francke re-

---

Fulbrook, *Religion and the Rise of Absolutism in England, Wüttemberg, and Prussia* (Cambridge: Cambridge University Press, 1983), 154; and Josef Neumann, "Die physische Erziehung des Kindes: Zum Verhältnis von Medizin und Pädagogik im Erziehungs-und Bildungskonzept von August Hermann Francke (1663-1727)," *Würzburger medizinhistorische Mitteilungen* 13 (1995): 267-85. Markus Meumann also describes the widespread suffering of poor children and orphans in German territories at the end of the late seventeenth century. See *Findelkinder, Waisenhäuser, Kindsmord*, 19.

20. Neumann, "Die physische Erziehung des Kindes," 271.

21. Pinson, *Pietism as a Factor in the Rise of German Nationalism*, 123.

22. Marianne Doerfel, "Pietistische Erziehung: Johann Christian Lerches Memorandum zu Reformbestrebungen am Pädagogium Regii in Halle," *Pietismus und Neuzeit* 20 (1994): 93.

23. Fulbrook, *Religion and the Rise of Absolutism in England, Wüttemberg, and Prussia*, 154.

24. Gustav Kramer says that there are no existing copies of these sermons but that Francke incorporated ideas from them into other texts. See *A. H. Francke's Pädagogische Schriften*, 2d edition, ed. Gustav Kramer (Langensalza: Hermann Beyer, 1885), xxxvii.

25. For an account of the establishment of these institutes, see Francke, *Die Fußstapfen des noch lebenden und waltenden liebreichen und getreuen Gottes* (1701), in *Werke in Auswahl*, ed. Erhard Peschke (Berlin: Luther Verlag, 1969), 30-55; and Thomas

ceived a large donation in a special offering box that he had designated for aid to the poor. Although the school began in his home, his endeavors were highly successful and attracted many students, both rich and poor. By the time of his death in 1727, he had built an orphanage and several schools that served over two thousand boys and girls,[26] between (roughly) six and fifteen years of age. More specifically, the schools included the following: (1) the *Pädagogium Regium*, which prepared sons of the nobility and the upper class for positions in the military and the government; (2) the Latin school, which prepared sons of ordinary citizens *(Bürgerkinder)* for the university and professions in law, medicine, and theology; and (3) the German school, which provided a general education for boys and girls to help them become good tradesmen and housewives. For a brief time, orphans and children of the poor (who paid no tuition or board) were taught separately in the orphanage, but they soon attended either the German or the Latin school.[27] Until 1740, the institutes also included a school for daughters of the nobility (the *Gynäceum*).[28] The schools were housed in separate buildings that included classrooms, dormitories, and infirmaries. In addition to the schools, the complex of buildings that made up the

---

Müller-Bahlke, "Die frühen Verwaltungstrukturen der Franckeschen Stiftungen," in *"Man hatte von ihm gute Hoffnung": Das Waisenalbum der Franckeschen Stiftungen, 1695-1749,* ed. Juliane Jacobi and Thomas Müller-Bahlke (Tübingen: Niemeyer, 1998), vii-xxii. Although the institutes included more than the orphanage, they are also sometimes referred to collectively as "the orphanage" (in German, *das Waisenhaus*).

26. According to Kramer, by 1727 there were 82 students in the *Pädagogium Regium,* 400 in the Latin school, 1,725 in the German school, and 134 in the orphanage; there were also 8 inspectors, 10 supervisors of the orphans, 167 male teachers, and 8 female teachers (see Kramer's introduction to *Pädagogische Schriften,* liii). Beyreuther states that out of approximately 2,300 students, 1,000 of them were girls; see *Geschichte des Pietismus,* 154. Müller-Bahlke states that the number of students in the orphanage during Francke's leadership was generally around 100 boys and 30 girls. See Müller-Bahlke, "Die frühen Verwaltungstrukturen der Franckeschen Stiftungen," xviii-xix. His article also provides the most recent and reliable statistics about the number of students in particular schools at various periods.

27. Müller-Bahlke, "Die frühen Verwaltungstrukturen der Franckeschen Stiftungen," xix.

28. According to Ulrike Witt, only about 100 girls were educated in the Gynäceum between 1698 and 1727, and it was closed in 1740 because there was not enough demand for this kind of education for girls at the time. Although Witt criticizes many aspects the *Gynäceum* and claims the standards of education there were lower than for boys in the *Pädagogium,* she still argues that it is an important institution in the history of the education of women. See Witt, "'Wahres Christentum' und weibliche Erfahrung: Bildung und Frömmigkeit im Piestimus des 17. und beginnenden 18. Jahrhunderts," in *Geschichte der Mädchen und Frauenbildung,* 2 vols., ed. Elke Kleinau and Claudia Opitz (Frankfurt/New York: Campus, 1996), 1:263-74.

institutes also included a print shop (which printed books, newsletters, pamphlets, and inexpensive Bibles) and bookstore (one of the largest in Germany at that time);[29] a pharmacy; a small home for widows; a library; a chemistry lab; a small museum of natural history; and a kitchen, washhouse, bathhouse, and brewery (collectively called the *Oeconomi*). The institutes also provided free meals for poor university students (the *Freitisch*). By 1721, the complex also included a pediatric hospital.[30]

In addition to providing at least some limited education for girls, Francke earnestly attempted to make another major educational innovation in the institutes: "to bridge educationally the social stratification of his day, which, at this particular time, required both vision and courage." Thus, although the schools were organized according to the rigid class system of the day, "lines between the various schools were fluid," and students were allowed to advance according to their ability and God-given gifts.[31] For example, there were always some sons of ordinary citizens in the *Pädagogium*, and early on a few orphans and sons of the poor even studied there.[32] Furthermore, many orphans and sons from poor families prepared for a university education in the Latin school. During the first fifteen years of the institutes, about 20 percent of them attended the Latin school, and thereafter this percentage rose to an average of between 30 and 40 percent.[33] In 1706, appar-

29. The print shop could print texts in German and Latin as well as print Greek, Hebrew, Syriac, Coptic, and Slavonic letters. The Bibles were sponsored by the Canstein Bible Society, and Francke was able to print them very cheaply. According to Oschlies, between 1713 and 1719, the print shop printed 80,000 Bibles and 110,000 copies of the New Testament, and by 1800 it had printed 2,770,282 Bibles or sections thereof; see *Die Arbeits- und Berufspädagogik August Hermann Franckes*, 31. According to Brecht, by 1717 the print shop's catalogue offered 300 titles by 70 authors, and between 1717 and 1723 no less than 350,000 copies of Francke's sermons were published; see "August Hermann Francke und der Hallische Pietismus," 1:485.

30. According to Paul Raabe, it was the first pediatric hospital in Germany. See Paul Raabe, "Einleitung," in *Schriften der Franckeschen Stiftungen* 10 (2000): 13.

31. Stoeffler, *German Pietism during the Eighteenth Century*, 26. Klaus Deppermann also claims that Francke's position toward class differences was far ahead of his time. See "Die Pädagogik August Hermann Franckes und ihre Bedeutung für die Gegenwart," in *Die Innere Mission* (September 1963): 286.

32. Müller-Bahlke, "Die frühen Verwaltungstrukturen der Franckeschen Stiftungen," xix.

33. Juliane Jacobi believes the rising percentages perhaps reflect a changing clientele of students who were intentionally seeking a good education. She also reminds us that the orphans (who had lost either a father or both parents) came from a range of social and economic situations, and some of the boys arrived with a fairly good educational background. However, a high percentage of female orphans always came from the lower classes. Jacobi also underscores the fact that records from this period show us how much social

ently an exceptional year, 60 out of 96 orphans were studying in the Latin school, while only 36 of them were learning a trade.[34]

Although in early eighteenth-century Germany churches typically bore the main responsibility for education and schools (with some support from states), Francke's institutes were funded by neither the church nor the Prussian state but rather by private donations and by revenue from the bookstore and the pharmacy. The Protestant church in Halle should have offered support, but it was dominated by orthodox Lutherans who were critical of Pietism and refused to support the institutes, even though many children from Halle attended Francke's schools. However, Francke did receive special tax privileges from the Prussian government and licenses to print books and sell medications. Furthermore, he found support among his colleagues at the University of Halle, which had been established by the Prussian government in 1694 as a counterbalance to the strongly orthodox Lutheran universities of Wittenberg and Leipzig,[35] and he used to his advantage the close proximity of the institutes to the university.[36] Philipp Jacob Spener (1635-1705), one of the central leaders of Pietism

---

mobility the institutes made possible for orphans. See Juliane Jacobi, "Zur sozial- und bildungsgeschichtlichen Bedeutung des Waisenalbums," in *"Man hatte von ihm gute Hoffnung,"* xxv, xxviii. A new project entitled *Franckes Schulen, 1695-1769* (directed by Jacobi, Müller-Bahlke, and Peter Menck) will be able to provide detailed statistics on the precise economic and educational backgrounds of students in Halle.

34. Stoeffler, *German Pietism during the Eighteenth Century,* 26; Beyreuther, *Geschichte des Pietismus,* 154; and Deppermann, "Die Pädagogik August Hermann Franckes," 287. I could not confirm the accuracy of the statistics provided by Stoeffler, Beyreuther, and Deppermann. However, according to Udo Sträter, director of the *Interdisziplinäres Zentrum für Pietismusforschung,* they could be accurate. Minutes from administrative conferences at this time indicate that a high number of orphans were studying Latin and Greek (and some even Hebrew), and that administrators wanted to investigate whether or not all of these orphans were gifted enough to be preparing for a university education. (See, for example, minutes from 12 August and 1 December 1705, cited in the archives as AFSt/W V/-/13 Bd. 1, pages 144, 178.) Even if the numbers for 1706 are not typical, Jacobi's percentages alone are striking for this period.

35. Fulbrook, *Religion and the Rise of Absolutism in England, Wüttemberg, and Prussia,* 154.

36. Most of the teachers Francke hired were university students at the school, who would receive free lunch at the *Freitisch* in exchange for teaching twelve hours a week. The students Francke chose participated in a training seminar for teachers (the *seminarium praeceptorum*), and the best students from this group (the *seminarium selectum praeceptorum*) were trained for two years and then taught for three years. This system of training seminars influenced the beginning of the academic training of teachers in eighteenth-century Germany; see Oschlies, *Die Arbeits- und Berufspädagogik August Hermann Franckes,* 223. Francke also hired several "inspectors" or directors for each school to supervise the teachers, to visit their classes, to meet with them once a week in order to discuss the progress of students and practical concerns, and to give monthly exams to the students.

256

in Germany, had helped to arrange the appointment of Francke and many other like-minded Pietist professors, and the university became the intellectual center of Pietism in Germany.

Grounds for Establishing the Institutes: Francke's View of Christian Faith and Life

One of the reasons that Francke created the institutes and devoted so much of his time and energy to them lies in his understanding of Christian faith and life.[37] He often spoke about faith in terms of "piety" or "godliness." For Francke and the Pietists in general, "piety" or "true faith" is a living, active faith that expresses itself in love and service to the neighbor, especially the poor. His notion of piety is built on Martin Luther's understanding of the relation between faith and love.[38] Luther believed that one is saved or justified by faith alone, not works — and yet this faith is manifested in works of love toward others. Francke emphasized this close relation between faith and works, often citing the following quotation from Luther:

> Faith is a divine work in us, which transforms us, grants us a new birth from God, and kills the old Adam; it fashions us into human beings who are entirely different in heart, soul, mind, and in all our powers; and it brings with it the Holy Spirit. Oh, faith is such a living, creative, active, powerful thing that it is impossible for it not to do good. It does not ask if there are good works to be done, rather even before the question is raised, faith has done them and is continually active.[39]

37. For a brief summary of his theological views translated into English, see his "Scriptural and Basic Introduction to True Christianity," translated by Gary R. Sattler in *God's Glory, Neighbor's Good: A Brief Introduction to the Life and Writings of August Hermann Francke* (Chicago: Covenant Press, 1982), 243-54. Important secondary sources on Francke's theology in German are the following texts by Erhard Peschke: *Studien zur Theologie August Hermann Franckes*, 2 vols. (Berlin: Evangelische Verlagsanstalt, 1964, 1966); *Bekehrung und Reform: Ansatz und Wurzeln der Theologie August Hermann Franckes* (Bielefeld: Luther-Verlag, 1977); and "Zur Struktur der Theologie A. H. Franckes," *Theologische Literaturzeitung* 86 (1961): 881-96.

38. For a discussion of some of the similarities and differences between the theologies of Luther and Francke, see Peschke, *Bekehrung und Reform*, 136-49.

39. Quoted in Erich Beyreuther, *Selbstzeugnisse August Hermann Franckes* (Marburg: Francke-Buchhandlung, 1963), 64; and from Luther's "Vorrede auf die Epistel S. Pauli an die Römer," in *D. Martin Luthers Deutsche Bibel: 1522-1546* (Weimar: Hermann Böhlaus Nachfolger, 1931), 7:10.

Although Francke builds on Luther's view of faith, he is more interested than Luther (and closer to Calvin here) in the kind of daily life and in the concrete works of love that result from faith. Francke, like other early Pietists, therefore pays more attention to the everyday behavior of the individual and expresses greater concern for social issues than Pietism's "Lutheran genesis."[40] He also clearly emphasizes that caring for the poor is a central part of living out the Christian faith. In a sermon entitled "The Duty to the Poor,"[41] for example, he claims that one of the main reasons Lutherans have neglected the care of the poor is that they have criticized the Catholic emphasis on works for so long that they think they do not need to do good at all. He points out that both the Old Testament and the New Testament emphasize love of the neighbor, especially widows, orphans, and all those in need. He also encourages members of his congregation to live simply and modestly (without pomp, arrogance, and useless material goods) so that they can use their financial resources to help the poor, and he urges them to get close to the poor, as Jesus did, by listening to their needs, helping them, and breaking bread with them.

This view of piety and concern for the poor fit Francke's own experience of radical conversion, which took place just after he had completed his university studies in 1687.[42] While preparing a sermon on John 20:31 about the nature of a true and living faith, he realized that he himself did not possess that kind of faith because he had serious doubts about God's existence and the truth of the Bible. In his state of doubt and anxiety, he prayed to God to help him and later reported, "As one turns one's hand, so all my doubts were gone. In my heart I was assured of the grace of God in Jesus Christ. I was able to call God not only God, but my Father. All sadness and restlessness of heart was taken away at once. However, I was suddenly overwhelmed by such a flood of joy that I thanked and praised God with all my heart for showing me such tremendous grace."[43] Through this experience, Francke felt empowered by God's grace to serve others. Throughout his writings he emphasizes his conviction that gratitude to God leads to a new way of life and to service to the neighbor, especially the underprivileged, and it is clear from his writings and actions that he himself "existentially identified with the poor" and felt deeply about their plight.[44]

Francke's view of piety, emphasis on love of neighbor, and experience of conversion are reflected in several specific themes that are foundational to his

---

40. Brown, *Understanding Pietism,* 136.

41. "Duty to the Poor" has been translated into English by Sattler in *God's Glory, Neighbor's Good,* 155-85.

42. See the account of his life in *"August Hermann Franckes Lebenslauf"* (1690/91), in *Werke in Auswahl,* ed. Peschke, 4-29.

43. *"August Hermann Franckes Lebenslauf,"* 22.

44. Stoeffler, *German Pietism during the Eighteenth Century,* 21.

theology. For example, he accentuates the themes of self-examination, repentance, and conversion. He claims that recognition of sin and repentance are often accompanied by a penitential struggle *(Busskampf)*, and he emphasizes the individual's experience of conversion *(Bekehrung)* by using more the language of "new birth" or "being born again" than of justification. Although this language highlights the experience of the individual believer, what is most important for Francke is not a particular experience of conversion but an individual's new relation to God, which leads to amendment of life and service to others.[45] Furthermore, he commonly speaks of those who have faith or the converted as "children of God" and opposes them to the "children of the world."[46] Although he says there can be no genuine community between the two, he insists that the "children of God" must associate with the "children of the world" and show compassion to them, as Jesus did. He also reminds believers to be humble and compassionate toward everyone because in many ways they are like the "children of the world": they are also sinners and need God's grace. This openness to the "children of the world" is also supported in his theology by his clear rejection of predestination and his belief that God is continually seeking out all people. Finally, Francke often speaks of faith as "childlike" in the sense that faith places trust in God as a loving father and is joyful, free of anxiety, and empowered by the Holy Spirit.[47]

Another central reason for Francke's deep commitment to his institutes is his belief that the education of children and young people and the care of the poor are the two best vehicles for improving church and society in all "realms" (the household, the school, the church, the government). In his "Great Essay," he laments the "universal corruption" or "depravity" *(Verderben)* that can be found in all areas of society — indeed, throughout the world. He claims that this corruption stems from two major sources: (1) the terrible education of young people and decay of the educational establishment, which includes the church and the school; and (2) the neglect of the poor.[48] For Francke, this corruption is evident in all areas of public and pri-

---

45. Stoeffler, *German Pietism during the Eighteenth Century*, 8.

46. See the sermon entitled *"Äusserlicher Umgang der Kinder Gottes mit den Kindern dieser Welt,"* (1695) in *Werke in Auswahl*, ed. Peschke, 293-303.

47. For his emphasis on "childlike faith" and "children of God," see, for example, his sermons entitled *"Die geistliche Seelen-Cur," "Die Wenigkeit der rechten Kinder Gottes,"* and *"Das rechte Lob Gottes,"* in *Sonn-Fest-und Apostel-Tags Predigten*, 5th ed. (Halle, 1715), 2:552-82, 2:583-609, and 3:151-70. Hereafter this work will be referred to as SFP (1715). See also Stoeffler, *German Pietism during the Eighteenth Century*, 20; and Brecht, "August Hermann Francke und der Hallische Pietismus," 1:464-66.

48. *Der Grosse Aufsatz: August Hermann Franckes Schrift über eine Reform des Erziehungs- und Bildungswesens als Ausgangspunkt einer geistlichen und sozialen Neu-*

vate life. Rulers oppress the poor and foster war. Family life is filled with affairs, lying, betrayal, stealing, drinking, and hatred. Within the schools and universities, students are crude, drunk, and unruly, and teachers do not take their work seriously. Within the church, pastors have no living relation to God and are more concerned about gaining wealth and fame than spreading the gospel. In all areas, the poor are neglected, resulting in thefts and violent crimes. Francke believes that since all pastors, teachers, and public officials are trained at schools and universities, a thoroughgoing revision of the entire educational system is the best way to address poverty and renew every area of public and private life.

The Aims of Education, the Nature of Children, and Breaking of the "Self-Will"

Because Francke was intensely engaged in establishing these institutes and strongly believed that a thoroughgoing revision of the educational system was the key to addressing poverty and other social problems, throughout his writings he articulated precise aims for education broadly understood to include not only formal education in the schools and the church but also child rearing in the home. He often summarizes the aim of education as the "honor" or "glory" of God (die Ehre Gottes).[49] He specifies this aim of education by saying that education should lead children to "genuine piety and true Christian wisdom" (Gottseligkeit und Klugheit).[50] Again, he understands "piety" to be a living faith that expresses itself in love and service to others, and he heightens his emphasis on serving others by saying that piety must be combined with "Christian wisdom," which involves avoiding temptations, knowing one's gifts, and possessing the knowledge and practical experience to be able to help others. Education that has as its purpose the "glory of God" therefore involves not only the formation of the intellect and Christian character but also the development of

---

ordnung der Evangelischen Kirche des 18. Jahrhunderts, ed. Otto Podczeck (Berlin: Akademie Verlag, 1962), 73, 76, 80. Gustav Kramer gave the essay the shortened title of Der Grosse Aufsatz in 1882, and it has been known by this title ever since; Francke's original title was Offenhertzige und gründliche Nachricht von der inneren Beschaffenheit und Wichtigkeit des Wercks des Herrn zu Halle im Hertzogthum Magedburg, sowohl wie es anitzo stehet, als was unter dem fernern Segen Gottes darvon zu hoffen. See Podczeck's introduction, 9.

49. Kurzer und einfältiger Unterricht, wie die Kinder zur wahren Gottseligkeit und christlichen Klugheit anzuführen sind (1702), in Werke in Auswahl, ed. Peschke, 124.

50. Kurzer und einfältiger Unterricht, 126.

practical skills and knowledge that help one serve others.[51] Francke contrasts this understanding of education to other views of the aims of education common in his own day: to achieve status, to get rich, to earn a living,[52] to feed one's vanity and ambition,[53] and to gain knowledge without using that knowledge to love and serve others.

In one of his most important texts on education, "A Short and Simple Guide on How Children Can Be Led to Genuine Piety and Christian Wisdom" (1702),[54] Francke claims that the way to foster genuine piety and Christian wisdom is through the care or cultivation of the "soul" or the "spirit" *("cultura animi"* or *"Gemüthspflege").*[55] He says the care of the soul includes attention to both the will and the understanding *(Wille und Verstand).*[56] This statement underscores his notion that education must address the entire person. However, he also claims that the cultivation of the soul "above all" involves the "breaking of the self-will" *(Eigen Wille),*[57] and he focuses most of his attention here and in other texts on this. Although "breaking of the self-will" initially sounds like a harsh process, throughout the text he describes it primarily in mild terms of

---

51. He also speaks of piety as a "living knowledge of God and Christ" and expresses the purpose of education in this way: "die Kinder vor allen Dingen zu einer lebendigen Erkenntnis Gottes und Christi und zu einem rechtschaffenen Christentum mögen wohl angeführet werden" (to lead children "to a lively [or living] knowledge of God and Christ and to upright Christianity"), 116; and "die Kinder zu einem wahren, lebendigen Erkenntnis Gottes und ihres Heilandes Jesu Christi zu bringen" ("to bring the children to a true, living knowledge of God and their savior, Jesus Christ"), 161. See *Ordnung und Lehrart, wie selbige in denen zum Waisenhause gehörigen Schulen eingeführet ist* (1702), in Kramer's edition of *Pädagogische Schriften*. In an appendix to this text, it states that the purpose of the orphanage is to "build up true piety" and help orphans "serve God and the neighbor" (176).

52. *Kurzer und einfältiger Unterricht,* 125.

53. *Von der Erziehung der Jugend* (1698), in *Werke in Auswahl,* ed. Peschke, 122.

54. *Kurzer und einfältiger Unterricht,* 124-50. Collections of Francke's main pedagogical writings include Kramer's *Pädagogische Schriften;* Richter's *Schriften über Erziehung und Unterricht; August Hermann Franckes wichtigste pädagogische Schriften,* ed. Johannes Gansen (Paderborn: Ferdinand Schöningh, 1891); and *Pädagogische Schriften,* 2d edition, ed. Hermann Lorenzen (Paderborn: Ferdinand Schöningh, 1964).

55. *Kurzer und einfältiger Unterricht,* 125. *Gemüth* is sometimes translated as "heart," although here Francke is clearly saying *Gemüth* includes the will and the understanding.

56. According to psychological teachings of the day and to several earlier theories, these are the two powers of the soul. See Peter Menck, *Die Erziehung der Jugend zur Ehre Gottes und zum Nutzen des Nächsten: Begründung und Intentionen der Pädagogik August Hermann Franckes* (Wuppertal: A. Henn Verlag, 1969), 29.

57. "Am meisten ist wohl daran gelegen dass der natürliche Eigen Wille gebrochen werde" (*Kurzer und einfältiger Unterricht,* 126).

"igniting a spark of true piety,"[58] "implanting piety,"[59] "instilling piety," "awakening faith and love,"[60] and "giving space and room for the working of God's grace."[61] Indeed, he uses the negative expression "breaking the self-will" only once in this essay, and throughout his discussion he consistently uses this milder language.

Francke's understanding of "breaking the self-will" and his more frequent use of the milder language of "instilling" or "awakening" piety can best be understood by examining his views of sin and grace and then outlining his concrete suggestions for "awakening piety." Like Augustine, Luther, Calvin, and others, Francke claims that the Fall has destroyed the power of human beings to love God and the neighbor without God's help. By nature (meaning fallen nature) human beings are turned in on themselves; their wills are stubborn and self-centered.[62] Thus, by "self-will" Francke means the natural (fallen) will of human beings that focuses on its own good and its own glory. He would agree with the *Augsburg Confession* that human beings are "full of evil lust and inclinations from their mother's wombs and are unable by nature to have true fear of God and true faith in God."[63] Francke also follows Augustine and the Pietist Johann Arndt in finding signs of this self-will evident even in small children.[64]

58. "zu einem Füncklein wahrer Andacht erwecken" (*Kurzer und einfältiger Unterricht*, 142).

59. "Einpflantzung der Gottseligkeit" (*Kurzer und einfältiger Unterricht*, 140).

60. "Glaube und Liebe erwecken" (*Kurzer und einfältiger Unterricht*, 144).

61. "der Wirkung der göttlichen Gnade Platz und Raum zu geben" (*Kurzer und einfältiger Unterricht*, 136).

62. Menck says that, for Francke, the self-will is the human will insofar as it is the "old man" (*Die Erziehung der Jugend zur Ehre Gottes und zum Nutzen des Nächsten*, 30). Menck also lists a number of quotations from Francke about the fallen nature of human beings. Gary Sattler also provides an extended treatment of Francke's view of sin and the self-will in English in *Nobler than the Angels, Lower than a Worm: The Pietist View of the Individual in the Writings of Heinrich Müller and August Hermann Francke* (Lanham, Md.: University Press of America, 1989).

63. *Augsburg Confession* (Article II), in *The Book of Concord*, trans. and ed. Theodore Tappert (Philadelphia: Fortress Press), 29.

64. Francke was highly influenced by Arndt and read and reread his *True Christianity*. Here Arndt clearly states that children are corrupt and depraved: "Look at a small child. Evil qualities arise at the moment of birth, particularly self-will and disobedience, and when the child grows up a little, an inherited self-love, self-honor, self-praise, self-righteousness, lying, and other things of the same kind break forth. Soon pride, arrogance, pomposity, despising God, cursing, swearing, evil desires, lies and deceptions, despising God and his Word, despising parents and authority, break forth. There follow wrath, antagonism, hatred, envy, enmity, desire for vengeance, murder, and all kind of abominations, particularly if external circumstances arise that awake the Adamic carnal qualities in man. . . . Who could have believed in the beginning that in so small, weak, and simple a

According to Francke, this "self-will" must be brought under obedience to God's will. Francke uses the notion of "breaking the self-will" to underscore the radical reorientation of the will that needs to take place in fallen human beings — from inordinate self-love to love of God and the neighbor. For Francke, it is the will, not the intellect, that is the seat of human egotism and self-centeredness and thus the source of evil deeds. It is this fallen will or self-centeredness that must be broken so that it will follow God's will of loving God and the neighbor.

From Francke's theological perspective, the only way to break the self-will, thereby allowing an individual to become a "new creature," is by God's grace and through God's Word. God forgives those who look to Christ and have faith in him. Through faith one is united with Christ and becomes a new creature who carries out his or her calling "joyfully and cheerfully" "to the glory of God" and "the neighbor's good."[65] Because Francke rejects predestination, he believes that everyone has access to this new life through the Word of God and the power of the Holy Spirit. The Holy Spirit works through the Word, which is the central means ordained by God to bring about new birth.[66] For Francke, this Word includes both the "law," which shows what one ought to do, reveals sin, and also instructs believers how to live out this new life in Christ; and the "gospel," which reveals God's love and forgiveness through Jesus Christ. Following Luther, Francke also believes that the sacraments (visible signs of the Word that offer forgiveness of sins) are another means to this new life in Christ. In regard to baptism, Francke supports infant baptism but emphasizes that one must always keep in mind the meaning of baptism and must renew the baptismal covenant through repentance and conversion and by living one's life according to God's will.[67]

Francke's understanding of the self-will, the need for radical conversion, and the role of the Word in this conversion help to illuminate his view of edu-

---

child there could lie hidden such a waste of all kinds of vices, so undoubtedly evil a heart, so abominable a worm and basilisk. Man himself demonstrates it in his life and walk, in his evil thoughts and activities from his youth on (Gen. 6:5). There is an evil root out of which so poisonous a tree grows, an evil seed of the serpent and of the vipers' generation out of which so despicable an image comes. Everything grows from the inside outward and is made much worse by external offenses. For this reason, the Lord Christ sternly forbade the offenses of youth because the seed of the serpent lies hidden in children. In it, much shame and evil rest and lie secretly hidden away, as poison in a serpent." See Johann Arndt, *True Christianity,* trans. Peter Erb (New York: Paulist Press, 1979), 34-35.

65. "Scriptural and Basic Introduction to True Christianity," 253.

66. Stoeffler, *German Pietism during the Eighteenth Century,* 16.

67. *"Von der H. Taufe Würde und Bedeutung,"* in *Predigten,* 2 vols., ed. Erhard Peschke (Berlin: Walter de Gruyter, 1987, 1989), 1:596-97. Peschke cites several other central texts on baptism in *Studien zur Theologie August Hermann Franckes,* 1:31-37.

cation and use of "breaking of the self-will." Francke believes that God alone can actually break the self-will and orient it toward God's will. The harsh language of "breaking" fits with Francke's own understanding of the radical reorientation of the will that is necessary to follow God's will and love others. However, because Francke believes that God works through the Word, he also claims that the main way in which a teacher, parent, or pastor can help "awaken" or "instill" piety within children is to expose them to the Word. This is the vehicle that God has given for bringing about conversion or the reorientation of the will. Thus, although the ultimate goal of education is to reorient the will and instill true piety, the central means to this goal is exposure to the Word. The mild language of "instilling," "implanting," "fostering," and "cultivating" piety fits with this focus on exposure to the Word.

Suggestions for Awakening Piety and Cultivating Christian Wisdom

It follows that all of the concrete suggestions Francke offers in his central texts on education for instilling piety within children are related to this emphasis on the Word, especially the gospel. For example, he claims that one central way that true piety is fostered in children is by reading the Bible and exposing them to the Word through the teachings and practices of the church (learning the catechism, singing hymns, praying, and worshipping). Francke encourages parents, especially fathers, to begin this approach right away with young children in the home by reading and discussing the Bible, teaching Luther's catechism, praying at meals, beginning and ending the day, if possible, with a prayer and a hymn, worshipping together, and preparing for worship on Saturday by reading the text for Sunday's sermon. Although he says that members of each family must do what is most comfortable for them in terms of these practices, he encourages the family to read through the whole Bible every two years and Luther's catechism every four weeks.[68] Furthermore, his writings on teaching methods and school regulations give a very detailed picture of the kind of exposure to the Word that students at his institutes received. Each school day included morning and afternoon devotions and a worship service.[69] Reading as-

68. *Glauchische Haus-Kirch-Ordnung oder Christlicher Unterricht Wie ein Haus-Vater mit seinen Kindern und Befinde das Wort Gottes und das Gebet in seinem Hause üben und Ihnen mit gutem Exempel vorleuchten soll* (Halle: Christian Henckeln, 1699).

69. Devotions were held at the beginning of morning and afternoon classes and included singing a hymn, saying prayers, reading a chapter of the Bible, repeating part of Martin Luther's catechism, and the offering of a blessing. Morning classes concluded with

signments also included passages from the Bible, and students were required to memorize and reflect on Luther's catechism.

Francke recommends that when exposing children to the Word, one should emphasize the promises of the gospel instead of the threat of God's punishment. One should stress that "godliness is valuable in every way, holding promises for this life and the next" (1 Tim. 4:8). Here Francke emphasizes not the promises of wealth or fame but rather the promises of a loving and faithful God who never abandons his children, of eternal life, and of the Kingdom of God, which is found in "righteousness and peace and joy in the Holy Spirit" (Rom. 14:17).[70] He does say that some children who consistently do wrong might need to be reminded of the threat of God's eternal punishment. However, he explicitly warns teachers not to attack children verbally and not to emphasize the punishment of God.

Another important way of exposing children to the Word and leading them to genuine piety is for parents, grandparents, teachers, and all those who have contact with children to be good examples. For Francke, a good example is someone with a living faith who is living out the Word: someone who follows Christ and God's will and exhibits humility, patience, kindness, and love of both enemies and neighbors, "especially the poor and those in need."[71] He believes that examples are especially powerful because children tend to imitate all that they see. He also emphasizes the importance of constant supervision of children in order to protect them from bad examples. In his institutes, many children stayed in the dormitories and were never without supervision. Inspectors ate with them, slept with them, and even read their private letters. Francke calls this strict supervision the "central nerve" of education.[72]

In relation to his understanding of a good example, Francke also says that it is "highly necessary" to teach children everything that belongs to true piety with "enthusiasm and love."[73] If one is to awaken faith and love in children, then they must be treated in a loving and friendly manner and guided by the

---

a prayer of thanks, the Lord's Prayer, and a hymn. The worship service or "prayer hour," held for all students at the end of afternoon classes, included singing hymns, reading a chapter of the Bible, listening to a meditation on Scripture, and saying prayers. Students attended classes six days a week and would meet before and after services on Sunday (even if they lived at home) to prepare for worship and discuss the sermon. For a description of the school schedule and its emphasis on exposure to the Word, see *Ordnung und Lehrart*, 119-54. If students lived in the orphanage, then they also had morning and evening prayers and prepared for Sunday worship with a service on Saturday.

70. *Kurzer und einfältiger Unterricht*, 135.

71. *Glauchische Haus-Kirch-Ordnung*, paragraph 4.

72. *Ordnung und Lehrart*, 179.

73. *Kurzer und einfältiger Unterricht*, 144.

"sweetness of the gospel" and not the "harshness of the law."[74] In texts on teaching, he specifically emphasizes this kind of approach to children in the schools and tells teachers that they should express the love of a father or mother to their students by teaching with friendliness, patience, tenderness, joy, and impartiality, and wishing the best for them all.[75] He contrasts treating children this way with the negative alternative: subjecting them to hate, violence, scolding, harshness, and anger, calling them terrible names (such as "ass" or "fool"), and being a taskmaster *(Zuchtmeister)*. For Francke, treating children with "gentleness and sweetness" *(Sanftmut* and *Süssigkeit)* instead of "strictness and harshness" *(Strenge* and *Härtigkeit)* is the best way "to present to them the love of God in Jesus Christ" and thus "to plant within their hearts a longing for and love of the Word of God" and "to awaken faith in them."[76] This kind of approach will "bend their hearts toward the good."[77]

In addition, Francke says that it is important to implant three particular virtues in children that he believes are central to an active faith and the Christian life: "the love of truth, the love of obedience, and the love of diligence."[78] He believes that the love of truth keeps the heart honest and open to all people. Parents and teachers should emphasize the seriousness of lying and not lie themselves. Obedience puts down the "self-will" and instills in children the virtues of humility, modesty, and friendliness. Although Francke claims that children should obey both parents and teachers, this does not mean that children should be treated like domestic servants or beaten into obedience. Children should also be taught not to obey anyone who would have them act in ways that do not glorify God. He reminds parents and teachers that true Christian obedience means that the "greater" serves the "lesser" in love, as Jesus did when he washed the feet of his disciples. Parents and teachers should also instill diligence in young children, which, for Francke, is related to his emphasis on piety and the love of neighbor. He fears that one of the biggest problems of young people is that they are "idle" not only in relation to work but also in relation to spiritual matters.[79] He believes that working diligently is important because through work one has the possibility to love the neighbor in concrete and practical ways.[80] However, he often warns

74. *Kurzer und einfältiger Unterricht,* 144.

75. *Ordnung und Lehrart,* 162-63, 187, 191.

76. *Ordnung und Lehrart,* 163.

77. *Ordnung und Lehrart,* 162.

78. "Liebe zur Wahrheit, Gehorsam, und Fleiss" (*Kurzer und einfältiger Unterricht,* 137).

79. *"Der Beruff Gottes nach dem unterschiedlichen Alter der Menschen,"* SFP (1715) 1:397.

80. In his *Lebens-Regeln,* Francke thoroughly discusses work and gives three reasons that human beings are to work: first, it is a command of God; second, it allows us to show

everyone to take a "middle road," neither being lazy nor working too much, which for him is also "godless" and "burdens the soul."[81] With children, too, parents and teachers should provide variety in school lessons, allow time for children to rest, and protect their health. Spiritual diligence is also central. Francke wants children to be diligent in terms of their relation to God, especially by industriously hearing the Word of God.[82]

Although Francke explains that in extreme emergencies it might be necessary to "use the rod," he warns against its misuse and praises God if it never has to be used at all.[83] He believes that corporal punishment usually drives children to hate their teachers and parents, causes them to perform good actions only out of fear, and even creates in them an aversion to "true piety." He does, however, leave room for using the rod as a "last resort" for a variety of reasons: it has basis in Scripture (and he mentions passages from Proverbs and the Psalms);[84] it can prevent children from growing up in wickedness and spare them from God's harsh judgment;[85] and it can be effective with children who have temperaments that do not respond to milder forms of discipline. However, he also limits the punishment based on biblical grounds (such as Deut. 25:2-3) and outlines in great detail the conditions under which corporal punishment should be carried out. For example, he believes that teachers should use corporal punishment only for serious offenses, such as stealing, and never for failing to understand course material. He also believes that girls and young children should not be subjected to corporal punishment. Teachers should ask God for guidance, show their students love and empathy, and avoid becoming angry. When correction seems warranted, teachers should warn students at least three times before resorting to the rod, and make sure students understand the reason for the punishment. They should also take care not to harm students.[86] Francke also strongly rejects several forms of severe punishment that must have been accepted in his time, such as locking children alone in dark rooms, hitting them until they bleed, and hitting them on the legs, head, and face. It was necessary to provide detailed instructions about physical punish-

---

love to the neighbor; and third, it helps address the needs of the body. He claims that even if people have enough money to provide for themselves and thus do not need to work, they should still work so they can use their money to help the poor. See *Lebens-Regeln*, ed. Georg Helbig (Berlin: Furche, 1938), chapter 6.

81. *Lebens-Regeln*, chapter 6, paragraph 5.

82. *"Der Beruff Gottes nach dem unterschiedlichen Alter der Menschen,"* SFP (1715) 1:397.

83. *Kurzer und einfältiger Unterricht*, 146.

84. *Ordnung und Lehrart*, 199-200.

85. *Kurzer und einfältiger Unterricht*, 146.

86. *Ordnung und Lehrart*, 163-64, 190-204.

ment because, according to minutes of teacher conferences at the school and according to Francke himself, some inexperienced teachers in his own institutes also inappropriately punished students.[87]

Although Francke devotes much of his writing on education to outlining these and other ways of "breaking the self-will" and instilling piety in children by exposing them to the Word in the variety of ways mentioned above, he also believes that it is important to address the intellect and to direct children to "Christian wisdom." Francke's suggestions for instilling wisdom are related to his emphasis on living out one's faith in concrete acts of love and service. As he sees it, a Christian needs "wisdom" to be able to act within a particular time and within his or her given context to the glory of God: "Christian wisdom" is knowing how to avoid temptations[88] and "having an eye for knowing what serves the greatest good and what protects from harm."[89] He believes that although some children may be highly educated or highly devout, they can still lack this practical sense to do what serves the greatest good in concrete ways.

For Francke, "Christian wisdom" is built on both knowledge and experience. In his institutes he tried to increase knowledge among students by offering courses in a number of disciplines, such as reading, writing, math, history, music, geometry, geography, astronomy, physics, botany, medicine (at the introductory level), Greek, Hebrew, French, and Latin. Francke also insisted that students understand the practical application of these subjects and built into the curriculum opportunities for practical experience in various areas. As Ernest Stoeffler points out, "For recreational as well as instructional purposes students were to visit regularly various workshops and art studios in the community. They were to have some insight into the physical sciences related to animals, herbs, trees, metals, stones, minerals, water, air, fire, etc. Furthermore, a certain elementary knowledge of basic trades such as carpentry, optics, etc. was mandatory."[90] The objects in the small natural history museum were also used in the curriculum.

Another important element of "Christian wisdom" for Francke is the ability to recognize one's God-given gifts and to develop them intentionally to serve the neighbor. Francke believes that every person has a special calling or vocation and unique gifts and abilities that should be used to glorify God and serve the neighbor.[91] In a text on teaching, he says that teachers must get to know their students individually and recognize their distinctive temperaments

---

87. Menck, *Die Erziehung der Jugend zur Ehre Gottes und zum Nutzen des Nächsten*, 48.

88. *"August Hermann Franckes Lebenslauf,"* 7-8.

89. *Kurzer und einfältiger Unterricht*, 150.

90. Stoeffler, *German Pietism during the Eighteenth Century*, 27.

91. *Ordnung und Lehrart*, 166-67.

and gifts. In this way teachers can best know how to treat individual students and help them recognize their God-given talents. Francke extends this application to poor children: he believed that even children who were beggars must recognize their gifts and be taught useful skills so that they would no longer need to beg but could rather serve the neighbor.[92]

Francke's heavy emphasis on recognizing each child's God-given gifts and talents suggests that he was highly sensitive not only to the individual abilities of children but also to stages in their development. Although he does not speak of stages of childhood in a systematic way, he certainly was attuned to various abilities and challenges at different levels of development. For example, he often distinguishes "children" *(Kinder)* who are under twelve from "young people" *(Jugend)* who are approximately twelve to fifteen years old.[93] He speaks about their special needs and abilities, including the specific difficulties young people face. His writings are filled with suggestions for addressing these various developmental stages in the treatment of children, such as telling parents not to lecture to young children or read too much to them at one time, and advising teachers to make the curriculum age-appropriate.

In addition to offering all of these suggestions for instilling piety and cultivating wisdom, Francke places great emphasis on praying with and for children. He encourages parents to let children pray in their own words, beginning when they are very young. He also claims that it is important for everyone who has contact with children to pray for them and to ask for God's wisdom to treat them rightly.[94] Francke admits that the upbringing and formal education of children is a difficult task and, in the end, requires the help of God. He also admits that it is difficult to discover a perfect way to raise children, and that obstacles will always stand in the way. Furthermore, he recognizes that it is sometimes difficult to know if one's efforts have done any good. However, he believes that God is gracious and merciful and will therefore hear those who pray for help.[95]

Francke believes that providing the kind of education that fosters piety and cultivates wisdom is the duty of everyone, and thus he directs many of his remarks on education not only to teachers but also to parents, grandparents,

92. *Ordnung und Lehrart,* 165.

93. For distinction of ages, see, for example, *"Der Beruff Gottes nach dem unterschiedlichen Alter der Menschen,"* SFP (1715) 1:387-405; *"August Hermann Franckes Lebenslauf,"* 8; or *Kurzer und einfältiger Unterricht,* 141-44.

94. See, for example, *"Der Beruff Gottes nach dem unterschiedlichen Alter der Menschen,"* SFP (1715) 1:396.

95. In one text, Francke reminds readers that God heard the prayers of Augustine's mother, Monica, and gives wisdom and understanding to those who ask for it. See *Von der Erziehung der Jugend,* 123.

and pastors. He especially wants this kind of education to take place in the home, recognizing the important role of parents. He urges them to take seriously their own responsibilities in their children's spiritual development and to reject the notion that this is the duty of only pastors and teachers.[96] However, he believes that many parents neglect their duties and do not even send their children to school or church. He also realizes that some parents are overprotective and criticize teachers who discipline their children. Other parents are simply bad examples and are obstacles to a good education.[97] Thus, the education of children must be a cooperative effort between church, home, and school, and the job of every teacher, pastor, parent, relative, and neighbor in regard to children is very much the same: to cultivate their souls and to foster in them a living faith that manifests itself in love of others.

Since Francke emphasizes the Word, helping children realize a vocation, and prayer, he often thinks of education, broadly understood, as creating a space for the Holy Spirit to work. Indeed, Francke sometimes speaks of schools (and this could apply to homes as well) as "workshops of the Holy Spirit."[98] He is not saying that education is the same as conversion, because conversion requires God's grace, the power of the Holy Spirit, and one's own acceptance of God's call. However, he does believe that the right kind of upbringing is crucial, because exposing children to the Word and helping them develop a sense of their gifts and vocation make room for the work of the Holy Spirit. An improper education or exposure to bad examples only creates obstacles to piety.

Francke also believes that it is almost easier for the Holy Spirit to move in the hearts of children than in the hearts of adults, and that children can have rich spiritual lives. He claims that through baptism the Holy Spirit is working in the lives of children, even if we do not always recognize it. Thus, children are able to accept the call of God at any time, even when they are young. Francke cites examples from church history to support this point. He also claims that the Holy Spirit finds fewer obstacles or resistance in children under twelve than in young people and adults who have had a bad upbringing, have developed habits and attitudes that keep their hearts turned from God, or who are distracted by worldly pursuits, such as fame, fortune, and vain pleasures.[99]

96. *Glauchische Haus-Kirch-Ordnung*, paragraphs 1-3.

97. *"Der Beruff Gottes nach dem unterschiedlichen Alter der Menschen,"* SFP (1715) 1:393-94. Several other references to Francke's critique of parents are summarized by Oschlies, *Die Arbeits- und Berufspädagogik August Hermann Franckes*, 109.

98. "Werkstätten des heiligen Geistes," in *Ordnung und Lehrart*, 204.

99. *"Der Beruff Gottes nach dem unterschiedlichen Alter der Menschen,"* SFP (1715) 1:392-98.

Envisioning the Child in a Class-Conscious Society: Evaluation of Francke and Comparison to Locke

Although Francke assumes that children are sinful and that their self-wills must be broken, and although he does accept corporal punishment of children as a "last resort," he clearly exhibits compassion toward children and does not display signs of the "poisonous pedagogy" that Miller and Greven outline in later forms of evangelicalism influenced by Pietism, such as treating children with severity and coldness, using force in the early years to break the will, and believing that parents are masters of their children.[100] As noted earlier, for Francke "breaking the will" is not a matter of destroying a child's will but rather of reorienting the will from inordinate self-love to the love of God and the neighbor. In addition, although Francke believes that obedience is a virtue, it is not the supreme principle in his view of education, and he does not require absolute obedience to parents, even when they are wrong, as some later forms of Protestant fundamentalism apparently did.[101] He is not preoccupied with obedience and punishment but rather focused on exposing children to the gospel and fostering in them a living and active faith that leads to service of others.

Furthermore, although Francke does not claim that the central goal of education is to foster a child's individuality or to develop critical thinking, as some of his critics might hope, his vision of education and child rearing does include room for attention to a child's individuality and for an appreciation of scholarship — but always within the context of love and service to the neighbor. He is interested in discovering a child's unique gifts and talents not for his or her own sake but rather so that the child can develop these talents to the glory of God and in service to the neighbor.[102] In the same way, Francke is also neither an anti-intellectual nor an enemy of scholarship, but he does want knowledge of the sciences, the arts, and languages to be used in concrete ways to the glory of God and for the neighbor's good.[103] He believes that the applica-

---

100. Miller, *For Your Own Good,* 59-60. In his *Spare the Child* and *The Protestant Temperament,* Greven speaks in great detail about several American Protestant thinkers who advocated the severe punishment of children, including infants.

101. Greven, *Spare the Child,* 198-99.

102. As H. Ahrbeck states, "The individual traits of children are not seen as valuable on their own but in their relation to the glory of God and the common good." Ahrbeck is quoted by Menck in *Die Erziehung der Jugend zur Ehre Gottes und zum Nutzen des Nächsten,* 65.

103. Menck, *Die Erziehung der Jugend zur Ehre Gottes und zum Nutzen des Nächsten,* 32-37. See, for example, Francke's view of learning in *Idea Studiosi Theologiae,* in *Pädagogische Schriften,* ed. Kramer, 405.

tion of knowledge is the measure of its worth.[104] It is true that his emphasis on the practical use of knowledge led him to underestimate the value of philosophy, but other areas of study greatly improved in Halle under the influence of Pietism, especially medicine. Theological studies also were strengthened through Francke's emphasis on biblical studies, ethics, preaching, and worship.[105]

It is beyond the scope of this essay to provide a detailed historical picture of how children were actually treated in Halle and how they experienced their education there or to examine in what way Francke's ideas precisely have influenced later proponents of a "poisonous pedagogy." More work in this area is just beginning to be done. In the current literature, most Francke scholars evaluate his own treatment of children positively. Although a few have judged his policy of constant supervision of children as harsh and even repressive, most believe that he followed the humane principles that he outlined in his writings and treated children with respect, sensitivity, and kindness.[106] Furthermore, they understand the strict supervision of children to be a necessary measure in a setting with a mixed group of children from a variety of social and economic backgrounds. Clearly, the schedule at the schools was rigorous.[107] Furthermore, because the schools were growing at a rapid rate and funds were scarce, the actual living conditions of the orphans were not always comfortable and did not consistently meet the guidelines outlined by Francke. For example, the sleeping hall for orphans could be drafty and cold in winter, and orphans did not always have enough clothing.[108] In addition, unlike Nicolas Ludwig von Zinzendorf (1700-1760), another important German Pietist and innovative educator who studied in Halle and later became the spiritual leader of the Moravians, Francke did not appreciate the importance of play in child development.[109] He also saw

---

104. Oschlies, *Die Arbeits- und Berufspädagogik August Hermann Franckes*, 76.

105. Stoeffler claims that Francke "prepared the way for the theological seminary of the future and the inclusion of 'practical theology' among its educational concerns" (*German Pietism during the Eighteenth Century*, 31). Beyreuther emphasizes Francke's appreciation of scholarly research in biblical studies (*Selbstzeugnisse August Hermann Franckes*, 7-8).

106. See, for example, Stoeffler, *German Pietism during the Eighteenth Century*, 28, 34.

107. For a precise description of the daily schedule, see Thomas Müller-Bahlke, "Kinder in den Glauchaer Anstalten zu Franckes Zeiten. Entsagung auf Teufel komm raus?" in *Schriften der Frankeschen Stiftungen* 10 (2000): 23.

108. Müller-Bahlke, "Kinder in den Glauchaer Anstalten zu Franckes Zeiten," 25-26. Apparently Francke was not always aware of these conditions because as the schools grew, so did his administrative duties, and thus his own direct contact with the children became minimal.

109. For an introduction to Zinzendorf and his view of children and youth, see O. Uttendörfer, *Zinzendorf und die Jugend* (Berlin: Furche-Verlag, 1923); John Weinlick,

little use for theater arts, dance, and fiction. Nevertheless, most scholars claim that the atmosphere at the schools was not oppressive,[110] and that Francke did provide children with many opportunities to sing, to play music, and to participate in physical activities as long as they served a useful purpose. Furthermore, his concern for the physical health of children and their proper medical care is considered exemplary for this period.[111]

However, most scholars agree that after Francke's death, some of his followers, including perhaps his own son, Gotthilf August, absolutized a few of Francke's principles. His followers apparently went in an anti-intellectual direction and overemphasized the struggle of repentance and conversion, creating a rigid and harsh environment for children and losing the sense of joy of a childlike faith.[112] Furthermore, even in evangelical movements today that have been influenced by Pietism, language about breaking the will and conversion is often connected to the harsh treatment of children. Certainly we should not judge Francke exclusively on the basis of later movements influenced by him or by Pietism in general, and it is important to remember that Pietism is a diverse movement and that its influence is complex and far-reaching, affecting fundamentalism and revivals of the eighteenth century as well as German Romanticism and liberal theologians of the nineteenth century, such as Friedrich Schleiermacher. However, perhaps the subsequent misunderstanding and misuse of his language of "breaking the self-will" can serve as an important warning: Even if a theologian clearly states that only God through the Word and the Holy Spirit can truly break the self-will (i.e., turn one's will away from inordinate self-love to proper love of self, God, and the neighbor), when the powerful language of "breaking the self-will" is used in the context of recommendations for child rearing and education, it can easily open a door to the notion that physical punishment breaks the self-will and thereby can create a space for the violent and abusive treatment of children.[113] How much difference would we have seen in later forms of Pietism

---

Count Zinzendorf (New York: Abingdon, 1956); and Henry Meyer, *Child Nature and Nurture according to Nicolaus von Zinzendorf* (New York: Abingdon, 1928).

110. See, for example, Beyreuther, *Geschichte des Pietismus,* 171, 181.

111. Neumann, "Die physische Erziehung des Kindes," 280.

112. Oschlies, *Die Arbeits- und Berufspädagogik August Hermann Franckes,* 51; Beyreuther, *Selbstzeugnisse August Hermann Franckes,* 146-55. The new research initiative, *Franckes Schulen, 1695-1769,* cited in footnote 33, will enable one to evaluate more accurately these long-held critiques of Francke's son and followers by providing a more detailed picture of the period after Francke's death.

113. In one unusual passage, Francke himself easily moves from emphasizing exposure to the Word as the vehicle for breaking the self-will to suggesting that it can be done through physical punishment. See *Glauchische Haus-Kirch-Ordnung,* paragraph 16.

and in the history of Christianity in terms of the treatment of children if parents and teachers had understood their central task not as breaking the self-will but as providing room for the Holy Spirit to work in the lives of children in all of the specific ways that Francke describes?

Even though language of breaking the self-will was later misused, clearly one of the greatest strengths and legacies of Francke's view of children and education is that his approach to children not only was humane for his time but also showed more openness than that of many of his contemporaries to the needs of the poor and marginalized in what was a highly class-conscious age. Of course, it is important to recognize that most of Francke's students in the end were not poor, and that he took for granted the class distinctions of his day. Nevertheless, at a time when poor children were primarily seen either as burdens or as a source of cheap labor, it is remarkable that Francke created a space for their education and allowed them to advance according to their abilities.[114] His own humane treatment of children and his striking commitment to all children can be seen by briefly comparing his ideas with those of a near contemporary who is often referred to as having "enlightened," "modern," and even "radical" views of children and education: John Locke.[115]

Although interpreters of Locke have commonly claimed that he believes children are shaped entirely by education and their environment, or that his ideas are "openly at odds" with conceptions of children as sinful,[116] his view of

114. Most scholars praise Francke for being among the first in Germany to reject sending poor children to workhouses in which they were used as forced labor and often had to work beside criminals. See, for example, Sattler, *God's Glory, Neighbor's Good,* 61; Beyreuther, *Geschichte des Pietismus,* 153; and Neumann, "Die physische Erziehung des Kindes," 272-77. In contrast, Sträter claims that although Francke's own orphanage was not connected to a "work house," he did not criticize orphanages that were. See "Pietismus und Sozialtätigkeit," 218-23.

115. Peter Gay claims that Locke in his time was denounced "as a radical, in education as in religion." See the introduction to *John Locke on Education,* ed. Peter Gay (New York: Columbia University, 1964), 15. J. H. Plumb states that Locke's attitude to child rearing and education was "modern" and that the goal of this new attitude, encapsulated in his *Some Thoughts Concerning Education,* "was to improve the lot of the child in the eighteenth century." See Plumb, "The New World of Children in Eighteenth-Century England," *Past and Present* 67 (1975): 67-68.

116. Hugh Cunningham claims, for example, that the "pessimistic view" of children conceived and born in sin is "openly at odds both with the Lockean conception of the child as tabula rasa, and with the more positively sentimental idea that children are the embodiment of innocence" (*Children of the Poor,* 48). As stated above (in footnote 18), Cunningham certainly recognizes that many figures do not fit neatly into one camp or the other, yet here he does suggest that Locke's own position is at odds with a view of children as sinful.

274

human nature is more complex than some recognize and in some ways congruent with Protestant ideas of fallen human nature, as W. M. Spellman has shown.[117] For example, although Locke rejects original sin and believes that children are neither virtuous nor evil by nature, he does think, as he claims in his popular *Some Thoughts concerning Education* (1693), that human beings have a "Natural Propensity to indulge Corporal and present Pleasure, and to avoid Pain."[118] Because of this tendency, children must be taught to deny themselves and the satisfaction of their own desires and follow what reason directs.[119] In this way they can serve the common good. Furthermore, as Spellman explains, Locke thinks that "our first actions are guided by self-love" and a natural love of "dominion" and that a child's unbridled quest for "propriety and possession" constitutes the root of almost all of the injustice and contention that disturb human life.[120]

Because Locke and Francke are both concerned about human selfishness and inordinate self-love, they share some similar ideas about the aims of education and the treatment of children. For example, Locke, like Francke, believes that good examples are crucial and that education must cultivate virtue and character and not merely impart knowledge. Locke also believes that adults need to guide or bend the will of children. "To keep their Wills right" is the "great Business" of education, he claims.[121] Although Locke clearly speaks of the will submitting to reason instead of God's will, in many writings Locke connects reason to the divine order. Like Francke, he also advocates the humane treatment of children and recommends physical punishment only as a "last resort." He also places great emphasis on practical knowledge and using education to help produce citizens who serve the common good. Although Locke does not emphasize one's relation to God or speak of the purpose of education as honoring God or awakening piety, he does say that one should instill in children "a true Notion of God" and "a Love and Reverence of this Supreme Being."[122] Children should also "learn perfectly by heart" the Lord's Prayer, the Ten Commandments, and the Creeds, and they should read and memorize

---

117. Spellman, *John Locke and the Problem of Depravity*. For a further discussion of Locke's view of human nature, see J. A. Passmore, "The Malleability of Man in Eighteenth-Century Thought," in *Aspects of the Eighteenth Century*, edited by Earl R. Wasserman (Baltimore: Johns Hopkins Press, 1965), 21-46.

118. John Locke, *Some Thoughts Concerning Education*, edited with introduction, notes, and critical apparatus by John W. Yolton and Jean S. Yolton (Oxford: Clarendon, 1989), 112.

119. Locke, *Some Thoughts Concerning Education*, 103.

120. Spellman, *John Locke and the Problem of Depravity*, 211.

121. Locke, *Some Thoughts Concerning Education*, 141.

122. Locke, *Some Thoughts Concerning Education*, 195.

"Fundamental Parts" of the Bible.[123] He also writes that human beings in general must pray to God for the "assistance of his Spirit" to enlighten our understanding and "subdue our corruptions" so that we can "show our faith by our works."[124]

Despite such similarities, Locke's vision for education is focused on upper-class children, mainly boys, and does not reveal the same compassion for the poor that one finds in Francke's work. In *Some Thoughts concerning Education*, Locke recommends that boys be taught at home by a private tutor.[125] Through private schooling, parents can more easily keep their children away from negative influences and avoid exposing them to the trickery and violence one finds among schoolboys. Girls are mentioned only in passing, and the poor never appear at all in this work. One might excuse Locke because this text was originally written to a close friend who had asked for advice about raising his young son. However, since the book does make some general claims about the nature of children and their education, Locke could have in principle included some remarks about poor children. In his report concerning Poor Laws (from 1697), he does speak directly about them,[126] and here his remarks, as the historian Peter Gay has said, seem "oddly out of place with his general humanitarianism" and "demonstrate that to seventeenth-century thinkers, even to radicals, the poor were barely human."[127] Locke says that beggars between the ages of three and fourteen should be "soundly whipped" and sent to "working schools" where they could learn some manual skills, "generally spinning or knitting," be introduced to "some sense of religion," and perhaps find employment when released.[128] Beyond this, Locke expected little for the poor.[129] He adds that since the children would earn their way with what they produced, their education would cost nothing. Gay excuses Locke's harsh remarks and his neglect of poor children in general by saying that during the seventeenth century, social hierarchies remained clear and class divisions were sharp, and it would be beyond "the wildest of Utopian dreams" for people of Locke's time to have imagined education for all because, at that time, the "poor did not count — not yet."[130]

Although Francke also lived in this highly class-conscious age, for him the poor obviously did "count," and recent research is helping to provide a more

---

123. Locke, *Some Thoughts Concerning Education*, 212-14.

124. Spellman, *John Locke and the Problem of Depravity*, 95.

125. Locke, *Some Thoughts Concerning Education*, 128-29.

126. "Report from the Select Committee on the Poor Laws," reprinted in H. R. Fox Bourne, *The Life of John Locke*, 2 vols. (New York: Harper and Brothers, 1876), 2:377-91.

127. Gay, *John Locke on Education*, 13.

128. Locke, "Report from the Select Committee on the Poor Laws," 381, 383-85.

129. Spellman, *John Locke and the Problem of Depravity*, 208.

130. Gay, *John Locke on Education*, 14-15.

accurate picture of attitudes toward the poor in this period.[131] Since Francke, like Locke, was very concerned about keeping children away from bad examples and negative influences, he could have easily chosen an approach to children that excluded some of them from his schools because of class (as Locke advised), gender (as was common at the time), or association with a particular religious community (as some thinkers advocated). Even Zinzendorf, for example, wanted the orphanage and school he established at Herrnhut to be exclusively for children of his congregation.[132] In contrast, many of Francke's central theological convictions that have been examined in this essay kept his doors open to all children. For example: (1) since true piety is expressed in service to others, especially the poor, we should serve all children; (2) since all people have God-given gifts to serve others, we should help all children discover those gifts and learn to use them; (3) since "the children of God" must love and serve "the children of the world," we should open doors to all children; (4) since Jesus embraced children, we should respect and love them all; (5) since all human beings are sinners, we should recognize our common humanity and remain humble and compassionate toward everyone; and (6) since God is seeking out all people, we should expose everyone to the Word.

Conclusion

The study of Francke's views of education not only provides a clearer understanding of his ideas about children and the "breaking of the self-will" but also contributes to a more detailed picture of conceptions of children among Pietists and representatives of the Enlightenment during the late seventeenth and early eighteenth centuries. Although Francke and Locke expressed distinct understandings of the nature of children and the precise aims of education, both of them advocated treating children humanely, paying attention to their individual gifts and talents, and helping them use their knowledge to serve others. Recognizing some of their differences and similarities reminds us that rela-

131. Although many scholars have claimed that concern for poor children began mainly in the nineteenth century, recent work on the history of poverty has shown that many initiatives took place much earlier, and that between 1650 and 1750 many orphanages, as distinct from workhouses, developed. See, for example, Meumann, *Findelkinder, Waisenhäuser, Kindsmord.*

132. Meyer, *Child Nature and Nurture according to Nicolaus von Zinzendorf,* 149, 156. A comparison of Francke and Zinzendorf regarding their view of children reveals several important differences and similarities that could not be addressed within the limits of this essay but that deserve further attention.

tionships between Enlightenment and Pietist views of children found in the early eighteenth century were more fluid than is often realized.[133]

Recognizing some of these similarities and Francke's inclusion of poor children and girls in his schools helps provide an important corrective to the common assumption that the notion of original sin was a central or even key obstacle to a more humane treatment of children in the eighteenth century and reminds us how complex the religious language of "depravity" can be, especially in relation to children. Any judgments about the effect of the idea of original sin on the treatment of children must be made cautiously and always within the context of a thinker's larger theological or philosophical framework. One must also be attentive to other assumptions and ideas that perhaps created greater obstacles to the humane and compassionate treatment of children, especially those who were poor, such as particular assumptions about class, gender, religion, and race. In the case of Francke, his view of original sin was set within a rich theological framework that, from several angles, supported a more humane treatment of children and attention to the poor. Precisely because of this theology and his understanding of sin, which provided a certain kind of egalitarian framework of thought, Francke was able to overcome some of the powerful assumptions in his highly class-conscious setting and to think seriously about the needs of poor children, to see them as individuals with gifts and talents that could be cultivated, and to respond creatively and effectively to their needs.

Francke's views of the nature and nurture of children challenge all of us to re-examine our own philosophical or theological assumptions and convictions and to see in what ways, if any, they encourage a concern for all children, regardless of class, gender, race, or religious affiliation. Taking this challenge seriously is an urgent task, especially today, when almost 20 percent of children in the United States live in poverty, when many poor children lack adequate educational opportunities, and when child poverty and child labor have become global issues. For those within the church, Francke's theology provides several foundations for concern for all children; and for those outside it, his ideas prompt reflection on additional grounds for child advocacy. Francke himself also serves for all of us as an important example of someone who opened his eyes to the needs of children in his midst and who tirelessly devoted his resources and energy to serving them.

133. For example, Francke had apparently read Locke's *Some Thoughts Concerning Education*, because Canstein discusses a translation of it in a letter to Francke. See *Der Briefwechsel Carl Hildebrand von Cansteins mit August Hermann Francke*, ed. Peter Schicketanz (Berlin: Gruyter, 1972), 74 (13 January 1700); see also 44 (22 October 1698).

10. John Wesley and Children

RICHARD P. HEITZENRATER

John Wesley, whose life spanned the eighteenth century (1703-91), was not an educational theorist himself and did not set any new trends in the area of child psychology. As the founder of Methodism and one of the important English theologians of his time, however, Wesley has had a continuing influence on one of the largest Protestant denominations worldwide.

Wesley's attitude toward children is often caricatured simply as a harsh reflection of his mother's dictum: "In order to form the minds of children, the first thing to be done is to conquer their will."[1] It is true that he did say, "Break their will, that you may save their soul,"[2] and the daily regimen for the students in his Kingswood School seems very harsh these days. Nevertheless, his views were very much in keeping with the prevailing English perspectives of the day. And his interactions with and concerns for children indicate a much more compassionate view than one might expect, given his writings on original sin and his strict regulations for Methodist schools.

1. Letter, Susanna Wesley to John Wesley (July 24, 1732), in *Susanna Wesley: The Complete Writings,* ed. Charles Wallace Jr. (New York: Oxford University Press, 1997), 370. See also John Wesley, the entry dated August 1, 1742, in *Journal and Diaries II,* ed. W. Reginald Ward and Richard P. Heitzenrater, in *The Bicentennial Edition of the Works of John Wesley* (Nashville: Abingdon, 1975-), 19:287 (hereinafter cited as *Works*).

2. John Wesley, Sermon 96, §9, in *Works,* 3:367.

Attitudes toward Children in Eighteenth-Century England

Although there is no consensus on the history of the concept of childhood, some analysts have felt that the idea that children were "little adults" was relatively common in medieval Europe.[3] Children were often portrayed as miniature adults, with small adult features, wearing small adult clothes, positioned in traditional adult stances. The art and literature of the period reflects a typical expectation that children should, as soon as possible, act like adults. Within this framework, success in child rearing could be measured by how early children actually did become "grown-up." According to Philippe Ariès, the "discovery of children" culminated in the eighteenth century.[4] This shift in view, however, was not necessarily a good thing for the children themselves. If the previous view put unnecessarily great expectations on young children, the new view gave them very little credit for any good possibilities. Children, now seen as inferior to adults and needing to be governed strictly by them, fell prey to a repressive and tyrannical concept of the family, typified by the harsh Puritan view.[5] Lloyd De Mause characterizes this eighteenth-century stage in the evolving treatment of children in Western civilization as "the intrusive mode."[6]

Behind these views of childhood, however, lies a theological debate on the nature of humanity that has consequences for the way young people were treated — are children by nature innocent, good beings, or are children by nature evil, depraved beings? Are children to be distinguished by their inherited corruption, marked by an inability to know or do what is "right" in a proper (adult) sense? Or are children characterized by a natural purity and innocence that provides a different conception of moral boundaries that should apply during their early years? The former view, characteristic of Puritans and evangelicals, could result in severe discipline as the parents tried to "bend the twig" into a religious shape. The latter view, attributed to Rousseau, might result in more allowance of "childish behavior" and a concomitant reduction of strictness.

Although Puritans and evangelicals typically stressed original sin and had a reputation for being hard on their children, the correlation of these views is neither simple nor universal. Nor are their attitudes toward children, in what-

---

3. Philippe Ariès, *Centuries of Childhood: A Social History of Family Life* (New York: Vintage, 1962), 33.

4. Ariès, *Centuries of Childhood*, 398-404; for criticisms of and alternatives to this view, see 12-13, 110, 120-21, and 162-63 in this volume.

5. See Linda Pollock, *Forgotten Children: Parent-Child Relations from 1500-1900* (London: Cambridge University Press, 1983), 1-3, characterizing Ariès's views.

6. Lloyd De Mause, *The History of Childhood* (New York: Harper & Row, 1975).

ever combination, necessarily new in the eighteenth century.[7] While many evangelicals could easily demonstrate total depravity, both theoretically and practically, in the lives of children, many others also held to the belief that even unbaptized children who died would go to heaven. And while a concern for salvation did seem to drive the stereotyped harshness of the attitudes within these groups toward child rearing, an idealized positive image of childhood also emerges within the traditional religious terminology of these groups — "to become as a little child," "to believe as a child," "teachable as a little child," "innocent as a child." These phrases, echoing biblical language, appear throughout Puritan and evangelical rhetoric.[8] In fact, this literature often refers to the soteriological goal in terms of one becoming "a child of God."

Although the publications of major writers within groups such as the Puritans during this period may reflect a particular view of children, the practices of the parents in that same group, as reflected in their private diaries, rely much less on theological argument and are less harsh than one might expect.[9] Even the use of total depravity to understand the child's inclination to rebellion might lead a parent to sympathize with the child's plight rather than to hate or punish the child.[10] The Puritans signal a new interest in children by giving non-traditional names to their children, such as Prudence, Chastity, and Tribulation, and by creating a separate body of literature for children.[11] In this literature, the Puritans explicitly stress the necessity of redemption and the rejection of worldliness, a perspective that, while it may have contrasted markedly with the Anglican inclination of the time to promote maintenance of the social order, was not exactly innovative.[12] And while the Puritan portrayal of children as exemplars of a true and living faith does in fact turn the tables on the view of children as "little adults" — in these cases, giving lessons to adults on the manner

---

7. A useful survey of these critiques is found in Susan Willhauck, "John Wesley's View of Children," Ph.D. diss. (Washington: The Catholic University of America, 1992), 68-71.

8. Wesley uses most of these terms, such as "teachable," "innocent," "helpless," "believeth as," "be directed as."

9. Pollock, *Forgotten Children*, 103, 148. Philip Greven makes a similar point in his study of American patterns of child rearing, pointing out that one should look at experience more closely than doctrine. See *The Protestant Temperament: Patterns of Child-Rearing, Religious Experience, and the Self in Early America* (New York: Alfred A. Knopf, 1977), 5.

10. C. John Sommerville, *The Rise and Fall of Childhood* (New York: Vintage, 1990), 127-30.

11. Sommerville, *The Rise and Fall of Childhood*, 125-26.

12. Willhauck, "John Wesley's View of Children," 88; Greven sees Anglican and Puritan (Evangelical) as the two main concepts of childhood during this period (*The Protestant Temperament*, 12-14).

of true religion[13] — it was not a totally new development in the evolving attitudes toward children.

In most cases, writers in this period who tried to explain proper methods of child rearing expressed major concern for two things: the education of children and the example provided by persons in contact with children. Most leaders felt that religious education did play an important role in the training of children and that parents were important in the process. As might be expected, however, one of the areas of dispute was the question of just what role religion might play in both situations — whether it should be the main feature of, or merely supplemental to, the educational process, and whether proper profession of faith by the parents was essential to their children's salvation.

The Puritan concern for children and their education resulted in the foundation of several educational institutions. Some of the Dissenting academies became well-known for their rigor and excellence. John Wesley's parents, Samuel and Susanna, were both raised in Dissenting ministers' families, and Samuel was educated at Dorchester School, one of the Dissenting academies. But both parents became staunch Anglicans in young adulthood, so that the family in which John was raised bore the influence of both traditions.

Susanna Wesley's Views on Child-Rearing Methods and Education

In his last years, Samuel Wesley indicated that his wife, Susanna, had given him "eighteen or nineteen children." One would have thought his count would have been more precise, he being both the father and the parish priest who was responsible for keeping the parish baptismal records. What is known for sure, however, is that ten of the Wesley children survived infancy. With the aid of wet nurses, maids, cooks, gardeners, butlers, and other help, the Wesley family managed to survive on the income of a country rector. The image of Susanna Wesley overwhelmed by the responsibility of taking care of nineteen children at any given time is by no means accurate. Of the ten who survived, no more than five or six resided at home during any given period.

Susanna's method of raising these children left a positive impression on her son John, and during his days as a tutor at Lincoln College, he solicited from her a description of her techniques and rules, which he published in his

13. See James Janeway's *Token for Children*, republished by JW (Bristol: Farley, 1749).

journal at her death.[14] This account, published as well in his *Arminian Magazine* in 1779, provides an important source for John's own views on child rearing and education.

Much of Susanna's method is a reflection of typical eighteenth-century theory, found in Locke and Milton.[15] Mrs. Wesley's primary interest in religious education fits very much into Milton's view of education, that the end of learning was to repair the ruins of our first parents by regaining the knowledge of God aright.[16] And Susanna's aim to "conquer the will" of children exhibits a similar intention as Locke's concern for the necessity of teaching children "compliance" to parental will.[17] Many of her specific instructions exhibit what might be called imposed formation. Pushing this point very hard over several paragraphs, she sees that an indulgent parent will lead to a headstrong child, which will result in sin and misery.[18] Although she recommends teaching children to "fear the rod," which she seems on occasion to have used, she does not appear to have been a severe disciplinarian.[19] And although Locke does assume

14. The entry dated August 1, 1742, in *Journal and Diaries II,* in *Works,* 19:286-91.

15. Alfred H. Body, *John Wesley and Education* (London: Epworth Press, 1936), 34, 49. "In order to form the minds of children, the first thing to be done is to conquer their will, and bring them to an obedient temper." See the entry dated August 1, 1742, in *Journal and Diaries II,* in *Works,* 19:287.

16. Body, *John Wesley and Education,* p. 34. See her comment that when the will is thoroughly conquered, "then a child is capable of being governed by the reason of its parents" (*Susanna Wesley,* 370), which is rather close to Locke's argument that obedience to parents is important, because by submitting "his will to the reason of others," the child prepares for adulthood, when he will "submit to his own reason, when he is of an age to make use of it." See John Locke, *Some Thoughts Concerning Education,* in *The Educational Writings of John Locke,* ed. James L. Axtell (Cambridge: Cambridge University Press, 1968), 145; see Hugh Cunningham, *Children and Childhood in Western Society since 1500* (London: Longman, 1995), 63.

17. Willhauck, "John Wesley's View of Children," 96. See also Locke, *Some Thoughts Concerning Education,* 147; and Philip Greven, *Child-Rearing Concepts, 1628-1861* (Itasca, Ill.: Peacock, 1973), 28.

18. "I cannot yet dismiss this subject. As self-will is the root of all sin and misery, so whatever cherishes this in children, insures their after-wretchedness and irreligion: Whatever checks and mortifies it, promotes their future happiness and piety" (*Susanna Wesley,* 370).

19. "Fear of the rod" is a common phrase used by many people, including Susanna Wesley and John Locke, to indicate a positive instrument of child rearing, but as Greven points out, firsthand accounts seldom indicate the actual practices used to conquer the children's wills (*The Protestant Temperament,* 38). Susanna Wesley does not, in fact, say how such fear was implemented or how often the rod might have actually been used. In a more recent work, Greven appears to have forgotten his earlier caution and portrays an exaggerated view of Susanna as an exceedingly cruel woman in whose home "beatings were a normal part of daily life." Given the lack of actual evidence (there are no firsthand accounts to indicate the

"correction by the rod" as an acceptable method of punishment, he seems to have more moderate views than Susanna on the propriety and frequency of corporal punishment.[20] Neither one, however, seems to have ignored the possibility that excessive punishment could result in what we now call child abuse.

Some of Susanna's regulations, such as expecting the children always to cry softly, may seem unreasonably harsh to us today, but they were in keeping with the traditional Puritan view of her day. Her feelings on the matter are often quoted: "When turned a year old (and some before), they were taught to fear the rod, and to cry softly; by which means they escaped abundance of correction they might otherwise have had; and that most odious noise of the crying of children was rarely heard in the house; but the family usually lived in as much quietness, as if there had not been a child among them."[21] Locke makes these points as well: "Crying is a fault that should not be tolerated in children. . . . [Obstinate crying] requires severity to silence it, and where a look or a positive command will not do it, blows must."[22] Susanna realized that the use of the rod was not acceptable to some parents, but she was convinced that the truly cruel parents were those who, "in the esteem of the world . . . pass for kind and indulgent." For, as she pointed out, allowing stubbornness and obstinacy to develop in a child would result in consequent punishment, the severity of which would be as painful to the parent as to the child.[23]

On the other hand, some of Susanna's ideas seem very modern, such as not punishing a child more than once for the same infraction and not succumbing to a child's desires in order to stop the crying.[24] Perhaps her most progressive design was to promote the education of the girls in the home on an equal footing with the boys. Susanna's eighth "by-law" was perhaps her most forward-looking: "That no girl be taught to work till she can read very well; and then that she be kept to her work with the same application, and for the same time, that she was held to in reading. This rule also is much to be observed; for the putting children to learn sewing before they can read perfectly is the very reason why so few women can read fit to be heard, and never to be well understood."[25]

---

actual daily practices in the Wesley household), his rhetoric is unjustifiably prejudicial: "her hostility toward her infant children," her "assaults and violence," her "persistent use of pain," etc. See *Spare the Child* (New York: Alfred A. Knopf, 1991), 19-20.

20. Locke, however, is much more explicit that corporal punishment should be used sparingly, for cases of obstinacy, and does not believe that "fear of the rod" results in long-term success; see *Some Thoughts Concerning Education*, 148-50.

21. *Susanna Wesley*, 369.

22. Locke, *Some Thoughts Concerning Education*, 218.

23. *Susanna Wesley*, 370.

24. *Susanna Wesley*, 370, 372.

25. *Susanna Wesley*, 373.

Typical of the period, Susanna was responsible for the education of the ten Wesley children in their home. Susanna began with her children on their fifth birthday, teaching them the alphabet and then teaching them to read the Bible. Although her own aptitude in foreign languages has been exaggerated, her learning was remarkable for the times and is best exhibited in the theological comments in her correspondence with her children.[26] This interest in learning she seems to have successfully transmitted to most of her children. John Wesley went on to Charterhouse School, and his brothers were both educated at Westminster School, these schools being among the finest in England. All three of the Wesley boys followed in their father's footsteps by attending Oxford University. Samuel Jr. became a schoolmaster at Blundell's School at Tiverton in Devon. His sister, Emily, became a schoolteacher in Lincoln and eventually opened her own school in Gainsborough. And another sister, Hetty, published poetry in at least four periodicals, including *The Poetical Register* and *The Gentleman's Magazine,* a leading London literary rag.[27]

John Wesley's Views on Child Rearing

John Wesley's views on child rearing appear to be largely derived from his mother.[28] His sermon "On Obedience to Parents" repeats her views on the necessity of obedience ("breaking the will") of the child in order to allow for learning. He seems convinced of the need for this conquest to happen as early as possible, most effectively by the age of two:

> Why did not you break their will from their infancy? At least, do it now; better late than never. It should have been done before they were two years old: It may be done at eight or ten, though with far more difficulty. However, do it now; and accept that difficulty as the just reward for your past neglect.[29]

26. For example, see *Letters I,* in *Works,* 25:159-60, 164-67, 172-73, 178-80, 183-85, etc.

27. Frederick E. Maser, *The Story of John Wesley's Sisters; or, Seven Sisters in Search of Love* (Rutland, Vt.: Academy Books, 1988), 22, 66.

28. Although he had no offspring himself, John Wesley incorporated the topic of raising children into several sermons, most notably Sermons 94-96: "On Obedience to Parents," "On the Education of Children," and "On Family Religion" (*Works,* 3:333-72). Although he follows many of his mother's ideas regarding child rearing and commends her for governing her children so well, Wesley states that he had never met a woman who could manage grandchildren, including his own mother, who "could never govern one grandchild" (*Works,* 3:358).

29. Wesley, Sermon 96, "On Obedience to Parents," II.5, in *Works,* 3:370. See also

Locke presents a very similar argument for early discipline when he talks of settling the authority of the parent over the child, keeping "a strict hand" over them "from the beginning." As he says, "Fear and awe ought to give you the first power over their minds." The resultant "compliance of their wills" will bring awe and respect in the beginning, but should hopefully evolve into love and friendship after the time for the correction of the rod is past.[30] But Wesley's view is much more explicitly directed toward the production of a good Christian than a fine gentleman, as was Locke's intention. Wesley's suggestions for child rearing are much more directed toward religious and spiritual growth of the child, as are his views on the education of children.

John Wesley's Educational Views

Since John Wesley married late in middle age and never had any children of his own, his ideas about the education of children must be derived from his writings about education and from the programs of education he established. Wesley produced several explicit publications on education. His "Thought on the Manner of Educating Children" (1783) stresses the importance of discipline and the significance of true religion to a good education. His sermon "On the Education of Children" (1783) is an extended comment on parental responsibilities for education in the family, reminiscent of his mother's letter on educational methods in the Epworth rectory. His "Address to the Clergy" (1756) outlines the necessary elements of a well-furnished mind for the clergy, echoing the tone and details of his father's "Letter to a Young Clergyman," which John published in 1735.[31] His *Plain Account of Kingswood School* is a combination of historical reflection and pedagogical comment. Wesley also wrote and published materials specifically for use in the educational process, including five grammars (in English, Greek, Latin, German, and French), a four-volume *Con-*

The Doctrine of Original Sin, in *The Works of the Rev. John Wesley,* 14 vols., ed. Thomas Jackson (London: Nichols, 1872), 9:232.

30. Locke, *Some Thoughts Concerning Education,* 146-47. When Locke recommends instilling "fear and awe" through "correction of the rod," does he thereby recommend "beating," as Greven would have us believe Susanna Wesley's use of such terminology would imply? It appears, in fact, that neither Locke nor Wesley ever actually recommended beating anyone of any age.

31. Under "*acquired* endowments" that Wesley feels are necessary, he lists knowledge of the ministerial office, of the Scriptures, of the original tongues, of profane history, of the sciences (logic, metaphysics, natural philosophy, geometry), of the Fathers, and of the world (of humankind). See *The Works of the Rev. John Wesley,* 10:482.

cise (!) *History of England,* a fifty-volume *Christian Library,* and a *Compendium of Logic,* as well as other textbooks for Kingswood School.[32]

In addition, Wesley published many other works that relate in one way or another to his educational program. In part, his monumental publishing enterprise itself was part of his educational mission. He published nearly five hundred works on all sorts of topics (many of them multivolume works), including *A Short History of Rome, Natural Philosophy* (three volumes), and many others. And he didn't have to publish all this in order to get tenure at Oxford. He was trying to educate his people. In his attempt to make these books available to all Methodists, his connection of preachers served as a network of colporteurs, each of them book agents in their local societies.

Wesley's interest in improving the mind (as part of the whole person) included an interest in both supporting and founding educational institutions. His early interest in charity schools is evidenced by his financial support of the Grey Coat School at Oxford in the 1720s. In the 1730s, he and his friends provided a schoolteacher and supplies for many of the orphans and poor children in Oxford in a school started by William Morgan, one of the Oxford Methodists. Wesley also showed interest in and provided support for a school in Georgia, encouraging his compatriot William Delamotte to teach the children. The conditions at many of the schools in England shocked Wesley. He saw several causes for the problems, such as the tendency for schools to be located in large cities, where corruption abounded. He also felt that most schools were not selective enough, either in choosing students who were not already corrupted or in choosing teachers who had adequate learning as well as virtue.[33] Unable to find a school "free from these palpable blemishes," Wesley decided to start one himself. His educational principles became embodied first in Kingswood School near Bristol, then in the Foundery day school in London, and later in a school at Woodhouse-Grove. His followers and compatriots also established schools with similar programs at Leytonstone (Mary Bosanquet, Ann Bolton, and so on), Trevecca (Lady Huntingdon), and High Wycombe (Hannah Ball).

A survey of the curriculum at Kingswood reveals Wesley's practical implementation of his principles in the area of secondary education. His intent was to include every area of "useful" learning, or practical studies. The main course of study was designed to teach reading, writing, and arithmetic; English, French, Latin, Greek, and Hebrew; history, geography, and chronology; rhetoric and logic; and geometry, algebra, physics, music, and ethics. Other topics were soon added, such as painting and astronomy. This scheme was based on the

32. He produced some two dozen works for Kingswood School.
33. Wesley delineates these problems in his *Plain Account of Kingswood School,* in *The Works of the Rev. John Wesley,* 13:290-92.

typical public-school curriculum, but added music, physics, Hebrew, religious biography, the Bible, and Christian classics. Many of the textbooks Wesley designated for dual use, both for reading and for translation.[34]

Although most of the students at Kingswood School started the program between the ages of six and nine,[35] Wesley also provided "a course of academical learning," which he considered to be comparable to a university curriculum. Wesley's own evaluation of this academical curriculum is unflinching: "Whoever carefully goes through this course will be a better scholar than nine in ten of the graduates at Oxford or Cambridge."[36] What others noticed, however, and what is most often remembered, is the strong element of religion, and the rigor of the schedule and discipline. The rules for the children at Kingswood meant rising at four A.M. and retiring at eight P.M.; starting the day with two hours of private and public devotion and ending the day with an hour of private devotion and an hour of public evening prayers; having no time during the day for play; and spending from seven to eleven A.M. and one to five P.M. "in school." Students should at all times be in the presence of a teacher and never be allowed to roam free or have contact with the colliers' children in the neighborhood.[37]

Wesley was, of course, criticized by some for his approach:

A gentleman with whom I was conversing a while ago . . . on the manner of educating children . . . objected strongly to the bringing them up too strictly; to the giving them more of religion than they liked; to the telling them of it too often, or pressing it upon them whether they will or no. . . . I knew [all this] was quite agreeable to the sentiments of Rousseau in his "Emilius;" the most empty, silly, injudicious thing that ever a self-conceited infidel wrote.[38]

But I knew it was quite contrary to the judgment of the wisest and best men I have known. I thought, If these things are so, how much mischief have we

34. This curriculum is charted in his "Short Account of the School in Kingswood," in *The Works of the Rev. John Wesley,* 13:287-88.

35. *A Plain Account of the People Called Methodists,* XIV.3, in *Works,* 9:278; and "Letter to Joseph Benson" (October 5, 1770), in *The Letters of the Rev. John Wesley,* 8 vols., ed. John Telford (London: Epworth Press, 1931), 5:202.

36. "Short Account of the School in Kingswood," in *The Works of the Rev. John Wesley,* 13:389. In the *Plain Account of Kingswood School,* he says, "And as to the knowledge of the tongues, and of arts and sciences, with whatever is termed academical learning; if those who have a tolerable capacity for them do not advance more here in three years, than the generality of students at Oxford or Cambridge do in seven, I will bear the blame for ever" (13:296).

37. *Minutes of the Methodist Conferences* (London: John Mason, 1862), 1:164.

38. In 1770 Wesley read Rousseau on education and commented, "How was I disappointed. Sure a more consummate coxcomb never saw the sun!" *Journal and Diaries V* (February 3, 1770), in *Works,* 22:214.

done unawares! . . . how much mischief has been done, and is now doing, at Kingswood, where (if this hypothesis be true) we are continually ruining fifty children at a time![39]

In spite of his critics, Wesley stuck by his plan:

> Meantime, I can only say, as a much greater man said, *Hier stehe ich: Gott hilffe mich!* By His help I have stood for these forty years, among the children of men, whose tongues are set on fire, who shoot out their arrows, even bitter words, and think therein they do God service. . . . Now, especially, I have no time to lose: If I slacked my pace, my grey hairs would testify against me. I have nothing to fear, I have nothing to hope for, here; only to finish my course with joy.[40]

On one of the touchstone issues of the day, Wesley was very firm — children could be ruined if allowed free rein to play. Here again he is following his mother's lead. Susanna was very clear that close supervision was absolutely necessary. She permitted no loud talking or playing during the hours when her children were being taught, and they were not to run out into the yard or street without permission: "Every one was kept close to their business, for the six hours of school."[41] The rules for the pupils at Kingswood were equally clear: "The children ought never to be alone, but always in the presence of a master" (otherwise they will "run up and down the wood"), and "They ought never to play."[42] Proper recreation for the children consisted of such activities as walking or working or singing, which gave them respite from their books but also had creative and useful ends.[43]

Another of Wesley's main principles was that education entails the joining of knowledge and piety, wisdom and holiness. This point is not always clearly understood, just as the phrases associated with this idea are not always accurately quoted: "Unite the pair so long disjoin'd, knowledge and vital piety." This Charles Wesley phrase is often misattributed to John Wesley, but does represent both of their views.[44]

---

39. "A Thought upon the Manner of Educating Children," in *The Works of the Rev. John Wesley*, 13:474.

40. *Plain Account of Kingswood School*, 13:300.

41. *Susanna Wesley*, 372.

42. *Minutes of the Methodist Conferences*, 1:164.

43. "Working" seems to have included such activities as gardening and carpentry. Apparently this rule forbidding play no longer applied at the university level. Wesley's diary reveals that he played all sorts of games after he reached twenty years of age, including backgammon, quoits, tennis, and a variety of card games.

44. The phrase comes from one of the hymns in Charles's *Hymns for Children*

The more important point, however, is what the Wesleys meant when they used the terms "knowledge" and "vital piety." Both terms conjure up recognizable caricatures — the thinker and the saint. For the Wesleys, however, there was no disjunction between the two. For them, knowledge is not a purely intellectual attribute but rather a channel of self-understanding, which is crucial for salvation. And vital piety entails not only a devotional stance based on love of God but also a social outreach exemplified by love of neighbor. Wesley reinforces this relationship between the two concepts when he reiterates the idea that "without love, all learning is but splendid ignorance."[45] John's own use of parallel phrases, such as "wisdom and holiness," also helps to reveal his understanding in this regard.[46]

Wesley's Program of Education

Wesley's approach to education also entailed a particular method and discipline. His program involved a set curriculum of study and strict rules of operation, not unlike the classical scheme of the English public schools but with some innovations. Seven aspects of his design went beyond the typical approach of his day. (1) Wesley's interest in epistemology was reflected in the stress that he placed on the students' understanding of the material they studied. To this end, he encouraged reflection and comprehension rather than rote learning.[47] (2) He also allowed for students of all ages, including "greyheaded" scholars. His interest in adult education was simply an extension of his own education, which continued throughout his lifetime.[48] (3) Following

---

(1763), entitled "At the Opening of a School in Kingswood" (v. 2 of #344 in the 1968 United Methodist Hymnal; v. 5 of #461 in the *Collection of Hymns, 1780*, in *Works*, 8:644).

45. Some scholars attribute this phrase to Augustine, but no one has yet identified the actual source. Wesley makes the point even stronger in a letter to Bishop Lowth (August 10, 1780): "My Lord, I do by no means despise learning: I know the value of it too well. But what is this, particularly in a Christian Minister, compared to piety? What is it in a man that has no religion? 'As a jewel in a swine's snout'" (*The Works of the Rev. John Wesley*, 13:143).

46. John Wesley uses this phrase at least six times in his writings, though he never quotes Charles's phrase.

47. This is a position in keeping with one of Locke's concerns; see *Some Thoughts Concerning Education*, 285-88.

48. In the last ten years of his life, Wesley's reading included descriptions of the interior of America and the Chinese empire, recent autobiographies by Voltaire and Olaudah Equiano, classics by Virgil and Dante, and works by William Shakespeare and Alexander Pope. See Richard Heitzenrater, *Faithful unto Death: Last Years and Legacy of John Wesley* (Dallas: Bridwell, 1991), 72-77.

his mother's lead, Wesley promoted female education. As the century wore on, the Methodist connection provided financial support for girls as well as boys who attended school.[49] (4) Wesley tried very hard to link parents to the educational process. They were expected to meet with the Stewards, or overseers, at school regularly to discuss their children's progress.[50] (5) The schools were to have a low student/teacher ratio (about 5 to 1) and to allow for the contact of students and teachers in extracurricular activities. (6) Besides boarding schools such as Kingswood, Wesley also started day schools for children who lived at home, such as the Foundery School in London. (7) And Wesley was concerned for children across the boundaries of social and economic class, and was willing to mix them together in the same schools. Wesley felt strongly that all people were children of God and that no one was beyond the need for learning.[51]

From the sources available, assessing the differences (assuming that there were differences) between the education provided to boys and to girls is difficult. The number of students supported each year after 1780 by the Methodist connection was nearly equally divided between the two sexes. And the cost per annum, as noted in the *Minutes* of the Wesleyan annual conferences, was equal for both — six pounds.[52] Evidence from the London charity schools indicates that 75 percent of the poor children, both boys and girls, were able to read.[53] Some individual benefactors of the charity schools had a persistent unease about teaching the poor how to read. They feared it might lead to upward mobility or unrest. But they were often assured that the poor children, when they

49. See *Minutes of the Methodist Conferences,* 1:114 (1774): "If any [daughters of preachers] were sent to M. Owen's school (perhaps the best boarding-school for girls in Great Britain), they would keep them at as small an expense as possible." Two girls were sent to M. Owen's school in 1775, but the next year the girls were sent to Publow School. By 1778, girls were admitted to Kingswood. After 1780, if there was no room at Kingswood for the preachers' children, they (both boys and girls) were given six pounds toward their education elsewhere; see *Minutes of the Methodist Conferences,* 119, 124, 135, 145, 156, 164.

50. The Stewards at Kingswood were instructed "every Wednesday morning to meet with and exhort [the students'] parents to train them up at home in the ways of God" (*A Plain Account of the People Called Methodists,* XIV.3, in *Works,* 9:279.

51. The radical nature of this assumption is underscored by Wesley's design to instruct the slaves on the plantations in America and his personal conversation with a young slave girl in South Carolina. See *Journal and Diaries I* (April 23-27, 1737), in *Works,* 18:180-81.

52. *Minutes of the Methodist Conferences,* 1:150, 220.

53. Victor E. Neuburg, *Popular Education in Eighteenth-Century England* (London: Woburn Press, 1971), 173. The figures were for the parish of St. Mary's, Islington, for the years 1767-1810.

were able to read the Bible, would learn to be pious, remain content with their station in life, and be grateful to their "betters."[54] Wesley, however, seems to have had no compunction about improving the lot of poor children, so long as they maintained a vital Christian life.

Wesley's approach to education focused on God but relied upon people as instruments of God's will and exemplars of godly minds and lives, as imitators of Christ.[55] The key individual in Wesley's formula was the teacher, who should be a person of piety and understanding.[56] In spite of all the lists of regulations for the schools, the emphasis was not so much on rules as upon virtues (we might say values). This combination of an obligation and a virtue ethic resulted in a perspective that allowed for decisions made not only on the basis of right and wrong but also on a scale of good to bad. A virtue approach is based on a model of the good, is impelled by imitation, and results in transformation. This process of spiritual and intellectual formation can be seen in many of the Methodist autobiographies of the period.[57]

Another feature of Wesley's educational program was that it involved changing the whole person — body, mind, and spirit.[58] Wesley wished that people would always push the boundaries of sin and ignorance, discovering the possibilities of what one might know and become. Self-knowledge is at the heart of this transformative process — people must know that they are ignorant and sinful before they can change. This approach is in tune with John Locke's ideas, as well as those of Johann Amos Comenius and John Milton.[59] Comenius, who also influenced August Hermann Francke and provided the

54. See, for example, the annual reports of the Society for Promoting Christian Knowledge, which supported many charity schools. "An Account of the Origin and Designs of the Society for Promoting Christian Knowledge," in John Heylyn, *A Sermon Preached at St. Sepulchre's* (London: J. Downing, 1734), 3, 15. See also Victor E. Neuburg, *Literacy and Society* (London: Woburn Press, 1971), vi.

55. "Having the mind that was in Christ and walking as he walked" (see Phil. 2:5; 1 John 2:6) was one of Wesley's continuing descriptive explanations of Christian Perfection (another echo of the combination of wisdom and love).

56. See his letter to Joseph Benson (December 26, 1769) in *The Letters of the Rev. John Wesley,* 5:166.

57. Wesley's *Arminian Magazine,* a monthly publication he founded in 1778, soon became filled with stories of holy living and holy dying by figures historic and contemporary who provided examples for his people to emulate.

58. In his sermon entitled "The Good Steward," Wesley points to this unity with poignant imagery in the midst of some questions that he suggests Christ might ask each believer at the final judgment, including whether he or she had presented his or her "soul and body, all thy thoughts, thy words, and actions, in *one flame of love,* as a holy sacrifice, glorifying [God] with thy body and thy spirit" (in *Works,* 2:296).

59. *Works,* 2:278.

model for Moravian education in Wesley's day,[60] like Milton, felt that the goal of education was to acquire not only knowledge but also virtue and piety. Wesley aligned himself with these forms of idealism when he quoted William Law's view that "education is to be considered as reason borrowed at second hand, which is, as far as it can, to supply the loss of original perfection."[61] Perfection or holiness, for Wesley, was pure love — love of God and neighbor, made possible by a total reordering of fallen human nature. Wesley never dropped this doctrine of perfection from his theology and never abandoned this ideal for his schools. Education can thus be seen as one means of grace by which the original perfection of creation (a creature of wisdom and holiness), lost in the Fall, could be restored.[62] The goal of this transformation in the believer is nothing less than a recovery of the image of God, the "one thing necessary."[63] As Wesley pointed out,

> Scripture, reason, and experience jointly testify that, inasmuch as the corruption of nature is earlier than our instructions can be, we should take all pains and care to counteract this corruption as early as possible. The bias of nature is set the wrong way. Education is designed to set it right.[64] This, by the grace of God, is to turn the bias from self-well, pride, anger, revenge, and the love of the world, to resignation, lowliness, meekness, and the love of God.[65]

For Wesley, then, the end of education is in some sense the same as the goal of religion. Knowledge and vital piety, wisdom and holiness, learning and love are essentially linked in his vision of God's purpose for humanity.

---

60. Body, *John Wesley and Education*, 49; see also the essay in this volume by Marcia Bunge, 248-49.

61. "On the Education of Children," in *Works*, 3:348, quoting Law's *A Serious Call to a Devout Life*.

62. "There was still wanting a creature of a higher rank, capable of wisdom and holiness. *Natus homo est.* So 'God created man in his own image; in the image of God created he him!'" (from the sermon entitled "The Fall of Man," in *Works*, 2:409). In Sermon 95, "On the Education of Children," §3, Wesley quotes William Law's *Serious Call* on this point: "The only end of education is, to restore our rational nature to its proper state" (*Works*, 3:348).

63. *Works*, 1:310.

64. See Locke's similar comment: "Few of Adam's children are so happy as not to be born with some byass in their natural temper, which it is the business of education either to take off or counter-balance" (*Some Thoughts Concerning Education*, 244); quoted by Sommerville, who, on this point, misinterprets the evangelical position, which also sees the corruption of nature in the Fall (*The Rise and Fall of Childhood*, 141).

65. "A Thought on the Manner of Educating Children," §7, in *The Works of the Rev. John Wesley*, 13:476.

Religious Experience among Methodist Children

Two of the questions that confronted Wesley concerning religious education and spiritual experience were these: What is the basic nature of children, and at what age could a child have a bona fide conversion experience?

Anglican theology taught that baptism, infant or otherwise, resulted in justification, forgiveness of sins, especially in the first instance the guilt of original sin. Therefore, the image of the terrible child as proof of original sin does not necessarily follow. But the alternate image — of childish innocence — also presents problems within a theology that speaks of being "justified and yet a sinner." Wesley does not have a consistently clear position on this matter. He does on occasion speak of evil in children, such as when he analyzes the question of suffering, which he sees as a penalty from God for human evil:

> Why do infants suffer? What sin have they to be cured thereby? If you say, "It is to heal the sin of their parents, who sympathize and suffer with them"; in a thousand instances this has no place; the parents are not the better, nor anyway likely to be the better, for all the sufferings of their children. Their sufferings, therefore, yea, and those of all mankind, which are entailed upon them by the sin of Adam, are not the result of mere mercy, but of justice also. In other words, they have in them the nature of punishments, even on us and on our children. Therefore, children themselves are not innocent before God. They suffer; therefore, they deserve to suffer.[66]

On the other hand, there are a few occasions when Wesley slips into the rhetoric of innocence. Take, for example, his observation at the home of an English gentleman and his family in Holland: "Here were four such children (I suppose seven, six, five, and three years old) as I never saw before in one family: Such inexpressible beauty and innocence shone together!"[67] These momentary expressions of anthropological optimism seem to be grounded more in the immediate impressions given by young personalities rather than in any consistent theological reflection on their soteriological condition by Wesley. In any case, based on his own experience, Wesley was convinced that any grace received by an infant at baptism would soon be sinned away, and the child would stand in need of God's forgiveness again: "I believe, till I was about ten years old, I had

---

66. *The Doctrine of Original Sin*, Part III, Sec. II, in *The Works of the Rev. John Wesley*, 9:318.

67. *Journal and Diaries VI* (June 15, 1783), in *Works*, 23:273-74. The previous day he also observed the women and children in Rotterdam, "who were surprisingly fair and had an inexpressible air of innocence in their countenance" (272).

not sinned away that 'washing of the Holy Ghost' which was given me in baptism."[68]

On the basis of firsthand observation and personal experience, Wesley presumes that a child can "know God" and thus be truly happy. Looking back on his years at school in London, when he was ten to seventeen years old, he observed that he was not then in such a state of assured salvation.[69] On the other hand, he records in his journal several accounts of children who have had what he considers to be an authentic religious experience by as early as the age of three.[70]

Occasionally revivals broke out among children in the Methodist societies and at Kingswood School. Elizabeth Blackwell sent Wesley an account of one such revival in Everton under John Berridge in 1759. Among those who experienced great spiritual struggle, and in some cases justification, were three young people, ages eight, ten, and twelve. The eight-year-old boy was said to have "roared above his fellows and seemed in his agony to struggle with the strength of a grown man."[71] John Walsh's account of this continuing revival a few weeks later includes notice of children, ages six and eight, who were "crying aloud to God for mercy."[72] He also notes that one eleven-year-old girl, "who had been counted one of the wickedest in Harston," was "exceedingly blessed with the consolations of God," and a "beggar-girl" of seven or eight "felt the word of God as a two-edged sword and mourned to be covered with Christ's righteousness."[73]

Young people were often the core of local revivals, and Wesley occasion-

68. *Journal and Diaries I* (May 24, 1738), in *Works*, 18:242-43.

69. He recalled that while he was at school, he was not in this condition, since he did not remember one week that he would have gladly repeated. See Sermon 77, "Spiritual Worship," III.2, in *Works*, 3:98.

70. See *Journal and Diaries III* (June 28, 1746), in *Works*, 20:143; see also 9:470-71. There are several similar accounts of children under age six, such as the following: "I buried, near the same place, one who had soon finished her course, going to God in the full assurance of faith, when she was little more than four years old" (20:39 [September 16, 1744]).

71. *Journal and Diaries IV* (May 30, 1759), in *Works*, 21:196. One account, describing the revival at Weardale, uses adult imagery to describe the demeanor of children who were converted: "Phebe Teatherstone, nine years and an half old, a child of uncommon understanding; Hannah Watson, ten years old, full of faith and love; Aaron Ridson, not eleven years old, but wise and stayed as a man; Sarah Smith, eight years and an half old, but as serious as a woman of fifty: Sarah Morris, fourteen years of age, is as a mother among them, always serious, always watching over the rest, and building them up in love." See *Journal and Diaries V* (June 5, 1772), in *Works*, 22:334.

72. *Journal and Diaries IV* (May 30, 1759), in *Works*, 21:214.

73. *Journal and Diaries IV* (May 30, 1759), in *Works*, 21:215, 219.

ally noted that their transformed lives became models for the adults. In February 1779 he notes in his journal that he preached at Lowestoft, where there had been "a great awakening, especially among youth and children; several of whom, between twelve and sixteen years of age, are a pattern to all about them."[74] Five years later, after describing the work of God in Epworth, he again emphasized his view that children often play a crucial role in revivals: "God begins his work in children. Thus it has been also in Cornwall, Manchester, and Epworth. Thus the flame spreads to those of riper years; till at length they all know him, and praise him from the least unto the greatest."[75]

Wesley's Views of Children in the Bible

Ironically, Wesley does not carry this view of the significant role of children in the Methodist revivals into his commentary on the New Testament,[76] even in places where there seems to be a natural opening for such observations. Wesley's comment on one central passage (Matt. 19:14: "Suffer the little children to come unto me, for of such is the kingdom of heaven") diffuses the possible impact by pointing to a possible double meaning of "children" — "either in a natural or spiritual sense."[77] His view of the sinfulness and ignorance of children is evident in his commentary on Matthew 18:4. Wesley there points out that, to enter the kingdom of heaven, we must become as little children, which he explains is to be "lowly in heart, knowing yourselves utterly ignorant and helpless, and hanging wholly on your Father who is in heaven for a supply of all your wants."[78] His comment on the nasty children in Luke 7:32 is also expectedly harsh: "So froward and perverse, that no contrivance can be found to please them." But he does not hold to such a view consistently. "In wickedness be ye infants" (1 Cor. 14:20) he understands to mean "Have all the innocence of that tender age."

In matters related to spiritual development, then, Wesley portrays a number of different views of the condition and role of children. But in matters of physical well-being, Wesley is consistently pro-active in trying to provide for their health and welfare.

74. *Journal and Diaries VI* (February 18, 1779), in *Works* 23:117.

75. *Journal and Diaries VI* (June 8, 1784), in *Works*, 23:315.

76. The following references can be found in his *Explanatory Notes upon the New Testament*, first published in 1755.

77. See also his comment on Mark 9:37 — "either in years, or in heart."

78. See also his comment on the parallel verse in Mark 10:15: "As a little child — as totally disclaiming all worthiness and fitness, as if he were but a week old."

Wesley's Programs to Assist Children

Children were, for Wesley, not only potential exhibits of both original sin and personal piety but also special targets of educational and revival activities. They were also a special object of his charitable activities. From the beginning of the Wesleyan movement at Oxford in the 1720s, children were one of the primary focuses of concern, primarily children of the poor. Wesley's financial accounts from 1725 to 1735 record that he contributed to the local charity schools, that he purchased wool and yarn for the children in the workhouses, that he paid a teacher to staff a school for children, that he visited children in prison, and that he bought food for poor families.

These activities became part of the Methodist program as the movement developed during the century. In addition to the establishment of schools for children, including Sunday schools, Wesley's broad interest in helping the poor in general also included the poor children in many specific ways. His medical clinic, loan program, subsidized housing, and collections of money, food, and clothing were primarily aimed at helping poor families. And these were not simply channels for dispensing resources to "others" — the poor were more often than not associated with the Methodist societies. Wesley felt it was very important to take the food and clothing directly to the poor, to visit them "in their hovels," to eat with them and come to know their plight firsthand.[79]

During his travels, Wesley often made a special effort to visit workhouses, orphanages, poorhouses, and prisons, as well as schools, to check on the plight of the children and poor families in those regions. His writing does not contain the typical vindictive rant of the period against the ineffectiveness of the parish charity system.[80] Rather, he directed his time and effort to soliciting funds from known benefactors (he called it "begging") in order to support his own program of activities to improve the lot of the poor.

79. This principle can be seen in his comments on the subsidized housing he established: "In this (commonly called The Poor House) we have now nine widows, one blind woman, two poor children, two upper servants, a maid and a man. I might add, four or five Preachers; for I myself, as well as the other Preachers who are in town, diet with the poor, on the same food, and at the same table; and we rejoice herein, as a comfortable earnest of our eating bread together in our Father's kingdom." See *A Plain Account of the People Called Methodists*, XIII.2, in *Works*, 9:277. See also his letter to Miss March (June 9, 1775) in *The Letters of the Rev. John Wesley*, 6:153.

80. There is a whole literature of criticism of the poor laws, workhouses, and other aspects of the parish charity system, typified by the pamphlet by a onetime Calvinist Methodist preacher named Joseph Townsend, *Dissertation on the Poor Laws, by a well-wisher to mankind* (London, 1786), and a more extensive work by William Bailey titled *A Treatise on the Better Employment, and more Comfortable Support, of the Poor in Workhouses* (London, 1758).

Conclusion

Although not a father himself, John Wesley took his work with children seriously. He was concerned enough about their intellectual and spiritual welfare that he also warned the Methodist preachers under his supervision either to spend regular time with the children in their societies or else to cease being Methodist preachers and go back to their trade.[81]

Wesley's view of children follows no previously established program or theory. Much of what he taught and practiced he learned at home as a child himself. Some of what he believed about children he had read or learned from colleagues. His views are not fully consistent or complete. He could as easily use children as empirical proof for the reality of sin as use them as models for the type of faith that Christ requires of us all. Wesley realized that children had limits, that they should not bear the burden of being considered the same as adults. And yet he also knew that some children had a capacity for knowledge and love that exceeded that of some adults.

Much of Wesley's terminology and methodology for discipline is presently out of vogue and frequently interpreted in exaggerated forms by modern eyes and norms. As is the case with many of the rules for his movement, however, the goals and principles of discipline and education should not be overlooked because of the dated nature of the practices used to implement them at that time.

The goal of Wesley's work was not simply to improve the level of education in England or to reduce the level of poverty. His main concern for child rearing was not so much to improve the psychological health of parents or to create a class of genteel adults in the country. His primary concern for children was the same as his concern for the rest of humankind — to help them know and love God. This knowledge and piety could result in children's and adults' lives that exhibited a faith that works through love. This goal was not part of an intellectual or doctrinal program that was primarily educational or social or religious. Wesley's actions were propelled by his own desire to love God and neighbor, which is simply the heart of what he called holiness or "Christian perfection."

Although Methodism today has largely lost this theological terminology, it continues to press the traditional Wesleyan program of educational and social programs that reflect this concern for all of God's children. Methodism in

---

81. His rule was for the preachers to spend at least an hour a week with the children, if there were at least ten in any society. If the preacher claimed he had no gift for that work, Wesley's response was, "Gift or no gift, you are to do it, else you are not called to be a Methodist Preacher." See *Minutes of the Methodist Conferences*, 1:69.

America, beginning early in the nineteenth century, became notable for its establishment of colleges and universities, hospitals and homes, and social programs for unfortunate and disadvantaged persons. One current program, for instance, known as the Bishops' Initiative for Children in Poverty, has provided a worldwide effort to improve the condition of children around the globe. This effort is just one of many, but is typical of the legacy of John Wesley.

11. Children of Wrath, Children of Grace: Jonathan Edwards and the Puritan Culture of Child Rearing

CATHERINE A. BREKUS

In 1735, Jonathan Edwards (1703-1758), the pastor of the Congregational Church in Northampton, Massachusetts, was summoned to the house of a four-year-old girl named Phebe Bartlet. According to her parents, who earnestly sought his spiritual counsel, Phebe had undergone a remarkable religious change. Influenced by her eleven-year-old brother, who recently had been "born again" during a conversion experience, Phebe had begun to disappear into her "closet" to pray and weep for salvation. "I pray, beg, pardon all my sins," she was heard crying loudly to God. As her parents confessed to Edwards, they had assumed that such a young child was "not capable of understanding" Christianity, but they had been deeply affected by her anxious prayers and sobs for mercy. One afternoon, despite her mother's attempts to soothe her, Phebe "continued exceedingly crying, and wreathing her body to and fro, like one in anguish of spirit," until she finally managed to put her fears into words. "I am afraid I shall go to hell!" she wept. After another bout of crying, however, she suddenly fell quiet. Turning to her mother with a smile, she proclaimed, "Mother, the kingdom of heaven is come to me!" In the hours and days afterward, Phebe seemed to have become a "new creature": she carefully recited her catechism, wept at the thought that her unconverted sisters might "go to hell," and, like Augustine, repented for stealing some fruit — a handful of plums — from a neighbor's tree.[1]

---

1. Jonathan Edwards, *A Faithful Narrative of the Surprising Work of God* (1742), in *The Works of Jonathan Edwards*, vol. 4: *The Great Awakening*, ed. C. C. Goen (New Haven:

The author would like to thank Kenneth P. Minkema and Harry S. Stout for their help with this essay.

As Edwards later explained in his book *A Faithful Narrative of the Surprising Work of God,* he was astonished by the "extraordinary change" that he saw in Phebe. On the one hand, he was hardly sentimental in his attitudes toward children. At a time when many moral philosophers, including Francis Hutcheson, questioned the Calvinist doctrines of predestination and original sin, he sternly insisted that "infants are not looked upon by God as sinless, but . . . are by nature children of wrath." Quoting from the Psalms, he preached, "The wicked are estranged from the womb: They go astray as soon as they be born, speaking lies." Yet on the other hand, Edwards also insisted that an all-powerful, sovereign God could transform even the youngest child into a paragon of Christian virtue. Although he feared that Phebe's story would be "most difficultly believed," he was absolutely convinced that she had been reborn in Christ.[2] Despite her youth, she was a symbol of God's extraordinary grace.

As the story of Phebe Bartlet illustrates, Jonathan Edwards viewed children as both sinners and saints: they were indelibly tainted with original sin, and yet also capable of genuine faith. As a Congregationalist, Edwards was the heir of both the Puritan and the Calvinist traditions, but besides defending the traditional view of children's depravity, he also subtly undermined it. To be sure, his hellfire sermons, his belief in the doctrine of infant damnation, and his staunch defense of the patriarchal family made him more conservative than almost all of the other theologians profiled in this book, including Augustine and Calvin. He frequently threatened children with eternal torments in hell if they failed to convert. Yet Edwards's thought moved in progressive as well as reactionary directions, and because of his belief in children's essential humanity, he took seriously their religious thoughts and questions. "Children of wrath," he insisted, could be reborn as "children of grace." Like earlier theologians, he was deeply influenced by the intellectual currents of his own place and time, and he bequeathed an ambivalent legacy to future Christians in search of a theology of

---

Yale University Press, 1972), 200, 201-5. For reasons that are not clear, Phebe Bartlet was not admitted to full membership in the Northampton church until 1754. Edwards had been dismissed from his pulpit four years earlier. Like many other people of her time, Bartlet joined the church shortly before her marriage. She died at the age of seventy-four in 1805. On Bartlet's later history, see Northampton Church Records, MSS volume, Joseph Hooker List of Admissions, First Church of Northampton; and James Russell Trumbull, "History of Northampton, Vol. III, Northampton Genealogies," unpublished typescript, Forbes Library, Northampton, 36-37, 40, 345. I am grateful to Kenneth P. Minkema for these two citations.

2. Edwards, *A Faithful Narrative,* 158; and Jonathan Edwards, *Doctrine of Original Sin Defended* (1758), in *The Works of Jonathan Edwards,* vol. 3: *Original Sin,* ed. Clyde A. Holbrook (New Haven: Yale University Press, 1970), 215, 267.

childhood. Studying his ideas can help us understand not only eighteenth-century views of children, but our own as well.

"More Hateful than Vipers": The Nature of Children

When Jonathan Edwards began his pastorate in Northampton in 1727 under the tutelage of his grandfather, Solomon Stoddard, he almost immediately began directing his sermons to the children and older "youth" of the congregation. Although he also hoped to convert the older people in his church, he lamented that their "dispositions to evil" had hardened with age. Children, in contrast, were far more malleable. Most important, like the first Puritan settlers who had fled to America a hundred years earlier, Edwards believed that God had chosen New England to be a "city on a hill" — a model of pure Christianity — and he saw children as the guardians of the future. Unless children accepted both the privilege and the burden of being God's "new Israel," the Puritans' mission into the wilderness would never endure.[3]

Although many historians have claimed that Puritans treated children as "miniature adults," Edwards clearly believed that children had distinct needs of their own. Following in the footsteps of earlier Christian theologians, he recognized three distinct stages of children's development: infancy (from birth to the age of six or seven), childhood (from seven to between fourteen and sixteen), and youth (from sixteen to twenty-five). For example, in a letter to Thomas Prince, Edwards explained that he had held special religious meetings for "children" who were "under the age of sixteen" as well as for "young people" between the ages of sixteen and twenty-six.[4] Anticipating the arguments of Jean Piaget and other twentieth-century psychologists, he and other Puritans assumed that children reached a crucial turning point around the age of seven in terms of their ability to "reason" and grasp abstract concepts. At this age, children were taken out of their

---

3. Edwards preached on Matthew 5:14 — "We are a City that is set on a hill & such a City Cant be hid" — in July 1736. See the "Sermon on Matthew 5:14, 34," Beinecke Library, Yale University, quoted in Gerald R. McDermott, *One Holy and Happy Society: The Public Theology of Jonathan Edwards* (University Park, Pa.: Pennsylvania State University Press, 1992), 21. On adult sinners, see Edwards, *Doctrine of Original Sin Defended*, 137; and Kenneth P. Minkema, "Old Age and Religion in the Writings and Life of Jonathan Edwards," manuscript in the author's possession. On Edwards's appeal to young people in Northampton, see Patricia J. Tracy, *Jonathan Edwards, Pastor: Religion and Society in Eighteenth-Century Northampton* (New York: Hill & Wang, 1979), 106.

4. Letter to the Reverend Thomas Prince of Boston (December 12, 1743), reprinted in *The Great Awakening*, ed. Goen, 546-47.

baby clothes and expected to help with chores. Edwards also shared the modern assumption that children experienced another significant transformation during puberty — a stage he identified as "youth" rather than "adolescence." Because he understood the differences between younger and older children, he tried to tailor his religious instruction to fit the unique needs of each group, carefully explaining the Bible in plain language. As one of Edwards's contemporaries explained, "Because of the weakness of their Understandings, and the narrowness of their Capacities, in their younger years, Pains must be us'd to convey Truth in such a manner as they may be able to *conceive* of it, and not meerly learn Things by rote."[5] Rather than seeing children as "miniature adults," Edwards and other Puritans believed their faith had to be carefully nurtured.

Despite his recognition of children's "weakness," however, Edwards preached a message of infant damnation and childhood depravity that strikes most modern-day Christians as harsh and unforgiving, if not cruel. In contrast to Thomas Aquinas, who suggested that unbaptized infants were sent to limbo, Edwards argued that an angry God would consign unconverted children to the flames. Although some people claimed that a merciful God would never condemn infants to eternal damnation, Edwards argued that it was "exceeding just" that "God should take the soul of a new-born infant and cast it into eternal torments."[6] Since infants inherited the stain of original sin, they were as guilty as adults. "As innocent as children seem to be to us," he explained, "if they are out of Christ, they are not so in God's sight, but are young vipers, and are infinitely more hateful than vipers. . . ."[7] Influenced by Augustine and especially John

---

5. Several historians have challenged the view that colonial children were treated as "miniature adults." See Ross W. Beales, "In Search of the Historical Child: Miniature Adulthood and Youth in Colonial New England," *American Quarterly* 27, no. 4 (October 1975): 379-98; and Gerald F. Moran and Maris A. Vinovskis, *Religion, Family, and the Life Course: Explorations in the Social History of Early America* (Ann Arbor: University of Michigan Press, 1992), 118. On Puritan understandings of children's development, see Kenneth Keniston, "Psychological Development and Historical Change," in *Growing Up in America: Historical Experiences,* ed. Harvey J. Graff (Detroit: Wayne State University Press, 1987), 64; Joseph F. Kett, "The Stages of Life," in *The American Family in Social-Historical Perspective,* 2d ed., ed. Michael Gordon (New York: St. Martin's Press, 1978), 166; and John Demos, *A Little Commonwealth: Family Life in Plymouth Colony* (New York: Oxford University Press, 1970), 131-44. The last quote is from William Williams, *The Duty and Interest of a People . . .* (Boston: S. Kneeland and T. Green, 1736), 63-64, quoted in Beales, "In Search of the Historical Child," 385.

6. On Aquinas, see the essay by Cristina Traina in this volume. The quotation is from *The "Miscellanies"* (entry nos. a-z, aa-zz, 1-500), vol. 13 of *The Works of Jonathan Edwards,* ed. Thomas A. Schafer (New Haven: Yale University Press), 169.

7. Edwards, *Some Thoughts Concerning the Present Revival* (1742), in *The Great Awakening,* ed. Goen, 394.

Calvin, Edwards insisted that even the youngest children were corrupt unless they had been "reborn" in Christ.[8]

Besides being influenced by the great Christian thinkers whom he had read as a young Yale student, Edwards was also shaped by his Puritan heritage. Although some scholars have portrayed him as a harbinger of modernity, an intellectual giant who was out of place in colonial America, he clearly shared traditional Puritan assumptions about children.[9] Theologically, the Puritans fed their children a steady diet of catechisms and books warning them not to provoke God's wrath. In the bestselling book *The Day of Doom*, which was published in 1662, Michael Wigglesworth imagined an angry God condemning sinners — even infants — to "endless pains, and scalding flames." (Echoing Augustine, however, he hastened to add that children would have "the easiest room in Hell.") John Cotton's popular morality tale, *Spiritual Milk for Boston Babes*, included the story of a "youth" who rebuffed Christ's gracious offer of salvation in order to pursue a life of frivolous "pleasure." Although he promised to become a Christian in his old age (after he could no longer enjoy the vanities of the world), Christ was so angered by his disobedience that he immediately struck him dead. "Thus end the days of woful youth,/Who won't obey nor mind the truth," Cotton concluded. "They in their youth go down to hell, Under eternal wrath to dwell. Many don't live out half their days, For cleaving unto sinful ways." The Puritans, as many historians have lamented, raised their children in a climate of fear.[10]

Yet even in comparison to the pronouncements of other Puritans, Edwards's emphasis on childhood depravity and infant damnation sounded particularly severe. Even though earlier Puritans had defended the doctrines of infant damnation and predestination, they had also offered a more comforting message. Indeed, many seem to have believed that their *own* children were safe from God's punishments. Identifying themselves as the "new Israel," they

8. Calvin argued that infants "bear their condemnation with them from their mother's womb" (quoted by Barbara Pitkin in her essay in this volume).

9. Perry Miller's view of Jonathan Edwards as a disciple of Locke and Newton has been challenged by many scholars. The classic text is Perry Miller, *Jonathan Edwards* (1949; reprint, Amherst: University of Massachusetts Press, 1981). For challenges, see Norman Fiering, *Jonathan Edwards's Moral Thought and Its British Context* (Chapel Hill: University of North Carolina Press, 1981); Conrad Cherry, *The Theology of Jonathan Edwards: A Reappraisal* (Bloomington: Indiana University Press, 1966); and James Hoopes, "Jonathan Edwards's Religious Psychology," *Journal of American History* 69, no. 4 (March 1983): 849-65.

10. See Michael Wigglesworth, *The Day of Doom: Or, A Poetical Description of the Great and Last Judgement* (1662; reprint, Tucson, Az.: American Eagle Publications, 1991), 30, 66; and John Cotton, *Spiritual Milk for Boston Babes in Either England: Drawn Out of the Breasts of Both Testaments* (Cambridge, Mass.: Hezekiah Usher, 1656).

claimed that God had entered into a special covenant with them that extended to their descendants as well. In theory, a sovereign God could choose to save or damn anyone he pleased, but according to seventeenth-century Puritan ministers, in practice he almost always decided to show compassion to the children of the covenant. As Cotton Mather explained, "The children of *Godly Parents,* we are bound in a *Judgment of Charity* to reckon, as much belonging upon the Lord, as *Themselves.*"[11] Softening the doctrine of infant depravity, Mather reassured "distressed parents" that grace, like original sin, was hereditary. As one historian has noted, "Although Puritan clergymen . . . allowed in their theology for the possibility, even the likelihood, that some infants were damned, when they discussed specific children the presumption was almost always made that heaven was the destination."[12] Proud of their status as God's chosen people, the Puritans reassured themselves that most (if not all) of their own children had been predestined for salvation while countless others had been sentenced to an eternity in hell.

Because parents were so anxious to bring their children under the protection of the church, Puritan clergymen decided to make baptism accessible to almost anyone who sought it — a striking reversal of their earlier history. In 1648 (almost twenty years after their arrival in Massachusetts Bay), the Puritans had made two innovations to ensure their religious purity: first, they had restricted full church membership to "visible saints" who could testify to a conversion experience, and second, they had tightly limited baptism to the "infant seed" of the godly.[13] By the middle of the seventeenth century, however, they decided to allow all those who publicly identified themselves as Puritans (and who promised to submit to church discipline) to bring their children to the baptismal font. Like Calvin, Puritan ministers never claimed that baptism was inherently

11. Cotton Mather, *Help for Distressed Parents* (Boston, 1695), 13, quoted in Peter Gregg Slater, *Children in the New England Mind* (Hamden, Conn.: Archon Books, 1977), 29. C. John Somerville, in *The Rise and Fall of Childhood* (Beverly Hills: Sage Publications, 1982), argues that seventeenth-century Puritans were less harsh in their attitudes toward children than their eighteenth-century descendants (124-25).

12. Slater, *Children in the New England Mind,* 40. As Harry S. Stout has reminded us in his book *The New England Soul: Preaching and Religious Culture in Colonial New England* (New York: Oxford University Press, 1986), printed sermons are not necessarily representative of what ministers actually said in the pulpit. Since there are thousands of unpublished Puritan sermons in archives, it is impossible to make definitive statements about them as a whole. Nevertheless, it is significant that clergy rarely spoke about infant damnation in their published sermons.

13. The Cambridge Platform of 1648 limited church membership to "visible saints" and their children. See Williston Walker, *The Creeds and Platforms of Congregationalism* (Boston: Pilgrim Press, 1960), 205-6.

salvific, but in order to soothe parents' fears, they elevated it as a symbol of God's covenantal relationship with his "New Israel."[14]

In contrast, Edwards used his sermons not to reassure parents but to shatter their complacency. Privately, he seemed to share Cotton Mather's assumption that "the infants of the godly that die in infancy are saved," but publicly, he warned parents not to underestimate God's hatred of sinners, no matter how young.[15] Even though he continued to allow large numbers of infants to be baptized, he sternly reminded parents not to confuse the *sign* of salvation with the thing itself. If they truly believed what they heard in church every Sunday — "that every one that has not been born again, whether he be young or old, is exposed every moment to eternal destruction, under the wrath of Almighty God" — then they had to face the possibility that their own children might be "the heirs of hell."[16]

In order to understand why Edwards spoke so harshly to both parents and children, it is important to situate him in the context of his own place and time. At a time of dramatic religious, social, and economic change, he seemed to be afraid that the traditional Puritan culture of his forefathers might soon collapse. Like many other eighteenth-century Americans, he was profoundly ambivalent about the transformations that were reshaping his world — the growth of a market economy, the breakdown of the patriarchal family, and especially the new Enlightenment faith in human reason — and he responded with a mixture of hope and anxiety. Although it would be a mistake to dismiss him as a mere reactionary, he clearly saw himself as the champion of an embattled Calvinist orthodoxy. By warning both parents and children not to forget their destiny as a chosen people, he hoped to preserve the Puritan way of life against the pressures of an increasingly modern world.

First, Edwards's view of children was colored by his worry that the Puritans had lost their earlier religious zeal. As he lamented from his pulpit, his congregation was filled with selfish "backsliders" who had "greatly departed from

14. On Puritan views of baptism, see Norman Pettit, *The Heart Prepared: Grace and Conversion in Puritan Spiritual Life*, 2d ed. (Middletown, Conn.: Wesleyan University Press, 1989); and E. Brooks Holifield, *The Covenant Sealed: The Development of Puritan Sacramental Theology in Old and New England, 1570-1720* (New Haven: Yale University Press, 1974). According to The Westminster Confession of Faith, "Altho' it be a great sin to contemn or neglect this ordinance, yet grace and salvation are not so inseparably annexed to it, as that no person can be regenerated or saved without it, or that all that are baptized are undoubtedly regenerated." See Westminster Assembly, *The Confession of Faith, Agreed Upon by the Assembly of Divines at Westminster, and the Larger and Shorter Catechism* (London, 1655), chapter 28, section 5.

15. Jonathan Edwards, "Miscellanies," no. 849, Beinecke Library, Yale University, quoted in *Original Sin*, ed. Holbrook, 27n.8.

16. Edwards, *Some Thoughts Concerning the Present Revival*, 394.

God." Instead of building a "new Israel," they had sacrificed "vital and experimental religion" for an empty, cold rationalism.[17] Perhaps, as many historians have argued, Edwards and other ministers exaggerated this "declension" in order to convince people to convert, but they also seem to have been gripped by genuine fear.[18] Unless children as well as adults lived as faithful Christians, God might punish them just as he had once punished the sinful Israelites. Even worse, he might decide to break his covenant with them, abandoning them in the wilderness.

Second, Edwards's concerns about children were also heightened by changes in the Puritan family. In the seventeenth century, ministers had identified the family as a "little commonwealth," a model for the hierarchical ordering of both church and state. Hoping to raise obedient, submissive children who would accept their subjection to parents, magistrates, and ultimately the king, the Puritans gave enormous power to parents, especially fathers. They controlled the family's property; they helped choose marriage partners for their children; and by law, they were allowed to administer "moderate correction" to unruly children and servants. They could also request that their children be punished by the courts. In several New England colonies (including Massachusetts Bay), children over the age of sixteen who cursed or struck their parents could be put to death. Significantly, no child was ever actually executed under this law, but it was a chilling reminder of paternal power in Puritan culture.[19]

By the mid-eighteenth century, however, as larger socio-economic forces began to reshape everyday life, men began to lose their authority over the family. Because of widespread land shortages, many fathers could no longer provide farms for their sons, and because of the growth of a new market-oriented economy, they lost control of children who moved away from home in search

17. Jonathan Edwards, MSS sermon on Jeremiah 2:5, April 1738, quoted in McDermott, *One Holy and Happy Society,* 22-23.

18. In his classic book titled *The New England Mind: From Colony to Province* (Cambridge: Harvard University Press, 1953), Perry Miller argued that Puritan religion "declined." In contrast, other historians have seen this "decline" as more rhetorical than real. See Stout, *The New England Soul,* and Sacvan Bercovitch, *The American Jeremiad* (Madison, Wis.: The University of Wisconsin Press, 1978).

19. Mary Beth Norton discusses the strength of "paternal power" in *Founding Mothers and Fathers: Gendered Power and the Forming of American Society* (New York: Alfred A. Knopf, 1996), 96-137. See also Demos, *A Little Commonwealth,* and Edmund S. Morgan, *The Puritan Family: Religion and Domestic Relations in Seventeenth-Century New England,* rev. ed. (New York: Harper & Row, 1966). One of the loopholes of this law was that it excluded parents who had been "very unchristianly negligent" in the education of their children. In other words, parents could save their children from execution by admitting their own child-rearing mistakes. See Norton, *Founding Mothers and Fathers,* 104.

of greater economic opportunities. Although they still tried to influence whom their children would marry, they had little success. As historians have shown, many couples seem to have realized that their best weapon against strong-willed fathers was pregnancy. By the 1740s and 1750s, the premarital pregnancy rate in New England had risen to as high as 40 percent.[20]

Whether or not Edwards understood the underlying historical forces that were changing the Puritan family, he was deeply disturbed by their effects. As he complained after arriving in Northampton, "family government did too much fail in the town." Instead of deferring to their elders, the "youth of the town" had become addicted to "frolicking," "frequenting the tavern," and such sinful, "lewd practices" as "bundling" — the New England custom of allowing young courting couples to sleep in the same bed with a "bundling board" between them.[21] In a sermon Edwards preached to young people, he condemned "taking such liberties as naturally tend to stir up lusts," including the "shameful custom of fondling women's breasts." By sternly admonishing parents to "keep their children at home," Edwards fought a losing battle to strengthen the traditional Puritan family.[22]

Third, and most important, Edwards's ideas about children were influenced by his resistance to the growing acceptance of humanitarianism and sentimentalism — the broad intellectual movement known as the "Age of Reason." In the late seventeenth and eighteenth centuries, prominent philosophers such as John Locke, the third Earl of Shaftesbury, David Hume, and Francis Hutcheson began to forge a new understanding of human nature that undermined older Christian interpretations. For example, Shaftesbury challenged the doctrine of original sin by claiming that humans are not naturally selfish but benevolent: they possess an inherent "moral sense" that helps them distinguish virtue from vice. Similarly, John Locke denied that a compassionate God would subject sinners to eternal tortures in hell, and John Tillotson rejected the Calvinist faith in predestination. "This doctrine cannot be of God," he protested, because "God is good and just." Struggling to create a more liberal understand-

---

20. On premarital pregnancy rates, see Daniel Scott Smith, "Parental Power and Marriage Patterns: An Analysis of Historical Trends in Hingham, Massachusetts," in *The American Family in Social-Historical Perspective,* ed. Michael Gordon, 255-68. On the breakdown of paternal authority, see Steven Mintz and Susan Kellogg, *Domestic Revolutions: A Social History of American Family Life* (New York: The Free Press), 17-21.

21. Edwards, *A Faithful Narrative,* 146.

22. Jonathan Edwards, MSS sermon on Job 14:2, quoted in Helen Petter Westra, "Cornerstones, Cannons, and Covenants: The Puritan Clergy as Cultural Guardians," *Pro Rege* (September 1990): 28. See also William J. Scheick, "Family, Conversion, and the Self in Jonathan Edwards' *A Faithful Narrative of the Surprising Work of God,*" in *Tennessee Studies in Literature* 19 (1974): 79-90.

ing of both humanity and God, these men criticized many traditional Christian beliefs as unfair or cruel.[23]

Although Edwards closely studied these philosophers (and even borrowed some of their ideas), he also saw them as a dangerous threat to Christianity. Deliberately rejecting the faith in "natural" human goodness, Edwards wrote several treatises defending orthodox Calvinist teachings. For example, in his *Freedom of the Will*, he argued that human beings had no free will of their own. In *The Nature of True Virtue*, he distinguished genuine virtue — which he defined as "love to Being in general" — from mere adherence to moral codes. And in his *Great Christian Doctrine of Original Sin Defended*, which he wrote as a critique of John Taylor's *The Scripture Doctrine of Original Sin Proposed to Free and Candid Examination*, he moved beyond the traditional view of "imputation" to offer a new interpretation of original sin. In contrast to Taylor, who questioned how a just God could hold all of humankind responsible for Adam's sin, Edwards insisted that all humans had been metaphysically present with Adam in the Garden of Eden. Just as a tree had many branches but was still one discrete organism, all of humanity was a single entity. There was "a real union between the root and branches of the world of mankind . . . established by the Author of the whole system of the universe," Edwards explained. As a result, *all* humans — whether young or old — fully shared Adam's guilt: "The sin of the apostasy is not theirs, merely because God *imputes* it to them," but because they, like Adam, had actually committed it.[24]

23. Tillotson is quoted in Fiering, *Jonathan Edwards's Moral Thought and Its British Context*, 228. See also *Sermons and Discourses, 1723-1729*, ed. Kenneth P. Minkema, vol. 14 of *The Works of Jonathan Edwards* (New Haven: Yale University Press, 1997), 29. On the growth of a new humanitarian sensibility in mid-eighteenth-century America, see Karen Haltunnen, "Humanitarianism and the Pornography of Pain in Anglo-American Culture," *American Historical Review* 100, no. 2 (April 1995): 303-34; Elizabeth B. Clark, "The Sacred Rights of the Weak: Pain, Sympathy, and the Culture of Individual Rights in Antebellum America," *Journal of American History* 82, no. 2 (September 1995): 463-93; and Ava Chamberlain, "The Theology of Cruelty: A New Look at the Rise of Arminianism in Eighteenth-Century New England," *Harvard Theological Review* 85, no. 3 (1992): 335-56.

24. Taylor's book was first published in either 1738 or 1740. On controversy over dating, see *Original Sin*, 2n. 5. The quotations are from Jonathan Edwards, *The Great Christian Doctrine of Original Sin Defended*, in *Original Sin*, ed. Holbrook, 408. For discussions of Edwards's understanding of sin, see Holbrook's introduction to *Original Sin*, 58-59; Slater, *Children in the New England Mind*, 60; and Cherry, *The Theology of Jonathan Edwards*, 196-202. Norman Fiering views Edwards's hellfire preaching as "an intentional affirmation of the orthodox teaching." See *Jonathan Edwards's Moral Thought and Its British Context*, 238. On Edwards's hostility to individualism, see Daniel Walker Howe, *Making the American Self: Jonathan Edwards to Abraham Lincoln* (Cambridge: Harvard University Press, 1997).

If not for his sensitive awareness of the changes that were transforming Puritan culture, Edwards might have said little about children, but in order to defend traditional Calvinist teachings against the Age of Reason, he was forced to articulate his assumptions about children's nature. For example, in response to John Taylor's argument that sin was the product of bad example, not inherent depravity, Edwards claimed that children's daily lives told a darker story. "The influence of bad example, without corruption of nature, will not account for children's universally committing sin, as soon as capable of it," he explained. Citing a long list of biblical examples, he argued that God, though compassionate, had never treated children as blameless innocents. For instance, during the destruction of Sodom, God had decided to rescue Lot, but he had allowed countless numbers of infants to perish. God had also destroyed thousands of children in the Flood, saving only Noah and his family, and he had slain all the firstborn children in Egypt. From Edwards's viewpoint, the evidence was irrefutable: the faith in children's innocence was not just misguided but blasphemous.[25]

Yet because Edwards insisted that humans were responsible for their own sinfulness, he never argued that infants were born essentially evil. Instead, influenced by Thomas Aquinas, he described sin as privative: it was the inevitable result of human frailty after Adam's fall. As Edwards explained, Adam had been created with divine as well as natural principles, but because of his sin, he had lost his holiness — and his ability to control his passions. As a result, infants came into the world without the "superior" principles that would have curbed their natural selfishness. They were morally *neutral* at birth, not corrupt, but without God's indwelling spirit, they began to sin as soon as they were "capable" of it. In other words, Edwards seems to have shared Augustine's view of infants as "non-innocent," but because of his deep sense of human frailty, he also insisted that children committed their first sin almost immediately after birth. Indeed, their "non-innocence" was so brief that is was virtually meaningless. As he explained, the "time of freedom from sin be so small" that it was "not worthy of notice."[26]

Although Edwards's view of children as both morally neutral and depraved may sound contradictory, he deliberately designed his theology to answer eighteenth-century debates over the "injustice" of original sin. According to many Enlightenment philosophers, Calvinists were guilty of portraying a moral God as the author of sin. Why, they asked, would a perfect and merciful

---

25. Edwards, *Doctrine of Original Sin Defended,* 200, 216, 217-18.

26. Edwards, *Doctrine of Original Sin Defended,* 134, 135-36n.2, and 50-51. See also Slater, *Children in the New England Mind,* 60-61. On Augustine, see the essay by Martha Stortz in this volume.

God create humans who were inherently flawed? In response, Edwards insisted that humans were solely responsible for their own sinfulness. Even though God did not create humans to be immoral, they persistently fell into corruption as soon as they had the opportunity to assert their wills.[27] Tragically, children repeated the sins of their parents because of their alienation from God. Even more tragically, their depravity was their own fault.

Perhaps no one in eighteenth-century America was more forceful than Edwards in decrying the sentimentalization of children. Yet, ironically, even *he* shied away from some of the bleaker implications of his thought. Since he was not only a pastor and a theologian but also the father of eleven children, he seems to have found it difficult to imagine his own sons and daughters as "young vipers." According to the Reverend Samuel Hopkins, he was a loving parent who took pains to raise his children as faithful Christians. Determined to save them from hell, he prayed with them, quizzed them on the Bible and the Westminster Shorter Catechism, and discouraged "frolicking." To his relief, several of his children experienced conversion at a young age, including his oldest daughter, Sarah, who was "born again" at the age of seven.[28] Nevertheless, Edwards was a devout Puritan, and he must have spent at least a few fearful nights fretting over whether all of his beloved children would be saved.

Whether because of his personal experiences as a parent or because of his close reading of Scottish commonsense philosophers, Edwards echoed the same rhetoric of children's goodness that he wanted to refute. In an ironic twist of history, the same man who is remembered for his biting criticism of Enlightenment thinkers also seems to have been subtly influenced by them. To be sure, he never claimed that children were "naturally" virtuous, and he saw their redemption as a product of God's grace, not their own righteousness. Nevertheless, he thought it was possible for God to choose even the tiniest infants for salvation. "As to the Time of bestowm[en]t of Conv[ersion]," he explained, "when G[od] hath a design of mercy, he sometimes bestows it on Persons when young or Even in childhood."[29] Even though infants or small children would not real-

---

27. The clearest explanation of Edwards's complicated understanding of original sin is given by Clyde A. Holbrook in his introduction to *Original Sin*.

28. Ola Elizabeth Winslow, *Jonathan Edwards, 1703-1758: A Biography* (New York: Macmillan, 1940), 164; Samuel Hopkins, "The Life and Character of the Late Reverend Mr. Jonathan Edwards" (1765), reprinted in *Jonathan Edwards: A Profile*, ed. David Levin (New York: Hill & Wang, 1969), 43-44.

29. Jonathan Edwards, "Sermon on John 3:8," December 1734, Edwards MSS, Beinecke Library, Yale University. Many scholars have argued that Edwards was influenced by Enlightenment thought. See Fiering, *Jonathan Edwards's Moral Thought and Its British Context*, and James Hoopes, "Jonathan Edwards's Religious Psychology," *Journal of American History* 69, no. 4 (March 1983): 849-65.

ize they had been spiritually reborn, they would learn to "exercise grace gradually as they exercise their reason."[30] As they grew to maturity, their virtuous actions would reveal them as God's elect.

In his personal devotional life, Edwards often meditated on the spiritual meaning of childhood. As he tried to define his own relationship to God, he imagined himself as a helpless, submissive child — an image that brought him immense comfort. "I very often think with sweetness, and longings, and pantings of soul, of being a little child, taking hold of Christ, to be led by him through the wilderness of the world," he wrote. If he could cling to Christ's strong hand, he would never be afraid of the darkness around him. Just as his own children looked up to him with utter trust and love, he yearned to "lie low before God, as in the dust; that I might be nothing, and that God might be ALL, that I might become as a little child." No other metaphor so perfectly captured his desire to lose himself in God.[31]

Despite his ambivalence about real, flesh-and-blood children, Edwards used images of them to symbolize ideal piety. For example, commenting on Mark 9:42 (the passage in which Christ warned his disciples not to "offend" his "little ones"), he reflected on the beauty of a childlike faith. "Christians are but babes and infants in this world," he wrote. "Christians must become as little children in humility, innocence, tenderheartedness, etc."[32] Given Edwards's other writings about children, it is astonishing that he chose to use the word "innocence," but despite his Calvinism, he thought children symbolized some of the best Christian qualities. Unlike adults, who had grown hardened in sin, they were not ashamed of their complete dependence on God. In that sense, they seemed endearingly "innocent."

Struggling to respond to the Age of Reason, the reorganization of the family, and the decline of religion (whether real or imagined), Edwards created a double image of children. On the surface, he presented himself as a defender of Puritan orthodoxy, a crusader against maudlin views of childhood innocence, but as we have seen, his underlying views were far more complicated — and far more ambivalent. Edwards certainly did not sentimentalize children, but he did not demonize them, either. Since children, like adults, were fully human, they had the potential to be full of sin, but also full of grace.

---

30. The "Miscellanies" (Entry Nos. a-z, aa-zz, 1-500), ed. Schafer, 389.

31. Jonathan Edwards, Personal Narrative, in Jonathan Edwards: Representative Selections, ed. Clarence H. Faust and Thomas N. Johnson, rev. ed. (New York: Hill & Wang, 1962), 67, 63-64.

32. Jonathan Edwards, "Notes on Scripture," Entry 31, in Notes on Scripture, vol. 15 of The Works of Jonathan Edwards, ed. Stephen J. Stein (New Haven: Yale University Press, 1998), 56.

"God Is Very Angry": Edwards's Sermons to Children

Today Edwards is usually remembered as a theologian, but he was also a pastor and a father who spent much of his life ministering to children. Rather than simply sitting in his study and thinking in abstract terms about children's nature, he watched them play, listened to their questions, and even held special religious meetings for them. Influenced by the example of Jesus, who had welcomed children into his arms, he gathered them together to teach them the gospel. Between 1739 and 1742, during the height of the revivals known as the "Great Awakening," he preached at least three sermons directed explicitly to children.[33]

Children's sermons would become a popular part of Protestant worship during the nineteenth and twentieth centuries, but they were much less common in Puritan New England. Although many Puritan ministers wrote catechisms for children, few (if any) seem to have held separate meetings for them. According to Thomas Hooker, a famous seventeenth-century divine, children were too irrational to understand "the mysteries of life and salvation." A ten- or twelve-year-old child, he claimed, lived the "life of a beast."[34]

In contrast, Edwards and other eighteenth-century revival preachers, including the Reverend Thomas Prince of Boston, insisted that children were capable of becoming faithful Christians. From reading the Bible, they were convinced that "God had perfect[ed] praise out of the mouths of babes and sucklings."[35] Although Edwards admitted that earlier Puritans had thought it was "a strange thing, when any seemed to be savingly wrought upon, and remarkably changed in their childhood," he defended children's conversions as a sign of God's extraordinary grace. Most of the converts in his Northampton congregation were "youth" between the ages of fourteen and twenty-five, but as he proudly reported, a large number of younger children also had been "savingly wrought upon." Besides the four-year-old Phebe Bartlet and two nine- or ten-year-olds, more than thirty children between the ages of ten and fourteen had been "born again."[36]

33. See *Sermons and Discourses, 1739-42*, vol. 17 of *The Works of Jonathan Edwards*, ed. Harry S. Stout and Nathan O. Hatch (New Haven: Yale University Press, forthcoming). On Edwards as a pastor, see Winslow, *Jonathan Edwards, 1703-1758*.

34. Thomas Hooker, *The Unbeleevers Preparing for Christ* (London, 1638), quoted in Beales, "In Search of the Historical Child," 386.

35. Edwards, *Some Thoughts Concerning the Present Revival*, 408.

36. Edwards, *A Faithful Narrative*, 158. See also his letter to Thomas Prince, where he marveled that "we had the most wonderful work among children that ever was in Northampton," in *The Great Awakening*, ed. Goen, 548. On the large numbers of "youth" who converted in Northampton, see Tracy, *Jonathan Edwards, Pastor*, 87. This pattern was

With the exception of the precocious Phebe Bartlet, however, very few children under the age of six seem to have participated in the revivals. According to Edwards, these children were still "infants," and although he rarely wrote about them, he seems to have assumed they were too young to recognize the signs of conversion. (Without more evidence, however, it is difficult to summarize his view.) Significantly, none of his own children experienced conversion until reaching the age of six or older. Perhaps he invited "infants" to his children's meetings, but it seems more likely that he directed his sermons to those between the ages of six and fourteen.

Edwards's ministry to children was one of the most striking results of his new theology of "religious affections." Unlike earlier Puritan ministers, who equated religion with a rational understanding of Scripture, Edwards claimed that true faith was a matter of the heart. "Our people don't so much need to have their heads stored, as to have their hearts touched," he wrote.[37] Although Edwards was certainly not anti-intellectual, he believed that even the humblest person — whether a slave, an uneducated farmer, or a child — was capable of understanding God's grace. Phebe Bartlet could not explain the intricacies of Puritan doctrine, but after her conversion, she had such a "new sense" of Christ's love that she wept with joy. Most important, her everyday behavior changed: she became more charitable, more devout, and more fearful of committing sin. Even though she did not yet have an intellectual appreciation of her faith, she had an intuitive, emotional understanding of her rebirth in Christ.[38]

---

true of the revivals in other New England towns as well. See Philip J. Greven Jr., "Youth, Maturity, and Religious Conversion: A Note on the Ages of Converts in Andover, Massachusetts, 1711-1749," *Essex Institute Historical Collections* 108 (1972): 119-34; and Stephen R. Grossbart, "Seeking the Divine Favor: Conversion and Church Admission in Eastern Connecticut, 1711-1832," *William and Mary Quarterly* 46 (1989): 696-740. Since Northampton's church records list only twenty members under the age of fourteen, Edwards may have exaggerated how many children converted. But it is also possible that some of them chose not to become full members. See Minkema, "Old Age and Religion in the Writings and Life of Jonathan Edwards," Table 1.

37. Edwards was quoting the famous seventeenth-century Puritan minister Thomas Shepard. See Edwards, *Some Thoughts Concerning the Present Revival,* 388. On Edwards's view of "religious affections," see Jonathan Edwards, *A Treatise Concerning Religious Affections,* in *Religious Affections,* vol. 2 of *The Works of Jonathan Edwards,* ed. John E. Smith (New Haven: Yale University Press, 1959), 93-461. On the older emphasis on rationality, see Teresa Toulouse, *The Art of Prophesying: New England Sermons and the Shaping of Belief* (Athens: University of Georgia Press, 1987).

38. Edwards, *A Faithful Narrative,* 202-3; Edwards, *A Treatise Concerning Religious Affections,* 40-42, 383-461. It is important to note that Edwards distinguished between "affections" and "passions." Unlike passions, affections involved a rational as well as an emotional understanding of the gospel.

In all of his sermons to children, Edwards mixed clear, logical explanations of the Bible with emotional appeals to the heart. Although he, like the apostle Paul, believed that faith must be nurtured by understanding, he did not want to clutter his sermons with arguments that children could not comprehend. For example, in his sermon "Children Ought to Love the Lord Jesus Christ above All," which was based on Matthew 10:37, he used clear, plain language to explain why they should love Christ more than their parents. Using simple images, he compared Christ to the brightest star, the loveliest flower, and the sweetest honey. "He is the delight of heaven," Edwards rejoiced. "There is nothing in heaven, that glorious world, that is brighter and more amiable and lovely than Christ." Best of all, Christ deeply loved children. Just as he had tenderly embraced and blessed the "little ones" who had crowded around him in Judea, he stood waiting for them in heaven "with the arms of his love open."[39]

After this blissful description of Christ's love and beauty, however, Edwards abruptly changed his tone. In case his young listeners had not been touched by his reflections on Christ's goodness, he decided to take a different tack. "If it had not been for Christ's preservation," he warned them, "they would have been in the grave, and there they would have been eaten up of worms long ago." With an immediacy that must have been alarming, he asked them to imagine what would happen if God suddenly withdrew his protection. At *that very moment,* as they were listening to his voice, devils would "immediately fall upon them and carry them away," dragging them away from their safe homes into hell. Without Christ, "they would have been burning in hell among devils long before this time."[40]

Unlike modern-day, liberal Christians who believe in fostering children's self-esteem, Edwards deliberately tried to strip away their feelings of pride, which he saw as inherently selfish. Theologically, he defined "true virtue" as selfless humility or, as he phrased it, "disinterested benevolence toward God."[41] In order to become faithful Christians, children had to learn how to renounce their own needs and desires, completely surrendering themselves to God. If they truly loved God, they would have "a great sense of their unworthiness."[42] Deference, not autonomy, was the mark of a true Christian.

To make children see their "unworthiness," Edwards did not hesitate to

39. Jonathan Edwards, "Children Ought to Love the Lord Jesus Christ above All" (1740), MSS sermon, Beinecke Library, Yale University, scheduled to be published in *Sermons and Discourses, 1739-42.*

40. Edwards, "Children Ought to Love the Lord Jesus Christ above All."

41. See Jonathan Edwards, *The Nature of True Virtue,* reprinted in *Jonathan Edwards: Representative Selections,* 349-71.

42. Unpublished letter of Jonathan Edwards to Benjamin Colman, dated May 30, 1735, reprinted in *The Great Awakening,* ed. Goen, 107.

use fear. Despite his modern reputation, he was not simply a hellfire preacher, and few theologians have written more lyrical descriptions of Christ's "sweetness," "beauty," and "excellence." Marveling at the "glorious *majesty* and *grace* of God," he exulted, "I seemed to see them both in a sweet conjunction; majesty and meekness joined together; it was as sweet, and gentle, and holy majesty; and also a majestic meekness; an awful sweetness; a high, and great, and holy gentleness."[43] Yet despite his "sweet sense" of Christ's beauty, Edwards also invoked terrifying images of divine wrath. For example, in a sermon that he preached in February of 1741, he harshly stated his main doctrine: "God is very angry at the sins of children." With blunt language that must have frightened them, he warned that a vengeful God would not only "correct" them but "cast 'em into hell to all eternity." Not only were they inherently "full of malice," but they had committed countless numbers of sins, including telling lies, disobeying their parents, quarreling with their brothers and sisters, and harboring "wicked thoughts [and] wicked desires." Unless they repented, they would "burn in hell forever."[44]

Although Edwards lived more than a century before the rise of modern psychology, he instinctively knew how to exploit common childhood fears of darkness, "monsters," abandonment, and death. Since as many as three out of every ten infants in New England did not survive to their first birthday (a death rate ten times higher than in the modern United States), he warned children to remember their mortality.[45] "'Tis not likely you will all live to grow up," he lamented. "If you should die while you are young, and death should come upon you and find you without any love to Christ, what will become of you?" Unless they repented, they would spend an eternity with the devil, a "roaring Lion that goes about seeking whom he may devour." Stirring up even deeper fears, Edwards insisted that unless they were "born again," their parents would stop loving them. On Judgment Day, as Christ sentenced them to eternal punishment in hell, their parents would not "be grieved," but would "praise God for his justice."[46] The same parents who had once tenderly embraced them, soothed their

43. Edwards, *Personal Narrative,* in *Jonathan Edwards: Representative Selections,* 60.

44. Jonathan Edwards, MSS sermon on 2 Kings 2:23-24 (1741), Beinecke Library, Yale University.

45. On mortality rates, see Moran and Vinovskis, *Religion, Family, and the Life Course,* 215. See also David E. Stannard, *The Puritan Way of Death: A Study in Religion, Culture, and Social Change* (New York: Oxford University Press, 1977), 44-71.

46. Jonathan Edwards, MSS sermon on 2 Kings 2:23-24. As he warned in another sermon as well, "When they shall behold you with a frightened, amazed countenance, trembling and astonished, and shall hear you groan and gnash your teeth; these things will not move them at all to pity you, but you will see them with a holy joyfulness in their countenances, and with songs in their mouths." See Jonathan Edwards, "The End of the

cries, and bandaged their cuts would rejoice to see them in torment. In other words, children's worst nightmares were not just fantasies but accurate depictions of their future agonies in hell. They would spend eternity in a dark pit; they would be tormented by monsters; and no matter how much they wept for mercy, they would be utterly alone, forsaken by their parents.

Yet at the same time as Edwards deliberately tried to frighten children, he also reassured them. No matter how much he emphasized God's anger, he always ended his sermons by imagining joyful children in heaven. Paradoxically, he plumbed the depths of hell in order to help them imagine the soaring beauty of God's grace — a beauty they could not fully see without the "new sense." His sermons were analogical: he showed children the ugly horrors of the "bottomless pit" in order to give them a brief taste of heaven's "sweetness." If they stubbornly refused to repent, they could be thrown into hell at any moment, but if they were born again, they would be safe in the shelter of Christ's love. They would sleep with angels watching over them; they would no longer fear thunder and lightning; they would "triumph over" the most horrible monster of all, the devil; and, most important, they would no longer be afraid of death. With plain, childlike language, Edwards promised them eternal life and magnificent rewards in heaven. As they feasted on sumptuous food, they would be crowned with a "glorious crown" that would be "a thousand times more excellent than the best crown that is worn by any king or queen."[47]

Without intending it, Edwards preached a potentially subversive message about children's value in the eyes of God. Undermining the traditional hierarchies of age and wealth, he insisted that Christ loved even the poorest or humblest child. "Christ is ready to receive little children into communion with him, even the poor children of poor parents," he promised. "Those that are despised in the world, Christ don't despise them." Quoting from Matthew 18:10, he vowed that God would punish anyone who disdained even "one little child that believes in him."[48] Although some adults — particularly those who had not yet been "saved" — measured children's worth according to their age or their social standing, Christ saw only their religious devotion.

God's world, according to Edwards, was a topsy-turvy world where children could be superior to adults. Ironically, even though he hoped to strengthen the traditional, patriarchal family, he also implicitly undermined it. On one hand, he insisted that "good" children would never tell lies, play on the

---

Wicked Contemplated by the Righteous: Or, the Torments of the Wicked in Hell, No Occasion of Grief to the Saints in Heaven," *Works* (1843), vol. 4, 296, quoted in Levin, *Jonathan Edwards*, 223. This sermon echoed Wigglesworth's *Day of Doom*.

47. Edwards, "Children Ought to Love the Lord Jesus Christ above All."
48. Edwards, "Children Ought to Love the Lord Jesus Christ above All."

Sabbath, or challenge the authority of their parents. Preaching a message of social control, he commanded them to be obedient. "Nothing has a greater tendency to bring a curse on persons, in this world, and on all their temporal concerns," he admonished, "than an undutiful, unsubmissive, disorderly behaviour
in children towards their parents."[49] At the same time, however, he also insisted
that God loved regenerate children much more than sinful adults. Despite children's youth, "many of them have more of that knowledge and wisdom, that
pleases him and renders their religious worship more acceptable, than many of
the great and learned men of the world."[50] Children could be wiser than their
parents.

In one of the most remarkable innovations of the revivals, Edwards allowed children to be admitted into full communion. During 1734-35, as historian Kenneth P. Minkema has shown, there were twenty children under the age
of fourteen whose names were added to Northampton's church records. Unlike
earlier ministers, who had not allowed children to participate in the Lord's Supper, Edwards thought they should be allowed to commemorate Christ's suffering and death on the cross. By passing the bread and cup to them, he treated
them as full spiritual equals. Although he decided to stop admitting children after 1740 because so many of them seemed to "backslide," losing their fervor as
the revivals waned, his brief experiment symbolized his deep appreciation of
children's piety.[51]

Many children seem to have been inspired by Edwards's theology. None
of their own letters or diaries have survived, but if Edwards's reports can be
trusted, large numbers of them forsook "frolicking" in favor of prayer meetings.
As he recounted, "A very considerable work of God appeared among those that
were very young, and the revival of religion continued to increase; so that in the
spring [of 1741] an engagedness of spirit about things of religion was become
very general amongst young people and children, and religious subjects almost
wholly took up their conversation when they were together."[52] Given the controversies swirling around the revivals, these children must have known that
people questioned their sincerity, but influenced by Edwards, they demanded
to be treated with respect.

Psychologically, some of the children who attended Edwards's meetings

49. Edwards, "Children Ought to Love the Lord Jesus Christ above All," and Jonathan Edwards, *Farewell Sermon,* in *Jonathan Edwards: Representative Selections,* 198.

50. Edwards, *Some Thoughts Concerning the Present Revival,* 408.

51. Minkema, "Old Age and Religion in the Writings and Life of Jonathan Edwards,"
Table 1.

52. Jonathan Edwards, "The State of Religion at Northampton in the County of
Hampshire, About a Hundred Miles Westward of Boston," in *The Great Awakening,* ed.
Goen, 545.

seem to have found them cathartic. As they listened to his horrifying descriptions of hell, they were able to express and ultimately conquer their deep-seated fears of darkness and death. Perhaps they welcomed the chance to express anxieties that other adults — even their own parents — impatiently dismissed as "childish." Not only did Edwards take their fears seriously, but, most important, he showed them how to overcome them. In response to their anxious questions about the devil, he always gave the same reassuring answer: even though they were too young and vulnerable to protect themselves, Christ would never allow any of his "chosen ones" to be harmed.

While some children were attracted to the reassurance of Edwards's sermons, others seem to have found them appealingly subversive. Taking his teachings to an extreme, they claimed to be spiritually superior to their parents or ministers. According to the Reverend Charles Chauncy, a vocal opponent of the revivals, the theology of "religious affections" had wreaked havoc in families. For example, when a father tried to offer religious advice to his fifteen-year-old daughter, she angrily responded that "all the Counsels he had ever given her, had no better a Tendency than to instruct her, how she should please the Devil." Reversing the roles in the father-daughter relationship, she claimed that *he*, not she, was "going Post-haste down to Hell."[53] Even though this girl was old enough to know the importance of obeying her father, she was so emboldened by the revivals that she openly defied him.

Most radically, a small number of children seem to have used the new emphasis on "religious affections" to justify their right to speak publicly during worship meetings. There is no evidence that Edwards himself ever allowed children to "testify" in public, but according to Charles Chauncy, other revival preachers were more permissive. As he complained, "babes in age as well as understanding" were allowed to harangue their elders.[54] Given Chauncy's animosity toward the revivals, he may have deliberately exaggerated children's participation, but his stories were echoed by more sympathetic ministers as well. For example, according to the pastor of a Massachusetts church, "children of five, six, seven years, and upward, would pray to admiration."[55] Because this minister assumed that children could be genuinely converted, he asked his entire congregation, even the adults, to listen to their raptures on God's grace.

Yet whatever the appeal of Edwards's ideas, he never answered the question that some of the children in his congregation may have desperately wanted

53. Charles Chauncy, *Seasonable Thoughts on the State of Religion in New England* (1743; reprint, New York: Regina Press, 1975), 169.

54. Chauncy, *Seasonable Thoughts on the State of Religion in New England*, 226.

55. *The Christian History*, vol. 11, 44, quoted in Sandford Fleming, *Children and Puritanism: The Place of Children in the Life and Thought of the New England Churches, 1620-1847* (New Haven: Yale University Press, 1933), 179.

to ask. If they were faithful Christians who loved God, were they still required to obey adults who had not been "born again"? Did they have to obey sinful parents who psychologically or physically abused them? Since Edwards had been raised in a family with a disturbing history of violence, he knew how much damage an abusive parent could inflict. His grandmother on his father's side, Elizabeth Tuttle, had been so physically violent and mentally unstable that his grandfather had finally convinced the court to grant him a divorce — a rare event in seventeenth-century Massachusetts. Even more troubling, his great-aunt (Elizabeth Tuttle's sister) had murdered her own son.[56] Given the stories he must have heard as a child, it is not surprising that as an adult, he insisted that Christians owed their first allegiance to God, not humankind. As he explained to children, real Christians should be willing to "leave mother and father and all things in the world" to be with Jesus.[57] Nevertheless, he was so committed to preserving "family government" that he refused to clarify children's individual rights. Like earlier Christian theologians, he knew there were children who lived in violent or dissolute families, but in a hierarchical world that took children's obedience for granted, he refused to explore the theological questions raised by their suffering.

Unfortunately, there were many children who found Edwards's theology neither cathartic nor empowering. Rather than using his ideas to expand their religious authority, they struggled with overwhelming feelings of anxiety and despair. Once again, the evidence comes from Edwards, who proudly reported that children broke down in tears while listening to his sermons. During one of his children's meetings, "the room was filled with cries," and afterward, groups of sobbing children "went home crying aloud through the streets, to all parts of the town."[58] Apparently Phebe Bartlet, who feared she might "go to hell," was not alone.

---

56. Winslow, *Jonathan Edwards, 1703-1758,* 18-20.

57. Edwards praised converted children for loving Christ more than their parents: "Some of them seem to be full of love to Christ and have expressed great longings after him and willingness to die, and leave mother and father and all things in the world to go to him, together with a great sense of their unworthiness and admiration at the free grace of God towards them" (Unpublished letter of Jonathan Edwards to Benjamin Colman, dated May 30, 1735, reprinted in *The Great Awakening,* ed. Goen, 107).

58. Jonathan Edwards, Letter to the Reverend Thomas Prince (1743), in *The Works of Jonathan Edwards,* vol. 16: *Letters and Personal Writings,* ed. George S. Claghorn (New Haven: Yale University Press, 1998), 117.

"Bring Them Up in the Nurture and Admonition of the Lord": Edwards's Sermons to Parents

Gratified by the conversion of more than thirty children in Northampton, Edwards believed his sermons to them had been a success. According to many parents, however, he had violated their trust by "frighting poor innocent children with talk of hell fire and eternal damnation."[59] Implicitly, to use more modern language, they accused him of subjecting their children to emotional and verbal abuse — a charge he angrily denied. As he complained, parents were so "blinded" by love for their children that they wanted him to sugarcoat the truth. But he, as an ordained minister, knew better. "A child that has a dangerous wound may need the painful lance as well as grown persons," he explained. "And that would be a foolish pity, in such a case, that would hold back the lance, and throw away the life." In other words, he believed there were times when children "needed" to be hurt. Indulgent parents thought they were being kind by concealing the horrors of hell, but in reality they were guilty of a far greater "Cruelty" than anything he had ever inflicted.[60] In the long run, "frighting" children was for their own good.

Since Edwards addressed several sermons to parents as well as to children, they knew firsthand how painful it was to be on the other side of his "lance." More than a hundred years before Horace Bushnell developed his theology of "Christian nurture," Edwards urged parents to raise their children as devout Christians. Unlike Bushnell, he never claimed that nurture could substitute for the climactic experience of conversion, but if parents reared their children on the Bible, they could prepare them to accept God's grace. Mothers and fathers had crucial religious responsibilities: they should read the Bible aloud to their children, help them memorize the Westminster Confession, lead family prayer every day, and serve as examples of Christian virtue. Edwards urged parents to be "as Carefull About the welfare of [children's] souls as you are about their bodies."[61]

Repeating the same strategies he had used with children, Edwards deliberately tried to frighten the adults in his congregation into becoming better parents — and better Christians. For example, in a sermon based on Ephesians 6:4 ("And, ye fathers, provoke not your children to wrath; but bring them up in the nurture and admonition of the Lord"), he asked them to imagine how they

59. Edwards, *Some Thoughts Concerning the Present Revival*, 394.

60. Edwards, *Some Thoughts Concerning the Present Revival*, 394. See also Jonathan Edwards, "Sermon on Ephesians 6:4," February 1748, Edwards MSS, Beinecke Library, Yale University.

61. "Sermon On Psalm 139:23," September 1733, Edwards MSS, Beinecke Library, Yale University.

would feel if their children died young. Would they be filled with remorse if they were suddenly forced to watch their "Children in their death bed in the sensible [visible] approaches of death . . . Gasping and dying"? If they had neglected the duties of family prayer or Bible reading, would they spend the rest of their lives in terror that their children had been "Cast, Gone down into Hell"?[62] Perhaps Edwards took a gentler tone during his private pastoral visits, but during his Sunday sermons, he tried to jolt parents into confronting the hard truths about sin and damnation.

Although some of the parents in Edwards's congregation seem to have appreciated his candor, others resented being characterized as overly fond and indulgent. Understandably, they bridled at his suggestion that they had shirked their parental responsibilities — or, even worse, that they did not love their children. Perhaps some were offended by his argument that if they did not warn their children to repent, they were as morally guilty — and as "bereft of reason" — as if they calmly allowed them to burn to death in a fire.[63] Although there is little evidence of their own theological understandings of childhood, some may have been influenced by the growing popularity of Enlightenment ideas. As moral philosophers debated over the possibility of human goodness, some parents may have refused to see their children as "young vipers."

Perhaps not surprisingly, the final rift between Edwards and his congregation involved — at least in part — another dispute about children. Because of his determination to strengthen religious orthodoxy, he decided to reverse nearly one hundred years of history by restricting access to the sacraments of baptism and the Lord's Supper. Like the first Puritan settlers, he argued that only full church members — those who publicly claimed to have been "born again" — were entitled to participate in the church's sacramental life. Even though "halfway" members made up the majority of his church, Edwards scorned them as hypocrites who cared more about social appearances than the substance of Christian faith. Indeed, he accused them of complacently attending Sunday services without ever striving for conversion. Worst of all, instead of viewing baptism as a "spiritual blessing," a symbol of their commitment to "give up their children to God," they "coveted" it as a "high honor and privilege."[64]

As historian David D. Hall has argued, Edwards's congregation objected to his attempts to limit communion, but they were especially angered by his decision to exclude large numbers of children from baptism. According to the

---

62. Edwards, "Sermon on Ephesians 6:4."

63. For this analogy, see Jonathan Edwards, *The Distinguishing Marks of a Work of the Spirit of God* (1741), in *The Great Awakening*, ed. Goen, 247.

64. Jonathan Edwards, *An Humble Inquiry* (1749), in *Ecclesiastical Writings*, ed. Hall, 318, 316.

Westminster Confession, baptism was not necessary for salvation, but at a time when infant mortality was high, many parents seem to have prized it as a form of protection. In Hall's words, they believed that "children within the covenant were better off because of being less threatened by the devil, more likely to obtain saving grace, and more apt to survive." Hoping to shield their infants from harm, most parents brought them to be baptized as soon as possible, often within two weeks of their birth, even if that meant carrying them through the snow and breaking the ice on the baptismal font.[65] Despite Edwards's insistence that baptism was only a "sign" of God's covenant, not a guarantee of salvation, parents continued to hope it might be inherently redemptive.

Although Edwards admitted there was "scarce any hope" of convincing his congregation to accept his view of baptism, he thought their fierce attachment to it was unscriptural and ultimately irrational.[66] Conversion, not baptism, was the only path to salvation, and yet parents foolishly thought they could rescue their children from damnation simply by performing the correct rituals. They calmly allowed their children to "go about the world in the most odious and dangerous state of soul, in reality the children of the devil, and condemned to eternal burnings," while at the same time, they shuddered to think of them being "disgraced by going without the honor of being baptized!" In a bold attempt to destroy this false sense of security, Edwards decided to limit access to baptism, depriving "halfway" members of one of their most cherished religious privileges. With characteristic bluntness, he announced that the children of unregenerate parents did not deserve to have "God's mark set upon them as some of his."[67]

Unfortunately for Edwards, he paid a high price for his devotion to religious purity. In June of 1750, after twenty-three years of ministry in Northampton, his congregation voted to dismiss him. Significantly, Edwards claimed that many "youths" continued to support him, but the majority of his church denounced him for his rigidity and harshness.[68] True to form, however,

65. David D. Hall, introduction to *Ecclesiastical Writings*, 37. See also Anne S. Brown and David D. Hall, "Family Strategies and Religious Practice: Baptism and the Lord's Supper in Early New England," in *Lived Religion in America: Toward a History of Practice*, ed. David D. Hall (Princeton: Princeton University Press, 1997), 41-68. From examining the early eighteenth-century church records from three Massachusetts towns, Brown and Hall found that 59 percent of children were baptized within the first two weeks of their birth (53).

66. See the letter from Edwards to the Reverend Thomas Foxcroft (dated May 24, 1749), in *Letters and Personal Writings*, ed. Claghorn, 283.

67. Edwards, *An Humble Inquiry*, 315.

68. See *The Life of President Edwards*, ed. Sereno E. Dwight, vol. 1 of *The Works of President Edwards* (New York: Converse, 1830), quoted in McDermott, *One Holy and Happy Society*, 169.

Edwards refused to soften his message during his farewell sermon — in fact, his words sounded particularly severe. Explicitly addressing the children in his audience — "the lambs of this flock," he called them — he lamented that so few of them had experienced conversion. Their future, unless they repented, was bleak. "I now leave you in a miserable condition, having no interest in Christ," he admonished, "and so under the awful displeasure and anger of God, and in danger of going down to the pit of eternal misery." Although promising to pray for them, he offered them far less reassurance than he had in earlier sermons. If they still ignored his warnings, they would be sentenced to "everlasting destruction."[69]

Remembering Edwards

After leaving Northampton in 1750, Edwards became a missionary to Native Americans in Stockbridge, Massachusetts, where he continued to defend Calvinism against Enlightenment "heresies." In 1758, at the age of fifty-four, he was called to the presidency of New Jersey College (now Princeton), but died only a few weeks later after receiving a smallpox vaccination. It was left to Samuel Hopkins, Joseph Bellamy, and his other followers, who were known as the "New Divinity" men, to perpetuate his theology in Revolutionary America.[70]

Yet despite the best efforts of his disciples, Edwards's understanding of human nature lost much of its appeal after the American Revolution, one of the most tumultuous periods in American history. Although scholars have argued over why there was such a profound religious transformation in early nineteenth-century America, they have agreed that it was at least partially linked to the growth of republican ideology. At a time when politicians celebrated the ability of "self-made" men to govern themselves, Edwards's faith in original sin, predestination, and childhood depravity seemed overly pessimistic, if not undemocratic. Although many nineteenth-century Protestant ministers revered Edwards, fighting over who could rightfully claim his mantle, they also modified his theology in order to give humans more agency in their salvation. Even Timothy Dwight, Edwards's grandson and the president of Yale, softened the

---

69. Edwards, *Farewell Sermon*, in *Jonathan Edwards: Representative Selections*, 196.

70. On the New Divinity, see Joseph A. Conforti, *Samuel Hopkins and the New Divinity Movement: Calvinism, the Congregational Ministry, and Reform in New England between the Great Awakenings* (Grand Rapids, Mich.: Christian University Press, 1981); and Mark R. Valeri, *Law and Providence in Joseph Bellamy's New England: The Origins of the New Divinity in Revolutionary America* (New York: Oxford University Press, 1994).

Calvinist understanding of original sin.[71] Just as Edwards had once feared, Calvinism had been both challenged and transformed by the "Age of Reason."

By 1847, the year that the Reverend Horace Bushnell published *Christian Nurture*, his treatise on childhood, many Protestants openly rejected Edwards's stark view of infant damnation and childhood depravity. Ironically, Bushnell was part of the same Congregational tradition that had molded Edwards, and he resembled him in more ways than he would have been willing to admit. Besides emphasizing the importance of parental guidance, he strongly denied "the radical goodness of human nature." Nevertheless, in a striking innovation, he argued that almost all children, if carefully nurtured, had the capacity to become faithful Christians. As he explained, a child could "grow up a Christian, and never know himself as being otherwise."[72] Rejecting the emphasis on conversion, he condemned Edwards and other Puritans for tormenting impressionable young children with threats of hell — a criticism that other liberals quickly echoed. Sarcastically, Oliver Wendell Holmes wondered whether Edwards had misread Christ's famous words as "Suffer little *vipers* to come unto me, and forbid them not."[73]

Today, as in the eighteenth and nineteenth centuries, Edwards's theology continues to cause controversy. Surprisingly, despite the predictions of earlier generations of liberals, his ideas have gained new currency as modern-day Christians have struggled to make sense of the violence of the twentieth century. In the wake of two world wars, the atom bomb, the Holocaust, and Vietnam, many Christians have questioned the liberal faith in human goodness, rejecting it as overly optimistic, if not naive. In this increasingly conservative religious climate, Edwards no longer seems like a reactionary who struggled against the forces of religious progress or "the last medieval American," as one historian described him, but like an unusually perceptive critic of religious sentimentality. Fascinated by his theology, scholars have published hundreds of dissertations, articles, and books about him since the 1950s. In addition, a dis-

71. On the changes in American religion after the American Revolution, see Nathan O. Hatch, *The Democratization of American Christianity* (New Haven: Yale University Press, 1989). On Edwards's influence on later theologians, see Mark A. Noll, "Jonathan Edwards and Nineteenth-Century Theology," in *Jonathan Edwards and the American Experience*, ed. Nathan O. Hatch and Harry S. Stout (New York: Oxford University Press, 1988), 260-87.

72. See Horace Bushnell, *Christian Nurture* (New York: Charles Scribner, 1861; reprint, Cleveland, Ohio: Pilgrim Press, 1994), 22, 10; and the essay by Margaret Lamberts Bendroth in this volume. The first, shorter edition of Bushnell's work was published as *Discourses on Christian Nurture* (Boston: Massachusetts Sabbath School Society, 1847).

73. Oliver Wendell Holmes, "Jonathan Edwards," in *Pages from an Old Volume of Life* (Boston, 1892), 393, quoted in Henry F. May, "Jonathan Edwards and America," in *Jonathan Edwards and the American Experience*, 23.

tinguished team of historians and philosophers have collaborated to edit his published and unpublished works, producing seventeen volumes between 1957 and the present, with ten more still in progress.[74]

Unfortunately, however, despite this growing interest in Edwards, very few scholars have written about his sermons to children. And, as one would anticipate, the few who have wrestled with his ideas have been sharply divided in their opinions. On the one hand, at least two historians have been openly sympathetic to his unflinching view of original sin. According to Peter Slater, for example, the Puritans' belief in childhood depravity may have helped parents cope with their inevitable feelings of impatience and frustration. Unlike nineteenth-century Romantics, who praised children as virtual angels, Edwards and other Puritans had a more realistic view of children's imperfections.[75] In an even more positive interpretation, Helen Westra, an evangelical scholar, has suggested that Edwards's style of firm discipline should be emulated by today's overly permissive parents. Influenced by contemporary debates over the loss of "family values," she has argued that Edwards "beheld and asserted truths about family, community, and society that no strong institution or nation can ignore without demoralizing effects."[76]

Yet in the midst of the "culture wars" between liberals and conservatives (battles that have often revolved around the best way to nurture and educate children), historians outside of the evangelical community have been far more critical of Edwards's theology. In a particularly stinging critique, Philip Greven has accused Edwards of helping to create a style of child rearing built on psychological and physical abuse. According to Greven, Edwards believed in "breaking the will" in order to force children to convert, and besides terrorizing children with images of hellfire, he also subjected them to brutal physical punishments. Citing fragmentary evidence, he argues that Edwards beat his own young children in order to make them more "Christian." Edwards, in his view, was not only "the most eloquent defender of divine punishments, pain, and torment in American history," but the father of modern-day evangelicals and fundamentalists who have defended child-beating as biblically sanctioned.[77]

74. On Edwards as the last "medieval" man, see Peter Gay, "Jonathan Edwards: An American Tragedy," in *Jonathan Edwards: A Profile*, ed. Levin, 231-51. The best guide to the voluminous scholarship on Edwards is M. X. Lesser, *Jonathan Edwards: A Reference Guide* (Boston: G. K. Hall, 1981).

75. Slater, *Children in the New England Mind*, 23.

76. Westra, "Cornerstones, Cannons, and Covenants," 31.

77. Philip Greven, *Spare the Child: The Religious Roots of Punishment and the Psychological Impact of Physical Abuse* (New York: Alfred A. Knopf, 1991), 57. See also Philip Greven, *The Protestant Temperament: Patterns of Child-Rearing, Religious Experience, and the Self in Early America* (New York: Alfred A. Knopf, 1977).

To be fair to Edwards, however, it is difficult to make definitive statements about his own child-rearing techniques. Many historians have argued that corporal punishment was common in colonial America, and Edwards certainly believed that children, like all sinners, needed "correction."[78] It is also clear that his adult daughter, Esther Edwards Burr, used corporal punishment to discipline her ten-month-old child. "I have begun to govourn Sally," she wrote to a friend. "She has been Whip'd once on *Old Adams* account."[79] Citing this letter, Greven argues that "Esther Burr surely was repeating the experiences she had had as a child herself."[80] But there is very little evidence of Edwards's own style of child rearing, and he himself does not seem to have used the phrase "breaking the will."[81] Even the single, brief account of his "government of his children" can be interpreted in contradictory ways. According to the Reverend Samuel Hopkins, Edwards was a remarkably patient father who taught his children to obey him through love, not fear. "He took special care to begin his government of them in season," Hopkins explained. "When they first discovered any considerable degree of will and stubbornness, he would attend to them till he had thoroughly subdued them and brought them to submit. And such prudent, thorough discipline, exercised with great calmness, and commonly without striking a blow, being repeated once or twice, was generally sufficient for that child; and effectually established his parental authority, and produced a cheerful obedience ever after."[82] While this account can be read as evidence that

78. Edwards compared the "correction" of children to the afflictions suffered by disobedient Christians: "That a child needs correction, and the benefit of correcting children, is a type of what is true with respect to God's children." See Jonathan Edwards, "Images of Divine Things," in *Typological Writings,* vol. 11 of *The Works of Jonathan Edwards,* ed. Wallace E. Anderson, Mason I. Lowance Jr., and David H. Watters (New Haven: Yale University Press, 1993), 97.

79. Two months later, when Sally was "very cross" after an illness, Esther wondered whether she would have to punish her again with "a whiping spel." See *The Journal of Esther Edwards Burr, 1754-1757,* ed. Carol F. Karlsen and Laurie Crumpacker (New Haven: Yale University Press, 1984), 95, 107.

80. Greven, *Spare the Child,* 21.

81. Since Edwards left thousands of manuscripts, many of which are still unpublished, it is impossible to make definitive statements about all of his essays, letters, notebooks, and treatises. But still, it is clear that this phrase was not a recurring one in his writings.

82. Hopkins, "The Life and Character of the Late Reverend Mr. Jonathan Edwards," 43. Cotton Mather, an influential seventeenth-century Puritan minister, had urged parents not to beat their children except in cases of extraordinary obstinacy: "The slavish way of education, carried on with raving and kicking and scourging (in schools as well as families) 'tis abominable, and a dreadful judgment of God upon the world." See Cotton Mather, "Some Special Points, Relating to the Education of My Children" (1706), reprinted in *Remarkable Providences: Readings on Early American History,* ed. John Demos, rev. ed. (Boston: Northeastern University Press, 1991), 148.

Edwards was a repressive, stern disciplinarian who sometimes (though not "commonly") beat his children, it also suggests that he was more gentle than other parents.

Despite the controversies over his legacy, Jonathan Edwards was neither as saintly nor as sinister as historians have depicted him. On the positive side, he recognized that children have spiritual lives that need to be nurtured. By urging parents to pray with their children and answer their religious questions, he taught them that even the youngest children were fully human and could be genuinely touched by grace. And although he exploited children's anxieties about death and abandonment, he may have also helped them give voice to their deepest and most terrifying fears. On the negative side, however, he and other Puritans tried to inculcate children with feelings of shame and anxiety, and by emphasizing the torments of hell, he may have made it hard for them to imagine a loving, merciful God. Whether or not Edwards advocated corporal punishment, many Christians today would see his hellfire sermons as psychologically harmful, even destructive.

Perhaps what Edwards offers Christians today is an opportunity to see our own attitudes toward children more clearly. Unfortunately, historians have often taken a condescending attitude toward the past, assuming that we are more progressive in our attitudes than those who lived before us. In the words of one historian, "The history of childhood is a nightmare from which we have only recently begun to awaken. The further back in history one goes, the lower the level of child care, and the more likely children are to be killed, abandoned, beaten, terrorized, and sexually abused."[83] Yet at the same time as we take pride in our enlightenment, we allow countless numbers of children to suffer unspeakable violence in their homes, their neighborhoods, and their schools. We also allow our children to be exposed to terrifying images of violence and murder on television — images that make Edwards's graphic, brutal descriptions of hell seem almost mild. We, like Edwards and the Puritans, raise our children in a climate of repression and fear. And we, like Edwards, have not yet managed to create a Christian theology that values children's spiritual needs. Although much has changed since Edwards preached to children in the eighteenth century, we have not yet fulfilled the best promises of the Christian faith — a faith built on Jesus's love for the oppressed, the forgotten, and the very young.

83. Lloyd de Mause, *The History of Childhood: The Untold Story of Child Abuse* (New York: Psychohistory Press, 1974), 1. For other examples of this progress narrative, see Mary Cable, *The Little Darlings: A History of Child Rearing in America* (New York: Charles Scribner's Sons, 1972); Joseph E. Illick, "Child-Rearing in Seventeenth-Century England and America," in *The History of Childhood*, ed. de Mause, pp. 303-50; and John F. Walzer, "A Period of Ambivalence: Eighteenth-Century American Childhood," in *The History of Childhood*, ed. de Mause, 351-82.

12. "Be Converted and Become as Little Children": Friedrich Schleiermacher on the Religious Significance of Childhood

DAWN DeVRIES

"We know nothing of childhood; and with our mistaken notions the further we advance the further we go astray."

Jean-Jacques Rousseau, *Émile*

"If only I knew the way back, the pleasant path to the land of childhood."

Klaus Groth, "Heimweh"

"I myself am become entirely a child again, luckily for me."

Joseph, in Schleiermacher's *The Celebration of Christmas*

In a letter written on his fortieth birthday (21 November 1808) to a friend, Friedrich Schleiermacher waxed eloquent about the joys of family life. Anticipating his coming marriage to a widow twenty years his junior, who would bring two young children to the marriage, he voiced his hope to raise them with love and understanding. But in the midst of these ruminations he stopped with a kind of confession: "I have taught so much about the beautiful and holy life of the family; now I must have the opportunity to show that all of this is more than just pretty and empty words."[1] If Schleiermacher's teaching about the family was to be

1. Friedrich Schleiermacher, *Aus Schleiermachers Leben in Briefen*, 4 vols. (Berlin: Georg Reimer, 1860; reprint, Berlin: Walter de Gruyter, 1974), 2:173. All translations are my own unless otherwise noted.

329

tested in the crucible of life, he had ample opportunity in his twenty-five years of marriage to Henriette von Mühlenfels, a union that produced four more children. However, his thoughts on children grew not only from his experience as a son, brother, uncle, and father, but also from his work as a private tutor, teacher, and catechist. In all of these roles, he was a keen observer of the lives of children and a thoughtful and sensitive theorist of their unique gifts and needs.

Friedrich Daniel Ernst Schleiermacher (1768-1834) is often referred to as the "father of modern theology." He was an ordained pastor in the Reformed Church and was active in promoting the union of the Reformed and Lutheran churches in Prussia. For a short time he served as a professor of theology and university preacher at the University of Halle. But for most of his career he was a professor of theology at the newly formed University of Berlin and co-pastor of the Holy Trinity Church in Berlin. Schleiermacher is surely the greatest Reformed systematic theologian between John Calvin and Karl Barth, and he did much to interpret this tradition for a modern world.[2]

While much has been written about Schleiermacher's views on women and his possible contributions to feminist thought, relatively little can be found about his views on children.[3] This is curious, because Schleiermacher

---

2. For further introduction to Schleiermacher's theological significance, see B. A. Gerrish, *Tradition and the Modern World: Reformed Theology in the Nineteenth Century* (Chicago: University of Chicago Press, 1978), esp. 13-48. Cf. three other volumes by Gerrish: *A Prince of the Church: Schleiermacher and the Beginnings of Modern Theology* (Philadelphia: Fortress Press, 1984); *The Old Protestantism and the New: Essays on the Reformation Heritage* (Chicago: University of Chicago Press, 1982); and *Continuing the Reformation: Essays on Modern Religious Thought* (Chicago: University of Chicago Press, 1993), esp. 147-216.

3. For Schleiermacher's views on women, see Marilyn Chapin Massey, *Feminine Soul: The Fate of an Ideal* (Boston: Beacon Press, 1985); Dawn DeVries, "Schleiermacher's *Christmas Eve Dialogue:* Bourgeois Ideology or Feminist Theology?" *Journal of Religion* 69, no. 2 (April 1989): 169-83; Ruth Drucilla Richardson, *The Role of Women in the Life and Thought of the Early Schleiermacher (1768-1806): An Historical Overview,* Schleiermacher Studies and Translations, vol. 7 (Lewiston, N.Y.: Edwin Mellen Press, 1991); *Schleiermacher and Feminism: Sources, Evaluations, and Responses,* Schleiermacher Studies and Translation, vol. 12, ed. Iain G. Nicol (Lewiston, N.Y.: Edwin Mellen Press, 1992); and Patricia Guenther-Gleason, *On Schleiermacher and Gender Politics,* Harvard Theological Studies, vol. 43 (Valley Forge, Pa.: Trinity Press International, 1997).

The fullest treatment of Schleiermacher's views on children can be found in Dietrich F. Seidel, "Schleiermacher on Marriage and Family" (Ph.D. diss., Toronto School of Theology, 1987). Cf. Karl Janssen, "Die Familie bei Schleiermacher und Wichern," in *Dienst unter dem Wort: Eine Festgabe für Prof. D. Helmuth Schreiner* (Gütersloh: Bertelsmann, 1953), 129-48. There is also helpful material in Andrew R. Osborn, *Schleiermacher and Religious Education* (London: Oxford University Press, 1934); and Karl Barth, "Schleiermacher's 'Celebration of Christmas,'" in *Theology and the Church: Shorter*

himself surely wrote as much about children as about women. From his early *Soliloquies* (1800) and *Celebration of Christmas* (1806) to his famous *Sermons on the Christian Household* (1820), he demonstrated a persistent interest in the subject of children. What is the child? What is the unique spiritual perspective of childhood? Must maturity alienate us from childhood? And how might parents best nurture their children and draw out the unique individuality that expresses itself in each of them? These are some of the key questions that he seeks to answer in his work. In what follows, I want to offer an initial outline of Schleiermacher's understanding of childhood. In the first section I attempt to sketch the context in which he developed his own thoughts about children. In the second section I look more closely at the way in which he defines the special gifts of childhood — the unique genius that characterizes this stage of human development. In the third section I analyze Schleiermacher's recommendations about child rearing. And in the final section I draw out the consequences of his views and discuss their continuing pertinence for Christian thinking.

Background to Schleiermacher's Views

The turn from the eighteenth to the nineteenth century marked an important shift in the history of the family in the German states. In the eighteenth century, the social order could still be described as feudal, in the sense that one's inherited social status was unalterable. A person was born into a station *(Stand)* — noble, townsman, peasant — which he or she would occupy from birth to death. The household, identified by its station, was the point of contact between the individual and wider society: it was a political, social, and economic unit, supplying most of the basic needs of its members. The household included more than the members of what we now call the "nuclear family": it encompassed extended family, servants, and workers. A strict legal code of appropriate relationships between superiors and inferiors was observed, and family relationships were bound to these broader social regulations.

By the turn of the century, the feudal order was finally breaking up in the

---

Writings, 1920-1928, trans. Louise Pettibone Smith (London: SCM, 1962), 136-58. Jürgen Fangmeier, in his essay "Theologische Anthropologie des Kindes," *Theologische Studien* 77 (1964): 1-22, notes that Schleiermacher's *Celebration of Christmas* is "in actual fact a theology of the child" (9), but he does little to explicate what he means by the phrase. For an account of life in Schleiermacher's household written by his stepson, see Ehrenfried von Willich, *Aus Schleiermachers Hause: Jugenderrinerungen seines Stiefsohnes* (Berlin: Reimer, 1909).

German states. In place of the stations, new class and gender distinctions were developing. The family was more and more seen as the nuclear family, and, unlike the household of the eighteenth century, the bourgeois family no longer participated directly in the political and economic spheres. Rather, the nuclear family was seen as a social institution, distinct from the political and commercial orders, and publicly represented in them through the work and citizenship of the father. The bourgeois family of the nineteenth century was a comfortable haven — a refuge from the turbulent public realm of politics and production.

These shifts in the conception of the family inevitably caused changes in the experience of children. For one thing, the roles of mothers and fathers became more sharply distinguished, and thus children's relationships with them changed. While previously education in the home had often been the work of fathers, it was now increasingly seen as solely the mother's work. Fathers, who were to compete in the world outside the home, were no longer to display strong emotions with their children, for the realm of emotions was deemed unmanly. Mothers, who had previously contributed to the economic life of the family directly, were now expected to devote themselves to hearth and home, while fathers alone were expected to earn wages. The extended family was no longer in the house, so children were not accustomed to receiving care from cousins, aunts, or grandparents. On the positive side, there was a greater emphasis on the importance of children's nurture and development through age-appropriate play and education. The rise of the bourgeois family corresponds to the development of the Kindergarten, children's literature, and children's toys.[4]

Schleiermacher lived through the transition from *ständische Häuser* to *bürgerliche Familien*, and his thinking about children bears the traces of both. He recognizes the old social stations, and he develops his educational theory with attention to them. But he can also paint a compelling picture of the typical Biedermeier family,[5] where the mother and children are the emotional heart of

4. For an excellent discussion of the social history of the family in Germany, see *Deutsche Kindheiten: Autobiographische Zeugnisse, 1700-1900*, ed. Irene Hardach-Pinke and Gerd Hardach (Kronberg: Athenäum Verlag, 1978), 1-59. See also the essays in *The German Family: Essays on the Social Hisory of the Family in Nineteenth- and Twentieth-Century Germany*, ed. Richard J. Evans and W. R. Lee (London: Croom Helm; Totowa, N.J.: Barnes & Noble, 1981). Interestingly, the shift to the bourgeois nuclear family was regarded with great suspicion by many contemporary social critics, who feared that it would lead to the demise of society. See the discussion in Peter Gay, *The Bourgeois Experience, Victoria to Freud*, vol. 1: *The Education of the Senses* (New York: Oxford University Press, 1984), 422-38.

5. Biedermeier culture is named for a style of furniture design that emphasized comfort and familial intimacy. Its symbol was the large round table in the living room, around which members of the family would gather each evening for games and conversa-

the home and the father its public face. Whether he accepted in every aspect the gender ideology that went along with the rise of the bourgeois family is debated.[6] But there can be no question that he was a powerful spokesperson for this new conception of family life.

Schleiermacher received his own early education among the Moravian Pietists, and their notions of family life also influenced his theories. In particular, he shared their emphasis on the family as a church within the church. The earliest religious formation of children, the Pietists argued, can be achieved only in the home, where pious experience can be recognized and nurtured. The magisterial reformers of the sixteenth century had emphasized the importance of a coordinated educational effort between home, church, and school, which would indoctrinate children in the Christian faith chiefly through catechism. Many Pietists found such indoctrination cold and formal, as likely to produce a dead legalism as living Christian faith. For them, then, the Christian home was to be a center of worship and Bible study in which children could actually experience the full range of Christian religious affections and come to a living faith in Christ. Only after such initial nurture could the clergy properly train young people to think about their faith in doctrinal terms.[7]

It was not only churchmen, however, who were thinking about changes in

tion. See James J. Sheehan, *German History, 1770-1866* (Oxford: Clarendon Press, 1989), 536-42.

6. For example, in his posthumously published *Lectures on Pedagogy,* Schleiermacher simply notes as a matter of fact that in his culture men and women have different roles in public life that require different sorts of education, but then goes on to claim, "Wenn wir auf den gegenwärtigen Zustand der Erziehung sehen, so müssten wir eigentlich auf ein Zurückbleiben des weiblichen Geschlecht schliessen" (Schleiermacher, *Ausgewählte Pädagogische Schriften,* ed. Ernst Lichtenstein [Paderborn: Ferdinand Schöningh, 1959], 187). How does one interpret such remarks? Is he anti-woman because he does not do enough to counter the prevailing cultural trends, or is he a proto-feminist because he recognizes that such arrangements are purely matters of cultural conditioning and not divinely ordained?

7. Schleiermacher expresses his commitments to the family as the basic center of religious formation already in his first book (1799). There he writes, "A family can be the most cultivated element and the truest picture of the universe. . . . We await a time at the end of our artful cultivation when no other preparatory society for religion will be needed except pious domesticity." See *Über die Religion: Reden an die Gebildeten unter ihren Verächtern,* 4th ed. (Berlin: Georg Reimer, 1831), in Friedrich Daniel Ernst Schleiermacher, *Kritische Gesamtausgabe,* ed. Hans Joachim Birkner et al. (Berlin: Walter de Gruyter, 1984-), I/12:213-214; hereafter cited as KGA, followed by division, book, and page number. The translation is from Friedrich Schleiermacher, *On Religion: Speeches to Its Cultured Despisers,* introduction, translation, and notes by Richard Crouter (Cambridge: Cambridge University Press, 1988), 186.

education in Schleiermacher's day. The publication in 1762 of Jean-Jacques Rousseau's *Émile ou de l'éducation* is one of the landmarks in what historian Philippe Ariès has called "the discovery of childhood."[8] Unlike earlier pedagogues, Rousseau started from the premise that children are not simply miniature or ill-behaved adults. In order to educate them well, Rousseau argued, we must know what children are capable of, but unfortunately the nature of childhood itself had not been well understood in the past.[9] He saw children as naturally innocent, not encumbered with the supposed inheritance of original sin that drove earlier pedagogues to speak about the need to break the sinful will of children.[10] Rather, it was the evil influences of society that spoiled the natural goodness of children. Thus a child should be raised according to the genius of nature: he or she should learn almost everything by immediate experience, through play and childlike experimentation. Books should not be introduced too early, and until the development of the child's own ability to control his or her lower instincts, he or she should learn to submit trustingly to the better judgment of the tutor (who will ideally be one of the parents).[11] The influence of Rousseau's ideas about education was powerful, and Schleiermacher, whose library contained the works of Rousseau, was undoubtedly instructed by him.[12]

8. See Ariès's groundbreaking study, *Centuries of Childhood: A Social History of Family Life*, trans. R. Baldick (New York: Alfred A. Knopf, 1962). For a discussion of Rousseau's conception of childhood, see Larry Wolff, "When I Imagine a Child: The Idea of Childhood and the Philosophy of Memory in the Enlightenment," *Eighteenth-Century Studies* 31 (1998): 377-401.

9. See the comments in the author's preface, from which I drew one of the epigraphs for this chapter (Jean-Jacques Rousseau, *Émile*, translated by Barbara Foxley, introduction by P. D. Jimack [London: J. M. Dent; Vermont: Charles E. Tuttle, 1993], 1-3). A helpful brief discussion of Rousseau's pedagogical perspective may be found in John Cleverley and D. C. Phillips, *Visions of Childhood: Influential Models from Locke to Spock* (New York: Teachers College Press, 1986), 34-38.

10. Of course, the received tradition on the need to "break the will" of sinful children is not as simple as Rousseau presents it. See the essays in this volume by Martha Stortz, Barbara Pitkin, Marcia Bunge, and Catherine Brekus.

11. Rousseau argued that boys and girls develop different faculties for controlling their passions or lower instincts: for boys the characteristic is reason, while for girls it is a sense of modesty or shame (Rousseau, *Émile*, 386). Schleiermacher, as we shall see below, accepts Rousseau's developmental view of childhood without taking over either his theological anthropology or his gender ideology. For an excellent discussion of Schleiermacher's critical exchange with contemporary gender ideology, see Ruth Drucilla Richardson, "Schleiermacher's 1800 'Versuch über die Schaamhaftigkeit': A Contribution Toward a Truly Human Ethic," in *Schleiermacher in Context: Papers from the 1988 International Symposium on Schleiermacher in Herrnhut, the German Democratic Republic* (Lewiston, N.Y.: Edwin Mellen Press, 1991), 65-108, esp. 74-77.

12. Schleiermacher does not refer to Rousseau's *Émile* in his posthumously pub-

This period of cultural transformation in Germany at the turn of the nineteenth century was the fertile soil in which Schleiermacher's views on childhood were formed. Yet his opinions cannot be reduced to any of the streams of thought that influenced him. As in the many other disciplines in which he labored, his appropriation of traditional understandings of childhood in the light of modern thought was nothing less than a groundbreaking creative achievement. And it is to the specific insights of that achievement that we now turn.

Early Writings on Childhood

In an endearing passage toward the end of his *Soliloquies* (1800), Schleiermacher pledges his allegiance to "eternal youth." The pledge comes in the final section of this ethical monograph, a section that discusses the relationship between youth and age, and it constitutes his earliest sustained reflection on the nature of youth.[13] He begins the argument by asking whether maturity requires the renunciation of youth, whether the two are incompatible opposites. In order to answer the question, he considers more carefully what distinguishes the two stages of human life. Youth is characterized by vitality and passion. It seeks for answers and self-expression. Age is the time of prudent circumspection, caution, the ability to weigh costs and benefits. He explicitly rejects any identification of the difference between youth and age with purely physical characteristics. Age is not merely about the decline of bodily powers, any more than youth is about their unbridled vitality. Rather, the two represent perspectives of the human spirit that belong together. Borrowing an organic metaphor, Schleiermacher sees youth and age as the flower and fruit of a plant, which follow each other in an unbroken circle of creative generativity. He concludes,

> He debases himself who wishes first to be young, and then old, who allows himself to be controlled first by what is called the spirit of youth, and only afterwards wishes to follow what is considered the counsel of maturity. Life cannot bear this separation of its elements. There is a two-fold activity of the spirit that should exist in its entirety at every time of life, and it is the perfec-

---

lished *Lectures on Pedagogy*. It is clear from references in his early writings, however, that he was reading Rousseau. See, for example, KGA I/1:30, 133.

13. Although the *Soliloquies* first appeared in 1800, I will cite the fourth German edition, *Monologen: Eine Neujahrsgabe* (Berlin: Georg Reimer, 1829), as it is given in the KGA I/12:323-93. The section on youth and age is located on pp. 384-93.

tion of human development ever to become more intimately and more clearly conscious of both its aspects, assigning to each its own peculiar and proper function.[14]

Schleiermacher's 1806 novella, *The Celebration of Christmas: A Conversation,* may perhaps be seen as a careful narrative presentation of this view of the relationship between childhood and maturity. The setting is the Christmas Eve celebration of a cultured Prussian family, who have gathered with friends to eat and drink, make music, open presents, and engage in conversation. The text falls into three sections. In the first, the celebration itself is described in detail, and the adults carry on conversations centering on the nature of children and women. In the second, the three women tell stories about Christmas celebrations they remember from the past. In the final section, the three men argue about the meaning of Christmas. In each of the sections, the subject of children figures significantly, but it is particularly the first section and the closing paragraphs that are important for our purposes.

As the story opens, attention almost immediately focuses on Sophie, the young daughter of the host and hostess of the party. After opening her present of Christmas music, she plays the piano and sings for the gathered guests, then invites them to her nursery to show them the complex diorama she has created, presenting scenes from the birth, life, death, and ascension of Christ, and the history of Christianity. Overcome by her feelings, Sophie exclaims that her mother might just as well have been the Mother of Christ. This statement provides the occasion for a subtle discussion among the adults about the nature of children and the best way to nurture their religious faith. Sophie's mother, Ernestine, admits that she is moved by the child's words, because she knows that they spring from a pure heart. She remarks, "Actually, I feel that she did not say too much when she said that I might well be the mother of the blessed child in this respect: I can in all humility honor the pure revelation of the divine in my daughter, as Mary did in her son, without thereby disturbing the proper relation of mother to child."[15] The other women agree that a mother's recogni-

---

14. KGA I/12:390. The translation is taken from *Schleiermacher's Soliloquies,* trans. Horace Leland Friess (1926; reprint, Chicago: Open Court Publishing Company, 1957), 98.

15. KGA I/5: 51. I cite the first edition, *Die Weihnachtsfeier: Ein Gespräch* (Halle: Schimmelpfennig und Kompagnie, 1806), as it is given in the KGA I/5:39-100. I use the English translation in *Christmas Eve: A Dialogue on the Incarnation,* translated and with an introduction and notes by Terrence N. Tice (Richmond, Va.: John Knox Press, 1967), 36; hereafter cited as *CE* (ET). The proper relationship between mother and child that Schleiermacher has in mind is the relationship of an authority providing limits and discipline for an immature person. He does not see an essential conflict between a reverence for the divine in children and a firm sense of their need for guidance and direction.

tion of the divine in her children is not about spoiling them. The men, however, emphasize the difference in the ways that men and women nurture children. Women are like the vestal virgins who watch over the sacred fire in the temple. They simply protect the spark of goodness and keep it from being extinguished. Men, on the other hand, are like pilgrims needing to recover the original goodness through penance and discipline. This theme is dropped for several pages, but taken up again in a discussion of the different ways in which men and women incorporate their own childhoods into their adult selves. Women are identified with children in the sense that the objects of girls' play are close to the objects of women's work. Men, on the other hand, go through a wild period, a "nothing," in which they become alienated from their childhoods and must be converted back to them. One of the women, Karoline, sums up by stating, "We have at last applied the correct interpretation to the old proverb that . . . women go right on being children while . . . men must first be converted to become so again."[16]

But what is the childlike nature that women seem to possess without interruption and that men are converted to? Sophie demonstrates it in everything she says and does at the party. She is spontaneous in expressing her feelings, and particularly her religious feelings. She does not question or judge them, but simply accepts and expresses the feelings that come to her. This quality in particular worries one of the men, Leonhardt, who is the Enlightenment skeptic of the party. He states that such inclinations will probably end badly, with Sophie refusing to marry and entering a Pietist convent. Her mother responds that Sophie's religious affections are no different than any of her other childish interests — she gives herself to all of them without reservation. A little later Leonhardt cross-examines Sophie about her feelings. He asks whether she would not rather be happy than sad. She responds, "Oh, that's hard to say. . . . I do not particularly favor one or the other. I always just like to be whatever I am at the moment." Leonhardt, not satisfied with her response, presses her. Is it a matter of indifference to her whether she is happy or sad? Sophie becomes flustered. What she likes is not a matter of indifference to her, she states, but she just likes to be what she is. She concludes, "I can be satisfied in one attitude or the other, and at present I feel extraordinarily fine without being in either one."[17] Once again it is Karoline who sums up the conversation: "She has clearly shown us . . . what the childlike attitude is without which one cannot enter into the kingdom of God. It is simply to accept each mood and feeling for itself and to desire only to have them pure and whole."[18]

16. KGA I/5:70-71; *CE* (ET), 55.
17. KGA I/5:68; *CE* (ET), 52.
18. KGA I/5:68; *CE* (ET), 53.

The ensuing conversation turns on the relationship between childhood and adulthood. Karoline notes that those who complain that they cannot enjoy things as they did when they were children probably did not have happy childhoods. Leonhardt sarcastically replies that for those who do not appreciate childish joys, nature has destined a return to childhood at the end of life. Another of the men, Ernst, replies that it is tragic to think that so many people will pass their lives this way — alienated from childhood, unable to attain the childlike joy in higher things. Their "return" to childhood at the end of life is not really a return: this second childhood is related to the first "as a contrary old dwarf is to a lovely and winsome child, or as the wavering flicker of a dying flame is to the embracing splendor and dancing form of one newly lit."[19] Now another of the women, Agnes, poses a key series of questions:

> Must the first childish objects of joy be lost in order for us to win the higher ones? Shouldn't there be some way of winning these things without letting go of the others? Does life, then, begin with a sheer illusion in which there is no truth, nothing lasting? What could that actually mean? Do the joys of the person who has come to a consciousness of himself and the world, and has found God, begin with struggle and warfare — with the extermination not of what is evil, but of what is innocent? For that is how we always characterize what is childlike, or childish if you prefer.[20]

The answer to these questions is given by Ernst, who comments that the Christmas celebration itself (*die Feier der Kindheit Jesu*) is nothing other than the acknowledgment of the "immediate union of the divine with the childlike, from which no further conversion is necessary."[21] In the Incarnation, childhood itself is affirmed as worthy by God.

The text proceeds through stories and speeches to a brief conclusion in which a late guest, Joseph, arrives at the party. He chides the men for intellectualizing about Christmas rather than singing carols or chatting with the women. He states,

> I can only laugh and exult like a child. Today all people are children to me, and are dear to me just for that reason. Smoothed of serious furrows, the years and worries for once are no longer written on their brows. Eyes sparkle and live again, the presentiment of a beautiful and grace-filled existence within. Also, I myself am become entirely a child again, luckily for me.[22]

19. KGA I/5:69; *CE* (ET), 54.
20. KGA I/5:69; *CE* (ET), 54.
21. KGA I/5:71; *CE* (ET), 55.
22. KGA I/5:97; *CE* (ET), 85. The last sentence of this passage is the third epigraph to this chapter.

The novella concludes with Joseph asking the others to bring in the child (Sophie) and to sing something pious and joyful.

The Celebration of Christmas is a complex text, and the parts of it highlighted here could not be taken as a thorough representation of the whole. I have tried to bring out what the text argues about the nature of childhood, and it would perhaps be useful to summarize the points here. First, childhood contains a "pure revelation of the divine" from which no conversion is necessary. Second, childhood's essence consists in the acceptance of the full range of emotional life without repression and a living in the present without regard to past or future. And third, for those who, through advancing years, have become alienated from the childlike, a conversion is necessary — a conversion to become as a little child.[23]

A similar discussion of the nature of the childlike faith to which adults must be converted can be found in Schleiermacher's 1834 homily on Mark 10:13-16. In exegeting the words "Whoever shall not receive the Kingdom of God as a little child, he shall not enter therein," he states, "The peculiar essence of the child is that he is altogether in the moment. . . . The past disappears for him, and of the future he knows nothing — each moment exists only for itself, and this accounts for the blessedness of a soul content in innocence."[24] This ability to be completely absorbed in the moment is a child's gift to adults, and it is the recovery of this perspective, Schleiermacher argues, that the Redeemer says is necessary for those who would enter the Kingdom of God. Living in communion with God through Christ in the present, without anxiety about past or future, is the essence of the eternal life that Christ promises to those who believe in him (John 11:25). Adults, then, must recover this childlike perception, as if by conversion.[25]

---

23. Karl Barth's reading of *The Celebration of Christmas* is as tendentious as most of what he has to say about Schleiermacher. He sees the chief meaning of the text as music and women as the "royal road to the divine." He faults Schleiermacher for presenting Christian faith without adequate emphasis on sin, conversion, and the in-breaking Word of God, thus making the higher life seem an endowment of nature ("Schleiermacher's 'Celebration of Christmas,'" 156-58). While I do not think Barth accurately interprets *The Celebration of Christmas* in his critique, I grant that Schleiermacher's presentation in this text *is* one-sided. The natural religious capacity of the child and the Christian life as marked by childlike faith are presented without a thoroughgoing exploration of the sin that makes redemption necessary. *The Celebration of Christmas* needs to be balanced by Schleiermacher's mature dogmatic system. Perhaps what Schleiermacher demonstrates here is the considerable risks associated with the attempt to present theological concepts in a narrative or fictional genre.

24. *Friedrich Schleiermachers sämmtliche Werke*, 31 vols. in three divisions (Berlin: Georg Reimer, 1834-1864), II/6:71-72; hereafter cited as SW, followed by division, volume, and page number.

25. SW II/6:72-73.

If this were all Schleiermacher had to say about childhood, however, we might be tempted to accuse him of romanticizing the child — forcing Rousseau's doctrine of original innocence into the language of Christian faith. But as we shall see below, Schleiermacher thought that, whatever the unique perspective on the religious life a child had by nature, it would not do to let the child develop "naturally." For nature had also implanted the inclinations and proclivities that could lead to human destruction. Bringing up a child "in the nurture and admonition of the Lord" (Eph. 6:4) required far more than the gentle guardianship of the "vestal virgins." It is to Schleiermacher's discussion of children's special needs that we now turn.

Nurturing Children: The 1818 Sermons on the Christian Household

By 1818, when Schleiermacher delivered his "Sermons on the Christian Household" in the Holy Trinity Church of Berlin, he was the father of five children. These sermons represent his fullest statement on how to raise children in a Christian family, and they are remarkable in the depth of psychological insight that they display.[26] Of the nine sermons in this series, three discuss child rearing.[27] The first takes as its text Colossians 3:21: "Fathers, do not provoke your children, lest they become discouraged." The second sermon centers on the parallel passage in Ephesians (6:4): "Fathers, do not provoke your children to anger, but bring them up in the discipline and admonition of the Lord." And the final sermon takes up the previous verses in Ephesians that command the obedience of children to their parents. Rather than summarizing the content of each of these sermons, I shall outline the major themes Schleiermacher takes up that relate to our topic.

A theme throughout these sermons is the wonderful blessing that children represent to the community of faith. They keep adults fresh and cheerful,

---

26. Schleiermacher's sermons are a contribution to a recognized genre of writing in early nineteenth-century Germany — the "Hausvater Bücher." These manuals, which drew on Scripture and catechisms, instructed Christian fathers about the best way to run their households. For a discussion of this literature, see Julius Hoffmann, *Die Hausväterliteratur und die Predigten über den christlichen Hausstand. Ein Beitrag zur Geschichte der Lehre vom Hause und der Bildung für das häusliche Leben im 16., 17. und 18. Jahrhundert* (Berlin: Julius Beltz, 1959).

27. These sermons are located in SW II/1:598-639; English translation, *The Christian Household: A Sermonic Treatise*, trans. Dietrich Seidel and Terrence N. Tice, Schleiermacher Studies and Translations, vol. 3 (Lewiston, N.Y.: Edwin Mellen Press, 1991), 36-90; hereafter *CH* (ET).

and they assist adults in advancing along the path of sanctification. Children remind us of the fact that God created humanity to live simply. They help adults to shed their obsession with the complexities of work and public life. Indeed, children draw adults back into the most basic of human relationships.[28] In spite of manifold adult failures, children are flexible and forgiving. Schleiermacher argues that to provoke children is actually rather difficult: it requires "bitter repetition of adverse experiences," and not just the inevitable mistakes that parents occasionally make.[29]

Children are not, however, perfect and sinless mediators of the higher life for adults. They are born with as much potential for sin as for salvation. Schleiermacher understands all human beings as possessing a lower and a higher consciousness. The lower — or sensible — self-consciousness represents the experience of the human as an animal, and includes basic sensations such as hunger, thirst, pain, pleasure, as well as basic drives and responses, such as competitiveness, sexuality, fear, and anger. The higher self-consciousness is the part of the human being that is capable of transcending animal instincts: it is the point of contact with God, the essence of distinctively human being, and the development and strengthening of a God-consciousness in each individual believer is the work of Christ for our salvation. When the God-consciousness dominates, humans are not alienated from God by their animal instincts and drives.[30] Schleiermacher elsewhere describes the relationship between the lower and the higher self-consciousness in the more familiar Pauline language of the struggle of the spirit to overcome the flesh.[31]

Children are born totally under the sway of the sensible self-consciousness. Hunger, fatigue, and basic emotional responses determine every aspect of their behavior. Moreover, the corrupting influence of the social structures into which they are born constantly threatens to extinguish any manifestations of the higher self-consciousness in them.[32] And yet, already in their relationship

28. SW II/1:606-9; *CH* (ET), 46-48.

29. SW II/1:611; *CH* (ET), 52.

30. See the discussion in the introduction to Schleiermacher's dogmatics, *Der christliche Glaube nach den Grundsätzen der evangelischen Kirche im Zusammenhange dargestellt*, 7th ed., based on the 2d German ed., ed. Martin Redeker, 2 vols. (Berlin: Walter de Gruyter, 1960), §§3-5; English translation, *The Christian Faith*, ed. H. R. Mackintosh and J. S. Stewart (Edinburgh: T. & T. Clark, 1928).

31. See, for example, *Die christliche Sitte nach den Grundsätzen der evangelischen Kirche im Zusammenhange dargestellt*, SW I/12:230.

32. Schleiermacher revises the traditional notion of original sin (German *Erbsünde*), which he understands not as corruption inherited from Adam and Eve but as the evil social structures into which individuals are born — even before they make any individual sinful choices. This corporate life of sinfulness, he argues, can be overcome only through the intervention of grace in the corporate life of blessedness (i.e., the church).

to mothers and fathers, children have some notion of basic dependence that will enable them later to understand their relationship to God.[33] Parents' duty is to nurture the higher self-consciousness in their children, which they do primarily through their own example, for religion cannot be taught like factual information.[34] Schleiermacher is clear that it is the whole manner of life in the home that teaches, and he does not hesitate to blame parents for their children's sins: "The older generation has lured the younger into sin." In very young children, whose conscience is not yet fully awakened, the higher self-consciousness cannot yet be developed, so parents' activity is limited to helping arouse the conscience.[35] In older children, parents should encourage whatever signs of strength they observe in their children's religious life.

Throughout these sermons Schleiermacher displays keen psychological insight into what damages children's emotional health. The most tragic consequence of parental failure is the child's loss of trust, he claims, and while such devastating damage is not easy to do, once done it is nearly impossible to repair.[36] How is this damage done? Schleiermacher argues that there are several culprits. First, parents can injure their children by failing to take their concerns and interests seriously, by convincing the children that the experiences of their daily lives are of little importance. Second, parents can wound children's psyches by failing to respond empathically to their emotions. If sadness is greeted with laughter, anger with belittlement, children will be provoked. Third, if parents are not in control of their own emotional responses, children will inevitably be hurt. The parent whose emotional life is chaotic or unreliable will drive her children to secrecy: "They close themselves off because of their anxious anticipation as to which . . . mood will manifest itself, and for each mood they have something or other carefully to conceal."[37] Finally, parents harm their children if they attempt to live their own dreams and aspirations through them.

Schleiermacher's understanding of original sin, then, makes contact with Rousseau's arguments about the evil influences of society. But while Rousseau thought he was able to do away with the doctrine of original sin, Schleiermacher saw these powerful and inescapable influences as of the essence of the collective sin that corrupts from birth and in this sense is "inherited" sin. See the discussion in *Der christliche Glaube*, §§70-72.

33. In his *Practical Theology*, Schleiermacher states, "Already in the child's first consciousness of his relationship to his parents is religion — it is the spiritual feeling of dependence, and religion is only an enhancement of that" (*Die praktische Theologie nach den Grundsätzen der evangelischen Kirche im Zusammenhange dargestellt*, SW I/13:412).

34. SWII/1:601; *CH* (ET), 40. See the discussion in the *Speeches on Religion* of the possibility of teaching religion (KGA I/12:150-80).

35. *Die christliche Sitte*, SW I/12:222-24.

36. SW II/1:604-5; *CH* (ET), 44.

37. SW II/1:608; *CH* (ET), 49.

Parents' love, on the contrary, should be self-sacrificing and should seek to nurture the unique individuality of children, which is God's gift.[38]

Nurturing the higher self-consciousness of the child cannot be accomplished through rewards and punishments. Schleiermacher rejects external enticements as inconsistent with Christian faith. In particular, he denounces the use of corporal punishment with children. Discipline is not about punishment but about promoting an ordered life. Until children are able to set and respect healthy boundaries for themselves, parents must assist them in doing so. But to exact compliance through fear of punishment only nurtures the lower self-consciousness, which naturally seeks to avoid painful experiences. Parents ought to instill in their children a love for the good, irrespective of rewards or punishments.[39]

Schleiermacher, like Rousseau, sees play as part of the learning activity of children. Thus, parents must be as concerned about the manner of play their children engage in as about their formal education. Companions who will assist children to grow in "wholesome self-knowledge" should be carefully chosen. Children should be exposed to all kinds of people and should learn to be tolerant of others. Play exercises different abilities in children, and "in their play they learn to use and control all those powers least called for in their work."[40]

The virtue of obedience should be cultivated in children from the very beginning. Schleiermacher argues that it is bad parenting to give in to children's demands for explanations. Obedience should be absolute, and no other reason should be required than that the parent demands something. This, to his mind,

---

38. SW II/1:598-99, 610, 617-18; *CH* (ET), 38, 51, 61.

39. SW II/1:614-18; *CH* (ET), 57-60. Cf. *Die christliche Sitte*, SW I/12:234-35.

40. SW II/1:619; *CH* (ET), 63. It is possible that Schleiermacher came by some of his pedagogical convictions from his own mother. In a letter to her brother, in which she discusses her own child-rearing practices, she states, "I think you will agree with us . . . that children must not be compelled to learn by punishment, but we should seek to teach them through play and through their striving for recognition. It seems to be a law of our nature that we should play during one period of our lives, and if we do not do so during the earliest part, we must do so afterwards" (*Aus Schleiermachers Leben in Briefen*, I:17). Schleiermacher defines play in his 1813/14 "Aphorisms on Pedagogy" as "being entirely in the present, the absolute negation of the future" (Schleiermacher, *Ausgewählte Pädagogische Schriften*, ed. Ernst Lichtenstein [Paderborn: Ferdinand Schöningh, 1983], 34). That is to say, play is an activity not directed toward something in the future but done for its own sake, for the present enjoyment of the activity. Count Nicolaus Ludwig von Zinzendorf (1700-1760), the leader of the Moravian Pietists, among whom Schleiermacher was educated as a young man, also emphasized the importance of play in the instruction of young children and built it into the schedule in his schools. See Henry Meyer, *Child Nature and Nurture According to Nicolaus Ludwig von Zinzendorf* (New York: Abingdon, 1928).

was the correct interpretation of the epistle writer's claim that obedience to parents is "right" or "fitting." Children who trust their parents will know instinctively that the parents have their best interests at heart. The importance of training in obedience is twofold. First, children learn to respect authority, and this is absolutely essential for both civil and religious life. Second and perhaps more important, obedience teaches children to honor a common good above their own desires. While children are young, parents stand in the place of some higher common will, and children's submission to parents leads them out of their egocentric view of the world.[41]

The way that children are educated in the Christian faith will have profound consequences on their future lives, both as individuals and as members of the Christian church. Schleiermacher argues that the Christian home is the first and irreplaceable school of faith. The religious formation of children in the home takes place primarily through family worship and Bible study, where children will take in the language of Christian faith in the same way that they learn their mother tongue.[42] That is to say, children will observe the religious faith of their parents, and under this attractive influence, they will be drawn into their own experience of Christian faith. Schleiermacher is critical of family worship when it becomes mechanical, for children can easily be shaped into protectors of dead ritual. Worship in the home should be marked by spontaneity and authenticity.[43]

Parents, however, do not undertake the religious formation of children alone. Pastors and schools also participate. During the years in which Schleiermacher lived and worked in Berlin, a movement began in which control of the schools was gradually shifted from the churches to the Prussian government. By 1825 a system of public schools had been established at both the elementary and secondary levels, and in these schools religious education was part of the required curriculum, as it had been in the old parochial schools. However, the aim of religious education in the public schools was not indoctrination into a particular religious communion but rather moral formation for business and citizenship.[44] Schleiermacher was a supporter of the newly developing system of public education and contributed to the thinking that went into the design of new schools.[45] But he realized that because the aims of public education were those of the state

41. SW II/1:630-38; *CH* (ET), 77-89.

42. *Die praktische Theologie,* SW I/13:348.

43. In *The Celebration of Christmas,* Eduard states that his family does not observe set hours for prayer or devotion; they simply follow their hearts (KGA I/5:54; *CE* [ET], 39).

44. See the discussion in Osborn, *Schleiermacher and Religious Education,* 157-61.

45. Schleiermacher's thoughts on the structure of educational systems and the philosophy of education cannot be fully explored within the limits of this essay. See his 1814 address to the Royal Prussian Academy of the Sciences entitled "Über den Beruf des Staates zur Erziehung," in *Ausgewählte Pädagogische Schriften,* 18-32.

and not of the church, the burden for the specifically *religious* formation of children had shifted more decisively to the home and the church. From his point of view, this was not a bad thing: the separation of church and state was a better arrangement. Moral formation for citizenship could be fostered in public schools, while pastors could do a great deal to form children for active participation in the church — chiefly through their work with confirmands. Catechisms, he thought, were not bad as educational tools, provided that they were rewritten frequently in the current language of children.[46] Ideally, a pastor should write a new instruction manual for each class of confirmands he teaches, for only in this way can the individuality of the learners be respected.

Schleiermacher sees children as capable of quite sophisticated theological questioning. Unlike some of his contemporaries, he saw no danger in teaching children the New Testament from a very early age. The argument against teaching Scripture, which Schleiermacher puts in the mouth of the skeptic Leonhardt in *The Celebration of Christmas,* is that children will form images and concepts based on stories understood like fairy tales, which they will later have to reject.[47] Better to protect them from such possible alienation from their childish faith, Leonhardt says. Schleiermacher roundly rejects this recommendation, stating that the heart of evangelical faith is the free use of Scripture, and children should not be prevented from it.[48] Indeed, he states, "A real life in the scripture is the foundation of all religious education [*Bildung*]."[49] The most important duty of a pastor in catechizing, then, is to lead children in developing sound and sophisticated abilities in reading and interpreting scripture. Such instruction might begin with memorizing Bible verses, but it should eventually lead to developing in children a way of thinking (*Gedankenerzeugungsprozess*) that can be applied to questions or situations that will arise when the catechizing process is over.[50]

---

46. *Die praktische Theologie,* SW I/13:375-76. Interestingly, Schleiermacher's stepson reports that his father did not use catechisms in his confirmation instruction (von Willich, *Aus Schleiermachers Hause,* 80-82).

47. "Listen, at a time when even the preachers are laudably zealous in dispensing with the Bible as much as possible in the pulpit, to put these books back in the hands of children, for whom they were never meant anyway, is the worst thing you could do. It would be better for these books — to use their own words against them — if a millstone were fastened round their neck and they were drowned in the depth of the sea than that they should give offense to the little ones. Who knows what may happen if they take in the sacred story with their other fairy tales?" (KGA I/5:57-8; I cite Tice's translation: *CE,* 42).

48. See his 1817 sermon entitled "Teaching the Reformation Faith to Our Children," SW II/4:68-72; the English translation can be found in *Servant of the Word: Selected Sermons of Friedrich Schleiermacher,* trans. and ed. Dawn DeVries (Philadelphia: Fortress Press, 1987), 90-94. Cf. SW II/1:621-27; *CH* (ET), 68-73.

49. *Die praktische Theologie,* SW I/13:399.

50. *Die praktische Theologie,* SW I/13:380-81.

If the capacity for religious experience is an innate capability of the child, fully formed Christian faith certainly is not. Schleiermacher states that the Socratic method of teaching cannot properly be applied to catechesis, because the Christian faith cannot be built from basic concepts that children already have. On the contrary, Christian faith rests on facts, and though one might be able to get to a sense of sin through Socratic recollection, and even perhaps to a vague sense of the need for help to overcome sin, one could not discover thereby that Christ is the Redeemer. This and other basic facts of Christian faith must be communicated to children through indoctrination.

Schleiermacher holds high expectations of the catechizing pastor. He states that when children who have been raised in the church lose their faith in adulthood, it is often because they have received poor catechetical instruction. Mindless repetition of correct answers will not sustain faith through the journey to adulthood.[51] Pastors should treat children as fellow seekers who will be no more satisfied with pat answers than adults. If there is a virtue to be developed in the teaching pastor, it is the virtue of humility, for teaching the faith is probably his most difficult task. Schleiermacher urges his ministry students always to consider their teaching a work in progress, and challenges them to be quick to admit their mistakes.[52]

What children need more than anything else is living faith in Christ. Parents, teachers, and pastors must devote all of their energy and enthusiasm to presenting Christ to their children. This is best achieved through the whole of life itself, lived with children. They should feel the love of adults as "reflecting the splendor of eternal love" in Christ.[53] Children who have received the Spirit

---

51. *Die praktische Theologie,* SW I/13:413. Schleiermacher writes out of his own bitter experience of going through a crisis of faith in his youth. The doctrine he learned from his pastor/father became a stumbling block for him, and for a while he thought he had lost his faith (*Aus Schleiermachers Leben in Briefen,* I:42-45). However, at a later time he confessed that he had not entirely lost the Pietist faith of his childhood, but had "become a Herrnhuter again, but of a higher order" (*Aus Schleiermachers Leben in Briefen,* I:295). Elsewhere, Schleiermacher claims that when people lose interest or faith in God, it is not God they have lost but only the prevailing doctrine about God. See, for example, Schleiermacher, *On the Glaubenslehre: Two Letters to Dr. Lücke,* trans. James Duke and Francis Fiorenza, AAR Texts and Translations, 3 (Chico, Ca.: Scholars Press, 1981). See also *Der christliche Glaube,* §172.2. The distinction between faith and doctrine, to which Schleiermacher frequently refers, is something he learned from the Pietists. Cf. Nicolaus Ludwig, Count von Zinzendorf, "Thoughts for the Learned and Yet Good-Willed Students of Truth" (1732), in *Pietists: Selected Writings,* edited and with an introduction by Peter C. Erb (New York: Paulist Press, 1983), 291-95.

52. *Die praktische Theologie,* SW I/13:384-85.

53. SW II/1:627; *CH* (ET), 73.

in baptism and who have been raised within the loving discipline of the Christian community give us reason to hope for the future.[54]

Schleiermacher the father was not spared the bitterest test that any parent could endure. In 1829 he preached the burial sermon at the graveside of his only biological son, nine-year-old Nathanael, who succumbed to diphtheria. The shattering grief of this loss never left him, and he followed his son in death just under five years later.[55] The sermon he preached is a telling last word. He remembers Nathanael's many endearing qualities, such as honesty, joy, and generosity. He quarrels with those who would comfort him by arguing that the child's early death was a blessing because he had been taken before the evils of the world could corrupt him. This way of thinking, Schleiermacher states, does not work for him, because he trusts the work of the Spirit in Christian children's lives. Moreover, he states, he had already seen the love of the Savior at work in his little boy's life:

> Why should I not have trusted securely that nothing would be able to tear him out of the hand of the Lord and Savior to whom he was dedicated, and whom he had already begun to love with his childlike heart — for one of his last rational responses in the days of his sickness was a warm affirmation to the question of his mother, whether he loved his Savior rightly. And this love, even if it was not fully developed, even if it had undergone fluctuations in him: why should I not indeed have believed that it would never be extinguished for him, that it someday would have possessed him wholly?[56]

In the innocent faith of the child is the piety of the man. As a father, Schleiermacher was not so much terrified of what would corrupt his son as eager to see what peculiar gifts of grace he would display. But that pleasure would not be granted him in this life. The sermon ends with a word of warning: "Let us all love one another as persons who could soon be separated."[57] For parents and children alike, the gift of loving, intimate communion is precious and fragile. Care must be taken to attend to these relationships in ways that will not cause lasting and bitter regrets.

---

54. SW II/1:608-9; *CH* (ET), 50.

55. A brief account of the effect of Nathanael's death on Schleiermacher is given in von Willich, *Aus Schleiermachers Hause*, 105-6.

56. *Servant of the Word*, 211.

57. *Servant of the Word*, 213.

The Significance of Childhood

For Schleiermacher, the religious significance of childhood has two sides. On the one hand, children *qua* children possess a spiritual perspective that is necessary for Christian faith. In their utter vulnerability and dependence, children mirror the relationship between God and humanity.[58] Trust and acceptance of dependence are natural in children, while most adults only grudgingly learn to accept their utter dependence on God. Moreover, children live in the moment, accepting their feelings and perceptions as they have them. Unlike adults, who are driven by their ambition to focus more and more on past and future, children have the gift of presence, or being-there. For Schleiermacher, eternal life is precisely such a communion with God in the present. Adults need to recover a childlike ability to be present in the moment if they are to experience the full blessing of Christian faith.

On the other hand, childhood forms the possibilities for the future life of faith. Children are vulnerable and dependent, and they will take in what the adults in their lives give them. If the influences and information are beneficent, they will blossom. But the opposite is also true: failures in child rearing can lead to pain and ultimately even to alienation from God. For this reason, the church neglects children at its own very significant peril. Schleiermacher, who served as a full-time pastor at the same time that he was a full-time professor, never believed the religious instruction of children was a task beneath him. He claimed to love the company of children, and he sought passionately to make the Christian faith accessible and attractive to them.

Some of what Schleiermacher thinks about children and their religious formation is difficult to translate into the twentieth-first century. His benign confidence in the bourgeois family was probably not warranted. Although he shows himself remarkably aware of aspects of what we would now call dysfunctional family systems, he felt sure that parents would do better if only they had better information. Further, the pressures attendant on the increasingly proscriptive gender roles of the bourgeois family undoubtedly account for some of the nostalgia for childhood expressed in the art and poetry of the nineteenth century. What man, under pressure to support an entire family economically and prohibited from displaying any of his fears or frustrations in the home, would not wish to be shown "the pleasant path to the land of childhood"?[59]

58. See n. 33 above.

59. My second epigraph to this chapter is a loose translation of a line from Klaus Groth's poem "Heimweh." The entire poem reads as follows: "O wüsst' ich doch den Weg zurück,/Den lieben Weg zum Kinderland!/O warum sucht' ich nach dem Glück/Und liess der Mutter Hand?/O wie mich sehnet auszuruhn,/Von keinem Streben aufgeweckt,/Die

Yet Schleiermacher may still have something to teach us. The utter seriousness with which he takes children is striking, and so, too, is his argument for the absolute value of the spiritual perspective of childhood. In a culture seduced by the totalizing discourse of the market, where children are valued as human capital — as goods to be consumed by the adults in their lives, or as investments whose worth will be measured by future payoff — we can learn from a view that values children as children and that speaks of adults' indebtedness to children.[60] It is also worth remembering that the Christian tradition is not a monolithic force turned against the health and welfare of children. Justification of child abuse and complicity in its execution are only part of the story: the work of theologians like Schleiermacher, who speak against violence and abuse, needs to be integrated into the story of Christianity's treatment of children.[61]

To be converted and become as little children is a hard saying for most adults. It is about more than a nostalgic longing for release from responsibility, more than infantile regression. Rather, it requires a return to the simplicity, openness, trust, and presence of childhood. In his "Aphorisms on Pedagogy," Schleiermacher states this general maxim: "Being a child should not prevent becoming an adult; becoming an adult should not prevent being a child."[62] The mutuality of children and adults, like the mutuality of men and women, is indispensable for the health of humanity.

---

müden Augen zuzutun,/Von Liebe sanft bedeckt!/Und nichts zu forschen, nichts zu spähn,/Und nur zu träumen leicht und lind,/Der Zeiten Wandel nicht zu sehn,/Zum zweiten mal ein Kind!/O zeigt mir doch den Weg zurück,/Den lieben Weg zum Kinderland!/ Vergebens such' ich nach dem Glück — /Ringsum ist öder Strand!" (*Das Oxforder Buch Deutscher Dichtung: Vom 12ten bis zum 20sten Jahrhundert,* ed. H. G. Fiedler (Oxford: Oxford University Press, 1952), 418. The nostalgia for a lost childhood is a common theme in literature of the period. It appears not only in poetry but also in literary memoirs. For example, Ehrenfried von Willich writes, "O selige Kinderzeit! . . . Wenn ich an diese Zeit zurück denke, so ist es mir wie ein Leben in Paradiese" (*Aus Schleiermachers Hause,* 10). Later he comments, "Es is etwas darin von dem Sehnen nach dem verlorenen Paradiese, von der Errinerung an das goldne Zeitalter, was in dem Verkehr mit Kindern sich in uns regt" (36). See the discussion in Wolff, "When I Imagine a Child," esp. 396-99.

60. See the discussion in Don S. Browning et al., *From Culture Wars to Common Ground: Religion and the American Family Debate* (Louisville, Ky.: Westminster/John Knox Press, 1997), 58-66, 247-68.

61. The work of scholars like historian Philip Greven and psychiatrist Alice Miller has been powerful in displaying the failures of religious communities to support the well-being of children. See, for example, Philip Greven, *Spare the Child: The Religious Roots of Punishment and the Psychological Impact of Physical Abuse* (New York: Vintage Books, 1990); and Alice Miller, *For Your Own Good: Hidden Cruelty in Child-Rearing and the Roots of Violence* (New York: Farrar, Straus, & Giroux, 1983).

62. *Ausgewählte Pädagogische Schriften,* 33.

13. *Horace Bushnell's* Christian Nurture

MARGARET BENDROTH

Horace Bushnell (1802-1876) was the quintessential American theologian of childhood. A leading Congregational pastor and scholar, his famous book entitled *Christian Nurture* (1847) was one of the first extended reflections on the religious lives of infants and young children. Arguing against extreme views of childhood sinfulness, Bushnell is perhaps best known for his memorable proposition that "the child is to grow up a Christian, and never know himself as being otherwise."[1]

This understanding of childhood faith as a gradual process of enlightenment was controversial in its time; however, Bushnell's views soon came to dominate Protestant conceptions of childhood, especially in the twentieth century. The now commonplace awareness that the home environment and family relationships may be instrumental in conversion — canonized in church nursery schools, religious education programs, and parachurch family organizations for much of the twentieth century — owes much to Bushnell's assertion that the seeds of faith exist in the heart even of a newborn child. And in a broader sense, Bushnell's systematic attentiveness to the emotional nuances of parent-child relationships places him at the center of a cultural shift in middle-class American family life. By the early twentieth century, the Victorian stress on gender roles and hierarchy had given way to a far more "Bushnellian" ideal that emphasized companionship, play, and emotional intimacy between parents and children.

---

1. Horace Bushnell, *Christian Nurture* (New York: Charles Scribner, 1861; reprint, Cleveland: Pilgrim Press, 1994), 10. For a recent general treatment of Bushnell, see Robert Edwards, *Of Singular Genius, of Singular Grace: A Biography of Horace Bushnell* (Cleveland: Pilgrim Press, 1992).

Although Bushnell was in some ways ahead of his time, he is still a nineteenth-century thinker; his ideas do not all translate well into a current conversation about children. On the most obvious level, his romantic, optimistic assumptions about childhood — which mark him as a typical middle-class Victorian — place him on the other side of an intellectual gulf rent by modern behaviorist and Freudian psychology. On our side of the ravine, we are far less sure that children naturally lean toward God — or even toward minimally civilized behavior. Most popular child-rearing literature, from Dr. Spock to Dr. Dobson, generally views childhood, especially the toddler years, as a time of undisciplined aggression. At best, they warn, parents can divert or channel those infamous grocery-store tantrums with a quick trip through the checkout line; not even the most well-behaved child is immune from an episode or two. We are also more deeply aware of the complicated, often negative aspects of parental influence. Since the early twentieth century, child-rearing experts have been warning mothers of the fine lines separating genuine nurture from harmful "smothering." Overzealous "momism" was said to have debilitated an entire generation of young boys in the World War II era, rendering them unfit for military service. In recent years, family therapists have deepened and nuanced our understanding of the ways in which "dysfunctional" relationships blight individual growth and happiness. Parenthood in these times has become a notoriously unscientific task with few sure chances of success — a fact all the more tragic as we understand more thoroughly the consequences of failure.

Still, there is much in Bushnell worthy of critical recovery. The fairly modest purpose of this essay is to suggest a few ways in which Bushnell's theology of childhood merits thoughtful retrieval. I will begin, however, with a summary of Bushnell's argument and then a broader discussion of *Christian Nurture* within its theological and larger social context.

Christian Nurture vs. "Ostrich Nurture"

Christian Nurture is still an accessible, highly readable book. In clear, engaging language, Bushnell combined practical advice on child rearing with forceful theological arguments on such abstract topics as the nature of sin and the efficacy of the sacraments. Initially appearing as a single essay on the faith of children, and then as a series of discourses published by the Massachusetts Sunday School Society, the volume grew as Bushnell attempted to stem the mounting controversy his essay had raised among his New England peers.

Central to Bushnell's argument was his critique of revivalism. In the hundred years beginning with the mid-eighteenth century transatlantic campaigns of great preachers like George Whitefield, the religious revival had emerged as a central feature of American Protestantism. From the steepled commons of New England to the backwoods of Kentucky and Tennessee, Protestants from a variety of traditions recognized its value in restoring spiritual vitality and garnering new converts. By Bushnell's day, the wild gyrations and spiritual agonies that often accompanied a camp-meeting conversion were less frequent, but religious emotions still occupied a pivotal role. Revivalism in principle insisted on a single emotional experience as the mark of true conversion.

Bushnell argued that this requirement spiritually disenfranchised children from the start. Revivalism, at least as he interpreted it, assumed that only a fully mature adult could undergo the emotional, intellectual, and physical rigors of conversion. By implication, then, children were in a kind of theological limbo, morally guilty of sin but incapable of achieving salvation. "They indoctrinate them soundly in respect to their need of a new heart," he explained, "tell them what conversion is, and how it comes to pass with grown people; pray that God will arrest them when they are old enough to be converted according to the manner; drill them, meantime, into all the constraints, separated from all the hopes and liberties of religion; turning all their little misdoings and bad tempers into evidences of their need of regeneration, and assuring them that all such signs must be upon them till after they have passed the change. Their nurture," Bushnell concluded, "is a nurture of despair; and the bread of life itself, held before them as a fruit to be looked upon, but not tasted, till they are old enough to have it as grown people do, finally becomes repulsive, just because they have been so long repelled and fenced away from it."[2]

Bushnell emphatically denounced such "ostrich nurture," comparing revivalism to an ostrich laying eggs, covering them up in the sand, and leaving them to hatch alone. (The biblical text in question was Lamentations 4:3: "The daughter of my people is become cruel, like the ostriches in the wilderness.") It encouraged dangerous passivity in parents and moral frustration — and, in some cases, outright venality — in children. Instead of guiding young children toward faith, evangelical Protestant parents concentrated their efforts on breaking a rebellious son's or daughter's will by harsh, sometimes abusive measures. Bushnell found it "monstrous" and "unnatural" to teach young children that they were depraved and fallen without offering them a genuine opportunity for conversion. To deny moral agency to infants and children was in his view "virtual abuse and cruelty."[3]

2. Bushnell, *Christian Nurture*, 74.
3. Bushnell, *Christian Nurture*, 72, 79. This is also the argument in Philip Greven, *The Protestant Temperament: Patterns of Child-Rearing, Religious Experience, and the Self in Early America* (New York: New American Library, 1977).

Revivalism in practice was of course more complicated than Bushnell painted it. By the 1820s and 1830s, as one revivalist noted, parents regularly took their children to such meetings, "'that they might be converted.'" The famous Cane Ridge Revival in 1800, as well as many that followed, featured converts of all ages: indeed, the younger the child, the more spectacular the miracle. As they became more routinized in the antebellum years, camp-meeting revivals also became places for families to strengthen their relational bonds with heavy doses of experiential religion, and to push children toward conversion. For all its power, however, revivalism could not guarantee results; Methodist parents, as Gregory Schneider writes, still had to depend on physical punishment to break the child's self-will, crafting an often unwieldy balance of terrible authority and a solicitous, easily wounded love.[4]

Bushnell envisioned true Christian nurture as a thoroughly natural process, the authentic sign of a godly home. Like most Protestants of his day, he assumed that every child would experience conversion at some point in early life. But, he argued, this need not be a sudden, cataclysmic event; rather, deep and permanent spiritual change came about as a gradual awakening of the soul to God. Parents, Bushnell argued, should "rather seek to teach a feeling than a doctrine; to bathe the child in their own feeling of love to God, and dependence on him, and contrition for wrong before him . . . ; to make what is good, happy and attractive, what is wrong, odious and hateful; then as understanding advances, to give it food suited to its capacity, opening upon it, gradually the more difficult views of Christian doctrine and experience."[5]

This process literally began at birth, when infants received their first intimations of the gospel through loving parental care. It continued on, well before any verbal communication could take place. In a truly godly parent, Bushnell argued, the gospel "beams out . . . as a living epistle, before it escapes from the lips, or is taught in words." Thus, in effect, years before a child could understand a Bible story or respond to a Sunday school lesson, the simple tasks of feeding, bathing, and participation in play could hold profound and permanent religious significance.[6]

Bushnell, both in theory and in practice, emphasized what he called an "organic" conception of family life. He was sharply critical of the individualism he saw in American society, particularly the way that it eroded civic and moral re-

---

4. A. Gregory Schneider, *The Way of the Cross Leads Home: The Domestication of American Methodism* (Bloomington: Indiana University Press, 1993), 74-75, 159-62. On children at revivals, see, for example, Bernard Weisberger, *They Gathered at the River: The Story of the Great Revivalists and Their Impact upon Religion in America* (Chicago: Quadrangle Books, [1958] 1966), 25, 29, 33, 37.

5. Bushnell, *Christian Nurture*, 51.

6. Bushnell, *Christian Nurture*, 22.

sponsibility. "A national life, a church life, a family life, is no longer conceived, or perhaps conceivable by many," he declared. ". . . We seem only to lie as seeds piled together, without any terms of connection, save the accident of proximity, or the fact that we all belong to the heap."[7] Bushnell's scheme of Christian nurture emphasized the powerful unseen bonds within a family, something far more than mere parental influence or didactic authority. The "atmosphere" of a Christian home — the "manners, personal views, prejudices, practical motives, and spirit of the house" — played a determinative role in the child's religious formation.[8]

Although the cultivation of proper feeling counted for much, especially in the child's earliest years, Christian nurture also demanded specific practices. Bushnell urged parents not to overfeed their children and to avoid sweets and stimulants. A "wrong feeding of children," he warned ". . . puts them under the body, teaches them to value bodily sensations, makes them sensual in every way, and sets them lusting in every kind of excess." Alternatively, food eaten in moderation, at regular intervals, and prefaced with a table blessing, could be a material means of grace. Even good manners, Bushnell argued, are "a sort of first-stage religion," protecting the child from temptations to coarse and selfish behavior.[9] Similarly, wise parents never lavished their children with expensive clothing or toys. "Dress your child for Christ, if you will have him a Christian," Bushnell advised; "bring every thing, in the training, even of his body, to this one aim, and it will be strange if the Christian body you give him does not contain a Christian soul."[10]

Bushnell also emphasized the importance of specific training in the creeds, Christian doctrine, and the content of Scripture, as long as the method and timing was sensitive to the child's needs and understanding. "It must be obvious," he wrote, "that very small children are more likely to be worried and drummed into apathy by dogmatic catechisms, than to get any profit from them. . . . Untimely intrusions of religion will only make it odious — the child cannot be crammed with doctrine." As an alternative, Bushnell counseled parents to interweave lessons with play and a variety of fun activities, and always to model the behaviors being taught. Their responsibility, he urged, was not to produce faith in their children but to nurture it, "presuming on a grace already and always given."[11]

Bushnell believed that each child came into the world as the recipient of a unique spiritual legacy. All parents bequeathed a range of prejudices — both

7. Bushnell, *Christian Nurture*, 91.
8. Bushnell, *Christian Nurture*, 94.
9. Bushnell, *Christian Nurture*, 276-84.
10. Bushnell, *Christian Nurture*, 293.
11. Bushnell, *Christian Nurture*, 358, 378, 381.

good and bad — to their children, even before birth. The child of pious parents who had cultivated Christian character all their lives inherited clear spiritual advantages — especially compared with the less fortunate child of debauched or "vicious" parents who came into the world with an inborn tendency toward evil ("morally weakened beforehand, in the womb of folly," as Bushnell put it). Any given child might have a range of moral predilections, but some were born with a greater will toward the good, strengthened by the Christian atmosphere of a decent home.[12]

The parents' time was short, however, for Bushnell believed that by the time the child had matured enough to exercise choice and free will — roughly age three, with the mastery of language — the die had been cast. His or her early experiences formed a repertoire of feelings and experiences for the child to carry through adulthood. But godly parents were not to worry unduly: under a regimen of solid Christian nurture, it would be all but impossible for any child to forsake the Christian faith.

Organic bonds also stretched between home and church, helping parents fulfill their covenantal responsibilities toward their children. These began with the sacrament of infant baptism, when the parents announced their presumption of the child's eventual salvation, a hope based on the organic bonds of connection between the child's inert faith and their own mature belief. The sacrament, Bushnell argued, "sees the child in the parent, counts him presumptively a believer and a Christian, and, with the parent, baptizes him also."[13]

But Bushnell was quick to deny any special form of grace in baptism. The baptized child and her parents all lived under the "known laws of character in the house." No "abrupt, fantastic, and therefore incredible grace" snatched them away from the daily incursions of bad temper or selfishness that marred even the most religious household. The organic unity of the family could, in fact, work both good or ill.[14]

But baptized children were still in a sense believers. Bushnell offered parents no guaranteed outcome, but, like Calvin, he identified the "seed faith" of children as an authentic — though still potential — response to grace. As a "rudimental being," a child could not be expected to have an adult faith; rather, Bushnell emphasized the developmental nature of spiritual understanding. Christ was "a Saviour for infants, and children, and youth, as truly as for the adult age; gathering them all into his fold together, there to be kept and nourished together, by gifts appropriate to their years."[15]

12. Bushnell, *Christian Nurture*, 94-110.
13. Bushnell, *Christian Nurture*, 40.
14. Bushnell, *Christian Nurture*, 116-17.
15. Bushnell, *Christian Nurture*, 54, 83.

Bushnell was careful to present his argument for infant baptism firmly within the historic and biblical traditions of the church, and he was sharply critical of the way that Protestants in his day had weakened its meaning. Invoking apostolic practice, he argued that infant baptism required a distinct obligation not just from parents but from the institutional church as well. Bushnell advocated a special form of non-voting membership in which the covenant child was not subject to church discipline but allowed full access to the Lord's Supper, in "sublime anticipation" of his or her future faith.[16] Baptized children, he argued, ought to be enrolled by name in church membership lists, "as composing a distinct class of candidate, or catechumen, members." Although the American Sunday school movement was still in its infancy when Bushnell composed his argument, the growth of denominational programs after the Civil War certainly owed much to his emphasis on the church's role in nurturing childhood faith. Bushnell may, however, have regretted the movement's institutional isolation of children from adult worship; he advocated their full participation in every aspect of church life, including more emphasis on singing in Sunday services, "that they may join their voices and play into expression of their own tribute of feeling and Christian sentiment."[17]

Still, the primary agent of grace was the family, not the church. "Religion never thoroughly penetrates life," Bushnell argued, "until it becomes domestic."[18] Christian nurture took its deepest root in the daily routines of family life, hour by hour, year by year, as the child absorbed the Christian atmosphere of the home and observed the tender, upright example of Christian parents. Bushnell saw families as "little churches," in many ways superior to formal religious gatherings, "as they are more private, closer to the life of infancy, and more completely blended with the common affairs of life."[19]

No summary of Bushnell's thought would be complete without noting that he enjoyed children for their own sake, because of — not in spite of — their inherent vulnerability. In his sermons to his Hartford congregation, he emphasized the heroic importance of "small things." "It requires less piety," he declared, ". . . to be a martyr for Christ than it does to . . . maintain a perfect and guileless integrity in the common transactions of life." Indeed, adults had much to gain by staying in touch with the humbleness and simplicity of childhood. "We love to do great things; our natural pride would be greatly pleased if God had made the sky taller, the world larger, and given us a moral royal style of life and duty," Bushnell observed, noting that God's "purpose is to heal our infir-

---

16. Bushnell, *Christian Nurture*, 168.
17. Bushnell, *Christian Nurture*, 192-93.
18. Bushnell, *Christian Nurture*, 63.
19. Bushnell, *Christian Nurture*, 406.

mity," and thus God "has ordained these humble spheres of action so that no ostentation, no great and striking explosions of godliness shall tempt our hearts."[20]

Bushnell's own family life testified to the authenticity of his convictions. One of his three daughters, Mary Bushnell Cheney, remembered him as a genuinely loving father, fond of "after-dinner romps" and impromptu picnics. He rarely lectured his family on religion. On Sunday evenings, Cheney wrote, the entire family gathered on the lawn for "conversation and discussion on religious topics." Each family member dropped a question into Bushnell's hat, and he picked out one or two to start things off. "We all said our say — and very comical commentaries they often were — leaving the final words to him. These words were few," Cheney recalled, "and were generally meant, not to settle the question, but to help us to do so, if that were possible, or, at least, to think them out as far as we could." Indeed, she concluded, "it was in family life that he shone the brightest. . . . My father was largest and most ideal to those who knew him in the nearness of family life and love. It is they who know most of his zest, his enthusiasm, . . . his delicate considerateness of those who were dear to him; of his great unexpressed and inexpressible tenderness; of the reasoning faith which beheld the unseen."[21]

Bushnell and the Victorian Family

Although Bushnell presented his arguments for Christian nurture against the backdrop of revivalism, there are other — and in the long run more significant — contexts for his work. In its social setting, Bushnell's thought reflects a shift in attitudes toward children taking place among middle-class Americans during the early nineteenth century. Until the late eighteenth century, most popular advice literature still depicted children as evil, "an innocent façade behind which lurked all kinds of wicked desires." Parents had a duty to restrain their children's bent toward sinning, if necessary by breaking their wills with harsh discipline. By the early nineteenth century, however, "the emphasis shifted from the certainty of their evil to the probability of their good, even the possibility of their perfection." Childhood was a time of special innocence and purity; the more enthusiastic proponents of this essen-

---

20. Bushnell, "Living to God in Small Things," in *Sermons for the New Life* (New York: Charles Scribner's Sons, 1904), 291-92.

21. Mary Bushnell Cheney, *Life and Letters of Horace Bushnell* (New York: Harper & Brothers, 1880), 452-53, 461, 468-69.

tially Romantic view saw children as more intuitively religious than people at any other stage of life.[22]

The structure of middle-class households both reflected and enabled this moral elevation of childhood. The Industrial Revolution of the late eighteenth and early nineteenth centuries had contributed to a growing social, economic, and spiritual divide between the worlds of home and work. As the outside world of politics, business, and war became the exclusive sphere of men, women took up mastery of the domestic realm. Although they often spoke of "woman's sphere" in patronizing, sentimental language, middle-class Victorians prized the security of this feminine world, for they believed it nurtured personal as well as civic morality. In a variety of ways, both practical and theoretical, the virtue of American society depended on the purity of each individual home.[23]

Within this private realm, mothers and children formed close emotional ties. Family size decreased across the nineteenth century, reflecting increasingly intense expectations for intimacy and maternal care. Indeed, most Victorians believed that children inherited characteristics from their parents; even a mother's emotional and spiritual state could permanently affect a child in utero.[24]

Bushnell's high expectations for parental influence certainly reflect this Victorian ethos, as does his faith in the near salvific power of a godly mother. In many ways he idealized the home as a protected moral sanctuary that could be effectively sealed off from noxious influences. There the mother's power over and her responsibility for the immortal souls of her children was virtually limitless. Anyone who has attempted to raise small children may well find Bushnell almost heartless: he warns mothers against showing temper with their children ("there is no place even for so much as a feeling of impatience"), against expecting too much as well as demanding too little, and, perhaps even more cruelly, against being overanxious.[25]

22. Peter Gregg Slater, *Children in the New England Mind: In Death and in Life* (Hamden, Conn.: Archon Books, 1977), 22; Priscilla Brewer, "'The Little Citizen': Images of Children in Early Nineteeth-Century America," *Journal of American Culture* 7 (Winter 1984): 45. See also Karin Calvert, *Children in the House: The Material Culture of Early Childhood, 1600-1900* (Boston: Northeastern University Press, 1992), 104-10.

23. Barbara Welter, "The Cult of True Womanhood: 1820-1860," *American Quarterly* 18 (1966): 151-74.

24. Frances E. Kobrin, "The Fall in Household Size and the Rise of the Primary Individual in the United States," in *The American Family in Social-Historical Perspective*, 2d ed., ed. Michael Gordon (New York: St. Martin's Press, 1978), 69-81. For a general history of American families, see Steven Mintz and Susan Kellogg, *Domestic Revolutions: A Social History of American Family Life* (New York: Free Press, 1988).

25. Bushnell, *Christian Nurture*, 296. See also Ann Taves, "Mothers and Children and the Legacy of Mid-Nineteenth-Century American Christianity," *Journal of Religion* 67, no. 2 (April 1987): 203-19. Compare with Nancy Pottishman Weiss, "Mother, the Inven-

Bushnell, especially in his later writings, clearly believed that children were special. While adults struggled with spiritual doubts, children, he said, "take in all most precious thoughts of God more easily. The very highest and most spiritual things are a great deal closer to them than to us." Bushnell admitted that, had he the chance to begin his career over, he would have preached first to children and only secondly to adults. "We get so fooled in our estimate of what we do," he declared, "that we call it coming down when we undertake the preaching to children; whereas it is coming up rather, out of the subterranean hells, darknesses, intricacies, dungeon-like profundities of old, grown-up sin, to speak to the bright day-light creatures of trust and sweet affinities and easy conviction."[26]

The Problem of the Sinful Child

Not surprisingly, Bushnell's critics worried that he had all but abandoned the possibility of childhood sin. Indeed, *Christian Nurture* is one link in a long and complex argument among American Calvinist theologians — a category that includes Bushnell — about the nature and scope of original sin, especially the doctrine's implications in regard to the primary innocence or evil of young children. In an age of high infant mortality, theological debates over infant damnation could be fraught with personal anguish. Could God punish an innocent child, one who had not yet had the opportunity for salvation, for a sin committed by Adam? By the time Bushnell published *Christian Nurture*, few New England theologians subscribed to any form of infant damnation — if indeed they ever had. By Bushnell's time, Calvinism was thoroughly on the defensive; Methodism, which emphasized human ability, and Unitarianism, which emphasized human rationality, seemed to fit the new order far better than an Augustinian understanding of corporate human guilt for Adam's original disobedience. But for early nineteenth-century Calvinists, the logical problem persisted; they understood intellectually, if not emotionally, that allowing children a "free pass" to heaven by virtue of their innocence would severely weaken the doctrine of human depravity — and of course, by extension, the necessity of supernatural salvation.[27]

---

tion of Necessity: Dr. Benjamin Spock's *Baby and Child Care*," *American Quarterly* 29 (1977): 519-46. Bushnell also opposed woman suffrage: see his *Women's Suffrage: The Reform against Nature* (New York: Charles Scribner, 1869).

26. Bushnell, *God's Thoughts Fit Bread for Children* (Boston: Nichols & Noyes, 1869), 25, 36.

27. For a general background, see Nathan Hatch, *The Democratization of American Christianity* (New Haven: Yale University Press, 1989); and Slater, *Children in the New England Mind*.

Thus, Congregationalist Bennet Tyler, one of Bushnell's major opponents in the *Christian Nurture* controversy, argued that scaling down the rigors of the conversion experience allowed children to believe in the "delusion" of their own righteousness. To Tyler, Bushnell's theology was thoroughly unrealistic about human nature, built on an airy notion of Christ as a mere "good example." "My dear Sir," he reprimanded Bushnell, "the only 'passions kindled' in the hearts of unrenewed man by a contemplation of the 'beauty and glory of God' as he is revealed in the scriptures, are the passions of hatred and disgust." Tyler argued that the real duty of Christian parents was to lead the child, "as soon as possible, to a knowledge of . . . the wickedness of his heart, and the necessity of a new heart to prepare him for heaven."[28]

Old School Presbyterian Charles Hodge similarly objected to the "false assumption" that "men are not by nature the children of wrath, that they are not involved in spiritual death, and consequently that they do not need to be quickened by that mighty power which wrought in Christ when it raised him from the dead." Although Hodge admired much about Bushnell's work, he was troubled by its "naturalistic" account of conversion as a process that might proceed without any supernatural intervention.[29]

Bushnell's critics had a point, of course, for at times his language seems to echo Rousseau more than Augustine. And in many ways, though Bushnell used Calvinist language of covenant and promise, he was a pioneering Protestant liberal, charting a theological path away from the metaphysical certainties of orthodox Calvinism. By the late nineteenth century, his normative emphasis on human experience, his "moral influence" view of Christ's atonement, and his symbolic understanding of religious language set him clearly apart from the main body of evangelical Protestants and, over the following century, marked him as an important innovator in the development of American religious thought.[30] Especially to conservative Calvinists, his arguments for nurturing faith in newborn infants sounded suspiciously Unitarian, if not overtly Pelagian — that is, dangerously presumptive of human moral ability.

Perhaps not surprisingly, Bushnell's understanding of childhood sin was

28. The first quotation is from Bennet Tyler, *Letter to the Rev. Horace Bushnell, D.D., Containing Strictures on His Book, Entitled "Views of Christian Nurture, and Subjects Adjacent Thereto"* (Hartford, Conn.: Brown & Parsons, 1848), 64, 68. The second quotation is from H. Shelton Smith, *Changing Conceptions of Original Sin: A Study in American Theology since 1750* (New York: Charles Scribner's Sons, 1955), 146.

29. Hodge, "Bushnell on Christian Nurture," *Biblical Repertory and Princeton Review* 19 (October 1847): 536, 529. On Bushnell's supernaturalism, see Robert Bruce Mullin, "Horace Bushnell and the Question of Miracles," *Church History* 58 (1989): 460-73.

30. Smith, *Changing Conceptions of Original Sin,* 149-63.

widely misinterpreted. Unitarian reviewers, as well as Old School Presbyterians like Charles Hodge, applauded his theory of Christian nurture for opposing reasons; indeed, Bushnell himself was not always systematic or clear in his explanation of sin's origins. By intellectual habit, he gravitated toward "comprehensive" answers that split the difference between two opposing sides. Thus, Bushnell did not believe sin was freely chosen or "natural necessity" for a child. Each new individual was in a sense a new Adam, coming into the world not morally perfect but morally innocent — that is, without any direct empirical knowledge of either good or evil. Adam's fall from grace and a child's first sinful act are the logical consequences of this inexperience. Neither *must* choose evil — as Bushnell said, "There is no reason why the first moral act of the child must be wrong rather than right" — but both certainly will. Bushnell did not believe that sin was in any sense imputed from one generation to the next, but his organic view of humanity and of the family meant that children simply could not avoid the effects of sin within the lives of their parents.[31]

But, taking his larger argument into account, Bushnell was not as dimissive of childhood sin as his rhetoric periodically implied. To the contrary, his scheme of Christian nurture introduced a stronger understanding of human fallenness than either revivalism or liberal rationalism could offer. Bushnell's theology in fact owed much to the "federal" theory of the Puritan divines and its emphasis on the corporate experience of human sin — a doctrine with "important truth," though "strangely misconceived" by nineteenth-century Protestants.[32] Federal theology rested on Paul's argument in Romans 5, that all of humanity received the sin of Adam because he was the first "head," or representative figure, of the human race; in a similar fashion, Paul explained, all of humanity would be saved through Christ, the second Adam. By the early nineteenth century, the theory had fallen into disuse, having come under concerted attack from Unitarian rationalists emphasizing the importance of individual choice and free will. Moreover, within the rising democratic ethos of American society, any concept of sin that did not arise from free choice seemed viciously unfair, if not downright absurd: how could God punish an entire race for one, long-dead individual's act of rebellion? Indeed, Nathaniel William Taylor, Bushnell's teacher at Yale, tried to moderate the problem by proposing that "the sin occurs in the sinning": although each individual shares a universal human condition, he or she becomes a sinner by an individual act of will.[33]

31. Bushnell, *Christian Nurture*, 39.

32. Again, see Smith, *Changing Conceptions of Original Sin*, for a summary of these and related arguments. See also Glenn Hewitt, *Regeneration and Morality: A Study of Charles Finney, Charles Hodge, John W. Nevin, and Horace Bushnell* (Brooklyn, N.Y.: Carlson Publishing, Inc., 1991).

33. Smith, *Changing Conceptions of Original Sin*, 106-8.

The main burden of Bushnell's argument was not to absolve children of sin but to distribute the responsibility more broadly across the family and society — to retrieve the doctrine from its increasingly individualistic application to the human condition. Although to some critics this lessened the seriousness of the situation, Bushnell was hardly a Pelagian or a Romantic when it came to the transmission of sin in families. As we have seen, he earnestly warned careless parents about the dangers of "ostrich nurture," of allowing a child to forge his or her own way toward heaven. *Christian Nurture* presents many lengthy descriptions of the ways in which parents wittingly or unwittingly introduced sin into the lives of their children, from the first moments of life onward. In fact, Bushnell's view of the family as thoroughly embedded in culture gave new complexity to the dynamics of sin and grace within the domestic sphere. He saw salvation as a thoroughly intergenerational process, taught and transmitted through human interactions within the family.[34]

Bushnell's understanding of sin and grace also reflects a Victorian emphasis on character. This means that at times his argument could be profoundly moral, calling for a thorough infusion of Christian teaching across American society; and at other times "Christian nurture" appears to be spectacularly trivial. Bushnell did, of course, denounce bigotry, sanctimony, and fanaticism as forms of "vice"; but he also inveighed against "intemperance" and "coarseness" (including personal slovenliness) as detriments to proper character. The true Christian and the proper Victorian gentleman or lady are at times hard to distinguish.

Bushnell's emphasis on character, especially in parents, also seemed to diminish children's spiritual responsibility. There are Pelagian echoes (and Lamarckian genetics) in his repeated emphasis on the failings of Christian parents and the "profound necessity" that they "make a thorough inspection of their morality itself, to find if there be any bad spot in it; knowing that, as certainly as there is, it will more or less fatally corrupt their children." To the objection that godly parents may for no discernible reason sometimes produce godless children, Bushnell observed that no religious character is without defect, especially in the home environment. "There are, in short, too many ways of accounting for the failure or success, in the family training of those who are remarkable for their piety, without being led to doubt the correctness of my argument in these discourses."[35] And if these warnings weren't enough, Bushnell

34. In this sense, Bushnell fully anticipated the social theories of both Durkheim and Freud. His insights on the interplay of culture and personality seem self-evident to us in the present only because they have become such a staple of social-science thinking. See Daniel Walker Howe, "The Social Science of Horace Bushnell," *Journal of American History* 70 (September 1983): 305-22.

35. Bushnell, *Christian Nurture*, 262, 52.

reminded his readers about the danger of eternal punishment: "And do not be surprised if these children when they meet you before the Judge of your and their life, have a more severe witness to give against you than if you had merely neglected their bodies."[36]

Bushnell's critics readily pointed out the psychological implications of such a demand. Tyler took particular issue with the way that Bushnell linked the piety of mothers and fathers to the salvation of their children. "I do not feel authorized to say," Tyler wrote, "that success is always in exact proportion to fidelity." Bushnell was asking parents "to be more faithful than Abraham, or Isaac, or Jacob, or Aaron, or Samuel, or David" — a long list of biblical parents whose children grew up to disappoint them. How could young, inexperienced Christian parents in the nineteenth century expect to do any better?[37] Tyler had a point: in the long run, a more individualistic, universal understanding of sin may be more humane toward children and less emotionally demanding of adults than an overconfidence of virtue on either side.[38] Depravity is, at least, a thoroughly democratic principle.

Being Bushnellian Today

Bushnell's view of the family as an instrument of grace has been sorely tested over the course of the twentieth century. From the popular media as well as the social sciences we have a more complex — and perhaps despairing — sense of the damage that families can inflict on their most vulnerable members. The therapeutic culture of the present day has traced the intricate ways in which family life can cause permanent pain in both parents and children; the best we can do, it seems, is to find ways to minimize the damage.

Bushnell's Victorian optimism and sentimentality are, to say the least, jarring within a modern setting. His scheme of Christian nurture rested on the confident assumption of moral congruence between home, neighborhood, church, and school; he saw these as a unified world of interlocking, mutually reinforcing social institutions. Such rarely exists for children today, who may confront a puzzling range of choices after playing in a friend's home, listening to a lesson at school, or going on an outing with the church youth group. Parents today do not have nearly the amount of moral control over their children's lives that Bushnell believed mid-nineteenth-century parents did; they manage their responsibility

36. Bushnell, *Christian Nurture*, 59.
37. Tyler, *Letter to the Rev. Horace Bushnell*, 25.
38. Slater, *Children in the New England Mind*, 22, 23.

for child rearing with help (or interference) from many others: doctors, teachers, coaches, and, of course, the ubiquitous media stars of professional sports and television. Television — and now the Internet — expose children to "every ugly secret of adulthood" with the touch of a button or the click of a mouse.[39]

Although Bushnell's morally integrated community is perhaps beyond retrieving (if indeed it ever existed), his critique of American society is still well-taken. The individualism that worried him in 1847 is now a fact of life; Americans today cannot assume that their families will sustain the kind of long-term stability and institutional order that underlaid Bushnell's model of Christian nurture. In response, Bushnell might point out the even stronger necessity of recognizing — and working to sustain — the pre-existent "organic bonds" between parents and children, those spiritual obligations that pre-empt individual choices or temporary social arrangements. Christian nurture in the present day would go far beyond the private, interpersonal issues that dominate child rearing today; fundamental to its logic is a concern not just for the individual child in one's family but for the welfare of children in general.

There is much about modern culture that Bushnell would find troubling — and perhaps familiar. He might even find a contemporary parallel to revivalism in the culture of consumerism and entertainment that has defined our social life for much of the twentieth century. Both require children in some sense to act as adults, pressuring them to make essentially grown-up decisions before they are psychologically and spiritually ready to do so. The regular bloodletting in children's television and movies is certainly more aimed at an adult moral sensibility (if any), denying children the moral simplicity that is owed them as the most vulnerable members of society. An advertiser pitching a product to a four-year-old is perhaps the logical extension of Bushnell's old-time revivalist manipulating the hellfire out of his young audience.

The careful modern reader might find in Bushnell a calm voice of sanity. Many children today are often left to fend for themselves on the street or in front of a television set, or they are shuttled around to a dizzying array of soccer games, ballet classes, and day-care providers. Even a mature adult would have difficulty finding a moral center in such an unstable setting. Raising good children, as Bushnell argues, is a long, slow, subtle process; it takes a lot of time and attention, many hours of being present, the effort to curb a sharp word, the energy to answer just one more question. Bushnell's emphasis on the moral efficacy of parents is perhaps a hard word to hear today, but it is still, without question, a wise and timely one.

---

39. Gary Alan Fine and Jay Mechling, "Minor Difficulties: Changing Children in the Late Twentieth Century," in *America at Century's End,* ed. Alan Wolfe (Berkeley and Los Angeles: University of California Press, 1991), 60.

14. African American Children, "The Hope of the Race": Mary Church Terrell, the Social Gospel, and the Work of the Black Women's Club Movement

MARCIA Y. RIGGS

Introduction

The nineteenth century was a time of transitions for the African American community. The lives of African Americans were forever changed by the social, political, and economic ramifications of emancipation, reconstruction, and urbanization. Those who had been slaves (approximately four million) found themselves thrust into a society for which they were ill-prepared — a society that was undecided about its obligations to African Americans. Consequently, both those African Americans who were free before the end of slavery and those recently emancipated found their lives further constrained as the society enforced overt and covert means of social control (e.g., disenfranchisement, exclusion from unions, scientific and religious ideologies of racial inferiority, increased lynchings)[1] upon African Americans as a racial caste.

African Americans responded to these transitions by creating parallel institutions that embodied philosophies of economic self-determination, moral development, self-help, and racial solidarity. These institutions included independent churches, schools, banks, insurance companies, and burial societies. Also important were the social reform movements. One of the most active and effective social reform movements was the club movement founded by African American women.

During the nineteenth century, African American women lived out their

---

1. The ideology of the black child/savage (deriving from social Darwinism) and the curse of Ham were particularly powerful scientific and religious ideologies operative at the time in support of the inferiority of African Americans as a social group.

faith through a variety of organized activities both within and outside of church structures. One of the most influential of these organized activities was the black women's club movement, which began in the late nineteenth century and lasted into the early twentieth century. Although the black women's club movement may be characterized by terms that are generally used to describe the club movement among both white and black women of the nineteenth century — that is, "nonsectarian" and "autonomous" (not an auxiliary of an organization under the leadership of men) — it can also be interpreted as a significant social reform movement under the leadership and membership of women who were sustained by a particular religious-ethical worldview[2] — a worldview that was derived from their experience in the church.[3] Two features of this religious-ethical worldview can be discerned as critically informing the club movement's work on behalf of children: (1) belief in both the justice of God and justice for blacks as a command of God; and (2) a sense of racial obligation and duty among blacks.

The black women's club movement was formally organized as the National Association of Colored Women (NACW) in 1896. The NACW was a socio-religious movement working for reform in society and uplift in the black community. The religious-ethical worldview of the women who formed the leadership of this movement was reflected in the constitution of the NACW — as Article II, which deals with the group's objective, indicates: "The object of this Association shall be by the help of God to secure harmony of action and cooperation among all women in raising to the highest plane, home, moral, and civic life."[4]

2. Marcia Y. Riggs, "The Socio-Religious Ethical Tradition of Black Women," in *Christian Issues and Moral Response*, 5th ed., ed. Paul Jersild and Dale Johnson (New York: Harcourt, Brace, Jovanovich, 1996), 128-39. In this essay I describe these features as central to the socio-religious ethical tradition of black women: an evaluation of the relation between economics and justice in American society; the recognition of an interrelationship between the oppression of blacks in America and other people of color; an awareness of the connection between the oppression of blacks and women in terms of misuse of power to subvert justice; an acknowledgment of distinctive aspects of oppression for black women; belief in both the justice of God and justice for blacks as a command of God; and a sense of racial obligation and duty among blacks.

3. Fannie Barrier Williams, "The Club Movement among Colored Women of America" (1900), in *Can I Get a Witness? Prophetic Religious Voices of African American Women: An Anthology*, ed. Marcia Y. Riggs (Maryknoll, N.Y.: Orbis Books, 1997). Williams states, "The training which enabled colored women to organize and successfully carry on club work was originally obtained in church work. . . . The meaning of unity of effort for the common good, the development of social sympathies grew into women's consciousness through the privileges of church work" (118).

4. Charles Harris Wesley, *The History of the National Association of Colored Women's Clubs* (Washington, D.C.: Mercury Press, 1984), 42.

This objective was incarnated in the programmatic emphases of the movement, one of which was the welfare of children. Specific aims of the programmatic emphasis on the welfare of children are outlined in the following excerpt from the address given by Josephine St. Pierre Ruffin (1842-1924) at the first national conference of black women (1895), which was the forerunner of the formation of the NACW:

> We need to talk over those things that are of especial interest to us as colored women, the training of our children, openings for our boys and girls, how they can be prepared for occupations and occupations may be found or opened for them, what we especially can do in the moral education and physical development, the home training it is necessary to give our children in order to prepare them to meet the peculiar conditions in which they shall find themselves, how to make the most of our own, to some extent, limited opportunities.[5]

In this essay, I will (1) describe the work of the club movement that was designed to fulfill the aims outlined above by Ruffin; (2) present significant ideas regarding children within the thought of Mary Church Terrell (the first president of the NACW, and a person who — I will contend — may appropriately be considered a practical theologian); and (3) offer an interpretation of the significance of this movement's work and thought for theological reflection and moral agency on behalf of children today. My methodology in this essay is to utilize primary source documents as the basis for the historical retrieval of insights that may serve as guides for the direction of current theological and ethical reflection. Because the source documents are unfamiliar and not readily available to most readers, I have chosen to quote from them somewhat extensively in order to give readers an opportunity to draw their own conclusions as well as evaluate those that I draw. Also, because I have allowed the documents to establish the parameters of the content of this essay, some topics (e.g., the baptism of children and the discipline of children) discussed in other essays in this volume are not found here.

The Work of the Black Women's Club Movement

In the passage quoted from the address of Josephine St. Pierre Ruffin, there were five general areas that established the basis for the movement's work on

---

5. Elizabeth Davis, *Lifting as They Climb: The National Association of Colored Women* (Washington, D.C.: National Association of Colored Women, 1933), 17-19.

behalf of children: (1) the need for educational opportunities, vocational training, and employment; (2) the importance of physical development; (3) the importance of moral education; (4) establishment of a secure home life; and (5) nurturance of overall capabilities to enable children to thrive in a social context that would place constraints on their lives because of their race. Although one need or another may have been the initial impetus for a particular program, in an important sense each program sought to address the needs of children in these five areas so that the well-being of children was nurtured comprehensively.[6] By 1900 there were approximately three hundred women's clubs throughout the United States, and almost every club addressed programmatically the needs of children.[7]

The following excerpts from the annual report of a local club and of the national organization from two different time periods describe the way in which the needs of children (e.g., for vocational training and better home environments) were understood and the kinds of programs (e.g., industrial schools, adult education for mothers and fathers) to be enacted:

Women's League of Wilmington, Del. (1897): Our League was organized Mar. 9, 1897 with a number of very earnest women. We now no. 83. Our object in organization was to establish an Industrial School for our girls. We feel the need of training the hand, as well as the head and especial to impress upon our girls that Labor is honorable. We therefore are trying to make it possible for them to learn the science of labor. We feel the oppression of the present condition of the laws of the South against our people. Indeed it is contagious for at times in the North, we find many obstacles. But this is an age of force, and the force that governs is the moral and intellectual force. And it is through and by the women that this event is to be brought about and the nation to whom the future belongs. What we need is men and women, History and Science filled with God as nature is full of God.[8]

The President's Statement (1930): The National Association of Colored Women is made to feel that as mothers, wives, sisters, and daughters of the men of the race, it should narrow its functions to combating the source of the evils that give the race the unenviable place it holds in the United States. We consider our deficiencies (the source of all our ills) as entirely within the home circle; we lack something of foundation which the race, as a whole, is not receiving at the proper time during childhood, something of beauty and culture that poor en-

6. For a full description of the club movement, see my book entitled *Awake, Arise, and Act: A Womanist Call for Black Liberation* (Cleveland: Pilgrim Press, 1994), chapter 4.
7. Williams, "The Club Movement among Colored Women of America," 117-31.
8. Subject Files, National Association of Colored Women, 1897-1962, Mary Church Terrell Papers, Manuscript Division, Library of Congress, Washington, D.C.

vironment is robbing our children of. . . . Consequently, at the Hot Springs meeting, 1930, the National Association of Colored Women took the fundamental step of narrowing the functions of the organization to the two departments of (1) Mother, Home, and Child, and (2) Negro Women in Industry. Through the department of Mother, Home, and Child, we would create better environments for colored children; would carry on a program of adult education for mothers and fathers; and encourage Negroes to love home, and to create homes (we do not mean mansions, but places in which children may be born and have the proper cultural background).[9]

In addition to starting industrial schools[10] and working to improve the home, establishing kindergartens was another means by which club women fulfilled their mission to children. In a discussion of the reasons for establishing kindergartens in the South, Mrs. A. H. Hunton (1866-1943), chair of the executive board of the Southern Federation of clubs in 1905, allows us to see a relationship between social factors and the club women's motivations for making children central to their agenda. She opens her article this way:

To those who believe that everything that contributes to the culture of right thought contributes also to the culture of right character, the kindergarten must hold a deep and active interest, since it is the most beautiful system of education extant for the training of those tender little human plants we call children in all of their relations to nature, man, and God.[11]

Mrs. Hunton goes on to discuss the great need for club women to undertake this work in the South because in only a few instances have kindergartens become part of the public school system for "any class of children." (In fact, some of the kindergartens were formed in association with black colleges.[12]) After noting

9. Davis, *Lifting as They Climb*, 88-89.

10. See August Meier, *Negro Thought in America, 1880-1915* (Ann Arbor, Mich.: Ann Arbor Paperbacks, 1966), 85-99. Industrial schools established by clubs were reflective of the programs of industrial education popular at the time. The philosophy of industrial education emphasized moral development, mental discipline, the development of manual skills, and learning trades. Among the skills and trades taught were shoemaking, bricklaying, masonry, carpentry, blacksmithing, cabinetmaking, farming, animal husbandry, printing for boys and domestic arts, sewing, dressmaking, and nursing for girls.

11. Mrs. A. H. Hunton, "Kindergarten Work in the South," *Alexander's Magazine* 2, no. 3 (July 1906): 29.

12. Hunton, "Kindergarten Work in the South," 30. There were kindergartens associated with Hampton Institute in Virginia; Atlanta University in Georgia; the State Normal School in Montgomery, Alabama; and Tuskegee Institute in Tuskegee, Alabama. Kindergartens such as these were supported financially by the institutions to which they were related; funds raised by individual clubs and the National Association were used to support others.

the benefits of kindergartens for the development of children ("through it the child enters the schoolroom with powers of observation quickened; ideas clear and ability to express them; with preparation that makes him advance more rapidly in writing, spelling, reading and numbers; and, last but not least, with a fit regard for the rights of others"), Mrs. Hunton asserts that there is a particular need for kindergartens that reach the "masses" of black children. In fact, she believes this last point informs most of the women's clubs, for whom kindergarten work is a priority: "It is in meeting this special need that our women have united their earnest efforts, for they know the value of this phase of education as a redeeming force in the world — and that in childhood alone lay our hopes for the future."[13] Indeed, the first department of the NACW was focused on the support of kindergartens through the sale of a pamphlet written by Mary Church Terrell entitled "The Progress of Colored Women."[14]

Mrs. Hunton concludes her article thus:

The kindergarten is peculiarly fitted to the needs of the Negro child —

1. Because home life for the masses is but in its formative period.

2. Because when the parent is laboring the tot is left to grow and develop alone — for the most part under vitiating influences.

3. Because the kindergarten takes away the need of reformatories and prisons.

4. Because the sweet faith truthfulness of childhood is protected and strengthened and the physical, mental and spiritual forces given the right trend.

5. Because in benefiting the child, the parent is also benefitted.

It is a source of regret that more philanthropy does not find its way to the kindergarten. In our large cities we need refuge for our young as we need nothing else. Let those who will study its beneficent effect, and there will not linger a shadow of a doubt as to its possibilities in the development of child nature.[15]

In sum, from the reports regarding the work of the black women's club movement on the behalf of children, these five ideas about children and the women's understanding of their obligations to them come to the fore:

1. Children are "human plants" who require proper environments and care in order to develop physically, mentally, and spiritually.

2. Children's nature is that of "sweet faith truthfulness," and this must be protected and strengthened.

13. Hunton, "Kindergarten Work in the South," 31.
14. Riggs, *Awake, Arise, and Act,* 75.
15. Hunton, "Kindergarten Work in the South," 32.

3. Children are gifts to the community (not simply to a single family) who represent that community's physical existence into the future as well as its theological raison d'être, its hope: promises unfulfilled for one generation will come to fruition in the next through the children.
4. The adult community has an obligation to provide the proper environments for the care, protection, and guidance of children as well as a duty to train adults to be adequate caregivers, protectors, and teachers.
5. By affecting the lives of children, both parents and the community are benefited: adults learn something about reciprocity in their relationships with children as their lives are extended into the future and thus given meaning.

Because the first president of the NACW, Mary Church Terrell, set the tone for the work on behalf of children, I will present her interpretation of these five ideas in a section below. I will first present a sketch of her personal and intellectual biography as the basis for the explication of her thought.

Mary Church Terrell (1863-1954)

Mary Eliza Church was born in 1863 to Robert R. Church (speculated to have been the first black millionaire in the South) and Louisa Ayers Church (owner of a fashionable hair salon) in Memphis, Tennessee.[16] Mary Church was born the year of the Emancipation Proclamation and did not know slavery herself, but both her parents had been slaves. These facts of her birth were to play an important role in the way her parents would raise her and how she came to see the world. In her autobiography, she would speak with pathos and anger about the impact of slavery on the lives of mothers and children — a pathos and anger that seem to ground her later thoughts about the impact of social circumstances upon children and the response that impact required of the community of adults.[17]

Because her parents wanted the best education for their daughter, Mary was sent to Ohio, where she attended the "Model School" connected to Antioch College. She graduated from Oberlin High School, and later earned a bachelor's

16. See *African American Women: A Biographical Dictionary,* ed. Dorothy C. Salem (New York: Garland Publishing, 1993), for an entry on Mary Church Terrell that gives a fuller biographical account and a list of bibliographic resources for further research into Terrell's life.

17. Mary Church Terrell, *A Colored Woman in a White World* (Washington, D.C.: Ransdall, Inc., 1940), 1, 5.

degree from Oberlin College in 1884 and a master's degree from the same institution between 1888 and 1890. She traveled and studied abroad in England, Belgium, Switzerland, France, and Germany. She taught at Wilberforce University and at a high school in Washington, D.C.

After marrying Robert H. Terrell (a Harvard graduate who was eventually appointed a municipal judge in Washington), Mary Church Terrell began an active career as a public lecturer in the United States and abroad, speaking on a wide range of topics — lynching in the United States, the convict lease system, world peace, the role of colored women in uplifting the race, segregation, and other social issues as they would arise. It is in her work as a public lecturer and three-time president of the National Association of Colored Women that her thought as a practical theologian[18] can be discerned.

As a practical theologian, Mary Church Terrell began with three practical questions: (1) how to address the pain that "colored" mothers felt for their children ("Seeing their children touched and seared and wounded by race prejudice is one of the heaviest crosses which colored women have to bear");[19] (2) how to inculcate adequate values and knowledge in children; and (3) how to create a social context in which children could flourish. These practical questions derived from her own experience as a mother who "sought to keep [her two daughters] from being humiliated by Jim Crow,"[20] the experiences of working-class mothers in relation to their needs for child care, and the impact of a legacy of slavery and segregation generally and the inadequacies of segregated educational systems in particular. Terrell's response to these practical questions was informed by her early religious training in the Christian Church in Yellow Springs, by her development as a member of the First Congregational Church of Oberlin while in high school and college, and by her studies at Oberlin College, a college that during the nineteenth century had "acquired unusual features such as coeducation, a policy of admitting Negroes, an intense and constant support for abolitionism and other moral and social-reform causes, adherence to a mild form of Christian perfectionism, and the leadership of the powerful evangelist Charles Grandison Finney."[21]

18. See Don S. Browning et al., *From Culture Wars to Common Ground: Religion and the American Family Debate* (Louisville, Ky.: Westminster/John Knox Press, 1997), 8. The authors give this definition of practical theology: "a style of doing theology that begins with practical questions, describes the situations from which the questions come, and searches the classic expressions of the Christian faith for guidance." This definition informs my description of Terrell as a practical theologian.

19. Terrell, *A Colored Woman in a White World*, 17.

20. Terrell, *A Colored Woman in a White World*, 239.

21. John Barnard, *From Evangelicalism to Progressivism at Oberlin College, 1866-1917* (Columbus: Ohio State University Press, 1969), 3.

It is not insignificant that Terrell received her degrees from Oberlin during the 1880s, the time of the college's theological transition from evangelicalism to progressivism. During the 1880s, students at Oberlin experienced "a social awakening," signifying a move toward a social-reform stance grounded upon a belief in both the reformation of the individual's character and structural changes in society.[22] In fact, the version of the Social Gospel advanced by Reverend Washington Gladden (1836-1918), who was associated with Oberlin at the time, "closely accorded with the idea of reform embraced by most Oberlin students."[23] Likewise, biblical studies and theology at Oberlin underwent changes related to scientific biblical criticism and an attempt to hold together a traditional conception of a personal God and the new liberal idea of God at work in the world with humans to better the world.[24] Terrell's thought reflects both of these transitions in the ethos and educational curriculum of Oberlin as well as emphases of the Social Gospel. Although I have not discovered direct references to the writings of Social Gospel forerunners such as Washington Gladden and Walter Rauschenbusch (1861-1918) in Terrell's papers, I think the connections that I will later draw in this essay between the thought of Terrell and Gladden are legitimate, given Gladden's participation in the life of Oberlin during the time of Terrell's education there.

The Social Gospel refers to a historical movement that flourished from the end of the Civil War through the end of World War I. On the one hand, the movement began in response to problems and issues deriving from the growth of industrialization and urbanization, including crime, poverty, unemployment, exploitative employment practices, slums, and disease. On the other hand, the movement represented an attempt "to bridge the chasm between action, criticism, and doctrine within the Protestant tradition."[25]

As a theological movement, the Social Gospel represented a social reinterpretation of Christianity that sought to bring together theology and sociology. There were four broad theological tenets of the Social Gospel: (1) social salvation based upon a dynamic interpretation of the kingdom of God; (2) the immanence of God; (3) "the fatherhood of God and the brotherhood of man";

22. Barnard, *From Evangelicalism to Progressivism at Oberlin College, 1866-1917*, 64-65.

23. Barnard, *From Evangelicalism to Progressivism at Oberlin College, 1866-1917*, 93. Gladden became closely associated with Oberlin when he was made pastor of the First Congregational Church in Columbus, Ohio, in 1882. He delivered lectures and sermons at the college, and his writings were studied in courses in practical sociology.

24. Barnard, *From Evangelicalism to Progressivism at Oberlin College, 1866-1917*, 76-77.

25. Richard D. Knudten, *The Systematic Thought of Washington Gladden* (New York: Humanities Press, 1968), 11.

and (4) an emphasis not simply on charity but on justice.[26] The corollaries of these tenets are as follows:

1. The principles of Jesus are reliable guides for personal and social life in any age.
2. It is important to have a strong belief in progress, conditional upon human response to divine leading.
3. Human beings can be educated to make the right choices and so contribute to the coming of God's kingdom on earth.
4. It is important to establish an ethics of the kingdom of God that puts great emphasis on the law of love, asserting that individual sin (primarily selfishness) and the corporate transmission of sin through human institutions can be overcome when individuals and institutions are subject to the law of love.[27]

The Reverend Washington Gladden is often referred to as the father of the Social Gospel.[28] Gladden was raised in the Presbyterian Church; but even as a boy, he questioned sermons that he heard there because they emphasized the fear rather than the love of God and did not address human life and its problems. Because of his questioning spirit and the later influence of a Congregational minister, Gladden joined the Congregational Church and began preparing for the ministry at Owego Academy in 1855, completing his education at Williams College in 1859. In 1860 Gladden was licensed to preach by the Susquehanna Association of Congregational Ministers. That year he began a pastoral ministry that would not end until his retirement from the First Congregational Church of Columbus, Ohio, in 1914.

Gladden's first and second pastorates both involved critical turning points for him. Gladden undertook his first pastorate in 1860, serving the First Congregational Methodist Church in Brooklyn, which was in the midst of a shift toward applied Christianity with respect to temperance and slavery issues. Gladden's second pastorate in Morrisania (1861-1866) afforded him the opportunity to read the New Theology of Horace Bushnell; Bushnell's theology became the basis for "his own interpretation of Calvinist-Congregational the-

26. Ronald C. White Jr., *Liberty and Justice for All: Racial Reform and the Social Gospel, 1877-1925* (San Francisco: Harper & Row, 1990), xix-xxii. See also Knudten, *The Systematic Thought of Washington Gladden*, 45-53.

27. Robert T. Handy, "Social Gospel," in *The Westminster Dictionary of Christian Ethics*, ed. James F. Childress and John Macquarrie (Philadelphia: Westminster Press, 1986), 593.

28. The following description of Gladden is based upon Knudten, *The Systematic Thought of Washington Gladden*, 21-42.

ology."[29] By the time that Gladden accepted the call to his last pastorate — the First Congregational Church of Columbus, Ohio — in 1882, he had honed his theology by serving hospitals during the Civil War, by serving as religion editor of the *New York Independent,* and by writing on socio-economic issues in light of the economic collapse of 1873. It was as pastor of the church in Columbus that Gladden became closely associated with Oberlin College; he delivered lectures and sermons at the college, and his writings were studied in courses in practical sociology.[30] Over the years, Gladden would be recognized as "a pioneer in three general fields — the popular exposition of new Biblical scholarship, the social application of the Gospel, and the presentation of liberal theology."[31]

Overall, the Social Gospel movement was operative among ministers and laypersons who carried out their work as pastors, educators, editors, and leaders in social-reform organizations. Among the social-reform efforts associated with this movement was that of racial reform, and a number of African American pastors and laity espoused the Social Gospel, including William N. DeBerry, Francis G. Grimke, George E. Haynes, Kelly Miller, Henry Hugh Proctor, Mary Church Terrell, Alexander Walters, and Ida B. Wells-Barnett.[32] In fact, reform organizations came to be interpreted by the Social Gospel as "'the church outside the churches.'"[33]

As important as it is that the religious roots of Terrell's thought can be found in the Social Gospel, it would be an oversight not to note that her thought is also informed by race-class ideologies among African Americans during the late nineteenth century. These ideologies emphasized racial solidarity, self-help, and group economy as the basis for racial advancement by means of economic and moral development. Debates about the strategies of racial advancement proposed by Booker T. Washington (accomodationist/integrationist) and W. E. B. DuBois (protest/nationalist) were a hallmark of the late nineteenth century. The positions for racial advancement espoused by Terrell and the NACW were considered to mediate between the ideologies and strategies of Washington and DuBois, thus sustaining the necessary link between the development of the African American as an individual and African Americans as a social group.

Although Terrell lived a very privileged life from birth through adulthood, it would be her own experiences with racial discrimination in spite of her privilege, a keen empathy for others, and a sharp mind for analyzing the roots

29. Knudten, *The Systematic Thought of Washington Gladden,* 26.

30. Barnard, *From Evangelicalism to Progressivism at Oberlin College, 1866-1917,* 93.

31. Knudten, *The Systematic Thought of Washington Gladden,* 41.

32. White, *Liberty and Justice for All,* xvii, xix. See also Calvin S. Morris, *Reverdy C. Ransom, Black Advocate of the Social Gospel* (Lanham, Md.: University Press of America, 1990), chapter 4.

33. See White, *Liberty and Justice for All,* chapter 14.

of social issues that would make her an effective spokesperson and moral agent for justice. As Gladys Byram Shepperd, an interpreter of her life, comments, "One source of her strength as a power for social reform was that her personality was a rare combination of the high intellectual in close understanding with the masses."[34] In the section that follows, I will explicate Terrell's thought.

Mary Church Terrell's Understanding of Work on Behalf of Children

In this explication, I will use the (previously listed) five ideas underlying the work of the club movement on behalf of children as key areas to highlight in Terrell's thought. I will also draw connections between Terrell's ideas and the Social Gospel, especially as found in the thought of Washington Gladden.[35]

1. *Children are "human plants" who require proper environments and care in order to develop physically, mentally, and spiritually.*

Terrell accepts this description of children and their needs because of the living conditions and social conditions of children that she observed. She describes children as having to tread "thorny paths of prejudice, temptation, and injustice," and goes on to assert that it is in "miserable hovels" that young criminals are bred. This is her description:

> Make a tour of the settlements of colored people, who in many cities are crowded into the most noisome sections permitted by the municipal government, and behold the mites of humanity who infest them. Here are our little ones, the future representatives of the race, fairly drinking in the pernicious example of their elders, coming in contact with nothing but ignorance and vice till, at the age of four, evil habits are formed which no amount of civilizing or Christianizing will ever completely break.[36]

---

34. Gladys Byram Shepperd, *Mary Church Terrell: Respectable Person* (Baltimore: Human Relations Press, 1959), 25.

35. The primary source document for this explication is an article by Mary Church Terrell entitled "The Duty of the National Association of Colored Women to the Race," *A.M.E. Church Review* 16, no. 3 (January 1900): 340-54. It is not insignificant that this essay was published in the journal of a historic black denomination, the African Methodist Episcopal Church.

36. Mary Church Terrell, "Club Work of Colored Women," *The Southern Workman* 30, no. 8 (August 1901): 438.

The more unfavorable the environments of children the more necessary is it that steps be taken to counteract baleful influences upon innocent victims.[37]

Thus Terrell insists on the kindergarten as a proper and needed environment. She remarks that through it "children have been cultivated and trained" — that it has the capacity to save them: "Through the kindergarten alone, which teaches its lesson in the most impressionable years of childhood, shall we be able to save countless thousands of our little ones who are going to destruction before our very eyes."[38]

Terrell's thought begins with the living conditions of children that one encounters in the settlements of colored people, which is a first indicator that she stands within the tradition of the Social Gospel, as author Ronald White points out: "The story of the embracing of a Social Gospel has a familiar if plaintive refrain. Personal encounter with human misery that, upon reflection, is seen to be not an individual problem but one of society is always a starting point."[39] Terrell's observations about the negative impact of settlement conditions and the suffering of children under such conditions are also indicative of the way that the Social Gospel understands social evil. Richard Knudten makes this point in his discussion of Washington Gladden:

> Since physical suffering is only a sympton of evil, men must work to alleviate the power of evil. "Suffering," Gladden commented, "is a consequence, and not a cause; and we often make a great mistake in trying to remove the consequence without touching the cause, — leaving the cause, indeed, actively at work to produce more suffering."[40]

Establishing kindergartens for needy children may be interpreted as a strong step toward eliminating the evil of poverty and race oppression that causes children's suffering — a task that the women's club movement undertook as part of the "church outside the churches."

37. Terrell, "Club Work of Colored Women."

38. Terrell, "The Duty of the National Association of Colored Women to the Race," 341, 342.

39. White, *Liberty and Justice for All,* xviii. White notes that Washington Gladden's encounter with the unemployed in Springfield, Massachusetts, provided the initial impetus for him.

40. Knudten, *The Systematic Thought of Washington Gladden,* 65.

2. *Children's nature is that of "sweet faith truthfulness," and this must be protected and strengthened.*

This assertion about children's nature is both affirmed and qualified in Terrell's thought. On the one hand, Terrell speaks of children as "innocent victims"[41] and appeals to clubs to establish day nurseries for the children of working mothers: "When one thinks of the slaughter of the innocents which is occurring with pitiless persistency every day, and reflects upon how many are maimed for life through neglect, how many there are whose intellects are clouded because of the treatment received during their helpless infancy, establishing day nurseries can seem neither unnecessary nor far-fetched; but must appeal directly to us all."[42] On the other hand, Terrell also seems to affirm the need for proper environments and care precisely because there is also within children's nature a tainted side that will come to dominate if not properly directed:

> The National Association of Colored Women is listening to the cry of children. So keenly alive is it to the necessity of rescuing the little ones, whose evil nature alone is encouraged to develop and whose noble qualities are deadened and dwarfed by the very atmosphere which they breathe, that its officers are trying to raise money with which to send out a kindergarten organizer, whose duty it shall be to arouse the conscience of our women and to establish kindergartens wherever means therefor[e] can be secured.[43]

This apparent tension in Terrell's thought regarding the nature of children ("innocent victims" versus "little ones" with an evil nature) seems less problematic when one considers two theological presuppositions from the Social Gospel that may inform her thought. First, Terrell's "innocent victims" are those children who live in racist, economically oppressed conditions; they are innocent victims of the social sin of race and class oppression. Second, when Terrell describes the children as having an evil nature, she acknowledges the capacity for individual sin within the human being that will thrive if the individual is not properly educated to make moral choices.

Terrell's ideas align with Gladden's understanding that humans have inherited moral tendencies — both negative tendencies (to sin, toward evil) and positive tendencies (toward goodness, truth, honor, fidelity). It is by personal resolve or participation in better environments that the negative tendencies do

---

41. Terrell, "Club Work of Colored Women," 438.
42. Terrell, "The Duty of the National Association of Colored Women to the Race," 344.
43. Terrell, "Club Work of Colored Women," 438.

not prevail. Gladden did not believe in total depravity; he believed that it is the environment in which the person is nurtured that is of critical importance. In Gladden's words, "'The main fact is that a good environment will prevail over a bad heredity.'"[44]

> 3. *Children are gifts to the community who represent that community's physical existence into the future as well as its theological raison d'être, its hope — promises unfulfilled for one generation will come to fruition in the next through the children.*

Terrell comes to affirm this idea through a struggle with the Old Testament idea of the "law of heredity" with regard to the transmission of sin from one generation to another and who she believes God to be. Recalling her study of the Bible as a college student, she notes, "I could not understand why a just and loving father [God] should make children suffer for the sins committed by their forefathers. The injustice of the law of heredity stunned me."[45] It seems that as Terrell matured (and perhaps because of her exposure to an emergent historical biblical criticism during her study of the Bible in college), she came to place a greater emphasis upon the fact that Scripture qualified upon whom the punishment would be inflicted — upon those who hated God. Thus, it became important to Terrell that black people avoid the penalty of the "law of heredity" by remembering the legacy of slavery in such a way that they not be determined by it or blame God for it. A mature Terrell, therefore, is able to affirm that God's justice orders the world, insisting that this should be the moral stance of black people: "Seeking no favors because of our color, nor patronage because of our needs, we knock at the bar of Justice and ask for an equal chance."[46] Here Terrell's ideas about God seem consistent with a Social Gospel understanding of God as "perfect justice, truth, benevolence, and purity."[47]

This theological affirmation of God's justice and the reminder to black people that they should not be determined by the legacy of slavery thus form the basis for believing in children as gifts to the community and the hope of the race. In 1900 Terrell rallied the NACW with these words emphasizing the promise of children:

44. Knudten, *The Systematic Thought of Washington Gladden*, 69.
45. Terrell, *A Colored Woman in a White World*, 42. She also said, "No verse came nearer shaking my faith in the justice of God than that one which states, 'I the Lord thy God am a jealous God, visiting the iniquity of the fathers upon the children unto the third and fourth generation of them that hate me, and showing mercy unto thousands of them that love me and keep my commandments'" (p. 42).
46. Terrell, "Club Work of Colored Women," 438.
47. Knudten, *The Systematic Thought of Washington Gladden*, 55-56.

Let us remember that we are banded together to do good, to work most vigorously and conscientiously upon that which will redound most to the welfare and progress of the race. If that be true, I recommend to you, I plead to you, for the children, for those who will soon represent us, for those by whom as a race we who shall soon stand or fall in the estimation of the world, for those upon whom the hope of every people must necessarily be built. As an Association, let us devote ourselves enthusiastically, conscientiously, to the children, with their warm little hearts, their susceptible little minds, their malleable, pliable characters. Through the children of to-day, we must build the foundation of the next generation upon such a rock of integrity, morality, and strength, both of body and mind, that the floods of prescription, prejudice, and persecution may descend upon it in torrents, and yet it will not be moved. We hear a great deal about the race problem, and how to solve it. This theory, that and the other, may be advanced, but the real solution of the race problem, both so far as we who are oppressed and those who oppress us are concerned, lies in the children.[48]

What seems most significant here is not that Terrell qualifies her interpretation of how the "sins of the fathers" are visited upon the children but that she moves constructively from a theological proposition about intergenerational sin to a theological affirmation about intergenerational hope.

4. *The adult community has an obligation to provide the proper environments for the care, protection, and guidance of children as well as a duty to train adults to be adequate caregivers, protectors, and teachers.*

In line with these ideas, Terrell sought to impress upon all women's clubs the necessity of finding the means to operate day nurseries, kindergartens, children's clubs, and mother's congresses. These programs offered "practical charity" to "imperative need."[49] She insisted that the "curriculum" of such programs include "telling and reading stories, teaching kindness to animals, politeness to elders, pity for the unfortunate and weak." The curriculum should be taught by adults who understood that they were working for a "revolution" whereby the children would provide capable leadership to the next generation

48. Terrell, "The Duty of the National Association of Colored Women to the Race," 345-46.

49. Terrell, "The Duty of the National Association of Colored Women to the Race," 343, 344. In her article Terrell underscores the imperative need to be addressed by citing some sad facts: that infants are often left in the inadequate care of older siblings or good-natured neighbors; that sometimes infants are left locked in a room, alone and dying; that in a particular case a baby of fourteen months had contracted rheumatism because the family was probably unable to heat their quarters and had nowhere else to go.

because they had learned to be "responsible for their thoughts" and to control their impulses toward evil.[50]

Furthermore, adults adequate to this task of effecting a revolution would themselves be trained to possess needful virtues that they would inculcate in children. For example, with reference to work, Terrell speaks of the need to have schools of domestic science. In these schools, adult women were to be taught skills and values to enhance their vocations, which would help them as well as their children. According to Terrell, "We are showing our women how fatal it will be to their highest, best interests and to the highest, best interests of their children, if the Negro does not soon build up a reputation for reliability and proficiency."[51]

"Practical charity" is the practice of love at the heart of the Social Gospel that compels Terrell to encourage club women to think of themselves as engaged in a "revolution" that will have both personal and social consequences. This also undergirds her insistence that the inculcation of virtues in children and adults is about the moral development of individuals and the social salvation of the black community. On the one hand, Terrell's admonishment to adults to become moral exemplars for children seems to capture the intent of a remark by Gladden: "'Children do not inherit their [parents'] sin; they inherit their example.'"[52] On the other hand, Terrell's understanding of the impact of this moral development upon how black people would be perceived and received by the larger society is a reflection of how her thought and work also embodied the features of the ideology for racial advancement operative at the time — the belief that inclusion in American society was contingent upon black people's ability to attain "respectability" according to middle-class norms and values.

5. *By affecting the lives of children, both parents and the community (humanity) are benefited: adults learn something about reciprocity in their relationships with children as their lives are extended into the future and thus given meaning.*

With this last idea, the overarching presupposition of Terrell's thought is set forth; she often speaks of the service being rendered to humanity and the race when the NACW fulfills its duty to children.[53] Her own relationship with

50. Terrell, "The Duty of the National Association of Colored Women to the Race," 345.

51. Mary Church Terrell, *The Progress of Colored Women* (n.p.: American Missionary Association, n.d.), 10.

52. Knudten, *The Systematic Thought of Washington Gladden*, 69-70.

53. See Terrell, "The Duty of the National Association of Colored Women to the Race," 344; and "Club Work of Colored Women," 437.

her daughters, as well as the relationship between black children and white children, seems the place to center this idea. Writing about her concern that her daughters not suffer the humiliation of Jim Crow, she speaks of teaching them how to get what is rightfully theirs:

> I taught my daughters that they were doing their Heavenly Father a service when they prevented anybody from treating His children with injustice, scorn or contempt solely on account of color or race. I taught them also they were justified in using any scheme, not actually criminal or illegal, to secure for themselves what representatives of other racial groups enjoyed, but of which they would be deprived on account of their African descent. I impressed upon them that they would perpetrate a great injustice upon themselves if they failed to take advantage of any good thing which they had a right to enjoy, simply because certain people had the power to deprive them of it by making arbitrary and unjust laws.[54]

Terrell is dismayed that she has to teach her children about the necessity of "subterfuge,"[55] but she is also acutely aware of the need to balance her aspirations for her children with the realities of the social world in which they must live. This is one way in which Terrell's thought demonstrates a reciprocity between children and adults: what we must teach our children in order to survive also chastens us about how in fact we must live.

As noted previously, Terrell affirms the belief that children are the hope for the future. When she turns to admonish white mothers about their role in raising children who will not continue the racist ways of the past and present, there is a point of departure for considering the relationship between the way we raise our children and the meaningfulness (or lack thereof) that our lives will hold in the future. Terrell writes,

> Let us . . . appeal directly to large-hearted, broad-minded women of the dominant race, and lay our case clearly before them. . . . Let us ask these women both to follow themselves, and teach their children, the lofty principles of humanity, charity and justice which they profess to observe. . . . Let the Association of colored women ask the white mothers of this country to teach their children that when they grow to be men and women, if they deliberately prevent their fellow creatures from earning their daily bread, by closing the doors of trade against them the Father of all men will hold them responsible for the crimes which are the result of their injustice, and for the human wrecks which the ruthless crushing of hope and ambition always makes. . . .

54. Terrell, *A Colored Woman in a White World*, 246.
55. Terrell, *A Colored Woman in a White World*, 246.

> In the name of justice and humanity, in the name of the innocence and help-lessness of childhood, black childhood, as well as white childhood, let us appeal to the white mothers of this country to do all in their power to make the future of our boys and girls as bright and promising as should be that of every child, born on this free American soil.[56]

This powerful quotation makes us mindful of the ultimate consequences of the morality or immorality of the way in which we raise our children.

Finally, Terrell offers this admonishment: "Let us not neglect, let us not forget, the children, remembering that when we love and protect the little ones, we follow in the footsteps of Him, who when He wished to paint the most beautiful picture of Beulah land it is possible for the human mind to conceive, pointed to the children and said — 'Of such is the kingdom of heaven.'"[57] This admonition shows Terrell's thought to be fully in line with a central tenet of the Social Gospel theology to which she was exposed: that it is finally the example of Jesus that gives us guidelines about our attitude and behavior toward children. Furthermore, her thought and the work of the clubs of the NACW on behalf of children reflected the Social Gospel's emphasis upon the potential of human beings to be educated to make moral choices and upon the fulfillment of divine purposes for reformation of injustices through both individuals and institutions operating from the law of love. In brief, the work of the club movement on behalf of children was work on behalf of the Kingdom of God.

Conclusion:
Significance of the Preceding for Theological Reflection and Moral Agency on Behalf of Children Today

In a book entitled *With Heart and Hand: The Black Church Working to Save Black Children,* these dire statistics are found:

> Every 46 seconds of the school day a black child drops out of school. Every 65 seconds a black teenager becomes sexually active. Every 104 seconds a black teenage girl becomes pregnant. Every 11 minutes a black child is arrested for

56. Terrell, "The Duty of the National Association of Colored Women to the Race," 350-51.
57. Terrell, "The Duty of the National Association of Colored Women to the Race," 346.

a violent crime. Every 20 hours a black child or young adult under twenty-five dies from causes related to HIV.[58]

Such a formidable list of issues affecting African American children has had two consequences. On the one hand, some churches and other agencies have been propelled into action, designing and implementing creative programs such as the ones described in the aforementioned book.[59] On the other hand, others of us both inside and outside of the church despair about what actual impact we might have upon the lives of African American children who seem captive to the values and ends of a racist, consumerist culture that, according to Cornel West, breeds "nihilism — the lived experience of coping with a life of horrifying meaninglessness, hopelessness, and lovelessness."[60]

When we turn to the thought of Mary Church Terrell and the work of the women's club movement, we are reminded that effective programs on behalf of African American children must be informed by the specific ethos and issues of the time in which we live. Just as the women's club reformers of the late nineteenth century analyzed and sought to address the collective needs of a people who had been emancipated from slavery for only thirty to forty years, so African Americans today must make contextually defined efforts on behalf of children. We must ask questions about the impact of public policy (e.g., welfare reform) on the lives of children as well as about what values (e.g., consumerism or compassion) they are being taught and by whom (e.g., the media or the church). Important points of departure for developing a theologically and ethically sound basis for contextually relevant work on behalf of African American children include these three that I have gleaned from Terrell and the club movement: (1) a particular view of God and sin; (2) the implications of moral education; and (3) the need for hopefulness.

The view of God as a God of justice and the view of sin as both personal and institutional were foundational to Terrell's thought and the work of the club movement. Neither of these emphases is new to current black and womanist theologies. However, Terrell's thought included criticism of practices and conditions internal to the black community, a criticism that sometimes gets slighted by contemporary theologians as we focus on the external structural realities that constrain African American life. We must be ever mindful

---

58. Susan D. Newman, *With Heart and Hand: The Black Church Working to Save Black Children* (Valley Forge, Pa.: Judson Press, 1994), vii.

59. Newman, *With Heart and Hand*. Programs in this book focus upon issues such as the adoption of black children, afterschool tutoring, living skills, career counseling, child care, homelessness, etc.

60. Cornel West, *Race Matters* (Boston: Beacon Press, 1993), 14.

that the God of justice makes claims upon all of us and that work on behalf of social salvation requires both personal and communal accountability.

This self-criticism of internal practices and conditions within the black community is most evident in Terrell's thought when she discusses the need for the moral training of adults who will be moral exemplars for children. Thus, the second area to which we must be attentive is moral education. Although the virtues (i.e., reliability and proficiency) that Terrell espoused may seem inadequate for our context, the fact is that she understood and sought to nurture a relationship between the practice of virtues and the reformation of the social context. Likewise, it is imperative that we think more concretely about the relationship between moral education and liberation, defined by both theological and social context. There is a sense in which we have become complacent about the moral nurture of African American children because the practices of oppression are more covert than overt, and we fail to even ask a critical question: What are the needful virtues for a liberated black humanity? While we may join in the current emphases upon character-building education, Terrell's thought reminds us that we must fine-tune these emphases to address the particular moral, spiritual, and social needs of African American children who continue to suffer racist, classist, and sexist assaults upon their minds, spirits, and bodies.[61]

Finally, Terrell's thought and the work of the club movement show that it is imperative to embrace anew African American children as *our hope.* We know that we will cease to exist physically as a social group without children. But Terrell and the club women remind us that the *soul* of African American people will cease to exist without our children.

---

61. For important discussions of the continuing emotional, spiritual, social, economic, and political plight of African Americn children, see Dr. Darlene Powell Hopson and Dr. Derek S. Hopson, *Different and Wonderful: Raising Black Children in a Race-Conscious Society* (New York: Simon & Schuster, 1990); James P. Commer, M.D., and Alvin F. Poussaint, M.D., *Raising Black Children* (New York: Penguin Books, 1992); and C. Eric Lincoln and Lawrence H. Mamiya, *The Black Church in the African American Experience* (Durham, N.C.: Duke University Press, 1990), chapter 11, "'In My Mother's House': The Black Church and Young People."

15. Reading Karl Barth on Children

WILLIAM WERPEHOWSKI

K arl Barth (1886-1968) was quite probably the greatest Protestant theologian of the twentieth century. Born in Basel, Switzerland, he decided to become a theologian at the age of fifteen on the eve of the day of his confirmation, "in the hope that through such a course of study I might reach a proper understanding of the creed in place of the rather hazy ideas that I had at that time."[1] Barth's second edition of his commentary on Paul's Epistle to the Romans[2] (1922) famously signaled a break with the legacy of nineteenth-century "liberalism," which, he believed, addressed not so much the utter sovereignty of God as the experience of the human religious quest. God is "wholly other" to any experiential route as such, and just so may be a truly *gracious* God who tells us a message of good news that we cannot tell ourselves. While he was a professor of systematic theology at Bonn (1930-35), Barth's convictions about the exclusive priority of God's revelation in Jesus Christ were put to work in his participation in the "Church Struggle" against Nazism's effort to co-opt German Christian witness by way of a racist and nationalist "natural theology." In May 1934 he played a major role in composing the Barmen Declaration of the German "Confessing Church"; it affirmed that "Jesus Christ, as he is attested to us in Holy Scripture, is the one word of God, whom we have to hear and whom we have to trust and obey in life and death. We condemn the false doctrine that

---

1. Karl Barth, quoted in Eberhard Busch, *Karl Barth: His Life from Letters and Autobiographical Texts* (Philadelphia: Fortress Press, 1975), 31.

2. Karl Barth, *The Epistle to the Romans* (Oxford: Oxford University Press, 1972).

Many thanks to Marcia Bunge, George Hunsinger, and Gilbert Meilaender for their great help as I was completing this essay.

the Church can and must recognize as God's revelation other events and powers, forms and truths, apart from and alongside this one Word of God."[3]

Barth was suspended from teaching when he refused to take the oath of loyalty to Hitler in November 1934, and by the following March he was forbidden by the Gestapo to speak in public. He returned to Switzerland and taught at the University of Basel until his retirement in 1962. During that time he also devoted himself to his greatest work, the *Church Dogmatics*. Spanning fourteen volumes (including unfinished "fragments"), the *Dogmatics* covers a vast range of theological topics. While Barth's commitments as a Reformed theologian led him to pay careful and groundbreaking attention to themes such as God's eternal election and an ethics of divine command, what distinguished his work, says Hans Frei, was the "startlingly consistent" identification of "universal divine action with divine action in Christ alone."[4] According to Frei, "Here God is present and known to us, and the only logical presupposition for this presence and this knowledge is — itself. For this unique thing there can be no set preconditions; it creates its own. No natural theology, no anthropology, no characterization of the human condition, no ideology or world view can set the conditions for theology or knowledge of God."[5] From this center Barth advanced a view of human existence encompassed and constituted by the *free grace* of the One who wills to be "*with* us, and in the same freedom to be not against us but, regardless and contrary to our desert, to be *for* us — [God in Jesus Christ] desires in fact to be humanity's partner and our omnipotent pitying Saviour."[6]

Barth's consideration of children in his work can be puzzling.[7] On the

---

3. Karl Barth, *Church Dogmatics,* II/1 (Edinburgh: T. & T. Clark, 1957), 172.

4. Hans W. Frei, *Theology and Narrative,* ed. George Hunsinger and William C. Placher (New York: Oxford University Press, 1993), 228.

5. Hans W. Frei, *Types of Christian Theology,* ed. George Hunsinger and William C. Placher (New Haven and London: Yale University Press, 1992), 154.

6. Karl Barth, "The Humanity of God," *Karl Barth: Theologian of Freedom,* ed. Clifford Green (Minneapolis: Fortress Press, 1991), 56. Green's volume is a good introductory collection of Barth's writings.

7. While it is beyond the scope of my study to connect Barth's theology concerning children with his own childhood and, more generally, his life with them, it is worth noting that these topics might also present a puzzle that awaits further study. Some recent scholarship has discussed Barth's difficult relationship with his mother, his discomfort around small children, and his relationship with his assistant, Charlotte von Kirschbaum, which brought great suffering to his wife and at least some of his children. Suzanne Selinger addresses these issues and sources in *Charlotte Von Kirschbaum and Karl Barth: A Study in Biography and the History of Theology* (University Park: Pennsylvania State University Press, 1998). But Eberhard Busch, relying on Barth's letters and autobiographical writings, makes a good case for Barth's great love of children, including the little ones, throughout his life, though in a context where work pulled him away from his family, and his wife,

one hand, he did not write much on the subject, and a good bit of what he did write was fragmentary or secondary to some other issue. In general, children hardly seemed to be at the core of his theological concerns. On the other hand, we have an extended section entitled "Parents and Children" in the *Church Dogmatics*[8] which, in combination with the other related reflections, affords a vantage point for rich and important insight. Perhaps some "reading between the lines" is necessary;[9] but the conviction underlying my *reading* or interpretation below is that *what Barth does say* about children offers a great look at his primary theological emphases and valuably contributes to the conversation that this volume of essays presents and hopes to further inspire.[10]

We can begin to understand the contribution by attending to a pair of "contrast cases," or striking examples of what Barth's approach to children *is not*. First, consider Augustine's well-known comments on his own infancy:

> Who can recall to me the sin I did in my infancy? *For in thy sight no one is clean of sin, not even the infant whose life is but one day upon earth.* . . . What, then, was my sin? Was it that I cried for more as I hung upon the breast? . . . Even in my infancy, therefore, I was doing something that deserved blame, but because I could not understand anyone who blamed me, custom and rea-

---

Nelly, assumed the major responsibility of childcare. For example, around the busy time when Barth was finishing his second edition of the Romans commentary, "he watched his children . . . growing up, with care and delight. He still had time, for example, to comb his son Christoph's hair every morning, 'more for my own pleasure than for his gain and satisfaction'" (Busch, *Karl Barth*, 121). On another front, Busch reports how Barth, during his years as pastor in the Swiss town of Safenwil (1911-21), immersed himself in his confirmation (and "pre-confirmation") classes, "told Bible stories to the twelve- to fourteen-year-olds in the so-called 'children's class' on Sundays after a sermon," and held weekly meetings for young people already confirmed. He felt strongly about what this instruction should be like: "It cannot merely be teaching and learning: we must discover each other personally and become good friends." Yet he also confessed that these tasks "were always a dreadful worry for me," that he often stood "awkwardly in front of bored faces," and usually he "simply ran out of steam, even in the most well-known things" (Busch, *Karl Barth*, 64-66). For a concise statement of the *theological* roots of Barth's spiritual and intellectual crisis in Safenwil, see Robert Jenson, "Karl Barth," in *The Modern Theologians*, ed. David F. Ford, 2d edition (Oxford: Blackwell, 1997), 21-22.

8. Karl Barth, *Church Dogmatics*, III/4 (Edinburgh: T. & T. Clark, 1961), 240-85.

9. Cf. Miller-McLemore's similar claim about feminist theology in her essay.

10. Frei discusses Barth's propensity to conceive the whole of his theology within each of its parts in *Types of Modern Theology*, 158. Gary Deddo analyzes the background logic of Barth's treatment of parents and children in *Karl Barth's Theology of Relations: Trinitarian, Christological, and Human: Towards an Ethic of the Family* (Frankfurt am Main: Peter Lang, 1999). The book came to my attention too late to consider it for the purposes of this essay.

son did not allow me to be blamed. . . . It is clear, indeed, that infants are harmless because of physical weakness, not because of any innocence of mind.[11]

As Stortz's contribution to this collection shows, we should proceed cautiously with a passage such as this, since Augustine appears to recognize that the "non-innocence" of infants falls short of their being guilty of specific sins (given their physical incapacity). Nevertheless, it also seems clear that (at least the later) Augustine claims that infants are born with evil tendencies by virtue of original sin, and that his view "fused biological ideas of heredity with the idea of the juridical liability of humanity."[12] Barth opposes this fusion, stressing instead that children are bearers of a promise of grace by virtue of God's will to make them, and all humanity, covenant partners in Jesus Christ. If he has anything at all to say about what is "proper" or "natural" to youngsters, it involves the readiness and capacity for a "beginner's" playful and therefore utterly objective freedom for God and with the neighbor. I will develop this and related themes in Part I below.

The second case has to do with the education of one Eric Blair, who between ages eight and thirteen attended "Crossgates," an English prep school "designed to prepare students for admission to schools like Harrow and Eton, where England's upper civil servants and leading professional men were trained."[13] Writing about this period over thirty years later under the name of George Orwell (1903-1950), he describes this part of his life in a way that is troubling but instructive.[14] "Learning" at Crossgates amounted to narrow preparation for qualifying exams on the one hand, and gaining a solid sense of Britain's hierarchical class system on the other. Blair's family was not rich; his intellectual promise brought him a scholarship along with the burden of performing well enough to make good on the school's investment and bring it credit. But his academic "success," for what that was worth, was degraded by the lessons of an environment that catered to the desires and expectations of wealthy, tuition-paying parents. Their kids were favored, were not disciplined, had birthday parties, were esteemed for what they *were*. In the end Eric came to

---

11. Augustine, *Confessions* I.7, trans. Rex Warner (New York: New American Library, 1963), 23-24.

12. Henry Chadwick, *Augustine* (New York and Oxford: Oxford University Press, 1986), 111.

13. Michael Walzer, *Spheres of Justice* (New York: Basic Books, 1983), 211.

14. George Orwell, "Such, Such Were the Joys . . ." in *A Collection of Essays* (New York and London: Harcourt, Brace & Company, 1946), 1-47. What Orwell has to say seriously concerns our prior issue of "original sin" in ways I cannot document here; see especially 1-6, 20.

see that he could not possibly bring credit to Crossgates. He was "not a good type of boy"; "in a world where the prime necessities were money, titled relatives, athleticism, tailor-made clothes, neatly brushed hair, a charming smile, I was no good."[15] Having won scholarships at Wellington and Eton, he departed prep school with an overwhelming conviction of failure and impending ruin.

This memoir discloses a palpable vision of the character of children's upbringing and the meaning of social justice with respect to them. Eric's growth was dictated by the commercial requirements of a corrupt educational system and a severely stratified workplace. He was repeatedly told that unless he won that scholarship, he was condemned to a life as "a little office-boy at forty pounds a year." In and out of class he was reminded that he was shamefully dependent and socially inferior. His greatest triumph really was just to "be an underling, a hanger-on of the people who really mattered."[16] Such instruction reflected norms of justice that were radically inegalitarian because of the tyranny of money.[17]

Rather than predicating a child's upbringing on the requirements of a social system, Karl Barth refers it first of all to the child's real invitation and opportunity to live joyfully for God. *All other disciplines — parental, social, economic, political — are relativized at their root by the discipline of God in the freedom of grace.* Social justice for children in God's world simply means securing social conditions that reflect the respect owed creatures beloved of their Creator, and hence speaking a word of hope to suffering fellow humanity. Where Blair/Orwell came away from Crossgates with a heart burdened by "the armies of unalterable law,"[18] we come away from Barth with a view of the world held up by the sovereign Creator and merciful Redeemer. I elaborate on this proposition in Part II.

I. Children's Being and Being a Child

Barth does not linger over the question of the specific "nature" or "being" of children. They, too, are creatures of God. Like all human creatures, they possess impulses and desires that must be respected and ordered to responsible existence. Under no circumstances should they be identified with an inherited strain of original sin. On this point we find, at once, a contrast to Augustine and

---

15. Orwell, "Such, Such Were the Joys . . ." 41-42.
16. Orwell, "Such, Such Were the Joys . . ." 32.
17. Cf. Walzer, *Spheres of Justice,* 95-128.
18. Orwell, "Such, Such Were the Joys . . ." 37.

others in the Christian tradition. Barth rejects outright hereditary transmission of sin as an "extremely unfortunate and mistaken" doctrine that would rule out a human agent's responsibility for the evil he or she does or becomes.[19]

Barth does accept "original sin" defined as "the voluntary and responsible life of every man . . . which by virtue of the judicial sentence passed on it in and with his reconciliation with God is the sin of every man, the corruption which he brings on himself so that as the one who does so . . . he is necessarily and inevitably corrupt."[20] A focus on voluntary decision does not exclude children from the range of this definition, unless one defines "children" exclusively as incapable of it; Barth, however, evidently sees no reason to single out what is at the very least a complicated case for purposes of analyzing the evil that youngsters do. He prefers to emphasize that the sin of humanity is really known *as it has already been set aside* by divine mercy in Christ. It is part of our past, not our future. Hence we discover the double contradiction of sin — it is a *fact* founded on a power that human creatures *do not have* as such, an "impossible possibility," what God, the source of all there is, *rejects*. And the contradictory being of sinful humanity is now once and for all put to death in Christ — yet still, absurdly, "lives."[21] Indeed, it has a supra-personal character in "lordless powers" that, though originally intrinsic to the self, "become spirits with a life and activity of their own."[22] Once all that is said, Barth believes himself prepared theologically to affirm the depth and terror of sin just because and as it maintains its absurd reality as fundamentally our human act, and never merely our inherited "fate." In summary, the theological pressure in this discussion of sin is directed toward honoring human creatures reconciled in Jesus Christ; human evil is taken with the greatest seriousness only in that context.

Note the related point that "what drives Barth's objection to infant baptism . . . is his insistence that the life of Christian discipleship 'cannot be inherited.'"[23] The focus here, however, is *social*. "No Christian environment, however genuine or sincere," he writes, "can transfer this [Christian] life to those who are in this environment. For these, too, the Christian life will and can begin

19. Karl Barth, *Church Dogmatics*, IV/1 (Edinburgh: T. & T. Clark, 1956), 500. Cf. John Webster, "'The Firmest Grasp of the Real': Barth on Original Sin," in John Webster, *Barth's Moral Theology* (Edinburgh: T. & T. Clark, 1998), 65-76.

20. Barth, *Church Dogmatics,* IV/1, 501.

21. Barth, *Church Dogmatics,* IV/1, 502-3.

22. Karl Barth, *The Christian Life: Church Dogmatics IV/4: Lecture Fragments* (Edinburgh: T. & T. Clark, 1981), 214. Cf. Webster, "'The Firmest Grasp of the Real': Barth on Original Sin," 74-75. These "lordless powers" include "Empire," "Mammon," and "ideologies." For the full discussion, see *The Christian Life*, 213-33.

23. John Webster, *Barth's Ethics of Reconciliation* (Cambridge: Cambridge University Press, 1995), 163.

only on the basis of their own liberation by God, their own decision." Baptism marks this beginning. Barth recognizes that infants and small children who have not yet reached the "age of discretion" continue to live in the light of objective, prevenient grace; but this is a "first chapter" of their history that should not be confused with a "second," their free movement of faith and obedience in response to God in Christ.[24]

In indirect yet unmistakeable ways, Barth is more alive to addressing not "children's being" but compelling conceptions of what it means to "be a child." These are recognizable, normative accounts, perhaps even "ideals," of a child's characteristic disposition or orientation. He presents at least the following three interrelated descriptions.

First, *children are needy beginners.* They are "inept, inexperienced, unskilled, and immature," but as such they may humbly acknowledge their need and assume a "sheer readiness to learn."[25] Barth writes this way about the fitting style of Christians, the children of God who *cry* to God their Father and who honor the Lord and their parents by being eager learners.[26] God wills that the whole life of God's dear children becomes an invocation aiming at recollection and renewal of a relationship of joyful intimacy and thanksgiving.

Second, *being a child is characteristically to be at play.* We discover this idea throughout Barth's rhapsodic writings on Wolfgang Amadeus Mozart. In his music, Mozart's *playing* reflects the absence of self-preoccupation. Unlike Beethoven, he is not focused on personal confession. He is not even about the "business" of communicating a message or doctrine (as Barth reads Bach). Mozart just "sounds and sings" with an objectivity that includes "an intuitive, childlike awareness of the essence or center — as also the beginning and end — of all things."[27] He does not *burden* his listeners, but in his modest freedom leaves them free to hear what he hears. What is Mozart's freedom? It is "an invitation to venture just a little out of the snail's shell of [one's] own subjectivity." It means immersing oneself in the activity at hand, which is no less than to witness and celebrate the glory of God through "a *turning* in which the light rises and the shadows fall, in which joy overtakes sorrow without extinguishing it, in which the Yea rings louder than the ever-present Nay."[28] Barth does not organize — let alone argue for — the facets of his description: self-forgetfulness,

---

24. Karl Barth, *Church Dogmatics,* IV/4 (Fragment) (Edinburgh: T. & T. Clark, 1969), 184, 181-82.

25. Barth, *The Christian Life,* 79-80. See Barth's brief parallel discussion in *Church Dogmatics,* IV/4 (Fragment), 180.

26. Barth, *Church Dogmatics,* III/4, 243, 245.

27. Karl Barth, *Wolfgang Amadeus Mozart,* trans. Clarence K. Pott (Grand Rapids, Mich.: Eerdmans, 1986), 16.

28. Barth, *Wolfgang Amadeus Mozart,* 55.

untoiling involvement, joyous objectivity, and clear-sighted cheerfulness not ignorant of darkness. It is no less striking and resonant for that.

The third portrayal is a bit more systematic, although it refers explicitly not to "being a child" but rather to "the young's" specific opportunity to realize their "freedom in limitation." Finite persons respond to God's call; they have a limited time and stand in a particular "vocation" or "place of responsibility." That place includes one's chronological stage of life. Barth repeats the theme that, whether we be "young," "mature," or "old," we are to respond to God's requirements for us "as if we were just setting out." Although he insists that we will do so as the same person we have become, he is just as resolute about our being also and especially "beginners" in our response to grace. The mature adult, however, makes this response by taking with relatively greater seriousness the fact that *now* is the time for bold ventures and good work to be done, following the preparations of youth. Still, he or she must not fail to venture still as a "child at play," a "student," or an "explorer," keeping a humble good humor.[29] The elderly person has the special opportunity "to discover that the Sovereign comes to meet him and to take him to Himself" — that is, to understand more deeply how indeed one's life of free decisions and deeds possess only such value as they gain from unmerited grace.[30] Understanding, though, should not be accompanied by the assumption that old age necessarily brings "undisturbed tranquility," "inactive reminiscence," or merely repetitive performance.

These moments of resolution and relinquishment apply to particular life periods while also coinhering with one another and with *youth's* special opportunity across the whole of life. Now what again is that? It is the *readiness to step into freedom* relatively unencumbered by the trappings of custom, habit, or an "established" past. The step presupposes a "youthful objectivity" that openly and in "fruitful astonishment" apprehends God's call at remove from any frozen portrait (or self-portrait) that gathers dust as it wins one's heart. Young people are to be an example to the older in this ever fresh hearing of the divine command.

The three descriptions of "being a child" develop from an elaborate theological vision. Barth sets them before his readers as part of the attempt to witness to God's Word, revealed in Jesus Christ and attested to in Holy Scripture. They are warranted for him by the way they fit within a full and faithful account of the identity of God and God's covenant with humanity, and not by a view of what is deemed "essential childhood" in, say, its natural access to the divine. The three together give us a glimpse of the Christian life as Barth often portrays it; moreover, though Barth himself does not tend to use these descrip-

---

29. Barth, *Church Dogmatics*, III/4, 613.
30. Barth, *Church Dogmatics*, III/4, 617.

tions as a basis for discussing our obligations to children, they offer some direction for our thought about children's nurturance and education. If "being a child" properly has to do with unashamed neediness, a beginner's readiness to learn, self-forgetting play, and youthful objectivity, then care and responsibility for them requires attention to need, encouragement of learning and learning anew, instruction in living by grace alone, and inspiration for stepping into freedom with hope and without fear. In the next section I will place these and other demands within the structure of Barth's extended discussion of the ethics of "parents and children."

II. "But Bring Them Up in the Discipline and Instruction of the Lord"

Two interests formally launch the discussion. The first is to specify Barth's dictum that "humanity is fellow-humanity." Elected in Christ to covenant partnership with God, human creatures correspond to that election by being made for covenant partnership with one another. Barth takes the differentiated relation of humanity as male and female to be normatively unavoidable and paradigmatic; the differentiation in the relation of parents and children is analogously compelling for him. Just as the "creaturely nature" of humanity encompasses existence as male or female, so too in a sequence of generations one exists as the child of one's (biological) parents. "To the extent that it is understood as fellow-humanity, our humanity necessarily has these two dimensions."[31] Barth's second interest, simply stated, is to explicate the divine commandment that children honor their mother and father.

We may discover the *content* of Barth's moral analysis by directing our attention to his passing commentaries on Ephesians 6:1-4: "Children, obey your parents in the Lord, for this is right. 'Honor your mother and father' (this is the first commandment with a promise), 'that it may be well with you and that you may live long on the earth.' Fathers, do not provoke your children to anger, but bring them up in the discipline and instruction of the Lord."[32] The first two sentences indicate the basis, limit, and meaning of parental authority and filial honor. Together with the subsequent injunction, the passage as a whole is a guide for the nurturance and education of children.

The essential basis of parental authority is not biological origin or seniority or assumed or established virtue. It consists in a divinely appointed spiritual

31. Barth, *Church Dogmatics*, III/4, 285.
32. Barth, *Church Dogmatics*, III/4, 242, 282-83.

mission to carry and mediate a promise of grace to one's children ("this is the first commandment with a promise"). Parents "from the standpoint of children have a Godward aspect, and are for them God's natural and primary representatives."[33] In their seniority, greater experience, and causal efficacy in bringing their children to be, they command their children's attention with special prominence, and may by divine grace correspond to God's being and act compatibly with their mission. Barth will not "invert this proposition . . . to say that parents should feel and act towards their children as God's representatives"; he warns against their succumbing "to a primitive and otherwise concealed desire to dictate and command."[34] Yet they are summoned as "elders" over their children to fit their action to the being and action of God, "to undertake the duty and dignity of being to [them] witnesses of this Word, and their work toward their children has thus the aim and the promise spoken of in Prov. 2:1-6: 'My son, if thou wilt receive my words, and hide my commandments with thee . . . then shalt thou understand the fear of the Lord, and find the knowledge of God. For the Lord giveth wisdom; out of his mouth come knowledge and understanding.'"[35]

A result of this position is that authority is both categorically affirmed and twice relativized. It is relativized, of course, "vertically" with reference to the being and action of God to which parents attest. That is, it is measured by the authority of God and cannot remain unchallenged by the requirements of the first commandment: "We have to do with the command of God when a young man knows that he is called to honor his parents for the sake of God and to His glory, to let himself be taught and guided by his parents in order to be the child of God. Only when we put the matter in this way does the command emerge in its true stature, independent of all natural impulses and social conventions."[36] Parents may be honored by exercising an authority over their children that is directed theocentrically away from itself.

But the exercise of this authority is also relativized "horizontally" or interpersonally in that the call to "elder" children covers a range of possibilities and situations. For instance, biological parents should be elders in a decisive but not exclusive sense; their responsibility should not insulate itself from the witness of others who may not be parents of this or that set of children but who can and should also instruct and edify them. Barth makes the point explicitly regarding married couples who, though "childless," may still be called to be el-

---

33. Barth, *Church Dogmatics*, III/4, 242, 245. Cf. what Barth says in his 1928 *Ethics*, trans. Geoffrey Bromiley (New York: Seabury, 1981), 241.

34. Barth, *Church Dogmatics*, III/4, 278-79.

35. Barth, *Church Dogmatics*, III/4, 247.

36. Barth, *Church Dogmatics*, III/4, 251-52.

ders "who in regard to all young people have the same task as physical parents have toward their physical offspring."[37] The "horizontal" move appears also to apply to adoptive mothers and fathers who are often unfairly stigmatized as not being their children's "real parents"; the stigma is possible because of a presumption that biological origin establishes an intrinsic importance independent of a required mission to help make of our children real children of God.[38]

The two qualifications establish a limit to a father's and mother's direction and self-understanding. Parents ought not to *dominate* their children as their "creator," their "senior," or their "teacher." Children "are not by nature their property, subjects, servants, or even pupils, but their apprentices, who are entrusted and subordinated to them in order that they might lead them into the way of life."[39] Clearly, instruction that gives pride of place to idols of family line or traditions is out. So is an isolated parenthood that has no use for the help of other witnesses to God's Word. And since parents must see to it that God should occupy for one's children "a firm and independent place," the possibility also exists that children may be called *out* of the history of the parent-child bond to assume "a special vocation to bear direct witness to God's eternal kingdom." Although this "orphaned state" ultimately would not destroy the bond but rather renew it, it may and will bring real and painful conflict.[40] The exceptional case may also apply to parents along these lines. Barth offers no specific scenario of what the ex-

37. Barth, *Church Dogmatics*, III/4, 268. I do not think that Barth is holding that the "motherliness" and "fatherliness" to which childless couples are called are identical to the mandate of "mothers" and "fathers" in the sense that they have the "same" authority to instruct my children as I have to instruct them. I believe he is saying that a number of folks may be "elders" to my children as witnesses to God's Word, and that my parenthood, however fittingly privileged in its "Godward" aspect by way of procreation, seniority, or (relative) wisdom, should be in solidarity with the calling of others who are distinct but not separate from me in their mission to care. My parenthood, moreover, ought not to embody the "indolent peace of a clannish warmth in relation to [my children], with its necessary implication of cold war against all others." See Barth, *Church Dogmatics*, IV/2, trans. G. W. Bromiley (Edinburgh: T. & T. Clark, 1958), 551. I am grateful to Gilbert Meilaender and Marcia Bunge for their help on this issue.

38. One can oppose the presumption and still hold that parents have a stringent (but not indefeasible) prima facie duty to raise their biological children. This surely seems to be Barth's view, though he could be clearer about its grounds. He also fails to highlight, despite his principled openness to adoption, the way in which a married couple's faithful love helps establish the loving fidelity and responsibility for the life and well-being of their children — even when the latter are not "biological." Here we might find another (Trinitarian?) "Godward" aspect that does not constitute parental authority but fittingly points to its source. On these matters, see William Werpehowski, "The Vocation of Parenthood," *Journal of Religious Ethics* 25, no. 1 (Spring 1997): 177-82.

39. Barth, *Church Dogmatics*, III/4, 243.

40. Barth, *Church Dogmatics*, III/4, 260-65.

ception entails; he is content to describe a borderline with warnings formally testing an agent's judgment that he or she has reached it.

If filial authority is rightly exercised by witnessing to God's gracious lordship, and if witness necessarily makes room for children's comprehension of God's prior and independent authority, then what does it mean *specifically* for a son or daughter to honor his or her parents? The answer depends on his or her stage of life and on the nature of parental care; but in all cases the goal remains *willingly to learn the freedom of obedience to God.*

The small child "must first learn to stand and walk," and is likely to need "simply to accept" parental guidance. It is an error to suppose, however, that the youngster is to behave merely as the object of parental wishes. Whenever possible, initiatives are to be encouraged, and parents must appeal to the child's budding freedom and responsibility by way of the "higher court" of divine jurisdiction. So "even the obedience of the little child is an honoring of its parents precisely in proportion as it is content to accept this intimation and to be challenged to adopt a mode of conduct which is in its own way voluntary and relatively independent of immediate parental directives."[41] Adolescence does not remove the need for some continuing parental heteronomy, but the child should continually learn that he "must already render his own account to this higher court, engaging in personal reflection on the meaning and purpose of what his parents expect of him, treading in his own ways and making his own judgments." The adult remains subject to the command to honor, though heteronomy has given way to personal autonomy in responsibility to God. One now "is to demonstrate in the power of the Spirit that he was not led and did not walk in vain along the way which had to begin . . . with sheer learning and obedience," *and hence* should heed parental counsel "in a way which is deeper, finer, and more worthy than anything which has perhaps preceded." There may be no evasion of the "bar of judgment" constituted by parental example and teaching.[42]

A poignant and perhaps more troubling test involves keeping the command in the face of parents' failures. Parents, too, are sinners who rely on God's mercy. The validity of the command does not and cannot depend "on the actualization of the notion of ideal parents," and children cannot decide to disqualify parents of their mission for poor performance. One hopes that in many cases, children, though "disturbed and troubled," are "not misled" by their parents in their representative role, and that they will accordingly honor them within the framework of their greater honoring of God. Even in the case where a child is convinced that his or her parents have failed outright in their duties,

---

41. Barth, *Church Dogmatics,* III/4, 253.
42. Barth, *Church Dogmatics,* III/4, 254-55.

the command is kept in refusing to imitate their failures, by avoiding self-righteous "cursing and mocking" of them, and by rushing to God's faithfulness all the more rather than transferring one's disillusionment to God. Finally, Barth asks that children, understanding their need for divine patience, witness to it by exercising patience "in the sense of continually taking them [their parents] with fresh seriousness in spite of everything, and therefore not ceasing to question them and to try to hear from them what a child should hear from its parents. Who knows how many erring parents might not have been helped, how many recalled to a sense of their mission, if they had not been too soon — and so long as they live there is always time for their conversion — abandoned as hopeless by their children and arbitrarily dismissed from their divinely appointed task?"[43] The command to honor is kept even in resisting an absolute decision that parents are and will be nothing but an offense.

Despite all of this attention to filial piety, we are justified in pressing a question about the shape, if you will, of *parental success*. What counts as good guidance and nurturance for Barth? How should children be cared for and raised? The guidelines about parents' "ambassadorial" function — their duty to attest to their children a divine promise that establishes both the priority of God's gracious authority and the goal of human freedom — does not *secure our understanding* so much as *prompt an inquiry* into details. What follows is the result of my own.

First, we should not be misled by Barth's requirement of *autonomy* as the purpose of the care and instruction of children. He is not speaking of an atomistic, abstract independence from social roles and relations. Freedom for God entails a divine permission for obedience to divine command. Interpersonal freedom is always for and with one's fellow in bonds of mutual assistance. Human freedom is also limited by time and our physical and social embodiment. Although Barth's ethics strongly endorse the unique particularity of individuals who answer to God as such, the demands of "obedient willing" concern neither self-absorbed isolation nor a laissez-faire indifference on others' part. Care and instruction of children, therefore, may be directed toward self-respecting sociality and valuing one's particular projects within creaturely limits.[44]

43. Barth, *Church Dogmatics*, III/4, 257.
44. For Barth on "obediently willing" one's particular identity and projects, see Gene Outka, "Universal Love and Impartiality," in *The Love Commandments*, ed. Edmund N. Santurri and William Werpehowski (Washington, D.C.: Georgetown University Press, 1992), 51-53. Cf. Kathryn Tanner, *The Politics of God* (Minneapolis: Fortress Press, 1992), 193-223; and William Werpehowski, "What Shall Parents Teach Their Children?" in *Why Are We Here? Everyday Questions and the Christian Life*, ed. Ronald F. Thiemann and William C. Placher (Harrisburg, Pa.: Trinity Press International, 1998), 118-24.

Second, parental love is distinguished from "every mimicry of love" by the way it communicates to children that their lives "are under the guardian-ship and guidance of the One who really undertakes for them." Positively, this means that love is "unconditional" as it points to God's love, which penetrates all roles, expectations, and worldly valuations in pursuit of the genuine good of the person in his or her irreplaceable identity. Negatively, parents cannot act in their children's best interests if they try "to clear away all obstacles to their progress," or if they attempt to mold the shape of their lives to conform as much as possible to their own, or if they see in them a good warranting ulti-mate sacrifices and exertions. In different ways these are all strategies for play-ing God — the Comforter, the Pattern, the Self-Sacrificing Victim — and so fall short. They cannot respond to real need or advance human wholeness.[45]

Third, the education of children cannot ignore exemplary social patterns to which children should adapt, just as it cannot escape concern for bringing up children to be independent individuals. Barth refers to a "stricter" and a "looser" discipline that should correspond to these considerations, respectively. The "crucial question" remains "whether parents themselves are genuinely and truly and radically disciplined, so that through their active self-discipline there may be seen the discipline which they themselves experience and which does not emanate either from the pattern or from the individual but the Subject of which is God Himself."[46] However a child is brought up to be "one's own" and also to "belong" to society and social traditions, he or she above all is to learn to be a child of God.

Fourth, "Christian exhortation as such can never point in the direction of disciplinary severity." To raise children "in the discipline and instruction of the Lord" excludes provoking them to the anger, resistance, and rebellion that emerges through the "assertion of Law, or the execution of judgment." Admo-nitions in the book of Proverbs not to spare the rod of correction must be transformed by the duty to know and correspond in thought and deed to grace, and *in that light* to summon children to repentance. A mother's and father's training and advice are to be a "joyful invitation to their children to rejoice with them"[47] in Jesus Christ. "To be joyful," Barth explains, "is to expect that life will reveal itself as God's gift of grace, that it will present and offer itself in provi-sional fulfillments of its meaning and intention as movement. To be joyful means to look out for opportunities for gratitude."[48] The work of parents is limited by time and a receding social space in which other influences on chil-

45. Barth, *Church Dogmatics*, III/4, 279.
46. Barth, *Church Dogmatics*, III/4, 280.
47. Barth, *Church Dogmatics*, III/4, 283.
48. Barth, *Church Dogmatics*, III/4, 378.

dren increasingly come into play. It is limited by the fact that parents cannot relieve their sons and daughters of personal responsibility. How much more vigorously must it be said that parents may nevertheless "give their children the opportunity to encounter the God who is present, operative and revealed in Jesus Christ, to know him and to learn to love and fear Him," and to that extent offer them a life that is joyful.[49]

Fifth, Christian instruction includes three practices which, with many others, accord roughly with the accounts of "being a child" presented in Part I. Parents and other "elders," for a start, should teach children to pray. At any age, invocation of God, giving thanks and praise "in unreserved acceptance of [one's] neediness" for God's free gifts, is constitutive of Christian life. We learn how to be children of God, eager listeners and needy beginners, in part through the practice of prayer. In fact, we learn to present ourselves joyfully before God as who we really are, putting aside our "roles," "masks," and "camouflages" for the sake of gratitude, repentance, and worship.[50]

Elders should also instruct youngsters in the practice of keeping the Sabbath day holy. This day of rest, its "interruption" of our worldly cares and affairs, gives a "temporal pause to reflect on God and his work." More, the command to keep this day "says that man's own work is to be performed as a work bounded by this continually recurring interruption," this opportunity to rejoice in free readiness for the Gospel. Barth writes in this connection of the need for a "renouncing faith" in God that gives up on trust in one's own work apart from God. This may be accomplished in communal Christian worship, and more generally in living this day without a program and without compulsion. An "infallible criterion of Sabbath observance" is "whether and how sincerely we are in a position to celebrate it as a true day of joy."[51] Another criterion is how our Sabbath rest carries over into the workweek, so that a definite "release from care," thankfulness, and openness to others combines with more nearly approaching our work as "play," a devoted, humble, childlike witness to grace in the service of our neighbors.[52] Barth comments, "He who has a self-renouncing faith on Sunday will have it also on a weekday. . . . As he is busy on the everyday, he will also be at peace; as he works on the everyday, he will also pray. At the same time, he will both grasp completely and let go completely. At bottom, he will never be anxious on the working day."[53]

49. Barth, *Church Dogmatics*, III/4, 284.

50. Barth, *Church Dogmatics*, III/4, 97-100; Barth, *The Christian Life*, 88.

51. Barth, *Church Dogmatics*, III/4, 50, 69.

52. Barth, *Church Dogmatics*, III/4, 71, 553.

53. Barth, *Church Dogmatics*, III/4, 72.

Finally, instruction includes teaching an active biblical literacy or, more precisely, a realistic understanding of the biblical story and its depiction of the identity of God in Christ, of the world created, fallen, and redeemed, and of human beings who live in that world. The new and surprising Word attested to in Holy Scripture enables readiness to "step into freedom" with "youthful objectivity"; for inasmuch as God and God's world are rendered in narratives or stories, to learn of them in faith is to begin to imagine how one may live in that world. To forgive and be able to let yourself be forgiven, to apply your talents in the service of God's kingdom, to love and accept love gratefully, to keep faith in the face of suffering and death, and to see that God stands with the poor and dispossessed are possibilities encountered in prodigal sons, merciful fathers, steadfast mothers, wise stewards, good samaritans and shepherds, and acts of deliverance both splashy and silent as night. Although the practice of learning the moral landscape of God's world in biblical narrative is not explicitly developed in Barth, much of his theology can justify the claim I am making, as does his tribute to Abel Burckhardt, a composer and editor of children's songs that young Karl learned in the 1890s:

> And what made an indelible impression on me was the homely naturalness with which these very modest compositions spoke of the events of Christmas, Palm Sunday, Good Friday, Easter, the Ascension and Pentecost as things which might take place any day in Basel or its environs like any other important happenings. History? Dogma? Doctrine? Myth? No — but things actually taking place, so that we could see and hear and lay up in our hearts. For as these songs were sung in the everyday language we were then beginning to hear and speak, and as we joined in singing, we took our mother's hand, as it were, and went to the stall at Bethlehem, and to the streets of Jerusalem where, greeted by children of a similar age, the Saviour made his entry, and to the dark hill of Golgotha, and as the sun rose to the garden of Joseph. . . . It was all present without needing to be made present. . . . Yes, it was very naïve, but perhaps in the very naivety there lay the deepest wisdom and greatest power.[54]

54. Barth, *Church Dogmatics*, IV/2, pp. 112-13. Cf. Barth on baptismal instruction, which should consist in imparting to candidates "a material and intelligible *narratio* of the great acts of God which is oriented to their future baptism," so that they are "set in a position and in readiness so to seek and desire baptism that they know what they are doing in the matter." See Barth, *Church Dogmatics*, IV/4 (Fragment), 152. For more on Barth and narrative, see David Ford, *Barth and God's Story: Biblical Narrative and the Theological Method of Karl Barth in the "Church Dogmatics"* (Frankfurt am Main: Peter Lang, 1981); Frei, *Theology and Narrative;* William C. Placher, *Unapologetic Theology: A Christian Voice in a Pluralistic Conversation* (Louisville, Ky.: Westminster John Knox, 1989); William Werpehowski, "Command and History in the Ethics of Karl Barth," *Journal of Religious*

Sixth, these three practices inspire a fourth in the struggle for human righteousness or justice. In learning and living the story of God in Jesus Christ, and in praying "thy kingdom come" with peaceful "renouncing faith," it may be that young folks will increasingly find themselves claimed for "kingdom-like" action on behalf of human beings — that is, action in support of their rights to live with one another as fellows in freedom, peace, and joy, and against their human dignity being "overlooked, forgotten, broken and trampled under the lordship of the released and lordless powers." The action corresponds with God's own kingdom only as it comes in Jesus Christ, yet it is "righteous in its own place and manner" and gives testimony to the kingdom out of gratitude and hope. Orwell's memoir can serve as an example here. He recounts how his prep school was dominated by class privilege; but efforts for justice oppose the "lordless power" of Mammon, "the material possessions, property, and resources that have become the idol of man, or rather his very mobile demon." Christians will thus offer hope and courage to wounded and suffering creatures in their "wrestling and fighting and suffering for a provisional bit of human right."[55] Of course, elders responsible for children may instruct them by their own exemplary and promising action in the name of justice, including justice for these and other children.

III. Review and Assessment

Karl Barth's mature theological writings on children are carefully focused on the one hand, and suggestively improvised on the other. We have seen that his accounts of filial honor and parents' "ambassadorial" role provide a formal framework for reflection about specific features of the care and education of children. Barth's more scattered comments about "being a child" and the Christian life present a rich and pleasing conceptual space for further improvisation about the interconnections between Christian practice and the identities of children, who both are and learn to become children of God. In this essay I have tried to be faithful to Barth, not just by way of careful explication but also by thinking within the former framework and playing in the latter space.

Barth's strengths on our topic are profound. His stress on the divine calling

Ethics 9, no. 2 (1981): 298-320; and William Werpehowski, "Narrative and Ethics in Barth," *Theology Today* 43, no. 3 (1986): 334-53.

55. Barth, *The Christian Life*, 266, 222, 270. For more on justice and Barth's political ethics, see William Werpehowski, "Karl Barth on Politics," in *The Cambridge Companion to Barth,* ed. John Webster (Cambridge: Cambridge University Press, 2000).

and mission of parents works to protect them from forms of self-justification based on the "success" of their work in raising their children. Parents establish themselves by deference and reflection, by pointing away from themselves and mirroring God's love, justice, and faithfulness; they have no claim to honor on any other ground, be it their genes or wit or sacrifice or virtue, be it their children's sports prowess or SAT scores or toughness or gentleness. Should their youngsters flourish, they do so as the ones who have learned freedom for obedience to God, under whom they stand with mom and dad, and with whom they pray humbly. How much damage can parents do when their destiny seems to them to hinge on their "legacy," their "hope for the future"? And how much are parents moved to hostility or despair toward their children and one another when things do not go their way, when various expectations are not met, when the thin envelope comes in the mail?

The structure of Barth's account also sets a curb to various sorts of neglect inspired by self-contempt, selfishness, or a misguided interest in promoting the autonomy of future generations. The presupposition of Barth's entire view is that parents have a wonderful and particular lesson to teach *that they keep learning* in moments of hope, self-giving, and faithfulness to Jesus Christ. Barth's "vertical" and "horizontal" relativizing of the parental calling works to clarify both its special importance and its freedom *from* independence and solitude.

Barth's theology preserves children from the pressures of conformity to any ideals besides those graciously given by God. This "freedom from" presupposes a certain "freedom for," and I like to think that teaching children to be free for joy is at the center of it. This especially includes the joy that responds to one's own accomplishments and achievements — and for Barth these must always be affirmed — thankfully and in community with others.[56] The ideal descriptions of "being a child," moreover, set up a "framework for attention" to children as well as norms of creaturely honor with respect to the Christian life. On the one hand, the portrayals highlight dimensions of young people's lives that command our notice in ways that may aid our care for them. Eager readiness to learn should not be destroyed by the way we teach. Vulnerability requires an answer that objectively fits the need in question and not our projections or fantasies. That children are "beginners" does not mean that they are to be kept in dependence on their elders; it implies that they may mature before God with a spirit of courage and cheerfulness, all the better to "step into freedom." That step, along with the freedom for play, suggests that a child's creaturely *self-possession* in pursuing projects and goals is *incompatible* with a restrictive *self-preoccupation*. After all, the latter often leads to picking up your ball and glumly leaving the game. On the other hand, Barth's threefold com-

---

56. See Werpehowski, "What Shall Parents Teach Their Children?" 118-20.

mendation of "being a child" makes a claim on elders to learn from children in ways that curb their (our) propensity for self-congratulation and self-pity.[57]

Problems in Barth's account begin with its schematic character. Although he does more than many twentieth-century theologians in covering our subject, and though I think my reading represents him reliably, it is true that there is a lack of detail in sections specifically devoted to children. Critics have made this point about much of Barth's ethics, and there may be considered reasons for his approach;[58] nonetheless, a fuller explication is desirable to advance central themes, apply them instructively to cases (for even Barth explicitly endorses a "practical casuistry"),[59] and clear up ambiguities.[60]

One ambiguity is the role that gender plays in his theological ethics. Barth endorses an order in marriage, a "succession" of "preceding and following." For example, he writes that "the business of woman, her task and function, is to actualize the fellowship in which man can only precede her, stimulating, leading and inspiring."[61] We do not know the consequences of this view, even were we to accept it, for parental responsibilities or the "patterned," adaptive dimension

57. Even youngsters who have not reached the "age of discretion" may, doing "more than they intend or know," respond to Jesus Christ in ways — childlike ways — that "might still be stronger than the movements of many who have reached years of discretion and decision." The responses might put the others to shame and within their limits "take on and have very high significance." See Barth, *Church Dogmatics,* IV/4 (Fragment), 182.

58. For example, Nigel Biggar offers evidence "that Barth conceived the specific task of the theological ethicist as that of drawing out the ethical implications of dogmatics, and that he considered the close analysis of particular moral problems as the province of another kind of ethicist." Barth's interesting but little-used distinction between "theological" and "Christian" ethics comes into play at this point. See Nigel Biggar, *The Hastening That Waits: Karl Barth's Ethics* (Oxford: Oxford University Press, 1993), p. 159.

59. Biggar may not acknowledge this quite enough in *The Hastening That Waits* (see 40-45). Cf. William Werpehowski, "Hearing the Divine Command," *Zeitschrift für dialektische Theologie* 15, no. 1 (1999): 64-74.

60. I wonder whether one basis of Barth's limited treatment is a reluctance to endorse any but the most qualified "pro-natalism" as over against, by his (perhaps mistaken) lights, Roman Catholic and Jewish thought. He insists that the primary aim of marriage is not to be an institution for the upbringing of children, that *post Christum natum* we may be freed of anxiety about posterity, and that a "homely and courageous confidence in life" is not invariably commanded of spouses as they consider their possible parenthood. He wants to stress that parenthood is a responsible choice and that childless marriages are not for that fact alone defective. Maybe a slighter treatise on children follows in the wake of these concerns. But Barth also says that procreation as the completion of marital union may be "an offer of divine goodness made by the one who even in this last time does not will that it should be all up with us," and that it must not be rejected out of arbitrariness or sloth. See *Church Dogmatics,* III/4, 267-73.

61. Barth, *Church Dogmatics,* III/4, 171. I try a critical analysis of this and other related texts in "The Order of Man and Woman: A Response to Suzanne Selinger" (unpublished).

of children's upbringing. Nor do we have an elaboration of Barth's passing comment that, though both mother and father are commanded to rejoice in the honor of participating in the creation of new life and to reckon seriously with their parental obligations, "it will be a proper and effective exchange if the mother is more conscious of the honor and therefore the joy, while the father feels more acutely the obligation and therefore the seriousness of the matter."[62] In these two cases it would have been helpful to hear more.

We also miss further attention to the intimate, preservative work of parents in tending to the needs of helpless infants and small children. As we have seen, so much in the account features issues of children's growth and education. It could be true, however, that a more discriminating and humanly embodied norm of parental love, imaging always the divine love, emerges out of consideration of this manner of parental practice, too.[63]

Nevertheless, our reading is, I propose, promising not only in theological substance but also in the deliberative approach to children that Barth recommends. He deems ethics to be an aid to hearing God's command "in the form of a series of questions which arise from the nature of the case and which we must all answer."[64] We should feel free to pose a host of questions to ourselves. Do I treat children as gifts who are promised God's friendship, and not as corrupt or neutral objects who exist for the sake of my control and fashioning? Does my care for them communicate hope and possibility rather than a sense of failure and ruin? Am I moved to witness good news to other children not my own who need to and by grace may hear it when they have enough to eat, or when they have an opportunity to learn and develop their own powers for responsible life with others? And with my own children, do I really place first their relation with God and my summons joyfully to invite them to rejoice with me in God, rather than first insisting that they mimic my life history or "make something of themselves"?[65] These are good questions, and Barth helps us ask them.

62. Barth, *Church Dogmatics*, III/4, 277.

63. Cf. Sara Ruddick, *Maternal Thinking* (Boston: Beacon Press, 1989). In a review of this essay, Gilbert Meilaender makes a structurally analogous point about how Barth's emphasis on joy and playfulness "may underrate a bit children's sin and the need for discipline" specifically directed against it. Nothing in Barth's treatment strictly denies this need, of course, unless childhood "sin" is identified with hereditary transmission.

64. Barth, *Church Dogmatics*, III/4, 66. Cf. Biggar, *The Hastening That Waits*, 7-45.

65. Werpehowski, "What Shall Parents Teach Their Children?" 119-20. Just before his eightieth birthday, Barth sketched a "Rule of life for older people in their relationship with the young." Eberhard Busch recounts the following words: "You must make it clear that our younger relations have the right to go their own way in accordance with their own principles, not yours. . . . In no circumstances should you give them up: rather, you should go along with them cheerfully, allowing them to be free, thinking the best of them and trusting in God, loving them and praying for them, whatever happens." See Busch, *Karl Barth*, 476.

16. *"Infinite Openness to the Infinite":*
Karl Rahner's Contribution to Modern
Catholic Thought on the Child

MARY ANN HINSDALE

Three ironies characterize modern Catholic thought on the child. First, despite its many statements on the family, Roman Catholic teaching has given little systematic consideration to the child.[1] Second, the person who potentially has the most to contribute to remedying this lacuna is Karl Rahner (1904-1984) — a thinker regarded by many as the most important Catholic theologian of the twentieth century. However, Rahner wrote comparatively little on children. Third, one essay in which Rahner discusses the theology of childhood is often cited for recognizing that Catholic teaching more or less *assumes* that everyone knows what a child is; however, the essay's content has not been sufficiently mined in terms of Rahner's own substantive contribution to this topic. This is doubly ironic, since the very foundation on which the essay rests — Rahner's theological anthropology — has had an enormous (though often unacknowledged) influence on contemporary Catholic approaches to the religious education of children.

This essay examines these three ironies in detail in order to underscore the need for a more coherent Catholic social teaching on children. In it I will investigate what Rahner's theology of childhood can contribute toward providing

---

1. In this essay, "official Roman Catholic teaching" refers to statements produced by the hierarchical *magisterium* (the teaching office of the pope and bishops) of the Catholic Church. These statements may be issued by ecumenical councils, synods, and individual popes and bishops. For an extended treatment of this topic, see Richard Gaillardetz, *Teaching with Authority: A Theology of the Magisterium in the Church* (Collegeville: Liturgical Press, 1997); Ladislas Örsy, *The Church: Learning and Teaching* (Wilmington, Del.: Michael Glazier, 1987); and Francis A. Sullivan, *Creative Fidelity: Weighing and Interpreting Documents of the Magisterium* (New York: Paulist Press, 1996).

a necessary theological foundation for our contemporary understanding of children and for discerning what our moral obligations should be toward them. Although its full import has not always been recognized, the theology of Karl Rahner has already significantly influenced Catholic religious education. An examination of Rahner's thinking on children therefore might provide important religious warrants for treating all children with respect and dignity, as well as serve as an impetus to develop better ways to foster and nourish the growth in Christian spiritual maturity of both children and adults.

This essay has three parts. In the first part I will highlight the neglect of children in official Roman Catholic teaching by examining the work of Todd Whitmore, a social ethicist. Whitmore provides an important summary of the fragmentary treatment of children in Roman Catholic social teaching and stresses the need for a more coherent teaching by illustrating how the dominant capitalist discourse of contemporary culture endangers children's welfare. In the second part, after situating Rahner's theology in the context of the paradigm shift that characterizes post–Vatican II Catholic theology, I will outline his important essay entitled "Ideas for a Theology of Childhood" as a potential resource for articulating an understanding of children that more adequately corresponds to the Christian vision. In this section I will also consider Rahner's views on original sin and baptism as they relate to children. In the third part of the essay I will draw attention to the indebtedness of modern Catholic religious education to Rahner's broader theological project, including his influence on the emergent field of "children's spirituality." By way of conclusion, I will summarize Rahner's contribution to modern Catholic thinking on children and will assess the extent to which his theology can provide a basis for a more coherent Catholic social teaching on children.

Children: A Neglected Theme in Catholic Social Teaching

In "Children: An Undeveloped Theme in Catholic Teaching," Todd Whitmore claims that in its many statements on the family, Catholic teaching has concentrated mainly on the duties of parents with respect to the procreation and education of children.[2] While referencing children in a familial context is consis-

2. Todd David Whitmore (with Tobias Winwright), "Children: An Undeveloped Theme in Catholic Teaching," in *The Challenge of Global Stewardship: Roman Catholic Responses,* ed. Maura A. Ryan and Todd David Whitmore (Notre Dame: University of Notre Dame, 1997), 161-85. See also Todd David Whitmore, "Children and the Problem of Formation in American Families," *The Annual of the Society of Christian Ethics* (1995): 263-74. The lack of theological reflection on the child in Catholic thought was noticed twenty-five

tent with Christian anthropology's understanding of the social nature of the person, Whitmore argues that Catholic social teaching lacks systematic reflection on what a child *is,* and thus children themselves remain an underdeveloped theme in Catholic teaching: "Although the rudiments are scattered here and there, there is no developed Catholic teaching on children like there is, say, on the conduct of war or the possession of private property. . . . [There is] the assumption that we all know who and what children are and why we should care about them. Historical shifts in social views of children indicate that such views cannot be taken for granted."[3]

In the first two sections of his essay, Whitmore highlights the urgent need to develop a stronger Catholic social teaching by synthesizing the scattered fragments that deal with children.[4] In section one he provides a descriptive overview of the state of children in today's world, noting both the "silent emergencies" (disease, malnutrition, AIDS, poverty, and so forth) and the "loud emergencies" (war, genocide, and an escalating "culture of violence") that characterize the plight of children today. In section two Whitmore reviews the two dominant discourses operative today that attempt to define who children are: (1) the rhetoric underlying much of the current children's rights discussion, which some neo-conservatives have called "the autonomy project";[5] and (2) the market logic of unrestrained capitalism.

---

years ago by liturgist Nathan Mitchell. See his excellent essay, which is heavily indebted to Rahner, entitled "The Once and Future Child: Towards a Theology of Childhood," *Living Light* 12 (1975): 423-37. Christine Gudorf also comments on the lack of systematic Catholic thought on children in *The New Dictionary of Catholic Social Thought,* s.v. "Children, rights of" (Collegeville, Minn.: Liturgical Press, 1994).

3. Whitmore, "Children: An Undeveloped Theme in Catholic Teaching," 175-76. For an excellent overview of the shifting cultural constructions of childhood represented in historiography, see Hugh Cunningham, "Histories of Childhood," *American Historical Review* 103 (1998): 1195-1207.

4. For those unfamiliar with the term, "Catholic social teaching" refers to those official statements of popes, bishops, synods, and councils that deal with the political, social, economic, and international order. Although the Catholic social tradition can be traced back to the Hebrew and Christian Scriptures and the writings of patristic and medieval theologians such as Augustine and Aquinas, modern "Catholic social teaching" is usually regarded to have begun with Pope Leo XIII's 1891 encyclical, *Rerum Novarum.* Encyclicals (papal letters addressed to the whole world) are the usual means of transmission for Catholic social teaching, although other ecclesial groups (episcopal conferences, synods, and councils) have also contributed to this body of thought.

5. See Bruce C. Hafen and Jonathan O. Haven, "Abandoning Children to Their Rights," *First Things* (August/September 1995): 18-24; and George Weigel, "What Really Happened at Cairo," *First Things,* (February 1995): 34-38. Although Whitmore acknowledges that it is debatable how deeply such logic characterizes the U.N. Convention on the Rights of the Child, he regards it as indisputable that advocates of this logic exist. See

Whitmore does not discuss the "autonomy project" in detail because he feels other authors already have provided an adequate assessment of it.[6] However, he provides a comprehensive analysis of the understanding of children that is implicit in the second discourse, arguing that the unrestrained economic liberalism that characterizes global capitalism is based upon a "market anthropology" which sees children as commodities, consumers, or burdens. Both discourses have enormously negative consequences for children, consequences that Whitmore regards as being in fundamental competition with a Christian — or, more specifically, a Catholic — understanding of the human person.[7]

In the prefatory remarks to this second section, Whitmore acknowledges that Pope John Paul II has cautiously endorsed market economies. However, he points out that the pope's encyclicals dealing with these matters stress the primacy of the whole person and the common good over individual interest. Furthermore, the market economies that the pope supports are "circumscribed with a strong juridical framework."[8] Whitmore intends to delineate the destructive potential that capitalist market anthropology bears toward children and illustrate how Catholic social teaching provides a critical resource to counter it.

According to Whitmore, unrestrained capitalism puts material objects and individual self-interest before the welfare of persons and the common good. The market economy's worldview understands all things in terms of exchange, so that even human persons become what Whitmore calls "fungible objects."[9] Thus, the first characteristic of market anthropology is that the person is a *commodity*. However, according to the teaching of the encyclical *Laborem exercens*, such instrumentalization and commodification (for example, expressions such as "workforce" and "cheap labor" are used by market economies as an impersonal force or a kind of "merchandise" that can be bought) are in direct conflict with Christian teaching.[10] A second characteristic

---

Whitmore, "Children: An Undeveloped Theme in Catholic Teaching," 182n. 8. For another critical assessment from a different political vantage point, see Christine Gudorf's excellent presentation on Catholic social teaching's position on the rights of children in *The New Dictionary of Catholic Social Thought*, s.v. "Children, rights of."

6. See n. 5.

7. Whitmore, "Children: An Undeveloped Theme in Catholic Teaching," 168.

8. Whitmore, "Children: An Undeveloped Theme in Catholic Teaching," 167-71. The primary encyclicals drawn upon here are *Laborem exercens* (1986) (English translation: *The Primacy of Labor*) and *Centesimus annus* (1991) (English translation: *One Hundred Years*).

9. Whitmore, "Children: An Undeveloped Theme in Catholic Teaching," 169.

10. See Pope John Paul II, *"Laborem exercens,"* in Gregory Baum, *The Priority of Labor* (New York: Paulist Press, 1982). In addition to the text of the encyclical, Baum provides an excellent commentary on this encyclical.

of market anthropology stresses that the person is a *consumer*. One has value in a consumer society only if one can purchase commodities, since the market can expand only if people buy products. Advertising fuels this process by telling people they do not have worth unless they buy certain products. The third characteristic of a market anthropology is that the person who cannot function as either a commodity or a consumer is a *burden*.

The implications of market logic for children seem obvious: they are either commodities and consumers — or burdens. In Whitmore's estimation, the rhetoric surrounding reproductive technologies, which views children in terms of cost-benefit analysis, provides a good illustration of this logic. He cites the high cost of producing a child through reproductive technology — over $50,000 per live birth from in vitro fertilization — as a factor reinforcing the view of a child as an "investment" from which parents can expect a "return" in the form of a "quality" product. Selection of embryos with desirable characteristics contributes to this market ethos, since failure to deliver "a product of suitable standard" can bring economic retaliation in the form of a legal suit.[11]

Another example of how market logic affects children's welfare is children's television. TV targets children as consumers by featuring programs with toys as main characters and hooking children into getting their parents to buy these commercial products. Even educational programming becomes marginalized by market-driven pressures, thus reducing the idea of public responsibility to profitability. According to the logic of the market, no person — child or adult — has "intrinsic worth." Children who are neither commodities nor consumers are "non-entities," and any claim they make on society is understood as a burden.[12]

Building upon the Thomistic *exitus et reditus* structure (that is, "everything comes forth from God and returns to God")[13] that characterizes Catholic social teaching in general, Whitmore attempts in the third and final part of his essay to formulate the foundations for a Catholic teaching on children by correlating Aquinas's structural dynamism of *exitus/reditus* with the theological virtues of faith, hope, and love. While it is beyond the scope of this essay to discuss in detail the documentary sources he uses,[14] three significant insights concern-

---

11. Whitmore, "Children: An Undeveloped Theme in Catholic Teaching," 171-72.

12. Whitmore, "Children: An Undeveloped Theme in Catholic Teaching," 175.

13. Derived from a neo-Platonic way of viewing the world, the *exitus/reditus* (exit and return) dynamic is the overarching structure that Thomas Aquinas gave to his *Summa theologiae*. The French Dominican Marie-Dominique Chenu (1895-1990) is credited with noticing the centrality and dynamism of this pattern. See Marie-Dominique Chenu, *Toward Understanding St. Thomas* (Chicago: Regnery, 1964); and Thomas F. O'Meara, *Thomas Aquinas: Theologian* (Notre Dame: University of Notre Dame Press, 1997), 53-63.

14. These sources include Leo XIII's *Immortale dei* (nos. 6, 20) and *Rerum Novarum*

410

ing children emerge from Whitmore's analysis. First, the idea of children as gifts of creation in the image of God follows from the belief that everything proceeds from God (the *exitus* dynamic). Recalling that children are created in the image of God thus relativizes the desires of prospective parents to have children in their image and creates, at the very minimum, a strong presumption against the practice of reproductive technology for profit, if it does not rule it out altogether. Second, children are signs of a future that extends beyond the self-interested desires of others, since the future toward which all human beings are headed is one with God at its center (the *reditus* dynamic). The view that children are "destined for union with God," Whitmore points out, "relativizes the immediate wants of adults." This accent on the future also places emphasis on the education and formation of children. Third, because children are gifts from God and destined to return to God, even our biological children are "ours only in trust" (including those children who are not our own biologically). Thus, according to Catholic social teaching, children are not "burdens" but blessings that call for our love in the form of present responsibility and stewardship.[15]

With the help of Catholic social teaching's principle of "subsidiarity,"[16] Whitmore delineates our stewardship of children by determining an *order* of responsibility for them. On the one hand, this principle argues against the direct intervention of large-scale institutions in family life, based upon the idea that "the best associations or institutions for providing care are those most proximate to the persons in question."[17] On the other hand, subsidiarity affirms that large institutions have an obligation to support the smaller ones. Thus, Catholic social teaching holds that family and society have complementary functions with respect to the stewardship of children.[18]

Whitmore has done a great service by examining modern Catholic social teaching on the child. Not only does he expose the danger presented by the lack of a developed Catholic tradition on the nature of children and our obligations toward them, but he also points out how certain aspects of Catholic teaching

---

(no. 11); Pius XII's 1942 "Christmas Address"; John XXIII's *Pacem in terris* (no. 121) and *Mater et magistra* (nos. 227-32); Vatican II's *Gaudiam et spes* (no. 52); Paul VI's *Octogesima adveniens* (nos. 16, 24), *Populorum progressio* (no. 15), and *Evangelii nuntiandi* (no. 29); John Paul II's *Dives in misericordia* (no. 13); *Laborem exercens* (no. 4); and *Familiaris consortio* (nos. 36-41, 45). See Whitmore, "Children: An Undeveloped Theme in Catholic Teaching," 185, n. 52, n. 53, n. 56, n. 61, n. 67.

15. Whitmore, "Children: An Undeveloped Theme in Catholic Teaching," 177-79.

16. The notion of subsidiarity was first defined in modern Catholic social teaching by Pope Pius XI in his encyclical *Quadragesimo anno* (1931) (English translation: "In the Fortieth Year").

17. Whitmore, "Children: An Undeveloped Theme in Catholic Teaching," 179.

18. See Pope John Paul II, *Familiaris consortio*, no. 45. But see also Gudorf's critique of this document. See n. 5 above.

could obscure the tradition or prevent it from operating with its full strength. For example, he finds "an excessive natalism" in Catholic tradition on children that tends to focus on the gift of creation expressed in procreation at the expense of how the child as "gift" might be manifested at other stages of life.[19] He admits that Catholic teaching never *denies* that the gift of creation is ongoing; yet, Catholic teaching tends to speak of children as "gifts of life" only when focusing on procreation, especially with respect to the issues of artificial reproduction, contraception, and abortion.[20] It is precisely this natalism, Whitmore argues, that drives couples to the extreme measures involved in conceiving through reproductive technologies: depleting their savings, mortgaging their homes, and, in the case of women, taking hormonal treatments that severely disrupt their metabolism.[21]

Todd Whitmore's discussion of children in Catholic teaching begins with an epigraph taken from Karl Rahner's essay entitled "Ideas for a Theology of Childhood," in which Rahner observes that Scripture and tradition alike presuppose "that we already know precisely what a child really *is* far more than they tell us explicitly or treat it as a distinct question."[22] At the end of his essay, Whitmore cites Rahner again and laments that, despite the extended treatment of procreative issues in Catholicism, there is no real consideration of children "as a distinct question." Ironically, Whitmore leaves aside the question of what Rahner's essay can contribute to the subject of Catholic teaching on children.[23]

19. Whitmore, "Children: An Undeveloped Theme in Catholic Teaching," 177. Whitmore does not discuss the possible reasons for this narrow emphasis; however, feminist theologians have suggested that much of the problem is due to the exclusion of women's — especially mothers' — experience and participation in the formulation of these teachings. See Bonnie Miller-McLemore's discussion in Chapter 17 of this volume. See also Christine Gudorf's discussion (above, n. 5) of the hierarchically ordered family model in Catholic teaching and its negative effects on children.

20. Whitmore has written more extensively on the implications of natalism in "Moral Methodology and Pastoral Responsiveness: The Case of Abortion and the Care of Children," *Theological Studies* 54 (1993): 316-38. See also the classic formulation of the late Joseph Cardinal Bernadin, *Consistent Ethic of Life* (Kansas City, Mo.: Sheed & Ward, 1988).

21. Whitmore, "Children: An Undeveloped Theme in Catholic Teaching," 177-78.

22. Karl Rahner, "Ideas for a Theology of Childhood," cited in Whitmore, "Children: An Undeveloped Theme in Catholic Teaching," 161.

23. This simply may be due to the fact that Whitmore is focusing on "official" teaching of the Catholic Church produced by the *magisterium* (councils, popes, and bishops) and not the "teaching" of *theologians*. However, there is no magisterial teaching that does not depend to some degree upon theology (illustrated, for example, in Whitmore's appreciation of the Thomistic structure of Catholic social teaching). And, as I am arguing in this essay, Rahner's theology has found its way into the pastoral practice of postconciliar Catholicism, even if it is not cited explicitly in the official pronouncements of the magisterium.

Before examining this question, however, it will prove helpful first to situate Rahner's theology in terms of the development of modern Catholic theology and to review some of the chief characteristics of his theology.

The Context for Rahner's Theology

The contribution of Karl Rahner to modern Catholic thought on the child must be viewed against the background of theology and church life that characterized Roman Catholicism for roughly the hundred years between 1850 and 1950. The dominant theological paradigm of this period is known as neo-scholasticism.[24] Neo-scholasticism was an attempt to return to the Scholastic tradition of the Middle Ages, especially to the perennial philosophy of Thomas Aquinas, as a means of fending off Enlightenment attacks on the compatibility of faith and reason and the authority of the Roman Catholic Church.[25] In his encyclical entitled "On the Restoration of Christian Philosophy," Pope Leo XIII decreed that the philosophy and theology of Thomas Aquinas would be the only framework for Catholic theological investigation.[26]

Unfortunately, this framework was provided not by the authentic Aquinas but by a simplified, static interpretation of his thought developed by later followers. Neo-scholasticism required that prescribed language with "correct" terms, good for all cultural circumstances, be used to transmit the message of Christianity and ethical instructions that would apply to all people for all time.[27] Questions and experiences that went beyond the framework of neo-Thomistic thought and language were assiduously prevented from being the subject of theological reflection. Informers denounced theological diver-

24. With few exceptions, the seminary education of priests and the religious instruction and preaching to which ordinary Catholics were exposed were dominated by neo-scholasticism at least until the early 1960s. The Second Vatican Council (1961-65) marked the definitive end of neo-scholastic hegemony in Catholic theology. See Gerald McCool, *Catholic Theology in the Nineteenth Century: The Quest for a Unitary Method* (New York: Seabury, 1977); and Benedict Ashley, s.v. "neoscholasticism," in *The Harper-Collins Encyclopedia of Catholicism*, ed. Richard P. McBrien (San Francisco: HarperCollins, 1995).

25. "Neo-scholasticism" is not synonymous with "neo-Thomism." The former term is the broader category, since Bonaventure and Scotus, along with Thomas Aquinas, can be classified as "scholastics." For an excellent discussion of neo-scholasticism in relationship to neo-Thomism, see O'Meara, *Thomas Aquinas: Theologian*, 167-75.

26. *Aeterni Patris* (August 4, 1879).

27. Herbert Vorgrimler, *Understanding Karl Rahner: An Introduction to His Life and Thought* (New York: Crossroad, 1986), 52-54.

gences to ecclesiastical superiors. Books considered dangerous to the faith were consigned to an "Index of Forbidden Books" and withdrawn from bookshops.[28] Local bishops employed harsh measures against dissident theologians, sometimes banishing them to monasteries and often requiring their "obedient silence." The pope was the only legitimate and competent preserver of the "deposit of faith." The role of the professional theologian consisted in defending the teaching of the church. As a result of neo-scholastic dominance, the period between the two World Wars was one of extreme rigidity in Catholic theology.

Rahner objected strenuously to the stultifying tendencies of neo-scholasticism. He called it "Pian monolithism," referring to the practices that entered the church after Pius IX (d. 1878) and reached their nadir with Pius XII (d. 1958).[29] In his estimation, these pontificates supported a system of thought that "threatened to make the church an immovable monolith, a mass of rock, an absolute monarchy, in which everything was governed and decided by the ruler down to the smallest detail."[30] Rahner also abhorred "integralism," a movement that bolstered neo-scholasticism in its demands that everything traditional must be kept, "simply because it is old." Integralists held that obedience to the authority of the Church was a supreme virtue and that the laity "were essentially on the receiving end of commands and have no real initiative."[31]

The place a child occupied in the Catholic world under the sway of neo-scholasticism was one of passive obedience. Like laity in general,[32] children

28. Vorgrimler, *Understanding Karl Rahner*, 53. The last official edition of the Index was issued in 1948 with a total of about 4,000 titles. The Index was abolished by Paul VI in the mid-1960s.

29. Rahner also used other terms for the kind of theology that predominated between Vatican I and Vatican II. For example, "Denzinger theology" referred to theological conclusions deduced from the *Enchiridion Symbolorum*, a comprehensive catalogue of official pronouncements of popes and councils, edited by Heinrich Joseph Denzinger in 1854. See Rahner's "The Prospects for Dogmatic Theology," *Theological Investigations*, vol. 1, trans. Cornelius Ernst, O.P. (New York: Seabury Press, 1974), 3. He also used the term "textbook theology" to describe the treatises used in seminary courses. The manuals, as they also were called, comprised a veritable theological genre that aimed to (1) "offer a defense of the Catholic faith against the rationalism inspired by the Enlightenment," and (2) "offer a systematic, internally coherent presentation of Catholic doctrine . . . alternative to the problematic systems inspired by philosophical idealism." See Richard Gaillardetz, "manualists," s.v., in *The HarperCollins Encyclopedia of Catholicism*.

30. Vorgrimler, *Understanding Karl Rahner*, 54.

31. Vorgrimler, *Understanding Karl Rahner*, 54.

32. In the nineteenth century, Lord Acton commented that the laity's role was to "pray, pay, and obey." Todd Whitmore notes that the laity are often characterized as "children" in Roman Catholic Church documents. See Todd Whitmore, "Children: An Undeveloped Theme in Catholic Teaching," 162.

were under the control of parents, clergy, and teachers. Paramount for Catholic families was that children be baptized as soon as possible after birth, lest "original sin remain upon their soul" and they be "deprived of eternal salvation."[33] Upon reaching "the age of reason" (around age seven), children were treated as miniature adults in terms of moral responsibility.[34] Education in the faith was carried out by means of the catechism, which ensured the uniformity of Catholic belief. As Michael Donnellan has pointed out, "By shaping the intelligibility of the Christian message for so many Catholics for so long a time, the catechism ultimately was better known than the Bible and more influential than any official Church document. The durability of the catechism was symbolic of the Church's own self-image as an unchanging society."[35]

Since Rahner grew up in Germany's Black Forest region at the turn of the twentieth century, his own childhood and education were stamped by this predominantly defensive attitude against the modern world.[36] But his early philosophical and theological studies as a Jesuit exposed him to a more authentic Thomism.[37] His studies with Martin Heidegger and his engagement with the transcendental Thomism of Joseph Maréchal, as well as other types of philosophy, enabled him to break through the stultifying rigidity of neo-scholasticism and reclaim Thomas the mystic, the Thomas who was "uncompromisingly progressive, if not actually revolutionary." The Scholastic theologian to whom

---

33. "Limbo," a theological postulate that never has been defined as a dogma by the Catholic Church, was developed to explain that those who through no fault of their own died unbaptized, such as infants, could still be saved from eternal damnation but would be deprived of the vision of God in some nebulous eternity "on the edge" (the literal meaning of "limbo") of heaven. See Cristina Traina's discussion of this topic in Aquinas's theology in this volume.

34. This concept is derived from Aquinas. Children were commonly thought to have reached the age of moral discretion at around the age of seven. See Cristina Traina's discussion of the Thomistic understanding of children's moral responsibility in this volume.

35. Michael Donnellan, "Bishops and Uniformity in Religious Education: Vatican I to Vatican II," in *Sourcebook for Modern Catechetics,* ed. Michael Warren (Winona, Minn.: Saint Mary's Press, 1997), 233.

36. Rahner describes his childhood as being ordinary, unremarkable, and typical of the German middle class at the turn of the twentieth century. See Karl Rahner, *I Remember: An Autobiographical Interview with Meinold Krauss* (New York: Crossroad, 1985), 20-34.

37. Rahner joined the Jesuits in Feldkirch (Voralberg, Austria) at age eighteen. For an account of his vocational decision and the nature of his philosophical and theological studies, see Karl Rahner, *I Remember,* 41-48. See also Karl Rahner in *Faith in a Wintry Season: Conversations and Interviews with Karl Rahner in the Last Years of His Life,* ed. Paul Imhof and Hubert Biallowons (New York: Crossroad, 1990), 15-38; in *Karl Rahner in Dialogue,* ed. Paul Imhof and Hubert Biallowons (New York: Crossroad, 1986), 12-15; 255.

Rahner was indebted was not "that potted version . . . produced under Pius X in the so-called 'Twenty Theses' published by the Congregation of Studies at Rome in 1914," but the Aquinas who "stands at the origins of that reflexive process in theology in which Christian faith explicitly recognizes the status of the world as autonomous and responsible for its own destiny."[38] Rahner's theology was profoundly influenced by Aquinas's understanding of God, a God whom he characterized as "not so much . . . him who inserts himself into the world, as it were perforating an otherwise closed system from without, but rather as the infinite incomprehensible mystery and absolute future, present intrinsically in the world all along as that which provides its ultimate consummation and so sustains its movement towards this from within."[39] If Rahner campaigned against neo-scholastic theology, it was because he wanted to liberate Scholastic theology.[40]

In breaking out of the defensive mentality of neo-scholasticism, Rahner belongs to a period of theological renewal in Catholic theology that reached a climax with the Second Vatican Council (1962-1965). The Council not only effectively marked the eclipse of neo-scholasticism but also ushered in a "paradigm shift" that the Catholic Church, to a great extent, is still negotiating.[41] According to his biographer and former assistant, Herbert Vorgrimler, Rahner belongs to the "second generation" of this renewal movement. Other theologians likewise consider Rahner a theologian more "of" the Second Vatican Council than one who prepared the way for it.[42]

38. Karl Rahner, "On Recognizing the Importance of Thomas Aquinas," *Theological Investigations,* vol. 13, trans. David Bourke (New York: Seabury Press, 1975), 3-12. See also the lengthy interview in which Rahner discusses his views on Aquinas and his interpreters, including Rahner's perceptions of liberation theology, in *Faith in a Wintry Season,* 41-58.

39. Rahner, "On Recognizing the Importance of Thomas Aquinas," 11.

40. "For my part I don't want to do much more than to release the inner dynamism that still exists in the ordinary, apparently sterile, homogeneous (in the pejorative sense) scholastic theology." See Karl Rahner, *Faith in a Wintry Season,* 17-18.

41. It is beyond the scope of this essay to give a complete account of Vatican II's impact on the Catholic Church. Rahner himself offered periodic assessments of the Council. See, for example, "Basic Theological Interpretation of the Second Vatican Council," *Theological Investigations,* vol. 20, trans. Edward Quinn (New York: Crossroad, 1981), 77-102; "Forgotten Dogmatic Initiatives of the Second Vatican Council," *Theological Investigations,* vol. 22, trans. Joseph Donceel, S.J. (New York: Crossroad, 1991), 97-105. Toward the end of his life, Rahner grew pessimistic about the way that some forces in Catholicism were attempting to short-circuit the reforms of Vatican II. See his reflections in *Faith in a Wintry Season,* 39, 74-78.

42. According to Thomas F. O'Meara, "The most important theologian of Vatican II was Yves Congar, for much of the agenda of the Council had been his agenda since the beginning of his ministry in 1932. The important theologian after the Council, however, has been Karl Rahner. The bibliography of writings by him and on him . . . indicate his broad,

Some Important Characteristics of Rahner's Theology

Although it is impossible to discuss Rahner's contributions to post–Vatican II Catholic theology in any detail here,[43] a review of some key themes and methodological concerns that characterize his theology will aid us in appreciating his thinking on children. Despite the unfamiliar philosophical terms and interminably long Germanic sentence structure that predominate in his writings, Rahner's theology is first of all a *pastoral* theology.[44] Pastoral theology, according to Rahner, is not so much a matter of concrete application as it is a consideration of the "demands" that the pastoral situation makes upon theology as a whole.[45] His former student, Johann Baptist Metz, observed that Rahner "held himself accountable to everyday believers, particularly those beset by the doubts engendered by the precarious existence of Christian faith in the secularized, scientific-industrial societies of European modernity."[46] In reflecting upon his life, Rahner commented, "Ultimately my theological work was really not motivated by scholarship and erudition as such, but by pastoral concerns. This likewise explains why a large part of my published work is filled with immediately religious, spiritual, and pastoral concerns."[47]

A second characteristic that flows directly from his pastoral concerns is

---

vast influence" ("Karl Rahner: Some Audiences and Sources for His Theology," *Communio* 18 [1991]: 237-38). Rahner seems to agree with O'Meara's assessment: "I did not exercise any great influence at the Council. . . . It is true that I attended almost all of the meetings of the Theological Commission and that I collaborated with the other theologians. As you know the most important schemata of this commission were on the Church and revelation. I was a member of certain sub-commissions that worked on these, but my contribution was not great." See *Karl Rahner in Dialogue*, 20.

43. It is estimated that Rahner authored more than four thousand written works. See the "Translator's Foreward" by Harvey Egan in *I Remember*, 1.

44. For an excellent overview of Rahner's pastoral theology, see Peter C. Phan, "Karl Rahner as Pastoral Theologian," *Living Light* 30 (1994): 3-12.

45. See "The New Claims Which Pastoral Theology Makes upon Theology as a Whole," *Theological Investigations*, vol. 11, trans. David Bourke (New York: Seabury Press, 1974), 115-36. For detailed examples of Rahner's pastoral theology, see the four-volume *Handbuch der Pastoraltheologie* (Freiburg: Herder, 1966), in which Rahner was a key collaborator. Rahner states that this handbook was developed precisely to combat the view that pastoral theology was confined to homiletics, catechetics, and pastoral liturgy. Rahner concurred with Friedrich Schleiermacher in preferring the term "practical theology" to describe the kind of theology he was engaged in, since the term "pastoral" suggests that it is only the clergy who are responsible for the Church's active work.

46. Cited in the introduction to Johann Baptist Metz, *A Passion for God: The Mystical-Political Dimension of Christianity*, trans. J. Matthew Ashley (New York: Paulist Press, 1998), 13.

47. *Karl Rahner in Dialogue*, 256.

the attention Rahner gives to fostering a new "mystagogy."[48] The "mystagogi-cal" character of theology, the idea that learning what faith means comes from within one's own existence and experience and not merely by indoctrination from without, is enormously important to Rahner.[49] As a consequence, much of his theology takes the form of sermons, prayers, and meditations.[50] For Rahner, all theology "must lead . . . into the presence of the one, same, and only all-embracing mystery of God."[51] With respect to children, as we shall see, Rahner is concerned with not only what a child *is* in the sight of God, but how God, as mystery, is revealed in the experience of childhood.

Rahner wrote often of "the mysticism of everyday life"[52] and challenged his audience to look at what "is implicit, hidden, anonymous, repressed, or bursting forth from the center of all we do."[53] By surrendering to the mystery that embraces all of life — including the mystery of childhood — one opens oneself to the encounter with God. As the "asymptotic goal" of human experi-ence, hidden in itself, the experience of God is not the privilege of the individ-ual mystic, Rahner argued, but is available to everyone:[54]

48. The term "mystagogy" is derived from the Greek *muein*, "to instruct in the mys-teries," and refers to the period after baptism when newly baptized Christians (neophytes) were instructed in how to live the Christian life. In the early church the "mystagogia" were instructions or homilies on the sacraments of baptism, anointing, and the Eucharist.

49. See James J. Bacik, *Apologetics and the Eclipse of Mystery: Mystagogy according to Karl Rahner* (Notre Dame: University of Notre Dame Press, 1980); William V. Dych, *Karl Rahner* (Collegeville, Minn.: Liturgical Press, 1992), 29; and Mary E. Hines, *The Transfor-mation of Dogma: An Introduction to Karl Rahner on Doctrine* (New York: Paulist Press, 1989), 119-22. For a history of Rahner's use of the term "mystagogy" and its importance for religious education, see Roman Bleistein, "Mystagogie und Religionspädigogik," in *Wagnis Theologie: Erfahrungen mit der Theologie Karl Rahners,* ed. Herbert Vorgrimler (Freiburg: Herder, 1979), 51-60; and Herbert Haslinger, "Der Gedanke der Mystagogie in der Theologie Karl Rahners," in *Sich Selbst entdecken — Gott erfahern: Für eine mystagogische Praxis kirchlicher Jugendarbeit* (Mainz: Mathias Grunewald Verlag, 1991), 41-62.

50. "I would say that I have always done theology with a view to kerygma, preach-ing, pastoral care. For that reason, I have written relatively many books on devotion in the standard sense such as the book *On Prayer* and *Watch and Pray with Me*" (*Karl Rahner in Dialogue*, 256). See also William Dych, *Karl Rahner*, 28; and Harvey D. Egan, *Karl Rahner: Mystic of Everyday Life* (New York: Crossroad, 1998), 80-104.

51. Rahner, *I Remember*, 57.

52. See Harvey Egan's discussion of this dimension of Rahner's thought in *Karl Rahner: Mystic of Everyday Life*, 57-77. See also Donald Buggert, "Grace and Religious Ex-perience: The Everyday Mysticism of Karl Rahner," in *Master of the Sacred Page*, ed. Keith Egan and Craig Morrison (Washington, D.C.: Carmelite Institute, 1997), 189-218.

53. Harvey Egan, *Karl Rahner*, 76-77.

54. Rahner acknowledged, however, that the process of reflecting upon this experi-ence "varies greatly from one individual to another in terms of force and clarity." See Karl

I think that people must understand that they have an implicit but true knowledge of God perhaps not reflected upon and not verbalized — or better expressed: a genuine experience of God, which is ultimately rooted in their spiritual existence, in their transcendentality, in their personality, or whatever you want to name it. It is not a really important question whether you call that "mystical" or not.[55]

Thirdly, in taking human experience as the starting point for theological reflection, Rahner makes use of a "transcendental method." Put simply, this means that Rahner wants to find the conditions for the possibility of experiencing God in human life. According to this method, human beings experience a fundamental openness (a self-transcendence) toward God in every truly human act. This unthematic, "transcendental" experience (as distinct from particular, "categorical" experience) lies at the very center of what it means to be human. It is the "horizon" for the offer of God's self-communication that is constitutive of human identity. A major theme that runs throughout all of Rahner's theology is that grace and revelation (the self-communication of God) are found in our human experience. As Harvey Egan explains,

> Central to Rahner's thinking is the notion that what is at the core of every person's deepest experience, what haunts every human heart, is a God whose mystery, light, and love have embraced the total person. God works in every person's life as the One to whom we say our inmost yes or no. We may deny this, ignore it, or repress it, but deep down we know that God is in love with us and we are all at least secretly in love with one another.[56]

Because the divine self-communication of God presents itself always as "offer," human freedom is respected, and God's grace and revelation remain gratuitous, thereby avoiding the pitfalls of the neo-scholastic nature/grace debate.[57]

A fourth aspect of Rahner's theology that is helpful for understanding his thinking on children is its indebtedness to the spirituality of St. Ignatius of

---

Rahner, "The Experience of God Today," *Theological Investigations*, vol. 11, 153. Also important for understanding Rahner's essay on the theology of childhood is his concept of "eternity" and its relationship to "temporal" existence. See "Eternity from Time," *Theological Investigations*, vol. 19, trans. Edward Quinn (New York: Crossroad, 1983), 169-77.

55. Rahner, *Faith in a Wintry Season*, 115.

56. Egan, "Translator's Foreward," in *I Remember*, 3.

57. A good summary of this debate, which includes the contributions of Henri de Lubac and Karl Rahner, can be found in Robert J. Hurley, *Hermeneutics and Catechesis: Biblical Interpretation in the Come to the Father Catechetical Series* (Lanham, Md.: University Press of America, 1997), 167-81.

Loyola.[58] Rahner was a Jesuit, so it is not surprising to find Ignatian themes in his theology; however, the extent of this influence is often overlooked by his interpreters.[59] Ignatian mysticism's emphasis on "joy in the world" and "finding God in all things" has a remarkable affinity with Rahner's reflections on childhood. Even if Rahner peferred to lay special stress on the *via negationis,* since it is here that the human spirit most often experiences its proper transcendence,[60] it is worth noting that he did not think a "burned-out," "tired and disillusioned heart" is closer to God than a young and happy one.[61]

Finally, a word about Rahner's style of theological reflection is also in order here. Jörg Splett comments that it was Rahner's practice in his writings to allow himself to be confronted by the questions on which he reflected. Thus, in his essays, Rahner typically begins by giving an overview of a problem, mentioning previous attempts made toward its solution. Then, unencumbered and without prejudice, he circumscribes the delimited question, thematizing his problems with it — often not so much to arrive at a solution to the problem as to disclose something deeper.[62] This indirect style of reflection gives Rahner's theology a meditative quality, in keeping with his mystagogical aims.[63]

---

58. See Karl Rahner, "Rede des Ignatius von Loyola an einen Jesuiten von heute," in Karl Rahner and Paul Imhof, *Ignatius von Loyola* (Freiburg: Herder, 1983), 9-38. In addition to this article, which Rahner regarded as his own "spiritual testament," see Jörg Splett, "Mystiches Christentum? Karl Rahner zur Zukunft des Glaubens," *Theologische Quartalschrift* 174 (1994): 263-66; Egan, *Karl Rahner,* 28-54; and Leo J. O'Donovan, "A Final Harvest: Karl Rahner's Last Theological Writings," *Religious Studies Review* 11 (1985): 360.

59. Exceptions include Donald Buggert, William Dych, Harvey Egan, Mary E. Hines, Leo O'Donovan, and Thomas O'Meara. In his later years Rahner commented, "In comparison with other philosophy and theology that influenced me, Ignatian spirituality was indeed more significant and important. . . . The spirituality of Ignatius himself, which one learned through the practice of prayer and religious formation, was more significant for me than all learned philosophy and theology inside and outside the order." See *Karl Rahner in Dialogue,* 191.

60. See, for example, "Reflections on the Experience of Grace," *Theological Investigations,* vol. 3, trans. Karl-H. and Boniface Kruger (Baltimore: Helicon Press, 1967), 86-87.

61. Harvey Egan, "Karl Rahner: Theologian of the Spiritual Exercises," *Thought* 67 (1992): 263.

62. Splett, "Mystisches Christentum?" 258.

63. This has been noted by Michael Langer, "Religionspädagogik im Horizont Transzendentaler Theologie: Karl Rahner's Beitrag zu Grundproblemen religiöser Sozialisation," in *Glauben Lernen — Leben Lernen,* ed. Konrad Baumgartner, Paul Wehrle, and Jürgen Werbick (St. Ottilien: Eos Verlag, 1985), 58-62. Harvey Egan has also drawn attention to the fact that Rahner's theology often begins and ends in prayer. See "Karl Rahner: Theologian of the Spiritual Exercises," 261.

Rahner's Theology of Childhood

Rahner's essay entitled "Ideas for a Theology of Childhood"[64] represents a major contribution to Catholic theology and to Christian thought on the child in general. His theological anthropology, according to which human persons — including children — are fundamentally oriented toward God, is much in evidence here. The aim of the essay is not directly to assist parents, teachers, or others who are engaged in caring for children, but to offer some foundational reflections on this theological question: "In the intention of the Creator and Redeemer of children what meaning does childhood have, and what task does it lay upon us for the perfecting and saving of humanity?" (33).

In the first section of the essay Rahner treats "the unsurpassable value of childhood" and presents childhood in terms of his transcendental theological anthropology and realized eschatology. In the second section Rahner interprets the understanding of childhood in Scripture and in the Christian tradition as being both *realistic* and *idealistic*. In the last section Rahner deals with the theological understanding of what it means to be a "child of God." In this essay Rahner's approach to childhood builds upon the central ideas that undergird his entire theological project: God as "incomprehensible, holy Mystery"; humanity as fundamentally graced; and "time" as a process revealing both possibility and limitation.

The Value of Childhood

For Rahner, a person's relationship with God is operative at *every* stage of human growth and development, childhood being no exception. However, modernity's tendency is to interpret temporal existence in a linear fashion, using physical/biological categories that view life as a sum total of a series of stages. In

---

64. Rahner's essay originated as a lecture he gave on October 1, 1962, at the Second International Conference of "SOS Children's Villages" in Hinterbühl, near Vienna, shortly before the opening of the Second Vatican Council. It was later published in the pastoral journal *Geist und Leben* 36 (1963): 104-14. The German version, "Gedanken zu einer theologie der Kindheit," is found in *Schriften zur Theologie*, 8 (Einsiedeln: Benziger Verlag, 1966), 313-29. I am following the English translation of David Bourke, "Ideas for a Theology of Childhood," in *Theological Investigations*, vol. 8 (London: Darton, Longman & Todd, 1971), 33-50. An edited, inclusive-language version of this essay can be found in *The Content of Faith: The Best of Karl Rahner's Theological Writings*, edited by Karl Lehmann and Albert Raffelt, translated and edited by Harvey D. Egan (New York: Crossroad, 1993), 123-29. Hereafter in this section, page references will be cited in the text. References are to the Bourke translation, unless otherwise noted.

this conceptual framework, human beings move through "phases" in such a way that, when one phase is exhausted, it leads on to the next, and the previous stage's meaning dissolves into it. Childhood and youth simply "prepare" for the "greater" part of life, the future that lies ahead. When this future arrives (presumably with maturity), childhood itself disappears. It is really only adult life that "counts."

Rahner finds this interpretation of human life-span particularly prevalent among Christians, which perhaps explains the Christian tendency to subordinate childhood to adult life. This view coincides with a commonly accepted concept of human history and time, and it is not necessarily without merit, since there is always the danger of becoming fixated in a particular stage of life. However, Rahner believes that this is only part of the truth about childhood. Far more important for Rahner is that a human being is a "subject." One is not just caught up inexorably in the sweep of time, but at every stage of human existence, one is able to grasp oneself as a whole. The past is retained as one moves toward a future, a future that is the result of what one has already worked out beforehand in the exercise of human freedom. To be a free human subject means that one can make present to oneself the *whole* of one's life — past, *present,* and future. And it is important for Rahner to remember that, according to the Christian view, the *totality* of existence is redeemed. Thus, eternity is not a final "stage" toward which we advance in time but the enduring validity of human existence lived in freedom. The goal toward which we advance (eternal life) is not "something added on" to this life. It is a gathering up of the *totality* of one's life, a gathering up in which one finds oneself. Temporal existence is not brought along behind oneself but is *made present* to oneself (34-36).[65]

For Rahner, this way of conceiving the relationship between human existence and eternal life is as appropriate to childhood as it is to any other individual phase of human life. However, of all the phases of human existence, it is childhood that most suffers from the impression of being merely provisional, existing simply to shape adult life. Rahner maintains that childhood is not merely a stage in one's past; it is an *abiding* reality. It endures as "that which is coming to meet us," an intrinsic element in the single and enduring completeness of our temporal existence considered as a unity: "the eternity of the human person saved and redeemed." According to this vision, human beings move *toward* the eternity of this childhood; we become the children we *were* as we gather up time into our eternity. Because the "decision" that eternity requires of us bears upon our life as a whole, we may still have to go on living

---

65. For Rahner's understanding of "eternity" and its relationship to "temporal" existence, see "Eternity from Time," 169-77.

through our own childhood.[66] Viewed in this way, childhood is something that we never leave behind completely. It continues to exercise an influence on us and remains an open question. Thus, Rahner concludes, "We do not move away from childhood in any definitive sense, but rather move toward the eternity of this childhood, to its definitive and enduring validity in God's sight" (35-36).

By now it should be clear that the experience of childhood in Rahner's thinking is "eschatological" as well as existential, since it enables us to appreciate the relationship of earthly life to eternal life. Childhood's significance is more than a matter of laying foundations for decisions that have eternal significance. Indeed, it is that aspect of our personal history that can only take place in childhood. Using the analogy of a field that bears fair flowers and ripe fruits, Rahner asserts that the experiences which take place in childhood are ones that "can only grow in *this* field and no other, and which will themselves be carried into the storehouses of eternity" (36). The grace of childhood is not merely the "pledge" of the grace of adulthood. This is his way of saying that "values of imperishability and eternity are attached to childhood . . . to be discovered anew in the ineffable future which is coming to meet us" (37). The "ineffable future" coming to meet us is nothing less than God's own Self, already present in our humanity.

For Christians, Rahner writes, the child is a human being from the very beginning of his or her existence. A child does not simply grow gradually into a human being; he or she *is* a human being (37). In the unfolding of one's personal history, one simply realizes what one already is. Furthermore, since in Rahner's theology being human implies an absolute immediacy to God, the child is intended to be, right from the start, a partner of God. Seeing the human being already present in the child, Christianity "protects the child while it is still in its mother's womb. . . . It has reverence for the child, for the child is a human being" (38).

In Rahner's thinking the state of childhood is considered the beginning of the state of the human condition: "Possessing itself yet exposed to the influence of the world and of history . . . it has still to become all things in the future. What is already present in the child has still to be realised, to become actual in experience." The connection between this beginning and one's full development is a mystery to which every one of us is subject and over which no one has control. Only when one's final completion is realized does one understand this origin of oneself (38-39).

---

66. Rahner's point is difficult to grasp unless one keeps in mind his overall transcendental theological project. He wants to emphasize that, due to the "situatedness" of human freedom (i.e., a childhood that can include deprivations such as poverty, violence, abuse, bad parenting, and so forth), even one who is an adult might still be working out eternally significant dimensions of childhood although one is biologically beyond that stage.

Childhood in Scripture and Tradition

Recognizing that an experience of duality permeates human existence,[67] Rahner argues that Christianity conceives of childhood as having a beginning in two different senses. In the first sense, the child is not a *pure* beginning, unaffected by what has gone before him or her, but is historically conditioned by the situation into which he or she is born. The human history of guilt and gracelessness that is a factor in every human individual history also affects the child. This is what theology traditionally has called "original sin." However, Rahner's view is considerably more optimistic than that of Augustine, the Reformers, or even the Council of Trent, since he recognizes also that although children are born into a history of sin, they are also in their origins "encompassed by God's love through the pledge of that grace, which in God's will to save all humankind, comes in all cases and to everyone from God in Christ Jesus" (39). Nevertheless, in contrast to Rousseau and other romantics,[68] Rahner does not view the child as "a sort of innocent arcadia, as a pure source which only becomes muddied at a later stage" (40). He accepts the Christian understanding of a child as

> already and inevitably the origin precisely of that person to whom guilt, death, suffering, and all the forces of bitterness in human life belong as conditions of his very existence. But . . . all this remains within the compass of God, of his greater grace and his greater compassion, therefore this realism with which Christianity reacts to the very origins of the human being in the child and its beginnings is far from being any kind of implicit cynicism. (40)

For Rahner, awareness of the guilt and tragedy that belong to the beginning of human existence comes about through a person's awareness of the blessedness of grace and the redemption that overcomes this guilt and tragedy. It is precisely this awareness that is brought about by the grace and redemption which a Christian experiences and to which he or she submits.

The second sense of "child" that Rahner considers is that what is said about children in Scripture presupposes that we already know what a child is. It is our own experience (our contacts with children as well as the experience of

---

67. The duality that Rahner refers to here is the lack of integration that is traditionally referred to as "concupiscence." Not to be confused with sin, it refers to the dissonance human beings experience in being unable to master or integrate all the elements that are given to us as a part of our reality prior to our free decisions. For further discussion of this idea, see James Bacik, "Rahner's Anthropology: The Basis for a Dialectic Spirituality," in *Being and Truth*, ed. Alistair Kee and Eugene T. Long (London: SCM Press Ltd., 1986), 172.

68. See Dawn DeVries's discussion of this view of children in her essay in this volume.

our own childhood) that the New Testament assumes in telling us that we must "become as children," or that we are "children of God by grace." This is not unproblematic, for, as Rahner recognizes, our experience is often "dark, complex, and conflicting in character" (40). His advice is "not to try to iron out the complexities, but to endure them," to be true to our own experience in arriving at an idea of what a child is. In so doing, we will remain true to the basic principle already articulated: that a child is a human being even in her incipient stages and, as such, she is divided within herself right from the beginning of her life, from the beginning onward.

According to Rahner, a genuinely Christian experience of childhood is both *realistic* and *idealistic.* Paul and Matthew both see the child as being immature and weak.[69] At the same time, "the little ones" (contrary to the prevailing wisdom of Jesus' own time) are used to exemplify the attitudes necessary for the reign of God: a lack of false ambition, not seeking dignities or honors; modesty; and a lack of artificiality. Again, the possession of these characteristics does not mean that children are "innocent." Rather, children are held up as examples because they are open and carefree in relation to God. Jesus points to children as those who know that they have nothing of themselves on which to base any claim to God's help, and yet who trust that his kindness and protection will be extended to them. When Jesus says, "Of such is the kingdom of heaven" (Matt. 19:14), he is not glorifying children but is saying he identifies with them. Children are those who know they have nothing on which to base their claim to God's help. They, like Jesus, expect everything from God (41-42).

In the last analysis, childhood is, for Rahner, a *mystery.* Along with being a beginning in the sense of being the absolute origin of the individual, a beginning that plunges its roots into a history over which the individual child has no control, childhood is the beginning of openness to God. Rahner calls this beginning "the future which comes to meet one" (42). But it is not until this future is recognized that the beginning which is childhood can be seen in its full significance. This beginning is actually given and "comes to its own realization, as a beginning which is open to the absolute beginning of God who is utter mystery" (42). If we are able to preserve this state of being delivered over to the mystery, "Life becomes for us a state in which our original childhood is preserved forever; a state in which we are open to expect the unexpected, to commit ourselves to the incalculable, a state which endows us with the power still to be able to play, to recognize that the powers presiding over existence are greater

69. For Paul, he cites 1 Corinthians 3:1; 13:11; and 14:28; Galatians 4:1-3; Ephesians 4:14; and Hebrews 5:13. See Matthew 11:16ff. for the parable of the children in the marketplace. See also Judith Gundry Volf's discussion of these biblical texts in her essay in this volume.

than our own designs, and to submit to their control as our deepest good" (42). This is the childhood, which characterizes the religious acts of adults, a spiritually mature state, a graced state that perdures even in its moments of sadness and struggle:

> Even in those cases in which we weep and are overcome by dejection . . . even these tears we accept as they are sent to us, recognizing that the sadness which they express is ultimately a redeemed sadness. And when our powers are at an end, we realize in a childlike spirit that our task too is at an end, since no one is tried beyond his own strength. When we take up this attitude, we make the mystery the protection and defense of our lives. We are content to commit them to the ineffable as sheltering and forgiving, to that which is unspeakably close to us with the closeness of love. (42)

For adults to attain the openness of children (which is what the kingdom of heaven requires), conversion is necessary. Yet, this conversion is only to become what we already are — children. Paradoxically, none of us know what childhood means at the beginning of our lives. It is only at the end of a lifetime of God-given repentance and conversion that we will be able to realize that childhood in which we receive the kingdom of God and thus become God's children. As Rahner says, "We only recognize the child at the beginning of life from the child of the future. And in the light of this, once more, we can understand that childhood involves a mystery, the mystery of our whole existence" (43).

Becoming Children of God: The Fullness of Childhood

Rahner insists that becoming a child of God involves more than a metaphorical application of the human experience of being a child to one's relationship with God (43). Contemporary depth psychology and transcendental philosophical analysis recognize that the experience of a secure childhood is necessary in order to have a basic trust in reality. This basic sense of trust has an impact upon our experience of God. While accepting the wisdom of this insight, Rahner cautions against exaggerating the necessity of a secure childhood for one's relationship with God. "It is perfectly possible," he points out, "that a lack of protection, a lack of that sheltering solicitude and security which comes from the love of one's parents, may actually serve to spur us on to the metaphysical quest for one who will provide us with our ultimate support, who will sustain us and protect us" (44). However, Rahner admits that only children who have been able to learn that the names "father" and "mother" stand for a protecting love will be able to use those names for God and be able to recognize in God the very source of their own existence, in whom they can be authentically themselves (45). He is aware that those who felt neglected or abandoned as children may interpret that experience in an ultimate and metaphysical sense. As a consequence, these persons often are not able to overcome subsequent experiences of life's hardships or psychological traumas by recourse to the experience of a secure childhood, which gives assent to meaning and life, but interpret such experiences as further projections of that experience of insecurity. Those who are engaged in religious education, spiritual direction, and clinical psychology know this only too well from their experience of dealing with people. This in itself underlines for Rahner how important the human experience of childhood is for understanding and experiencing the realities expressed by the transferred concepts of "child of God," "God the Father," "God the Mother," and so on (46-47).

Childhood is not a state that applies only to the first phase of our biological lives but is "a basic condition," always appropriate to human existence lived rightly. As an inherent factor in our lives, childhood

> must take the form of trust, of openness, of expectation, of readiness to be controlled by another, of interior harmony with the unpredictable forces with which the individual finds himself confronted. It must manifest itself as freedom . . . as receptivity, as hope which is still not disillusioned. This is the childhood that must be present and active as an effective force at the very roots of our being. . . . The childhood which belongs to the child in the biological sense is only the beginning, the prelude, the foretaste and the promise of this other childhood, which is the childhood proved and tested and at the same time assailed, which is present in the mature man. (47)

It is the childhood of the mature person that is "the true and proper childhood" for Rahner; it is the fullness of that *former* childhood, the childhood of immaturity. What brings about the unity between these two childhoods is that both entail orientation to God. As I noted above, this orientation is not merely metaphorical, the transference of a word from a biological context to a religious context. Rather, in the *reality* of human childhood — in its openness, its trusting dependence on others, its courage to face fresh horizons — one encounters as "already *ipso facto* an achieved and present fact": that transcendence of faith, hope, and love in which the ultimate essence of the basic act of religion precisely consists (48). Rahner offers this explanation:

> In the last analysis, therefore, human childhood is not transferred by some dubious process of metaphorical or poetic transference to a quite different reality which we called childhood of God, but rather has its ultimate basis in

this itself, so that the latter is always and right from the first contained in the former, and finds expression in it. . . . Childhood is only truly understood, only realises the ultimate depths of its own nature, when it is seen as based upon the foundation of childhood of God. (49-50)

These acts of transcendence (which are typical of the state of childhood), according to Rahner's theological anthropology, are characteristic of the fundamental religious orientation of the human person. They can be elevated to religious acts, and the ideas through which we apprehend the world can be elevated to the level of prayer. It belongs to the essence of such an act "that it should not come to rest at any other point except that of total self-abandonment to the incomprehensible infinitude of the ineffable mystery" (48). Thus, for Rahner, adults who maintain childhood as an elemental factor in their nature and allow it to develop to the fullest and without limitation are truly religious.

In summary, Rahner defines human childhood as "infinite openness."[70] Embracing the mature childhood of the adult, that "attitude in which we bravely and trustfully maintain an infinite openness in all circumstances . . . despite the experiences of life which seem to invite us to close ourselves," is essential for developing an authentic religious existence. But the ability to maintain such an attitude is always a matter of the "self-bestowal of God," or what in theological language is called "grace." The adventure of being human, as Rahner describes it, begins with being a child in the biological sense and continues in "remaining a child forever, becoming a child to an ever-increasing extent, making [one's] childhood of God real and effective in this childhood" (50).

Original Sin and Infant Baptism

Rahner's thinking on original sin and baptism has become extremely influential in post–Vatican II Catholic theology.[71] The neo-scholastic textbooks had

---

70. In Nathan Mitchell's estimation, Rahner views a child as "a sacrament of that radical openness to the future which is a characteristic posture of the Christian believer precisely because the child reveals not only what we once were, but what we will be." See Mitchell, "The Once and Future Child," 428.

71. See, for example, Thomas A. Smith's assessment in *The HarperCollins Encyclopedia of Catholicism*, s.v. "original sin." Rahner's theology has exerted great influence on both Catholic sacramental theology and liberation theology. See, for example, Mark O'Keefe, *What Are They Saying about Social Sin?* (New York: Paulist Press, 1990).

428

taken it for granted that an unbaptized child was guilty of original sin and that baptism was necessary for salvation because it "took away original sin." Rahner's brief allusion to the existence of original sin in "Toward a Theology of Childhood" indicates that he also held that children were affected by original sin as part of the universal human condition. However, he stressed that the divine self-communication of God, "who alone is essentially holy, is grace *antecedent* to the free decision of a creature who is ambivalent and therefore not holy by his very essence"[72] (emphasis mine).

Rahner lamented the atrophy of the doctrine of original sin. He felt that the doctrine had largely become "a catechism truth" for modern people, a topic mentioned at its proper place in religious instruction and then forgotten in daily life and average preaching. Original sin did not have much formative influence in a contemporary person's conception of reality, in which death and concupiscence were construed as "natural" parts of human experience. Rahner also realized that, for most Catholics, baptism was regarded as "annulling original sin more or less in such a way that the latter is only felt to be a vital problem as regards unbaptized children."[73]

Rahner's response to this modern pastoral situation was to explain that original sin is only "sin" in an analogous sense.[74] It is not sin in the same sense as personal sin.[75] However, since it involves something "that should not be," it ought to be regarded as sin.[76] The doctrine of original sin is an attempt to express the role that sin plays in a human life *prior* to one's exercise of freedom. In this sense, every human being is "situated" in a condition of prior human sinfulness that affects his or her free decisions. To put it another way, Rahner would say that every human person is born into the world under the influence of two competing forces: the power of God's redeeming love in Christ and the power of sin opposed to Christ. However, although these two forces are fundamental, they are not equal.[77] Original sin is *not prior in time* to Christ's redemp-

---

72. Karl Rahner, "Original Sin," in *Encyclopedia of Theology: The Concise Sacramentum Mundi* (New York: Seabury Press, 1975), 330.

73. Karl Rahner, "Original Sin," 329.

74. Karl Rahner, *Foundations of Christian Faith* (New York: Seabury Press, 1978), 106-15.

75. While there are clearly basic similarities between them, here Rahner ultimately differs from Augustine, who never sufficiently differentiated between original sin and the voluntary, personal sin for which one can be held accountable.

76. Karl Rahner, "Anonymous Christianity," *Theological Investigations*, vol. 12, trans. David Bourke (New York: Seabury Press, 1974), 164.

77. For a helpful commentary on Rahner's understanding of original sin, see Brian McDermott, "The Bonds of Freedom," in *A World of Grace: An Introduction to the Themes and Foundations of Karl Rahner's Theology*, ed. Leo J. O'Donovan (New York: Seabury Press, 1980), 50-63.

tive action. Therefore "original sin" cannot be regarded as more universal and efficacious than the effects of "original redemption" deriving from Christ. (Romans 5:15-17 is cited as scriptural evidence.) For Rahner, nevertheless, they are two "existentials"[78] of the human situation with regard to salvation which at all times determine human existence.[79] Human beings lack God's sanctifying Spirit precisely because they are members of a sinful human race. However, since it is God's will that humans should have this sanctifying Spirit, the absence of the Spirit is contrary to God's will. But this *lack which ought not to exist* is sin only in an analogous sense, as the "state of what ought not to be."[80]

Rahner's theology emphasizes baptism as a sacramental entrance into the Church and thus into the fullness of Christian life.[81] Baptism "imparts that life which God gives us through his self-communication . . . in order to make us capable of eternal life in immediate unity and community with God."[82] Again, Rahner recognized that a number of modern persons are troubled by baptism. "They ask why baptism, and even baptism of infants, exists, when we know, or at least hope, that God leads to eternal salvation every person of good will, hence also non-Christians, 'heathens,' and even atheists (if they obey the voice of conscience)."[83]

Rahner uses the example of the relationship between "dispositions" and "gestures" to explain why the universal offer of grace to humanity does not negate the importance of baptism. He observes that the love of one person for another, considered as an inner disposition, differs from the glance, the gesture, the caress, with which one might express one's love. Yet, the inner disposition of love fully develops only if it is also expressed and "embodied" in bodily gestures. So, too, the solidarity that several people might feel is an inner disposition. But that solidarity can become wholly itself only when these people share a common meal.[84] Following upon these analogies, for Rahner, the refusal of baptism when it is possible to be baptized is like a person refusing to grow, because it is said that even as an embryo one is already a human being. It is like re-

---

78. Rahner borrows this terminology from Heidegger to refer to the general characteristics of human existence. See Bacik, "Rahner's Anthropology," 168-82.

79. Rahner, "Original Sin," 330.

80. Rahner, "Original Sin," 330. See also "The 'State of Fallen Nature,'" *Theological Investigations,* vol. 19, 39-53.

81. It is interesting to note that although the revised Rite of Baptism for Children provides a ritual "in case of danger of death," it also includes the "Rite of Bringing a Baptized Child to the Church," which should be celebrated if the infant survives.

82. Karl Rahner, "Baptism and the Renewal of Faith," *Theological Investigations,* vol. 23 (New York: Crossroad, 1992), 195. See also *Foundations of Christian Faith,* 411-15.

83. Rahner, "Baptism and the Renewal of Faith," 195-96.

84. Rahner, "Baptism and the Renewal of Faith," 196.

fusing a concrete act of love while at the same time affirming one's love. Baptism, then, in Rahner's thinking, is also an *effect* of grace, since the baptized person brings the grace of God that he or she has already freely accepted. This viewpoint creates a problem, of course, in the case of children.

In defending the practice of infant baptism, Rahner reviews the history of Catholic theological arguments, moving from the Council of Trent's pronouncement against the Anabaptists (no re-baptism or ratification of baptism is required when children reach the age of reason), to the argument from analogy (which held that just as original sin was contracted without personal fault, so the faith underlying infant baptism was the "alien" faith of parents, sponsors, or the whole church), to a further clarification which recognizes that even the capacity for faith is always the gift of God's grace. It is this insight which solves the problem for Rahner:

> The whole matter is settled once we perceive that we are graciously enabled to perform free, salutary acts by God's pure gift, which in fact precedes all human activity, though not necessarily by a priority of time. This salvific will of God for each individual, which must first bestow life before life can develop and fulfil itself, is addressed to the child at his baptism, as a gift and an obligation, in terms that are historically and ecclesially tangible, because the reality of that gift and obligation does not derive from the assent of his faith.[85]

Rahner would not maintain, as some would, that if baptism makes one a member of a visible church, then one ought to be able to choose such membership freely, something a child cannot do. Rahner's reply is that when we are born,

> we may accept or we may hate our existence, but we cannot get rid of it. Human freedom is always unquestionably a reaction to something that we have not chosen. . . . So if in baptism that which a human person really is becomes manifest — namely the creature loved by God, destined to receive divine life — then freedom does not suffer any injustice, because, with regard to God and the world, it is always a responsive freedom that never has the first word.[86]

The Church understands herself as the historical and social manifestation of the fact that all persons are called by God. To say that in baptism one becomes a member of the Church simply concretizes the standing invitation addressed to everyone by God. Certainly, the inner presence of grace can exist without the

85. Karl Rahner and Herbert Vorgrimler, *Theological Dictionary*, s.v. "Infant Baptism" (New York: Herder & Herder, 1965).
86. Rahner, "Baptism and the Renewal of Faith," 201.

appropriate outer embodiment and manifestation (that is, in "baptism of desire" and "perfect contrition"), but this does not mean that it is "something left up to individuals."[87]

Rahner admits that the New Testament does not mention baptism of children, but notes that the Church has clung to the correctness and meaningfulness of this practice. This is not the same as saying that one is "obliged" to baptize children. However, if in baptism what a human person really is becomes manifest, "namely, the creature loved by God, destined to receive divine life," then it becomes important that parents be committed to accepting responsibility for enabling their children to accept in faith, hope, and love the love of God that is offered to them throughout their lives. The position of the Catholic Church — that it does not allow a child to be baptized (except "in danger of death") unless there is a guarantee of his or her Christian upbringing — is based upon this understanding of baptism.[88]

With regard to the fate of unbaptized children, Rahner adamantly rejected the doctrine of "limbo," a theory that, even as recently as the Second Vatican Council, conservative neo-scholastic theologians wanted to define as church dogma.[89] Rahner was incredulous that the authors of the preconciliar schema could profess to know with such certainty what eternal reward awaited unbaptized children and was especially incensed about the pastoral difficulties created by such reasoning.[90]

87. Rahner, "Baptism and the Renewal of Faith," 197.

88. Rahner and Vorgrimler, "Infant Baptism," 230. See also Mark Searle's discussion of the role of parents and the family in infant baptism in "Infant Baptism Reconsidered," in *Living Water, Sealing Spirit: Readings on Christian Initiation,* ed. Maxwell E. Johnson (Collegeville, Minn.: Liturgical Press, 1995), 404-8.

89. Rahner possibly was helpful in forestalling the attempt of conservative members of the Roman curia to define limbo as a dogma of the Church at Vatican II. See the account of his advisory work on the Council's preparatory texts for Cardinal König: "Konzilsgutachten," in *Karl Rahner — Sehnsucht nach dem geheimnisvollen Gott,* ed. Herbert Vorgrimler (Freiburg: Herder, 1990), 104-6. For a complete account of the neo-scholastic origin of these drafts and the reactions to them, see Klaus Wittstadt, "On the Eve of the Second Vatican Council (July 1–October 10, 1962)," in *History of Vatican II,* vol. 1, ed. Giusseppe Alberigo and Joseph A. Komonchak (Maryknoll, N.Y.: Orbis Books, 1995), 410-29.

90. Rahner wrote to König, "How does one help people of today understand that God — who surely has a universal, saving will — in the time before Christ would allow children who died as infants into heaven, but since the New Covenant, through no fault of theirs or others, simply because He has gotten into a bind with his baptismal command, refuses them entrance? How is one to make clear to people today that the authentic, universal saving will of God is available to children, if one is doomed to founder on an obstacle that God Himself and his saving will has created?" See Rahner, "Konzilsgutachten," 106-7. I am grateful to Eckhard Bernstein for his help in translating Rahner's German here.

According to Rahner, as an *invitation* to accept God's love, the baptism of children reaches its real meaning and completion when eventually they accept this love of God that is offered to them in faith, hope, and love on a daily basis in their adult lives:

> The decisive question is not whether, through the love and fidelity of their ordinary Christian life, they accept God's self-donation offered to them when they were children or whether, time and again, explicitly in Christian freedom, they ratify the baptism they received as children. The ultimate and decisive acceptance of baptism in personal freedom takes place throughout the length and breadth of human and Christian life.[91]

Rahner and the Religious Education of Children

One of the legacies of Rahner's theology is the impact that his theological anthropology and his rethinking of the relationship between nature and grace has had on the contemporary renewal of catechetics in Roman Catholicism. A brief historical overview of approaches to the religious education of Catholic children in the twentieth century will help contextualize Rahner's contribution, as well as provide important background for the rich resource that this aspect of pastoral practice offers for a more fully developed Catholic teaching on children.

Catechetics in Recent Catholic History

The history of catechetical renewal in twentieth-century Roman Catholicism is bound up with several other renewal movements in the Church that both paved the way for and were legitimized by the Second Vatican Council. The liturgical and biblical movements, the social movement known as "Catholic Action," the *nouvelle Theologie,* which emphasized a return to patristic sources *(ressourcement)* — all played a key role in reforming catechetics.[92] At the beginning of

91. Rahner, "Baptism and the Renewal of Faith," 202.
92. For a brief but excellent history of how these movements influenced Catholic catechetics in the twentieth century, see Berard Marthaler, "The Modern Catechetical Movement in Roman Catholicism: Issues and Personalities," in *Sourcebook for Modern Catechetics,* 275-89. See also Mary Charles Bryce, "Evolution of Catechesis from the Catholic Reformation to the Present," in *A Faithful Church: Issues in the History of Catechesis,* ed. John H. Westerhoff III and O. C. Edwards Jr. (Wilton, Conn.: Morehouse-Balow Co., Inc., 1981), 204-35.

the twentieth century, outside of Sunday preaching, catechetics in most of the Catholic world was centered upon children. Question-and-answer catechisms were the chief means of "passing on the faith." Robert Hurley describes this as a "magisterial process" because it assumed that "verifiable information would be taught in a didactic fashion by a competent instructor":

> Catechisms had evolved into doctrinal summaries that were replete with abstractions, far beyond the psychological capacities of children in primary and elementary grades. These texts, tending towards rationalism and legalism, were often tainted with anti-Protestant polemics. The catechetical process was cut off from the child's family life and was most often considered the task of professionals in the field, such as priests, sisters, brothers and lay teachers. Moreover, catechesis had become estranged both from the parish and from the rhythms of the liturgical year.[93]

The catechetical renewal that began shortly after the turn of the century had three phases.[94] The first was occupied with the quest for more effective *methods*. In German-speaking countries the "Munich Method" was popular. Based upon insights from German educational psychology, it never really caught on in the United States because of its emphasis on passive learning. In France, Bishop Ladrieux, the bishop of Dijon, wrote a pastoral letter in 1922 that became a kind of manifesto for a catechetical renewal there. He observed wryly that "instead of going in directly by the open doors of the child's imagination and sense perception, we waste our time knocking on the still bolted doors of his understanding and his judgment."[95] A few years later Chanoine Dupont set forth the outline of a catechism session:

> The point of departure should be a picture shown to the children or a story told to them. They should then be asked to express themselves freely and let their hearts speak up. Little by little, with delicacy and tact, they should be guided toward the discovery of the catechism formula or the prayer text which the picture shown to them at the beginning suggested in the concrete.[96]

A pedagogical method that had been developed earlier, known as the "activity school," was appropriated by French catechists in the mid-1930s. They

---

93. Hurley, *Hermeneutics and Catechesis*, 22.

94. Marthaler, "The Modern Catechetical Movement in Roman Catholicism," 276.

95. P. Ranwez, as cited in *Shaping the Christian Message: Essays in Religious Education*, ed. Gerard S. Sloyan (Glen Rock, N.J.: Paulist Press, 1963), 120.

96. Dupont's method was published in Belgium under the title *Pour apprendre la religion aux petits* (Tamines: Duculot, 1929).

advocated group work, singing, recitation of verse, and games or projects. Involving the children in preparing the equipment needed for the lesson was also viewed as valuable, since "a truth can be understood only in so far is it is personally experienced."[97] Another innovation involved getting the children to enter into the spirit of the liturgical season, "for example by having them work together on the staging of a show based on the mysteries of Christmas or Easter."[98]

Madame Lubienska de Lenval's approach to Christian formation involved a system of teaching in which gestures and attitudes inspired by both Bible and liturgy were designed to foster the awakening of a balanced religious sense. Similarly, Madame Damez brought out very strongly the need to arouse "the essential religious activity, prayer." She argued that catechism teachers ought to guide their four- or five-year-old pupils toward a meeting with God. By praying in their presence and with them, by creating an atmosphere of silence, and by preserving an attitude of reverence, teachers can "set free the flight of the Christian child toward God."[99]

In this first phase, the attempts to find more effective methods of religious education focused on making the teaching of religion something active: by introducing various activities to sustain a child's interest (drawing, singing, acting out scenes); by introducing the child to liturgical life; and, most especially, by awakening that supreme religious activity, prayer. Even the "Munich method," though not entirely successful, signaled the beginning of a defection from the defensive attitudes of the Counter-Reformation that characterized Catholic religious education before Vatican II.

The second phase of catechetical renewal developed somewhat in reaction to the first phase. During this period — which also saw the convergence of the catechetical, liturgical, and kerygmatic movements, each of which sought to "return to Christ" as the central focus of Christianity — there was more emphasis on *content*. A name that stands out in this period is Josef Jungmann, S.J. (1889-1975). Although better known for his contribution to liturgical studies, Jungmann became identified with the "kerygmatic theology" movement, so named because its followers stressed the "Christian message" (kerygma). Welcoming the kerygma as "good news" was thought to be more important than the orthodox interpretation of certain doctrines and proper teaching methods. Not surprisingly, Jungmann's views were considered suspect by the Vatican's Holy Office, and his book, *Die Frohbotschaft und unsere Glaubensverkündigung*

---

97. This was the approach of Marie Fargues, *Les méthodes actives dans l'enseignment religieux* (Paris: Edition du Cerf, 1934).

98. Françoise Derkenne, *La vie et la joie au catéchisme* (Paris: de Gigord, 1935).

99. P. Ranwez, as cited in Sloyan, *Shaping the Christian Message*, 121.

(1936), was withdrawn from circulation. As a result, it did not appear in English until 1962. In the United States his writings were made known through the lectures of visiting scholars, especially Johannes Hofinger. Since Jungmann taught at Innsbruck during the same period as Rahner, there has been speculation about whether his thinking in any way influenced Rahner.

In fact, Rahner clearly distanced himself from "kerygmatic theology," although some authors recently have proposed that the situation might be more complicated than this.[100] However one might construe his relationship to Jungmann, Rahner's objection to kerygmatic theology needs to be understood in the context of the discussions concerning the reform of seminary education that were being carried on at the time. Rahner himself explains:

> There was a time, in the 1930s, when a theory was developed in Innsbruck which advocated a dual education for future priests: there would be a "kerygmatic theology" which would directly serve the task of preparing priests to preach. There would also be another scholarly theology based more upon philosophical and theological reflection. I never accepted this theory, although I grant in practice there can be variations in theology and pedagogy.[101]

It is true that Herbert Vorgrimler is willing to use the term "kerygmatic" to describe Rahner's theology, if that simply means that it is always wholly concerned with the religious basis of the human situation:

> Seen from this standpoint, his theology may be described as "kerygmatic theology," but the term is liable to be misunderstood. For Rahner it does not mean that alongside the necessarily abstract and dry, strictly scientific theology, there must be a diluted form "for wider circles"; nor does it mean that he is opposed to subtle, highly specialized theological studies. It is simply a difference of horizon.[102]

Other reactions against the kerygmatic approach came primarily from missionaries and catechists in the developing nations who did not doubt that the Word of God was "good news," but who advocated the inculturation of preaching, catechesis, and liturgy. A series of "International Catechetical Study Weeks" was organized under the direction of Johannes Hofinger between 1959

100. This is the view of Georg Baudler in "Göttliche Gnade und menschliches Leben: Religionspädigogische Aspecte der Offerbarungs-und Gnadentheologie Karl Rahners," in *Wagnis Theologie*, 39-40.

101. Rahner, *Faith in a Wintry Season*, 9.

102. Vorgrimler, *Karl Rahner: His Life, Thought, and Works* (Glen Rock, N.J.: Paulist Press, 1966), 7.

and 1968.[103] The last one, which was held in Medellín, challenged catechetics to address the political and socio-economic order that shapes religious attitudes. It also called for the endorsement of pluralism as a positive value in catechetical activity and enacted a resolution that this principle be recognized in *The General Catechetical Directory.*[104]

The third phase of catechetical renewal, which corresponds to the present, postconciliar period, involves a broadening of educational ministries. These include retreats, youth ministry, adult education, and preschool religion programs based on Montessori methods. These various ministries make use of new instructional technologies (such as educational television and video) and increasingly emphasize the role of the community brought about by the Rite of Christian Initiation of Adults (RCIA). Today the debates over content and method are not as heated, perhaps because of increased emphasis on adult religious formation.[105]

Rahner's Particular Contribution

Rahner himself wrote very little about the practical and existential situation of children in the family, church, and society. Yet, his own early pastoral experience[106] and the overarching pastoral concerns of his theology that I have discussed above indicate his awareness of the challenges facing those entrusted with passing on the faith to the next generation. In a few interviews Rahner talked with adolescents (of high-school age), and he wrote a series of letters to young adults about the concrete challenges of contemporary Chris-

---

103. These seminars took place in Nijmegen (1959), Eichstätt (1960), Bangkok (1962), Katigondo (1964), Manila (1967), and Medellín (1968).

104. Marthaler, "The Modern Catechetical Movement in Roman Catholicism," 281. *Sharing the Light of Faith (The General Catechetical Directory)* was a document of the U.S. bishops that gives principles for Catholic religious education.

105. It is beyond the scope of this essay to give an assessment of the contemporary state of religious education in the Roman Catholic Church. However, as a college professor who teaches mainly Catholic undergraduates, I, along with many of my colleagues, have become increasingly concerned about the imperiled state of children and youth catechesis. Many baptized and confirmed Catholic students arrive at college theology courses today without even a rudimentary understanding of "the Christian story," let alone an understanding of the Bible and church tradition. Ironically, although more emphasis is being put on parental responsibility for the religious education of children, local parishes and dioceses have cut budgets for adult religious education.

106. Rahner spent most of the war years (1938-1945) as a member of the diocesan Pastoral Institute in Vienna. During the last year of this period he served as a parish priest in the Bavarian village of Mariakirchen.

tian life.[107] His Christmas meditations[108] reflect upon the coming of God as a child, although they center more on the doctrine of the Incarnation than on the child in any existential sense.[109] However, two essays, one written several years before Vatican II and the other in 1970, provide evidence that Rahner was concerned about children's religious development.

In the 1970 essay entitled "Faith and the Stages of Life,"[110] Rahner addresses the needs of younger children and questions whether a catechism is the appropriate medium for the religious initiation of a child. Here Rahner shows himself to be fairly astute about issues of child development and suggests that content in religious education should be approached more carefully:

107. Rahner's *Faith in a Wintry Season* contains three conversations in which Rahner was interviewed by young women students at Munich's Gymnasium am Anger (1983), by students in Augsburg (1984), and by young women at the BVM Institute at St. Pölten (1983). A series of letters from young adults and Rahner's replies to them was published as *Mein Problem: Karl Rahner antworte jungen Menschen* (Freiburg: Herder, 1982); the English translation is *Is Christianity Possible Today?* (Denville, N.J.: Dimension Books, 1984). Lawrence James discusses some of these letters in "Karl Rahner Answers Young People," *The Living Light* 30 (1994): 13-17.

108. See Karl Rahner, *The Eternal Year* (Baltimore: Helicon, 1964), 19-55; "Christmas, The Festival of Eternal Youth," in *Theological Investigations*, vol. 7, trans. David Bourke (London: Darton, Longman & Todd, 1971), 121-26; "Holy Night," in *Theological Investigations*, vol. 7, 127-31; "Weihnachten: Fest der Geschichte," in *Herausforderung des Christen: Meditationen — Reflexionen — Interviews* (Freiburg: Herder, 1975), 33-35; *Gott ist Mensch Gewordern: Meditationen* (Freiburg: Herder, 1975); and *Die Gabe der Weihnacht* (Freiburg: Herder, 1980). In addition, see the selections from "The Christmas Season" in *The Great Church Year: The Best of Karl Rahner's Homilies, Sermons, and Meditations,* edited by Albert Raffelt, translation edited by Harvey Egan (New York: Crossroad, 1993), 47-106.

109. Rahner's Christmas meditations remind one of Schleiermacher, who also used Christmas as an occasion for reflecting on human experience as the locus of divine encounter. See Dawn DeVries's discussion of *The Celebration of Christmas: A Conversation* in her essay in this volume. Although Rahner nowhere acknowledges Schleiermacher as an influence on his theology, this similarity has been noticed by others such as Daniel Donovan. Donovan, for example, in reviewing volumes 17 and 20 of the English editions of Rahner's *Theological Investigations*, says, "In spite of all the obvious differences, there is much . . . that is reminiscent of Schleiermacher. Rahner's philosophical categories are certainly not those of his great Protestant predecessor. The experience, however, to which he points, the primacy that he attributes to it, even the formulations that he uses to evoke it in his more personal and spiritual writings, bear a striking resemblance to what lay at the heart of Schleiermacher's theological revolution." See Daniel Donovan, "Vintage Rahner," *Cross Currents* 33 (1983-84): 387. Francis Schüssler Fiorenza also has noted the similarity of the two thinkers. See his forthcoming article in *Modern Theology.*

110. Karl Rahner, "Faith and the Stages of Life," in *The Practice of Faith: A Handbook of Contemporary Spirituality,* ed. Karl Lehmann and Albert Raffelt (New York: Crossroad, 1984), 124.

When religious education is conducted in such a way that ten- to twelve-year-old children have already heard everything once, what they can actually assimilate existentially has not been presented in adequate depth and vitality, nor with the promise of anything *new* still to come in their faith experience or in religious instruction in later stages of development. It is scarcely any wonder, then, if this age marks the beginning of a period of decline in a knowledge of the faith.[111]

Concerned that children were being forced to become miniature adults in the area of religion, and that adults were instructing them this way "simply for fear of not being able to reach them later," Rahner recommends that certain biblical passages (for example, the Genesis stories) be presented to children only when they can better appreciate the poetic-mythical character of the narratives, when they are able to distinguish content from form. Similarly, he sees disadvantages in introducing children to certain religious customs, such as altar serving or singing in the choir. He worries that these activities will be regarded as "children's activities," ones that will be outgrown eventually and put aside. Rahner suggests that these activities be presented as "privileges" for which a child one day becomes "old enough."[112]

Some years ago, Michael Langer, a German religious educator, discussed Rahner's writings that had relevance for the religious socialization of youth in an increasingly secularized culture.[113] Although the majority of these writings are more oriented to ministry with young adults rather than children, Langer praises Rahner's boldness in addressing the pastoral needs of the young. He singles out for special mention the earlier of Rahner's two essays referred to above, "The Sacrifice of the Mass and an Ascesis for Youth."[114] Despite the fact that it was written in 1957 and employs pre-conciliar terms that are no longer meaningful to most Catholics,[115] this essay demonstrates Rahner's abiding concern for youth catechesis. For example, Rahner warned against putting too much emphasis on the Mass for young people. He encouraged the development of a "Mass of life," or a "people's Mass," that would be age-specific and more appropriate for those under twenty-five. The essay reveals clearly how, early on, Rahner understood that there were stages of religious development that correspond to the stages in human biological devel-

---

111. Rahner, "Faith and the Stages of Life," 124-30.

112. Rahner, "Faith and the Stages of Life," 125.

113. Langer, "Religionspädagogik im Horizont Transzendentaler Theologie," 45-77.

114. "The Sacrifice of the Mass and an Ascesis for Youth," *Mission and Grace: Essays in Pastoral Theology*, vol. 1 (London: Sheed & Ward, 1963), 203-54. The German original appeared in 1957.

115. For example, "ascesis for youth" might better be rendered "spirituality" today.

opment. Thus, he encouraged the coordination of the presentation of religious truths according to these phases of development and voiced the regret that, aside from a few requirements of Canon Law from which one is exempted before age seven and before age twenty-one, "as soon as children cease to be children in the narrower sense they begin to be regarded simply as undifferentiated Christian people."[116]

Langer also observes that from 1964 through 1977, Rahner undertook the composition of what he called "short formulas of faith." In these brief credal statements he attempted to express Christian faith in a way that corresponded to the present cultural situation. Several "short formulas" are included in the epilogue to *Foundations of Christian Faith*.[117] Although these were probably not intended for small children, Langer encourages religious educators to follow Rahner's example and employ such "short formulas" as a way of overcoming the "faith deficit" that young people experience.[118]

The Impact of Rahner's Theology

More significant than any individual writings on the catechesis of children and youth, however, is the impact that Rahner's whole theological project had on Catholic religious education after Vatican II. He is seldom mentioned by name in this connection,[119] but Rahner's theology, when taken as a whole, particularly his central focus on God's self-communication in human experience and his concern for "a new mystagogy," deserves greater recognition from Catholic religious educators. It may well be that his ideas have so permeated modern Catholic theology that they have become part of the very air religious educators breathe.

Maria Harris, for example, recalls the early days of post–Vatican II religious education in the United States and the enormous impact of Rahner's theology. In the mid-1960s she joined the religious education staff of the Catholic

116. Rahner, "The Sacrifice of the Mass and an Ascesis for Youth," 227.

117. Rahner, *Foundations of Christian Faith*, 448-59.

118. Langer, "Religionspädagogik im Horizont Transzendentaler Theologie," 71. Langer also endorses Rahner's recommendation that his book of meditations, *Encounters with Silence*, might serve as a fitting "commentary" on the short formulas.

119. Although many authors have commented on the pastoral thrust of Rahner's theology, in my research I could find only two sources in English that discuss the implications of Rahner's thought for religious education. See James B. Dunning, "Human Creativity: A Symbol of Transcendence in Contemporary Psychology and the Theology of Karl Rahner: Implications for Religious Education" (Ph.D. diss., The Catholic University of America, 1973); and Hurley, *Hermeneutics and Catechesis*.

diocese of Rockville Centre, New York, where her major work was in-service education with directors of religious education (DREs). She saw their number grow from four in 1967 to one hundred seventy-eight in 1973. Reflecting on how today these men and women fill every conceivable pastoral role, she notes in particular the influence of Karl Rahner:

> Back then . . . especially in Catholic circles, the majority of people in individual parishes were only at the start of a world shaking awareness of new possibilities for being "Spirit in the world" — a phrase of Karl Rahner's. Women and men were signing up for masters programs like the one our diocese was initiating and were reading Rahner. . . . The laity were crowding the many educational programs we were running because they were experiencing a new kind of community. They wanted deeper theological understanding for themselves and yearned for non-rote teaching and a broader religious education for their children.[120]

While Harris merely suggests that Rahner's thought helped spark a new era among U.S. Catholic religious educators, Georg Baudler adamantly insists that "the *entire* renewal of religious education, especially that documented by the [German] synod's final document on religious instruction in the schools, would be unthinkable without Karl Rahner's renewed formulation of the relationship between nature and grace."[121] Baudler maintains that without the new horizon of theological reflection (often called "the anthropological turn") that is exemplified in Karl Rahner's theology of revelation and grace, recent pedagogical theories adopted by religious educators would not be possible.[122]

Likewise, Roman Bleistein,[123] another German religious educator, cites Rahner's vision of a "new mystagogy" as an illustration of how Rahner realized long ago what many religious educators are coming to understand only today: namely, that the cultivation of a sense of *mystery* (in the sense of mystagogy) is essential for children's religious education and for fostering their spirituality. A prime example is the work of David Hay, the director of the British Children's

---

120. Maria Harris and Gabriel Moran, *Reshaping Religious Education: Conversations on Contemporary Practice* (Louisville: Westminster/John Knox, 1998), 1.

121. The German original: "Ich mochte hier jedoch die These vertreten, dass der *gesamte* Neuansatz der Religionspädagogik, wie er sich besonders im Synodenbeschluss über den Religionsunterricht an der Schule dokumentiert, ohne die Neubestimmung des Natur-Gnade-Verhältnisses durch Karl Rahner undenkbar wäre." See Baudler, "Göttliche Gnade und menschliches Leben," 38. The translation in the text is mine.

122. Baudler, "Göttliche Gnade und menschliches Leben," 38.

123. Bleistein, "Mystagogie und Religionspädagogik," 51-60. See also Herbert Haslinger, *Sich selbst entdecken — Gott Erfarhen*, 41-62.

Spirituality Project at Nottingham University, who has used Rahner's theology to ground his research into the spirituality of children.[124]

Hay and his colleagues are challenging the dominance of cognitive developmental theory (that of Piaget,[125] Goldman,[126] and Kohlberg[127]) in the field of religious education. They believe it "come[s] close to dissolving religion into reason, and childhood religion into a form of deficit or inadequacy."[128] Instead, they endorse the spiritual potentiality within every child, no matter what the child's ability or cultural context: "Our position is akin to that of Rahner. We conceive of an innate spiritual capacity in childhood, but recognise that this may focus in particular ways and take different and changing forms as the child's other capacities develop."[129]

Hay takes issue with developmentalists who are "stuck at the level of God-talk" in their exploration of children and religion. These researchers focus on the language that children use as the criterion for identifying religious experience. Hay objects to considering only what children *say* about God (which leads to the conclusion that childhood religion is immature and inadequate) because language, like all conceptual reflections, always fails to capture the experience.[130] Researchers, Hay argues, need to take a different direction. They need to focus on children's perceptions, their awareness of and responses to those ordinary activities that Peter Berger calls "signals of transcendence."[131] Given the lack of such a research tradition, Hay and his colleagues find resonance in Rahner's transcendental theology. They frequently cite the following

124. See David Hay with Rebecca Nye, *The Spirit of the Child* (London: HarperCollins, 1998); David Hay, "Children and God," *The Tablet* 249 (1995): 1270-71; David Hay, Rebecca Nye, and Roger Murphy, "Thinking about Childhood," in *Research in Religious Education*, ed. Leslie J. Francis, William K. Kay, and William S. Campbell (Macon, Ga.: Smyth and Helwys Publishing Co., 1996), 47-71. In addition, see *Education, Spirituality, and the Whole Child*, ed. Ron Best (New York: Cassell, 1996); Robert Coles, *The Spiritual Life of Children* (Boston: Houghton Mifflin, 1990); Margaret Crompton, *Children, Spirituality, Religion, and Social Work* (Brookfield, Vt.: Ashgate, 1998); M. McClure, "How Children's Faith Develops," in *The Spirituality of Children: The Way* (Supplement) 86 (1996): 5-13.

125. Jean Piaget, *The Language and Thought of the Child* (New York: Harcourt Brace, 1926).

126. Ronald Goldman, *Religious Thinking from Childhood to Adolescence* (New York: Routledge, 1964).

127. Lawrence Kohlberg, *The Philosophy of Moral Development: Moral Stages and the Idea of Justice* (San Francisco: Harper & Row, 1981).

128. Hay, "Children and God," 1270.

129. Hay, Nye, and Murphy, "Thinking about Childhood," 60.

130. A compelling example that Hay et al. use is the profound faith of people who are mentally retarded. See Hay, Nye, and Murphy, "Thinking about Childhood," 56.

131. David Hay with Rebecca Nye, *The Spirit of the Child*, 54.

passage from Rahner in order to substantiate the difference between religious "knowing" and the ability to capture spiritual experience in words:

> And even if this term [God] were ever to be forgotten, even then in the decisive moments of our lives we should still be constantly encompassed by this nameless mystery of our existence. . . . Even supposing that the realities which we call religions . . . were to totally disappear . . . the transcendentality inherent in human life is such that [we] would still reach out towards that mystery which lies outside [our] control.[132]

Hay believes that because modern technological society ignores the spiritual dimension of children's lives, in time this dimension will become repressed. Rahner's theology is therefore extremely relevant for parents, preachers, and religious educators, who, according to Hay, must direct children's attention to areas of experience that are ignored, misinterpreted, or trivialized by the surrounding culture.

Conclusion

This examination of Rahner's theology of the child, as well as his reflections on original sin, infant baptism, and children's religious development, lead me to the following observations and conclusions concerning his contribution to a more coherent Catholic teaching on children.

First, Rahner provides a twofold view of childhood: (1) he contributes an important definition of the child as "infinite openness to the infinite"; and (2) he understands childhood as an abiding quality of human existence that, when entered into and embraced, makes us receptive to Jesus' vision of the realm of God. Already as a child, a human being is a "subject" who enjoys an immediate relationship with God that is actual and not merely potential. As Rahner sees it, childhood is the beginning of human transcendentality, and thus constitutes both the quality that enables us to love and to be responsible, *and* the state of spiritual maturity that characterizes our participation in the interior life of God and makes possible the experience of genuine human community.

Second, according to Rahner, being a child has value in its own right and is not simply a stage one passes through on the way to becoming an adult. This view stands in sharp contrast to the market anthropology of late twentieth-

---

132. Karl Rahner, "The Experience of God Today," *Theological Investigations*, vol. 9, 149-65. Cited in David Hay, *The Spirit of the Child*, 19-20.

century capitalism, which regards children as commodities or consumers and evaluates their worth according to cost-benefit analyses. The implication of Rahner's theological anthropology of the child is clear. Children are not objects to be bought, sold, or used. Rather, according to the example given by Jesus in the Gospels, they are the paradigm for a new ethos characterized by mutual trust and interdependence.

Third, Rahner's understanding of childhood as a "basic condition" or "existential"[133] that remains throughout the whole of one's life provides a needed corrective to the "excessive natalism" of much official Catholic teaching that focuses solely on the incipient stages of human life. The definition of the child as a full human being from his or her very beginning implies that a child is a "sacred trust" to be nurtured and protected at *every* stage of his or her existence. Therefore, an important implication for Catholic social teaching, which derives from Rahner's transcendental notion of enduring childhood, is the promotion of the dignity and welfare of children as an ethical demand that is equal in importance to the protection of fetal life. In particular, the basic openness that characterizes the essence of a child must not be compromised or betrayed by those who have been entrusted with the care of the child. Violations of this trust not only injure the child but, as Rahner points out, can have tragic, long-term effects on the adult: his or her basic sense of openness and trust can be destroyed.[134]

Fourth, while Rahner's theology has begun to be more widely appreciated by religious educators for breaking through the abstract, defensive, neo-scholastic overemphasis on content to a more "subject-centered" (in the sense of child-centered) catechesis, researchers in the emerging field of children's spirituality are forging a new application of his insights. They have recognized that the cultivation of the child's natural sense of wonder about such fundamental human experiences as friendship, love, death, sex, sadness, joy, success, failure, and so forth — experiences that contemporary culture trivializes, misinterprets, or ignores — is vital to the encounter with the "gracious mystery" that, for Rahner, characterizes both the experience of God and the experience of the self.[135] Today, this aspect of Rahner's theology is being utilized to advocate the development of the child's innate spirituality and to re-envision children's religious education as "a new way of seeing" in a world that is becoming increasingly devoid of mystery.

133. See Bacik, "Rahner's Anthropology," 168-72, and above, n. 78, for a review of Rahner's concept of "existential."

134. This is borne out by contemporary clinical practitioners' interest in adult recovery of the "inner child."

135. For a fuller treatment of Rahner's understanding of the unity of the experience of self and the experience of God, see his "Experience of Self and Experience of God," *Theological Investigations*, vol. 13, 122-32.

Finally, in much the same way that the *exitus/reditus* dynamic functioned for Thomas Aquinas in the *Summa Theologiae,* Rahner's notion of the child as "infinite openness to the infinite" and his concept of childhood as an inherent human disposition offer a profoundly important theological anthropology for a Catholic social teaching on children. Rahner's theological anthropology reminds us not only that our obligation is to nurture the children who are given to us and all that belongs to them as children, but that each one of us, again and again, must become that child we were in the beginning. It invites those of us who are adults to allow our childhood trust, openness, expectation, and willingness to be dependent upon others to be released, "not as a fond or bitter memory, but as a facet of what we hope to become."[136] As Rahner reminds us,

> It is only in the child that the child in the simple and absolute sense of the term really begins. And that is the dignity of the child, his task and his claim upon us all that we can and must help him in this task. In serving the child in this way, therefore, there can be no question of any petty sentimentality. Rather it is the eternal value and dignity of [the human being], who must become a child, that we are concerned with, [the human being] who only becomes a sharer in God's interior life in that he becomes that child which he only begins to be in his own childhood.[137]

---

136. This phrasing belongs to Nathan Mitchell, "The Once and Future Child," 427.
137. Karl Rahner, "Ideas for a Theology of Childhood," 50.

17. "Let the Children Come" Revisited: Contemporary Feminist Theologians on Children

BONNIE J. MILLER-McLEMORE

While widespread concern for children has generated an interest in children on a number of academic fronts in the past several years, research on children has not exactly proliferated in either theology or women's studies. A library word-search combining the terms "feminism," "religion," and "children" does not turn up many articles or books. More disturbing, a recent *Dictionary of Feminist Theologies*, edited by Letty Russell and J. Shannon Clarkson, skips from "character" to "Christ, Jesus," leaving out an entry on children.[1] Unfortunately, some people assume that when it comes to religious values and children, feminists have focused solely on women's right to choose abortion. Such quick appraisals only feed the common suspicion that feminists, including feminist theologians, are anti-child and anti-family.

Yet, these random observations should not mislead us. Feminist theologians have said more on children than one might suppose at first glance. That the *Dictionary of Feminist Theologies* does contain entries on "family" and "mother/motherhood" tells us a great deal about the current state of the discussion: Feminist theologians have attended directly to both motherhood and family and indirectly, through these interests, to children. Thus, reading between the lines for ways in which feminist theologians have understood the nature of children, their education and formation, and adult responsibilities and obligations for the nurture of children is a far more fruitful project than the usual carping about feminist oversights.

In undertaking this task, we will find that many feminist scholars in religion

---

1. *Dictionary of Feminist Theologies*, ed. Letty Russell and J. Shannon Clarkson (Louisville: Westminster John Knox Press, 1996).

have given more attention to children's needs from a wide range of academic, religious, and ethnic perspectives than other contemporary theologians. In the first two sections of this essay, I will attempt to situate the feminist theological discussion in the context of the mid- to late-twentieth-century, characterizing three sorts of groups that have emerged. In the final section, drawing on the work in each group, I will characterize what feminist theologians have said about children, concluding with a brief appraisal of the implications of feminist theology for an enriched theological discussion. Among their primary contributions, I will argue, are a material appreciation for the labors of love, a psychological grappling with early developmental issues, a spiritual understanding of the gifts of children, and a political declaration of the vulnerabilities and rights of children.

As American society reconsiders the needs of children and as parents and congregations struggle to care for them, feminist theologians remind us not to lose sight of these important material, psychological, spiritual, and political realities. Many feminist theologians have not only thought about children; they have acted as primary caregivers of children. It is from this vantage point in part that they have distinctive contributions to make. Because feminist theology has addressed the issue of children more indirectly than directly, I will argue that it needs to make a bolder articulation of its indirect remarks about children and to provide a fuller theological vision of children and our obligations to them for the sake of children and for the sake of the vitality of theology itself. Modern theological anthropology, centered largely on adult cognition and volition, has become a hollow, narrow rendition of the lively unpredictability of human life with children.

The Contemporary American Context

In Western culture, during the period from the eighteenth to the mid-nineteenth century, the movement of men out of the home and into the workplace had a powerful impact on American family life that has been well documented. Broadly speaking, men had less immediate involvement with domestic life and hence with children. In matters of education and spiritual formation, children had fewer male role models readily available. The impact on children of working women, especially among the lower classes, received less attention until the more recent alarm over the employment of white middle-class women. Between 1948 and 1993, the percentage of married women in the workforce with children under six rose from 10.8 percent to 59.6 percent.[2] Unfortunately, pa-

2. Children's Defense Fund, *The State of America's Children Yearbook: 1994* (Washington, D.C.: Children's Defense Fund, 1994), 76.

ternal involvement in child care and household chores has not increased proportionately. As a result of these and many other interconnecting factors,[3] the care and religious formation of children have been under increasing duress in the last century.

Yet scholarship on children has not been a high priority in twentieth-century theology, even though congregations and denominations have maintained important ministries for children. As Todd Whitmore observes, the associated institutions of the U.S. Catholic Church have written documents and provided services, but "there is no *developed* teaching on children" by the church itself.[4] A similar indictment could be made of the lack of theological deliberation in Protestant denominational policy statements and in the work of Protestant theologians.

In feminist theology there are understandable reasons for the silence. As I have argued in an earlier essay on children, "On children women have much to say but little time, less energy, and almost no means of voice. Children rapidly consume these elements. This essay itself was hammered out in small pieces between minor crises in tending my children."[5] The passions of maternity and all the work that comes with attending to children can fracture or destroy the focus required for second-level erudite deliberations. These impediments are magnified by cultural presumptions and social structures that discourage women's creative passions beyond their children.

Another powerful reason has also been operative: feminists in general have worked hard to undermine the "inexorable tie between mothers and children."[6] Unlike first-wave feminism in the nineteenth century, second-wave feminism of the twentieth century deeply disturbed the U.S. public precisely because it contested assumptions at the heart of American home life: a man's domestic headship and the subordination of a woman's desires and power in relationship to her husband and children. Women and mothers, feminists asserted, have needs independent of and sometimes in immediate conflict with the needs of children and men. Housework and childcare ought not to con-

---

3. For a more developed exploration of the multiple factors influencing families, see chapter 2 in Don Browning, Bonnie J. Miller-McLemore, Pamela Couture, K. Brynolf Lyon, and Robert M. Franklin, *From Culture Wars to Common Ground: Religion and the American Family Debate* (Westminster John Knox Press, 1997).

4. Todd David Whitmore, "Children and the Problem of Formation in American Families," *The Annual of the Society of Christian Ethics* (1995): 273, emphasis in text.

5. Bonnie J. Miller-McLemore, "Let the Children Come," *Second Opinion* 17, no. 1 (July 1991): 12.

6. Ann Snitow, "Feminism and Motherhood: An American Reading," *Feminist Review* 40 (Spring 1992): 36; see also Barbara Easton, "Feminism and Contemporary Family," *Marxist Perspectives* 1, no. 1 (1993): 11-36.

sume the mother's very lifeblood. Certain texts, such as Shulamith Firestone's *The Dialectic of Sex,* have been especially "demonized, apologized for, endlessly quoted out of context," often to protest that the feminism of the late sixties and early seventies was, among other negative family sentiments, anti-children.[7]

Finally, the hotly debated issue of women's right to procreative choice claimed a great deal of attention. Battles over a variety of religious issues, such as the moral authority of women, the participation of women in ministry, and celibate views of sexuality, became narrowly focused around abortion. Conflict between U.S. Catholic feminists and the Vatican, for example, came to a head when ninety-seven prominent Catholics, including twenty-six nuns, signed a *New York Times* ad that ran on October 7, 1984, claiming that a diversity of opinions existed on the morality of abortion.[8] Perhaps no other issue has caused such splits, with religious women taking polar opposite sides. For many feminists across the moral spectrum, however, the emphasis fell on the labors of raising children, recognizing overtly, perhaps for the first time, not only the blessing of children but the real costs of caring for them. Feminist concern with the welfare of *born* children raised problems for Christian theological reflection on human nature and responsibility that remain unsolved. Undoubtedly, hidden behind many anti-abortionists' love of children lay misogyny or hatred of women. Hidden behind many abortion advocates' words was a love of women and already existing children. According to Maura Ryan, the fight represents "nothing less than a demand for a new social order, one in which women define rather than are defined by their reproductive contribution."[9]

Initially the visibility of the "demon" texts and particular hot issues overshadowed differences among feminists and the variegated claims about women and children. In the past two decades, however, the voices of women of color and the writings of postmodernity made the diversity of women's childbearing experiences more apparent. Partly as a result, a shift from liberal feminist to women-centered feminist approaches has occurred, making motherhood a more acceptable topic.

This shift is most clearly marked by three pivotal texts of the late seventies: Adrienne Rich's *Of Women Born* (1976), Nancy Chodorow's *The Reproduction of Mothering* (1978), and Sara Ruddick's *Maternal Thinking* (1980). All three have had an immense influence on understandings of mothers. But they did not change the general public perception of the women's movement as an-

---

7. Snitow, "Feminism and Motherhood," 35.

8. Rosemary Radford Ruether, "Catholic Women in North America," in *In Our Own Voices: Four Centuries of American Women's Religious Writing,* ed. Rosemary Radford Ruether and Rosemary Skinner Keller (New York: HarperCollins, 1995), 30.

9. Maura A. Ryan, "Abortion," in *Dictionary of Feminist Theologies,* 2.

tagonistic toward families and, for the most part, did not reflect the experiences of women outside the white middle-class. Some feminist critics have worried about the impact on feminist politics of the more recent pronatalist and profamily leanings of certain prominent feminists, such as Betty Friedan and Germaine Greer.[10] Moreover, children themselves have yet to receive the same level of attention as mothers. If some people question whether a focus on mothering subverts feminist politics, they will be sure to quarrel with a focus on the primacy of children.

The Contemporary Feminist Theological Discussion

Where have feminist theologians stood in these debates? From the beginning, feminists in theology recognized their importance in the critique of the patriarchal family and the critique of Christian tenets that support it. They disputed religiously endorsed assumptions that men are ordained "heads" of households and that all women desire and, indeed, need motherhood to become fully human according to their "special nature." Some, such as Rita Nakashima Brock, see many Christian doctrines as a form of the patriarchal family writ large: God the father symbolizes male dominance, and traditional portrayals of the cross condone child abuse. In this view, the "major key" to unraveling patriarchal power lies with the family.[11] Many feminist theologians have argued for the biblical and theological appropriateness of the redistribution of power in families and for the adequacy of the choice not to have children or to live alone.[12]

Among many issues, arguments for the appropriateness of childlessness and shared responsibilities in families have had to contend with powerful connections between the maintenance of strong families and the survival of a religious tradition or ethnic group. This is most apparent in particular communities such as the Jewish community,[13] fundamentalist Christian groups,[14] and

10. See Judith Stacey, "Are Feminists Afraid to Leave Home? The Challenge of Conservative Pro-Family Feminism," in *What Is Feminism? A Reexamination,* ed. Juliet Mitchell and Ann Oakley (New York: Pantheon, 1986), 208-37; and Barbara Ehrenrich, "On Feminism, Family and Community," *Dissent* (Winter 1983): 103-9.

11. Rita Nakashima Brock, *Journeys by Heart: A Christology of Erotic Power* (New York: Crossroad, 1988), 3.

12. See Margaret R. Miles, "The Courage to Be Alone — In and Out of Marriage," in *The Feminist Mystic,* ed. Mary Giles (New York: Crossroad, 1982), 84-102.

13. Martha A. Ackelsberg, "Families and the Jewish Community: A Feminist Perspective," *Response* 48 (Spring 1985): 10.

14. Margaret Lamberts Bendroth, *Fundamentalism and Gender: 1875 to the Present*

African American families.[15] But beyond these particular instances, religion in general has frequently equated the maintenance of distinct gender and child-bearing roles in patriarchal families with the survival of a religious faith community.

Theology has also tended to lump women and children together as subordinate to and dependent on men. As early as the Gospel of Matthew — "not counting women and children" (Matt. 14:21) — women and children have often been dismissed *en masse*. Hence, even when children remained a personal or communal priority, for the initial feminist project in religion to become involved with children threatened its already precarious position in a public world heretofore defined by men, exclusive of women and children. As relative newcomers to the study of religion in the sixties and seventies, feminists had plenty of other work to do, challenging truncated and harmful understandings of women and central theological doctrines. Feminists may simply not have realized the extent to which redefining our position and value as women requires a redefinition of the lower status of children.

Nonetheless, feminist theologians have taken a different tack toward children than secular feminists. Unlike the authors of the "demon texts," most feminist theologians have avoided inflammatory statements that blamed children for women's plight. Connections to religious history and practices have acted as a partial restraint. Feminist theologians are related to a rich heritage of women's long-standing religious commitments to families and children. From the late nineteenth to the early twentieth century, women of faith in a variety of contexts championed the needs and rights of children through a proliferation of women's organizations and the founding of community institutions like orphanages and schools.[16] In their characterization of the history of African-American Christian women, Jualyne E. Dodson and Cheryl Townsend Gilkes observe, "More often than not, it was the consciousness con[c]erning their chil-

---

(New Haven: Yale University Press, 1993); and Betty A. DeBerg, *Ungodly Women: Gender and the First Wave of American Fundamentalism* (Minneapolis: Augsburg Fortress, 1990), especially chapters 2 and 3.

15. Toinette M. Eugene, "Sometimes I Feel Like a Motherless Child: The Call and Response for a Liberational Ethic of Care by Black Feminists," in *Who Cares: Theory, Research, and Educational Implications of Care,* ed. Mary M. Brabeck (New York: Praeger, 1989), 46-48. See also Bonnie Thorton Dill, "Our Mother's Grief: Racial Ethnic Women and the Maintenance of Families," *Journal of Family History* 13, no. 4 (1988): 415-31.

16. Anne Firor Scott, *Natural Allies: Women's Associations in American History* (Urbana: University of Illinois Press, 1991), 13-20; Evelyn Brooks Higginbotham, *Righteous Discontent: The Women's Movement in the Black Baptist Church, 1880-1920* (Cambridge: Harvard University Press, 1993), 149-63; and the National Council of Jewish Women, *The First Fifty Years* (New York: National Council of Jewish Women, 1943), 32-38, cited in *In Our Own Voices,* 69, 120, 160.

dren . . . that fueled careers in public activism."[17] Such concern is still evident. A statement on children by the Women's Division of the United Methodist Church's Board of Global Ministries is a wonderful example of the only acceptable Christian response to the double bind for women who love children: "We continue to face the historical dilemma which assigns only to women the concern for ministries with women, children and youth. We must continue to make these 'women's concerns' our priority because the larger church and the society are reluctant to take the lead."[18]

With such important practical commitments in the background, the feminist theological treatment of children can be seen in a new light. Regard for children in feminist theology actually began before the turn to motherhood in secular gynocentric feminism in the 1970s and 1980s and also received new energy from this shift. Although sustained, systematic study of children remains to be done, distinguishable groups of feminist theologians have considered children in the midst of their ardent promotion of three related causes: (1) motherhood and God; (2) family and the common good; and (3) social, economic, and political justice. In each group, to a greater or lesser extent, children — although not the main text — are an important subtext.

1. Motherhood and God

Oddly enough, most easily overlooked is material by the "motherhood group." Interest in mothers arose partly in response to the shift toward gynocentric feminist theory and has generated in work in both theological and religious studies. Many of the texts in theology, such as Anglican Margaret Hebblethwaite's *Motherhood and God,* do not enjoy wide circulation and readership. Although not overtly feminist in orientation, Hebblethwaite takes up the task of "finding motherhood in God," which resembles the feminist project of Sallie McFague and others. However, Hebblethwaite adds a second purpose that is seldom explored: "finding God in motherhood." She draws on the "frustrating material details of everyday life" with three small children to make theological observations about the divine-human relationship and

17. Jualyne E. Dodson and Cheryl Townsend Gilkes, "Something Within: Social Change and Collective Endurance in the Sacred World of Black Women," in *Women and Religion in America: 1900-1968,* vol. 3, ed. Rosemary Radford Reuther and Rosemary Skinner Keller (San Francisco: Harper & Row, 1986), 81.

18. "Ministries with Women and Ministries with Children and Youth: A Gift for the Whole Church," policy statement of the Women's Division (Cincinnati: General Board of Global Ministries, United Methodist Church, 1993), 2, cited in *In Our Own Voices,* 104-5.

spiritual judgments about domestic devotional practices.[19] Problems with conception teach humility before God's creative power, labor and delivery teach trust, and children bring simultaneous joy, frustration, and desperation that hint at the mystery of God's love for us and our necessary reliance upon it in raising children.

In one of the earliest feminist collections in theology, both Valerie Saiving and Carol Christ also identified the fruits of maternal experience. According to Saiving, the minutia of mothering leads women toward both self-transcending love and destructive self-loss.[20] According to Christ — and Penelope Washbourne, who devoted an entire book to women's development — birthing itself and the mother-daughter bond deserve celebration as creative, life-giving activities that Western body-denying religion has disregarded and denounced.[21] Soon after, Beverly Wildung Harrison contended that deterring the world's self-destruction rests on embracing a feminist ethic grounded precisely in the maternal power of tending the personal bonds of community.[22]

More recently, my own work on maternal knowledge, Tikva Frymer-Kensky's recreation of childbirth literature, and Cristina Traina's research on maternal sexuality give some of these early themes new interpretations.[23] Whereas Saiving's 1960 essay begins with her declaring that "I am a student of theology; I am also a woman," my book, *Also a Mother,* cries out for serious attention to experiences of mothering and their implications for theology, religious practice, and women's lives. Mothers have access to certain invaluable

19. Margaret Hebblethwaite, *Motherhood and God* (London: Geoffrey Chapman, 1984), 1.

20. Valerie Saiving, "The Human Situation: A Feminine View," *Journal of Religion* (April 1960); reprinted in *Womanspirit Rising: A Feminist Reader in Religion,* ed. Carol P. Christ and Judith Plaskow (San Francisco: Harper & Row, 1979), 25-42; and Penelope Washbourne, *Becoming Woman: The Quest for Wholeness in Female Experience* (New York: Harper & Row, 1977).

21. Carol P. Christ, "Spiritual Quest and Women's Experience," in *Womanspirit Rising,* 228-45.

22. Beverly Wildung Harrison, "The Power of Anger in the Work of Love: Christian Ethics for Women and Other Strangers," *Union Seminary Quarterly Review* 36 (1981): 47.

23. See Bonnie J. Miller-McLemore, *Also a Mother: Work and Family as Theological Dilemma* (Nashville: Abingdon, 1994); and Tikva Frymer-Kensky, *Motherprayer: The Pregnant Woman's Spiritual Companion* (New York: Putnam Press, 1995); for Frymer-Kensky's reflections on the development of her thought, see "Birth Silence and Motherprayer," *Criterion* (Spring/Summer 1995): 28-34. See also Cristina Traina, "Maternal Experience and the Boundaries of Christian Sexual Ethics," *Signs: Journal of Women in Culture and Society* 25, no. 2 (Winter 2000): 369-405; "Passionate Mothering: Toward an Ethic of Appropriate Parent-Child Intimacy," *Annual of Christian Ethics* 18 (1998): 177-96; and "Set Afire: Images of Maternity in Medieval 'Theoeroticism,'" paper delivered at the American Academy of Religion, November 23, 1997.

ways of knowing, particularly bodily knowing, that are avenues to the creation of personhood; children themselves yield revelatory insights. *Motherprayer*, Frymer-Kensky's retrieval of meditations on pregnancy and childbirth, also emerges from her own maternal experiences and frustrations with the stark limits of a religious tradition and theological academy afraid to celebrate biological life processes as occasions for spiritual growth. Similarly, through careful study of the connections between sexual arousal and maternal response, Traina declares that ethicists can no longer remain silent about the meaning and moral status of the sensual pleasures experienced by many mothers in birthing, nursing, and caring for children.

Womanist theologians Toinette Eugene, Delores Williams, and Teresa Snorton, Ghananian theologian Mercy Amba Oduyoye, and Mujerista theologian Ada María Isasi-Díaz develop related themes. From the perspective of communities marginalized by race, class, and gender, women theologians of color also raise particular questions about the oversight of mothers and children in early liberal feminism. Endorsements of motherhood question the outright denunciation of housework and childcare in much of early feminist thought. The home has an invaluable place in sustaining particular communities; theology and religious congregations must recognize and respond to the distinct vulnerability of children of color. Motherhood enjoys special sanctity, although this regard is not without internal ambiguities and tensions. Isasi-Díaz captures the ambivalence. She identifies family as one of a few key themes in which she has further theological investment. The family, she says, is the "heart of Latino culture." But almost in the same breath she admits her own trepidation about picking up such a divisive and volatile issue: The "politics . . . are extremely complicated."[24]

Yet, in general, women theologians of color recognize that the value of motherhood extends well beyond procreation to the survival and sustenance of the community.[25] Biological and social motherhood empower women precisely through the flourishing of children and the extension of self through family. This conviction disputes the conventional moral polarity between love of self and love of others. Moreover, while patriarchy presents severe challenges for women and children, men, particularly husbands and fathers,

24. Ada María Isasi-Díaz, *Mujerista Theology: A Theology for the Twenty-First Century* (Maryknoll, N.Y.: Orbis Books, 1996), 204.

25. Eugene, "Sometimes I Feel Like a Motherless Child," 46-48; Delores S. Williams, *Sisters in the Wilderness: The Challenge of Womanist God-Talk* (Maryknoll, N.Y.: Orbis Books, 1993), 34-59; Teresa E. Snorton, "The Legacy of the African-American Matriarch: New Perspectives for Pastoral Care," in *Through the Eyes of Women: Insights for Pastoral Care*, ed. Jeanne Stevenson Moessner (Minneapolis: Augsburg Fortress, 1996), 50-65; Mercy Amba Oduyoye, "Poverty and Motherhood," *Concilium* 206 (1989): 23-30.

remain extremely significant partners in communal liberation and familial stability.

Research on motherhood and children by feminist scholars in religious studies is harder to classify. Most of this research falls into diverse and sometimes narrower interdisciplinary schools of thought, such as the writings of Kathryn Rabuzzi in literature and religion or Diane Jonte-Pace in the psychology of religion. Trying to revive a sense of the sacred in her post-Christian world, Rabuzzi takes an intensely mother-focused approach in her books, absorbed with the mythic, gynocentric journey into maternal selfhood. She celebrates childbirth as an "instrument of self-transformation" and a religious practice, but children themselves do not figure prominently in her work, even if they hold personal importance for her. Her belief that salvation comes through selfhood almost completely overshadows moral questions of responsibility for children. As she puts it, the question "Do I *want* to become a mother?" must replace that of "*Should* I have a baby?"[26] She is more determined to oppose the tendency in Western religious tradition to denigrate childbearing and the childbearer than to contest the devaluation of children, even though the two are intricately interrelated.

From the different perspective of the psychology of religion, Jonte-Pace brings together object relations and feminist theory to underscore the importance of the early mother-child relationship for the development of religious sentiment, ritual, and god imagery in adulthood. In particular, she draws on psychoanalyst Ana Maria Rizzuto's pivotal work on the role of preoedipal relationships in the formation of god imagery to rethink the function of religion in the human psyche.[27] The voice of the mother-with-child allows Jonte-Pace to interrogate cherished psychoanalytic explanations of religion, in particular Freud's fascination with paternal power in the family and his reduction of religious formation to a pathological resolution of father-son conflicts. A feminist psychology of religion embraces and challenges rather than rejects motherhood. Study of the preoedipal relationship between the mother and the child provides fresh ways to understand the religious yearnings of adults for mutual dependency and relationship.

While eclectic in method and orientation, the "mother group" focuses on the social, interpersonal, and intrapsychic dimensions of childbearing, the

26. Kathryn Allen Rabuzzi, *Motherself: A Mythic Analysis of Motherhood* (Bloomington: Indiana University Press, 1988), 2, emphasis added; see also Rabuzzi, *Mother with Child: Transformations through Childbirth* (Bloomington: Indiana University Press, 1994), ix-xx.

27. Diane Jonte-Pace, "Object Relations Theory, Mothering, and Religion: Toward a Feminist Psychology of Religion," *Horizons* 14, no. 2 (1987): 310-27. See also Ana Maria Rizzuto, *The Birth of the Living God* (Chicago: University of Chicago Press, 1979).

preoedipal mother-child relationship, and existential ethical and spiritual issues of child rearing. Children offer a rich source of personal and spiritual fulfillment. They shed light on the dynamics of adult development and religious behavior. These scholars clearly celebrate the fruits of children, the value of children in and of themselves, and maternal experiences of children, while remaining aware of the twin dangers of the demise of the mother's subjectivity in her caretaking role and the temptation to use children as a means to secure adult happiness.

2. Family and the Common Good

Following wider cultural trends toward increased concern about families, a second group appeared in the last decade and shifted the focus of feminist theology from the phenomena of mothering to the family. The "family group" has a more visible commitment to children than the other two groups. Yet even here the decisive passion is not exactly children or even mothers but the promotion of civil society and the common good. In moving away from women's experiences of oppression, this group sometimes submerges or reshapes the feminist political agenda in their work. Greater effort is made to plumb theological and philosophical traditions. From a distinctly Catholic and biblical perspective, for example, theological ethicist Lisa Sowle Cahill would find Rabuzzi's focus on personal fulfillment exemplary of a liberal tendency to neglect the social and communal interconnections linking sex, commitment, and parenthood. For Cahill, childbearing is not so much personally transformative as transforming of social connections: it is a "specifically *sexual* mode of social participation." The desire to have a child (Rabuzzi's main focus) and moral obligations to extend altruistic care to all children belong together as companion considerations. Thus procreation needs institutionalization in "family forms which are stable and beneficent toward children."[28]

Jean Bethke Elshtain adopts the latter agenda with particular zest. Her remarks were sparked initially by discontent with the disregard for the family in feminist and radical circles and more recently by concern for the plight of children outside stable, two-parent families. Children disappear in a market-driven society where the ultimate measures of value are utility and self-interest. Elshtain's pointed protest brings the needs of children — the "protection of vulnerable human life" — into sharp focus. She states unequivocally, "Social feminism of the sort I propose places children in the center of its concern."

28. Lisa Sowle Cahill, *Sex, Gender, and Christian Ethics* (Cambridge: Cambridge University Press, 1996), 201, 214; emphasis in text.

456

Children need attachment to specific committed adults as a "prerequisite for authentic human existence."[29] More recently, she has strengthened her case in support of the family in civic life and the importance of mothers and fathers to the life of the child and the life of the church and community. To learn the basics of democracy, including responsibility and reciprocity, children require a clear structure of external authority and limited freedom different from that practiced more widely in a civil society of democratic politics of equality among citizens. They need attachment to particular adults who keep the lines of parental moral supremacy clear. Stable families are the source of "nothing less than our capacity for sociality."[30]

Not surprisingly, at various times in the past two decades Elshtain has found herself under strong attack by other feminists for her subtle and sometimes not-so-subtle anti-feminist sentiments. Her critics have reason to signal their concerns. Her remarks on families come packaged with reproaches about feminist blunders and, initially at least, a romanticized longing for a pre-market family that preserves "feminine virtues" where the working-class woman "would prefer to be [home] with her children" rather than work under less-than-optimal conditions.[31] Her advocacy for children is sometimes overshadowed by a predilection for traditional parental structures with their values of hierarchy, inequality, and subordination. Support for women and concern about the gendered division of labor in the workplace and in families occupies a conspicuous backseat to other social values. Rather than understanding pressures that have led to increased family diversity or arguing for conditions that might better sustain equality in marriage, Elshtain focuses predominantly on the greater status and normativity of procreative heterosexual unions over "every ad hoc collection of persons who happen to be under one roof."[32]

Nonetheless, broadly speaking, in their concern for the common good, the "family group" offers a distinct feminist approach to children that is largely absent in the motherhood group. Children demand a modification of liberal premises about individual freedom. Responsibilities for children assume paramount importance. Embracing the revitalization of family life and community is seen as one way to break the destructive hold of social, moral, and religious

29. Jean Bethke Elshtain, "Feminism, Family, and Community," *Dissent* (Fall 1982): 447-48. See also Elshtain, *Public Man, Private Woman: Women in Social and Political Thought* (Princeton: Princeton University Press, 1981).

30. Jean Bethke Elshtain, "The Family and Civic Life," in *Rebuilding the Nest: A New Commitment to the American Family,* ed. David Blankenhorn, Jean Bethke Elshtain, and Steve Bayme (Milwaukee: Family Service America, 1990), 121-22; and "Family Matters: The Plight of America's Children," *The Christian Century,* 14-21 July 1993, 711.

31. Elshtain, "Feminism, Family, and Community," 448.

32. Elshtain, "Feminism, Family, and Community," 448.

problems that arose when values of individualism, deconstructivism, capitalism, and liberalism were taken to destructive extremes of solipsism, nihilistic relativism, materialism, and unrestrained libertinism.

3. Social, Economic, and Political Justice

A third category of scholarship has consistently received more attention than the other two, although not necessarily for its attention to children. This group arose earliest and continues to flourish. It includes some of the most prominent theologians in feminist studies, such as Rosemary Radford Ruether and Beverly Harrison, and some women more recently published, such as Paula Cooey, Pamela Couture, Christine Gudorf, myself, and others. The unity of this group lies in a common concern about the interconnections between theological ideas and social practices, particularly the complex constellations related to sexism, classism, racism, heterosexism, and ecological destruction. Ruether and Harrison represent well many of the widely shared assumptions. For both of them, the gospel is a social and political message of liberation from injustice, oppression, and destruction. Initially both Harrison's and Ruether's thinking on children involved the application of this interpretation to the question of reproductive rights.[33] Contrary to common perception, however, advocacy for procreative choice is based on a concern for the care of children rather than their neglect. Harrison, for example, grounds her argument in a "real concern for human dignity and the social conditions for personhood and the values of human relationship."[34] Choice entails not a devaluation of procreation but a fresh estimation of its seriousness. As she explains,

> Women understand what many men cannot seem to grasp — that the birth of a child requires that some person must be prepared to care, without interruption, for this infant, provide material resources and energy-draining amounts of time and attention for it. . . . Women bear the brunt of this reality and know its full implications. . . . No historical interpretation of abortion as

33. See Rosemary Radford Ruether, "The Development of My Theology," in "Rosemary Radford Ruether: Retrospective," *Religious Studies Review* 15, no. 1 (January 1989): 2. See also Beverly Harrison, *Our Right to Choose: Toward a New Ethic of Abortion* (Boston: Beacon, 1983); and, more recently, "Special Issue: Rhetoric, Rituals and Conflicts Over Women's Reproductive Power," ed. Beverly Harrison, *Journal of Feminist Studies in Religion* 11, no. 2 (Fall 1995): 1-93.

34. Beverly Wildung Harrison with Shirley Cloyes, "Theology and Morality of Procreative Choice," in *Making the Connections: Essays in Feminist Social Ethics*, ed. Carol S. Robb (Boston: Beacon, 1985), 119.

a moral issue that ignores these matters deserves moral standing in the present debate.[35]

Although Harrison has a different agenda from the "family group," she makes a similar claim: childbearing is not a capricious, individualistic matter but a complex, demanding activity accountable to the moral claims of the community.[36]

The "justice group" promotes the welfare of children by addressing related acute social and economic ills, including the poverty of mothers and children, child abuse, disdain for the bodily rights of children, rhetoric over "family values," and unfriendly public and governmental practices.[37] Christine Gudorf, for example, champions the critical import of a child's assertion of her "bodyright" or bodily integrity and control as a means to empower her to resist abuse and as morally appropriate in itself. The premise of the sanctity of embodiment rests on a child's claim as a worthy creation of God. Moreover, sexual pleasure and the body can operate as a conduit of divine reality and should be respected as such. The claim of a child's embodied worthiness is often overlooked by adults and inadequately supported by theology. Adults must understand children as "sufficiently important to warrant the adult spending time to explain" what is happening and why, for example, they must undress for the doctor, wear appropriate clothes, and express physical affection to a relative. Recognition of bodyright dictates that the child's wishes "should be solicited, heard, and considered in any decision about the child's bodyself," and a range of options offered relative to the child's maturity.[38] As with those in the motherhood group, Gudorf's own maternal thought and experience enrich her arguments, but her intent is less maternal exploration than social action.

Scholars in this group invoke an eschatological image in which all are welcomed to the table of God. An overriding concern in the work of Pamela Couture on women's poverty, Ruether and myself on work and family roles, and Paula Cooey on family values is stated nicely by Cooey: Christians are obliged to create a world in which "every child who wants might learn to dance."[39] Stated more formally, "Christians need to be at the forefront of advo-

---

35. Harrison, "Theology and Morality of Procreative Choice," 123.

36. Harrison, "Theology and Morality of Procreative Choice," 130.

37. See Pamela D. Couture, *Blessed Are the Poor? Women's Poverty, Family Policy, and Practical Theology* (Nashville: Abingdon, 1991); Christine E. Gudorf, *Body, Sex, and Pleasure: Reconstructing Christian Sexual Ethics* (Cleveland: Pilgrim, 1994); Rosemary Ruether, "Politics and the Family: Recapturing a Lost Issue," *Christianity and Crisis,* 29 September 1980, 261-66; Paula M. Cooey, *Family, Freedom, and Faith: Building Community Today* (Louisville: Westminster John Knox, 1996); and Marian Wright Edelman, *Families in Peril: An Agenda for Social Change* (Cambridge: Harvard University Press, 1987).

38. Gudorf, *Body, Sex, and Pleasure,* 193, 203.

39. Paula M. Cooey, "That Every Child Who Wants Might Learn to Dance," *Cross*

cating for the protection of all children, regardless of what kind of household, religious or otherwise, they come from."[40] Dance becomes a metaphor for a joy-filled engagement with life that defies injustice and subverts the false opposition between self-fulfillment and self-sacrifice. In general, the "justice group" makes full personhood and moral agency fundamental prerequisites to the good life and calls for justice for the "least of these" (Matt. 25:40). Feminists in this group criticize liberals as much as conservatives for the tendency to advocate for special interests, individual rights, and large social programs to the neglect of diverse and needy families. Children suffer from the same or related social and cultural distortions of human rights and public policies that women have encountered for decades. Like women, they are gifts of God's good creation, and even if not yet adults, they are "persons rather than property of their parents, and as persons, worthy of rights and capable of taking responsibility commensurate with their development."[41] Ultimately, in Margaret Farley's words, people are called "to make the family, as every other institution, a place of justice."[42]

*   *

This schematic categorization of three types of feminist theological reflection on children helps us sort through the richness of the feminist theological discussion. Of course, the boundaries between these three groups are not as distinct as this typology suggests. Feminists with interests in mothering share interests in justice and in families and vice versa. My own work, for example, sometimes cuts across all three groups. In fact, I would take this observation one step further and offer it as a constructive thesis about necessary directions for future feminist theological reflection: that is, the strongest feminist theological position on children would incorporate the strengths of all three categories, honoring maternal experiences, recognizing the value of stable family structures for the common good, and affirming the prerequisite of justice amid diversity in family life.

Currents: The Journal of the Association for Religion and Intellectual Life 48, no. 2 (Summer 1998): 185-97. For a similar stance, see Rosemary Radford Ruether, *New Woman, New Earth: Sexist Ideologies and Human Liberation* (New York: Seabury, 1975), 207-11.

40. Cooey, *Family, Freedom, and Faith*, 101.

41. Cooey, *Family, Freedom, and Faith*, 103. See also Rosemary Radford Ruether, "An Unrealized Revolution: Searching Scripture for a Model of the Family," *Christianity and Crisis*, 31 October 1983, 399-404.

42. Margaret A. Farley, "The Church and Family: An Ethical Task," *Horizons* 10, no. 1 (Spring 1983): 70.

In most cases the approach to children is funneled through a broader overarching agenda. This prioritizing of other concerns — mothers, civil society, justice — can and does sometimes eventuate in the benign neglect of children. But I would like to suggest that in all three groups, in general, feminist theologians have often sought a mediating position, attempting to a greater or lesser extent to reconcile two critical values often seen as competing: the welfare of children *and* the well-being of women. This position sometimes harbors idealistic assumptions and ignores the often irresolvable conflicts between freedom and community, individual autonomy and the social good. As Harrison admits, "The social policy I propose is highly utopic. Even to imagine a society that would function to prevent a trade-off between fetal life and women's well-being is difficult."[43] Sometimes feminist theologians simply put these ideals into a fertile Christian eschatological framework as something for which to hope with the coming of God's realm. In a word, the goal of feminist theological reflection on children is to work toward a redemptive community that encompasses all people and rights the wrongs they formerly inflicted upon each other.

Perspectives on Children

The threefold schema of categorizing trends in feminist reflection on children, religion, and theology demonstrates the rich diversity and major thematic contributions commonly overlooked in current family debates and in theological discussion. The bolder feminist theological position on children that I am advocating requires a more explicit and careful consideration of at least the following three areas: the nature of children, their education and formation, and adult responsibilities and duties. While this essay does not attempt to develop such a position in full, it lays the rudimentary groundwork by illuminating some of the contributions of the feminist discussion thus far. In the exploration below, it is interesting to note that despite the differences in political and religious agendas, all three groups make many of the same claims about the nature and nurture of children.

Equally notable is that many of the claims are largely unprecedented in theological history. The devaluation of nurturance and the lack of child-centered theological anthropology go hand in hand with the distance of most men from the intricate daily routines of providing for children in the last two centuries. As we will see, feminist theologians who sometimes carry the fruits

43. Harrison, *Our Right to Choose*, 31.

of their proximity to children into their theological reflection have greater access to insights that children themselves have to offer.

1. The Nature of Children

Contemporary feminist theologians such as Mary Pellauer, Marie Fortune, and others have raised the thorny question of the close connections between patriarchal Christianity and domestic violence and abuse.[44] Underlying and informing this analysis is an experiential grasp of the utter vulnerability of children before the adults that create and shape their world. This portrayal of the trusting innocence of children contrasts sharply with some traditional Christian perceptions of children's inherent sinfulness and greed. As a rule, feminist theologians believe that children may harbor evil thoughts, but that the depth and extent of their corrupt behavior is in direct proportion to the actions of the adults in their midst. Because they possess such incredible trust in and love for their parents, sometimes in the midst of the most horrible circumstances, they stand in need of adult advocacy and parental protection. Many feminist theologians plead for children and their embodied sanctity precisely because they write out of their own extremely painful personal history and seek to create a world in which no child will ever experience the same atrocities they did. This first and fundamental insight about the nature of children has important implications for the next two topics: education and parental responsibility for the nurture of children.

Feminist theologians also see children as more virtuous and dependent than do classic theological interpreters, sometimes to the extreme of identifying parents, particularly domineering fathers, as the loci of evil and wrongdoing. Rita Nakashima Brock, for example, builds her theology from the perspective of the disempowered child and, drawing on the psychological theory of Alice Miller, depicts the destructive ways in which parents use their children to satisfy their own immature narcissistic needs.

44. See *Christianity, Patriarcy, and Abuse: A Feminist Critique,* ed. Joanne Carlson Brown and Carole R. Bohn (New York: Pilgrim, 1989); Annie Imbens and Ineke Jonker, *Christianity and Incest* (Minneapolis: Fortress Press, 1992); *Violence against Women and Children: A Christian Theological Sourcebook,* ed. Carol J. Adams and Marie M. Fortune (New York: Continuum, 1995); Marie M. Fortune, *Violence in the Family: A Workshop Curriculum for Clergy and Other Helpers* (Cleveland: Pilgrim, 1991); Carolyn Holderread Heggen, *Sexual Abuse in Christian Homes and Churches* (Scottsdale, Ariz.: Herald Press, 1993); *Abuse and Religion: When Praying Isn't Enough,* ed. Anne L. Horton and Judith A. Williamson (Lexington, Mass.: Lexington Books, 1988); and *Sexual Assault and Abuse: A Handbook for Clergy and Religious Professionals,* ed. Mary D. Pellauer, Barbara Chester, and Jane A. Boyajian (San Francisco: Harper & Row, 1987).

On the other hand, without wanting to negate the problem of abusive parents, others such as Christine Gudorf draw upon their maternal experiences to recognize that children have more power over their parents than is commonly believed. Gudorf writes, "My husband and I were never in control of the relationship with either of [our] children, and are not now. . . . The children were in control, not only of themselves, but of us, a[t] least as much as we were. They dictated where we went and didn't, what we ate, all home activities, whom we saw, even how much sleep we got."[45]

Even though Brock and Gudorf appear to disagree on the surface, their differing arguments have a similar end in mind: both promote a fresh view of the child as a fully recognized human creation of God, deserving of immense respect and empathy all too often unjustly and wrongly denied them. Society has tended to infantilize children as fundamentally incapable of constructive thought and action. While children are not adults in body or mind, in their potential personhood they deserve the same recognition as adults.

Feminist theologians are concerned that children not be held unfairly responsible for inappropriate and destructive adult behavior, a concern that appears most overtly in the restraint surrounding and even the avoidance of the topic of children and sin. As a result of feminist theologizing, definitions of sin have received radically new interpretations in general. Feminist theologians have challenged the equation of sin with Eve, women, sexuality, lust, and bodily regeneration. More specifically, for Valerie Saiving, Judith Plaskow, and others, the besetting sin for women is triviality and self-denigration rather than pride and self-assertion. When they consider sin, they first of all redefine it in strikingly adult ways, as a human activity that rests on adult proclivities and powers — leanings and control that most children have not yet acquired. In her book *Family, Freedom, and Faith,* in a chapter on human creation in the image of God, Paula Cooey defines sin as the "warping of difference into division based on skewed power, exemplified in Adam's rule over Eve."[46] The "real sin," in Rosemary Ruether's eyes, is sexism or the "distortion of the self-other relationship into the good-evil, superior-inferior dualism" of male and female.[47] Little speculation has arisen on the distinctiveness of children and sin, although the ideas that failure to become a self is sinful and that distorted relational hierarchies are sinful could both easily be extended to self-development in children.

45. Christine E. Gudorf, "Parenting, Mutual Love, and Sacrifice," in *Women's Consciousness and Women's Conscience: A Reader in Feminist Ethics,* ed. Barbara Hilkert Andolsen, Christine E. Gudorf, and Mary D. Pellauer (San Francisco: Harper & Row, 1985), 177.

46. Cooey, *Family, Freedom, and Faith,* 67.

47. Rosemary Radford Ruether, *Sexism and God-Talk: Toward a Feminist Theology* (Boston: Beacon Press, 1983), 163.

Sin pertains as much to the social sphere of oppression as to personal acts. Again, this idea can be extended to the social context that limits and harms the lives of children. Sin, then, is not just the disparagement of women but the diminution of children as well. Sin is more something to which children fall victim than something they engage in as culprits.

Understandings of the vulnerability, relative innocence, and relative power of children trade on popular social and cultural perspectives. This is exemplified in the general appeal among many feminist theologians of Alice Miller's attacks on narcissistic parenting and the denial of the needs and desires of children. But feminist theology has also protested the common cultural assumptions of a capitalistic society in which children are seen as either possessions or impediments to economic progress. Children are named gifts of God that promise delight, bewilderment, and enlightenment.

As gifts, children have the capacity to create in those involved in their intimate, proximate care a hermeneutic of charity toward other children and humanity at large. Children instruct adults in the practices of nurture — what Beverly Harrison calls "a formidable power," "less dramatic, but every bit as awesome, as our technological power," that literally draws the other into being.[48] To learn to nurture through the act of parenting is to acquire an essential human virtue and even to perfect one's life of faith in Christ. To care for all children, and not simply one's own child, then becomes key to the good Christian life.

Besides serving as a crucial aid in Christian sanctification, children have an unprecedented role in informing theological reflection. Gudorf claims, "My experience of [my] children has been basic for my understanding of human nature."[49] In my own exploration, I note, "Having children has forever changed my ways of knowing and thinking. . . . Parting the passions in order to articulate those ways comes less easily."[50]

Finally, the claim of child as gift raises hard ethical questions, perhaps best illustrated but not exhausted by dilemmas in reproductive technology and genetic testing. Some of the conventional motivations for parenthood, in which the child is reduced to a means, "an extension of the self," or "a thing" rather than respected as an end in herself, are strikingly problematic when viewed from this perspective. As Gudorf remarks, infertility does not "represent an intolerable deprivation"; it provides impetus to renewed struggle with the question of what we seek through parenthood.[51] In a way unprecedented in human

48. Harrison, "The Power of Anger in the Work of Love," 47-48.
49. Gudorf, "Parenting, Mutual Love, and Sacrifice," 177.
50. Miller-McLemore, *Also a Mother*, 146.
51. Christine Gudorf, "Dissecting Parenthood: Infertility, in Vitro, and Other Lessons in Why and How We Parent," *Conscience* 15, no. 3 (Autumn 1994): 20.

history, as a result of new technologies and the population explosion, parents can no longer enter into parenthood blithely and unreflectively. People must now weigh carefully the validity and merits of their often preconscious and sometimes rather self-centered motives to reproduce themselves. Gudorf and other feminist theologians have made clear that the choice to have children is not simply a personal choice but a matter of social responsibility influencing the future of entire groups within society.

In many respects, parenthood is an institution under siege. This is partly because social institutions, such as schools and the workplace, and community structures, such as suburban neighborhoods, have evolved in the midst of benign neglect of children's perceptions and needs. Heretofore theology has done little or nothing to contest the oversight of children, since children as subjects in their own right have figured so little in theological rumination about human nature and salvation in the past century. Theologians in general, it would seem, have a great deal more to learn about the nature of children, and, as feminist theologians imply, the very survival of the world may depend on it.

2. The Education and Formation of Children

While we do not find a heavy emphasis on formation of children per se among feminist theologians themselves, the problems of deformation and abuse under patriarchy receive extraordinary and essential attention.[52] The emphasis is as much on protection and education for the sake of prevention as on religious and spiritual formation. The goal is often immediate implementation and change in ministerial and family situations that threaten children, rather than Christian formation in nonviolent, nonabusive Christian homes. Nevertheless, Christian ethical claims about the importance of a child's "bodyright" radically shift the goal of child-rearing practices from achieving socially desired behavior through requiring obedience to authority to transferring power and responsibility to children, commensurate with their ability to handle it safely and well. "Bodily integrity," Harrison asserts, is a basic moral requirement for women and children. That is, control over one's own body and protection from bodily violation is a moral condition of human well-being that the community owes its members.[53] Children learn bodily integrity through adults who practice it.

---

52. See footnote 44 above.

53. Harrison, "Theology and Morality of Procreative Choice," 129-30. See also Janet R. Jokobsen, "Struggles for Women's Bodily Integrity in the United States and the Limits of Liberal Legal Theory," *Journal of Feminist Studies in Religion* 11, no. 2 (Fall 1995): 5-26.

And men and fathers are not the only audience addressed in this call to recognize children; that mothers also abuse their children raises particularly complex problems for feminist theology.[54]

Unlike theologians prior to the twentieth century, feminist theologians have also benefited from developmental theory in psychology, education, and sociology. In particular, many have turned to the research, done by Nancy Chodorow and others, on early preoedipal mother-child interactions in order to understand the ways in which gendered, sexist, misogynist, and heterosexist behavior and character are reproduced when only mothers mother. For example, taking seriously social-studies findings that boys grow through separation and devaluation of women, while girls grow through attachment and self-diminishment, means that Christian formation must subvert the perpetuation of patterns of dominance and subordinance in mothering and fathering and encourage a broader range of sexual and spiritual self-understandings beyond the stereotypical masculine and feminine dichotomies. Recognition of the relationality of human nature, supported by recent social-science research, also requires raising children with different ideals than those commonly promoted by Christian views of adulthood. A child should be encouraged toward interdependence or mutual dependence on others rather than independence and autonomy. Connections to others and a fluid selfhood are prized over views of the self as separate and self-sufficient.

A few scholars, such as Diane Jonte-Pace, have explored the implications of the "maternal-infant matrix of religious experience" for religious formation. A child's healthy attachment and gradual transformation in relationship to a primary caregiver lays a rich foundation for further spiritual developments in adult life. This analysis contests Freud's view that religious faith is merely a result of castration anxiety, guilt, and repressed aggression toward the father in the oedipal stage of development. This father-dominated psychological interpretation is replaced by interpretations sensitive to the role of the mother and experiences of the infant and toddler in preoedipal development. Attachment to the mother and transmutations of this attachment in relationship to transitional objects, such as the beloved blanket, stuffed animal, or doll, foster rich images of a loving God and human attributes such as hope, creativity, and empathy. In this view, early parenting of young children assumes a new importance in the formation of religious ideas. This invites further exploration that may continue to challenge more reductive psychological views of religion.

According to the research of Mary Ellen Ross and Cheryl Lynn Ross, these

---

54. Paula M. Cooey, "Bad Women: The Limits of Theory and Theology," in *Horizons in Feminist Theology: Identity, Tradition, and Norms,* ed. Robecca S. Chopp and Sheila Greeve Davaney (Minneapolis: Augsburg Fortress, 1997), 137-53.

fresh understandings of the important role of the mother-child bond in preoedipal interactions shift the focus from the pathological analysis of previous psychoanalytic assessments of religion as illusion, delusion, and neurosis. They begin to explain the nonpathological creative and playful elements in religious rituals. As examples, Ross and Ross describe the ways in which Catholic mass creates what Victor Turner describes as *communitas,* and the ways in which worshippers, who unite their voices to confess their faith or who share the Eucharistic meal, foster what D. W. Winnicott calls potential transitional space.[55] The creation of such a transitional space, or a space that functions as a symbolic substitution for the solace provided by the mother and yet can be controlled and reshaped, is crucial to the development of essential psychological and spiritual characteristics.

3. The Responsibilities and Obligations of Parents and the Community

Of our three areas, the theme of parental and communal responsibility receives the most extensive consideration on several fronts. Beyond the critical emphasis already noted on speaking out about and arresting abuse, most striking is the promotion of what might be called "nonparent-parenting." This concern has two components. Bearing and rearing children are not absolutely requisite for human fulfillment or Christian service, *and* the responsibility of parenting includes and depends on wider circles of care that extend beyond the immediate biological parents. The first claim is perhaps best put in a positive way by Beverly Harrison, who declares, "Noncoercion in childbearing is a foundational social good."[56] In terms of the second claim, womanists have the most explicit traditions of "othermothers" within congregation and community. Many members of African American congregations regularly "adopt" children and regard themselves as accountable to a wide range of children and youth. In this and other contexts of social oppression and even genocide, biological and social reproduction function as dramatic acts of resistance.[57] Margaret Farley generalizes this sentiment: in a time such as ours, in which an apocalypse of ecological and political destruction seems very real, "one of the greatest acts of radical hope and signs of belief in a possible future (both a future that transcends this world and a future within this world) can be the choice to bear chil-

---

55. Mary Ellen Ross and Cheryl Lynn Ross, "Mothers, Infants, and the Psychoanalytic Study of Ritual," *Signs: Journal of Women in Culture and Society* 9, no. 1 (1983): 26-39.

56. Harrison, *Our Right to Choose,* 17.

57. See Katharina von Kellenbach, "Reproduction and Resistance during the Holocaust," in *Women and the Holocaust: Narrative and Representation,* ed. Esther Fuchs (Lanham, Md.: University Press of America, 1999), 19-32.

dren."[58] Not all feminists would agree with her. Christine Gudorf, for example, argues that the population explosion necessitates an immediate curtailing of current rates of reproduction.

Regardless of the differences, many feminist theologians would agree that we need to take more seriously the theological task of widening the communal parameters of adult accountability in bearing and rearing children in terms of the roles of both the church and the state. More specifically, within the congregation we must retrieve the motif of adoption, so evident in the Hebrew scriptures and in some streams of Christian practice, that transcends common structures of family and community through covenants of extra-biological, extra-legal kinship.[59] In addition to adoption, Paula Cooey suggests a reinstitutionalization of the practice of naming godparents. Godparents should be willing to take on certain responsibilities along with the honor — responsibilities that ought to include training in parental skills, sustained, committed involvement with the biological parents early on in the lives of the children, intervention in times of crisis, and so forth.[60]

Feminist theologians ask not only for a wider sharing of the labor of parenting in the church and local community. They also strive to break silences about parental struggles and family strife within the congregation. This endeavor alone disturbs the overt peace that tends to cover over the acute family dilemmas faced by almost everyone within the congregation.

Underlying and informing these concrete suggestions is a conviction about parental instincts that extend beyond biological children to the wider community, including the state. Biological parenting can become the source of broader communal and social concern. At the same time, biological parenting alone is not sufficient to meet the need for wider care for the next generation. As Mercy Amba Oduyoye declares, "I am not a mother but I have children."[61] Both Farley and Gudorf — and most feminist theologians — would agree with the second principle of feminist ethics as defined by Eleanor Humes Haney: Feminists are called to nurture life "in whatever form it appears."[62]

Advocacy for greater communal responsibilities has focused on the responsibilities of the state as well. Beyond breaking silences within the congregation, feminist theologians also follow the general premise of the early feminist

58. Farley, "The Church and Family: An Ethical Task," 60.

59. See Pamela D. Couture, "Single Parents and Poverty: A Challenge to Pastoral Theological Method," in *Pastoral Care and Social Conflict*, ed. Pamela D. Couture and Rodney Hunter (Nashville: Abingdon, 1995), 57-70.

60. Cooey, *Family, Freedom, and Faith*, 102.

61. Oduyoye, "Poverty and Motherhood," 23.

62. Eleanor Humes Haney, "What Is Feminist Ethics? A Proposal for Continuing Discussion," *Journal of Religious Ethics* 8, no. 1 (1980): 121.

movement in its belief that the "personal is political." As already mentioned, the perpetuation of violence and abuse against women and children makes vigilant protection, protest, and public advocacy for children among the most critical duties of both the church and the state. Those concerned about the poverty of women, such as Couture and Harrison, are naturally also advocates for children threatened by the hardships of impoverishment.

Broadly speaking, religious commitment calls for serious engagement with public policies on welfare, abortion, poverty, childcare, health-care benefits for families, parental rights, parental leaves, and other pressing issues. Harrison's earliest work on reproductive rights as well as the work of several other scholars, such as Cooey and Couture, demonstrates serious deliberation about the important role of the state in securing the welfare of families. None of these three Protestant scholars spends much time adjudicating the lines between state and church responsibility. With the Catholic principle of subsidiarity behind her, Lisa Sowle Cahill is perhaps the most careful about delineating the relative importance of the state in relationship to the local community and the family. The family, the church, and the state each have unique and distinctive spheres of influence; the state ought not to interfere in matters for which the family itself is the best resource. At the same time, the state has a responsibility to create an environment supportive of all families, including the most vulnerable.

Moving from communal to familial realms, feminist theologians have argued consistently for radical revision of paternal responsibility. The reality of the burden of the domestic labor of love for children and its grossly unequal distribution worldwide becomes a significant theological consideration for Rosemary Ruether, Beverly Harrison, Barbara Andolsen, myself, and others. Reproduction is not a "natural" value-free process but a profoundly ethical, religious, and political event. As the boundaries set by nature shift, mothers are seen as no more or less bound to children by their created nature than men. Instead, both mothers and fathers are bound in different ways. Obligations to children and family ought to be shared equitably between parents, despite primary physiological differences in birthing and nursing. Quite simply, as Ruether points out, transforming sexism requires "real solidarity" between men and women, which means, practically speaking, that a man "shares housework and child care."[63]

---

63. Ruether, *Sexism and God-Talk,* 191. See also Barbara Hilkert Andolsen, "A Woman's Work Is Never Done: Unpaid Household Labor as a Social Justice Issue," in *Women's Consciousness and Women's Conscience: A Reader in Feminist Ethics,* ed. Barbara Hilkert Andolsen, Christine E. Gudorf, and Mary D. Pellauer (San Francisco: Harper & Row, 1985), 3-18.

In turn, the nature and dynamics of parental love are receiving fresh interpretation. Parents have legitimate and inevitable needs in relation to children. Rather than striving for the unconditional love of children, feminist theologians point out, parents must face the more complex challenge of recognizing the inevitable intersection of their own interests in the flourishing of their children.[64] Moreover, rather than advocating for the priority of universalizable love, feminist theologians recognize that the very particularity of love for a distinctive child has the power to foster a generalizable practice of love that extends to other children as well as to the child in other adults.[65] In relation to children, parents are not to presume a permanent hierarchy but to hope for the evolution of mutuality. In these reinterpretations of the nature of Christian love, there is a central interconnection and interpenetration of the well-being of mother and child. Harrison simply states, "I take the task of *feminist* ethics to contribute to that almost endless reconstruction of inherited moral traditions in a direction that seeks to assume that women's well-being genuinely matters and that the well-being of the children that women bear matter[s]." These two conjoint concerns define the parameters of Christian responsibility and, if logically extended, actually include the "well-being of everybody,"[66] including men and the larger society.

Finally, bearing and raising children is celebrated as a vibrant spiritual discipline by Margaret Hebblethwaite, myself, and others. Spiritual or religious dimensions of the care of children have largely been disregarded in most previous conceptions of the contemplative life as the celibate life. Gudorf recognizes parenting as harboring the potential to spark adult maturation. Indeed, a child's successful growth depends in part on parental development and the ability of parents to resolve residual conflicts in their own families of origin.[67] Kathryn Rabuzzi's entire project could be summarized as an effort to proclaim that motherhood has a sacred dimension. To be a mother, she says, is "to be 'graced.'"[68] Contrary to social assumptions, parenthood is a vocation for both women and men, not an avocation or pastime. The very meticulous, repetitive labors that parenting requires have enriching, beneficial potential. Oduyoye ar-

64. Miller-McLemore, *Also a Mother,* 162-67; Gudorf, "Parenting, Mutual Love, and Sacrifice," 181-86.

65. Sally Purvis, "Mothers, Neighbors, and Strangers: Another Look at Agape," *Journal of Feminist Studies in Religion* 7, no. 1 (Spring 1991): 21, 23, 34.

66. Beverly Wildung Harrison, "Situating the Dilemma of Abortion Historically," *Conscience: A Newsjournal of Prochoice Catholic Opinion* 11, no. 2 (March/April 1990): 15.

67. See Christine E. Gudorf, "Sacrifice and Parental Spiritualities," in *Religion, Feminism, and the Family,* ed. Anne Carr and Mary Stewart Van Leeuwen (Louisville: Westminster John Knox), 295-99; and "Dissecting Parenthood," 20-21.

68. Rabuzzi, *Mother with Child,* xv. See also Elizabeth Dodson Gray, *Sacred Dimensions of Women's Experience* (Wellesley, Mass.: Roundtable Press, 1988).

gues that mothering, "biological or otherwise, calls for a life of letting go, a readiness to share resources and to receive with appreciation what others offer for the good of the community."[69] This reclamation of the importance of family and parenthood fundamentally challenges a powerful stream in the Christian tradition that has relativized parenting and parental sexuality as less conducive than the celibate life to total devotion to God.

The theme of adult responsibilities toward children has received extended attention in feminist theology because dramatic changes have occurred in the past few decades in the roles of parents in relationship to one another and in relationship to their children, as well as in the role of children themselves. While major questions about the parameters of parental and communal obligation remain, this overview indicates that feminist theologians might now need to turn their attention to the prior questions of the nature of children and their needs for education and formation. Further concerted exploration of these two related themes could provide some of the knowledge needed to arbitrate more justly the distribution and sharing of responsibilities within the family and society in their care of children.

Enriching Contemporary Views and the Theological Discussion

When we look at the wider discussion, it becomes clear that feminist theologians have said a great deal about children, putting children and adult responsibilities in a new light. Even though prior to my research I knew feminist theologians had written amply on mothers, families, and justice, perhaps one of my biggest surprises was discovering just how much of this material pertained to children once I began to read with this in mind. Reflection on children comes through and remains intricately related to concern about other primary subjects, such as motherhood, families, and social justice. Thus the research task requires moving from general remarks on mothers, families, and social justice toward a bolder articulation of some of the more indirect remarks on children. This essay is in no way exhaustive of the possible readings of this diverse movement. I have only scratched the surface of a rich trajectory that promises further developments. I have given an impressionistic representation of some of the evolving themes.

69. Oduyoye, "Poverty and Motherhood," 24. See also Laurie Zoloth-Dorfman, "Traveling with Children: Mothering and the Ethics of the Ordinary World," *Tikkun* (July/ August 1995): 25-29.

Roughly speaking, at least four significant implications emerge for enriching contemporary discussion. As already discussed in some detail, among the primary contributions of feminist theologians to current debates on the welfare of children are a material appreciation for the intense labors of love, a psychological grappling with early developmental issues, a spiritual understanding of the gifts of children, and a political declaration of the vulnerabilities and rights of children. Appreciation for the labors of love includes both concern about the consequences of the impoverishment of women and children within the public economic sphere and concern about the injustice of worldwide inequities in the distribution of domestic labor within the home. Fresh psychological insights into the construction of gender during childhood and the spiritual gifts received in attending to children challenge cultural models of adulthood and provide alternative Christian ideals. Finally, political activism on behalf of children forces renewed discussion of justice. The concept of justice takes on new meanings when raised in relationship to children and put in the context of family structure, roles and distribution of power in the family, family stability, and family violence.

The study and appreciation of children in feminist theology exemplify the immense benefits of some of the basic presuppositions of feminist theological method: the incorporation of daily life as a central analytical category and respect for the voices of the underside, the marginalized, and the outcast as a central guiding norm. Children are a large part of daily life for many women and a rich source of theological inspiration for some scholars. And children represent one of the least heard of all marginalized groups. Feminist reflection on children embodies the theological conviction that the divine manifests itself in the mundane and that genuine liberation must occur in the most commonplace of places — in the embodied life of the child.

In the past several decades, little concerted thought in theology has gone into understanding the nature of children or adult responsibilities for their nurture. It is almost as if concern for children in theology has followed the same path as the care of children more generally. Over the last century, care of children gradually became devalued as something that one does on the side in one's spare time, not valued as a critically important part of individual life and collective survival. Similarly, Christian thought on children became a subject relegated to the margins, something that those in Christian education or pastoral care might consider, but of little relevance for serious theological reflection. For the most part, women cared for children; men did not. Mothers with children did not often aspire to write theology; the men who did had less investment in writing theologies that took children into account. Doctrines of human nature, salvation, and God remained amazingly adult-centered, forgetting that all people begin their lives as children and that many people spend a large portion of their adult lives responsible for children in some way. Unfortunately, theological neglect coincided with a broader societal negligence. Theology played little or no role in calling society to account for its attitudes and actions toward children.

Changes have occurred both on the theological scene and in contemporary society. The dire consequences of neglect of children in social and familial circles and in theological reflection have become increasingly apparent. In society, many people have pointed to social indicators such as teen pregnancy, violence, and suicide as reason for concern. In theology, many people have complained about the production of theological treatises removed from the rhythms of daily life. More women, including mothers with children, have followed a vocational call into the academy of theology and have refused to set aside their care for children in their theological writings.

The contributions of recent feminist theology on families, mothers, and children are manifold. First, the interior lives of parents, particularly mothers, have suddenly become an essential consideration in the welfare of children. One cannot secure the welfare of children without securing the interests of women and mothers. Birthing and parenting are full of religious potential both for adult spiritual development and for renewal of God imagery. Children themselves go through complex developmental changes that deserve respect and attention. Second, feminists concerned about civil society have demonstrated the costs for children of a rampant liberal pursuit of individual benefit. Choices in childbearing should not be seen as strictly personal and private. How individuals birth and raise children holds critical social and moral implications for society at large. Finally, those feminist theologians most concerned about social justice have pleaded for increased appreciation for the potential personhood and rights of children as full human beings. Such appreciation makes apparent the moral turpitude of child sexual abuse, violence, poverty, and other social and familial ills.

Although few feminist theologians have made children the immediate subject of their research, many have discussed the needs and rights of children in relation to critical concerns about mothers, women, families, and a just social order. On this score, feminist theologians have spoken volumes where theology, more broadly speaking, has remained silent. The challenge now is to articulate even more boldly and directly a stronger and fuller theological vision of children and our obligations toward them. This vision must draw on the wealth of diverse positions on mothers, civil society, and justice already operative within current feminist theological discussions. One would hope that scholars in theology will never again have to prove that the nature and nurture of children are vital and credible topics, worthy of more careful and intentional theological exploration.

Select Bibliography

I. Select Bibliography by Chapter

Chapter 1: The Least and the Greatest: Children in the New Testament

Primary Sources

Jesus' healing of children
Mark 5:35-43
Mark 7:24-30
Mark 9:14-29

Jesus' teaching on children
Mark 9:33-37 (parr. Matt. 18:1-2, 4-5; Luke 9:46-48)
Mark 10:13-16 (parr. Matt. 19:13-15; Luke 18:15-17)
Matt. 21:14-16

Children in the Epistles
The household codes
Col. 3:20-21
Eph. 6:1-4
The Pastorals
1 Tim. 3:4, 12
Titus 1:6

For texts and translations of classical works, consult the *Oxford Classical Dictionary* under the name of the author.

Secondary Sources

Barton, Stephen C. "Jesus — Friend of Little Children?" In *The Contours of Christian Education,* edited by Jeff Astley and David Day, 30-40. Great Wakering, Essex: McCrimmons, 1992.

Beasley-Murray, George R. "Church and Child in the New Testament." *Baptist Quarterly* 21 (1965-66): 206-18.

Crossan, John Dominic. *The Historical Jesus: The Life of a Mediterranean Jewish Peasant.* San Francisco: Harper SanFrancisco, 1991.

Dixon, Suzanne. *The Roman Family.* Baltimore: The Johns Hopkins University Press, 1992.

Dunn, James D. G. "The Household Rules in the New Testament." In *The Family in Theological Perspective,* edited by Stephen C. Barton, 43-63. Edinburgh: T. & T. Clark, 1996.

Garnsey, Peter, and Richard Saller. *The Roman Empire: Economy, Society, and Culture.* Berkeley and Los Angeles: University of California Press, 1987.

Jeremias, Joachim. *Infant Baptism in the First Four Centuries.* Philadelphia: Westminster, 1960.

Légasse, S. *Jésus et L'Enfant: "Enfant," "Petits" et "Simples" dans la Tradition Synoptique.* Paris: Lecoffre, 1969.

Müller, Peter. *In der Mitte der Gemeinde: Kinder im Neuen Testament.* Neukirchen-Vluyn: Neukirchener, 1992.

Rawson, Beryl, ed. *The Family in Ancient Rome: New Perspectives.* Ithaca, N.Y.: Cornell University Press, 1986.

Schroeder, Hans-Hartmut. *Eltern und Kinder in der Verkündigung Jesu: Eine hermeneutische und exegetische Untersuchung. Theologische Forschung* 53 (1972).

Semeia 29 (1983).

Weber, Hans-Ruedi. *Jesus and the Children: Biblical Resources for Study and Preaching.* Geneva: World Council of Churches, 1979.

Wiedemann, Thomas. *Adults and Children in the Roman Empire.* New Haven and London: Yale University Press, 1989.

Chapter 2: The Ecclesial Family: John Chrysostom on Parenthood and Children

Primary Sources

John Chrysostom. *An Address on Vainglory and the Right Way for Parents to Bring Up Their Children.* Appended to *Christianity and Pagan Culture in the Later Roman Empire,* by M. L. W. Laistner, 77-122. Ithaca, N.Y.: Cornell University Press, 1967.

————. *A Comparison between a King and a Monk/Against the Opponents of the Monastic Life: Two Treatises.* Translated by David G. Hunter. Lewiston, N.Y.: Edward Mellen Press, 1988.

————. *On Marriage and Family Life.* Translated by Catherine P. Roth and David Anderson. Crestwood, N.Y.: St. Valdimir's Seminary Press, 1986.

Secondary Sources

Campenhausen, Hans von. *The Fathers of the Greek Church.* New York: Pantheon Books, 1959.

Guroian, Vigen. *Ethics after Christendom: Toward an Ecclesial Christian Ethic.* Grand Rapids, Mich.: Eerdmans, 1994.

————. *Incarnate Love: Essays in Orthodox Ethics.* Notre Dame: University of Notre Dame Press, 1987.

Kelly, J. N. D. *Golden Mouth: The Story of John Chrysostom: Ascetic, Preacher, Bishop.* Ithaca, N.Y.: Cornell University Press, 1995; Grand Rapids, Mich.: Baker Book House, 1998.

Chapter 3: "Where or When Was Your Servant Innocent?": Augustine on Childhood

Primary Sources

Augustine. *Concerning the City of God against the Pagans.* Edited by David Knowles. Translated by Henry Bettenson. New York: Penguin Books, 1972.

————. *Confessions.* Translated by Henry Chadwick. New York: Oxford University Press, 1991.

————. "Eighty-Three Different Questions." In *The Fathers of the Church,* vol. 70, translated by David L. Mosher, 3-220. Washington, D.C.: Catholic University of America Press, 1982.

————. "The Literal Meaning of Genesis." Translated by John Hammond Taylor, S.J. In *Ancient Christian Writers,* vols. 41-42, edited by Johannes Quasten, Walter J. Burghardt, and Thomas Comerford Lawler. New York: Newman Press, 1982.

————. "On Catechising the Uninstructed." In *The Works of Aurelius Augustine, Bishop of Hippo,* vol. 9, edited by Marcus Dods, 261-336. Edinburgh: T. & T. Clark, 1892.

————. "On Marriage and Concupiscence." In *St. Augustin: Anti-Pelagian Writings,* 258-309, in volume 5 of *The Nicene and Post-Nicene Fathers,* First Series, edited by Philip Schaff. New York: Christian Literature Company, 1887.

————. "The Punishment and Forgiveness of Sin and the Baptism of Little Ones." In *Answer to the Pelagians,* translated by Roland J. Teske, S.J., 17-137. In Part I, vol. 23 of *The Works of St. Augustine,* edited by John E. Rotelle, O.S.A. Hyde Park, N.Y.: New City Press, 1997.

————. *St. Augustine on Marriage and Sexuality.* Edited by Elizabeth Clark. Washington, D.C.: Catholic University Press of America, 1996.

————. *Teaching Christianity.* Translated by Edmund Hill, O.P. In Part 1, vol. 11 of *The Works of St. Augustine,* edited by John E. Rotelle, O.S.A. Hyde Park, N.Y.: New City Press, 1996.

————. "To Jerome." In *Letters of St. Augustine,* edited and translated by John Leinenweber, 190-91. Tarrytown, N.Y.: Triumph Books, 1992.

————. "To Simplician — On Various Questions." In *Augustine: Earlier Writings,* edited and translated by John H. S. Burleigh, 370-406. In vol. 6 of *The Library of Christian Classics.* Philadelphia: Westminster Press, 1953.

Pelagius. *Pelagius's Commentary on St. Paul's Epistle to the Romans.* Edited and translated by Theodore De Bruyn. Oxford: Clarendon Press, 1993.

Secondary Sources

Brown, Peter. *Augustine of Hippo: A Biography.* Berkeley and Los Angeles: University of California Press, 1969.

476

Clark, Gillian. "The Fathers and the Children." In *The Church and Childhood,* edited by Diana Wood, 1-28. Oxford: Blackwell Publishers, 1994.

Fisher, J. D. C. *Christian Initiation: Baptism in the Medieval West: A Study in the Disintegration of the Primitive Rite of Initiation.* London: SPCK, 1965.

————. *Christian Initiation: The Reformation: Some Early Reformed Rites of Baptism and Confirmation and Their Contemporary Documents.* London: SPCK, 1970.

Harmless, William, S.J. *Augustine and the Catechumenate.* Collegeville, Minn.: Liturgical Press, 1995.

Hayward, Paul A. "Suffering and Innocence in Latin Sermons for the Feast of the Holy Innocents, c. 400-800." In *The Church and Childhood,* edited by Diana Wood, 67-80. Oxford: Blackwell Publishers, 1994.

Kevane, Eugene. *Augustine the Educator: A Study in the Fundamentals of Christian Formation.* Westminster, Md.: Newman Press, 1964.

Laquer, Thomas. *Making Sex: Body and Gender from the Greeks to Freud.* Cambridge: Harvard University Press, 1990.

Miles, Margaret R. *Desire and Delight: A New Reading of Augustine's "Confessions."* New York: Crossroad, 1992.

————. "Infancy, Parenting, and Nourishment in Augustine's *Confessions.*" *Journal of the American Academy of Religion* 50 (1983): 349-64.

Pellauer, Mary. "Augustine on Rape: One Chapter in the Theological Traditions." In *Violence against Women and Children: A Christian Theological Sourcebook,* edited by Carol J. Adams and Marie M. Fortune, 207-41. New York: Continuum, 1995.

Powers, Kim. "*Sed unam tamen:* Augustine and His Concubine." *Augustinian Studies* 23 (1992): 49-76.

Rousselle, Aline. *Porneia: On Desire and the Body in Antiquity.* Translated by Felicia Pheasant. Oxford: Basil Blackwell, 1988.

Chapter 4: A Person in the Making:
Thomas Aquinas on Children and Childhood

Primary Sources

Thomas Aquinas. *Commentary on Saint Paul's Epistle to the Ephesians.* Translated and introduced by Matthew L. Lamb, O.C.S.O. Aquinas Scripture Series, vol. 2. Albany, N.Y.: Magi Books, 1966.

————. *Commentary on Saint Paul's Epistle to the Galatians.* Translated by Fabian R. Larcher, O.P., and introduced by Richard T. A. Murphy, O.P. Aquinas Scripture Series, vol. 1. Albany, N.Y.: Magi Books, 1966.

————. *Commentary on Saint Paul's First Letter to the Thessalonians and the Letter to the Philippians.* Translated by Fabian R. Larcher and Michael Duffy. Aquinas Scripture Series, vol. 3. Albany, N.Y.: Magi Books, 1969.

————. *Commentary on the Gospel of St. John,* Part I. Translated by James A. Weisheipl, O.P., S.T.M., and Fabian R. Larcher, O.P. Aquinas Scripture Series, vol. 4. Albany, N.Y.: Magi Books, 1980.

————. *The Literal Exposition on Job: A Scriptural Commentary Concerning Providence.*

Translated by Anthony Damico. Classics in Religious Studies, no. 7. Atlanta: Scholars Press, 1989.

————. *On the Truth of the Catholic Faith: Summa Contra Gentiles*. Book Two: *Creation*. Translated by James F. Anderson. Garden City, N.Y.: Hanover House, 1956.

————. *Quaestiones Disputatae et Quaestiones Duodecim Quodlibetales*. Vol. 5 of *Quaestiones Quodlibetales*. Rome: Domus Editoriales Marietti, 1942.

————. *The Sermon-Conferences of St. Thomas Aquinas on the Apostles' Creed*. Edited and translated by Nicholas Ayo, C.S.C. Notre Dame: University of Notre Dame Press, 1988.

————. *Summa Theologica*. 3 vols. Translated by the Fathers of the English Dominican Province. New York: Benziger Brothers, 1947-1948. Reprint in 5 vols. by Christian Classics (Westminster, Md., 1981).

Secondary Sources

Finnis, John. *Aquinas: Moral, Political, and Legal Theory*. Oxford: Oxford University Press, 1998.

Foster, Kenelm, O.P., editor and translator. *The Life of St. Thomas Aquinas: Biographical Documents*. London: Longmans, Green; Baltimore: Helicon Press, 1959.

Shahar, Shulamith. *Childhood in the Middle Ages*. London: Routledge, 1990.

Weisheipl, James A., O.P. *Friar Thomas D'Aquino: His Life, Thought, and Work*. Garden City, N.Y.: Doubleday, 1974.

Chapter 5: The Child in Luther's Theology: "For What Purpose Do We Older Folks Exist, Other Than to Care for . . . the Young?"

Primary Sources

Luther, Martin. *Luther's Works*. American edition. 55 vols. Edited by Jaroslav Pelikan and Helmut Lehmann. St. Louis: Concordia; Philadelphia: Fortress, 1955-1986.

Secondary Sources

Erikson, Erik. *Young Man Luther: A Study in Psychoanalysis and History*. New York: W. W. Norton, 1958.

Lazareth, William H. *Luther on the Christian Home: An Application of the Social Ethics of the Reformation*. Philadelphia: Muhlenberg Press, 1960.

Oxford Encyclopedia of the Reformation. 4 vols. Edited by Hans J. Hillerbrand. New York: Oxford University Press, 1996.

Ozment, Steven. *When Fathers Ruled: Family Life in Reformation Europe*. Cambridge: Harvard University Press, 1983.

Strauss, Gerald. *Luther's House of Learning: Indoctrination of the Young in the German Reformation*. Baltimore: The Johns Hopkins University Press, 1978.

Tappert, Theodore G., trans. and ed. *The Book of Concord: The Confessions of the Evangelical Lutheran Church*. Philadelphia: Fortress Press, 1959.

Wengert, Timothy J. "Luther on Children: Baptism and the Fourth Commandment." *Dialog* 37, no. 3 (Summer 1998): 185-89.

Wiesner, Merry E. *Women and Gender in Early Modern Europe.* Cambridge: Cambridge University Press, 1993.

Wingren, Gustaf. *Luther on Vocation.* Translated by Carl C. Rasmussen. Philadelphia: Muhlenberg Press, 1957.

Chapter 6: "The Heritage of the Lord": Children in the Theology of John Calvin

Primary Sources

Calvin, John. *Brief Instruction . . . Against the Errors of the Common Sect of the Anabaptists* (1544). In *Treatises against the Anabaptists,* edited and translated by Benjamin Wirt Farley, 44-56. Grand Rapids, Mich.: Baker Books, 1982.

————. *Calvin's Commentaries.* 46 vols. Edinburgh: Calvin Translation Society, 1843-1855. Reprint in 22 vols. by Baker Books (Grand Rapids, Mich., 1989).

————. *Institutes of the Christian Religion* (1559). Edited by John McNeill and translated by Ford Lewis Battles. Vols. 20-21 of the Library of Christian Classics. Philadelphia: Westminster Press, 1960.

————. *Institutes of the Christian Religion: 1536 Edition.* Translated by Ford Lewis Battles. Grand Rapids, Mich.: Eerdmans, 1975.

————. *Ioannis Calvini Opera Quae Supersunt Omnia.* Edited by G. Baum, E. Cunitz, and E. Reuss. 59 vols. *Corpus Reformatorum,* vols. 29-87. Brunswick and Berlin: C. A. Schwetschke and Son (M. Bruhn), 1863-1900.

————. *Ioannis Calvini Opera Selecta.* 5 vols. Edited by Peter Barth. Munich: Christian Kaiser, 1952-1962.

————. *Letters of John Calvin.* 4 vols. Edited by Jules Bonnet. Vols. 1 and 2 translated by David Constable. Vols. 3 and 4 translated by Marcus Gilchrist. Edinburgh: Thomas Constable & Co., 1855-1858. Reprint, New York: Burt Franklin, 1972.

Secondary Sources

Blacketer, Raymond Andrew. "*L'École de Dieu:* Pedagogy and Rhetoric in Calvin's Interpretation of Deuteronomy." Ph.D. dissertation, Calvin Theological Seminary, 1998.

Brouwer, Arnie R. "Calvin's Doctrine of Children in the Covenant: Foundation for Christian Education." *The Reformed Review* 18, no. 4 (May 1965): 17-29.

DeJong, Peter Y. "Calvin's Contributions to Christian Education." *Calvin Theological Journal* 2, no. 2 (November 1967): 162-201.

Edwards, Charles Eugene. "Calvin on Infant Salvation." *Bibliotheca Sacra* 88 (1931): 316-28.

Kingdon, Robert M. *Adultery and Divorce in Calvin's Geneva.* Cambridge: Harvard University Press, 1995.

————. "Calvin and the Family: The Work of the Consistory in Geneva." In *Articles on Calvin and Calvinism,* edited by Richard C. Gamble, 13:93-106. Hamden, Conn.: Garland Publishing, 1992.

Millet, Olivier. "Rendre raison de la foi: Le Catéchisme de Calvin (1542)." In *Aux origines du catéchisme en France,* edited by P. Colin et al., 188-207. Tournai: Desclée, 1989.

Naphy, William G. "Baptisms, Church Riots, and Social Unrest in Calvin's Geneva." *Sixteenth Century Journal* 26, no. 1 (Spring 1995): 87-97.

———. "The Reformation and the Evolution of Geneva's Schools." In *Reformations Old and New: Essays on the Socio-Economic Impact of Religious Change, c. 1470-1630,* edited by Beat Kümin, 183-94. Brookfield, Vt.: Ashgate Publishing Co., 1996.

Peter, R. "L'abécédaire genevois ou catéchisme élémentaire de Calvin." *Revue d'Histoire et de Philosophie religieuses* 45 (1965): 11-45.

Witte, John Jr. "Between Sacrament and Contract: Marriage as Covenant in John Calvin's Geneva." *Calvin Theological Journal* 33, no. 1 (April 1998): 9-75.

Chapter 7: Complex Innocence, Obligatory Nurturance, and Parental Vigilance: "The Child" in the Work of Menno Simons

Primary Sources

Braght, Thieleman J. van. *The Bloody Theater or Martyrs Mirror of the Defenseless Christians.* 13th ed. Scottdale, Pa.: Herald Press, 1982.

Riedeman, Peter. *Account of Our Religion, Doctrine, and Faith* (1545). London, 1970; 2d ed., Rifton, N.Y.: Plough Publishing House, 1970.

Simons, Menno. *The Complete Writings of Menno Simons.* Translated by Leonard Verduin and edited by J. C. Wenger. Scottdale, Pa.: Herald Press, 1956.

Secondary Sources

Clasen, Claus-Peter. *Anabaptism: A Social History, 1525-1618: Switzerland, Austria, Moravia, South and Central Germany.* Ithaca, N.Y.: Cornell University Press, 1972.

Erb, Betti. "Reading the Source: Menno Simons on Women, Marriage, Children, and the Family." *Conrad Grebel Review* 8, no. 3 (Fall 1990): 301-20.

Kauffman, J. Howard, and Leo Driedger. *The Mennonite Mosaic: Identity and Modernization.* Scottdale, Pa.: Herald Press, 1991.

Klassen, John. "Women and the Family among Dutch Anabaptist Martyrs." *Mennonite Quarterly Review* 60, no. 4 (October 1986): 548-71.

Klassen, William. "The Role of the Child in Anabaptism." In *Mennonite Images: Historical, Cultural, and Literary Essays Dealing with Mennonite Issues,* edited by Harry Loewen, 17-32. Winnipeg: Hyperion Press Ltd., 1980.

Kreitzer, Beth. "Menno Simons and the Bride of Christ." *Mennonite Quarterly Review* 70, no. 3 (July 1996): 299-318.

Wohlers, William R. "The Anabaptist View of the Family in Its Relationship to the Church." Ph.D. dissertation, University of Nebraska-Lincoln, 1976.

Chapter 8: "Wonderful Affection": Seventeenth-Century Missionaries to New France on Children and Childhood

Primary Sources

The Jesuit Relations and Allied Documents. Edited by Reuben Gold Thwaites. Cleveland: Burrows Bros., 1896-1901.

Marie of the Incarnation: Selected Writings. Edited by Irene Mahoney. New York and Mahwah, N.J.: Paulist Press, 1989.

Secondary Sources

Atkinson, Clarissa W. *The Oldest Vocation: Christian Motherhood in the Middle Ages.* Ithaca, N.Y.: Cornell University Press, 1991.

Brodeur, Raymond, and Nive Voisine. "Nouvelle France, Nouveau catéchisme: La reproduction d'un modèle européen par le catéchisme en Amerique française." In *Aux Origines du Catéchisme en France,* edited by P. Colin et al., 247-60. Paris: Relais-Desclée, 1989.

Campeau, Lucien. *La Mission des Jésuites chez des Hurons, 1634-1650.* Montreal: Éditions Bellarmin, 1987.

Chartier, Roger, Dominique Julia, and Marie-Madeleine Compere. *L'Éducation en France du XVIe au XVIIIe Siécle.* Paris: Société d'Édition d'Enseignement superieur, 1976.

Choquette, Leslie. "'Ces Amazones du Grand Dieu': Women and Mission in Seventeenth-Century Canada." *French Historical Studies* 17 (1992): 627-55.

Deslandres, Dominique. "Femmes Missionaires en Nouvelle-France." In *La Religion de ma Mére: Les Femmes et la Transmission de la Foi,* edited by Jean Delumeau, 209-24. Paris: Éditions du Cerf, 1992.

Goddard, Peter. "Augustine and the Amerindians in Seventeenth-Century New France." *Church History* 67, no. 4 (1998): 662-81.

———. "Converting the *Sauvage:* Jesuit and Montagnais in Seventeenth-Century New France." *Catholic Historical Review* 84 (1998): 209-24.

Jaenen, Cornelius J. *Friend and Foe: Aspects of French-Amerindian Cultural Contact in the Sixteenth and Seventeenth Centuries.* New York: Columbia University Press, and Toronto: McClelland and Stewart, Ltd., 1976.

Mali, Anya. *Mystic in the New World: Marie de l'Incarnation.* Leiden: E. J. Brill, 1996.

Martin, A. Lynn. *The Jesuit Mind: The Mentality of an Elite in Early Modern France.* Ithaca, N.Y.: Cornell University Press, 1988.

O'Malley, John W. *The First Jesuits.* Cambridge: Harvard University Press, 1993.

Trigger, Bruce G. *The Children of Aataentsic: A History of the Huron People to 1660.* 1976; reprint, Kingston, Ont.: McGill-Queen's University Press, 1987.

———. *Natives and Newcomers: Canada's "Heroic Age" Reconsidered.* Kingston, Ont.: McGill-Queen's University Press, 1985.

Wolff, Lawrence. "Parents and Children in the Sermons of Père Bourdaloue: A Jesuit Perspective on the Early Modern Family." In *The Jesuit Tradition in Education and Mission: A 450-Year Perspective,* edited by C. Chapple, 81-94. Scranton: University of Scranton Press, 1993.

Zemon Davis, Natalie. *Women on the Margins: Three Seventeenth-Century Lives.* Cambridge: Harvard University Press, 1995.

Chapter 9: Education and the Child in Eighteenth-Century German Pietism: Perspectives from the Work of A. H. Francke

Primary Sources

Francke, August Hermann. *A. H. Francke's Pädagogische Schriften.* Edited by Gustav Kramer. 2d ed. Langensalza: Hermann Beyer, 1885; Osnabruck: Biblio-Verlag, 1966.
————. *Catechismus-Predigten.* Halle: Verlegung des Waysenhauses, 1726.
————. *Glauchische Haus-Kirch-Ordnung oder Christlicher Unterricht Wie ein Haus-Vater mit seinen Kindern und Befinde das Wort Gottes und das Gebet in seinem Hause üben und Ihnen mit gutem Exempel vorleuchten soll.* Halle: Christian Henckeln, 1699.
————. *Der Grosse Aufsatz: August Hermann Franckes Schrift über eine Reform des Erziehungs- und Bildungswesens als Ausgangspunkt einer geistlichen und sozialen Neuordnung der Evangelischen Kirche des 18. Jahrhunderts.* Edited by Otto Podczeck. Berlin: Akademie Verlag, 1962.
————. *Pädagogische Schriften.* Edited by Hermann Lorenzen. 1957. 2d ed. Paderborn: Ferdinand Schöningh, 1964.
————. *Predigten.* 2 vols. Edited by Erhard Peschke. Berlin: Walter de Gruyter, 1987, 1989.
————. *Sonn-Fest-und Apostel-Tags Predigten.* 5th ed. Halle, 1715.
————. *Werke in Auswahl.* Edited by Erhard Peschke. Berlin: Luther Verlag, 1969.
Locke, John. *Some Thoughts concerning Education.* Edited by John W. Yolton and Jean S. Yolton. Oxford: Clarendon, 1989.

Secondary Sources

Beyreuther, Erich. *Geschichte des Pietismus.* Stuttgart: Steinkopf, 1978.
Brecht, Martin, ed. *Der Pietismus von siebzehnten bis zum frühen achtzehnten Jahrhundert.* Vol. 1 of *Geschichte des Pietismus.* Göttingen: Vandenhoeck & Ruprecht, 1993.
Deppermann, Klaus. "August Hermann Francke." In *Orthodoxie und Pietismus,* edited by Martin Greschat, 241-60. Stuttgart: Kohlhammer, 1982.
Jacobi, Juliane, and Thomas Müller-Bahlke, eds. *"Man hatte von ihm gute Hoffnung": Das Waisenalbum der Franckeschen Stiftungen, 1695-1749.* Tübingen: Niemeyer, 1998.
Kramer, Gustav. *August Hermann Francke: Ein Lebensbild.* 2 vols. Halle: Buchhandlung des Waisenhauses, 1880-82.
Menck, Peter. *Die Erziehung der Jugend zur Ehre Gottes und zum Nutzen des Nächsten: Begründung und Intentionen der Pädagogik August Hermann Franckes.* Wuppertal: A. Henn Verlag, 1969.
Oschlies, Wolf. *Die Arbeits- und Berufspädagogik August Hermann Franckes (1663-1727): Schule und Leben im Menschenbild des Hauptvertreters des halleschen Pietismus.* Wittenberg: Luther-Verlag, 1969.
Peschke, Erhard. *Bekehrung und Reform: Ansatz und Wurzeln der Theologie August Hermann Franckes.* Bielefeld: Luther-Verlag, 1977.

———. *Studien zur Theologie August Hermann Franckes.* 2 vols. Berlin: Evangelische Verlagsanstalt, 1964, 1966.

Sattler, Gary R. *God's Glory, Neighbor's Good: A Brief Introduction to the Life and Writings of August Hermann Francke.* Chicago: Covenant Press, 1982.

Spellman, W. M. *John Locke and the Problem of Depravity.* Oxford: Clarendon, 1988.

Stoeffler, F. Ernest. *German Pietism during the Eighteenth Century.* Leiden: Brill, 1973.

Chapter 10: John Wesley and Children

Primary Sources

Arminian Magazine. Vols. 1-14. London: Hawes et al., 1778-91.

Locke, John. *The Educational Writings of John Locke: A Critical Edition with Introduction and Notes.* Edited by James L. Axtell. Cambridge: Cambridge University Press, 1968.

Minutes of the Methodist Conferences. Vol. 1. London: John Mason, 1862.

Wesley, John. *The Bicentennial Edition of the Works of John Wesley.* 35 vols. Nashville: Abingdon, 1975-.

———. *Explanatory Notes upon the New Testament.* London: William Bowyer, 1755.

———. *The Letters of the Rev. John Wesley.* 8 vols. Edited by John Telford. London: Epworth Press, 1931.

———. *The Works of the Rev. John Wesley.* 14 vols. Edited by Thomas Jackson. London: Nichols, 1872.

Wesley, Susanna. *Susanna Wesley: The Complete Writings.* Edited by Charles Wallace Jr. New York: Oxford University Press, 1997.

Secondary Sources

Body, Alfred H. *John Wesley and Education.* London: Epworth Press, 1936.

Heitzenrater, Richard. *Faithful unto Death: Last Years and Legacy of John Wesley.* Dallas: Bridwell, 1991.

Maser, Frederick E. *The Story of John Wesley's Sisters, or Seven Sisters in Search of Love.* Rutland, Vt.: Academy Books, 1988.

Willhauck, Susan. "John Wesley's View of Children." Ph.D. dissertation, The Catholic University of America, 1992.

Chapter 11: Children of Wrath, Children of Grace: Jonathan Edwards and the Puritan Culture of Child Rearing

Primary Sources

Edwards, Jonathan. "Collection, 1696-1972." Beinecke Rare Book and Manuscript Library, Yale University, New Haven, Connecticut.

———. *Jonathan Edwards: A Profile.* Edited by David Levin. New York: Hill & Wang, 1969.

Jonathan Edwards: Representative Selections. Edited by Clarence H. Faust and Thomas N. Johnson. Revised edition. New York: Hill & Wang, 1962.

———. *Sermons and Discourses, 1739-42*. In *The Works of Jonathan Edwards*, edited by Harry S. Stout and Nathan O. Hatch. New Haven: Yale University Press, forthcoming.

———. *The Works of Jonathan Edwards*. Harry S. Stout, general editor. 17 vols. New Haven: Yale University Press, 1957-1999.

Secondary Sources

Brown, Anne S., and David D. Hall. "Family Strategies and Religious Practice: Baptism and the Lord's Supper in Early New England." In *Lived Religion in America: Toward a History of Practice*, edited by David D. Hall, 41-68. Princeton: Princeton University Press, 1997.

Cherry, Conrad. *The Theology of Jonathan Edwards: A Reappraisal.* 1966; reprint (with a new introduction), Bloomington: Indiana University Press, 1990.

Conforti, Joseph A. *Jonathan Edwards, Religious Tradition, and American Culture.* Chapel Hill: University of North Carolina Press, 1995.

Fiering, Norman. *Jonathan Edwards's Moral Thought and Its British Context.* Chapel Hill: University of North Carolina Press, 1981.

Greven, Philip J., Jr. *The Protestant Temperament: Patterns of Child-Rearing, Religious Experience, and the Self in Early America.* New York: Alfred A. Knopf, 1977.

———. *Spare the Child: The Religious Roots of Punishment and the Psychological Impact of Physical Abuse.* New York: Alfred A. Knopf, 1990.

Hatch, Nathan O., and Harry S. Stout, eds. *Jonathan Edwards and the American Experience.* New York: Oxford University Press, 1988.

Lesser, M. X. *Jonathan Edwards: A Reference Guide.* Boston: G. K. Hall, 1981.

McDermott, Gerald R. *One Holy and Happy Society: The Public Theology of Jonathan Edwards.* University Park, Pa.: The Pennsylvania State University Press, 1992.

Scheick, William J., ed. *Critical Essays on Jonathan Edwards.* Boston: G. K. Hall, 1980.

Stein, Stephen J., ed. *Jonathan Edwards's Writings: Text, Context, Interpretation.* Bloomington: Indiana University Press, 1996.

Tracy, Patricia J. *Jonathan Edwards, Pastor: Religion and Society in Eighteenth-Century Northampton.* New York: Hill & Wang, 1979.

Winslow, Ola Elizabeth. *Jonathan Edwards, 1703-1758: A Biography.* New York: MacMillan, 1940.

Chapter 12: "Be Converted and Become as Little Children": Friedrich Schleiermacher on the Religious Significance of Childhood

Primary Sources

Schleiermacher, Friedrich Daniel Ernst. *The Christian Household: A Sermonic Treatise.* Schleiermacher Studies and Translations, vol. 3. Translated by Dietrich Seidel and Terrence N. Tice. Lewiston, N.Y.: Edwin Mellen Press, 1991.

———. *Christmas Eve: A Dialogue on the Incarnation.* Translated by Terrence N. Tice. Richmond, Va.: John Knox Press, 1967.

———. *Friedrich Schleiermachers Sämmtliche Werke.* 31 vols. in three divisions. Berlin: Georg Reimer, 1834-1864.

———. *Kritische Gesamtausgabe*. Edited by Hans Joachim Birkner et al. Berlin: Walter DeGruyter, 1980-.

———. *On Religion: Speeches to Its Cultured Despisers*. Translated by Richard Crouter. Cambridge: Cambridge University Press, 1988.

———. *Schleiermacher's Soliloquies*. Translated by Horace Leland Friess. 1926; reprint, Chicago: Open Court Publishing Company, 1957.

Secondary Sources

Evans, Richard J., and W. R. Lee, eds. *The German Family: Essays on the Social History of the Family in Nineteenth- and Twentieth-Century Germany*. London: Croom Helm, 1981.

Gay, Peter. *The Bourgeois Experience: Victoria to Freud*. Vol. 1 of *The Education of the Senses*. New York: Oxford University Press, 1984.

Gerrish, B. A. *A Prince of the Church: Schleiermacher and the Beginnings of Modern Theology*. Philadelphia: Fortress Press, 1984.

Hardach-Pinke, Irene, and Gerd Hardach, eds. *Deutsche Kindheiten: Autobiographische Zeugnisse, 1700-1900*. Kronberg: Athenäum Verlag, 1978.

Hoffmann, Julius. *Die Hausväterliteratur und die Predigten über den christlichen Hausstand. Ein Beitrag zur Geschichte der Lehre vom Hause und der Bildung für das häusliche Leben im 16., 17. und 18. Jahrhundert*. Berlin: Julius Beltz, 1959.

Osborn, Andrew R. *Schleiermacher and Religious Education*. London: Oxford University Press, 1934.

Seidel, Dietrich. "Schleiermacher on Marriage and Family." Ph.D. dissertation, Toronto School of Theology, 1987.

Chapter 13: *Horace Bushnell's* Christian Nurture

Primary Sources

Bushnell, Horace. *Christian Nurture*. New York: Charles Scribner, 1861. Reprint, Cleveland: Pilgrim Press, 1994.

———. *God's Thoughts Fit Bread for Children*. Boston: Nichols & Noyes, 1869.

———. *Horace Bushnell: Sermons*. Edited by Conrad Cherry. New York: Paulist Press, 1985.

———. *Life and Letters of Horace Bushnell*. Edited by Mary Bushnell Cheney. New York: Harper & Brothers, 1880.

———. *Sermons for the New Life*. New York: Charles Scribner's Sons, 1904.

———. *Sermons on Living Subjects*. New York: Charles Scribner's Sons, 1883.

———. *Women's Suffrage: The Reform against Nature*. New York: Charles Scribner's Sons, 1869.

Secondary Sources

Edwards, Robert. *Of Singular Genius, of Singular Grace: A Biography of Horace Bushnell*. Cleveland: Pilgrim Press, 1992.

Hewitt, Glenn. *Regeneration and Morality: A Study of Charles Finney, Charles Hodge, John W. Nevin, and Horace Bushnell.* Brooklyn, N.Y.: Carlson Publishing, Inc., 1991.

Hodge, Charles. "Bushnell on Christian Nurture." *Biblical Repertory and Princeton Review* 19 (October 1847): 502-39.

Mintz, Steven, and Susan Kellogg. *Domestic Revolutions: A Social History of American Family Life.* New York: Free Press, 1988.

Schneider, A. Gregory. *The Way of the Cross Leads Home: The Domestication of American Methodism.* Bloomington: Indiana University Press, 1993.

Slater, Peter. *Children in the New England Mind: In Death and in Life.* Hamden, Conn.: Archon Books, 1977.

Smith, H. Shelton. *Changing Conceptions of Original Sin: A Study in American Theology since 1750.* New York: Charles Scribner's Sons, 1955.

————, ed. *Horace Bushnell.* New York: Oxford University Press, 1965.

Taves, Ann. "Mothers and Children and the Legacy of Mid-Nineteenth-Century American Christianity." *Journal of Religion* 67, no. 2 (April 1987): 203-19.

Tyler, Bennet. *Letter to the Rev. Horace Bushnell, D.D., Containing Strictures on His Book, Entitled "Views of Christian Nurture, and Subjects Adjacent Thereto."* Hartford, Conn.: Brown & Parsons, 1848.

Chapter 14: African American Children, "The Hope of the Race": Mary Church Terrell, the Social Gospel, and the Work of the Black Women's Club Movement

Primary Sources

Hunton, Mrs. A. H. "Kindergarten Work in the South." *Alexander's Magazine* 2, no. 3 (July 1906): 29-32.

Knudten, Richard D. *The Systematic Thought of Washington Gladden.* New York: Humanities Press, 1968.

Terrell, Mary Church. "Club Work of Colored Women." *The Southern Workman* 30, no. 8 (August 1901): 438-41.

————. *A Colored Woman in a White World.* Washington, D.C.: Ransdall, Inc., 1940.

————. "The Duty of the National Association of Colored Women to the Race." *A.M.E. Church Review* 16, no. 3 (January 1900): 340-54.

Secondary Sources

Davis, Elizabeth. *Lifting as They Climb: The National Association of Colored Women.* Washington, D.C.: National Association of Colored Women, 1933.

Harley, Sharon. "Mary Church Terrell: Genteel Militant." In *Black Leaders of the Nineteenth Century,* edited by Leon Litwack and August Meier, 307-21. Urbana: University of Illinois Press, 1988.

Morris, Calvin S. *Reverdy C. Ransom: Black Advocate of the Social Gospel.* Lanham, Md.: University Press of America, 1990.

Riggs, Marcia Y. *Awake, Arise, and Act: A Womanist Call for Black Liberation.* Cleveland: Pilgrim Press, 1994.

————, ed. *Can I Get a Witness? Prophetic Religious Voices of African American Women: An Anthology.* Maryknoll, N.Y.: Orbis Books, 1997.

Shepperd, Gladys Byram. *Mary Church Terrell: Respectable Person.* Baltimore: Human Relations Press, 1959.

Wesley, Charles Harris. *The History of the National Association of Colored Women's Clubs.* Washington, D.C.: Mercury Press, 1984.

White, Ronald C., Jr. *Liberty and Justice for All: Racial Reform and the Social Gospel, 1877-1925.* San Francisco: Harper & Row, 1990.

Chapter 15: Reading Karl Barth on Children

Primary Sources

Barth, Karl. *The Christian Life: Church Dogmatics IV/4: Lecture Fragments.* Edinburgh: T. & T. Clark, 1981.

————. *Church Dogmatics III/4.* Edinburgh: T. & T. Clark, 1961.

————. *The Humanity of God.* Atlanta: John Knox Press, 1960.

————. *Karl Barth: Theologian of Freedom.* Edited by Clifford J. Green. Minneapolis: Fortress Press, 1991.

————. *Wolfgang Amadeus Mozart.* Trans. Clarence K. Pott. Grand Rapids, Mich.: Eerdmans, 1986.

Secondary Sources

Biggar, Nigel. *The Hastening That Waits: Karl Barth's Ethics.* Oxford: Oxford University Press, 1993.

Ford, David. *Barth and God's Story: Biblical Narrative and the Theological Method of Karl Barth in the "Church Dogmatics."* Frankfurt am Main: Peter Lang, 1981.

Placher, William C. *Unapologetic Theology: A Christian Voice in a Pluralistic Conversation.* Louisville, Ky.: Westminster John Knox Press, 1989.

Selinger, Suzanne. *Charlotte Von Kirschbaum and Karl Barth: A Study in Biography and the History of Theology.* University Park: Pennsylvania State University Press, 1998.

Webster, John B. *Barth's Moral Theology.* Edinburgh: T. & T. Clark, 1998.

Werpehowski, William. "Narrative and Ethics in Barth." *Theology Today* 43, no. 3 (1986): 334-53.

Chapter 16: "Infinite Openness to the Infinite": Karl Rahner's Contribution to Modern Catholic Thought on the Child

Primary Sources

Rahner, Karl. *The Content of Faith: The Best of Karl Rahner's Theological Writings.* Edited by Karl Lehmann and Albert Raffelt. Translation edited by Harvey D. Egan. New York: Crossroad, 1993.

————. *Faith in a Wintry Season: Conversations and Interviews with Karl Rahner in the*

Last Years of His Life. Edited by Paul Imhof and Hubert Biallowons. Translation edited by Harvey D. Egan. New York: Crossroad, 1990.

————. *The Great Church Year: The Best of Karl Rahner's Homilies, Sermons, and Meditations.* Edited by Albert Raffelt. Translation edited by Harvey D. Egan. New York: Crossroad, 1993.

"Ideas for a Theology of Childhood." In *Theological Investigations,* vol. 8: *Further Theology of the Spiritual Life 2.* Translated by David Bourke. New York: Herder & Herder, 1971.

————. *I Remember: An Autobiographical Interview with Meinold Krauss.* Translated by Harvey D. Egan. New York: Crossroad, 1985.

————. *Mission and Grace: Essays in Pastoral Theology.* 3 vols. London: Sheed & Ward, 1963-66.

————. *The Practice of Faith: A Handbook of Contemporary Spirituality.* Edited by Karl Lehmann and Albert Raffelt. New York: Crossroad, 1983.

Secondary Sources

Baudler, Georg. "Göttliche Gnade und menschliches Leben: Religionspädadogische Aspeckte der Offenbarungs — und Gnadentheologie Karl Rahners." In *Wagnis Theologie: Erfahrungen mit der Theologie Karl Rahners,* edited by Herbert Vorgrimler, 35-49. Freiburg: Herder, 1979.

Best, Ron, ed. *Education, Spirituality, and the Whole Child.* New York: Cassell, 1996.

Bleistein, Roman. "Mystagogie und Religionspädagogik." In *Wagnis Theologie: Erfahrungen mit der Theologie Karl Rahners,* edited by Herbert Vorgrimler, 51-60. Freiburg: Herder, 1979.

Dych, William V. *Karl Rahner.* Collegeville, Minn.: Liturgical Press, 1992.

Egan, Harvey D. *Karl Rahner: Mystic of Everyday Life.* New York: Crossroad, 1998.

Hay, David, with Rebecca Nye. *The Spirit of the Child.* London: HarperCollins, 1998.

Phan, Peter C. "Karl Rahner as Pastoral Theologian." *Living Light* 30 (1994): 3-12.

Vorgrimler, Herbert. *Karl Rahner: His Life, Thought, and Works.* London: Burns & Oates, 1963; Glen Rock, N.J.: Paulist Press, 1966.

————. *Understanding Karl Rahner: An Introduction to His Life and Thought.* New York: Crossroad, 1986.

Warren, Michael, ed. *Sourcebook for Modern Catechetics.* Winona, Minn.: Saint Mary's Press, 1983, 1997.

Whitmore, Todd David, with Tobias Winright. "Children: An Undeveloped Theme in Catholic Teaching." In *The Challenge of Global Stewardship: Roman Catholic Responses,* edited by Maura A. Ryan and Todd David Whitmore, 161-85. Notre Dame: University of Notre Dame Press, 1997.

Chapter 17: *"Let the Children Come" Revisited: Contemporary Feminist Theologians on Children*

Primary Sources

Cahill, Lisa Sowle. *Sex, Gender, and Christian Ethics.* Cambridge: Cambridge University Press, 1996.

Cooey, Paula M. *Family, Freedom, and Faith: Building Community Today.* Louisville: Westminster John Knox Press, 1996.

————. "That Every Child Who Wants Might Learn to Dance." *Cross Currents: The Journal of the Association for Religion and Intellectual Life* 48, no. 2 (Summer 1998): 185-97.

Elshtain, Jean Bethke. "The Family and Civic Life." In *Rebuilding the Nest: A New Commitment to the American Family,* edited by David Blankenhorn, Jean Bethke Elshtain, and Steven Bayme, 119-32. Milwaukee: Family Service America, 1990.

————. "Family Matters: The Plight of America's Children." *The Christian Century,* 14-21 July 1993, pp. 710-12.

————. *Public Man, Private Woman: Women in Social and Political Thought.* Princeton: Princeton University Press, 1981.

Eugene, Toinette M. "Sometimes I Feel Like a Motherless Child: The Call and Response for a Liberational Ethic of Care by Black Feminists." In *Who Cares: Theory, Research, and Educational Implications of Care,* edited by Mary M. Brabeck, 44-62. New York: Praeger, 1989.

Gudorf, Christine E. *Body, Sex, and Pleasure: Reconstructing Christian Sexual Ethics.* Cleveland: Pilgrim, 1994.

————. "Dissecting Parenthood: Infertility, in Vitro, and Other Lessons in Why and How We Parent." *Conscience* 15, no. 3 (Autumn 1994): 15-22.

————. "Parenting, Mutual Love, and Sacrifice." In *Women's Consciousness and Women's Conscience: A Reader in Feminist Ethics,* edited by Barbara Hilkert Andolsen, Christine E. Gudorf, and Mary D. Pellauer, 175-92. San Francisco: Harper & Row, 1985.

————. "Sacrifice and Parental Spiritualities." In *Religion, Feminism, and the Family,* edited by Anne Carr and Mary Stewart Van Leeuwen, 294-309. Louisville, Ky.: Westminster John Knox, 1996.

Harrison, Beverly. *Our Right to Choose: Toward a New Ethic of Abortion.* Boston: Beacon, 1983.

Hebblethwaite, Margaret. *Motherhood and God.* London: Geoffrey Chapman, 1984.

Isasi-Díaz, Ada María. *Mujerista Theology: A Theology for the Twenty-First Century.* Maryknoll, N.Y.: Orbis Books, 1996.

Jonte-Pace, Diane. "Object Relations Theory, Mothering, and Religion: Toward a Feminist Psychology of Religion." *Horizons* 14, no. 2 (1987): 310-27.

Miller-McLemore, Bonnie J. *Also a Mother: Work and Family as Theological Dilemma.* Nashville: Abingdon, 1994.

————. "Let the Children Come." *Second Opinion* 17, no. 1 (July 1991): 10-25.

Oduyoye, Mercy Amba. "Poverty and Motherhood." *Concilium* 206 (1989): 23-30.

Pellauer, Mary D., Barbara Chester, and Jane A. Boyajian, eds. *Sexual Assault and Abuse: A Handbook for Clergy and Religious Professionals.* San Francisco: Harper & Row, 1987.

Rabuzzi, Kathryn Allen. *Motherself: A Mythic Analysis of Motherhood.* Bloomington: Indiana University Press, 1988.

————. *Mother with Child: Transformations through Childbirth.* Bloomington: Indiana University Press, 1994.

Ross, Mary Ellen, and Cheryl Lynn Ross. "Mothers, Infants, and the Psychoanalytic Study of Ritual." *Signs: Journal of Women in Culture and Society* 9, no. 1 (1983): 26-39.

Ruether, Rosemary Radford. "Church and Family I-V." *New Blackfriars* (January-May 1984).

————. *Sexism and God-talk: Toward a Feminist Theology.* Boston: Beacon Press, 1983.

Williams, Delores S. *Sisters in the Wilderness: The Challenge of Womanist God-Talk.* Maryknoll, N.Y.: Orbis Books, 1993.

Secondary Sources

Browning, Don S., Bonnie J. Miller-McLemore, Pamela D. Couture, K. Brynolf Lyon, and Robert M. Franklin. *From Culture Wars to Common Ground: Religion and the American Family Debate.* Louisville: Westminster John Knox Press, 1997.

II. Select General Bibliography on the History of Childhood and Contemporary Issues Regarding Children

Adams, Carol, and Marie M. Fortune, eds. *Violence against Women and Children: A Christian Theological Sourcebook.* New York: Continuum, 1995.

Airhart, Phyllis D., and Margaret Lamberts Bendroth, eds. *Faith Traditions and the Family.* Louisville: Westminster John Knox Press, 1996.

Alefeld, Yvonne-Patricia. *Göttliche Kinder: Die Kindheitsideologie in der Romantik.* Paderborn: Schöningh, 1996.

Alexandre-Bidon, Danièle, and Didier Lett. *Les Enfants au Moyen Age: V^e-XVe Siècles.* Rev. ed. Paris: Hachette Littératures, 1997.

Amato, Paul R., and Alan Booth. *A Generation at Risk: Growing Up in an Era of Family Upheaval.* Cambridge: Harvard University Press, 1997.

Amidei, Nancy. "Child Advocacy: Let's Get the Job Done." *Dissent* (Spring 1993): 213-20.

Anderson, Herbert, Don Browning, Ian S. Evison, and Mary Stewart Van Leeuwen, eds. *The Family Handbook.* Louisville: Westminster John Knox Press, 1998.

Anderson, Herbert, and Susan B. W. Johnson. *Regarding Children: A New Respect for Childhood and Families.* Louisville: Westminster John Knox Press, 1994.

Anderson, Michael. *Approaches to the History of the Western Family, 1500-1914.* Cambridge: Cambridge University Press, 1995.

Ariès, Philippe. *Centuries of Childhood: A Social History of Family Life.* Translated by Robert Baldick. New York: Vintage Books, 1962. Originally published as *L'enfant et la vie familiale sous l'Ancien Régime.* Paris: Librairie Plon, 1960.

Arnold, Klaus. *Kind und Gesellschaft in Mittelalter und Renaissance.* Paderborn: Schöningh, 1980.

Atkinson, Clarissa. *The Oldest Vocation: Christian Motherhood in the Middle Ages.* Ithaca, N.Y.: Cornell University Press, 1991.

Baudach, Frank. *Planeten der Unschuld — Kinder der Natur: Die Naturstandsutopie in der deutschen und westeuropäischen Literatur des 17. und 18. Jahrhunderts.* Tübingen: Niemeyer, 1993.

Berryman, Jerome W. *Godly Play: An Imaginative Approach to Religious Education.* San Francisco: HarperSanFrancisco, 1991; Minneapolis: Augsburg Fortress, 1995.

———. *Teaching Godly Play: The Sunday Morning Handbook.* Nashville: Abingdon Press, 1995.

Blankenhorn, David. *Fatherless America: Confronting Our Most Urgent Social Problem.* New York: Basic Books, 1995.

Blankenhorn, David, Jean Bethke Elshtain, and Steven M. Bayme, eds. *Rebuilding the Nest: A New Commitment to the American Family.* Milwaukee: Family Service America, 1990.

Boswell, John. *The Kindness of Strangers: The Abandonment of Children in Western Europe from Late Antiquity to the Renaissance.* New York: Pantheon Books, 1988.

Brown, Robin, ed. *Children in Crisis.* New York: H. W. Wilson Co., 1994.

Browning, Carol, and Don S. Browning. "Better Family Values: A New Paradigm for Family Policy Can Bridge the Partisan Gap." *Christianity Today* 6 (February 1995): 29-32.

———. "The Church and the Family Crisis: A New Love Ethic." *The Christian Century,* 7-14 August 1991, pp. 746-49.

Browning, Don S. "Christian Ethics and the Family Debate: An Overview." *Annual of the Society of Christian Ethics* (1995): 251-66.

———. "The Family and the Male Problematic." *Dialog* (Spring 1995): 123-30.

———. "Practical Theology and the American Family Debate: An Overview." *International Journal of Practical Theology* 1 (1997): 136-60.

———. "The Religion, Culture, and Family Project." *Criterion* (Spring 1993): 5-11.

Browning, Don S., Bonnie J. Miller-McLemore, Pamela D. Couture, K. Brynolf Lyon, and Robert M. Franklin. *From Culture Wars to Common Ground: Religion and the American Family Debate.* The Family, Religion, and Culture Series, edited by Don S. Browning and Ian S. Evison. Louisville: Westminster John Knox Press, 1997.

Brueggemann, Walter. "Will Our Faith Have Children?" *Word and World* (1983): 272-83.

Cable, Mary. *The Little Darlings: A History of Child Rearing in America.* New York: Charles Scribner's Sons, 1975.

Calvert, Karin. *Children in the House: The Material Culture of Early Childhood: 1600-1900.* Boston: Northeastern University Press, 1992.

Canada, Geoffrey. *Fist Stick Knife Gun: A Personal History of Violence in America.* Boston: Beacon Press, 1995.

Capps, Donald. *The Child's Song: The Religious Abuse of Children.* Louisville: Westminster John Knox Press, 1995.

———. "Religion and Child Abuse: Perfect Together." *Journal for the Scientific Study of Religion* 31, no. 1 (1992): 1-14.

Carlson, Eric Josef. *Marriage and the English Reformation.* Oxford: Blackwell, 1994.

Carr, Anne, and Mary Stewart Van Leeuwen, eds. *Religion, Feminism, and the Family.* Louisville: Westminster John Knox, 1996.

Cavalletti, Sofia. *The Religious Potential of the Child.* New York: Paulist Press, 1983.

"Children." Special issue. *Dialog* 37 (Summer 1998).

"Children." Special issue. *Word and World* 15 (Winter 1995).

Cleverley, John F., and D. C. Phillips. *Visions of Childhood: Influential Models from Locke to Spock*. Rev. ed. New York: Teachers College Press, 1986.

Clinton, Hillary Rodham. *It Takes a Village, and Other Lessons Children Teach Us*. New York: Simon & Schuster, 1996.

Coles, Robert. *The Moral Intelligence of Children: How to Raise a Moral Child*. New York: Plume, 1997.

————. *The Moral Life of Children*. Boston and New York: Atlantic Monthly Press, 1986.

————. *The Spiritual Life of Children*. Boston: Houghton Mifflin Company, 1990.

————. "Struggling toward Childhood: An Interview with Robert Coles." *Second Opinion* 18, no. 4 (April 1993): 58-71.

Coontz, Stephanie. *The Way We Never Were: American Families and the Nostalgia Trap*. New York: Basic Books, 1992.

Couture, Pamela. *Blessed Are the Poor? Women's Poverty, Family Poverty, and Practical Theology*. Nashville: Abingdon Press, 1991.

Cunningham, Hugh. *Children and Childhood in Western Society since 1500*. New York: Longman Publishing, 1995.

————. "Histories of Childhood." *The American Historical Review* 103, no. 4 (October 1998): 1195-1208.

Damon, William. *Greater Expectations: Overcoming the Culture of Indulgence in Our Homes and Schools*. New York: Free Press Paperbacks, 1995.

————. *The Moral Child: Nurturing Children's Natural Moral Growth*. New York: Free Press, 1988.

Dawn, Marva J. *Is It a Lost Cause? Having the Heart of God for the Church's Children*. Grand Rapids, Mich.: Eerdmans, 1997.

De Jong, Mayke. *In Samuel's Image: Child Oblation in the Early Medieval West*. New York: E. J. Brill, 1996.

DeMause, Lloyd. *The History of Childhood*. New York: Psychohistory Press, 1974.

Denzler, Alice. *Jugendfürsorge in der alten Eidgenossenschaft: ihre Entwicklung in den Kantonen Zürich, Luzern, Freiburg, St. Gallen und Genf bis 1798*. Zurich: Verlag des Zentralsekretariates Pro Juventute, 1925.

Edelman, Marian Wright. "A Call for Compassion and Justice: Rescuing Our Nation's Children and Their Families." *Review and Expositor* 91 (Summer 1994): 309-24.

————. *Families in Peril: An Agenda for Social Change*. Cambridge: Harvard University Press, 1987.

————. *Guide My Feet: Prayers and Meditations on Loving and Working for Children*. Boston: Beacon Press, 1995.

————. *The Measure of Our Success: A Letter to My Children and Yours*. Boston: Beacon Press, 1992.

Elkind, David. *The Hurried Child: Growing Up Too Fast Too Soon*. Rev. ed. Reading, Mass.: Addison-Wesley Publishing Co., 1988.

————. *Ties that Stress: The New Family Imbalance*. Cambridge: Harvard University Press, 1994.

Elshtain, Jean Bethke. "Family Matters: The Plight of America's Children." *Christian Century*, 14-21 July 1993, pp. 710-12.

————. "Political Children." *Criterion* (Spring-Summer 1994): 2-15.

————, ed. *The Family in Political Thought*. Amherst: University of Massachusetts Press, 1982.

Erikson, Erik. *Childhood and Society.* 2d edition. New York: W. W. Norton, 1963.

"The Family and Feminist Theory." Special issue. *Hypatia* 11, no. 1 (Winter 1996).

Fisher, J. D. C. *Christian Initiation: Baptism in the Medieval West: A Study in the Disintegration of the Primitive Rite of Initiation.* London: SPCK, 1965.

————. *Christian Initiation: The Reformation: Some Early Reformed Rites of Baptism and Confirmation and Their Contemporary Documents.* London: SPCK, 1970.

Fliegelman, Jay. *Prodigals and Pilgrims: The American Revolution against Patriarchal Authority, 1750-1800.* London: Cambridge University Press, 1982.

Fowler, James. *Faithful Change: The Personal and Public Challenges of Postmodern Life.* Nashville: Abingdon Press, 1996.

————. *Stages of Faith: The Psychology of Human Development and the Quest for Meaning.* San Francisco: Harper & Row, 1981.

Friedich, Laura Dean Ford. *Putting Children and Their Families First: A Planning Handbook for Congregations.* New York: United Methodist Church, 1996.

Fuchs-Kreimer, Nancy. *Parenting as a Spiritual Journey: Deepening Ordinary and Extraordinary Events into Sacred Occasions.* Woodstock, Vt.: Jewish Lights Publishing, 1996.

Goodich, Michael E. *From Birth to Old Age: The Human Life Cycle in Medieval Thought, 1250-1350.* Lanham: University Press of America, 1989.

Greven, Philip. *The Protestant Temperament: Patterns of Child-Rearing, Religious Experience, and the Self in Early America.* New York: Alfred A. Knopf, 1977.

————. *Spare the Child: The Religious Roots of Punishment and the Psychological Impact of Physical Abuse.* New York: Alfred A. Knopf, 1991.

————, ed. *Child-rearing Concepts, 1628-1861: Historical Sources.* Itasca, Ill.: Peacock, 1973.

Gudorf, Christine E. "Dissecting Parenthood: Infertility, in Vitro, and Other Lessons in Why and How We Parent." *Conscience* 15, no. 3 (Autumn 1994): 15-22.

————. "Parenting, Mutual Love, and Sacrifice." In *Women's Consciousness and Women's Conscience: A Reader in Feminist Ethics,* edited by Barbara Hilkert Andolsen, Christine E. Gudorf, and Mary Pellauer, 175-92. San Francisco: Harper & Row, 1985.

Guroian, Vigen. *Tending the Heart of Virtue: How Classic Stories Awaken a Child's Moral Imagination.* New York: Oxford University Press, 1998.

Gutman, Herbert. *The Black Family in Slavery and Freedom, 1750-1925.* New York: Pantheon Books, 1976.

Guy, Kathleen A. *Welcome the Child: A Child Advocacy Guide for Churches.* Washington, D.C.: Children's Defense Fund, 1991.

Haas, Louis. *The Renaissance Man and His Children: Childbirth and Early Childhood in Renaissance Florence, 1300-1600.* New York: St. Martin's Press, 1998.

Hawes, Joseph M., and N. Ray Hiner, eds. *American Childhood: A Research Guide and Historical Handbook.* Westport, Conn.: Greenwood Press, 1985.

————. *Children in Historical and Comparative Perspective: An International Handbook and Research Guide.* New York: Greenwood Press, 1991.

————. *Growing Up in America: Children in Historical Perspective.* Urbana: University of Illinois Press, 1985.

Heller, David. *The Children's God.* Chicago: University of Chicago Press, 1986.

————. *Talking to Your Child about God: A Book for Families of All Faiths.* New York: Berkley Publishing, 1994.

Herlihy, David. "Medieval Children." In *Essays on Medieval Civilization,* edited by Bede

493

Karl Lackner and Kenneth Roy Philp, 109-41. The Walter Prescott Webb Memorial Lectures, XII. Austin: University of Texas Press, 1978.

Herrmann, Ulrich. *Aufklärung und Erziehung: Studien zur Funktion der Erziehung im Konstitutionsprozess der bürgerlichen Gesellschaft im 18. und frühen 19. Jahrhundert in Deutschland.* Weinheim: Deutscher Studien Verlag, 1993.

Hewlett, Sylvia Ann, and Cornel West. *The War against Parents: What We Can Do for America's Beleaguered Moms and Dads.* Boston: Houghton Mifflin, 1998.

Hull, John M. *God-talk with Young Children: Notes for Parents and Teachers.* Philadelphia: Trinity Press International, 1991.

Juengst, Sara Covin. *Sharing the Faith with Children: Rethinking the Children's Sermon.* Louisville: Westminster John Knox Press, 1994.

Kagan, Jerome, and Sharon Lamb, eds. *The Emergence of Morality in Young Children.* Chicago: University of Chicago Press, 1987.

Kincaid, James Russell. *Child-loving: The Erotic Child and Victorian Culture.* New York: Routledge, 1992.

———. *Erotic Innocence: The Culture of Child Molesting.* Durham, N.C.: Duke University Press, 1998.

King, Wilma. *Stolen Childhood: Slave Youth in Nineteenth-Century America.* Bloomington: Indiana University Press, 1995.

Kingdon, Robert M. *Adultery and Divorce in Calvin's Geneva.* Cambridge: Harvard University Press, 1995.

———. "Social Welfare in Calvin's Geneva." *The American Historical Review* 76 (1971). Reprinted as chapter 6 of R. M. Kingdon, *Church and Society in Reformation Europe.* London: Variorum Reprints, 1985.

Kozol, Jonathan. *Amazing Grace: The Lives of Children and the Conscience of a Nation.* New York: Crown Publishers, Inc., 1995.

———. *Savage Inequalities: Children in America's Schools.* New York: Crown Publishers, Inc., 1991.

Lazareth, William H. *Luther on the Christian Home: An Application of the Social Ethics of the Reformation.* Philadelphia: Muhlenberg Press, 1960.

Levenson, Jon D. *The Death and Resurrection of the Beloved Son: The Transformation of Child Sacrifice in Judaism and Christianity.* New Haven: Yale University Press, 1993.

Levi, Giovanni, and Jean-Claude Schmitt, eds. *Ancient and Medieval Rites of Passage.* Vol. 1 of *A History of Young People in the West.* Translated by Camille Naish. London and Cambridge, Mass.: The Belknap Press of Harvard University Press, 1997.

———. *Stormy Evolution to Modern Times.* Vol. 2 of *A History of Young People in the West.* Translated by Carol Volk. London and Cambridge, Mass.: The Belknap Press of Harvard University Press, 1997.

Lincoln, C. Eric, and Lawrence H. Mamiya. *The Black Church in the African-American Experience.* Durham, N.C.: Duke University Press, 1990.

Lipman, Matthew, ed. *Thinking Children and Education.* Dubuque, Ia.: Kendall Hunt, 1993.

Lipman, Matthew, Ann M. Sharp, and Frederick Oscanyan, eds. *Growing Up with Philosophy.* Philadelphia: Temple University Press, 1978.

Luke, Carmen. *Pedagogy, Printing, and Protestantism: The Discourse on Childhood.* Albany, N.Y.: SUNY Press, 1989.

Matthews, Gareth. "Concept Formation and Moral Development." In *Philosophical Per-*

spectives on Developmental Psychology, edited by James Russell. Oxford: Basil Blackwell, 1987.

———. *Dialogues with Children.* Cambridge: Harvard University Press, 1984.

———. *Philosophy and the Young Child.* Cambridge: Harvard University Press, 1980.

———. *The Philosophy of Childhood.* Cambridge: Harvard University Press, 1994.

Meilaender, Gilbert. "What Are Families For?" *First Things* 6 (October 1990): 34-41.

Metz, René. *La Femme et L'Enfant dans le Droit Canonique Médiéval.* London: Variorum Reprints, 1985.

Meumann, Markus. *Findelkinder, Waisenhäuser, Kindsmord: Unversorgte Kinder in der frühneuzeitlichen Gesellschaft.* Münich: Oldenbourg, 1995.

Miller, Alice. *For Your Own Good: Hidden Cruelty in Child-Rearing and the Roots of Violence.* Translated by Hildegarde Hannum and Hunter Hannum. New York: Noonday Press, 1983.

———. *Thou Shalt Not Be Aware: Society's Betrayal of the Child.* New York: Farrar, Straus & Giroux, 1984.

Miller-McLemore, Bonnie J. *Also a Mother: Work and Family as Theological Dilemma.* Nashville: Abingdon, 1994.

———. "Let the Children Come." *Second Opinion* 17, no. 1 (July 1991): 10-25.

———. "Will the Real Pro-Family Contestant Please Stand Up? Another Look at Families and Pastoral Care." *Journal of Pastoral Care,* Spring 1995, 61-72.

Naphy, William G. *Calvin and the Consolidation of the Genevan Reformation.* Manchester and New York: Manchester University Press, 1994.

Neumann, Josef N., and Udo Sträter, eds. *Das Kind in Pietismus und Aufklärung.* Halle/Tübingen: Verlag der Franckeschen Stiftungen im Max Niemeyer Verlag Tübingen, 2000.

Newman, Barbara. "'Crueel Corage': Child Sacrifice and the Maternal Martyr in Hagiography and Romance." In *From Virile Woman to WomanChrist: Studies in Medieval Religion and Literature,* 76-107. Middle Ages Series. Philadelphia: University of Pennsylvania Press, 1995.

Oehme, Johannes, ed. *Das Kind im 18. Jahrhundert: Beiträge zur Sozialgeschichte des Kindes.* Lübeck: Hansisches Verlagskontor H. Scheffler, 1988.

Okin, Susan Moller. *Justice, Gender, and the Family.* New York: Basic Books, 1989.

Osiek, Carolyn, and David L. Balch. *Families in the New Testament World: Households and House Churches.* Louisville: Westminster John Knox Press, 1997.

Ozment, Steven. *When Fathers Ruled: Family Life in Reformation Europe.* Cambridge: Harvard University Press, 1983.

Pais, Janet. *Suffer the Children: A Theology of Liberation by a Victim of Child Abuse.* New York: Paulist Press, 1991.

Perdue, Leo G., Joseph Blenkinsopp, John J. Collins, and Carol Meyers. *Families in Ancient Israel.* The Family, Religion, and Culture Series, edited by Don S. Browning and Ian S. Evison. Louisville: Westminster John Knox Press, 1997.

Peters, Ted. *For the Love of Children: Genetic Technology and the Future of the Family.* Louisville: Westminster John Knox Press, 1996.

Piaget, Jean. *The Child's Conception of the World.* London: Kegan Paul, 1929.

———. *The Moral Judgment of the Child.* 1932; reprint, New York: Free Press, 1965.

Piercy, Sandra Lee. "The Cradle of Salvation: Children in Late Sixteenth and Seventeenth Century England." Ph.D. dissertation, University of California, Santa Barbara, 1982.

Pipher, Mary. *Reviving Ophelia: Saving the Selves of Adolescent Girls.* New York: Putnam, 1994.

Pollock, Linda. *Forgotten Children: Parent-Child Relations from 1500 to 1900.* New York: Cambridge University Press, 1983.

———. *A Lasting Relationship: Parents and Children over Three Centuries.* London: Fourth Estate, 1987.

Popenoe, David. *Disturbing the Nest: Family Change and Decline in Modern Societies.* Hawthorne, N.Y.: Aldine De Gruyter, 1988.

———. *Life without Father: Compelling New Evidence That Fatherhood and Marriage Are Indispensable for the Good of Children and Society.* New York: Free Press, 1996.

Popenoe, David, Jean Bethke Elshtain, and David Blankenhorn, eds. *Promises to Keep: Decline and Renewal of Marriage in America.* Lanham, Md.: Rowman and Littlefield Publishers, Inc., 1996.

Postman, Neil. *The Disappearance of Childhood.* New York: Vintage Books, 1994.

Pritchard, Michael S. *On Becoming Responsible.* Lawrence, Kans.: University Press of Kansas, 1985.

———. *Philosophical Adventures with Children.* Lanham, Md.: University Press of America, 1985.

Quinn, Patricia A. *Better than the Sons of Kings: Boys and Monks in the Early Middle Ages.* Studies in History and Culture, vol. 2. New York: Peter Lang, 1989.

Ratcliff, Donald. "Baby Faith: Infants, Toddlers, and Religion." *Religious Education* 87, no. 1 (Winter 1992): 117-26.

Rich, Adrienne. *Of Woman Born: Motherhood as Experience and Institution.* New York: W. W. Norton, 1976.

Robinson, Edward. *The Original Vision: A Study of the Religious Experience of Childhood.* Oxford: Religious Experience Research Unit, Manchester College, 1977.

Scales, Peter C., and Nancy Leffert. *Developmental Assets: A Synthesis of the Scientific Research on Adolescent Development.* Minneapolis: Search Institute, 1999.

Schindler, Stephan K. *Das Kind als Subjekt: Die Erfindung der Kindheit im Roman des 18. Jahrhunderts.* Berlin: Erich Schmidt, 1994.

Schmitt, Jean-Claude. *The Holy Greyhound: Guinefort: Healer of Children since the Thirteenth Century.* Translated by Martin Thom. New York: Cambridge University Press, 1983.

Schultz, James A. *The Knowledge of Childhood in the German Middle Ages, 1100-1350.* Middle Ages Series. Philadelphia: University of Pennsylvania Press, 1995.

Shahar, Shulamith. *Childhood in the Middle Ages.* London: Routledge, 1990.

Slater, Peter. *Children in the New England Mind: In Death and in Life.* Hamden, Conn.: Shoe String Press, 1977.

Snyders, Georges. *Die grosse Wende der Pädagogik: Die Entdeckung des Kindes und die Revolution der Erziehung im 17. und 18. Jahrhundert in Frankreich.* Paderborn: Schöningh, 1971.

Sommerville, C. John. *The Rise and Fall of Childhood.* Rev. ed. New York: Vintage Books, 1990.

Stackhouse, Max L. *Covenant and Commitments: Faith, Family, and Economic Life.* The Family, Religion, and Culture Series, edited by Don S. Browning and Ian S. Evison. Louisville: Westminster John Knox Press, 1997.

Steedman, Carolyn. *Strange Dislocations: Childhood and the Idea of Human Interiority, 1780-1930.* Cambridge: Harvard University Press, 1995.

Stone, Lawrence. *The Family, Sex, and Marriage: England, 1500-1800.* London: Weidenfeld & Nicolson, 1977.

Strauss, Gerald. *Luther's House of Learning: Indoctrination of the Young in the German Reformation.* Baltimore: The Johns Hopkins University Press, 1978.

Strommen, Merton, and Richard Hardel. *Passing on the Faith: A Radical New Model for Youth and Family Ministry.* Winona, Minn.: St. Mary's Press, 2000.

Sturm, Douglas. "On the Suffering and Rights of Children: Toward a Theology of Childhood Liberation." *Cross Currents* 42, no. 2 (Summer 1992): 149-73.

Taves, Ann. "Mothers and Children and the Legacy of Mid–Nineteenth-Century American Christianity." *Journal of Religion* 67, no. 2 (April 1987): 203-19.

Theology Today. Special millennium issue devoted to the subject of children. Vol. 56, no. 4 (January 2000).

Thompson, Marjorie J. *Family: The Forming Center.* Rev. ed. Nashville: Upper Room Books, 1996.

Tranvik, Mark D. "The Other Sacrament: The Doctrine of Baptism in the Late Lutheran Reformation." Th.D. dissertation, Luther Northwestern Theological Seminary, 1992.

Wall, James M. "Family Values, Christian Values." *Christian Century* 31 (January 1996): 104-14.

————. "The New Middle Ground in the Family Debate: A Report on the 1994 Conference of the Religion, Culture, and Family Project." *Criterion* (Fall 1994): 24-31.

Wasting America's Future: The Children's Defense Fund's Report on the Costs of Child Poverty. Report by The Children's Defense Fund. Boston: Beacon Press, 1994.

Wetzel, Michael. *MIGNON: Die Kindsbraut als Phantasma der Goethezeit.* Münich: Wilhelm Fink, 1999.

Whitmore, Todd David. "Children and the Problem of Formation in American Families." *The Annual of the Society of Christian Ethics* (1995).

Whitmore, Todd David, with Tobias Winright. "Children: An Undeveloped Theme in Catholic Teaching." In *The Challenge of Global Stewardship: Roman Catholic Responses,* edited by Maura A. Ryan and Todd David Whitmore, 161-85. Notre Dame: University of Notre Dame Press, 1997.

Wiesner-Hanks, Merry. "Family, Household, and Community." In *The Handbook of European History, 1400-1600: Late Middle Ages, Renaissance, and Reformation,* 2 vols., edited by T. A. Brady, H. A. Oberman, and J. D. Tracy, 1:51-78. Leiden and New York: E. J. Brill, 1994.

Wishy, Bernard. *The Child and the Republic: The Dawn of Modern American Child Nurture.* Philadelphia: University of Pennsylvania Press, 1968.

Witte, John Jr. *From Sacrament to Contract: Marriage, Religion, and Law in the Western Tradition.* The Family, Religion, and Culture Series, edited by Don S. Browning and Ian S. Evison. Louisville: Westminster John Knox Press, 1997.

Wood, Diana, ed. *The Church and Childhood.* Studies in Church History, vol. 31. Oxford: Blackwell, 1994.

Zelizer, Viviana. *Pricing the Priceless Child: The Changing Social Value of Children.* 1985; reprint, Princeton: Princeton University Press, 1994.

Zuck, Roy B. *Precious in His Sight: Childhood and Children in the Bible.* Grand Rapids, Mich.: Baker Books, 1996.

Contributors

Clarissa W. Atkinson
Associate Dean for Academic Affairs
The Divinity School, Harvard University

Margaret Bendroth
Professor of History
Calvin College

Catherine A. Brekus
Assistant Professor of the History of Christianity
The Divinity School, University of Chicago

Marcia J. Bunge
Associate Professor of Theology and Humanities
Christ College, Valparaiso University

Dawn DeVries
John Newton Thomas Professor of Systematic Theology
Union Theological Seminary and the Presbyterian School of Christian
    Education

Keith Graber Miller
Professor of Bible, Religion, and Philosophy
Goshen College

Judith M. Gundry-Volf
Associate Professor (Adjunct) of New Testament; Senior Research Scholar
Yale University Divinity School

Contributors

Vigen Guroian
Professor of Theology and Ethics
Loyola College in Maryland

Richard P. Heitzenrater
William Kellon Quick Professor of Church History and Wesley Studies
The Divinity School, Duke University

Mary Ann Hinsdale
Associate Professor of Theology and Director of the Institute of Religious
    Education and Pastoral Ministry
Boston College

Bonnie J. Miller-McLemore
Professor of Pastoral Theology
The Divinity School, Vanderbilt University

Barbara Pitkin
Acting Assistant Professor of Religious Studies
Stanford University

Marcia Y. Riggs
Associate Professor of Christian Ethics
Columbia Theological Seminary

Martha Ellen Stortz
Professor of Historical Theology and Ethics
Pacific Lutheran Theological Seminary

Jane E. Strohl
Associate Professor of Reformation History and Theology
Pacific Lutheran Theological Seminary

Cristina L. H. Traina
Associate Professor of Religion
Northwestern University

William Werpehowski
Professor of Theology and Director of the Center for Peace and Justice
    Education
Villanova University

Index of Subjects

Abandonment of children, 80, 83, 87, 116, 120-21, 123, 124-25, 132. *See also* Infanticide

Abortion, 4, 36, 412, 446, 449. *See also* Reproductive choice

Abuse: of children, 4-5, 7, 10, 16, 251, 284, 349, 450, 459; Edwards and, 320, 321, 326; patriarchy and, 462, 465-66. *See also* Corporal punishment

Adolescence, 84-85, 113n.37, 119-20, 165, 303, 397. *See also* Childhood: stages of

Adoption, 25, 83n.21, 129, 132, 396, 396n.38, 467, 468

African Americans: children of, 369-70, 376-77, 381-85; and concern for children, 450-51, 451-52, 467; nineteenth-century situation of, 365-66; race-class ideologies among, 375, 381. *See also* Black women's club movement; Racism; Womanist theology

Anabaptists: central convictions of, 195; critique of, 183, 185, 186, 190, 192, 431; family life of, 196-98; Hutterites, 195, 205, 219-20; persecution of, 197-98, 217-18, 221-23; Swiss, 201, 210-11. *See also* Baptism: adult (or believers'); Mennonites; Simons, Menno

Baptism: adult (or believers'), 17, 195, 198-201, 203-7, 225, 242-43, 244-45, 391-92, 401-402n.54; and analogy to circumcision, 184, 186, 200n.18; Augustine on, 78-80, 91, 94-99, 100, 102; of desire, 114, 117-18; of the fetus, 94, 115n.45; of Huron Indians, 242-45; infant, 16-17, 37n.34, 59, 69-70, 114-15, 116, 141-43, 171, 181-86, 193, 243-45, 263, 294-95, 305-6, 322-23, 355-56, 415, 428-33; naming of children at, 177-78; without parental consent, 115-16, 244

Black women's club movement, 26, 59, 365-71, 376-85

Catechesis, 97-98, 116, 186-89, 193, 344-47, 433-43, 444-45. *See also* Childrearing; Education

Catechism: and Bushnell, 354; by Calvin, 162, 172, 187-89; by Luther, 144-49, 264-65; among missionaries in Canada, 229n.5, 231, 233; and the Roman Catholic Church, 415, 434, 438; and Schleiermacher, 345, 345n.46; Westminster, 311. *See also* Catechesis; Education

Celibacy, 20, 53, 63n.3, 139, 145, 156, 217, 240, 470-71

Index of Names

Index of Scripture References